ROUTLEDGE LIBRARY EDITIONS:
ACCOUNTING HISTORY

Volume 12

THE BOOK-KEEPER AND
AMERICAN COUNTING-ROOM, VOLUME 4

THE BOOK-KEEPER AND
AMERICAN COUNTING-ROOM, VOLUME 4

January, 1884–December, 1884

Edited by
RICHARD P. BRIEF

Routledge
Taylor & Francis Group

LONDON AND NEW YORK

First published in 1989 by Garland Publishing, Inc.

This edition first published in 2021
by Routledge
2 Park Square, Milton Park, Abingdon, Oxon OX14 4RN

and by Routledge
52 Vanderbilt Avenue, New York, NY 10017

Routledge is an imprint of the Taylor & Francis Group, an informa business

British Library Cataloguing in Publication Data
A catalogue record for this book is available from the British Library

ISBN: 978-0-367-33564-9 (Set)
ISBN: 978-1-00-304636-3 (Set) (ebk)
ISBN: 978-0-367-51400-6 (Volume 12) (hbk)
ISBN: 978-0-367-51414-3 (Volume 12) (pbk)
ISBN: 978-1-00-305372-9 (Volume 12) (ebk)

Publisher's Note
The publisher has gone to great lengths to ensure the quality of this reprint but points out that some imperfections in the original copies may be apparent.

Disclaimer
The publisher has made every effort to trace copyright holders and would welcome correspondence from those they have been unable to trace.

The Book-Keeper and American Counting-Room

In Four Volumes

Volume 4
January, 1884-December, 1884

GARLAND PUBLISHING, INC.

NEW YORK & LONDON 1989

For a list of Garland's publications in accounting,
see the final pages of this volume.

These volumes have been reproduced from copies in the
American Institute of Certified Public Accounting.

Library of Congress Cataloging in Publication

■ ■
The Book keeper and American counting-room, 1880–1884.
(Foundations of accounting)
Includes index.
Contents: v.1. July, 1880–December, 1881—v.2. January, 1882–June,
1883—[etc.]
1. Bookkeeping—United States—History—19th century. 2. Account-
ing—United States—History—19th century. 3. Finance, Public—
United States—Accounting—History—19th century. I. Book keeper
(New York, N.Y.). II. American counting-room. III. Series.
HF5616.U5B65 1989   657'.0973   88-33588
ISBN 0-8240-6141-1 (set)

Design by Renata Gomes

The volumes in this series are printed on
acid-free, 250-year-life paper.

Printed in the United States of America

Editor's Note

The *Book-keeper* was first published in New York City on July 20, 1880 and continued until June 19, 1883 when its name was changed to *The American Counting Room*, the latter being published from July 1883 to June 1884. The editor of the first issue was Selden R. Hopkins whose notice in the August 3 issue announced that he

> Will give counsel upon improved methods of keeping the accounts
> of Incorporated Companies. Assists bookkeepers and business men
> in straightening out intricate and improperly kept books. Adjusts
> complicated partnership accounts. Examines books for stockholders
> and creditors. [p. 31-32]

The August 31 issue indicated that Charles E. Sprague, author of the accounting classic, *Philosophy of Accounts* (1907), had become co-editor. In its advertisement in this issue, the periodical asserted that "'The Book-keeper' is the First[1] and only Publication of its Character in the World," dealing with the following subjects: "Historical reviews of methods and systems in all ages and by all nations. Elucidations of accounts, introducing new and simplified features of accounting. Problems from the counting-room discussed and explained. Instructive notes upon plans and methods of book-keeping in every department of trade, commerce and industry. Biographical sketches. Personal and news items."

In his paper, "Public Accountancy in the United States," which was published in The American Institute of Accountants *Fiftieth Anniversary Celebration, 1937,* and reprinted by Garland Publishing in 1982, Norman E. Webster commented that "Historically this [*The Book-keeper*] is an important item of source material" on public accountancy in America. Webster indicates[2] that the publication was the first of its kind in America and estimates a circulation of more than 3, 000.

After more than one hundred years, *The Book-keeper* is being reprinted. This journal is a primary source for students interested in the history of accounting in the United States. The reprint edition will make this material more widely available.

Richard P. Brief
New York
April 1, 1988

Notes

[1] A slight exaggeration. In October 1874, *The Accountant* began publication in London.
[2] *The American Association of Public Accountants: Its First Twenty Years 1886-1906* (New York: American Institute of Accountants, 1954, pp. 10-11.)

AMERICAN COUNTING-ROOM.

Vol. VIII.   JANUARY, 1884.   No. 1.

THE RISE AND FALL OF A MILLIONAIRE.

It is a rare page in history upon which are recorded facts concerning the life of a man who, within a decade, is seen an humble employé, a millionaire, the controller of the fortunes of a hundred others as wealthy as himself, and again shorn of his riches and reduced to moderate circumstances. This, it is believed, is not an exaggeration of the history of one of whom we purpose here to recall. There came to this country from England about twelve years ago a young man who was well connected in the country of his birth, and the possessor of a reasonable fortune. Among the cities he visited, and where he made friends and acquaintances, Boston was, perhaps, the most prominent. While sojourning in Boston this young man became impressed with the idea of investing some portion of his fortune in American securities, or properties, which it seemed probable would yield a better return than investments in his own country. He was introduced to a gentleman who was reccommended to. him as a suitable person to act as his agent, and invest for him such moneys as he might deem best to place in this country. As a result, an agreement between the two was entered into. The young Englishman was married while in this country, and with his bride returned to England. From his home he sent from time to time to his agent in this country moneys for investment in such securities as his agent might deem proper, and which he believed would prove the most remunerative. According to terms of agreement the agent was to receive, in addition to the stipulated

amount for his services, a certain per cent. of the profits resulting from the investments of his principal's capital.

At that time railroad securities were looked upon as among the favored channels for profitable investments of capital, and consequently by far the largest part of the money invested for the English capitalist was used in purchasing various railroad stocks and bonds. There had been organized in Wisconsin a company to build and operate a road now known as the Wisconsin Central Railroad. The bonds of this company were placed upon the market, and the agent of the English investor became acquainted with the officers of the railroad company, and with the value of the company's securities. It was agreed between various interested parties, and among them the agent referred to, that a syndicate should be formed, to take up and dispose of a large amount of bonds for the Wisconsin company. This arrangement was carried into effect, and the agent was one of the persons who formed the syndicate, and soon after bent his way to Europe for the purpose of finding purchasers in Holland and the Netherlands for the securities which he and his colleague had agreed to place upon the market. Before taking his departure, however, he transferred to his English principal a large amount of the syndicate's securities, thus demonstrating to the company and to other capitalists the salability of the bonds. While in Europe he made many acquaintances with wealthy capitalists, and, possessing all the qualities of an industrious, intelligent, and persevering financier, and a gentleman of culture and refinement, he won supporters and admirers among his newly-made acquaintances. He was successful in his efforts, and proved himself capable of carrying through his project which he had assisted in organizing in America. His success in this direction led him into avenues of wider range and greater opportunities.

Not long after his return from Europe to this country he became one of the active operators in the Oregon Transcontinental Company—an organization which, although of a local character at the time of its inception, but with an aim in view that looked forward to a great transcontinental route, uniting the Atlantic with the Pacific on the northern border of the United States. Before engaging in this last enterprise, the agent of the English capitalist had rendered an account of his stewardship, and had turned over to his principal the securities, consisting of bonds and stock—chief among which were bonds of the Wisconsin Central Railroad Company. This agent of the English capitalist, and who now had become a prominent railroad magnate, was no less a person than Mr. Henry Villard.

To carry out the gigantic schemes formulated under the management of the now celebrated Oregon Transcontinental Company there was formed a "blind pool," the capital of which was ten million dollars. Mr. Villard was the financier into whose charge this immense amount of money was placed, and, too, with the perfect confidence of its contributors. Previous to the time we have mentioned, when an acquaintance was formed between Mr. Villard and the gentleman from England whom he represented, Mr. Villard was unknown in the great financial circles of the country, in which, during the past few years, he has acted so prominent a part.

During the month of December just past, the name of Mr. Villard, and the reports of his schemes and operations as president of the Northern Pacific Railway and of the Oregon Transcontinental Company, has attracted the attention of the financial world, both in this country and in Europe. The announcement of his resignation from the presidency of the great corporations over which he presided, and of his financial troubles and failure, produced a consternation in the money centers of the country which has seldom been equaled in recent financial history. His wealth had been estimated at ten million dollars, and the greater portion of this, it was known, he must have accumulated within the past five years.

How a man, however shrewd or whatever his possibilities for the acquirement of wealth, even as the managing magnate of such corporations as those which Mr. Villard had under his control, could manage to accumulate wealth at the rate of two million dollars a year, was a puzzling question, not only to those who find it difficult with many advantages in their favor—with intelligence, shrewdness, and sagacity in business affairs—and yet barely able to secure a moderate share of the luxuries of life, but as well to those kings of money-makers who seemingly hold the purses of the persons with whom they have business dealings.

As the facts appear now on the surface, it seems that there was not so much cause for surprise as many had been forced to believe. Had his revenues been legitimate and proper, had the wealth he was reputed to possess been actual rather than supposed, it would not be necessary to chronicle at this time not only his retirement from the management of the extended corporations he controlled, but the release of nearly all the valuable estate, including a new and magnificent mansion he was supposed to possess. What rather seems now to be the mystery is, not how Mr. Villard could have accumulated wealth with such rapidity, but how it was possible for him and his associates to so manipulate the finances of such an institution as a corporation worth, in the aggregate, many millions of dollars, to their own personal advantage, and apparently as if the wealth of the corporation was but their own private assets. Previous to the resignation of Mr. Villard as president of the Oregon Transcontinental and the Oregon Railroad and Navigation Company an investigation of the financial condition of those corporations was reported to have been made and reported upon as being satisfactory. However, since the facts have come to light, the question is raised if the purported investigation actually took place, or if the information given by the investigation was not furnished by some person or persons directly interested in having a favorable report made. As to whether the person selected to make the investigation was competent, or whether he employed competent persons to act with him—persons recognized as accountants, whose ability would enable them to determine the financial status of the corporation—we are not at present advised; but from what has since transpired it may be reasonable to infer that no competent accountant was employed for the purpose. It is too often the case where persons are entrusted to perform a duty requiring a special education or technical knowledge of the trust confided to them that they accept statements of those in charge of the accounts it is their duty to examine, instead of making personal examinations and employing competent persons to assist them in doing so. As the finances of the Oregon Transcontinental Company began to drift into a state of restless anxiety, it was resolved by the stockholders and the executive committee that the affairs of that corporation should be thoroughly investigated; and accordingly a committee for that purpose was appointed. This committee consisted principally of a subcommittee of the executive committee of the Board of Directors of the company, and the following is a portion of their report:

To the Executive Committee of the Board of Directors of the Oregon and Transcontinental Company :

The committee appointed by the Executive Committee of the Oregon and Transcontinental Company to examine the assets and liabilities of the company and report thereon would respectfully represent to your committee that, in response to a suggestion in which they heartily concurred, Mr. R. G. Rolston was by them requested to join the committee and take part in the investigation. The committee was organized by the appointment of Mr. E. P. Fabbri as chairman and secretary, and at the earliest moment proceeded to an investigation of the company's affairs. The matter of the investigation being of an intricate character, and requiring many meetings, much time has necessarily been taken by the committee in arriving at the substance of their report. Inasmuch as the business and affairs of the company had been largely under the control and management of President Villard, his absence, in consequence of severe illness, during the examination, has greatly interfered with the committee's labors and has prevented their making a report as satisfactory in detail as they would have desired.

The liabilities of the company from the best sources at the committee's hands are shown to be as follows :

Bills-payable....................... .... $10,562,500.00
Credited vouchers, as reported by treasurer...   396,733.33
Oregon Railway and Navigation Company...   48,895.41

The committee are informed that the bonds yet to be received from branch lines will meet the requirements for construction. Your committee has deemed it proper to state the assets at their face or share value, not considering it within their province or desirable to affix market values which are constantly liable to fluctuation.

In closing the report the committee desire to express their appreciation of the readiness on the part of the officers and employees of the company to facilitate as much as lay in their power the task assigned to the committee.

E. P. FABBRI.
WILLIAM ENDICOTT, JR.
R. G. ROLSTON.

NEW YORK, MONDAY, DEC. 31, 1883.

This report furnishes some evidence of the looseness in which the affairs of the company had been managed. The fact that it required many meetings and much time, and that because of the unavoidable absence of President Villard, the committee was prevented from making a report satisfactory in all particulars —that is to say, that, owing to these difficulties, the committee were unable to arrive at the facts which would enable them to report fully and intelligently upon all affairs connected with the finances of the company. Had the business of the company been properly conducted, and books of account properly kept, the work should not have been intricate, nor should it have been in any way essential that the president of the company should have assisted in an examination of the financial condition of the corporation. It is shown by the report that the liabilities of the company in bills-payable alone are over ten and a-half millions of dollars, and that the total liabilities exceed eleven million dollars. The assets are shown to be made up of shares of stock of various railway and other corporations; the item of "Second mortgage bonds," to the amount of two million dollars, is the only one reported among the securities in which it would appear that the assets bore anything more than a speculative value; and this one of second mortgage bonds may properly be considered a questionable asset. Municipal corporations in numbers, all over the country, are to-day the owners of second mortgage bonds of railroad companies which are worth no more than the paper upon which they are printed. Those mentioned in the report may have a similar value.

In commenting upon Mr. Villard's failure, a leading city paper says:

The report of the committee on the O. T. Company, and Mr. Villard's letter resigning the presidency of the Northern Pacific, the final abdication of all his former power, have been leading subjects of discussion. The expression of personal feeling in the letter touched a like chord of personal feeling in its readers, and while many, perhaps, yet sore from their losses, could not feel otherwise than resentful, there was still a feeling of sympathy for the man whose brief and striking career had ended in so sudden and complete ruin. Even Wall Street was moved at the cry of anguish from the fallen man, prostrated in mind and body, the costly surroundings erected to his glory only making his fall more conspicuous to the world, and laying down his office with words of bitterness : " This is the unjust result." All had been sacrificed to avert failure, and in the end there was failure, utter and disastrous. It is the hard experience of life that we are made to pay for our mistakes as cruelly as for our conscious misdeeds. Mr. Villard has had to pay hard for his, for it is not enough to intend to do right ; it is necessary to know how to do it. Every man who has given thought to his own life sees that for the errors done from want of strength, or want of knowledge, or want of fortitude, there is no more mercy than for the wrong-doing done in actual viciousness. Indeed, that thing which may bring the harshest punishment is often something done unwillingly, despite our mental protest, but under a press of circumstances too great for our strength. Yet for this there is no mercy, because the errors of incompetence are always most fatal in their effects. It is the incompetent general who sacrifices the most men ; and Mr. Villard has gone down because the things he undertook to do were more then he knew how to do.

In addition to the debt of eleven million dollars, according to the report of the committee, it has been stated that, shortly before the investigation, the company had reduced its indebtedness about nine million dollars, which would show that not more than a few months ago it owed at least twenty millions; and this fact, it seems now to appear, was a surprise to the general body of stockholders.

It has been generously stated that Mr. Villard, in his management of the companies over which he presided, was made the scapegoat of friends who shared with him in the speculations that were transacted through the companies whose finances they controlled. The losses suffered by those financially interested in the several classes of security, which have been known in the market as the "Villard stocks," should accept this remarkable case as a reminder of their duty in other enterprises in which they may in the future take part.

A thorough examination, quarterly or semi-annually, by competent accountants, who, it is known, would faithfully discharge their duties and render true and unvarnished reports of the financial situation of these unfortunate corporations, would, it may reasonably be believed, have averted the direful calamity which cast its shadow upon the financial situation during the last month of the year just closed. *S. R. H.*

PUBLIC MONEYS AND ACCOUNTS.
THIRD ARTICLE.

MUNICIPAL CORPORATIONS — COLLECTION OF TAXES — *Continued.*

In the ledgerized form for tax assessment rolls (which were given in the preceding article, page 329, No. 6, Vol. I.), it will be observed that instead of arranging the book in alphabetical order, as to the names, the plan is followed of having all the property in each street appear on the rolls consecutively, according to numbers. A page of ordinary size would contain, in the form given, the records of four or, perhaps, five separate pieces of property. It would, therefore, be advisable, where a street is of such length as to have a thousand or more numbers, lots, or distinct divisions of property, to use one or, perhaps, more books for a single street. One thousand divisions of property will, in the form given, occupy a book of five hundred pages, and this book will last from eight to twelve years. Rather than increasing the size of the book, where the number of pieces of property are large, it would be advisable, as stated, to use another, or even several other books, if found necessary. The street may be divided into sections, or one book may be made to contain records of all property on one side of the street only, while another would be used for those on the opposite side. There are but few cities having streets of such length as to require more space than would be given in a book of five hundred pages. Then again, the requirements of property in short streets may be so combined that those of two or more streets may be grouped together in a single book. By this plan, the requirements of any particular piece of property may be readily referred to without reference to the name in which it is assessed.

A plan which to some extent has been introduced is that of dividing the city or town into districts, and using books in which these districts are represented in map form, to correspond with the various pieces of property assessed. These maps have, in some instances, been gotten up in an elaborate style with colored charts, and carefully drawn diagrams, representing boundary lines. They have not been very extensively used.

When the tax-rolls have been made up, it should be the duty of the collector of taxes to make out, ready for the signature, all receipts for them ready for delivery to the tax-payer when the time arrives for the collection of the taxes. Where the rolls are made out in the ordinary form — that is, arranged alphabetically, according to the names of tax-payers — the receipt should be made out in books to correspond with the rolls, each letter of the alphabet having one or more separate tax receipt-books. The receipt-book could be improved by having the names arranged under a vowelized system, so that it would require

comparatively little labor to find any particular receipt; circumstances would govern. If from the list of names the tax-books were cumbersome, the objection may be overcome by using either a cabinet letter-file, or a set of properly constructed pigeon-holes for filing receipts.*

Where the ledgerized form of tax-rolls is in use, the books of blank tax-receipts would be arranged to correspond with the rolls by having blank receipt-books for the different streets. As the numbers would run consecutively through the tax receipt-books, the receipt of any particular piece of property could be found without a moment's hesitation or delay. The tax-payer coming into the office of the collector to pay his taxes would give the street upon which his property was situated and the numbers, and this would be all the information desired by the collector to enable him to place his hand at once upon the required receipt, made out and proved, ready for his signature, and the tax-payer would not be kept waiting for the collector to make out his receipt. It is customary, in most places at least, for the collector to fill out the tax-receipts after the tax-payer calls to make payment. At certain times there is a great rush of work, and the collector is taxed to his utmost to meet the demands of those who are desirous of escaping the penalty placed upon delinquents. Inexperienced help must, at times, be depended upon, and the liability of error in filling out tax-bills, during times of excitement and haste, is very much increased. Where the bills are made out beforehand, and nothing remains but to attach the signature and receive the money, there need arise no occasion for undue haste or error in collections. Attached to each tax-receipt should be a stub, upon which would appear a memorandum of the receipt, specifying the property and the amount collected. As the receipt is given to the tax-payer, the stub should be placed on some sort of convenient file from which, at the close of the day's work, it could be taken and

* For the arrangement of pigeon-holes or indexes to meet any requirement of this kind see table on page 167 of the COUNTING-ROOM, Vol. VII.

entered upon the tax-rolls. The footing of the stub should, of course, tally with the cash receipts.

One of the important advantages in having the receipts of property made out beforehand—that is, before the time arrives for the collection of taxes—is the facility the plan will afford for determining delinquents when the time arrives for the addition of the penalties attached, according to law, for the non-payment within a prescribed time. As soon as the prescribed limits have expired, before the penalty is to be added, it should be the duty of the collector to then go over all tax-receipts remaining at that time in his hands, adding thereto the penalty for non-payment, where the line opposite the charge in the tax-rolls which was made, or supposed to have been made at the time the tax was paid, shows that there is a great liability of errors in such a system. It is not unusual, where such systems are in vogue, for the tax-collector to include erroneously in his list of taxes to be sold for non-payment, properties upon which the taxes have been paid, and receipts for the same properly given. In some cases I have known of property thus erroneously reported by the collector to have been sold for taxes, and in that manner the city government to incur a large, needless expense for advertising and costs of sale.

The form of receipt given in this con-

REGISTER OF

Date.	Title of Account Credited and General Notes upon Receipts.	Receipts from Collections of Current Taxes.				Redempt'n o Property Sol for Taxes.
		City.	County.	City Interest and Penalty.	County Int'st and Penalty.	

penalty is made a certain percentage of the principal tax. In cases where the law provides that a certain rate per cent. per annum shall be added to all delinquent taxes, this penalty cannot be added until the taxes are paid, or are sold for non-payment. The tax-receipts remaining unsigned in the hands of the collector are always evidence, or should be at least, that the taxes which they represent have not been paid. They will, therefore, furnish, in a very systematic manner, the basis for a list of properties to be offered for sale for non-payment of taxes. Instances that I am familiar with, where the tax-receipts are made out on loose blanks, and the only record remaining in the office of the tax-collector showing that taxes have been paid is a memorandum or notation on a nection is not offered as a perfect model of what an improved tax-receipt should be; but rather as a suggestion of a form showing the stub with certain notations. There are, as will be seen, two perforated lines—one, separating the receipt from the stub; the other, the stub from the book. When the receipt has been signed and cancelled with the stamp of the office, and passed to the tax-payers, the stub should then be detached and placed upon file as before described. A plan which may, in some cases, be considered an improvement on this would be that of making the receipt in duplicates by the use of carbon paper. This is, perhaps, the most accurate, and would prove in many ways much the most serviceable to an accounting-officer. While the cost of the receipts or receipt books would be somewhat increased by the use of duplicates, the loss would be more than compensated through a saving of time required for filling out the stub, as illustrated in the accompanying diagram. By the duplicate system it would be necessary only to place a sheet of carbon paper between two receipts at the time of making, and one writing would give a receipt for the tax-payer, and its duplicate to be retained in the office of the collector, thus obviating the necessity of a stub, and the labor of filling it out. It would, also, diminish liability of error. No advantage of the duplicate system would be found, in entering up the receipts for the day, where it was necessary to carry out to the

work of a city treasurer, it is assumed that this official acts in the capacity of a tax-collector, as well as city treasurer. This special routine will not, therefore, be found universally applicable. In some States city treasurers have no part in the work of collecting taxes, that duty being performed by a county treasurer, or an official chosen especially for the purpose. The accompanying form will serve to show the various sources from which moneys reach the hands of those city treasurers who also act as tax-collectors. The form is one that was devised to meet the requirements of a certain city charter. This charter provided that the treasurer, who was also collector of taxes, should deposit each

ASH RECEIPTS.

Receipt Account of Returned Taxes from City Attorney.				Receipts from Chamberlain.			Miscellaneous.	
City.	County.	City Int. and Percentages.	Interest on County Taxes	Licenses.	Fines.	Rents & Sales	Receipts.	Deposits.

credit of the various accounts the amounts of daily collections.

GENERAL RECEIPTS OF CITY TREASURER.

In the first article on this subject, the difficulties lying in the path of one who undertakes to review the methods in use, and to formulate a course of advice, or suggest improvements in connection with the system of public accounts which are in vogue, were briefly intimated. In describing the work belonging to any public official, where that description touches special technical parts of the duties, it is necessary to understand precisely what duties are necessary to be performed. In describing here, the duties, and illustrating the

day in such bank or banks as might be designated by the city counsel, all moneys coming into his hands. A classification of the sources of revenue showed there were five currents through which moneys would, or could, properly reach the treasury. These were:

(1) Receipts from the collection of current taxes.

(2) Receipts from redemption of property which had been sold for taxes.

(3) Receipts from the city attorney on account of taxes placed in his hands for collection.

(4) Receipts from the city chamberlain or clerk.

(5) Receipts from the sales of public property, and those not otherwise specified, which would properly be termed miscellaneous.

Under the heads of receipts from the collection of current taxes would be found four special sources. These were:

(1) City taxes.
(2) County and State taxes.
(3) Penalties and interest on city taxes.
(4) Penalties and interest on county taxes.

Under the head of receipts from the city attorney on account of return taxes were also four special sources, the same as those above described.

Under the head of receipts from city chamberlain or clerk were three special sources, namely:

(1) Licenses.
(2) Fines.
(3) Rents and sales.

The city charter alluded to provides that the city attorney should collect delinquent taxes. That when the time for a payment of taxes had expired in which to collect, without the addition of a penalty, it was the duty of the city treasurer to make up a statement of all delinquent taxes, report them to the city counsel, and they were then placed in the hands of the city attorney for collection. It is hardly necessary to say that such a practice or system led to serious disturbances in the accounting department of the city government. The arrangement, also, whereby the city clerk or chamberlain was made the receiver of moneys, while not so objectionable as dividing up between different officials the duty of collecting taxes, is one that has no points of merit to recommend its adoption.   *S. R. H.*

STUB.   FORM OF RECEIPT.

CITY OF IMAGINATION.

OFFICE OF COLLECTOR OF TAXES.

GETHROW STITCHBACK, *Collector.*

IMAGINATION, *January 20th, 5884.*

RECEIVED in payment of taxes, special assessments, penalties and interest for delinquency, being the amounts due the CITY OF IMAGINATION for city, county, state, and other taxes levied and assessed, *November 15th, 5883,* as per the following statement, the total of which is *One hundred thirty-five and 60/100 dollars.*   *Gethrow Stitchback,* Collector.

MYSTIC AVENUE, 208.

GEORGE B. PACKER.

Date of payment.....................
Cash page ....
Tax-roll page.........

City taxes...................... 99.60
State and County 36.00
     Total tax 135.60
Penalty, ... %................
Interest, ... months,... days,
     ☞ .... %................
         Total *135.60*

Description of property:
     Brick residence;
     208 Mystic Avenue.

Assessed to
George B. Packer.

{ Stamp of office. }

City Contingent...............	18	..
Lamps and Lighting....... ..	15	..
Streets and Highways....:.....	5	40
Principal Public Debt..........	36	..
Interest of Public Debt	6	..
Public School..................	14	40
Public Alms......	4	80
Special......	..	..
Total City...............	99	60
State and County	36	..
Total Tax...............	135	60
Penalty .... %.........		
Interest, ... months, ... days,		
☞ .... %....................		
Total.....................	135	60

[*To be continued.*]

MINES AND MINING COMPANIES.

"In the morning," said my informant after we had finished our supper and he had lighted his pipe, "the boss left the other mine, and put a strong guard to watch the two levels of the 'Lone Jack' at the intersection. There wasn't much done during the day, but the next night we had war sure enough. The fighting commenced in the lower level of the 'Lone Jack' when their men undertook to break through the barricade. From the lower level the fighting spread to the upper level, and from there to the top of our main shaft. They tried to take possession of our works and shaft, but we proved too much for 'em. One of their men was killed, and two was wounded at our shaft. In the levels, three of our men was wounded, two of their's — one so badly that he did not recover for months, and came near dying. The next day both of us got reinforcements, and the men was paid ten dollars a day. The fighting was terrible the next night. One of our guard at the main shaft was killed, and two more was wounded, and they all had to retreat and leave the enemy in possession of the shaft. But our boss was awful quick-witted, for, while the guard was being driven away from our shaft, he was mustering more men, and made an attack on the 'Lone Jack' shaft, and captured it. They had only a few men on guard, and did not expect an attack. Our boss sent one of the men down in the levels of the 'Lone Jack,' and gave the report to their men that he had taken possession of the property, and that if they wanted to get out alive they must come up at once, as he intended to blow up the works, and would cut off all chance of their getting out at all. The 'Lone Jack' men in the mines then surrendered, and before the fellows who took possession of our shaft could get down to the men in the lower workings who was holding the 'Lone Jack' boys at bay, (that's where I was),

our boss got word to us of the situation, and we then guarded the shaft coming down from 'Maryann.' Three men there with plenty of ammunition and good rifles could keep out a regiment. So, you see, when morning came we was in possession of the 'Lone Jack,' and our enemies had the 'Maryann.'"

The narrator then went on. Pausing for a moment, and giving his pipe a fresh light there seemed to come a shadowed thought, then a long sigh; and apparently wishing to change the subject, the miner looked me in the face, and shaking his closely cropped head he gravely muttered:

"It was a terrible time, you just bet. Why, Mister, all that has ever been taken out of this camp, and all the money put into it wouldn't amount to a lump of dirt in a ton of ore towards paying for the loss of life in them two days. And besides that, it was a foolish, hot-headed affair, and could have been avoided just as well as not. If them rich rich men in New York and other cities, who was making money out of the stock, had been the ones to shoulder the guns and risk their lives for ten dollars a day, there wouldn't been nobody killed around this camp you may bet your head for a football."

Then the narrator concluded the interesting story by telling how a cessation of hostilities was brought about, and how the two companies finally consolidated and formed the present organization — the Oxyoke Consolidated Mining Company. The history of a number of instances where war of this kind had been waged between contestants to mining claims was related to me during my stay at the camp. Many of the stories — and their truth was well vouched for, and much of what happened appeared in the public prints at the time — were really thrilling narratives. The case I have thus lightly pictured will serve, in a measure only, to show the extent to which lawlessness and a disregard for law and order prevailed. When people thought the law was weak they took it into their own hands. I was told of certain cases, and saw the properties, where litigation over titles had cost several hundred thousand dollars. The properties were, of course, very valuable, or such sums of money would not have been thus expended; but it is doubtful if the mines in all similar cases were ever found to be worth half the money required to secure their control.

And now I come to the result of my investigation of titles, and the organization of the company. I have traced each property from its discovery to its absorption by the consolidated company. The consolidation was effected between the company which owned the "Maryann," viz., the "Maryann" Mining Company, and the individual owners of the "Lone Jack," which had been worked under lease by two of the owners. The terms of the consolidation were that the new company should be organized with a capital-stock of $800,000. Shares to the amount of $350,000 should go to the "Maryann" Mining Company, and to the amount of $250,000 should be given to the individual owners of the "Lone Jack," according to their respective interests; the remaining $200,000 to form a fund for developing the property and increasing the operating capacity. Some months after the consolidation had taken place, the capital-stock was increased to a million dollars.

When I looked into the accounts, the first peculiarity which attracted my attention was the fact that the capital-stock account stood credited with $900,000, when I knew $1,000,000 in stock had been issued. The explanation given for this was that the $200,000 of stock disposed of to form a fund for the development of the property had been sold at fifty dollars a share, and, therefore, only $100,000 had been realized from it, which, as the book-keeper said, "left capital-stock a hundred thousand short." Continuing the inspection, I found an account entitled "Mines," to the debit of which was $600,000. In the journal I saw the explanatory entry showing that

at the time the consolidation had taken place the account of "Mines" was debited, and "Capital-stock" credited, for the amount of stock issued to the consolidating companies. This was taking an exceedingly short cut to wipe out the difficulties of a complicated transaction. In many instances I observed that postings had been made to the ledger accounts, in the form of original entries, no records or memoranda of them appearing in any other place. A general account entitled "Mining" I found to be a common receptacle for almost all sorts of items. Supplies, such as fuse, powder, drills, candles, ropes, together with charges for improvements, mining, machinery, timber, and the like, were all bunched together in the carry-all account.

The first day I devoted to work in the office I learned something that was really interesting to know. It was simply the purposes and objects in mining company accounts of an "Improvement Fund." I had supposed it to represent capital set aside to be used solely and especially for improving and developing the property; but I ascertained here that the stock declared to be set aside as an "Improvement Fund" had been sold, and the money used to pay dividends for the purpose of "bulling" the stock market in the New York Exchange. Large dividends had been paid out of this "Improvement Fund" stock at times when it required several thousand dollars to mine the ore in excess of the product. At first I could not understand how it was possible to declare dividends and pay them if the accounts did not show that the property was making money. Looking at the Profit and Loss account I found everything apparently properly carried out, and a sufficient amount with which to declare dividends carried to the dividend account. Going back still further, I peered into the catch-all account, entitled, "Mining." I found at the close of the year, when the annual statements were made up, that a large amount had each year been carried to the credit of "Loss and Gain." The amount had been closed in regular form, having been credited by inventory. This, at first sight, looked to be all right, as I supposed the inventory had been properly made out and passed upon by the Board of Trustees as correct before having been credited to the account. But I was inquisitive to get at the bottom facts, and called for the original inventory from which the crediting entry had been made. The book-keeper informed me that he knew nothing about it; that there was, or had been, an inventory made out each year, and that he had entered from it the credit as shown by the mining account. A thorough search in and about the premises — through pigeon-holes, boxes, desks, powder-cans, in tool-chests—failed to furnish me the desired information. The original inventories were nowhere to be found. I then set to work to prepare inventories from the information I was able to obtain from the books, vouchers and papers in my possession. In this way I discovered that there was an estimated value placed upon the product of the mine, which remained in hand at the time the inventory was made; but this estimate was clearly many thousand dollars too high, and the amount credited to the mining account was, I learned, in a great measure fictitious. It was not a *bona fide* inventory of assets, values or property on hand at the time the books were closed.

By carrying to the credit of the mining account a sum something like fifty thousand or sixty thousand dollars in excess of the *bona fide* inventory, the managers were able to make it appear from the books that a profit had been made, and furnished them a handsome dividend account upon which to declare dividends to stockholders. The money which it was supposed had been safely laid aside for future developments of the property had been used to pay off the forced dividends, and thus bolster up the stock market. By a careful examination I learned, also, that the managers had used of the company's funds large sums in prospecting and seeking titles to other mining properties in the adjoining district. Then came the work correcting the errors, and introducing the improved methods in keeping the accounts. Through the introduction of a book called the "Ore Register" we were enabled to determine every week the exact output of the mine, together with the cost of developing, and the amount expended for labor in mining. The plan of using pay-checks was adopted, and arrangements were made with merchants and others with whom the miners had dealings that the checks should be received by them without discount. A complete system of vouchers was introduced from which a careful audit of accounts could be made at any time. A new board of managers was appointed, and the superintendent put in charge of the property who performed his duties with one eye to the interests of the stockholders, and it was not many months before the property was found in a paying condition, making money for the stockholders.

Richard Rufus.

THE NEW YORK STOCK EXCHANGE.

This institution is an unincorporated association, existing under a written constitution and by-laws. The history of the Exchange may be traced back to the year 1817, when an organization was formed for the purpose of dealing in securities, principally the indebtedness of the Government growing out of the War of 1812. The constitution adopted at that time is no longer in existence, having been destroyed in the great fire of 1835. The present constitution was adopted in May, 1869, upon the consolidation of the "Government Department" and the "Open Board of Stock-brokers"— two associations of similar character—with the New York Stock Exchange; and under the constitution the government of the Exchange is vested entirely in a committee of forty-two, consisting of the president, treasurer, and forty of the members, called the "Governing Committee."

Every applicant for membership must

be a citizen of the United States, and at least twenty-one years of age.

As fixed by the constitution, the inition fee for members, admitted by election, is twenty-thousand dollars, and that for members admitted by transfer is one thousand dollars; but as the membership is limited to 1,100, and that limit has been reached, the actual market value of a seat at the present time ranges from twenty-five to thirty thousand dollars.

Transactions in the Exchange are confined to such stocks, bonds and securities as are listed, and are all conducted through the mediumship of a member, called a broker. Members only are permitted upon the floor of the Exchange.

A person being desirous of buying certain stock — one hundred shares of Western Union, for example—will give an order to his broker to buy that amount of stock. This order may restrict the broker as to the price at which he may purchase, or as to the terms, or it may leave it entirely to his discretion as to the price he will pay. The broker then proceeds to execute the order. On the floor of the Exchange will be found various groups of members, each group dealing in some particular stock, and by custom these various groups are always congregated in about the same spot upon the floor. He goes to the Western Union group and makes a bid a little below the market-price, using his discretion at what figures to close the purchase. If 80½ is asked he will probably offer 80¼, and if there are more sellers than buyers he may obtain it at that offer. If, on the other hand, there happens to be a demand for that stock, he will have to pay what is asked. Now, there are three classes of sales: "cash," "regular," and "time"; and this transaction may belong to either one or the other of these classes. Where no special agreement is made as to the kind of sale, the transaction is deemed "regular."

If the transaction is a "cash" sale, the stock must be delivered before a quarter past two p. m. on the very day the sale is made, and it must be paid for by that time; and if either party fails—

the seller to deliver, or the buyer to pay for, the stock—the party not in default may buy over again or sell out the stock, as the case may be, to fix a difference to be settled in the future.

In the "regular" sale, the delivery and payment need not be made till a quarter past two of the following day, and on the default of either party the proceedings are the same as in a "cash" sale.

Of the "time" sales there are several varieties: "buyer's option," 3, 5, 10, 15, 30, and 60 days, and "seller's option" for the same periods. In "buyer's 3," as it is expressed, the buyer has three days within which to pay for the stock, but has the option to call for its immediate delivery at any time short of the three days. In "seller's 3" the option is with the seller to deliver at any time within the three days. In "buyer's 5," 10, 15, etc., the buyer has the option of calling for its delivery at any intermediate period on giving one day's notice to the seller, and in "seller's 5," etc., the seller can likewise deliver at any intervening period on a like notice of one day.

Where the delivery is postponed for any longer period than three days, the buyer has to pay interest at the rate of 6% per annum until delivery, and this, whether the delivery is at his option or at the option of the seller.

When stock is sold at buyer's option, it is nearly always in favor of the buyer and on the offer of the seller. If the seller cannot get his price, say of 80½, for Western Union on a cash or regular sale, as an additional inducement he will offer it at "buyer's 3," or "buyer's 5"; and on the other hand, if the buyer who wants to pay 80¼ cannot obtain the stock at this figure on a cash or regular sale, he will bid 80¼ "seller's 3," or "seller's 5."

The sale being consummated, each broker makes a memorandum of its terms, in an abbreviated form, upon a little pad or tag which he carries, and this is immediately dispatched to his office for entry upon his books. The seller's tag would probably read:

S. Jones, 100.W. U., 80⅛.   (Signed) Smith.

meaning that he had sold to Jones 100

shares of Western Union at that figure, while the buyer's tag would be as follows:

B. Smith, 100 W. U., 80¼. (Signed) Jones.

Before reporting the purchase or sale to the customer it is usual to make what is called a "comparison," to guard against error. A boy is dispatched to the office of the broker who sold the stock, and also a boy to the buyer's office, with what is called a " comparison ticket." The ticket issued from the buyer's office would read:

We have bought 100 shares of Western Union at 80¼ regular. (Signed) Jones Bros.

and containing a line,

If not correct, please report immediately.

This is left at the seller's office, for comparison with his books, and a corresponding ticket is left by the seller at the buyer's office.

If there is an error it is at once detected. In case of a dispute, an amicable settlement, if possible, is arrived at, and witnesses are sought to throw light upon the point in controversy. If an agreement is not arrived at, the disagreement is appealed to the chairman of the Exchange for discussion, and on an appeal from his decision, seconded by two members, he calls the Board to order, and takes a vote of all those who witnessed the transaction. If there seems to be some uncertainty, and the question is of some moment, the party would not submit it to a vote, but would go through the form of buying in or selling out the stock to fix a difference to be settled in the future. The dispute is then laid before the Arbitration Committee, who hear the witnesses and render a decision. If there are no witnesses, however, it is useless to take it before the Arbitration Committee, and a compromise is generally effected by a division of the loss.

Where stock is sold for future delivery either party has the right, under the rules of the Exchange, to call upon the other to deposit ten per cent. of the agreed price with some Trust company, as security against any fluctuation, on making a deposit of a similar amount; and when the market changes so as to reduce the margin of this deposit either way below five per cent., another deposit of ten per cent. may be called for. In practice, where the firms dealing are responsible, this is seldom resorted to, as the party in whose favor the market stands is obliged to put up a similar amount, for which he receives but a small rate of interest—2½ per cent. In case either party fails to comply with a demand for such deposit, the party calling, after having given due notice, will report the default to an officer of the Exchange, who therefore re-purchases or re-sells the security forthwith in the Exchange, and any difference is paid over to the party entitled to it. Whenever a difference of opinion exists as to the place of deposit, the rules of the Exchange designate the New York Life and Trust Company.

No contract for the purchase or sale of securities beyond sixty days is valid in the Exchange. The stock, on delivery, must be paid for either in money or a certified check; and if anything else is tendered in payment it can be refused.

The commissions of the broker are fixed by the rules of the Exchange, and the minimum rates on securities other than gold, government bonds and exchange, are as follows:

One eighth of one per cent. of the par value upon both buying and selling, where the transaction is for a party not a member of the Exchange; and one thirty-second of one per cent. where the party is a member of the Exchange.

In many cases the transactions are carried on entirely upon what are called "margins"—that is, the broker advances the money to purchase, or furnishes the stocks for sale, only requiring from his customer a deposit of a sum of money sufficient to cover any fluctuation in the market-price of the stock and his commissions. This deposit is called "margin." This margin is generally fixed at ten per cent. of the current market value of the stock; but it may be less, or no margin need be advanced, at the option of the broker.

For example: A customer wishes to

purchase 100 shares of Western Union, which is quoted at 80. By depositing with his broker a margin of, say, $500, the broker will advance the money and hold the stock for his customer, whose account with the broker will now stand:

Dr. $8,000 + Commission, $12.50 $8,012.50
Cr. $500 + 100 shares of Western Union.

The market, so far as Western Union is concerned, having a downward tendency, the stock falls to 75½, which leaves to his credit, after deducting an additional $12.50 anticipated commission, when the same is sold, but $25. His broker will give his customer a notice to put up more margin, and in case of his failure the stock will be sold; and after deducting commissions, he will receive, or be obliged to pay, whatever balance may exist either in his or the broker's favor.

But if instead of declining the market in Western Union advances until 84 is reached, and at this point he directs his broker to sell, the account will stand:

Dr. $8,000 + Commissions, 25............ 8,025
Cr. $500 margin + proceeds of sale of stock, 8,400
    Total, 8,900.   Bal. to his credit, $875.

In a transaction of this kind, the broker is said to "carry the stock" for his customer.

"Short sales" are frequently made upon margin. A "Short sale" is one, if the sale be for future delivery, where the seller does not own or possess the stock at the time the transaction is entered into, but anticipates a fall in the price which will enable him to buy at a less figure when the time for delivery arrives; or if the sale be "regular," where he borrows the stock from some third person, anticipating a fall in the price before the time for returning the stock to the lender. This borrowing transaction is in form a sale, but the entries upon the books of the brokers treat it as a loan. The seller is then known as a "bear."

A person is said to be "long" of stocks when a purchase has been made and the stocks are being carried, anticipating a rise in the price. He is then called a "bull,"

A "corner" in stocks arises where the "bulls"—*i. e.*, the owners or holders of the stocks—combine together and refuse to loan stocks to the "bears," or those "short" of stocks, to enable them to carry out their "short" contracts, and the "bears" are compelled to go into the market and buy the stocks at whatever price they can obtain them.

These transactions are all carried on in the name of the broker, the name of the principal rarely being divulged. Where the broker "carries the stock" for his principal, the principal is chargeable with legal interest upon the amount which the broker has advanced, and is also liable to pay any extra interest which the broker is compelled to pay for carrying the stock caused by a stringency of the money market. The principal is also liable for any assessment which may be made upon the stock, and is credited with any dividend paid upon it while it is being carried for him.

In the course of dealing in stocks, contracts are frequently made whereby, for a consideration, one party has the right of calling for the delivery from, or delivering to, another party, at a certain time, for a certain price, a specified stock.

Thus a "call" is a contract by which one party, for a consideration, agrees to deliver, at the option of another party, within a certain time, a specified stock at an agreed price. The following is a copy of the common form of a "call" contract:

NEW YORK, January 21, 1884.

For value received, the bearer may call on me for 100 shares of the stock of the Western Union Telegraph Company, at 80 per cent., at any time within ten days from date. The bearer is entitled to all dividends or extra dividends declared during the time.
Expires January 31, at 1¼ P. M.
    (Signed)   JOHN SMITH.

A "put" is a similar contract, wherein the party who holds it has the option of delivering stock to the maker. It is as follows:

NEW YORK, January 21, 1884.

For value received the bearer may deliver me 100 shares of the stock of the Western Union Telegraph Company, at 80 per cent., at any time within ten days from date. The undersigned is entitled to all dividends or extra dividends declared during time.
Expires January 31, 1¼ P. M.
    (Signed)   THOMAS JONES.

There is also a contract called a "straddle," or "spread eagle," which combines the advantage of a "put" and a "call," the holder having the advantage of either delivering or receiving at his option stocks therein specified. The following is a form of "straddle" contract:

NEW YORK, January 20, 1884.

For value received the bearer may call on the undersigned for 100 shares of the stock of the Western Union Telegraph Company, at 80 per cent., at any time in ten days from date. Or the bearer may, at his option, deliver the same to the undersigned, at 80 per cent., at any time within the period named. All dividends or extra dividends declared during the time are to go with the stock in either case; and this instrument is to be surrendered upon the stock being either called or delivered.

Expires January 30, at 1¼ P. M.

(Signed)   JAMES ROBINSON.

Such is the course of dealing, stated briefly, in the New York Stock Exchange, and although many of the transactions would seem from their nature to be illegal, they have been in most cases sanctioned and upheld by the Courts.   *T. B. P.*

A REVIEW OF BUSINESS.

Nearly every one who has given any attention to the subject realizes that the present condition of business throughout the United States is inactive, and most observers content themselves with ascribing that fact to over-production. Few have either the disposition or the opportunity to trace this over-production to general causes. This has been done with care and a truly scientific generalization by the *Railroad Gazette* in its issue of Dec. 28, and those who care for more than a superficial knowledge of the situation would do well not only to examine but to study the statements therein contained. The conclusions reached are the more valuable, because they confirm those based on the history of 1882, and announced at the close of that year.

The tendency of modern trade to move through periods of activity in which the demands of the future are unduly anticipated, capacity for production is unduly increased, and available is converted into fixed capital to succeeding periods of reaction in which manufacturing production is checked, accumulated stocks are consumed, original or agricultural production is allowed to advance, and the demand for secondary products overtakes the supply, has long been recognized, and for at least twenty years back this tendency has been constantly more carefully studied, and its development more accurately defined. According to the *Gazette* the last of these periods of inaction came to an end in 1877. For the seven years ending with 1878, the cultivated acreage of the country steadily advanced—that of grain at an average of 8 per cent. a year, and that of cotton at an average of 7 per cent. From 1877 to 1880 there were exceptionally great crops. The proceeds of these crops naturally increased the capacity of consumption. Production other than agricultural was greatly stimulated and continued at very profitable prices up to and including 1880.

Then began the reaction. The crops of 1881 were very light. There was a war of rates between the railways, which checked profits in these enterprises. Speculation fell off. Trade became dull. The increase in cultivated acreage since 1879 has been but 9 1-4 per cent.; of cotton production but 4 per cent.; in cereal production there has been a decrease of 5 per cent. The railway building and the manufacturing has gone on, but at a gradually lessening rate. Forty per cent. of mileage has been added to the railroads in four years, but 39 per cent. less in 1883 than in 1882. Manufactures of all sorts, and particularly those dependent on railway construction, have been lessening their output, reducing wages, working on half-time, or suspending altogether. The process was inevitable. The question is whether it has been possible to accomplish it with sufficient moderation and soon enough to avoid that sudden breakdown which is called panic. On this point the *Gazette* says: "The gradual reduction of prices and the great reduction in profits since 1880 have led most business men, probably, to believe that the country has escaped the danger of a panic at this time, but must submit to a somewhat protracted but not violent industrial depression. Whether this general impression is correct we do not feel able to say. The extent to which production is 'balanced,' as indicated by the statistics we have given, is sufficient to cause anxiety and alarm, but a long continuance of the downward tendency of prices and very low prices and very low rates of interest have never, we believe, preceded an industrial crisis heretofore."

A curious and striking comparison between the crops and population with the mileage of railways within the last four years is made by the *Gazette*. There was one mile of railroad in 1880 to 34,-818 pounds of cotton; in 1881 to 25,416 pounds; in 1882 to 30,000 pounds; in 1883 to 24,066 pounds. There was one mile of railroad in 1880 to 29,408 bushels grain; in 1881 to 20,000 bushels; in 1882 to 23,724 bushels, and in 1883 to 21,000 bushels. There was one mile of road in 1880 to 554 inhabitants; in 1881 to 518; in 1882 to 481; in 1883 to 466. It will be seen that the sources of business for the roads are markedly less now than four years since. These are facts to which speculation will be compelled to yield. Yet they are by no means discouraging. The process of recovery is as sure and as inevitable as the process of shrinking, and there is considerable evidence that it has already begun. The immediate future is not promising to those who are in haste to get rich. It is, perhaps, on that account more encouraging to those who are content with moderate gains honorably made.

—*N. Y. Times.*

GOING INTO BUSINESS.

Downright ignorance, and lack of system account for the failure of many traders. There are hundreds of men starting as shop-keepers every year who will acknowledge that to learn to shoe a horse requires training, that even to mix drinks behind a bar requires some practice and skill; but the ability to buy and sell goods, they think, "comes by Natur'." Hence they act upon the belief that no training, no experience—almost no knowledge—is needed to become a successful shop-keeper, and they plunge into that business. Some people have an idea that it does not cost anything to "run" a store when you get your wife or son to stand behind the counter, or when you happen to own the premises and can do your own "clerking."

This recklessness or simple-mindedness on the part of traders is manifested in all parts of the country. It was remarked recently by a New York mercantile journal which quoted the case of a Quebec woman whose failure arose from carelessness: "The shiftlessness of doing business without method or record is not peculiar to Canadians or women. Many men in trade to-day without question think their business is prospering. They are happy, they handle a good deal of money, they have a good run of custom. But if an expert were to unravel their accounts, write up their books and give them the result, they would call a halt at once to cut down expenses, and if possible increase profits to avoid a sheriff's sale."

—*Monetary Times.*

THE VALUE OF AN ACCOUNTANT'S BALANCE–SHEET.

The why and the wherefor for the title of this writing must be ascribed to my patriarchal anxiety that young aspirants for the responsibilities of business life should profit by the perusal of the trials and tribulations and ultimate success of my early business career.

My pen having gone thus far, who should come into my sanctum sanctorum but my old friend Mark Checkup. Said he, "Good Morning, Father Whitehead." Said I, "Good morning, old Gift of the Gab. Of all the persons in the world you are just the man I wanted to see."

"Wanted to see *me* — Mark Checkup, *if you please* — did you? Well, here I am. What is it about?"

"It is about telling a story, Mr. Checkup — I want to tell a story. I have read several of your yarns — I beg pardon, I meant to say, stories — in the AMERICAN COUNTING-ROOM and in THE BOOK-KEEPER, and I thought you would be just the man to put me right when I was going wrong in saying what I want to say. I have looked upon you, my dear Mark, as an apostle of story-tellers, gifted with an inspiration in that line."

"Mark Checkup an inspired apostle of story-tellers! What next, Mr. White-head! That's enough for the present. Any more such compliments would stop the digestion of my breakfast."

"I can assure you, Mr. Checkup, that I am perfectly sincere when I say that your mental lucidity fully entitles you to be considered as an inspired story-telling apostle; and in proof of my sincerity I shall esteem it a favor if you will listen to my story, and interrupt me in its narration as often as you may deem advisable to keep my tongue within the line of your inspired ability."

"Anything in the world to oblige you, Father Whitehead. But what kind of a story have *you* in your head?"

"Well, Mark, I'll begin it, and you'll soon see its drift. It is now nearly forty years since I essayed, with a large amount of youthful precocity, to tramp the stones of London as a business man. Yes, Mark, the stones of London! They are the hardest in the world to tramp — competition is so tremendously keen there.

"I was but twenty-three, but, as a mechanic, in my line I flattered myself that if I could but get a start in business I should succeed. For many months I had been forecasting events, and before very long my predictions were realized by my forming a partnership with an old schoolfellow whose friendship, name and family influence I valued personally, and also as an aid to business.

"Our united capital was small — too small, said my father, uncles, and other matured business friends. I heeded not their opinion, for I fully believed that a deficiency of capital would be amply made up by hard work and rigid economy. My partner thought so, too. The start was made right in the heart of London city, and as the business was a mechanical one a by-street was selected as our location, mainly because the premises were suitable and obtainable at a very low rent. The necessary plant was purchased, mechanics were engaged, and the first Saturday's pay-roll footed a considerable figure.

"I was the practical man, and my partner undertook to keep the books, manage cash matters, attend to correspondence, etc. In temperament he was as lethargic as I was energetic. Things went along smoothly—financially—for a few weeks. Then he told me that he did not see how Saturday's pay-roll, with other necessary payments, was to be met. I said; the men must be paid whoever went unpaid. To this he agreed. Consequently the pay-roll was regularly met, and as I did not hear anything to the contrary I supposed he was gradually appeasing outside claims by payments on account. He had taken the responsibility of financing, and I kept him to it, thinking that if anything would rouse him from his wonted inactivity and make him useful as a business man the surmounting of financial difficulties would. He reported to me that the profits were good, that we were more than paying expenses, and that collections—though they might have been better—were fair. With this state of things I was satisfied. Before very long, however, my partner fell sick, and then the financial as well as the mechanical duties of the business devolved upon me. True, if I had had but little experience —and that little limited to what I had seen in my father's business—in bookkeeping, my respected partner's knowledge, judging from the condition in which I found his books, of keeping accounts was far less than mine. Every book was a cobweb of figures—as mathematically untrue as the little insect's web was geometrically true. Consequently those books were a problem which the most astute Philadelphia lawyer would have failed in solving. I at once saw that, by hook or by crook, I must raise some additional capital. I applied for assistance to those who, at the start, had predicted that our united capital would be insufficient for the business which was certain to fall into our hands."

"Of course your friends favorably responded to your request?" interrupted Mr. Checkup, with a sarcastic twinkle in his right eye.

"Well, the fact is, Mr. M. C.—'M. C.,' Mr. Checkup, as you know, stands for 'Master of the Ceremonies'"——

"That's something new to me; but why should you dub me with 'M. C.'? I want no such title. I always thought I was of a most *retiring* disposition."

"I hope you are not angry. I did not mean that you were ever in anyway officious. On the contrary, my dear Mr. Checkup, I have always considered, in listening to you—as the financial head of the great mercantile house of Glamorgan, Checkup & Co.—when solving, with a lucidity of intellect which is very remarkable, difficult matters of business, that you were so thoroughly master of the situation that you were a veritable 'Master of the Ceremonies.'"

"Taking the 'M. C.' in that light, Father Whitehead, I take it as a compliment. Please go on with your account of how you 'raised the wind' from your friends."

"They received my application very kindly, sympathized with me, hoped that my partner would soon be again attending to his responsible duties, and talked as if they were there and then ready to grant me the necessary aid. But when I mentioned £200—I wished afterward I had said £1200—as the sum I needed, they thought it so trifling an amount that I had better try and pull through by making very close collections."

"Just the advice I should have given you," said Mark, kindly.

"As soon as my partner was able to resume his duties I told him I could not understand the state of our finances. He thanked me for my efforts, during his absence, in carrying on the business. By borrowing some small sums of money on my own private account I had appeased the clamor of several creditors, and his mind was relieved to that extent. He promised to keep things financially straight. That, however, with him was an impossibility: his books were figurative cobwebs. For over two years we struggled along as best as we could. I was continually being called upon to raise more money. At last I said, 'Partner, I in no way doubt your integrity, but tell me how it is, when you have always represented to me that the business was making good profits, and that there have been few bad debts—and then only for insignificant amounts— that we are always so hard up for money.' His reply was so incoherent that I was sorry for him, and I did not press the inquiry further. Very soon after this he proposed to retire from the concern. I acceded to his terms with the proviso that as to his name was attached a fair amount of credit, I should keep the name of the firm as it was until I saw my way clear, financially, to relieve him from all pecuniary responsibility. To this he agreed, and I took the business into my own hands.

"Immediately I called in professional accountants, handed over to them all books, accounts and papers, and told them to get a new set of books, and, meanwhile, to put me in the way of seeing, week by week, how I stood. After the second week they assured me that there was life in the business. I told them I should remodel its connections by seeking new customers and discarding several old ones whose work was alike troublesome and unprofitable. This I did so successfully that my spirits revived more quickly than they had drooped. My accountants had supplied me one book, which was so columnized that it served for entering orders, the cost of all work, the total charge—the difference between the cost and the charge columns being the approximate net profit. At the close of each week these columns were accurately footed, and the profit found to be very encouraging. Indeed, so much so, that long before the accountants had perfected their balance-sheet of the condition of the business at the time of the dissolution of partnership, they assured me that I had a splendid trade and could easily get matters straight.

"It took the accountants four weeks to complete their statement, and when they presented it to me, as the best they could do with the material at command, I was stunned with the fact that the liabilities, over every available asset, were *eighteen hundred and eighty-three pounds, eighteen shillings, and sixpence!* and that, too, in only twenty-seven months' trading. Those prodigious figures were the figures of professional accountants—not of a book-keeper—and could not be gainsayed.

"In three months, having kept the new books with which they had supplied me, they gave me a second balance-sheet, which showed that I had wiped off a large amount of indebtedness, and they predicated that at the end of twelve months from that time I should be well out of the wood, even if the balance-sheet did not show a surplus."

"That must have been an awfully anxious time for you, Father Whitehead."

"It was, indeed, friend Checkup; but, as the sequel of my story will prove, the game was worth the candle."

"I'm all impatience for the sequel; so let's have it as soon as you can."

"I will, Mark. The accountants were young men like myself, and they seemed to take an especial interest in my affairs. They were most careful in fully estimating the wear and tear of machinery so as to keep the plant at its proper value, and they discarded every doubtful account from the assets. They also included in the expenses of the business a good round sum as salary for my services, and itemized it among the wages. Thus you will see, Mr. Checkup, that the profits shown upon the balance-sheet were profits indeed."

"That was a novel idea. I have always considered it was *the* thing in business not to charge a business with salaries for partners, but rather to make the profits of a concern appear as large as possible by the partners taking the equivalent for their services out of the profits shown by the balance-sheet. I see, now, how much fairer, from a strict business view, was the plan of your accountants."

"Well, then, if naught else comes of this story-telling interview, you will at least admit that the inspired apostle of American mercantile affairs has learnt something valuable from a London accountant."

"And I shall profit by it, I can tell you," said Mark, tapping his head as if he were trying to find, in the already over-crowded mental portion of his cranium, a place wherein to deposit the new inspiration.

"Now to cut a long story short, I will drive at once to the real gist of this writing.

"As my accountants predicted, at the end of the first twelve months of my trading alone, I was just financially even. In eighteen months I had a surplus of £300. In two years that was increased to over £1000, and at the end of the third year I was over £2000 to the good over and above every possible liability.

"Then, one day, quite unexpectedly a young man, who wanted to purchase an interest in a similar business to mine, was introduced to me. At first I did not give him the slightest encouragement. In a few days he called again to ask me if I was still in the same mind. I told him that since his first interview I had mentioned the matter to some friends, who advised me that as I had had a hard time of it for the past three years it would be well for me to seek a little relaxation, providing I could sell a half interest in my business on my own terms."

"'If you please, Mr. Reynolds, will you state your terms?' said my newly introduced friend.

"'Providing your references are satisfactory, and you are satisfied with mine, my terms are, that you should bring to the business an amount of capital equal to mine—£2253—and that you shall pay me £500 for a half-share of the goodwill of the business.' To the former he did not object, but to the latter amount he rather shrugged his shoulders. I was firm as to both requirements for I was in a position to be independent.

"He said he should have to refer the matter to his guardians, and would communicate with me in a few days. On the third day he came: said he had seen his guardians, but as one was a doctor of divinity and not accustomed to business transactions he should refer me to his other guardian—Mr. Kinglake, of Moorgate Street. With this gentleman an appointment was made. And to my surprise when I called at his office I found he was a lawyer. By one of his clerks I sent in my card. Presently Mr. Kinglake came out of his private room. After surveying me from head to foot he said: 'Yes, Mr. Reynolds, my ward has spoken to me about this business. I am very much engaged just now, and shall therefore only ask you two or three questions.' Looking at me straight in the eyes—my eyes straightened to his— he said:

"'Have you a balance-sheet?'

"'Yes, sir, I have several.'

"'Prepared by yourself or by an accountant.'

"'By professional accountants.'

"'Please name them.'

"'Messrs. Caldwell and Kennock, of 23 Coleman Street.'

"'Oh, I know them. Do you refer me to them?'

"'I do, sir.'

"'What are your terms?'

"'My terms are that your ward should bring into the business an equal amount to that which I have in it, and that he should pay me £500 for half-share of the goodwill of the business.'

"'Please write them down; give them to my managing clerk, and he will hand them to me. This is Tuesday; for an answer you can call on Friday at noon.'

"Apologizing for the hurried manner in which he had received me, he withdrew to his private office.

"On Friday at noon I saw Mr. Kinglake. He said he was very much pressed by other engagements, and simply remarked:

"'I have seen your balance-sheets and your accountants. I am satisfied with their representations of your business, and I have advised my ward to accept your terms. He will call upon you and arrange time for the signing of the deed of partnership and the payment of the money.'

"In due course everything was settled, and the new firm of Reynolds & Roberts was announced in legal form by advertisement."

"Is that *your* story?" said Mr. Checkup, directly I had ceased speaking.

"Yes; certainly."

"Well, then," said Mr. Mark Checkup, M. C., "all I have to say is, that as you, Father Whitehead, have dubbed me as being *the* apostle of story-tellers, I shall most certainly dub you as *the* prince of those apostles. Good-day, Mr. Whitehead. I sha'n't forget this morning's interview."

To all business men the moral of this true story will be found in its title — "*The Value of an Accountant's Balance-sheet.*"

Father Franklin.

THE PUBLIC DEBT AND THE IMPERILLED NATIONAL BANKS.*

At the outset let us concede that the public welfare is the sole consideration at issue. It then remains to discover what is good public policy, and, when discovered, to pursue it.

To avoid one point of controversey, we shall also concede that if our National banking system is to depend for ever upon the existence of a National debt, the National bank is doomed.

We may safely assume that the public cannot dispense with the business of banking. The banking business of the country should, therefore, be conducted with the greatest possible safety to the public. In the United States, three systems for this conduct exists, i. e., the National bank, the State bank, and the private banker.

On behalf of the National bank we submit that among the more than 2000 National banks in existence during the two and a-half years to November, 1882, employing in all an average capital and surplus of about $600,000,000, there have been only three failures. Of the 2752 National banks organized for business during the twenty years to that date, the failures among them have numbered, all told, but eighty-seven. Among these insolvent banks forty have paid their creditors seventy-five per cent., and twenty-one have paid their creditors in full. In no instance, of course, has the National bank-note failed of payment. To this element of public safety, in the method prescribed by National charter for the conduct of this indispensable business, add the advantages which an everywhere-existing, uniform and easily understood system of banking must confer upon the public, and it would appear wise, in the public behalf, to preserve the National bank, if it can be done at no great public cost.

But recount the features of this pre-scribed conduct to which in largest measure the infrequency and non-disastrous nature of failures among the National banks is due, and it will be discovered that the effect of these features upon the minds of those who contemplate the system with a view to organize or continue business under it, is repellent rather than attractive.

The method prescribed for the conduct of National banks includes the provision of a central control for all, at Washington, and involves the right to visit and examine at unexpected intervals. It provides for public displays of actual condition upon demand of the Controller, and at dates of his own selecting; the requirement of a lawful money reserve against deposits, and the requirement as to accumulating surplus capital; the restriction as to amount and the securities for loans, and as to the payment of unearned dividends; the prohibition as to loaning on pledge of any of the circulating medium of the country, and as to the over-certification of checks; the prescribed minimum of capital permitted any bank, and the additional liability of stockholders for all debts, contracts and engagements to an extent equal to the par value of their stock: and, further, the penalties attached to misdemeanor and malfeasance in office, with the fact patent that the whole power of the general Government is at command to enforce them.

The upright, of course, are in no dread of law, but it may be assumed that men will not be eager to organize or continue under this National system for any personal gratification which officers and directors and shareholders can discover in all these provisions, though these same provisions are found to constitute the public safeguard. It would thus appear that in this, as in every other busi-

* The first portion of this article containing a plan of legislation for the relief of the banks was read by its author Mr. William P. St. John, President of the Mercantile National Bank of New York, at the recent Bankers' Convention. He revised the Paper, and added an argument in support of his plan. Published in the *Banker's Magazine*.

ness, *inducement* must be permanent if the National banks are to be preserved and multiplied.

The prevailing inducement to organize and continue under National charter has been the profit on the issue of circulating notes. This is evidently true of the National banks of the non-reserve cities —the so-called "country banks." The National charter requirement of reserve against deposits, a portion of which reserve may be placed on cash deposit in National banks of the reserve cities, is of no special avail to these said "country banks." Let these country banks withdraw from the system, and then the National banks of the seventeen reserve cities, other than New York, will no longer be indebted to their National charter for what country bank balances they may thereafter employ. Next, let these seventeen reserve cities' banks withdraw, and then the National banks of New York City also will owe nothing to this reserve requirement for any out-of-town banks' balances which they may thereafter have the use of, the profitable employment of which is now their prime inducement to continue under National charter. That the inducement of profit on note issue should prevail hereafter, is, therefore, of public importance, because vital, perhaps, to the future of the National banks. But the public has another and more immediate interest in the preservation of this system, now in measure threatened by the continued retirement of the three per cent. bonds. Last year's surplus revenues applicable to the reduction of the public debt amounted to about $155,000,000. This year's applicable surplus is safely estimated at $120,000,000. At this latter rate of Government income the entire $300,000,000 of three per cents. might be retired within three years, and $200,000,000 of these bonds are on pledge for the circulating notes of National banks. The present high prices for the fixed-date bonds appear to preclude the hope that the banks will purchase them to replace their pledged three per cents. as called. If none shall be replaced by purchase, two-thirds in amount being pledged for the bank-note issue, the public must prepare for a currency contraction of some $60,000,000 within the year.

At this point we ask attention to certain circulars, emanating from a highly respectable firm of Government-bond dealers, displaying profit on the circulation at present prices for fixed-date bonds. These circulars used to issue on the basis of a six per cent. employment of money. They now appear on a five-per-cent. basis, and when next they issue a lower rate may be assumed as a satisfactory employment of money, in order that everything additional may appear as "profit on circulation." The unusual investment assumed for the calculation —$1,000,000—is also noteworthy. The result, of course, is a goodly array of figures. If, however, they be accurate, these figures merely serve to show that the investment, for "circulation," in the better-paying bonds of all, the four per cents., at present market prices, 122 per cent., will furnish something over five per cent. per annum as the entire earning on any sum thus invested; further, that with the present tax on circulation removed the entire annual earning on the money thus employed is but six and eighty-eight-one-hundredths per cent.

But imagine a National bank possessed of $1,000,000 capital being authorized to issue $800,000 of circulating notes at a purchase and pledge of $899,000 of bonds, and buying four per cents at 122 per cent. There must then appear at debit of premium account the startling sum of $195,000. In recognition of the conservative element in its community of dealers, the bank is a rarity indeed that would issue and circulate its reports of condition at such a showing for the temptation of a five per cent. or fifteen per cent. per annum employment of its means.

This view, with the likelihood of enhanced market prices, were any general purchasing movement for the fixed-date bonds begun, would seem to dispose of the suggestion that the removal of the present tax on circulation would afford the sufficient inducement required. But better than theory to support our view, we observe that for the year, to October, 1883, the increase of National-bank holdings of the high-priced four per cents. has been about $1,000,000, against the increase of $7,500,000 of the four and-a-half per cents; the four per cents. all the time offering the much better profit on circulation.

With this aversion to a premium account thus manifest, let it be further observed that the newer localities, smaller cities and country towns, offer the highest interest rates for the employment of money; then, in this connection, to question the profit inducement to take out or to continue circulation, attention is directed to the last annual report of the Controller of the Currency, from which it appears that of the $315,000,000 National-bank notes outstanding, $227,000,000 were the issues of the country banks. If there be no sufficient inducement at something over five per cent. per annum to these banks to purchase the fixed-date bonds, then if not at once, yet at the first advance in market, there may appear sufficient temptation to those of them who now pledge four per cents. and four and a-half per cents. to sell their bonds for the better employment of their means. If this selling movement were begun and persisted in, we should have, in addition to the fairly estimated $60,000,000, currency contraction reasonably to be counted upon, a thus made *sudden* contraction of the currency, the possibilities of which are appalling.

But these selling banks are not in jeopardy. They profit if they sell. This apprehension, if warranted, is thus a *public* peril.

It is in the public behalf, therefore, that we ask immediate relief.

It has been proposed that the Government income be diminished. Some advocate tariff amendment for this purpose; others demand the total repeal of internal taxation; others, again, denounce any attempt to impede the steady reduction of the National debt, and are ready to treat any such attempt as a step to antagonize the public and the banks.

Therefore, whether or not it be wise to continue our past or present rate of debt-reducing, it would at least appear certain that the question of tariff reform and internal-revenue repeal may wisely be avoided for the moment, if it be possible to accomplish our purpose by a method distinct from either.

The demand for immediate results further prohibits the hope that attention can be had for anything new in theory, at present, aimed at the perpetuation of the National banks. Within two and a-half years the banks have been required to substitute their five per cents. and six per cents. for three and a-half per cents., and next for three per cents., until now these three per cents. have become the basis of $200,000,000 of the circulation. It need thus occasion no surprise that in these numerous substitutions the rapidity of the change should promise us a crisis when suddenly these three per cents. are now to be retired. Multitudes cannot be educated in a day. Therefore, with the endeavor to discover a plan of relief along the line with which the public is familiar, we offer the following suggestion for the Government proceeding, viz.:

To the National banks now pledging three per cents. or four and a-half per cent. bonds as security for their circulating notes, issue in exchange at par, if desired, twenty-year two-per-cent. bonds, and upon the ninety per cent. of notes allowed on pledge of these two per cents. remit the tax on circulation.

Next, extend this privilege of exchange, when desired ·to banks now pledging four per cents. or currency six per cents. for this purpose, the Government to purchase these bonds at prices which shall amply provide these banks in the exchange their present annual earning on circulation for the period of twenty years; provided that this exchange shall be made only when and so long as the surplus revenues applicable will admit.

Next, extend this privilege, if desired, to owners in general of the fixed-date bonds: for the four and a-half per cents. at par, and for the four per cents. and six per cents. at prices determined for the aforesaid banks, and only when and so long as the surplus applicable will admit.

Thereafter, apply any remaining applicable surplus to purchases of fixed-date bonds, or to the retirement of three per cents. while any remain and as may appear expedient in the discretion of the Secretary of the Treasury. And thereafter let debt-reducing proceed with all convenient dispatch by purchase of outstanding bonds.

Then all these proposed two per cent. bonds must bear the same date of issue, that all may mature at one time, and the Act must provide the assurance that the privilege of an untaxed note issue against these bonds, to the extent of ninety per cent. of their face, shall continue in force during the entire twenty years.

For the three per cents. the exchange proposed, on the terms named, would be desirable on any possible estimate of the remaining life of these bonds. For the four and a-half per cents. at par and the four per cents. and six per cents. at purchase prices required, the following will display the measure of the inducement to exchange. Assuming an interest rate for the calculation — say six per cent. per annum—and $10,000 of bonds, without allowance for redemption, it will appear that the

Twenty-year two per cent., for *untaxed* note issue, is worth a present premium of	$1,618.03
Six-and-a-half-year four and a-half per cent., *tax on* circulation is worth.....	1,595.26
Longest date, fifteen-year, currency six per cents., *tax on*, is worth..........	4,021.45
Twenty-three-and-a-half-year four per cents., *tax on*, is worth..............	3,128.15

Thus the four and a half per cents. may be surrendered in the exchange at par at a saving of premium of 22 $\tfrac{77}{100}$ per $10,-000, say at a quarter per cent. profit. The longest date currency six per cents. must be bought at the difference of premium between $4021.45 and $1618.03, say $2403.42, i. e., at 124 per cent., the market price being 138 per cent. The four per cents., at $3128.15, less $1618.03, say $1510.10, must thus be purchased by the Government in the exchange at 115½ per cent., the present market price being 122 per cent. In view of the three and a-half years longer life of the four per cents. than of the proposed two per cents., 115½ per cent. might be paid for the four per cents. in the proposed exchange. The fact that there is no promise of the continuance of the privi-

lege of note issue against these four per cents. during all the life of the bonds will further serve to make the exchange attractive. And, besides, their refusal to exchange would thereafter leave these four per cent. and six per cent. holders to face the contingencies of the future as a small minority among the National banks. An additional incentive, applicable also to both, is the release of premium to the extent of the price of the Government purchase of these bonds. These prices for purchases of four per cents. and six per cents. must, of course, be lowered as the bonds approach maturity.

To estimate the Government's profit or loss in these several transactions for the proposed exchange, it will be fair, first to assume that if the Government is a borrower at all for the term of twenty years, two per cent. per annum is preferable to a three, four, four and a-half, or six per cent. rate of interest for its loans. Therefore, the issue of a two per cent. bond at par in substitution and retirement of a bond bearing a higher rate of interest would appear profitable to the Government without doubt.

For the longest-date currency six per cents. the estimate would appear as follows:

Present Government obligation is fifteen years' interest, at six per cent.............................	$9,000	
Less fifteen years' *tax* on circulation	1,350	
		$7,650
Face of the bond...............	..	10,000
Present total obligation to pay...	..	$17,650
Against premium to be paid on $10,000 bond at 124 per cent.....	$2,400	
Twenty-year interest payments at two per cent....................	4,000	
Face of the bond at maturity (twenty years hence)................	10,000	
Total proposed obligation........		$16,400
Net cash gain to the Government by the purchase and exchange...	..	$1,250

For the four per cents. the estimate would appear as follows:

The existing obligation for $10,000 of these bonds is interest at four per cent. for twenty-three and a-half years....................	$9,400	
Less twenty-three and a-half years' tax on circulation..............	1,800	$7,600
Face of bond at maturity........	..	10,000

Total obligation to pay........... ..		$17,600
Against premium on the four per cents. at 115¾ per cent., say,.....	$1,550	
Twenty years' interest at two per cent..........................	4,000	
Face of the bond at maturity....	10,000	
Total proposed obligation.........		$15,550
Actual gain to the Government... ..		$2,050

If the suggestion that the Government purchase any of its bonds from banks at a premium is obnoxious to some, it may be replied that the present rate of annual income, if it should continue, would insure the complete retirement of the three per cents. within three years as already stated. Thereafter, debt-reducing must proceed by purchase of outstanding bonds, and without the influence upon the market price which our plan provides in the remaining $100,000,000 of the three per cents. left outstanding and subject to Treasury calls. Besides, this plan would afford the opportunity to retire these bank-held four per cents. at seven per cent. less, and the six per cents. at fourteen per cent. less than current market prices for these bonds. This, in view of the probable enhancement of price to take place when the Government must needs become a purchaser, would seem finally to silence this objection.

There is a second objection which might weigh with some, *i. e.*, a seeming discrimination against owners of three per cents., other than National banks. This, however, would appear free from the taint of injustice, their present status considered, and the result of our plan might serve even to profit these other holders by a longer deferred retirement of their bonds. And supposing there be no real delay in this retirement for these holders, then the objection, at its worst, must disappear in the public gain to be secured by the important results achieved.

In suggesting twenty years as the life of the proposed two per cent. bond, we have been influenced, *first*, by the recent Congressional enactment of provision for charter extension of the National banks, which was for this period of twenty years; *second*, the bank-held four and one-half per cents. are thus sure to be attracted to the exchange *at par;*

third, this being the case, no purchase of bank bonds at a premium at all need be made in order to forestall all present danger of currency contraction, or to preserve the National banking system for twenty years to come. So much of our plan as provides for the purchases of bank-held bonds, is therefore in the public behalf primarily. The Government would profit by the transaction. Secondarily, however, this part of the plan is important, in order to attract to a single basis of security for their note issues the whole number of the National banks. Thereafter all would be prepared to discuss new theories for the perpetuation of the system from the point of a common interest in results to affect them all alike.

As to the effect on debt reducing, let it be observed that the proposed exchange of fixed-date bonds for the twenty-year two per cents. on the terms named, though profitable for the purpose of an untaxed note issue, as against the present taxed note issue, would not be profitable to the ordinary investor at the purchase prices proposed. Then the entire ownings of National banks, for security of their circulating notes, are in all only $360,000,000 of bonds, out of the total $1,200,000,000 Government bonded debt remaining. Further, it may be said that while the profit on circulation, which our plan provides, will tend to attract those about to organize for the banking business to select the National system, there is no sufficient profit provided to induce organization for the sole purpose of issuing circulating notes.

To recapitulate, then, we would advocate this plan of Government proceeding:

First.— Because it distinctly waives the issues of "tariff amendment" and "whisky-tax repeal," and thereby affords the hope of *prompt* relief from present perils of currency contraction.

Second.— It imposes no actual impediment upon the steady reduction of the public debt.

Third.— It appears to offer attraction to the whole community of the National banks. It would thus, if adopted, induce them all to a single basis of security for their note issues, as a common ground of interest in any measure thereafter proposed pertaining to the future of the National banks.

Fourth.— It provides for the preservation and multiplication of the National banks for the period of twenty years, the time limit of their original charter.

Fifth.— It offers the inducement of profit to organize and continue under this system in preference to the other systems of banking named.

Sixth.— It offers to the banks this sufficient inducement of profit on circulation without actual cost to the Government.

Seventh.— It affords this profit without the objectionable necessity of a high premium on the bonds required.

Our plan, if adopted, will thus serve to retire some $200,000,000 of three per cents.; $100,000,000 of four per cents.; $40,000,000 of four and a half per cents.; $3,000,000 of currency six per cents., and instead the United States will have issued the like amount of its twenty-year two per cent. bonds at par, and sure to be maintained in market at never less than par. No diminishing of the public revenue will have been required. No impediment upon the steady reduction of the public debt will have been imposed, and we shall have dispelled all fears of currency contraction by means which effect, for twenty years, the preservation and multiplication of the National banks.

A QUAINT OLD OFFICE.

Not long since I wandered into a strange, old-fashioned office. Stepping over the threshold I felt those subtle whisperings of fancy which come to a man when he treads among byways now given over solely to memories of past days, incidents laid away in the sacred archives of time. From the ceiling— cracked and stained by the ravages of decay and dilapidation—grim cobwebs swung to and fro as the slight draught came through the open doorway. The small, diamond-shaped panes, covered with dust, sifted the straggling sunrays, causing them to assume a softened, mellowed hue as they played upon the floor.

There, in the corner, groaning underneath a massive pile of yellow, dust-laden papers, was the desk, once the pride of some faithful knight of the quill, whose bones have long since crumbled into dust. And arranged along the sides of the room in regular rotation are the old ledgers: their backs are well worn, and their leaves are dog-eared. Upon a shelf stands the old sand-box, now only an object of curiosity to the observer.

Above me I hear the ceaseless clatter of hurrying footsteps. The rumble of wheels and the clang of iron hoofs reach my ears. 'Tis the business, the never ceasing business ebb and flow; and I am here, alone in the quaint old office, surrounded by the things of by-gone days, yet all associated with the growth of the to-day's great flood of commercial life.

Dare I raise the lid of the old desk? Can I, without removing the mass of papers piled upon it? Slowly, inch by inch, I lift the lid, and—the papers tumble to the floor. A thick cloud of dust arises from the disturbed mass, and I am, as it were, surrounded by the halo of old times. The rustling papers seem to whisper to me, in soft, low tones, words of reproach; they seem to chide me for having disturbed them from their long rest. However, I secured one glance of the interior of the desk, which fully repaid me. In one corner was a basket of letters, dainty and yellow, like the old papers. The packet was tied with a faded ribbon. Not for the world would I penetrate the secrets those old letters told; for they concern only two—the man and woman whose lives were bound together for two-score years and more— the sweet old couple now lying side by side in Greenwood. I saw a bunch of quills—stubbed, inky, ragged, and useless. What messages they must have told, long, long ago! They have told of men's credit, and, mayhap, have signed the death-warrant of some of the old-time commercial giants. Life was as full of romance in their days as it is now, and love may have engaged more than a passing fancy from the quills.

After restoring the papers to their place upon the desk, I seat myself in a leather-cushioned chair opposite the tallest pile of ledgers, and am lost in that mystic realm of Fancy's visitation, so strange to he who dwells among it — so unreasonable to him who cannot comprehend its meaning.

The very lowest ledger of the pile moves from its place and stands upright upon the floor. Slowly and softly the covers are pulled apart by some invisible hands. The leaves are turned back; and as their faint rustling greets me, the sound seems like some human voice speaking to me from afar.

"Here's Miles Standish — the staunch one of old—the grand, the noble man of Manhattan's Isle. 'Tis with pride that I point this great old gentleman out to you. Here his figures are traced, fine and clear. Here you see the god-like hero of the grand old days, the noblest American of them all — George Washington. And upon the opposite page is Arnold: he whom the States detested for his treachery; whom they respected for his bravery ere the tempter's foul tongue blasted his fame. Burr, the incomprehensible: the man of the gifted tongue, the fascinator of women, and the slayer of the State's greatest financier. This noble one opposite, Hamilton. The unwritten history of these men is contained among these old, yellow pages; business, business, business, about which the world cares but little in connection with the historic lights placed before your gaze."

Slowly, as though crippled with rheumatism, the old ledger hobbled back to the pile and slid into its place as its fellows raised themselves up. Ah! what is that? There in the center of the room, with his double chin folded in two layers upon his silk stock, is a short, stumpy, old man. In front of him is his great, great grandson, now a middle-aged man of wonderful business qualities.

"Well, my boy, how many vessels have you got upon the seas?" asked the little old man.

"Twenty-four."

"Bless my stars! So many? *I* thought two were enough to keep me busy," said the little old man as he lifted his hands in astonishment. Then he asked:

"How many clerks?"

"Two hundred and forty."

"What? I had three. Well, well, business has grown, to be sure. What has become of the *nest-egg* I left to this house?"

"It came to me — ten millions of dollars. I shall leave it to my son — double ten millions."

"This completely staggered the little old man. He gazed upon his great grandson as though he doubted his words. Finally, with a sigh, he said:

"It is a great change. Once this room was the honored office of a great house. When *I* was in it it was the meeting-place of commercial giants. If those jolly old chaps were here *now*, and could hear you speak of millions as they spoke of thousands, they would feel like puppets in comparison to you, my honored prince of commerce. Since my little nest-egg is lost among your millions, I will take my departure. Allow me to bid you a very good afternoon."

With a polite bow, the little old man tipped his hat, took a pinch of snuff, and sneezed himself away.

Was it a fancy, I wondered? While I was trying to unsolve the mystery, a hand was laid upon my shoulder, and a voice said:

"Well, young man, haven't you been among the old things long enough?" It was the janitor.

"Who was the old fellow?" I asked.

"What old fellow?"

I saw that he did not understand, and I said no more. Wrapped in thought I turned my back upon the quaint place — forever.

H. S. Keller.

COUNTING-ROOM CHATS.

Printed Letter-headings.

From G. F. Brown, Ogden, Utah.

Could you offer, through the columns of your magazine, any suggestions that would aid a subscriber in the use of printed letter-headings where it frequently occurs that more than one or two pages are required in a single correspondence ? It has often occurred to me that the use of duplicate sheets of printed headings in a single letter was not altogether good taste, or in accord with strict business economy.

REPLY.— Since printed letter-headings have come into such general use the question presented by our correspondent is only one of many which have arisen concerning the style, form, and economy of letter-headings. An endless variety of tastes may be observed by looking over the headings of letters of correspondents. On some appear a profusion of fancy types covering about one-third of the sheet; on others, only a line or two of miniature print will be seen delicately tucked up in the left-hand corner; while, again, others will take the medium between the two extremes. Some will be found printed plainly in black; others, in brown, carmine, purple, or some attractive color ; while others will present all the varied shades of the rainbow, resembling a decorated poster of a comic opera, or the fantastic pictures of a Humpty Dumpty primer. Some will appear printed from type; others will be elaborately engraved, presenting finely drawn pictures of buildings or establishments. Where two or more sheets are necessary for containing the communication, it seems like an uncalled-for waste of labor and material to use duplicates of elaborately printed headings ; and not only *that*, but it may look to some like a desire, on the part of the writer, to crowd upon the attention of his correspondent an advertisement of the writer's business. Especially may this be the case where the writer uses only one

28

side of the paper, and that the side printed or engraved upon. We have observed that some correspondents, to avoid this seeming intrusion, turn the second and subsequent sheets over, using the plain side for their writing.

This objection raised by our correspondent is overcome by having sheets of plain paper, corresponding in size and quality to the printed headings, for the duplicates. In cases where it is necessary that the sheets should be copied in a letter-press, the plan adopted by many mercantile houses, of printing across the top of the blank sheets a line to be filled in with the name of the person addressed, and the date of the communication, may be accepted as a model.

A style that prevails to some extent, but more in England than here, is to use full sheets of note-paper, with the printed headings on the fourth page. This allows the writer more space on each heading, and also avoids an accumulation of waste paper with those to whom the letter is written. If the letter is short, only a half sheet need be used ; if it is long, a full sheet may be covered, and there is but little waste of space in headings. In copying, the sheet is opened out, and the two pages appear side by side in the letter-book.

Where paper is of sufficient thickness for both sides to be written upon with legibility, there can be no objection in ordinary correspondence to that being done. Speaking for ourselves, we would prefer to receive a letter written upon two pages of a single sheet than upon two separate sheets of paper. If the communication is expected to go into the hands of a printer, the case is altered. Printers do not like a manuscript written upon both sides of the paper, because the side lying upon the case, while the other is being set, is apt to become disfigured and rendered illegible by the metal of the types.

One advantage in writing upon both sides of

the paper, for ordinary correspondence, is the saving of space required in filing. Duplicate sheets of paper, written only on one side, are cumbersome and fill up the letter-file with waste paper. There is no greater trouble in copying both sides of a letter-sheet at once than of copying two sheets—the only disadvantage being that the two pages will not be side by side, but on opposite pages of the book. This, however, is not a serious objection.

Certified Checks.

From PACIFICUS, New York.

I was very glad to see the subject of certification again under discussion; especially as to the comparative merits of the New York plan of stamping the check as good; and, on the other hand, the Boston plan of taking up the check and issuing in its stead the check of the cashier on the bank itself.

Long ago, in an ancient periodical called, I believe, THE BOOK-KEEPER, which was issued in the infancy of counting-room journalism, I tried to make a discussion of the question, but nobody replied. Either my article was too convincing or too tedious—take your choice. Then, as now, I was an adherent of the New York school, but desirous of learning the reasons for the other practice and its advantages.

I have read with great interest Mr. Cochran's defense of the cashier's check; but I think it leaves much to be said. I join with him in the wish that some practical banker will enlighten us. Especially do I hope some Pittsburgh banker who has, as Mr. Cochran says, become a convert to what he calls the "new" doctrine, but which I always believed to be older than

certification. I know what practical bankers in New York will say, for I have asked several, and their unanimous opinion is that the New York volume of business could never be done on the cashier's check plan. What we want is an argument from the other side.

In the first place, I quite agree with Mr. Cochran that certification without immediately debiting the depositor's account is a most dangerous and censurable practice. And all I shall say will be on the assumption that when the paying-teller marks the check as good, he instantly makes an entry, the effect of which will be, when it reaches the ledger,

Depositor | Certified Checks.

No New York bank would dream of any other procedure than debiting the dealer and crediting certified checks' account. By the way, I find that the Chase National has a very neat system which supplies the voucher for posting, and Mr. C. rightly declares it to be a necessity. (I took the liberty of calling at the Chase after reading the article in your September number, and brought away a lot of new wrinkles not therein described.) The paying-teller has a padded blank, on which he records the name of the depositor and the amount of the check, draft or note certified, the amounts being columnized as belonging to the various ledgers, "National" "State," "Individual A to K," etc. This slip goes to the book-keeper as the voucher or slip from which all the postings are made. I will send you a copy of the slip, and if the printer can work in an imitation of it he is welcome to do so. So *that* difficulty is disposed of.

The first reason given for preferring the

CHASE NATIONAL BANK,	CHECKS CERTIFIED.	188				
No.	Name.	P'st'g	Individuals.	National Banks.	State Banks.	When Paid.
	Individuals..... National Banks. State Banks.....					
First Teller	Total					

cashier's check is, if I understand aright, to make the transaction similar to the one where the depositor purchases exchange on New York, paying with his own check for the banker's draft on a New York bank. But, *first,* why is it desirable to do two different things in a similar way? why enforce uniformity at the expense of convenience? *Secondly:* If it is advisable to testify by issuing a second obligation, why does not the drawee of a bill of exchange, instead of accepting, issue a promissory note for the amount? This would be on the same principle. And as a third answer, some country banks are adopting the sensible plan (according to my view) of stamping their depositor's own check at his request, "Payable at the National Park Bank of New York," thus applying the certifying principles to inland exchange. I have known this to be done by a Wilmington bank in drawing on Philadelphia, and by a Concord (N. H.) bank on Boston.

As to the subject of safety, I cannot see wherein it is any more difficult to forge a cashier's check than a certified one. One correspondent says he never heard of a forged cashier's check. Well, I have. I have handled two: Boston and Baltimore. And about a year ago I received a circular saying that an organized gang was operating entirely with what purported to be cashiers' checks.

As to the other side, I think one check is easier to write than two, and that it is more logical to unite in one voucher all the successive parts of a transaction than to split it into several. The indorsement of a check is a valuable receipt; the drawer loses this vital advantage if he takes a cashier's check. He might as well take the money, and I know that he frequently would. The Boston banks have to use much more currency than the New York banks; a State bank (no circulation) could not live in Boston, and there is not a single one there. Often the holder of a check, not the drawer, wants to have it certified for safety, and then indorse it over so as to preserve the connected history of the whole affair on one piece of paper. Notes are certified, too, when due. This is a convenience. In short, the whole tendency of the New York method is to concentrate all the transactions into the exchanges at the Clearing-house, and the more this is done the greater the economy of time and labor, as shown by experience.

It seems to me that the Boston-Pittsburgh

plan has one use—perhaps not intended—that of avoiding the law against over-certification. Congress, in its wisdom, legislated against over-certification, but did not prohibit overpayment. Why not pay, then, with a cashier's check? That the Wall Street banks did not adopt this easy means of evasion is another proof that they considered it so awkward as to be impracticable.

Labor-saving Device for Posting.
From T. L. PALMER, Des Moines, Iowa.

The device described by Mr. Jaffards, I supposed, until I read his article, was known and used only by myself. In 1880 I had occasion to have a desk built, and incorporated as a part of it an arrangement so very similar to the one described by your correspondent that I saw at once how it was that "great minds often run in the same channel." I think the plan I had for the smaller part, or the ledger desk which stood at right angles with the main part, was somewhat more perfect than that described by Mr. J., as mine was made so as to revolve easily, being made somewhat after the plan of an office-stool or similar to the little revolving tables often seen in hotels for holding the great register. The device is, as Mr. Jaffards says, an important affair for saving labor where large books are in use. It is much easier to get at two books when lying at angles to each other than to move back and forth and to be continually twisting the books into a more convenient position. The device needs only to be tried to be appreciated.

The Real Author of Ware's Method Heard From.
From J. S. RUSSELL, Lowell, Mass.

In the July number of AMERICAN COUNTING-ROOM C. E. Cady asks: "Can any one tell who is the author of it?"—that is, a certain method of averaging accounts which he assumes to criticise. His criticism seems to me to be open to criticism. But I will first speak to his question.

Some years ago a friend informed me that a prize of $10,000 had been offered for the best method of averaging accounts, and that his daughter said she wished Mr. Russell knew of the offer. This was within about a week of the time set for the decision. I supposed the limited time would prevent my entering the competition; but I immediately concocted a method and forwarded it directly to Prof. Ware, instead of to the Committee. At a meeting of the parties it was said there was a disagreement in regard to the kind of funds of which the award was to consist; the result of which was that $1000 in cash should be the award, and the decision deferred to another time, when, lo, and behold! the prize was awarded to Prof. Ware himself!

On examining Prof. Ware's method, the likeness to my own method was so complete that I could not avoid the conclusion that my rights had not been properly respected. The slight modifications of my method, I think, were not improvements.

Mr. Cady adduces three examples worked by the method under consideration—two of which he says are certainly wrong. Now, if the incorrectness which he finds is the result of his working the problem, what becomes of his criticism of the *method?*

As I work his first example by this method, the average date falls between five and six o'clock on the morning of December 18th, which, Mr. Cady says, is the correct date. Where, then, is any error? An excess of a fraction over even days may well be allowed to carry the average date over to the next day. Here, as also in his second example, I find the average date on the morning of May 2d, where he fixes the date. Hence Mr. Cady, rather than Prof. Ware, should shoulder the error.

The items in this example are so large that a fraction of a day becomes important when absolute correctness is required. There is a possible moment in the second day of May, which, if Mr. Cady should use in his proof, his balance would be all right.

His third example, correctly worked by this method, gives the average date 16 days 9 hours into December, or at 9 o'clock on the morning of the 17th; and not on the 16th day, as Mr. Cady's working by this method fixes the date.

Mr. Cady's objection to this method, that it ignores the inequality of calendar months, is not tenable; for when time is given in months, calendar months are used. But time is generally required in days, which are distributed by calendar months.

The results worked by this method may be as accurate as desired; and the ease of counting the time and counting the interest are sufficient to recommend it above all other methods.

Aluminum Pens.

From M. S., Portsmouth, O.

Can you inform me where the Aluminum pen can be found? It is stamped

MYERS'
ALUMINUM
Birmingham.

What is a Dozen?

From J. G. C., Santa Fe, N. M.

A question has arisen here which involves the definition of a dozen. A customer ordered a dozen jugs, and was supplied with three—the dealer claiming that three of the size ordered were a dozen. Will you state what is customary?

REPLY.—To most persons a dozen would appear to be a definite quantity, and if the inquiry were made, How many constitute a dozen? the answer would unhesitatingly be, twelve. Some might make an exception, and say that thirteen constituted a baker's dozen. The sense in which it is employed in some parts of the world, however, gives a very different view of the case. In the Staffordshire potteries, and in the English earthenware trade, a dozen represents that number of any special article which can be offered at a fixed price. In this trade the prices remain fixed, while the number of pieces furnished for the price varies according to circumstances. The number to the dozen varies. For instance, jugs are sold as 2, 3, 4, 6, 9, 12, 18, 24, 30, and 36 pieces to the dozen, depending upon the size of the pieces and the condition of the market—the price for a dozen remaining constant. The ordinary size holding a quart is called a "twelve,"— signifying twelve to the dozen—while the size holding a pint will be twenty-five to the dozen; and is so designated in the trade. Few of the articles in the earthenware trade are sold in dozens of twelve. Plates are, to a certain extent, handled in this way; and yet there are exceptions among them, for in some cases they are sold sixty to the dozen.

I. A. & B. C. M. U. S. N. A.

From NAPOLEON TAYLOR, Secretary.

I beg to intermit de report ob the previus meetin ob dis Institoot.

De meetin ware called to ordah wid the president in de chare. De minits of de last previus meetin habin been red and reproved, a slite discushin follered on de recurrense at de last meetin aforsaid between brudders Caradam Smith and Cheesit Pumroy. De sense ob de meetin, as declarated by de president, was dat de way in which brudder Smith was sot on by brudder Pumroy was not in accordance wid de rules of de duells, as rekognized by de gilded yuthes ob de age, and dat nothin short ob an abject apology and de offer of a large watermillion from de next plantin could wipe out de disgrace. Brudder Pumroy, in his usual elementary manner, said dat so far as de meetin was konserned he heahby tendered his apology fur de interrupshun. But at de same time he hoped dat no udder member would tempt him agin in de like manner. Nuthin, he sed, plezed him more dan it did to imprint on de mind of a common brudder of de organizashun de rectitude wid which he should conport hisself in de presence of his souperieors. Continuin, he sed dat he wanted to warn all, dare and den, dat he would not be reprehonsible for de konsequenses if such another occashun should oppertuniate. So far as brudder Smith was konserned, he willinly apologized to him for not havin conflicted more obstreperous instigation. De brudder said dat he konsidered dat a man, and even a member ob dis Instiloot, whom was so enviable ob his feller benighted assosheates wasn't kalculated to have much existense, and dat dare would be okashun to hang craip on de door ob de Smith manshun de next time de same sirkumstances was reperpetuated. Brudder Pumroy den sat down, and for a minit dare was such silence dat you could heah a crowbar drop. Den de hole Instiloot, wid de ekseption of brudder P., rose up and sed: "Mr President!" and de noise was so deefenin dat for about a minit de President could not make hisself herd. Bein a powerful man, however, wid de assistunse ob a gablle about fore feet long, he rekonsiled de most domicilatory ob de members, and at last redused de meetin to its poleval state. He den vigorusly remarked dat de langwage of de brudder was so onbareable dat he called on de members for an impression ob de feelins which de remarks occurred.

Brudder Pineapple sed dat he konsidered de entire bizness tempestuous in de extreme. De brudder den moved dat Cheesit Pumroy be obliterated from de membership. De mo-

tion ware declared to be suffishently punctilius dat it dit not hab to be seconded, and was put to vote, and ware pusilanimously carried. Derefore, the name ob de honurable Cheesit Pumroy was spunged from de parchment. De expostulated member done left de room by saying dat Brudder Pineapple would be waltzed home before mornin on a shutter. De brudder referred to, however, took his aperature early, sayin dat a sea-sick wife required his divulgence at home. He ware unobsearved to go out de reer doah.

Brudder Brown, ob de Examinin Committee, reported progress on de names propozed for members, and said dey seemed to know a good deal about book-keepin—espeshally borrered ones. Dey ware all elekted, but, bein short ob cash, de Examinin Committee reported a large stok ob turnups on hand, which it was desided to sell cheap fur de money. When it ware diskovered dat de new members was elekted, de sekretary ware ordahed to uniform dem ob de fac, and enklose a bill for de inishiashun fee wid dews fur de las six months.

No furder business comin up, all discussion was declared in ordah, and Brudder Brown led off. He said dat de idea ob postin from anythin but de slate was absorbed—dat he would like to know what de slate was fur. Brudder Jones interrupted him by sayin dat he thought de brudder ought to know, as he had seen his name several times on de one kept at de corner. Brudder Jones was fined fifteen cents for interruptin de meetin, and settled by givin his note ob hand, on demand wid interest.

Brudder Brown went on to say dat if de slate was not to post from, what was de use ob de slate? Ef you was gwine to post from pieces ob paper, dat you might jist as well not hab any slate at all—jist put it down on de slip of paper in de fust place.

Brudder G. Washington Jones den rose and said: "Mr. President and feller members of de instiloot! de gemman as has succeded me, takes the ground dat he can't post from nothin but de slate—dat may suit him. As fur me, I would be willin never to see a slate agen. When I was a small chile, durin my infancy, de fust thing I had to figger on wus a slate; when I didn't know my lesson in de school I ware batted ober de hed wid a slate. Since den, when in a fit of substraction, I hab gone out widout payin for de purchas; and when I went to de place agen I found my name on de slate. At de last primery meetin, we made up a slate wid de names ob dose in de ring as candidates; but owin to a slite misunderstandin between two ob de members, de slate was broke, and we ware all left in de kold. No, brudders! let us leave de slate; and, havin our vouchments in a propper state ob disintegration, boldly post our ledgers, and den tare up de slips—dus avoidin any back postin."

ITEMS AND ACCOUNTS.	SALES A.	SALES B.	SALES C.	SALES D.	AMOUNT.
Smith & Post.........	.. ..	.. ..	50 ..	.. .	50 ..
Sweet & Olds.........	.. ..	60 ..	.. ..	.. ..	60 ..
.. "..........	.. ..	.. ..	10 ..	.. .	10 ..
John & Jones.........	.. ..	.. ..	.. ..	30 ..	30 ..
Kent & Kent	5 ..	.. ..	.. ..	.. ..	5 ..
* * *	5 ..	60 ..	50 ..	40 ..	
5%.............	.. 25	3 ..	2 50	2 ..	

De president heah remarked dat de brudders had stated de case freely and perplexedly, and as it was gittin late, and as sum ob de members libed in Jersey, he would call for de sense ob de meetin—de question bein: Is it proper to post into de ledger direct from de slate, or should de proper vouchments be made out and used in journal form? It bein decided dat it was, de meetin adjourned, and de members permeated to dere homes.

NAPOLEON TAYLOR, Sec'y.

Commissions Subject to Special Terms.
From H. FRIEDBURG, Toledo, O.

Referring to the inquiry of Mr. Mathews, of Dayton, O., on page 289 (November number), I would suggest that he should have in the cash-book a number of columns in which to enter the amount, according to a classification of sales, as shown in the above illustration. These commissions should be journalized at the close of the week or month, as might be most desirable.

₊ It does not appear to us that the information desired by the Dayton correspondent is fully furnished in the above communication. The point which occasioned the inquiry is, probably, that involved in the advisability of crediting-up commissions before they are due, coupled with a plan for treating notes, a portion of which, when collected, belong to an agent. To make the case plainer, we will suppose Henry Ruble, of McGregor, Iowa, is agent for B. Altman & Co., of Mansfield, O. Mr. Ruble sells a threshing-machine for $600; $100 is paid down, and the balance is arranged to be paid in notes. The commission is

twenty per cent. Of the $100 paid in cash the agent retains $20, and sends $80 to his principal; he also sends the notes for $500. As these notes are paid, 20% belongs to Mr. Ruble.

It is evident that it would be improper for Messrs. Altman & Co. to charge Bills-receivable and credit their sales or accounts with the full amount of the notes. Would it not be best to credit only their proportion of the notes to their operative accounts, whatever it might be, and place to the credit of a Commission Fund the amount which, when the notes are paid, will go to the credit of the agent? In the case cited, and including the full transaction, the entries would then be thus:

FIRST PART.

Cash............. 100 | Threshing-Machine 480
Bills-receivable .... 500 | Commission Fund.. 120

SECOND PART.

Henry Ruble.. ... 20 | Cash............. 20

Now, when the purchaser of the machine pays his first note, which, suppose, is $100, and interest, $8, the entry would be:

FIRST PART.

Cash............. 108 | Bills-receivable 100
| Interest.......... 8

SECOND PART.

Commission Fund.. 20 | Henry Ruble...... 20

It is possible that our views of Mr. Mathews's question are incorrect; but be that as it may, the above is offered only as a suggestion for the use of those who may feel disposed to give the correspondent the benefit of their knowledge and experience. Mr. Friedberg may be —and, no doubt, is—correct in his plan for the purpose intended; but if we are clear in our theory of the question, the reply he gives does not cover the ground upon which information is wanted. Mr. M. may be able to enlighten us.

Premiums of Life Insurance.
From JOSEPH COURAND, Castroville, Tex.

I have made it a practice to have premiums

of my life insurance, when paid, charged to my personal account. This, it seems to me, would make it appear on the books as a loss to my business, which I think is not a proper showing. I shall be thankful for your own or the views of your readers on this point.

*** There seem to be two questions involved, of which the more important is, Shall insurance premiums be considered as an asset? The affirmative were, at least in theory, true. The company owes the policy-holder a specified amount, if certain conditions be complied with, payable at a period certain but unknown, yet forfeitable on certain other contingences. What the value of the asset may be is an actuarial question. A fire insurance premium, on the other hand, is an expense — a minor loss voluntarily submitted to, to provide against a loss which might be ruinous. But we do not agree with our correspondent that charging his personal account would have the effect of representing the premium as a business loss. It would rather be a withdrawal of capital for private use.

Classification of Items.

From I. R. A., Poughkeepsie, N. Y.

Replying to Pendy's question, on page 356 of the December COUNTING-ROOM, he should charge office-furniture, fixtures, and petty expenses to the "General Expense" account, but he should keep a distinct "Horse and Wagon" account. This account should be opened by taking an inventory of horses, wagons, and harness on hand—the amount of which should be placed to the debit of the account; to the Horse and Wagon account should be charged amounts paid for horses, wagons, fodder, repairs, shoeing, wages of teamsters, and every other item specially connected with that department. At the end of the year inventory should be taken of stock on hand and amount of same brought down as a balance. The remaining amount, showing net cost of the department, can then be carried to "Profit and Loss"·—or, in the case of a manufacturing concern, to the account representing aggregate cost of the manufactured article.

From BETA, St. Louis.

In reply to "Pendy," page 356 in last number, I say that in no case is it proper or right to charge Expense account with expenditures in office-fixtures, horses, wagons, and such other

articles having a marketable value attached to them, which are necessary in the proper conduct of a business. If "Pendy" has no snch account, I would suggest his opening one and call it, "Movables and Fixtures," and charge that account with all purchases of the nature I mention and for repairs of same; and in the case of a sale of any articles credit the account with the proceeds; and at the general stock-taking and closing of the books, by making proper allowances for depreciation, etc., the account will speak for itself, just the same as the Merchandise account will do. In this way a clear and distinct history is had of that class of property which is too often neglected by book-keepers.

As to petty expenses, this term is too indefinite to give any intelligible reply. I would not allow such an account to creep into a set of books; no matter how small the amount may be, there is a proper place for it. I would sub-divide Expense account under the following heads: Insurance, Gas and Fuel, Salaries, Stationery and Postage (Freight is not expense), or any other source of outgo of a fluctuating nature; but anything of a fixed nature, as rent and taxes, I would charge direct to Expense account. In this way there would be no difficulty, I think, in placing any item of expenditure.

Scope of the Accountant's Art.

From ***, New York.

The following extract from the circular of an eminent firm of accountants, well-known both here and in Europe, so admirably defines the sphere of the profession as to leave no argument for its necessity to be desired.

The full scope of the business comprises:

The designing of books of accounts for any special trade, business, or purpose, and the opening, balancing and closing of the same.

The auditing of the books of accounts of all corporations, including railroad companies, banking and insurance corporations, municipal corporations, water-works and gas-works, iron and other works, public, mercantile and manufacturing coporations, and of private individuals and firms.

Examining into the financial relations existing between all corporations, their branches and agencies.

Auditing and certifying statements of corporations to stockholders, or for the use of directors, managers and trustees, or as a basis of reports to State officials.

Auditing and certifying reports made by agents to principals or parent companies in other States or foreign countries.

The liquidation of the affairs of individuals, private firms and public corporations.

The investigation and adjustment of disputed accounts and of partnership and joint accounts.

Examining and reporting upon the statements, facts and financial conditions, upon the strength of which it is proposed to found commercial, manufacturing, mining, financial or other undertakings.

Examining and reporting on receivers' and trustees' accounts for settlement and acceptance in court.

Searching books of account by order of court for the purpose of establishing evidence of facts, or for testing probable theories.

Examining and reporting upon the accounts of insolvents, and upon the value of their assets.

Estimating and reporting on the value of securities, and comparing them with vouchers and entries upon account-books.

Supervising and directing inventories of stock and assets, and the proper balancing of sets of books, so as to show the real state of affairs of a business or coporation.

Examining the affairs of embarrassed but solvent debtors, and of insolvent debtors.

Arbitrations.

The preparation of the accounts of executors and administrators, and trustees; ascertaining the respective interests of legatees and other beneficiaries in the estates of deceased persons, both as to principal and income, and their apportionment.

Overhauling old books of account for stating the interests of minor children, or absent parties,.and for final settlement.

Searching for errors, intentional or otherwise, in accounts, and correcting the same.

Defining a Trial-balance.

From A. A. ROCKWOOD, Olean, N. Y.

A correspondent asks for a definition of a trial-balance. Its usual office is a proof of the ledger. It is not positive proof, however, as two contra errors in posting would leave the ledger accounts in balance, and yet two errors would exist. I have found much satisfaction

in making a classified trial-balance. The method of doing this is as follows:

Before crediting to the merchandise account the amount of the inventory, take off the ledger balances in a classified form. To illustrate:

John Brown owes us 20.00		20.00
Labor for the month 200.00		
Coal " " 100.00		
Expense " " 200.00		
Raw material, cost 1000.00		1500.00
Total		1520.00
Bills-payable		1000.00
Mdse. sales for month		520.00
Total		1520.00
Inventory of goods on hand..... ..		200.00

By the above it is shown that raw material, labor and expense for the month cost..1500.00

The sales of merchandise		520.00
Inventory		200.00
Total		720.00
Then what has cost 1500.00		
Is worth only 720.00		
Hence the loss 780.00		

This, then, is common-sense in accounts irrespective of double-entry. The same information could be obtained through single-entry, but the proof would not be so conclusive or reliable.

Having ascertained that the loss was 780.00 the inventory may now be credited to the ledger. Then Merchandise should be closed into Loss and Gain, and Loss and Gain into Stock, or partners' accounts. From the face of the ledger make a statement of Resources and Liabilities; the books are then in readiness for the new month. The statement of Resources and Liabilities proving equal, another trial-balance is thus produced.

The advantage of a classified trial-balance is, that while proving the ledger you determine, with much more promptness and facility, the results of the business, and are able to make a showing much quicker.

Titles for Class Accounts.

From PENDY, Detroit, Mich.

What is the proper title for those classes of accounts comprising the individual accounts due the concern, and the individual accounts of those to whom the concern is indebted? Is it

"Accounts-receivable" and "Accounts-payable," respectively, or is it simply "Personal accounts" for both kinds under one general heading?

REPLY.—The class of personal or individual accounts — meaning accounts with persons, firms or corporations, which represent the concern's debtors, is properly designated as "Accounts-receivable"; and the class representing persons, firms or corporations indebted to the concern, is properly styled "Accounts-payable." In making up financial statements it is frequently advisable to combine with the personal accounts the account of bills, either receivable or payable, according to the class; and in such case the proper titles are, "Accounts and Bills Receivable," respectively. In using the term "personal accounts," it is intended to express all that class of accounts outside of those representing property values, or which show results of the business; as for instance, various accounts which designate the profits and losses. It is used to denote both "Accounts-receivable" and "Accounts-payable."

Another title sometimes made use of for denoting personal accounts due the concern, combined with bills receivable, is, "Anticipated Resources"— meaning accounts which are classified and treated as resources or assets, but which in reality represent only resources in *anticipation*, and not in actual possession. People who have had much experience in business know that there is a certain distinction between a resource account, such as "cash" or "goods," and one like "John Smithers." Cash represents a value that may be positively relied upon, while the account of Mr. Smithers may, perhaps, never prove of any tangible value. It represents a tangible asset, which is expected to be received at some future time, but which may never prove of any value beyond the alluring anticipation. On the other hand, the class we have designated as "Accounts and Bills-payable" are sometimes termed "Contracted Liabilities." In every case of indebtedness a contract is either expressed or implied. To make a debt is to "contract" it —that is, giving either an expressed or implied obligation to pay; hence the designating title.

Advanced Methods for Bank Book-keeping.
From M. C., South Bend, Ind.

I was interested in the article in your Sep-

tember number, entitled, "Advanced Methods in Bank Book-keeping," which I heartily applaud for use in city banks, but do not think practical for use in country banks. Methods in banks in commercial centers, and those in towns with only local depositors, must differ very materially in details; so much so, that what is just the thing for one may not suggest even a starting point for the other. How would it do to extend a general invitation to bank book-keepers in cities of *60,000 and under* to prepare short, concise papers on bank book-keeping and practice in all departments, from the time the doors are open in the morning until the last man is ready to leave at night; only two of such papers — those which offer the more *new* and *good* points — to be published at your direction; writers to give their methods with the thought that, while many or all of their ideas may not be new or original with them, yet they may place others on higher ground, and furnish material for discussion, thereby drawing out new and, probably, improved methods from others. You will bear in mind that the book-keeper in a country bank does not have the same facility for comparing ideas with his co-workers that is open to those in cities, and many not over-burdened with originality plod along in the paths their grandfathers trod, doing much unnecessary work, and leaving undone much which should be done.

*** We should be very glad to have just such an interchange of experience as you suggest. Consider the invitation extended to all, and be the first to accept it. We will, if the suggestion is favorably received, be able to make a summary of all the material thus collected, which will be very interesting.

In the early days of THE BOOK-KEEPER we published an invitation to our readers in banks to assist us in making such a comparison of methods. We were not successful in drawing them out, for, besides the smallness of their number, their was at that time a bashfulness about appearing in print which our periodical has succeeded in overcoming. Our invitation contained a sketch of the plan of such reports which may even now be suggestive. We proposed the following list of questions: What are the principal books used in your bank? What is the arrangement and use of each? What course is taken by each of the following transactions in passing through the book — a deposit, a check, a remittance (*to New York*), a draft, a certificate of deposit, a certification (*if you certify*), a discount, a loan, a collection?

Accounts with Cash Customers.

From DEVONSHIRE BOOK-KEEPERS, Boston, Mass.

In our business we have a great many cash transactions requiring treatment similar to credit entries. For cash sales we make out regular bills, copy and receipt them. Our copying-books are kept carefully indexed and posted up. An examination of the copying-books will show exactly what has been sold any day—the items as well as amounts. The proprietors, it seems to us, are rather notional about some things, and especially about these cash transactions. They insist upon having a journal entry made explanatory of each and every of the many petty cash sales, and those entries posted to ledger-accounts the same as though they were credit sales.

This entails a large amount of what appears to us as unnecessary labor, and encumbers the ledger with a vast number of accounts with strictly cash purchasers.

Should like to hear from your readers as to whether the practice demanded of us is customary, and if in their opinion there could exist any reasonable need of it?

_**_*The question raised here is scarcely worthy of discussion, except on the ground that the practice referred to is one that is occasionally insisted upon by proprietors who are more captious and exacting than intelligent. The only reason for the rule, at least in the cases where we have observed it in force, is that the ledger shall show the names of all persons with whom business is done. That it is important to have a record of the firm's customers, and the names of those to whom sales are made, where the goods sold were of sufficient consequence to demand a receipted bill, no good business man can doubt. It is important, too, that provision should be made for a ready reference to transactions, through either an index of names or index of goods. It is often a special necessity in mercantile houses to be able to ascertain the cash customers, what they have purchased, and what prices were charged them.

If a good cash customer comes into the store and says he wants a dozen pairs of sheep-shears or elephants' tails of the same make and quality to those purchased last June, though he has forgotten the brand, it is a very pleasant situation to the proprietor to be able to know precisely what is wanted, and a very embarrassing predicament if he is unable to tell anything about it. It is often these little conveniences that enable merchants to secure customers and hold them.

But the correspondents say that in their case this convenience is provided for by an indexed copying-book containing all cash sales, an examination of which will at any time furnish the desired information. If the book contains *fac-simile* copies of all bills sold, and these are carefully indexed, we can see no good reason for demanding a ledger account to be kept with cash purchasers. There must be some other reason than the one we have referred to. One little improvement might be suggested. Would it not be well to have two copying-books for bills of sales—one for credit, and the other for cash bills? It is true that this would not be as convenient for reference, by the proprietor, as a regular ledger account containing the items as well as dates and amounts. There appears, as we advance, abundance of room for something to be said, and we shall await the response of our readers.

Improved Stock-ledger.

From WILLOW RELLEF, Canton, O.

In your reply to "E. E. G." upon the subject of stock-company book-keeping, in the December number, you say, "If a book of stock-certificates is properly made it can be used to take the place of a stock-ledger." Will you kindly give an illustration?

REPLY.—For the paper use sheets that will make a page about nine inches wide by twelve inches long. Perforate the page crosswise about five inches from the outer end, thus leaving for the certificate a sheet five inches in width by nine inches in length. The stub will be seven inches in width by nine in length. The front part of the stub from which the certificate is detached will form the credit side of the ledger account — the back of the stub forming the debit side of the following account. When the certificates are issued and detached, the stubs will form a neat ledger, with ample space for all the entries that would be required during a number of years. The stubs of the sheets should be ruled in ledger form, and any specially desired style of ruling may be adopted.

FORM I.— FACE OF CERTIFICATE AND CREDIT OF LEDGER.

CERTIFICATE No. *5000.*

Jan.	10	Cash in full of 100 shares........	..	..	10,000	..
July	1	Dividend No. 1..................	500	..		
Jan.	1	" No. 2..................	300	..		
July	10	" No. 3..............	700	..		

Perforated line

CERTIFICATE OF STOCK No. *5000*
OF THE
MERCURY and MOON AIR LINE RAILROAD CO.

No. of Shares,

This is to certify that Man-in-the-Moon, or the holder hereof, etc., etc.

FORM II.— BACK OF CERTIFICATE AND DEBIT OF LEDGER.

Transferred, without recourse, to
HUMPTY DUMPTY,

July 1, 2146.

....
....
....

Man-in-the-Moon, Lunar City.

Jan.	1	100 shares, at par value of $100.	..	..	10,000
July	8	Cash...	500	..	
Jan.	5	"	300	..	
July	1	Transferred to Humpty Dumpty			
	15	Cash...........................	700	..	

If the certificates are issued before the stock is paid in full, and therefore subject to future calls, there should be double money columns upon both the debit and credit pages — one column for the stock, and the other for dividends. If, however, the stock is paid in full before the certificates are issued, single money columns only would be required, as the only entries to be made after the first would pertain to dividends.

When a stockholder sells a part of his shares, surrendering his certificates and asking for new certificates, the account with the first certificate is closed and new ones are opened with the certificates last issued. In cases of transfers of the stock in blocks, without the requirement of new certificates, the transfer may be noted in the ledger account without the necessity of opening a new account. The index may be made to form a part of the book, or an index independent of the stock-certificate ledger may be used. The illustrations herewith will probably serve to give a fair idea of the formular arrangement.

Collections of Traveling Salesmen Again.
From H. J. CARR, Grand Rapids, Mich.

Noting the "advice" of Mr. Beach in December number, and the editorial comments following, upon the above-named subject, and as the writer of one of the mentioned three communications in the November number, I may say, that as a matter of business policy I have no exception to take to the rule laid down by Mr. Beach ; I believe it a sound rule, and that the "advice" is good. But as accountants, we are usually expected to do as our employers wish, rather than to *advise* or *dictate* to them as 'to what they shall or shall not do in their business practice. If they prefer to have their travelers collect of customers, it is certainly their right ; and we are simply called upon to keep account of the same in the best and most feasible way. In that belief and spirit did I understand the original question to have been asked, and hence answered accordingly.

Certified Checks.
From A COUNTRY BANKER.

Your Pittsburgh correspondent asks in your last number for the views of a practical banker on the subject of "Cashiers' Checks *vs.* Certified Checks." I therefore venture to give mine.

It requires much less time and is much less trouble to certify a check and make a memorandum of it than to draw and record a cashier's check. And in the press of business, during the hours a bank is open to the public, time and trouble saved count no little. On the customer's part the certified check is more satisfactory, because he ultimately receives it back as a voucher with indorsements on it that make it a voucher again to him for money paid.

In practice there is no difficulty found in the want of the veritable voucher. A simple memorandum is made at the time by the teller, for example, thus : *

CR.

CERTIFIED CHECKS.

John A. Jones, $1,275.00.

This is used first as credit-ticket for certified checks ; then put on the check file, charged to the customer, and filed with his checks. When the account comes to be balanced the checks are usually in hand, in which case the memorandums are destroyed ; otherwise, they are delivered with other vouchers ; the depositor, understanding the transaction, knows just what they represent, and that he will receive the original vouchers at some future time.

I also use cashiers' checks, but generally issue them for transient deposits to represent opening petty accounts ; also, in payment of loans to occasional borrowers and similar purposes.

I conclude, then, that the certified check accomplishes what the other would—and a little more for the customer--is less trouble, and equally as satisfactory to the bank.

You will understand, though, that I speak as a country banker, being sensible that the experience of such offers no parallel to that of his fellows of the great cities, where the magnitude of the business, the larger clerical force, and the consequent division of labor and details, make the conditions so very different that with them a reverse opinion might follow.

Cannot we hear from some of the city brethren?

---

* These memorandums are from a pad used as credit-tickets, and are about the size of a postal-card.

Legal Miscellany.

PARTNERSHIP PROPOSITION.— SUFFICIENT ACCEPTANCE.

Plaintiff and defendant were co-partners doing business as brewers under the name of Winslow, Moore & Co. On or about December 21st, 1880, defendants made the following proposition to plaintiff: "We hereby offer to sell and transfer to Charles Winslow all of our right, title and interest in and to the partnership property and assets of the firm of Winslow, Moore & Co., of which we are members, for the sum of $7,800, to be paid when the conveyance of our said interest is made, he to fully protect us and save us harmless of and from all the outstanding liabilities and indebtedness now existing against said firm. In case he does not accept said offer, we hereby offer to him, for his interest in said firm, the sum of twenty-five hundred dollars in cash, on his conveying the same to us, and to fully protect and save him harmless from all the liabilities and indebtedness now existing against said firm. This offer to be accepted on or before the 1st of January, 1881." On the 30th of December, 1880, plaintiff signed and delivered to each of the makers of this proposition the following acceptance:

"Gentlemen—I hereby accept your offer to sell your interest, assets and property of Winslow, Moore & Co., for $7,800. I will be prepared to accept the transfer, and pay the money, etc., at W. & J. D. Kernan's office, on Friday, December 31st, 1880, at 2 p. m."

Defendants refused to carry out their proposition, and plaintiff brought this action to compel performance. The claim made by defendants was that the paper delivered by plaintiff was not a sufficient acceptance, it containing merely an acceptance of the offer to sell, and not of the proposition to save them harmless, etc., and that the designation by plaintiff of the office was a different place of performance than the law would have fixed—to wit, the place of business of the parties.

Judgment was given for the plaintiff, and on appeal it was sustained, and it was

Held, that the acceptance was an unconditional and unqualified acceptance of all the terms of the offer. *Winslow* vs. *Moore et al.,* N. Y. Supreme Court, General Term, Fourth Dept., June, 1883.

ADULTERATED TEAS.— ENJOINING SALE.

The Health Department of the City of New York brought an action against James Purdon and others in the Superior Court of the City of New York, to restrain the sale of a quantity of teas which the Health officers alleged to be adulterated, unfit for use, and unwholesome. These teas had been announced and offered for sale at auction in May last, and were green teas of the kind known in the market as "Pingsuey teas."

Judge O'Gorman has recently handed down an opinion, admitting the fact of adulteration to be clearly proved, but denying the application for an injunction on the ground that there was not sufficient proof to establish the fact that the effect of such adulteration would be to render the tea seriously detrimental to health, and unwholesome as an article of human drink, without which proof no sufficient ground would exist to enjoin their sale.

In his opinion, the Judge says: "Pingsuey teas are a low and coarse grade of teas grown near Shanghai, in a district where the soil is too poor to raise a finished leaf. Of late years, the 'Pingsuey' teas have been steadily deteriorating, from the fact that the growers have raised too much of these teas, until they have now become the coarsest and commonest teas in the market. The average 'Pingsuey' tea should not be classed as tea at all, but as an imitation of tea. The teas in suit are the poorest of all of these 'Pingsuey' teas yet seen in this market. They are found to be colored green heavily by means of mineral matter composed of Prussian blue. They contain soapstone (ground to powder), clay (called *terra alba* or *gypsum*), sand or gravel, and ash, and, in many instances, 'lie tea,' which is a substance made to imitate tea, and composed of unsound, exhausted and rotten leaves, filth, the sweepings of factory floors, and rubbish of all kinds, cemented together with starch or other adhesive substance, and made into particles resembling tea."

The question of adulteration being conclusively settled in the affirmative, the Judge goes on to consider the question of whether such adulteration is injurious or detrimental to public health. Upon this point, he says: "Competent experts — chemists of recognized ability and reputation — officers of the Board of Health, on whom are imposed the important duties of protecting the inhabitants of the city from the use of unwholesome food, as well as reputable merchants long engaged in the tea trade, and conversant with the values, quantities, composition, and mode of manufacture of the different grades of teas, have testified at length, and assigning, as I have endeavored to do, to the testimony of each witness, such weight and credit as it was fairly entitled to. I cannot say, from the evidence laid before me, that any serious danger to human life, or detriment to health is to be reasonably apprehended from the use of the teas in suit, which would justify the issuing of a perpetual injunction to prevent their sale. . . . .

"Without placing too much reliance, however, on such opinions or surmises, it is clear that the burden of proving that the sale of these teas threatens serious danger of injury to the public health is on the plaintiffs in this action, and they have not, in my opinion, succeeded in making out a case so clear and free from doubt as to warrant a Court of Equity in stopping or interfering with the transactions of a large and important traffic necessarily involving the use of large capital, and affecting the consumption of a beverage, which, although adulterated and deficient in the element of nutrition which genuine tea is said to possess, is yet cheap, and perhaps safer and less likely to injure public health than many other beverages to which the public, if deprived of this, might be inclined to resort." *Health Department* vs. *Purdon et. al.*, N. Y. Superior Court, Special Term, decided November 30th, 1883.

INSURANCE AGAINST ACCIDENT.

On September 6th, 1880, one Leonard Burkhard, a traveling salesman about to start upon a railroad journey, purchased from the Traveler's Insurance Company what is known as an "accident ticket." By this ticket the company agreed to insure Burkhard for a period of thirty days, in the sum of $3,000 against accidental death, and it contained the following condition:

"No claim shall be made under this ticket when the death or injury may have been caused by voluntary exposure to unnecessary danger, hazard or perilous adventure, or by walking or being on the road-bed or bridge of any railway."

On September 12th, 1880, Burkhard left Cincinnati, Ohio, for Louisville, Ky., upon the Ohio & Mississippi Railroad, due in Louisville at 11.40 p. m. of the same day. The train reached the Ohio river bridge, which is only a few squares from the Louisville depot, shortly after midnight, and was obliged to come to a stop upon the bridge, owing to the draw being open to admit the passage of a canal boat. While the train was at a standstill, Burkhard left his seat, walked out upon the platform of the car, down the steps, and alighting, went directly through a hole in the bridge, and falling a distance of 100 feet, was instantly killed. This hole had been opened by some workmen who were making repairs to the bridge, and had been left uncovered. Several other passengers had got out of the car, some of them in advance of the assured. The bridge, with the exception of this hole, was well covered with plank, and entirely safe. At the time that Burkhard alighted, several of the passengers were standing on the footwalk of the bridge, and the brakeman was sitting on a pile of timber on the footwalk, holding his lantern in such a position that the timber cast a shadow over the hole.

The company refused to pay the ticket, and in a suit brought against them the lower Court sustained their refusal, finding that "to leave a railway train in the obscurity of the night while it is standing on a railway track over a river" was a voluntary exposure to danger within the meaning of the contract, and also that the deceased "violated the prohibition against being on the track or bridge."

Plaintiff appealed, and the higher Court *Held* (1st), That there was not such a voluntary exposure to danger as to fairly bring the act of the insured within the meaning of the exception. (2d), That there was not such a walking or being on the bridge as to bring the case within the meaning of the prohibition contained in the contract; the purpose of such prohibition being not to avoid liability for injuries resulting from being on bridges unsafe in themselves, but to exempt the company from responsibility for damages caused by trains moving thereon.

The judgment of the lower Court was, therefore, reversed, and judgment for the plaintiff ordered. *Burkhard* vs. *Travelers' Insurance Company*, Supreme Court of Pennsylvania, decided October, 1883.

NOTES AND COMMENTS.

In a very learned article on "Defective Eyesight" Mr. Samuel York at Lee furnishes the readers of the *Popular Science Monthly* much valuable information concerning the results of investigations and experiments, both in our own and foreign countries, upon the subject of Myopia. According to the statements of the learned gentleman — which are, of course, all based on actual investigations — the school-children of the whole country are affected, more or less, with some form or another of this ever-spreading and rapidly increasing derangement. The investigations go to prove that, as school-children advance from grade to grade, the organ of sight grows weaker. It is stated by Prof. Calhoun, of Atlanta Medical College, "that in the interior of the eye there is an elastic muscle by which the sight is graduated to different distances. In the normal eye, the contractions and expansions of this muscle are not noticed by us. But in the near-sighted, or over-sighted, eye, the changes are violent, and sometimes painful, and eventually the action of this muscle is spasmodic and so weakened that the sight is permanently injured. "Near-sightedness," he remarks, "seldom begins until the sixth year, when children commence using the eye on school-books." According to "records of examinations of the eyes of forty-five thousand schoolchildren, of all ages and grades, white and colored," it is proved that near-sightedness increases gradually as the students advance.

"The causes to which this deterioration of eyesight has been attributed are alleged to be cross-lights from opposite windows, light shining directly on the face, insufficient light, small type, and to the position of the desk, forcing the scholar to bend over and bring the eyes too close to the book or writing-paper, etc. But were all these defects remedied, the integrity of the eye would not be restored, nor its deterioration prevented. The chief causes of the evil would still remain. These are the colors of the paper and ink. White paper and black ink are ruining the eyesight of all reading nations." It is the belief of the learned writer that our very common white paper and black type, or white paper and black ink, are in direct opposition to the suggestions of optical science.

Is it not possible that such argument as this will have a strong tendency to create, among the enlightened and educated people of the land, a demand for something less injurious to the eye than white paper and black ink? People who have so much to do with white paper and black ink as those who pore over ledgers, statements, and accounts, are, above all persons those most interested in improvements or changes that will save their vision. There is no reason why softly-tinted papers should not be used extensively in the manufacture of account-books and stationery. It is argued by Mr. Yorke at Lee that green paper is far preferable. A celebrated French Psychologist, in a chapter entitled "Sensations" says: "Green is the softest of colors, the most permanently grateful; that which least fatigues the eyes, and on which they will longest and most willingly repose. Accordingly, nature has been profuse of green in the coloring of all plants, and she has in some sort dyed of this color the greater part of the surface of the globe."

Let us, then, inaugurate a new era by demanding of our stationers and paper manufactures that they furnish us, upon which to write our accounts, and with which to print our books, green, rather than white, paper.

With this number we commence a new volume—one that we hope will not only give us much pleasure and satisfaction, but will prove of value and unusual interest to our readers. We shall aim so to conduct the magazine that it shall continue to be recognized in the future — as we feel assured it has been in the past — an authority on subjects of commercial science, business economy, and counting-room work.

———

Fully appreciating the broad field which it becomes our duty to survey we shall lay before our patrons what we believe to be the choicest and the best attainable information on those subjects which it is our special province to discuss; and during the coming year the magazine will contain a number of very important articles on topics of finance, trade, and the conduct of business affairs. Our articles on " Public Moneys and Accounts" will be carried through several numbers, and it is expected that when completed they will form a valuable treatise on the work and duties of various public officials and others holding positions where their services require a knowledge of not alone what they do, but what others, holding similar positions, have found expedient and practicable.

———

The departments of banking and manufacturing furnish, for study and experiment, fields of thought which, through the exposition of methods of practice and means used in the transaction of these important classes of commercial science, it shall be among our aims to bring out and fully demonstrate.

———

We shall endeavor from time to time to place before our readers reports of such lectures and public discussions as will add to their fund of information on subjects of business economy and accounts. We heartily solicit co-operation of thought and talent in enabling us to build up in the magazine the department of correspondence, which, we have every assurance, has been very kindly received, and is attracting the attention of many hundreds of our readers. There is scarcely a person enrolled among our list of subscribers, so far as we are able to judge, but who may be of service in eliciting some new idea that will tend to promote friendly discussion among a large class of readers. We shall, in this department, make every effort to bring about a freedom of thought and expression, by the means of which all may be more or less benefited.

The article which appears elsewhere under the title of " The Value of an Accountant's Balance-sheet " is suggestive of very many things we are continually prompted to speak of to our readers. The writer is a man who has had long experience in the business affairs of a very busy city. He is an Englishman, and in his native country was taught to appreciate the value of accurate book-keeping. In England much more attention is given to the subject of book-keeping than is the case in this country. The duties of a professional accountant in England became a positive necessity fifty years ago when the passing of the Bankruptcy Act compelled the filing of proper balance-sheets with the Bankruptcy Court before adjudication was entered upon; consequently those duties are, as a rule, quite dissimilar to anything that people on this side are familiar with. The plan inaugurated by Father Franklin's accountants of charging to the Expense account a stipulated or certain amount, regularly, for the services of the proprietor, is a practice that is well worthy of consideration. It is not entirely unknown in commercial houses on this side, but it is a plan that has not been adopted to the extent it should be. In a business where the proprietorship is invested in one or more individuals, and each devotes his whole time to it, there should be charged to the expenses of conducting the business a stated amount for the services of each proprietor. ———

As a theory, the business is, of course, as much indebted to the proprietor for his services, if he is dependent upon the business for an income, and devotes his time to it, as it is to any employee; and there is sufficient force in the argument to warrant book-keepers in following this practice, unless forbidden to do so by the proprietor himself. Some people are exceedingly notional, and for a book-keeper to undertake to adopt such a practice with an eccentric character, to whom the theory might appear absurd, might be worth the price of his position.

———

The chief point — and it is an invaluable one — made by Father Franklin is, that a balance-sheet prepared by the book-keeper of an English business house is valueless as compared with that prepared by a professional accountant, and indorsed with his name as a guarantee of its correctness. Other points are worthy of careful thought — not only by accountants, but by business men and business managers as well. It is, we take it, in no way belittling to a book-keeper for a proprietor to secure the services of an accountant to come in at stated periods, or at such times as he may think proper, and examine the books. It would really be an advantage to book-keepers if this practice were almost universally adopted.

Mr. S. S. Packard has kindly consented to furnish for our Febuary number an article embodying the chief features of the lecture he delivered before the Institute of Accountants and Book-keepers of New York, at their December meeting. Such an article may be made to set forth the ideas in a more comprehensive form than could be elicited from a report of a blackboard lecture, such as he favored the Institute with. It will enable the lecturer to incorporate many very valuable thoughts and experiences which could not well be brought out in a brief talk before an assemblage of patient listners.

We have received the Ninth Annual Report of the Board of Managers of the Book-keepers' Beneficial Association of Philadelphia, for the year ending December 3d, 1883. According to the report, the membership of the Society at present is 250. There were elected during the year 1883 forty members. There was a decrease of ten in the membership, namely, by death, four; by withdrawal, one; by striking from the roll, five. In his report, the President expresses his gratification with the substantial growth and prosperity of the organization. "Our membership," he says, "has largely increased, and our financial condition, notwithstanding our losses, is stronger. The stated meetings have been better sustained by the members. Harmony and goodwill have prevailed, and continued prosperity and success seem assured to us. With a noble aim in view, let us endeavor to put forth more earnest efforts for the best interests of our association by striving in every way to promote its welfare and success, and as the history of each succeeding year is recorded, let each and all endeavor to make it

a history of solid advancement and enduring prosperity." The very worthy secretary, in his annual report, urges upon the members a united action in aiding each other to promote their well-being. He reports that several members have accepted positions in other cities, but with all of them a steady correspondence is maintained, and they manifest no less interest in the organization than when they were residents of Philadelphia, and could attend the meetings. "Their eulogies of our thriving little organization," he says, "have doubtless aroused an enthusiasm among the fraternity in the West, as within the last six months associations similar to ours have been formed in Cleveland, St. Louis, and Chicago." The officers of the Philadelphia association are: *President*, John D. Ford; *Vice-president*, Horace A. Reeves; *Treasurer*, Watson De Puy; *Secretary*, Jas. G. Keys. The Directors are: Messrs. J. J. McLaughlin, John C. Garland, C. W. Sparhawk, Theo. B. Keys, R. C. Zebley, E. H. D. Farley, Elijah Baker.

Information continues to reach us concerning the subject of certified checks or cashiers' checks. A slight controversy seems to have arisen between several of our correspondents as to the merits of the two plans. A cashier of a small bank in Pennsylvania, a short time ago, was unable, through the use of cashiers' checks, to "accommodate" a friend who was in need of capital for conducting the business. Through the use of these cashiers' checks the friend so accommodated was enabled, for a length of time, to conduct his business on the credit of the bank; but the time came when the credit of the bank was not sufficient. Something more substantial was called for, and a collapse followed. The directors and stockholders of the bank mentioned are not at all in favor with the system of cashiers' checks. The sort of checks they seem inclined to most need are checks on the cashier. It is possible that the accommodating cashier would have been able to show his generosity for his friend through the system of certification equally as well as the manner in which he did. Over-certification of checks would invariably produce as direful results as an over-issue of cashiers' checks.

THE LIBRARY.

THE MODERN STENOGRAPHER. By Geo. H. Thornton. New York: D. Appleton & Co.

A very plain and simple exposition of one of the many slight modifications of Pitman's phonography. Care is taken to avoid the common fault of making the system too elaborate and complex. It is called a "light-line" system, but this consists merely, as far as we can see, in telling the advanced pupil to drop the shading of consonants. To give him a stylograph would serve the same purpose.

*AMES'S NEW COMPENDIUM OF PRAC-
TICAL AND ARTISTIC PENMANSHIP.
Giving more than twenty entire alphabets, with
numerous designs for engrossed Resolutions, Testimonials, Title-pages, Certificates, Monograms,
Miscellaneous Designs, etc., for the use of Pen-
men and Artists.* Daniel T. Ames, Author and Publisher, 205 Broadway, New York.

This is an excellent large work of just what is set forth in its title page. The illustrations are fac-similes of pen-productions. They are, therefore, far better specimens of real pen-work than are those which have been trimmed and toned over by the engraver's art. These specimen-sheets having been printed from photo-engraved or photo-litho-graphed plates produced from actual pen-produc-tions are the true evidences of what in the hands of the skilled artist the pen is capable of accomplish-ing. As an art-production the work is entitled to a place in the studio, the library, and the parlor. The opening pages are devoted to concise though comprehensive information on practical writing, in which is to be found many valuable suggestions and sufficient of the general rules and instruction upon the subject to make the treatise valuable in the hands of the learner. As an elegant birthday or holiday gift it would be difficult to find an article more appropriate to be presented to the young than one of these beautiful compendiums of true artistic merit.

Vick's Floral Guide.—Here it is again, brighter and better than ever ; the cover alone, with its del-icate tinted background and its dish of gracefully arranged flowers, would entitle it to a permanent place in every home. The book contains three beautiful colored plates, is full of illustrations, printed on the best of paper, and is filled with just such information as is required by the gardener, the farmer, those growing plants, and every one need-ing seeds or plants. The price, only ten cents, can be deducted from the first order sent for goods. All parties any way interested in this subject should send at once to James Vick, Rochester, N. Y., for the Floral Guide.

Latine is published during the present year by the Appletons. It is greatly enlarged and im-proved. All the features which made the first volume so attractive to those who take pleasure in keeping up their classical taste, are retained, with many new ones. A model lesson for beginners (for the suggestion of which Prof. Shumway gives us credit) proceeds on the plan of teaching by les-ser sentences all the words and instructions in-volved in some long sentence, which, when intro-duced *after* all this patient preparation, seems easy and familiar. We hope to hear the idea critically discussed by practical teachers.

Magazines for January.

The *Popular Science Monthly* opens with a discus-sion upon "The Classical Question in Germany," by Edmund J. Jones, Ph.D., Professor of Finance and Administration in the University of Penn-sylvania. Every person interested in this vital question should read what Professor James has said in this Paper. "Nowhere," he says, "has the struggle between the adherents of the old classical curriculum and the representatives of modern cul-ture been carried on with more bitterness than in Germany. In no other land have the respective antagonists shown more narrowness and bigotry, or been less inclined to allow their opponents the possession of common sense, or pure motives." But it is in that country, we are informed, that both parties are gradually receding from their extreme positions, and coming to approach each other with a more harmonious feeling. "This dis-cussion," says Mr. James, "which in one form or another has appeared in every civilized nation, has been everywhere marked by bitterness and preju-dice, and has resulted in a slowly growing victory for modern cultu e. The question has attracted renewed and wide attention in this country of late, owing to Mr. Charles Francis Adams's attack upon the requisition of Greek as a part of the course in Harvard College. The old weapons on both sides have been brought out and burnished, and made to do valiant service in the good cause. The result of the criticism and counter criticism has been to demonstrate pretty clearly that, however we may feel about it, the fact is that the cause of the ' mod-ernists' is gaining ground." We regret, exceed-ingly, that we are unable to give a more extended review of what this able writer has said upon the important subject, and would advise our readers—at least all who are in any way interested—to procure the Paper. The third article on "The Morality of Happiness," by Thomas Foster, is entitled, "The Evolution of Conduct," and is worthy of a careful and candid perusal. The second of two lectures delivered at the Philosophical Institution at Edinburgh, last November, under the title of "Female Education, from a Medical Point of View," is given in this number, and is an excellent contribution to science and education. "The Control of Circumstances," by William A. Eddy, is an interesting Paper. "Religious Retrospect and Prospect," by Herbert Spencer, a Paper, which, the author says, "will eventually form the closing chapter of 'Ecclesiastical Institutions.'" Part VI. of "The Principles of Sociology" is one of Mr. Spencer's strongest contributions to popular science. The interesting Paper, by Samuel Yorke at Lee, on "Defective Eyesight" will well repay perusal. "Catching Cold" is an instructive Paper, by Dr. Page. "The Source of Muscular Energy," by Professor Stillman, is an admirable contribution. "Idiosyncrasy," by Prof. Grant Allen, should have a careful examination. A large number of other very useful and instructive articles complete the number.

The *Century* furnishes as its frontispiece for the January number a most admirable portrait of Gen. Sherman, engraved by T. Johnson, after a photograph by George M. Bell. The accompanying article is from the pen of E. V. Smalley, and the writer acknowledges his indebtedness particularly to Gen. Grant and to Gen. Sherman for their information and for the revision of his proofs. The article, which covers twelve pages, is exceedingly interesting, though, of course, giving only a glimpse of the great General—his habits, and his very memorable career as one of the grandest soldiers the world has ever known. The opening article is from the pen of Andrew Lang, entitled, "Edinboro, Old Town"; the illustrations accompanying the Paper are magnificent. They were drawn by Mr. James Pennell, and engraved by a staff of noted artists, who have contributed largely to beautiful previous numbers of this magazine. The famous story of "The Bread-winners," begun last August, is concluded in this number. The very characteristic Paper, by C. C. Buel, entitled, "Log of an Ocean Studio," is superbly illustrated, and is written in a pleasing and attractive style. "An Average Man," by Robert Grant, begun in the December number, is continued. "The Forty Immortals," in connection with which thirteen handsome portraits of eminent French scholars and writers appear, is well worthy of its prominent place in this prominent periodical. The extracts from a journal of a trip to Europe in 1897, by the late President Garfield, entitled, "Gar-

field in London," is especially noteworthy. "Husbandry in Colony Times," by Edward Eggleston, with illustrations, forms a prominent feature of the number.

The January *Atlantic* may be referred to as an evidence that this popular periodical is keeping fully abreast with the times. The announcement of the publishers for the year 1884 gives assurance of some rare treats in the way of elegant literary dishes, prepared by the best authors and writers. "In War Times" is the title of a very fascinating story, by S. Wier Mitchell, complete in this number. "H. H." contributes a short, brilliant story, entitled, "Chester Streets." "The Bishop's Vagabond" is by Octave Thanet. "Iwan Turgenieff" is from the pen of Henry James. Mr. A. P. Peabody discusses the study of Greek, favoring its retention in the curriculm of higher education. Mr. Richard Grant White gives "A Sequel to Mr. Washington Adams" in a letter from Mr. Mansfield Humphreys. Mr. E. V. Smalley contributes a Paper on "The Political Field." The usual amount of serial stories, interesting short sketches, communications in "The Contributors' Club," etc., are found in the number.

Lippincott's Magazine for January gives its readers as a frontispiece a beautiful representation of the new City Hall in Philadelphia. The illustrated article with which the number opens, entitled, "Philadelphia's Hotel de Ville," from the pen of Edward V. Bruce, forms an admirable contribution both to literature and art. "Sebia's Tangled Web" is the title of a serial story, by Lizzie W. Champney. Next in this number Belle Osbourne has furnished a very characteristic production under the title, "Hawaii Ponoi." "Notes of Conversations with Emerson," by Pendleton King, covers a few pages, and might very acceptably have been enlarged upon. "Under-Graduate Life at Oxford" is from the pen of Norman Pearson. Under the title of "A Floury City" Mr. F. E. Curtis gives an interesting description of the beautiful city of Minneapolis, in which he thoroughly discusses the manufacture of flour, for which that city has become so renowned. "Matthew Arnold in America" is a brief sketch by Louis Judson Swinburne. "Healthy Homes," from the pen of Dr. Oswald—one of the best authorities of this country—is the title of a series of Papers to be given the readers of this magazine.

The *Phrenological Journal*, under the title of "Some Distinguished Visitors," gives brief sketches of Lord Chief-Justice Coleridge, Matthew Arnold, and Henry Irving, accompanied by handsome portraits of these prominent persons. "The Oratorical Type of Character" is a very able Paper, and deserving of close study. "China, its Age, Government and Social Customs" is a contribution by Mr. Albert L. Dunham, which is replete with valuable information concerning that peculiar people.

In the *Banker's Magazine*, among the very important subjects discussed, are, "Bank Deposits as a Circulating Medium," "International Movement of Money," "Annuities," "Judge Kelly's Silver Bill," "New Demands for Money," "Domestic and Foreign Trade and Finance," "Relative Populations," "Small Circulating Notes," "Political Economy in Germany," etc. The number is replete with valuable information for persons interested in financial and commercial subjects.

PUBLISHERS' DEPARTMENT.

We have received from Messrs. B. Lowenbach & Son, Milwaukee, Wis., a sample of their combined letter-sheet and envelope, for letter, note and billheads, statements, circulars, and the like, for which a patent was issued on October 30th, 1883. It is a very simple, yet neat and convenient, device, as it enables one not only to preserve the communication, but also to keep the envelope in which it comes in connection with, and attached to, the letter. The envelope part is formed by cutting down nearly one-third of the length from each end, through the centre of a sheet of full-sized letter-paper, and forming at the outer edge a circular projection, which laps over and seals the sheet when folded.

Messrs. Campbell & Smith, 110 and 112 Nassau St., New York city, manufacture the National Safety Paper, which is largely used in all parts of the country to prevent the alteration of checks, drafts, and other commercial documents. The cost of the Safety Paper is but a trifle in addition to the ordinary quality, and those engaged in business cannot afford to take the risk of having their notes or other papers altered or forged, when a means so simple and also so inexpensive is placed within their reach for preventing it. Specimen paper will be furnished by the manufacturers. Address requests to Mr. George La Monte, superintendent, 110 Nassau Street, New York city.

In the advertising pages our readers will observe the card of Mr. Thomas B. Paton, attorney and counselor-at-law; office, 23 Union Square, New York city. Mr. Paton makes the incorporation of firms and companies a specialty in his practice. We most heartily commend him to those of our readers who may desire the assistance of an able and straightforward lawyer.

Professor Thomas A. Rice, of St. Louis, Missouri, advertises in this magazine his work, entitled, "Prevention, Detection, and Correction of Errors in Trial-balances." Mr. Rice has had many years of practical experience as a book-keeper and accountant, and has evidently given the subject upon which he treats very long and careful attention. The work is highly reccommended by those who have had ample opportunity to test its merits. The price is $1.50, and the address of the publishers is 210 North Fourth Street, St. Louis, Mo.

The business of Ivison, Blakeman, Taylor & Co., New York has been increasing to immense proportions since occupying their new quarters at 753 and 755 Broadway. The firm is well known throughout the country as publishers of some of the best textbooks in existence. They enjoy a large and constantly increasing trade in almost all kinds of school-books and supplies, and are now extensive manufacturers of inks and pens. Their Spencerian Blue-Black Fluid is specially adapted to the use of accountants and office-work generally. It flows freely; never corrodes, nor oxidizes steel-pens; turns intensely black soon after being used, and does not fade. The various grades of Spencerian pens have already become great favorites. Those desiring to test the quality of these pens will be supplied with samples by sending to the manufacturers a three-cent stamp for postage. Samples of ink may be found in all first-class stationery establishments, and will be ordered by stationers or forwarded direct from the manufacturers.

Messrs. C. L. Downs & Co., of 320 Broadway, New York, manufacture a stylographic pen which retails at $1. It is highly reccommended, can be carried with safety in the pocket, and possesses many features of marked superiority. Their advertisement, to which attention is directed, appears elsewhere.

The Stokes Automatic Shading Pen which is manufactured and sold by J. D. Whitmore & Co., 41 Beekman St., New York city, is an instrument that no office should be without. It is exceedingly convenient for addressing packages, writes a peculiar and attractive style, and is very easily manipulated. It requires no special skill to become quite expert in printing with this peculiarly constructed pen. It writes and shades with one stroke. For particulars, direct as above, and also see advertisement in the advertising department.

Many of our readers will be glad to know where they can send an order, and have it promptly filled, for almost anything in the line of counting-room supplies. The Keystone Stationery Company make counting-room supplies a specialty. Their place of business is Lansdale, Montgomery County, Pennsylvania, near Philadelphia. The company carries in stock a line of goods that book-keepers, business-managers, and office-men are constantly using. They supply almost everything, from a box of pens or a paper-weight to an elegant counting-room desk or a fire-proof safe. They possess special facilities for packing and shipping goods to all parts of the United States and foreign countries, and from our knowledge of the concern we believe that any order placed in their hands will receive careful and prompt attention. The proprietor, Mr. C. H. Ahlum, is himself an old office-manager, and has had large experience in selecting goods for others. The advertisement, which appears in our advertising pages, will be found to give further information concerning the goods handled by the company, and we would recommend all in need of supplies of this kind to send for their illustrated catalogue and price-list, which will be mailed free upon application.

We wish to call the attention of our readers to the advertisement of the Fidelity and Casualty Company, of New York. It is the business of this company to issue bonds of suretyship, in which they become bondsmen for persons holding positions of trust, either in private or public concerns. Every person who has gone through the painful ordeal of calling on friends to become responsible for his acts, while in the discharge of important financial and commercial duties, cannot but hail with a sense of gladness the advent of a company organized for this especial purpose, The officers of the company are: Mr. Wm. M. Richards, *president;* John M. Crane, *secretary;* Robert J. Hillas, *assistant-secretary.* The principal office is at 179 Broadway, New York city. The Board of Directors consists of some of the best-known business men of the country. From our personal knowledge of the work done by the company we are prepared to say that it has not only proved to be a concern of great financial advantage, but a boon to many hundreds who have sought its aid, and been benefited by its organization.

Our readers, as a class, are persons who understand better than almost any other the value of good paper in books of account, and other articles of stationery. Almost every person who knows very much of the manufacture of paper is familiar with the name of Crane Bros., Westfield, Mass. Their papers are in use in almost every part of the civilized world, having been awarded prizes at four of the most important world's fairs. If, when ordering stationery or books, the specification is made for Crane's papers, it may be relied upon that the quality will be satisfactory. Persons using any considerable quantity of paper should not fail to have one of Messrs. Crane Brothers' sample-books, which can be obtained without cost by writing direct to the manufacturers at Westfield, Mass.

It is needless for us to mention to our readers the necessity of having none but a first-class, *permanent* ink about their stores or offices. Documents are often signed, contracts written, or papers filled out that involve a large amount of money, and are required to last for several decades. All sensible book-keepers (and what book-keeper is not sensible) feel this. But there is a point to which we wish to call their attention, and that is, that Carter, Dinsmore & Co., manufacturers of the justly celebrated "Carter's Inks," make enough *kinds* of ink to suit *all tastes,* and that *all inks* bearing their name are *permanent and reliable* inks. We are led to make these remarks from having just received samples of their Koal-Black Ink, and Arabin—two new products—the results of long and persistent labor and research. The "Koal-Black" is a very black ink when first put on the paper, and is much sought after by all persons wishing an ink that can be readily seen when written. Most book-keepers prefer "Carter's Writing Fluid"; but still, for ornamental or card-writing, billing, or outside work, we should think the "Koal-Black" would be the ink wanted. It is admirable for stylographic pens, being an intense black, and still fluid and non-corrosive. Their "Arabin" is a very fine article of mucilage. It is made from pure gum, with all extraneous matter eliminated, so that it is clear as crystal, and nothing is left but the sticking qualities. It is nearly equal to glue, in mending articles, and being so pure and clean is cheapest in the end, although a more costly product than their mucilage. It is a pleasure to use this, as well as their other goods, and we would say to our readers that if they have not tested these products to do so at once and be happy. Any information as to these inks will be given on application to Carter, Dinsmore & Co., 35 Batterymarch St., Boston, Mass., or 36 Dey St., New York City.

The title of a very comprehensive work on book-keeping is "Short Roads to Results in Book-keeping," of which Mr. O. C. West, of Syracuse, N. Y., is the author. The book sets forth a system of accounts which Mr. West has had in practical use for some time, thoroughly testing its merits, and is very handsomely bound and neatly printed. A more complete description may be found in a prospectus which will be mailed to any address upon application to the author.

BUSINESS REVERSES.

Banks, Brokers, etc.

Bank of Pike County, Pittsfield, Ill., assigned; paid-up capital, $50,000; deposits, $65,000.

B. C. Wickham & Co., Tioga, Pa., bankers; judgments for $125,000 issued.

H. S. Gilbert & Co., Ottawa, Ill., grain and bankers; confessed judgment, $43,000.

C. P. Crawford, Silver City, N. M.; assigned debts, $300,000; assets, $400,000.

Lamborn & Gray, Alliance, O., bankers, assigned.

The Grant Co. Bank, Silver City, N. M.; assignee appointed.

The Manufacturers' Bank, Amsterdam, N. Y., suspended; assets, $120,000; liabilities, $135,000. M. L. Stover appointed receiver.

Books and Stationery.

Geo. McDowell & Co., Philadelphia, Pa.; execution issued for $21,000; also, against Geo. McDowell for $20,000.

Boots and Shoes.

Arrington Bros., Boston, Mass., offer 50 cents; debts, $27,000; assets, $24,000.

Coal.

The Kankakee Coal Co., Kankakee, Ill., confessed judgment for $12,000.

Clothing.

Samuel Isaac, Mattoon, Ill., confessed judgment for $15,000.

Thomas Cunningham, New York city, manufacturer of skirts, assigned; liabilities, $28,000.

E. Langsdorf & Co., New York city, assigned on December 3d; debts reported at $80,000.

John Paret & Co., New York city, assigned; debts reported at from $250,000 to $275,000.

Sattler Bros., St. Paul, Minn.; debts, $80,000.

L. Rothenberg, Denver, Col., assigned; debts, $35,000.

Lesser & Wisotzky, Ishpeming, Mich., assigned; debts, $40,000.

Samuel Shapiro, New York city, assigned; debts, $25,000.

Cotton, Silk, and Woolen Manufacturers.

Edward Heald, Philadelphia, Pa., cotton goods; debts, $41,000; offers 50 cents to compromise.

Amos D. Smith & Co., Providence, R. I., cotton goods, assigned on 26th inst.; liabilities estimated at $1,500,000.

The Franklin Manufacturing Co., The Groton Manufacturing Co., and The Providence Steam Mill Co., have all assigned.

The Dover Silk Manufacturing Co., Paterson and Dover, N. J., in hands of receiver: capital of $26,000 paid in; debts reported at $102,000.

Clark & Kline, Amsterdam, N. J., knit goods, assigned Dec. 3d; debts estimated at $200,000.

S. M. Meyenberg & Co., New York city, silk manufacturers (factory at Hoboken, N. J.); liabilities reported at $225,000.

Russell Murry, New York city, silk yarns, suspended; debts, $102,000; assets, $77,000.

Geo. W. Stead, Philadelphia, cotton and woolen yarns, closed out by sheriff; debts, $25 000.

Slack & Gavett, Rushville, Ill., woolen mills, closed by sheriff; bill of sale to bank, $45,000.

A. & W. Potter, Danielsonville, Conn., casimeres, suspended.

Joseph Mullen, East Brookfield, Mass., woolens, failed.

Mrs. A. W. Kline, Amsterdam, N. Y. (H. P. Kline, agt.), knit goods, assigned; debts, $100,000.

Dry Goods and Notions.

G. L. Florence & Co., Atchison, Kas., notions, assigned; debts, $11,600.

Ludwig Schiff, Newark, N. J., dry goods, transferred stock to H. B. Claflin & Co., for $10,000; debts, $18,000.

D. M. & E. G. Halbert, dry goods; debts reported at $250,000; assets supposed to be less than $100,000.

Bomann & Von Bernuth, New York city, worsteds and trimmings, assigned; debts, $150,000.

J. McGough & Co., Columbus, Ga., assigned; debts, $55,000; assets, $30,000.

Cameron & Mareau, Chicago, Ill., closed by sheriff on judgment for $22,000.

Wm. B. Schoen, Litchfield, Ill., assigned; debts, $20,000.

M. Hammer, Matoon, Ill., confessed judgment for $9,000.

A. W. Turner, Brazil, Ind., failed; debts, $25,000.

Donald Gordon, assigned; debts estimated at $250,000.

C. A. Contant & Co., Chicago, Ill., fancy goods and notions, confessed judgment for $35,000.

Simon Henry, Chicago, Ill., offers forty cents; debts, $48,000.

Joseph Levi, Rock Island, Ill., failed; debts, $14,000.

McManus, Haire & Doolin, Providence, R. I., assigned; debts estimated at $125,000; assets at $160,000.

General Store.

T. A. Wickham, Tioga, Pa., failed; judgments for $40,000 entered.

John Garland, Aberdeen. Dak.; debts, $17,000; offers 60 cents.

F. H. Gasque, Marion, S. C., compromised at 50 cents; debts, $45,000.

John Munro, Sr., South Arn, Mich., assigned; debts, $35,000.

Kirkpatrick Bro's, Dillon, Mont., assigned; debts estimated at $30,000.

Grocers, and Grocers' Supplies.

Geo. L. Aggers, Denver, Col., assigned to G. C. Corning, a silent partner.

Black Bro's, Philadelphia, canned goods, failed; liabilities, $30,000.

Wright Gillies & Bro., New York city, wholesale coffees and teas, closed by sheriff. Judgments filed, $33,000.

French & McKnight, Erie, Pa., grocers; judgments entered for $31,000.

Hats.

Chas. Fox's Son & Co., New York city, assigned, giving preference for $92,781.

John Rowland & Sons, New York city, assigned; debts, $41,626; actual assets, $15,543.

Iron and Iron Manufacturers.

Coates & Brother, Baltimore, Md., rolling mill, assigned on Dec. 4th; debts reported at $75,000.

Jewelry.

L. A. Rivert & Co., Chicago, Ill.; bill of sale and judgment; debts, $12,000; assets, $9,000.

Lumber.

Geo. D. Emery, Chelsea, Mass., mahogany lumber, assigned; liabilities, 254,757.

The H. S. Falter Manufacturing Company, St. Louis, Mo., sash, doors, etc., assigned on Dec. 6th, assets, $25,000.

Millinery.

Benjamin Bronner, Syracuse, N. Y., assigned; debts estimated at $53,000.

Millers.

Gordon, Baker & Co., Sparta, Ill., assigned; debts, $100,000.

Paper and Paper-hangings.

Seaman Jones, Jr., & Co., New York city, paper-hangings, assigned on December 6th; preferences for $6,726.

Produce and Grain.

Lane & Son, New York city, commission grain, assigned; liabilities reported at $100,000.

Dillworth, Maxwell & Co., Hicksville, O., grain, embarrassed; debts, $15,000.

Publishers and Printers.

Miller & Umbdenstock, Chicago, Ill., printers, confessed judgment for $6,224, and closed.

J. L. Peters, St. Louis, Mo., music, compromised with his creditors; claims assets, $55,000, and debts, $25,000.

C. E. Southard, Chicago, Ill., printer, assigned; debts, $21,000.

The Leonard Scott Publishing Company, New York city, attached by C. M. Green.

Miscellaneous.

Porter, Crofut & Hodgkinson, Orange, N. J., hat manufacturers; debts, $25,000.

Wm. Carroll & Co., New York city, hat manufacturers, failed; indebtedness, together with the debts of the firm of Carroll & Co., are placed at $200,000.

Higgins & Fowler, New York city, soap manufacturers; liabilities, $30,000.

The Hartford Engineering Company, Hartford, Conn., closed by sheriff and received appointed capital, $200,000.

Kamspeck & Green, Atlanta, Ga., fertilizers, suspended; debts, $75,000.

J. W. Woolfolk, Columbus, Ga., warehouse, assigned; debts, $100,000.

The Enterprise Machine Company, Geneva, O., assigned; authorized capital, $200,000; debts, reported, $70,000.

Baerman & Gersfeld, New York city, manufacturers of children's cloaks, assigned; debts, $17,000; actual assets, $10,000.

J. P. Billups & Co., New York city, cotton commission and export, suspended; liabilities, reported, $600,000.

Fabric Ornamenting and Manufacturing Company, New York city, failed and attached; capital-stock, $100,000.

Thomas Kirwin, Bradford, Penn., oil producer, assigned; debts, $52,000; nominal assets, $65,000.

DECEMBER TRADE REVIEW.

THE MONEY MARKET AND FINANCIAL SITUATION. —The month of December showed but little change in the general commercial and financial situation. Profits have been exceedingly small in almost every line of business, with the exception of the net earnings of railroads, which are larger proportionately than in business of other kinds. The rule of small profits is the result of the general decline in prices of all commodities during the past two years, which has been caused by "over-production." The plethoric condition of the money market and the low rates for money are the result of the decrease of enterprises and the cessation in the further expansion of the scope of commercial transactions that leaves a larger proportion of capital unemployed. As merchants and manufacturers are not making money, they have less surplus to invest in interest-paying securities and investments, which are consequently in less demand. The depreciation of values, however, seems to have reached the lowest extreme, and the hope is that the condition of affairs may improve with the new year. In connection with the general movement of products in the West there has been some improvement, but the general features of the market remain unchanged. Money continues plentiful on call, at 2 and 2½ per cent.

FOREIGN EXCHANGE.—The market for sterling was dull and the business small for the first half of the month, but during the last half of December it was somewhat unsettled and advanced.

UNITED STATES BONDS.—The tone of the Government-bond market has been firm and steadily advancing throughout the month.

STATE AND RAILROAD BONDS.—There has been something of a reaction in the investment in railroad bonds. The movement of capital for investment, which has been a feature for several months past, evidently received a check during the past month, and though the market continued active, prices in many instances declined. Trouble in the railroad pools, arising out of increasing competition and the recent extension of new lines into the territories of those already in existence, has had a tendency to depress stocks and make capitalists more cautious in bonds of roads so affected. At the close of the month the market was feverish, though prices were firm.

RAILROAD AND MISCELLANEOUS STOCK.—The stock market was depressed throughout the whole month, occasioned by troubles in the various pools, the resignation of Mr. Villard from the presidency of the Oregon and Trans-Continental and Oregon Railway and Navigation Company, and the appointment of a committee to examine into their financial condition, and rumors affecting the New York Central and the Northwestern. Prices showed a pretty general decline.

COMMERCIAL.—General trade has been dull, and the tendency of prices has been, in nearly all cases, to cover figures, and a very unsettled condition of affairs has prevailed.

PROVISIONS.—The speculation in lard has been liberal. Lard and pork have sympathized with the strong Chicago advices regarding corn. A selling movement to realize profits brought about some irregularity, but the market was generally firm. Speculation in lard was quite active during the last week of the month, and prices advanced.

RIO COFFEE was dull during the early part of the month, and options were active at higher prices. During the last week Rio coffee was active on the spot and advanced.

TEA was steady and firm, showing some activity during the latter half of the month.

SUGARS.—Raw sugars were active at a decline during the month. Refined sold at a decline.

COTTON for future delivery showed considerable activity during the month—at times there being a tendency of prices to advance, but increased receipts generally caused a reaction. Cotton on the spot was dull.

FLOUR was, on a rule, dull and depressed. The receipts were large, foreign demand light, and prices declined.

WHEAT was quiet for export throughout the month, but fairly active on speculation until after the second week, when the transactions were on a comparatively moderate scale. There was an effort to bull the market on account of the probability of the Franco-Chinese war, but without any noteworthy effect. Latterly the decreased trading and a further increase in the visible supply in the country, as well as the quantity afloat for Europe, in connection with the sluggish state of the foreign market, caused a decline.

INDIAN CORN showed considerable speculative activity, but was quiet for export. The market has been irregular and feverish. The Agricultural Bureau report confirmed the previous statement respecting the poor condition of a large proportion of the crop. During the latter part of the month the trading in options showed a sharp falling off, and prices, which had previously displayed a little strength, took a downward turn.

RYE, during the first week of the month, was in moderate demand, but it grew more active at an advance in the second week, and then continued steady.

OATS, during the first quarter of the month, were fairly active on speculation, but sympathized with corn and wheat, and the latter part of the month showed a steady market with moderate demand.

IRON AND STEEL.—The market for American pig-iron has been dull during the past month, but prices have remained nominally the same. Sales have been light. More furnaces have shut down. It is the general opinion, however, that prices have reached bottom, though it is not probable an advance will be made for some time. Out of 417 furnaces in blast at the opening of 1883, 270 are now out of blast. Stocks are lower than ever, and are declining; and as makers are adverse to listening to offers upon the market the result must sooner or later be a revival in demand and price. Bessemer steel has continued dull; sales have been made at $20—a cut of fifty cents. Manufactured iron has been stagnant. The nail market showed some additional strength, owing to the stoppage of some Western mills. Steel rails remained steady at $35 for 1884 delivery at mill. Scotch pig has been dull, with light demand.

MARKETS AND EXCHANGES.

(When no Figures are Given the Price Remains the Same as Last Quotation.)

Foreign Exchange.—Closing Rates for each Day in December.

	1.	3.	4.	5.	6.	7.	8.	10.	11.	12.	13.	14.	15.	17.	18.	19.	20.	21.	22.	24.	25.	26.	27.	28.	29.	31.
London ....60 days	483	....	....	....	....	....	....	482½	482	....	....	482½	....	....	....	....	....	483	....	482½	Holiday	....	....	....	....	....
" ....3 "	485½	....	....	....	....	....	....	....	485	....	485½	....	....	....	....	....	....	486	....	485½		....	....	....	....	....
Paris, francs ....60 "	520⅝	....	....	....	....	....	....	....	....	....	....	....	....	....	....	....	....	....	....	....		....	521¼	....	....	....
" " ....3 "	517½	....	....	....	....	....	....	....	....	....	....	....	....	....	....	....	....	....	....	....		....	518⅛	....	....	....
Geneva ....60 "	520	....	....	....	....	....	....	....	....	....	....	....	....	....	....	....	....	....	....	....		....	520⅝	....	....	....
" ....3 "	516⅞	....	....	....	....	....	....	....	....	....	....	....	....	....	....	....	....	....	....	....		....	517½	....	....	....
Berlin, reichmarks ....60 "	94⅞	....	....	....	....	....	....	....	....	....	....	....	....	....	....	....	....	....	....	....		....	....	....	....	....
" " ....3 "	95¼	....	....	....	....	....	....	....	....	....	....	....	....	....	....	....	....	....	....	....		....	....	....	....	....
Amsterdam, guilders ....60 "	40⅛	....	....	....	....	....	....	....	....	....	....	....	....	....	....	....	....	....	....	....		....	....	....	....	....
" " ....3 "	40⅜	....	....	....	....	....	....	....	....	....	....	....	....	....	....	....	....	....	....	....		....	....	....	....	....

Government Bonds and Currency.—Closing Prices at the New York Board during December.

	Interest Periods.	1.	3.	4.	5.	6.	7.	8.	10.	11.	12.	13.	14.	15.	17.	18.	19.	20.	21.	22.	24.	25.	26.	27.	28.	29.	31.
4½s, 1891 ....reg.	Q.-Mar.	114	....	....	....	113⅞	114	114⅜	114	114¼	....	114½	....	114⅜	114½	114⅝	....	114¼	114⅝	114½	114⅝	Holiday	114⅝	114⅞	....	115	114⅝
4½s, 1891 ....coup.	Q.-Mar.	114	....	....	113⅞	114	....	114⅛	114	114¼	....	114½	....	114¼	114⅝	114⅝	114½	....	114⅝	114½	114⅝		114⅝	114⅞	....	....	....
4s, 1907 ....reg.	Q.-Jan.	122	....	....	122⅛	122½	122¼	122⅞	....	122⅞	122⅞	123	....	....	123⅛	123½	123⅛	....	123½	123⅝	123⅛		124	123⅞	124	....	....
4s, 1907 ....coup.	Q.-Jan.	123	....	....	123⅜	123¼	....	123⅜	123⅜	....	123⅞	124	124¼	124	124½	124½	124½	124½	124⅝	....	124⅝		124⅜	125	125⅜	124⅞	....
3s, option U. S. ....reg.	Q.-Feb.	100¼	....	100⅞	....	....	100⅞	101	....	....	101⅛	....	101½	....	101¼	....	101⅜	....	....	101½	101		....	....	102	....	....
6s, cur'cy, 1895 ....reg.	J. & J.	129¼	....	127¼	....	....	127	127½	....	....	....	....	....	....	....	127½	....	....	128	....	....		....	....	....	....	....
6s, cur'cy, 1896 ....reg.	J. & J.	131¼	....	129¼	....	....	129	129¼	....	....	....	....	....	....	....	129⅝	....	....	130	....	....		....	....	....	....	....
6s, cur'cy, 1897 ....reg.	J. & J.	133¼	....	131¼	....	....	131	131¼	....	....	....	....	....	....	....	131⅝	....	....	132	....	....		....	....	....	....	....
6s, cur'cy, 1898 ....reg.	J. & J.	134¼	134	133⅞	....	133¼	131	133⅞	133¼	....	....	....	133⅞	133¼	....	133⅞	....	....	134	....	....		....	134¼	134	....	....
6s, cur'cy, 1899 ....reg.	J. & J.	136¼	....	134⅞	134⅞	134¼	134	134⅞	134¼	....	....	....	134⅞	134¼	....	134⅞	....	....	135	....	....		....	135¼	135	....	....

New York Stock Exchange.—Daily Highest Prices for December.

STOCKS.	1.	3.	4.	5.	6.	7.	8.	10.	11.	12.	13.	14.	15.	17.	18.	19.	20.	21.	22.	24.	25.	26.	27.	28.	29.	31.
RAILROADS.																										
Atchison, Topeka & S. F.	82	....	79⅞	....	....	....	....	....	....	....	....	....	....	....	....	....	....	....	....	....	Holiday	....	....	....	....	....
Boston Air-Line, pref.	82	....	....	....	....	....	....	....	....	....	....	....	....	....	....	....	....	....	....	....		....	82½	....	....	83
Bur., Cedar Rap. & No.	85	....	....	....	....	....	....	83	....	....	....	....	....	82	....	....	81	....	....	....		....	....	....	85	....
Canadian Pacific	59½	59⅞	58½	57¾	57⅞	57⅞	57⅞	57½	57	56⅞	56⅞	56⅞	56	56½	55⅞	55½	....	55⅝	54⅞	54½		53	54	55	55⅝	54⅞
Canada Southern	57½	....	56½	57⅛	56⅜	56½	56⅜	56½	56	55⅝	55⅝	55	54½	54⅞	55	54½	....	54⅞	54	....		52⅞	53½	53	52⅞	52⅞
Central of New Jersey	84¼	84½	83¾	83⅞	83¼	85⅝	....	84¼	84⅞	....	85½	....	84¼	85	....	84⅛	85	84¼	....	84		83¼	83⅞	83⅝	85	84
Central Pacific	66	....	67⅞	67⅞	67⅞	67¼	67⅞	67¼	67½	66⅛	66⅞	66½	65⅞	66⅞	66½	66⅞	....	66¼	65½	65		64⅞	64⅞	64⅝	64½	64½
Chesapeake & Ohio	16	16¼	....	....	....	10⅞	15½	....	16	15	15½	15	16	....	15⅛	....	14⅛	....	14⅞	14½		14½	15	14½	15	15⅛
Do 1st pref.	27¾	27⅞	....	....	29	28	....	26⅜	26⅜	27½	27⅛	....	25⅜	27	....	....	26⅜	27	25	....		....	....	27	28	27
Do 2d pref.	18½	18½	....	18	18½	....	....	18	17½	18	....	....	....	17½	18½	17	....	18	....	16⅜		....	18	17½	17½	....
Chicago & Alton	134	133⅞	134	....	133¼	132½	133¼	133	132⅞	132⅞	133	133¼	132⅞	134½	134	....	....	....	....	132⅛		133½	....	....	134	....
Chicago, Bur. & Quincy	125⅞	126¼	124¼	125	124½	124	123⅞	123½	122¼	121¼	....	121	....	121⅞	122½	121⅞	122¼	121½	120¼	120¼		121	120⅜	121½	....	....
Chicago, Mil. & St. Paul	99⅝	99⅞	98¼	99½	98⅞	98	97⅞	98⅞	98	96⅞	96⅞	95⅞	95⅞	95⅞	96½	....	96⅜	96¼	94⅞	94		93⅞	93½	94⅞	....	....
Do pref.	118¼	118	....	....	....	....	....	....	....	117¼	118	117¼	116¼	117	....	117¼	117	116	....	....		116⅝	116½	117	....	....
Chicago & Northwest	127½	....	126	....	124¼	119⅞	....	119⅜	119	117¼	117⅞	116⅞	117⅞	119	119¼	119¼	119⅞	119½	118	116⅝		117	117⅛	117½	....	....
Do pref.	148¼	149¼	148¼	148⅜	147⅞	144	144⅞	....	144	143⅞	143⅜	143½	142½	144	144½	143¼	144	143½	142⅞	143		142	144	143	....	....
Chicago, R. I. & P.	122	122⅜	122	121⅞	121	120½	119⅜	120	119	....	....	118⅞	....	118¼	....	....	118⅜	118⅞	119	118		....	119	119⅞	....	....

Holiday

- Chicago, St. Louis & Pitts.
- Do pref.
- Chicago, St. P., M. & O.
- Do pref.
- Cincinnati, Sand. & Cleve.
- Cleveland, Col., Cinn. & Ind.
- Cleveland & Pittsburg, guar.
- Columbus, Chic. & Ind. Cen.
- Delaware, Lack. & West.
- Denver & Rio Grande.
- East Tenn., Va. & Ga.
- Do pref.
- Evansville & Terre Haute.
- Green Bay, Winona & St. P.
- Hannibal & St. Joseph.
- Do pref.
- Harlem.
- Houston & Texas Central.
- Illinois Central.
- Do leased line.
- Indiana, Bloom'n & Western.
- Lake Erie & Western.
- Lake Shore.
- Long Island.
- Louisiana & Missouri River.
- Louisville & Nashville.
- Louisville, N. Alb. & Chic.
- Manhattan Elevated.
- Do 1st pref.
- Do common.
- Manhattan Beach Co.
- Memphis & Charleston.
- Metropolitan Elevated.
- Michigan Central.
- Mil., L. Sh. & West.
- Minneapolis & St. P.
- Do pref.
- Missouri, Kansas & Texas.
- Missouri Pacific.
- Mobile & Ohio.
- Morris & Essex.
- Nashville, Chat. & St. L.
- N. Y. Central & Hdson.
- N. Y., Chic. & St. Louis.
- Do pref.
- New York Elevated.
- N. Y., Lack. & Western.
- N. Y., Lake Erie & W.
- Do pref.
- N. Y. & New England.
- N. Y., New Haven & Hart.
- N. Y., Ontario & Western.
- N. Y., Susq. & Western.
- Do pref.
- Norfolk & Western.
- Do pref.
- Northern Pacific.
- Do pref.
- Ohio Central.
- Ohio & Mississippi.
- Do pref.
- Ohio Southern.

[Continued on next page.]

New York Stock Exchange.— Daily Highest Prices for December.— *Continued.*

STOCKS.	1.	3.	4.	5.	6.	7.	8.	10.	11.	12.	13.	14.	15.	17.	18.	19.	20.	21.	22.	24.	25.	26.	27.	28.	29.	31.
RAILROADS.																										
Oregon & Trans-Continental																					*Holiday.*					
Peoria, Decatur & Evansville																										
Philadelphia & Reading																										
Pittsburg, Ft. Wayne & Chic.																										
Richmond & Allegheny																										
Richmond & Danville																										
Richmond & West Point																										
Rochester & Pittsburg																										
St. Louis, Alton & T. H. pref.																										
St. Louis & San Fran. pref.																										
Do 1st pref.																										
St. Paul & Duluth pref.																										
Do pref.																										
St. Paul, Minneap. & Man.																										
Texas & Pacific																										
Union Pacific																										
Wabash, St. L. & Pac.																										
Do pref.																										
MISCELLANEOUS.																										
American Tel. & Cable Co																										
Bankers' & Merchants' Tel																										
Colorado Coal & Iron																										
Delaware & Hudson Canal																										
Mutual Union Telegraph																										
New Central Coal																										
N. Y. & Tex. Land Co																										
Oregon Improvem't Co																										
Oregon R'way & Nav. Co.																										
Pacific Mail																										
Pullman Palace Car																										
Quicksilver Mining																										
Do pref.																										
Standard Consol. Mining																										
Western Union Telegraph																										
EXPRESS.																										
Adams																										
American																										
United States																										
Wells, Fargo & Co.																										

Petroleum.— Prices for each Day in December.

	1.	3.	4.	5.	6.	7.	8.	10.	11.	12.	13.	14.	15.	17.	18.	19.	20.	21.	22.	24.	25.	26.	27.	28.	29.	31.
Pipe Line Certific's—highest																					*Holiday.*					
" lowest																										
Crude in bbls																										
Naphtha																										
Refined, cargo lots, 110 deg																										
" 70 deg. Abel test																										

Grain.— Highest Prices for Future Delivery for each Day in December.

WHEAT—	1.	3.	4.	5.	6.	7.	8.	10.	11.	12.	13.	14.	15.	17.	18.	19.	20.	21.	22.	24.	25.	26.	27.	28.	29.	31.
December	111⅞	110⅝	111½	111	111½	110¾	111⅜	112⅜	....	111	111½	112	....	112½	112¾	112⅝	113	112¼	....	Holiday.	Holiday.	112⅝	111⅝	111½	111	Holiday.
January	113⅜	112⅝	113½	112⅞	112⅜	112⅜	113⅜	114⅞	114¼	113⅜	113½	....	113⅜	114¼	114¼	113⅜	....	113¼	113			....	112	111⅜	111½	
February	115⅝	114⅝	115½	115	114¾	114¼	115½	117	116⅜	116	115⅝	115½	117⅜	116⅜	116⅝	115⅜	....	115⅝	113½			115	114⅛	113⅜	113¾	
May	120¼	120	120½	120	119⅝	112½	120⅜	122	121⅞	121½	120¼	120⅝	121⅛	122¼	122¾	121⅜	121⅝	121¼	121			120⅛	120	119½	115¼	
CORN—																										
December	63⅝	63½	64	63⅞	64⅛	....	65½	68	67⅛	67½	65¼	....	64½	64⅝	64½	64¼	64⅝	64½	64¼	Holiday.	Holiday.	....	64⅛	64	63¼	Holiday.
January	64⅝	64⅛	65	64⅞	65⅛	65½	66½	69⅛	68⅝	68¼	66⅝	66⅝	65½	65⅝	65¼	64¼	65⅛	65½	65			65½	64½	64⅛	64	
February	65½	64⅛	65½	65⅝	65¼	65⅝	67⅞	70⅝	69⅝	69⅝	67⅞	67½	66⅝	66½	66¼	66½	....	66⅝	66½			66⅝	65⅝	65⅝	65¼	
May	66¼	66	67⅞	....	67⅝	....	69¼	72	72⅞	72	70¼	70¼	69⅞	69⅝	....	69⅝	69⅞	69⅛	69½			69¼	68⅝	....	65⅛	
OATS—																										
December	37⅞	....	37½	....	37⅝	37½	38¼	40	40⅝	40	....	....	....	40¼	40⅝	....	40¼	....	40⅝	Holiday.	Holiday.	..	40½	....	..	Holiday.
January	38¼	38⅝	38¾	38⅝	38⅞	....	39¼	41	41½	40⅝	40¼	40⅝	40⅞	41	41⅛	41	41⅛	41	....			....	40⅝	40¼	40⅝	
February	39⅛	39¼	40	39⅞	39⅞	39⅞	40⅛	42½	42⅛	....	41⅞	....	41⅞	42⅛	....	42	42⅛	42	43			42⅛	41⅜	41⅛	41⅛	
May	41⅞	41⅛	42⅛	....	....	42⅛	43⅜	45⅞	45⅞	45⅛	44⅞	44⅛	....	45	....	44⅞	45	....	44⅞			44⅞	44⅛	44⅛	42⅛	

Flour.— Closing Prices.

	First Quarter.	Second Quarter.	Third Quarter.	Fourth Quarter.
No. 2 spring .... per bbl.	$2.20 @ 2.75	$.... @	$2.00 @ 2.75	$.... @ ....
No. 2 winter	2.50 3.00	....	....	....
Superfine	2.75 3.40	....	2.60 3.40	2.60 3.30
Spring wheat extras	3.75 5.00	....	3.50 5.00	....
Minn. clear and straight	4.00 5.75	....	....	....
Winter shipping extras	3.45 3.90	....	....	3.35 3.75
Winter clear and straight	4.25 6.00	....	....	....
Patents, spring	5.50 7.00	....	....	....
Patents, winter	5.50 7.00	....	5.50 6.75	5.25 6.75

	First Quarter.	Second Quarter.	Third Quarter.	Fourth Quarter.
City shipping extras .... per bbl.	$5.10 @ 5.65	$.... @	$.... @	$5.10 @ 5.50
South'n bakers' and family brands	4.62½ 6.62½	....	4.62½ 6.50	....
Southern shipping extras	3.75 5.50	....	....	....
Rye flour, superfine	3.50 3.90	3.50 4.00	3.40 3.85	3.40 3.75
Corn Meal—				
Western, etc	3.00 3.35	....	....	3.00 3.40
Brandywine, etc	3.35 3.40	....	3.35 3.50	3.35 3.45
Buckwheat flour .... per 100 lbs.	3.50 3.75	3.00 3.50	3.00 3.60	3.00 3.50

New York Coffee Exchange.— Spot Quotations on Rio Coffee for each Day in December.

	1.	3.	4.	5.	6.	7.	8.	10.	11.	12.	13.	14.	15.	17.	18.	19.	20.	21.	22.	24.	25.	26.	27.	28.	29.	31.
Prime	12.50	....	....	12.25	....	12.00	....	....	....	11.75	....	....	....	....	....	11.90	12.00	....	....	Holiday	Holiday	12.50	....	....	....	....
Good	12.25	....	....	12.00	....	11.75	....	....	....	11.50	....	....	....	....	....	11.65	11.75	....	....			12.25	....	....	....	....
Fair	12.00	....	....	11.75	....	11.50	....	....	....	11.25	....	....	....	....	....	11.40	11.50	....	....			12.00	....	....	....	....
Low Fair	11.70	....	....	11.40	....	11.15	....	....	....	10.95	....	....	....	....	....	11.10	11.20	....	....			11.70	....	....	....	....
G'd Ordi'y	11.55	....	....	11.15	....	10.90	....	....	....	10.60	....	....	....	....	....	10.75	10.85	....	....			11.35	....	....	....	....
Ordinary	11.25	....	....	10.80	....	10.50	....	....	....	10.25	....	....	....	....	....	10.40	10.50	....	....			11.00	....	....	....	....
LowOrd'y	10.80	....	....	10.35	....	10.10	....	....	....	9.75	....	....	....	....	....	9.90	10.00	....	....			10.50	....	....	....	....
St. G.Com.	10.45	....	....	9.95	....	9.70	....	....	....	9.25	....	....	....	....	....	9.40	9.50	....	....			10.00	....	....	....	....
Good Com.	9.95	....	....	9.45	....	9.30	....	....	....	8.85	....	....	....	....	....	9.00	9.10	....	....			9.50	....	....	....	....
Common	9.30	....	....	8.95	....	9.00	....	....	....	8.50	....	....	....	....	....	8.65	8.75	....	....			9.25	....	....	....	....

Sugar.—Highest Prices at Closing of each Day in December.

	1.	3.	4.	5.	6.	7.	8.	10.	11.	12.	13.	14.	15.	17.	18.	19.	20.	21.	22.	24.	25.	26.	27.	28.	29.	31.
RAW SUGAR.																										
Com. to good refi. Cuba	6⅜	....	....	....	....	6⅜	....	....	....	....	....	....	....	....	....	....	....	....	....	Holiday	Holiday	....	....	....	....	Holiday
Com. to good refi. Porto Rico	6⅜	....	....	....	....	6¼	....	....	....	....	....	....	....	....	....	....	....	....	....			....	....	....	....	
Centrifugal	7¼	....	....	....	....	7¼	....	....	....	....	....	....	....	....	....	....	....	....	....			....	....	....	....	
Manilla	6⅜	....	....	....	....	....	....	....	....	....	....	....	....	....	....	....	....	....	....			....	....	....	....	
Pernams	6½	....	....	....	....	....	....	....	....	....	....	....	....	....	....	....	....	....	....			....	....	....	....	
Bahia	6	....	....	....	....	....	....	....	....	....	....	....	....	....	....	....	....	....	....			....	....	....	....	
Melado	....	....	....	....	....	....	....	....	....	....	....	....	....	....	....	....	....	....	....			....	....	....	....	
REFINED SUGAR.																										
Cut loaf	9	....	....	....	....	....	....	....	....	....	....	....	8⅞	....	....	....	....	....	8⅞			....	....	....	....	
Crushed	9	....	....	....	....	....	....	....	....	8⅜	....	....	....	....	....	....	....	....	8⅞			....	....	....	....	
Cubes	8½	....	....	....	....	....	....	....	....	....	....	....	8⅛	....	....	....	....	....	....			....	....	....	....	
Powdered	8⅜	....	....	....	....	....	....	....	....	....	....	8⅛	8½	8⅛	....	....	....	....	8⅛			....	....	....	....	
Granulated	8 1/16	....	....	....	8⅛	....	....	8 1/16	....	....	....	....	8	....	....	7.94	7⅞	....	....			7 13/16	....	....	....	
Mould "A"	8	....	....	....	....	8⅛	8	....	....	7⅞	....	....	....	....	....	7⅞	....	....	....			....	....	7⅞	....	
Confectioners' "A"	7¾	....	7 13/16	7⅞	....	....	....	....	7 13/16	....	....	7⅞	....	....	....	7 13/16	7⅝	....	....			....	7.56	7 9/16	....	
Coffee "A" standard	7⅝	7 9/16	....	....	7⅝	....	....	7 1/16	....	....	....	7½	....	....	....	7⅝	....	....	....			....	....	7⅝	....	
Coffee off "A"	7⅝	....	....	....	....	....	....	....	....	....	7½	7⅝	7½	....	....	....	....	....	....			....	....	....	....	
White extra "C"	7	....	....	....	....	....	....	....	6⅝	6⅞	....	....	6⅞	....	....	....	....	....	6⅝			....	....	....	....	
Extra "C"	6⅞	....	....	....	....	....	....	....	....	....	....	....	6⅛	....	....	....	....	....	....			....	....	....	....	
"C"	6½	....	....	....	....	....	....	....	....	6⅜	....	....	6	....	....	....	....	....	....			....	....	....	....	
Yellow	6	....	....	....	....	....	....	....	....	5⅞	....	....	5⅞	....	....	....	....	....	....			....	....	....	....	
Yellow "C"	....	....	....	....	....	....	....	....	....	....	....	....	....	....	....	....	....	....	....			....	....	....	....	

Lard.—Highest Price for Future Delivery for each Day in December.

	1.	3.	4.	5.	6.	7.	8.	10.	11.	12.	13.	14.	15.	17.	18.	19.	20.	21.	22.	24.	25.	26.	27.	28.	29.	31.
December	8.55	8.53	8.73	8.82	....	8.77	9.00	9.33	9.28	9.00	8.97	....	9.10	9.15	9.20	9.22	9.25	9.20	....	Holiday	Holiday	9.07	8.95	8.75	....	Holiday
January	8.60	8.63	8.83	8.87	8.92	8.90	9.15	9.41	9.34	9.20	9.06	9.05	9.15	9.26	....	9.25	9.38	9.32	9.28			9.12	9.13	9.12	9.03	
February	8.70	8.75	8.93	8.98	9.02	9.00	9.25	9.51	9.44	9.34	9.15	9.14	9.28	9.38	9.36	9.39	9.47	9.42	9.36			9.21	9.20	....	9.10	
March	8.75	8.87	9.03	9.06	9.12	9.07	9.35	9.60	9.50	9.38	9.20	9.25	9.37	9.45	9.48	9.46	9.56	9.51	9.47			9.30	9.27	9.30	9.21	
April	9.10	9.00	9.12	9.15	9.20	....	9.45	9.70	9.57½	9.45	9.30	9.33	9.45	9.53	9.51	9.60	9.63	9.60	9.56			9.40	9.36	....	9.30	
May	9.10	9.05	9.20	9.25	9.30	9.25	9.55	9.80	9.68	9.55	9.43	....	9.56	9.66	9.63	9.65	9.75	9.70	9.65			9.50	9.47	9.46	9.41	

Pork.—Highest Spot Prices for each Day in December.

	1.	3.	4.	5.	6.	7.	8.	10.	11.	12.	13.	14.	15.	17.	18.	19.	20.	21.	22.	24.	25.	26.	27.	28.	29.	31.
Mess	14.25	....	....	....	....	....	14.50	15.00	....	....	....	....	....	15.25	....	....	15.50	....	....	Holiday	Holiday	14.75	15.00	....	....	Holiday
Extra Prime	12.00	....	....	....	....	12.50	....	13.00	....	....	....	....	....	....	....	....	13.50	....	....			....	....	....	....	
Prime Mess	15.50	....	....	....	....	....	....	....	....	....	....	....	....	....	....	....	....	....	....			....	....	....	15.00	
Clear Back	17.00	....	....	....	....	18.00	....	....	....	....	....	....	....	....	....	....	18.50	....	....			....	....	....	18.00	
Family	15.00	....	....	....	....	15.50	16.00	....	....	....	....	....	....	....	....	....	16.00	....	....			....	....	....	....	

Cotton.—Current Prices for each Day in December.

	1.	3.	4.	5.	6.	7.	8.	10.	11.	12.	13.	14.	15.	17.	18.	19.	20.	21.	22.	24.	25.	26.	27.	28.	29.	31.
UPLANDS.																										
Ordinary...........per lb.	8 7/8									8 3/8		8 7/8				8 3/8				*Holiday*	*Holiday*			8 7/8		*Holiday*
Strict Ordinary.	8 7/8									8 7/8		8 3/8				8 7/8								8 3/8		
Good Ordinary.	9 1/4									9 1/4		9 1/4				9 1/4								9 3/4		
Strict Good Ordinary.	9 5/8									9 3/4		10 1/8				9 3/8								9 3/4		
Low Middling.	10 1/8									10 1/8		10 1/8				10								10 1/8		
Strict Low Middling.	10 1/4									11 1/8		10 1/4				10 3/8								10 3/8		
Middling.	10 3/8									10 3/8		10 3/8				10 3/8								10 3/8		
Good Middling.	10 3/8									10 5/8		10 5/8				10 3/8								10 3/8		
Strict Good Middling.	10 5/8									11		11				11								11		
Middling Fair.	11 1/8									11 3/8		11 1/4				11 1/4								11 1/4		
Fair.	12 1/8									12 1/4		12 1/4				12								12 1/4		
NEW ORLEANS.																										
Ordinary...........per lb.	8 7/8									8 3/8		8 7/8				8 3/8								8 7/8		
Strict Ordinary.	9									8 7/8		8 3/8				8 3/8								8 3/8		
Good Ordinary.	9 3/8									9		9 1/4				9 1/4								9 1/4		
Strict Good Ordinary.	10 1/8									10 1/8		10 1/8				10								10 1/8		
Low Middling.	10 1/4									10 3/8		10 3/8				10 3/8								10 3/8		
Strict Low Middling.	10 3/8									11		10 3/8				10 3/8								10 1/4		
Middling.	10 5/8									11		10 3/8				10 3/8								10 3/8		
Good Middling.	11 1/8									11		11				11								11		
Strict Good Middling.	11 1/2									11 1/4		11 1/4				11 1/4								11 1/4		
Middling Fair.	11 3/4									11 3/4		11 3/4				11 3/4								11 3/4		
Fair.	12 3/4									12 3/8		12 3/8				12 3/8								12 3/8		
TEXAS.																										
Ordinary...........per lb.	8 7/8									8 3/8		8 7/8				8 3/8								8 7/8		
Strict Ordinary.	9									8 7/8		8 3/8				8 3/8								8 3/8		
Good Ordinary.	9 3/8									9		9 1/4				9 1/4								9 3/8		
Strict Good Ordinary.	10 1/8									10 1/8		10 1/8				10								10 1/8		
Low Middling.	10 1/4									10 3/8		10 3/8				10 5/8								10 3/8		
Strict Low Middling.	10 3/8									11		10 3/8				10 3/8								10 3/8		
Middling.	10 5/8									11		10 3/8				10 3/8								10 3/8		
Good Middling.	11 1/8									11		11				11								11		
Strict Good Middling.	11 1/2									11 1/4		11 1/4				11 1/4								11 1/4		
Middling Fair.	11 3/4									11 3/4		11 3/4				11 3/4								11 3/4		
Fair.	12 3/4									12 3/8		12 3/8				12 3/8								12 3/8		
STAINED.																										
Good Ordinary...........per lb.	7 3/8									7 3/8		7 3/8				7 3/8								7 3/8		
Strict Good Ordinary.	8 3/8									8 7/8		8 3/8				8 1/8								8 3/8		
Low Middling.	9 3/8									9		9 3/8				9								9 3/8		
Middling.	10 3/8									10 3/8		10 3/8				10								10 3/8		

UNITED STATES MAILS TO FOREIGN COUNTRIES.

Schedule of Steamers Appointed to Convey the United States Mails to Foreign Countries During the Month of January, 1884.

TRANS-ATLANTIC MAILS.

Date of Sailing.	Name of Steamer.	Name of Line.	Port of Destination and Intermed'te Ports of Call.	Hour of Clos'g Mail at P.O. at Port of Departure.	Mails to be Conveyed.
			FROM NEW YORK.		
Jan. 1	Nevada	Williams & Guion	Queenstown	4.00 A. M.	Mails for Great Britain and Ireland; also German, Austrian, French, Belgian, Netherlands, Swiss, Italian, Spanish, Portuguese, Russian, Turkish, Danish, Swedish, and Norwegian closed mails.
" 2	Pavonia	Cunard	Queenstown	5.00 "	Mails for Great Britain and Ireland; also Belgian, Netherlands, Swiss, Italian, Spanish, Portuguese, Russian and Turkish closed mails; *also specially addressed correspondence for France, Germany, Austria, Denmark, Sweden, and Norway.*
" 2	St. Laurent	General Trans-Atlantic	Havre	5.00 "	Mails for France direct.
" 2	Maasdam	Netherlands Steam Nav. Co	Rotterdam	5.00 "	Mails for the Netherlands direct.
" 2	Habsburg	North German Lloyd	Bremen	11.30 "	*Specially addressed correspondence for Germany, Austria, Denmark, Sweden and Norway.*
" 3	City of Montreal	Inman	Queenstown	6.00 "	Mails for Ireland; *also specially addressed correspondence for Great Britain and other European countries.*
" 3	Wieland	Hamburg Am. Packet Co	Plymouth and Hamburg	7.30 "	Mails for Great Britain and Ireland; also German, Austrian, French, Belgian, Netherlands, Swiss, Italian, Spanish, Portuguese, Russian, and Turkish closed mails via Plymouth; mails for Germany direct; also Austrian, Danish, Swedish, and Norwegian closed mails via Hamburg.
" 5	Britannic	White Star	Queenstown	7.30 "	Mails for Great Britain and Ireland; also French, Belgian, Netherlands, Swiss, Italian, Spanish, Portuguese, Russian, and Turkish closed mails; *also specially addressed correspondence for Germany, Austria, Denmark, Sweden, and Norway.*
" 5	Belgravia	Anchor	Glasgow	7.30 "	*Specially addressed correspondence for Scotland.*
" 5	Westerland	Red Star	Antwerp	7.30 "	Mails for Belgium direct.
" 5	Donau	North German Lloyd	Southampton and Bremen	11.00 "	Mails for Great Britain and Ireland; also German, Austrian, French, Belgian, Netherlands, Swiss, Italian, Spanish, Portuguese, Russian, Turkish, and Swedish closed mails via Southampton; mails for Germany direct; also Austrian, Danish, and Norwegian closed mails via Bremen.
" 8	Wyoming	Williams & Guion	Queenstown	10.30 P. M.	Mails for Great Britain and Ireland, etc. (Same as Nevada.)
" 9	Gallia	Cunard	Queenstown	11.30 "	Mails for Great Britain and Ireland, etc.; also German, Austrian, Belgian, Netherlands, Swiss, Italian, Spanish, Portuguese, Russian, Turkish, Danish, Swedish, and Norwegian closed mails via Bremen.
" 9	Edam	Netherlands Steam Nav. Co	Amsterdam	1.00 P. M.	Mails for the Netherlands direct.
" 9	Amerique	General Trans-Atlantic	Havre	1.00 "	Mails for France direct.
" 10	Rugia	Hamburg Am. Packet Co	Plymouth and Hamburg	11.00 A. M.	Mails for Germany and Austria via Plymouth; mails for Germany direct; also Austrian, Danish, Swedish, and Norwegian closed mails via Hamburg; *also specially addressed correspondence for Great Britain and other European countries.*
" 10	Republic	White Star	Queenstown	11.30 "	Mails for Great Britain and Ireland, etc. (Same as Britannic.)
" 12	City of Chester	Inman	Queenstown	2.30 "	Mails for Great Britain and Ireland, etc. (Same as Britannic.)
" 12	Bolivia	Anchor	Glasgow	2.30 "	*Specially addressed correspondence for Scotland.*
" 12	Switzerland	Red Star	Antwerp	2.30 "	Mails for Belgium direct.
" 12	Neckar	North German Lloyd	Southampton and Bremen	1.00 "	Mails for Great Britain and Ireland, etc.
" 15	Alaska	Williams & Guion	Queenstown	4.00 "	Mails for Great Britain and Ireland, etc. (Same as Donau.)
" 16	Scythia	Cunard	Queenstown	5.30 "	Mails for Great Britain and Ireland, etc. (Same as Nevada.)
" 16	Havre	General Trans-Atlantic	Havre	5.30 "	Mails for France direct.
" 16	P. Caland	Netherlands Steam Nav. Co	Rotterdam	5.30 "	Mails for the Netherlands direct.
" 16	Celtic	White Star	Queenstown	6.00 "	Mails for Great Britain and Ireland, etc. (Same as Wieland.)
" 17	Frisia	Hamburg Am. Packet Co	Plymouth and Hamburg	7.00 "	Mails for Great Britain and Ireland, etc. (Same as Wieland.)
" 19	City of Chicago	Inman	Queenstown	7.30 "	Mails for Great Britain and Ireland, etc. (Same as Britannic.)

Date	Steamer	Line	Destination	Time	Remarks
Jan. 19	Waesland	Red Star	Antwerp	7.30 A.M.	Mails for Belgium direct.
" 19	Devonia	Anchor	Glasgow	7.30 "	*Specially addressed correspondence for Scotland.*
" 19	Oder	North German Lloyd	Southampton and Bremen	11.00 "	Mails for Great Britain and Ireland, etc. (Same as Donau.)
" 22	Wisconsin	Williams & Guion	Queenstown	9.30 "	Mails for Great Britain and Ireland, etc. (Same as Nevada.)
" 23	Cephalonia	Cunard	Queenstown	10.30 "	Mails for Great Britain and Ireland, etc. (Same as Nevada.)
" 23	General Werder	North German Lloyd	Southampton and Bremen	11.00	Mails for Germany, Austria, Swiss, Italian, Spanish, Portuguese, Russian, and Turkish closed mails; *also specially addressed correspondence for France, Germany, Austria, Denmark, Sweden, and Norway.* Mails for Germany, Austria, and Sweden via Southampton; mails for Germany direct; also Austrian, Danish, and Norwegian closed mails via Bremen; *also specially addressed correspondence for Great Britain and other European countries.*

FROM BOSTON.

Date	Steamer	Line	Destination	Time	Remarks
" 23	St. Germain	General Trans-Atlantic	Havre	11.00	Mails for France direct.
" 23	Amsterdam	Netherlands Steam Nav. Co	Amsterdam	11.00 "	Mails for the Netherlands direct.
" 24	City of Richmond	Inman	Queenstown	11.00 "	Mails for Great Britain and Ireland, etc. (Same as Britannic.)
" 24	Circassia	Anchor	Glasgow	4.00 "	Mails for Scotland direct.
" 26	Main	North German Lloyd	Southampton and Bremen	11.00 "	Mails for Germany, Austria, and Sweden, etc. (Same as General Werder.)
" 26	Germanic	White Star	Queenstown	11.30 "	Mails for Great Britain and Ireland, etc. (Same as Britannic.)
" 26	Nederland	Red Star	Antwerp	3.00 P.M.	Mails for Belgium direct.
" 29	Arizona	Williams & Guion	Queenstown	3.00 A.M.	Mails for Great Britain and Ireland, etc. (Same as Nevada.)
" 30	Bothnia	Cunard	Queenstown	4.30 "	Mails for Great Britain and Ireland, etc. (Same as Gallia.)
" 30	France	General Trans-Atlantic	Havre	4.30 "	Mails for France direct.
" 31	W. A. Scholten	Netherlands Steam Nav. Co	Rotterdam	6.00 "	Mails for the Netherlands direct.
" 31	Baltic	White Star	Queenstown	4.30 "	Mails for Great Britain and Ireland, etc. (Same as Britannic.)
" 31	Westphalia	Hamburg Am. Packet Co	Plymouth and Hamburg	5.30 "	Mails for Great Britain and Ireland, etc. (Same as Wieland.)

FROM BOSTON.

Date	Steamer	Line	Destination	Time	Remarks
Jan. 5	Samaria	Cunard	Queenstown and Liverpool	11.00	Mails for Great Britain and Ireland; also closed mails for Belgium and France.
" 19	Catalonia	Cunard	Queenstown and Liverpool	12.00 M.	Mails for Great Britain and Ireland; also closed mails for Belgium and France.

FROM PHILADELPHIA.

Date	Steamer	Line	Destination	Time	Remarks
Jan. 9	Illinois	American Steamship Co	Queenstown and Liverpool	4.30 A.M.	Mails for Great Britain and Ireland.
" 10	Pennsylvania	American Steamship Co	Queenstown and Liverpool	4.30 "	Mails for Great Britain and Ireland.
" 23	Zeeland	Red Star	Antwerp	4.30 "	Mails for Belgium direct.
" 30	Ohio	American Steamship Co	Queenstown and Liverpool	8.30 "	Mails for Great Britain and Ireland.

FROM BALTIMORE.

Date	Steamer	Line	Destination	Time	Remarks
Jan. 10	America	North German Lloyd	Bremen	2.00 P.M.	Mails for Germany.
" 31	Nurnberg	North German Lloyd	Bremen	2.00 "	Mails for Germany.

MAILS FOR CANADA AND NEWFOUNDLAND.

FROM BOSTON.

Date	Steamer	Line	Destination	Time	Remarks
Jan. 1	Cleopatra	Nova Scotia Steamship Co	Yarmouth	7.00 A.M.	Mails for Nova Scotia.
" 5	Carroll	Boston, Halifax, and Prince Edward Island	Halifax	" "	Mails for Nova Scotia.
" 8	Cleopatra	Nova Scotia Steamship Co	Yarmouth	11.00	Mails for Nova Scotia.
" 12	Carroll	Boston, Halifax, and Prince Edward Island	Halifax	7.00	Mails for Nova Scotia.
" 15	Cleopatra	Nova Scotia Steamship Co	Yarmouth	11.00	Mails for Nova Scotia, Newfoundland, and Miquelon.
" 19	Carroll	Boston, Halifax, and Prince Edward Island	Halifax	7.00	Mails for Nova Scotia.
" 22	Cleopatra	Nova Scotia Steamship Co	Yarmouth	11.00	Mails for Nova Scotia.
" 26	Carroll	Boston, Halifax, and Prince Edward Island	Halifax	7.00	Mails for Nova Scotia, Newfoundland, and Miquelon.

FROM SAN FRANCISCO.

Date	Steamer	Line	Destination	Time	Remarks
Jan. 7	Mexico	Pacific Coast Steamship Co	Victoria	9.00	Mails for British Columbia.
" 15	Geo. W. Elder	Pacific Coast Steamship Co	Victoria	9.00 "	Mails for British Columbia.
" 23	Mexico	Pacific Coast Steamship Co	Victoria	9.00 "	Mails for British Columbia.
" 31	Geo. W. Elder	Pacific Coast Steamship Co	Victoria	9.00 "	Mails for British Columbia.

[Continued on next page.]

MAILS FOR THE WEST INDIES, MEXICO, CENTRAL AND SOUTH AMERICA.

Date of Sailing.	Name of Steamer.	Name of Line.	Port of Destination and Intermed'te Ports of Call.	Hour of Closg Mail at P.O. of Departure.	Mails to be Conveyed.
			FROM NEW YORK.		
Jan. 3	Alvena	Atlas	Port au Prince	1.00 P.M.	Mails for Hayti.
" 3	Antillas	Atlas	St. John's	1.00 "	Mails for Porto Rico direct.
" 3	Santiago	New York and Cuba Mail	Nassau and Santiago	1.00 "	Mails for the Bahama Islands, and for Santiago and Cienfuegos, Cuba.
" 3	British Empire	N.Y., Hav., & Mex. Mail	Havana, etc.	1.30 "	Mails for Cuba, and for the West Indies and Mexico via Havana.
" 4	Valencia	Red D	Puerto Cabello, Laguayra, Maracaibo, and Curaçoa.		Mails for Venezuela and Curaçoa.
" 4	Muriel	Quebec Steamship Co.	Barbadoes	10.00 A.M.	Mails for the Windward Islands.
" "	Niagara	New York and Cuba Mail	Havana	1.00 P.M.	Mails for Cuba, and for Porto Rico via Havana.
" 8	Athos	Atlas	Kingston, Port au Prince, Port Limon, and Savanilla	1.30 "	Mails for Jamaica, Hayti, Port Limon, and the United States of Colombia, except Aspinwall and Panama.
" 10	Colon	Pacific Mail	Aspinwall	1 00 "	Mails for the South Pacific and Central American ports, and for the West Coast of Mexico via Aspinwall
" 10	City of Puebla	N.Y., Hav., & Mex. Mail	Havana	10.00 A.M.	Mails for Cuba, and for Porto Rico and Mexico via Havana.
" 10	Orinoco	Quebec Steamship Co.	Hamilton	1.30 P.M.	Mails for Bermuda.
" 12	Glenfyne	Red D	Puerto Cabello, Laguayra, Maracaibo, and Curaçoa.	1.30	Mails for Venezuela and Curaçoa.
" 12	Flamborough	Quebec Steamship Co.	Barbadoes	10.00 A.M.	Mails for the Windward Islands.
" 12	Newport	New York and Cuba Mail	Havana	1.00 P.M.	Mails for Cuba, and for Porto Rico via Havana.
" 15	Advance	U.S. and Brazil Mail	St. Thomas, Para, Maranham, Pernambuco, Bahia, and Rio de Janeiro	1.00 A.M.	Mails for the West Indies via St. Thomas, for Brazil, and for the Argentine Republic, Uruguay, and Paraguay via Brazil. Steamer receives mails from New York and Baltimore at Newport News, Va.
" 15	Bermuda	Quebec Steamship Co.	Barbadoes	1.00 P.M.	Mails for the Windward Islands.
" 17	Cienfuegos	New York and Cuba Mail	Nassau and Santiago	1.30 "	Mails for the Bahama Islands, and for Santiago and Cienfuegos, Cuba.
" 17	City of Alexandria	N.Y., Hav., & Mex. Mail	Havana	1.30 "	Mails for Cuba, and for the West Indies and Mexico via Havana.
" 18	Alps	Atlas	St. John's	1.00 "	Mails for Porto Rico direct.
" 20	Saratoga	New York and Cuba Mail	Havana	1.30 "	Mails for Cuba, and for Porto Rico via Havana.
" 21	City of Para	Pacific Mail	Aspinwall	10.00 A.M.	Mails for the South Pacific, etc. (Same as Colon.)
" 22	George W. Clyde	Clyde	Cape Hayti, Puerto Plata, Samana, St. Domingo City, and Grand Turk	1.00 P.M.	Mails for Cape Hayti, Saint Domingo, and Turk's Island.
" 22	Ailsa	Atlas	Kingston, Port au Prince, Port Limon, and Savanilla	1.00 "	Mails for Jamaica, etc. (Same as Athos.)
" 24	Caracas	Red D	Puerto Cabello, Laguayra, Maracaibo, and Curaçoa.	10.00 A.M.	Mails for Venezuela and Curaçoa.
" 24	Orinoco	Quebec Steamship Co.	Hamilton	1.30 P.M.	Mails for Bermuda
" 24	City of Washington	N.Y. Hav., & Mex. Mail	Havana	1.30 "	Mails for Cuba, and for Porto Rico and Mexico via Havana.
" 26	Niagara	New York and Cuba Mail	Havana	1.00 "	Mails for Cuba, and for Porto Rico via Havana.
" 30	Alvo	Atlas	Port au Prince	1.00 "	Mails for Hayti.
" 31	City of Merida	N.Y., Hav., & Mex. Mail	Havana	1.30 "	Mails for Cuba, and for Porto Rico and Mexico via Havana.
			FROM NEW ORLEANS.		
J'n. 1	Whitney	Morgan Line	Vera Cruz	6.15 A.M.	Mails for Mexico.
" 1	Morgan	Morgan Line	Havana	7.00 "	Mails for Cuba.
" 3	City of Dallas	Royal Mail Steamship Co.	Belize, Puerto Cortez, and Livingston		Mails for British and Spanish Honduras, and Guatemala.
" 5	City of Mexico	New York, Havana, and Mexican Mail	Vera Cruz via Bagdad, Tampico, and Tuxpan	10.00 "	Mails for Mexico.
" 7	E. B. Ward, Jr.	Oteri's Pioneer Line	Ruatan and Truxillo.	7.00 :	Mails for Spanish Honduras and Bay Islands.
" 10	Hutchinson	Morgan Line	Havana	8.00 :	Mails for Cuba.
" 16	Whitney	Morgan Line	Vera Cruz.	7.00 :	Mails for Cuba.
" 17	Morgan	Morgan Line	Havana.	6.15 :	Mails for Cuba.
" 17	Lucy P. Miller	Royal Mail Steamship Co.	Belize, Puerto Cortez, etc.	10.00 :	Mails for British and Spanish Honduras, and Guatemala.

Date	Steamer	Line	From / Route	Time	Description
" 24	Hutchinson	Morgan Line	Havana	7.00 A.M.	Mails for Cuba.
" 25	E. B. Ward, Jr.	Oteri's Pioneer Line	Ruatan and Truxillo	8.00 "	Mails for Spanish Honduras and Bay Islands.
" 26	City of Dallas	Royal Mail Steamship Co	Belize, Puerto Cortez, etc.	10.00 "	Mails for British and Spanish Honduras, and Guatemala.
" 27	City of Mexico	N. Y., Hav., & Mex. Mail	Vera Cruz via Bagdad, etc.	7.00 "	Mails for Mexico.
" 31	Morgan	Morgan Line	Havana	7.00 "	Mails for Cuba.
			FROM GALVESTON, Tex.		
Jan. 8	Whitney	Morgan Line	Vera Cruz	....	Mails for Mexico.
" 17	Whitney	Morgan Line	Vera Cruz	....	Mails for Mexico.
			FROM KEY WEST, Fla.		
Jan. 6	Morgan	Morgan Line	Havana	....	Mails for Cuba.
" 13	Hutchinson	Morgan Line	Havana	....	Mails for Cuba.
" 20	Morgan	Morgan Line	Havana	....	Mails for Cuba.
" 27	Hutchinson	Morgan Line	Havana	....	Mails for Cuba.
			FROM BALTIMORE, Md.		
Jan. 15	Advance	U. S. and Brazil Mail	St. Thomas, Para, etc.	4.00 A.M.	Mails for the West Indies, etc. (Same as Advance above.)
			FROM SAN FRANCISCO		
Jan. 5	Newbern	Cal. and Mexican SS. Co.	Ensenada, Cape St. Lucas, Magdalena Bay, La Paz, Mazatlan, and Guaymas	11.00 A.M.	Mails for the West Coast of Mexico.
" 15	San Blas	Pacific Mail	Panama and Way Ports	8.30 "	Mails for Mexico, and for the South Pacific and Central American ports.

TRANS-PACIFIC MAILS.

Date	Steamer	Line	From / Route	Time	Description
			FROM SAN FRANCISCO		
Jan. 1	Mariposa	French Contract Line	Papeiti	2.00 P.M.	Mails for Tahiti and Marquesas Islands. Mails close 4 p. m., December 31.
" 1		Oceanic Steamship Co	Honolulu	....	Mails for the Sandwich Islands.
" 9	C of Rio de Janeiro	Pacific Mail	Yokohama and Hong Kong	10.30 A.M.	Mails for Japan, Shanghai, Hong Kong and dependent Chinese ports, and the East Indies, except British India.
" 15	Alameda	Oceanic Steamship Co	Honolulu	2.00 P.M.	Mails for the Sandwich Islands.
" 18	Zealandia	Pacific Mail	Honolulu, Sydney, Auck'd	....	Mails for the Sandwich Islands, New Zealand, and Australia; for Fiji and Samoan Islands, and New Caledonia via Sydney, New South Wales.
" 23	City of Tokio	Pacific Mail	Yokohama and Kong Kong	10.30 A.M.	Mails for Japan, etc. (Same as City of Rio de Janeiro.)

In case of accident to any steamer booked for departure at a particular date, another one is substituted to carry the mail at the time specified.

TELEGRAPHIC CABLE RATES.

Tariff to Great Britain, Ireland, France, and Germany.

Per word.

From New York City, Brooklyn, and Yonkers in New York, the New England States, New Brunswick, Nova Scotia, Ontario and Quebec.......... 50 cents.

From New York (except New York City, Brooklyn and Yonkers), New Jersey, Pennsylvania, Delaware, Maryland and District of Columbia....... 53 cents.

From Virginia, West Virginia, Ohio, Michigan, Kentucky, Indiana, Illinois, St. Louis in Missouri, and Milwaukee, Wisconsin.................. 55 cents.

From North Carolina, South Carolina, Georgia, Alabama, Mississippi, New Orleans in Louisiana,

Per word.

Tennessee, Denver and Leadville in Colorado, and Western Union offices in Florida........... 60 cents.

From Louisiana (except New Orleans), Texas, Wisconsin (except Milwaukee), Iowa, Missouri (except St. Louis), Arkansas, Minnesota, Dakota, Manitoba, Kansas, Nebraska, and Indian Territory.... 65 cents.

From Colorado (except Denver and Leadville), Wyoming, Utah, New Mexico, Idaho, Montana, Nevada, California, Arizona, Oregon and Washington Territory................................. 70 cents.

From British Columbia.......... .... 75 cents.

Senders can insure their messages being forwarded by any particular route, such as "via Siberia," "via Santander," "via Teheran," etc., by inserting the indication of route in the "Check." The indication is transmitted free of charge.

Messages destined for places beyond the lines of telegraph must contain instructions from the sender as to the name of the place from which they are to be posted. The postage to be charged is thirty-seven cents.

Rules for Atlantic Cable Business.

(1) The maximum length of a chargeable word will be fixed at ten letters. Should a word contain more than ten letters, every ten or fraction of ten letters will be counted as a word.

(2) Code messages must be composed of words in the English, French, German, Spanish, Italian, Dutch, Portuguese, and Latin languages. Proper names (*i. e.*, names of persons and places) will not be allowed in the text of Code Messages, except in the manner they are used in ordinary private messages.

(3) Groups of figures or letters will be counted at the rate of three figures or letters to a word, plus one word for any excess.

Rates from New York to	PER WORD	Rates from New York to	PER WORD	Rates from New York to	PER WORD
Aden, Arabia ...	$1.43	Siberian rate shall be collected for messages to Japan.		from London : Rio de Janeiro and places north in Brazil, $2.41 per word ; places south in Brazil, $2.61 per word. The words via *Government land lines* must be included and paid for.	
" via Bombay	2.20	Luxemburg	$ .56		
Africa—		Madeira, (Madeira Islands)	.88		
Delagoa Bay	2.65	Malacca	2.05		
Mozambique	2.65	Malta	.64		
Zanzibar	2.40	Mauritius—Telegrams for the Island of, can be posted at Aden.		Uruguay—	
Africa (South)—				Montevedio	$3.21
Durban	2.65	Montenegro	.62	All other places in Uruguay..	3.21
All other places in South Africa	2.75	New Zealand	3.40	Argentine Republic—	
Algeria	.58	Norway	.60	Buenos Ayres	2.94
" via Falmouth	.77	Orkney Islands—Rules and rates same as Great Britain.		All other places in Arg'ne Rep	2.94
Australia, via Falm'th or Teheran	3.15			Chili	3.11
" via Siberia	4.55	Penang, via Falmouth or Teheran	1.85	Peru—	
Austria	.61	" via Siberia	3.50	Arica	5.20
Belgium	.56	Persia	.90	Arequipa	5.58
Beloochistan	1.50	Phillipine Island, Luzon.	2.95	Callao	6.10
Benghazi — Messages posted at Malta.		Portugal	.65	Islay	5.58
		" via Santander	.68	Iquique	4.83
Burmah, Further India	1.80	Roumania	.62	Lima	6.30
" " via Penang	2.30	Russia in Europe	.68	Molendo	5.58
Bushire	1.18	Russia, Caucasus	.75	Puno	5.58
Cape Verde Islands. St. Vincent.	1.48	Russia in Asia, west of Verkhnee Oudinsk	.90	Tacna	5.20
Ceylon, via Falmouth or Teheran	1.75	Russia in Asia, east of Verkhnee Oudinsk	1.15	Bolivia, Antofagasta ...	4.83
Channel Islands—Rules and rates same as London.		St. Vincent, Cape Verde Island .	1.48	Messages for South America can also be sent via the West Indies.	
Channel Islands via France.	.59	Scilly Islands. Same as London.		Spain, via Falmouth or Santander	.66
China	2.55	Servia	.62	" via Gibraltar.	.75
Cochin China—		Sicily	.59	" via Marseilles.	.65
Saigon, via Falm'th or Teheran	2.30	Sardinia	.59	Sweden	.64
" via Siberia	3.15	Shetland Islands—Rules and rates same as Great Britain.		Switzerland	.56
Corfu	.64	Singapore, via Falm'th or Teheran	2.08	Tripoli	.79
Corsica	.59	" via Siberia	3.25	Turkey in Europe	.64
Cyprus	.95	South America, via cable from Europe:		" via Falmouth.	.83
Denmark	.60	Brazil—		" Asia—Seaports	.70
Egypt—		Maranham	3.52	" " via Falm'h	.88
Alexandria	.84	Para	3.81	" " Inland	.74
All other places in Egypt	.81	Pernambuco	2.70	" " " via Falm'th	.93
Gibraltar	.68	Bahia and Rio de Janeiro	2.61	Turkish Islands	.74
Greece	.66	Santos	3.11	" via Falmouth	.93
Greek Islands	.70	Santa Catherina	3.11	Turkey, via Russia and Odessa Cable—Messages must be marked "via Indo," and sent via London. Rates are as follows:	
Heligoland	.65	Rio Grande do Sul	3.11		
Holland	.58	Other places in Brazil, north.	2.91	Turkey in Europe	.83
Hungary	.61	" " " south.	3.11	" Asia—Seaports	.89
India, via Falmouth or Teheran..	1.75	Messages for Brazil can also be sent via Government land lines in Brazil at following rates *per word*		" " Inland	.93
Italy	.59			" " Archipelago	.93
Java, via Falmouth or Teheran ..	2.20			Tunisia	.58
" via Siberia	3.50			" via Falmouth	.77
Japan, via Falmouth or Teheran .	3.50				
" via Siberia	2.80				
Unless specially directed, the					

To Cuba and West Indies.

Via Cable to Havana, Cuba.

From New York City to the Following Places at the Rate of 50 Cents per Word:

Havana, Cuba	Consolacion*	Ciego de Avila*	Manzanillo‡	St. Dom'go (Coloniado*)
Batabano, " *	Colon*	Guanaja*	Mariel*	Sagua*
Bajucal, " *	Cardenas*	Guines*	Pinar del Roi*	Santiago‡
Bemba, " *	Cienfuegos‡	Guantanamo‡	Puerte Principe*	Santo-Spiritu*
Bayamo*	Caibarien*	Jignani*	Remedios*	Trinidad*
Bahia Honda*	Cabanas*	Matanzas*	San Antonio*	....

* Add to the rate of 50 cents per word 40 cents for each ten, or fraction of ten, words.

† Add to the rate of 44 cents per word $2.25 for first ten words or less, and 22 cents for each word over ten.

‡ Add to the rate of 44 cents per word $3 for first ten words or less, and 30 cents for each word over ten.

From New York City to

Per word.		Per word.		Per word.		Per word.
Antigua.............$2.41	Grenada $2.83	Porto Rico, San Juan $2.18	St. Lucia..............2.66
Barbadoes 2.84	Guadaloupe 2.51	" Other places 2.14	St. Vincent 2.73
Berbice 3.38	" Basse Terre. 2.49	St. Croix...............2.22	Trinidad, Port of Spain. 2.94
Demerara 3.36	Kingston (Jamaica).... 1.35	St. Thomas 2.17	" Other places.. 2.96
Dominica..............2.55	Martinique 2.60	St. Kitts 2.35	....

To Mexico.

From New York City.

Messages to all places, except towns near the boundary line between the United States and Mexico, will be sent via cables of the Mexican Telegraph Company from Galveston, Texas. Important towns in Mexico near the frontier, sent via Western Union offices. For other places rates are as follows:

To Tampico, Mexico, $3.75 for ten words, and 33 cents for each word over ten.

To Vera Cruz, Mexico, $4.75 for ten words, and 43 cents for each word over ten.

To City of Mexico, Mexico, $5.25 for ten words, and 48 cents for each word over ten.

To Goatzacoalcos, Mexico, 62 cents per word.   To Salina Cruz, Mexico, 72 cents per word.

To Aspinwall, Colon, $1.00 per word.   To Panama, $1.00 per word.

To all other points in Mexico, on Mexican Government lines, the rate to Vera Cruz (no reliable inland line from Tampico) will be charged, and the Mexican Government rate will be added, as follows: 50 cents for ten words, and 5 cents for each word over ten.

To points on State or Private Line Stations, beyond the Government lines, the State or Private Line rate will be added to the Government rate.

The Date, Address and Signature are free.

To Central and South America.

Via Central and South American Cables.

Salvador.—La Libertad, 75 cents per word. Other offices in Salvador, 80 cents per word.

Guatemala.—All offices in Guatemala, 80 cents per word.   **Honduras.**—All offices in Honduras, 80 cents per word.

Costa Rica.—All offices in Costa Rica, $1.05 per word.

Nicaraugua.—San Juan del Sur, $1.00 per word. Other offices in Nicaraugua, $1.05 per word.

South America.

Panama, $1.00 per word.   **From New York City.**   Aspinwall, Colon, $1.00 per word.

U. S. Columbia.—Buenaventura, $1.52 per word. Bogota and other offices, $1.57 per word.

Ecuador.—St. Elena Bay, $1.77 per word. Guayaquil, $1.77 per word.   Bolivia.—Antofagasta, $2.72 per word.

PERU.

Per word.		Per word.		Per word.		Per word.
Arica.............$2.52	Huanillos.............$2.68	Mollendo.............$2.47	Pisaqua $2.68
Arequipa 2.69	Iquique 2.57	Pabullon de Pica........2.68	Tacna................2.67
Callao................2.17	Lima 2.17	Payta................1.92	....

CHILI.

Per word.		Per word.		Per word.		Per word.
Caldera.............$2.82	Copiapo $2.93	Huasco...............$2.93	Taltal...............2.92
Carrizal 3.03	Coquimbo 3.03	Lota 3.18	Talcahuano 3.18
Chillan 3.18	Famaya 3.51	Ovalle 3.03	Tocopilla 2.83
Chanaral 2.93	Freirina 3.03	Santiago 3.18	Valdivia 3.18
Cobija 2.83	Guavacan 3.03	Serena 2.92	Vallenar 3.03
Concepcion 3.18	Higuera 3.43	Talca 3.18	Valparaiso............3.07

To **Buenos Ayres** and other places in the Argentine Republic, $2.92 per word from New York.

To **Montevideo** and all other places in Uruguay, $3.00 per word from New York.

BRAZIL.

Per word.		Per word.		Per word.		Per word.
Bahia................$2.91	Para.................$3.80	Rio..................$2.91	Santos............... $3.11
Pernambuco....... 2.70	Maranham.............3.50	Rio Grande.............3.11	Santa Catharina.. .... 3.11

All inland stations 15 cents per word in addition to tariff from nearest coast line station.

Love's Young Dream.

I wooed her when the grass was young,
  And earth put on her robe of flowers;
My love, wild as March winds, I sung;
  As fickle she as April showers.

Her troth she plighted when the moon
  Was grand and full; the air's caresses
Full freighted with the sweets of June
  Waved to and fro her golden tresses.

Oh, happy were the passing hours,
  The sweetest days that I remember;
The coming frost possessed no powers
  To cast a blight in bright September.

But when the ground was white with snow,
  Ere bleak November days were over,
She told me calmly I could go:
  She deemed me but a summer lover.

'Twas years ago. Could I forget
  I gave my young love to her only?
My heart was crushed with vain regret
  And I grieved desolate and lonely.

Where is she now? I little reck,
  What "might have been" has long been
    mended;
Another young love came on deck
  And thus the boyhood dream was ended.
              Harry J. Shellman.

Pen-wipers.

Hard to beat — stones.

Artists are designing creatures.

Knights of the Middle Ages — those from forty to fifty years old.

A big salary is unusual to a choir; but it is sometimes obtained by chants.

When pedestrians are afflicted with bad colds, their walking-match becomes a hoarse-race.

When twins are born, a father's responsibilities become two apparent; at least so they are apt to appear to a parent.

What is the difference between the moonshiner troubles and a man who posts placards? One is a still bicker and the other a bill sticker.

"Punctuality requires no undue exertion" if you are ahead of time, for you can sit down and wait; but if one only happens to have about five minutes to walk a mile and catch a train, a fellow generally finds it necessary to hump himself in order to be prompt.

A Matter of Feeling.

"What do you think of that young lady?" asked one gentleman of another, at a party.

"Why, she made quite an impression on me," he replied, as he felt of his favorite corn on which she had accidentally stepped.

"I suppose she wanted to make sure of your footing before she was introduced."

"Well, she certainly arrived at an understanding."

Quite a Breeze.

"Waitaw, I will weally have to wemove to anothaw table. There appeaws to be a terwible dwaft heaw."

"Tain't no draff heah, no how, Mr. La Dude. Dah aint no win' 'tall 'cept wat dat yer lady am makin' wid her fan."

"Aw, that's it. I knew there was a dwaft. It nearly blew me away. Weally, now, couldn't you ask her to stop?"

AMERICAN COUNTING-ROOM.

Vol. VIII.   FEBRUARY, 1884.   No. 2.

BUILDING AND LOAN ASSOCIATIONS.
I.

Philadelphia, the great city of homes, owes much of its justly-earned celebrity in this respect to the wide-spread results of building associations. But familiar as is the idea to most of its people, there are comparatively few, even among those who are members of some one or other of the hundreds of such bodies, who are *intimately* acquainted with the practical workings of their own organization, and still fewer who have made the general subject, and the respective merits or demerits of the varied plans of working of building associations, a study. Such being the case in that home of these societies, it is no wonder that in other places, where no such attempts at combining funds for mutual benefit have ever been tried, there should be still less information in reference to them. In fact, in many places they had never been heard mentioned; and as there appears to be a growing desire manifested by letters of inquiry from widely separated communities to learn something about their true inwardness, modes of organizing and working, and, what is of far more importance, perhaps, as deserving a place in this journal, the mode in which the accounts connected with them are managed, this article is written; not intended to be, by any means, an exhaustive analysis of the subject, but to give a general outline sketch of the principal ideas sought to be attained; the inducements held out by rival associations; the value that may be derived by a community from such an organization; the rocks upon which they may be split, and the risks that may be incurred.

The principal idea of a building asso-
Vol. VIII.—5.

ciation is, that a number of persons may, by combining their means in equal periodic sums, help each other to obtain for themselves homes. There has been added to this the other idea that some who do not want to purchase or build may want to use money in some other way—under some other security. Hence they became building and loan associations.

Still a third idea in them is, that others—some who do not want either to buy, build or borrow—may want to invest money, they to reap their share of the benefits arising from the use of the funds by the borrowers.

It is manifest from this statement of the fundamental ideas of these bodies that there must be an agreed-upon completed value to a share, and that there must be an agreed-upon rate and period of paying-in, and of selling or loaning, the funds.

The completed value of shares of, I believe, all associations in Philadelphia, and wherever its systems have been adopted, is two hundred dollars, paid in monthly dues, or instalments of one dollar each. If there were no earnings, it would take $16\frac{2}{3}$ years to complete the full paid value. In any well-regulated society, carefully and honestly managed, it will "run out" in about ten years, more or less, according to the demand and the rates of premium paid for the use of money. Some have "run out" in less than eight years. Whether such extraordinary prosperity is a healthy condition of affairs or not depends upon other causes, which it is not my province here to discuss, but belongs, with the discussion of similar problems, to the political economist.

The accumulated funds derived each month from the payment of dues and other sources of income (to be treated of hereafter) are put up at auction, and sold to the highest bidder, according to the peculiarities of the system under which they may be working. The amount of money for which the would-be borrower bids is so many multiples of $200 as he may want, or there may be to sell. The bid having been recognized as the highest, the matter is referred to a committee, to whom is submitted, for their inspection, the security the bidder has to offer; on which they report subsequently. If favorable, the title is examined, and the necessary papers drawn by the solicitor; the order is drawn on the treasurer, and the borrower gets his money, subject to certain conditions, which being fulfilled until his shares have attained a value of $200 each, his securities are released, and so far as that transaction is concerned the matter is ended. Such, in brief outline, is the ground-work of all building associations, and on this foundation the various superstructures are erected which distinguish one plan of working from another.

The most prominent of these are:

I. *The premium-full-paid plan;* which again is subdivided between "*the interest paid upon the full value*" and "*the interest paid upon the reduced value.*"

II. *The interest-in-advance-plan;* and

III. *The premium-paid-monthly plan.*

Each of these have various modifications, according to the fancy of those organizing the association. Each, of course, claims for itself superiority over every other plan, and each, of course, has some peculiar merit to recommend it to the attention of the public. The judgment, however, of the best informed among the experts in this class of accounts is, that, under ordinary circumstances, and fairly administered, there is not much difference as to the results; between nine and ten years is the normal life of a series. (Here again is a distinction under each of these kinds; some are, "one series" associations,

while others are "many series.") While such is the case as to general results, it does not by any means follow that the practical workings under each is the same to every borrower, either under the system governing his own association, or as between that and some other plan, as will more fully appear when the workings of each of these comes to be considered.

Let us suppose a building association is about to be started, and those favorable thereto have met for the purpose of organizing one, say, on the first-mentioned plan ("Premium-full-paid," which was the original one); they have decided upon a name, have applied for a charter, and adopted a constitution, which sets forth—

(1) *Its Title and Object.* — This last being "the accumulation of a fund by monthly instalments, interest on loans, premiums and fines, to enable stockholders to purchase real estate, erect buildings, or to use in such ways as they may deem for their best interest," etc. The stock shall be limited (say, to five thousand shares).

(2) *Stockholders.* — Describing who may or may not become such.

(3) *Officers.* — These are, usually, a president, vice-president, treasurer, secretary, solicitor (or conveyancer), directors (usually seven or nine), and auditors (generally three).

(4) *Meetings.* — Time of monthly and annual.

   a. of Stockholders and quorum.
   b. of Directors.
   c. of Special; how convened, etc.

(5) *Dues, Fines, etc.*—This, generally, provides for an extra assessment on each share of stock (say, of 25 cents, for instance) to provide for organization expenses, regular dues, fines for non-payment of dues (this is limited by law in Pennsylvania to two per cent., as formerly it used to be ten per cent., and the burden got to be oppressive to delinquents) provides for action in case persistent non-payment of dues either of a borrower or non-borrower (usually, in the case of a borrower, six months is the limit).

(6) *Loans.* — Sec. *1*. Each stockholder is *entitled* to receive a loan of two hun

dred dollars on each share. *Sec. 2.* The mode of disposing it shall be in open session, and the highest bidder (under this plan) to be entitled to it, etc. *Sec. 3.* How low bids may be made (in some States laws govern this, and any bid, if the highest, whether or not it reaches the limit set by the association, must be accepted. When money is very easy, the associations with a high limit run a risk of not being able to sell their funds. *Sec. 4* provides for the deduction of the premium bid from the principal, the securing of the association on the loan, etc. *Sec. 5* provides for loans made upon stock collateral.

(7) *Deceased Stockholders' Rights.* — (Generally there is some State law which has to be considered in this connection).

(8) *Seal.*

(9) *Certificates of Stock.* —Some associations issue certificates, and some do not. Where they do, provision is made for their issue, transfer, cancellation, and re-issue, in case of loss, putting whatever safeguards they deem best around this. (N. B.—The importance of this last is not always sufficiently apprehended, and is worthy of careful consideration.)

(10) Provides for Articles of Agreement—that, is, an agreement to be written out, in due form, in a book provided for the signature and address of every member.

(11) Shows how its term of life.— either as a series or association—shall be determined.

(12) *By-laws.* — Providing
1. For elections.
2. Duties of officers.
3. Duties of directors.
4. Meetings of directors.
5. Fines, forfeitures, withdrawals, etc.
6. Change or cancellation of securities.
7. Salaries.
8. Amendments, etc., to by-laws.
9. Order of business. Usually,
   (1) Roll-call of officers.
   (2) Roll-call of association, when each member, answering to his name, comes forward paying his dues, etc.
   (3) Reading minutes.
   (4) Reports of committees.
   (5) Other business.
   (6) Second roll-call of members.
   (7) New business.
   (8) Sale of money—usually at some fixed hour.
   (9) Appointment of committees, etc.

In different societies the practice varies in reference to the mode of receiving the dues of the association. Some appoint a committee of two to receive as members come in, or as their names may be called by the secretary. These two are to be others than either the secretary or treasurer. The secretary notes, on his record, how much ought to have been received; having given credit to each member as the committee announces, compares the result with the committee's records, and takes the treasurer's acknowledgment for the amount received, which he then records in the minutes. Others are less formal, less careful, and run more risk.

Having adopted our constitution and by-laws, and elected our officers, we are now ready to proceed to business.

The president, having called the association to order, announces that before opening regularly for the main business of the association there are some preliminaries necessary to be considered and acted upon, so he is ready for a motion.

Mr. Keen, who has as his pet hobby the "one series" idea, immediately rises and says: "Mr. President, I move that this association be a "one series" one; and in making this motion I desire—"

President: "One moment, Mr. Keen. Is that motion seconded?"

"I second that motion."

President: "It has been moved and seconded that this association be limited to one series. Are you ready for the question?"

"Mr. President!" "Mr. President!" "Mr. President."

President: "Mr. Keen is entitled to the floor."

Mr. Keen: "I desire to present the reasons which to my mind are conclusive why this or any other building association should be limited to one series. In the first place and chiefly the members are all placed on an equal footing; any burdens that are to be borne are shared alike; there is no room for dispute as to the division of profits; and, lastly, there is more certainty when the end is reached."

Mr. Sharp: " Mr. President. I am opposed to this motion, and desire, before resuming my seat, to move an amendment by saying it be *not* limited to any definite number of series; and for the following reasons good and sufficient to me, and, when you have duly considered them, I trust, to you all. A one series association is apt to start well and flourish, perhaps, for a year or two—possibly three; then, as the life of the association seems nearer to its close, borrowers become fewer, as there is less advantage in paying premiums for five years or less than the same, or even a proportionately greater, for eight or nine. Again; there can be little inducement held out, as the time rolls on, for bringing in new members when they are brought to face the fact that they must pay up, not only the back dues, but the increased value. Still further; in advocacy of the amendment which I now offer, new series started every year or six months brings in new blood, more money, more borrowers, divides the weight of expenses among a greater number, replaces withdrawals, and insures combined prosperity."

The amendment having been seconded, the argument progresses, ringing the changes upon these and other arguments, when the question is put to a final vote and is decided.

Let us say in favor of a many series— more for the purpose of explaining here how the operations are conducted and of showing the working of the accounts thereunder—as in explaining this the " one series " system will be equally well understood. For, of course, we start with " Series 1," and for the first six months at least there is no difference. Say we have started with one hundred members and six hundred shares. Each member comes forward and pays one dollar per share, and twenty-five cents per share assessment, as before explained, for initiatory expenses. Our receipts have thus been $750. Each member receives a book containing a

printed copy of constitution and by-laws, with additional blank pages sufficient for twelve years, ruled something like one of the following forms:

BUILDING AND LOAN ASSOCIATION..

DATE.	DUES.	INTEREST.	FINES.	TOTAL.
Sept. 18				$
Received, $				*Secretary.*
Oct. 18				$
Received, $				*Secretary.*
Nov. 18				$
Received, $				*Secretary.*

BUILDING AND LOAN ASSOCIATION.

Jan.	Cash	
Feb.	Cash	
March.	Cash	
April.	Cash	
May.	Cash	
June.	Cash	
July.	Cash	
August.	Cash	
Sept.	Cash	
Oct.	Cash	
Nov.	Cash	
Dec.	Cash	

There are many other forms, and still others can be adopted to suit the convenience or fancy—the object, however, being to furnish the stockholder with an acknowledgment of some competent authority—either the secretary or a director appointed to receive, as before explained — binding the association to account to him for so much moneys and their product.

The secretary having recorded the names, and the amounts corresponding, has taken the treasurer's acknowledgment. Bills are presented for books, charter, fees, stationery, and the other expenses incidental to the opening. These will, probably, be found to approach, say, three hundred dollars, not necessarily all to be counted as expenses of the first year or first series, but can be, and justly ought to be, distributed through a series of years, say, in tenths. There will then be four hundred dollars for sale. The president announces the fact and says he is open to receive bids on one share ($200) with the privilege of (say five, as the receipts of the next evening being probably six hundred more, will enable them to loan one thousand dollars by the time the loan is ready to be made.) Ten per cent. is bid; 15, 20, and, if demand is active and borrowers enthusiastic, as they are apt to be in a new organization, 25 or even more; and the money is knocked down to Mr. Ready, who says he will take on five shares. The president appoints a committee to examine the security offered, and orders a special meeting of the Board (if thought necessary) prior to next regular monthly meeting, to hear the report of the committee and take such further steps in the premises as may be required.

Mr. Ready fills up the blank form of application, which may be somewhat after the following form:

No........   *Account No........*
........................*188*

To the President and Directors of the Building
and Loan Association of————:
GENTLEMEN:

Having bid for an advance on........shares of the Association in No......series, I offer you the property herein described by me, as security for the payments, in accordance with the constitution and by-laws.

....

Residence......................

The property consits of a lot of ground situated on.........Street, being No.........Street, in the.......of————, ——. The size thereof is ....feet front on.........Street, by..... ....feet deep...........on which is erected...... ....the size of which is .... built and finished in the year............

The property is subject to ....held by .... Insured perpetually in the office of the..............in the sum of..............

The property is rented, and brings $........per annum.

...shares No...series, @...per cent. per share premium. Par value of loan, $....

N. B.—Send this to the Chairman of the Committee on Property on or before the............. day of..............A. D., 188

This is handed to the committee, who make their examination, and fill up a form of report something like this:

........................*188*
To the President and Directors of the Building
and Loan Association of————:
GENTLEMEN:

We have viewed the property described in the application of Mr..............as security for an advance on......shares, and, in our opinion, an advance upon......shares in No....series can be safely made thereon. We therefore recommend that an advance to the amount of.............. dollars, upon......shares in No...series be made to Mr..............upon the property described.

A perpetual Policy of Insurance for the sum of ....dollars being first assigned by ....to the Association as collateral security for the payment of all dues and fines. And also.......................................
We estimate the value of the property to be $.....

....
..................⎫ *Committee.*
..................⎭

The Board having met to hear the report of the committee, generally coincide with their views, unless some member's knowledge is adverse; and, if favorable, it is referred to the solicitor on a form something like the following:

........................*188*
To................Esq.,
Solicitor of the Building and Loan Association, of ——.

SIR:—You are hereby directed to examine the title, make searches, draw bond and mortgage for ....dollars, and other necessary papers, and, if all proves correct, attest by signing the report below.   ....*President.*
..................*Secretary.*

for his examination as to title and incumbrances, and he reports as he finds.

*To Mr..............Secretary of the Building and
Loan Association, of————:*

I certify that I have caused searches to be made in the proper offices, and that there are no incumbrances on the real estate described in the foregoing application, except.........................
and that the said..............has a good and perfect title to the said real estate described by him, and that he has executed a bond and mortgage to THE BUILDING AND LOAN ASSOCIATION OF————, in the sum of $.............which is on record.... ....and assigned a perpetual Policy of Insurance on the same to said Association, in the sum of..................

.......................A. D. 188

....*Solicitor.*

Everything being correct, the solicitor reports to the secretary, when the subject is presented at next meeting, and on motion an order is drawn on the treas-

Account No......

Building and Loan Association
OF ————.

REPORT OF THE

No......

COMMITTEE on PROPERTY,

OFFERED AS SECURITY BY

Mr..
Located No.............................Street,
in the ....Ward, ————, ——.
...............shares, No...............series.
Loan...........shares, par value, $............
As per order No........
Dated.......................188
See minutes dated......................188

urer for one thousand dollars less the amount of premium. If twenty-five per cent., his order is for seven hundred and fifty dollars. His bond and mort-

gage is for one thousand dollars, and he is to pay each month five dollars dues and five dollars interest (a six per cent. rate). These forms are all in one sheet, with a backing, same as form herewith, which the secretary fills and files all with his papers.

Here comes in the first variation referred to before in plan similar to this in every other respect, except that the interest, instead of being on $1,000 as above, is on the net amount *received*. In the case before us, $750, or $3.75.

I hear some one say here, "You quoted approvingly the judgment of some that there was not much difference in results," and is there not considerable difference both to the payer and payee between $10 per month and $8.75 per month? Truly there is; but this is just one of the conundrums connected with associations of this kind, and if you want to argue the question I will find you plenty of men who will take either side you do not take, and debate for hours together and yet.

R. B. Keys.

[*To be continued.*]

IS CHARACTER AFFECTED BY PECUNIARY CONDITIONS?

Webster tells us that poverty is a relative term: what is poverty to a gentleman would be competence for a day-laborer. I shall, in this argument, regard the term *poverty* not as meaning extreme indigence, or a lack of the actual necessities of life, but, rather, as a lack of the good things of life, and, especially, the lack of as much money as one might fancy would contribute most fully to their happiness. That poverty which makes one count the cost before making a purchase, and compels one, in every case, if such a thing were possible, to make one dollar do the work of two. Positive want will certainly have a disastrous effect upon character, narrowing it down until but one thing can find a place in the mind—where to get means to keep body and soul together. God help the very poor! No wonder they wander so soon from the paths of recti-

tude and become steeped in sin and wickedness. But there are those who, while having the wherewithal to feed and clothe themselves, yet find life in some sort a struggle, and oftentimes feel the pinching hand of want. These latter frequently suffer in silence, when those around them suppose they have plenty to supply their need. Such privation as this will have various effects upon character. Some people in the world—and doubtless they form a large class too—are spoiled by the trials and deprivations, which, in the course of a life-time, they are called upon to endure. Who has not met with the querulous man or woman, often, but not always, advanced in life, who is dissatisfied with all their surroundings? The prosperity of their neighbors is sufficient reason for them to pour forth complaints concerning their hard fate · everything which happens they regard only as an added opportunity for bewailing their unfortunate lot in life. Jealousy and discontent have so long been their constant companions that they can see no good thing in aught that occurs. But may not such a one have been a pessimist from the beginning, and so have found, in the peculiar circumstances of his life, an excellent opportunity to cherish that petulance or peevishness, which was natural to him, until he has actually become so disagreeable that no one would willingly choose him for a companion? Trials come to all who live; none are exempt, and those who would learn the lesson of life rightly must rise superior to them. There is no condition so distressing but that we may find a silver lining to the cloud if we are disposed to look for it, and, if accepted in the proper spirit, I maintain that poverty elevates the character far more than riches. It is said that temperance, fortitude, discreet silence, and other virtues became common in Sparta in consequence of the scarcity of ready money. At any rate, in all ages of the world's history men who have made their mark have, in an overwhelming number of instances, known what it was to be very poor in early life. Poverty sharpens the wits, brings out whatever talents are possessed, and compels one to make the most of themselves. It makes people more tender-hearted, too; for their own sad experience teaches them to sympathize with the sufferings of their fellow creatures. Many a parent, son, daughter, brother or sister, have learned, in the bitter school of adversity, the lesson of self-denial, which will ennoble any character. On the other hand, the rich man fares sumptuously every day; he has no special need to make use of the talents God has given him, and so, very often, they lie dormant. He knows nothing by experience of the innumerable trials which form part of the poor man's daily life, and cannot sympathize with what he has never felt. In the very abundance which surrounds him, lies his danger; the innate selfishness which is common to the whole human family is nursed into vigorous life when one has means to gratify every desire. Energy and ambition seem numbed, and, if a man possesses riches, more often than not he will spend his life in the pursuit of pleasure. Of course, there are countless exceptions on either hand. Samuel Johnson's whole character was warped, and his entire after life embittered, by the hardships of his youth. Very many noble philanthropists are to be found among the wealthy classes, who devote much of their time and money to relieving the wants of their poorer brethren; but in nine cases out of ten, I think it will be found that even those have risen through their own exertions, and are living examples of the wonderful effect which poverty has in developing the character. If asked which we would *prefer*, poverty or riches, the answer would be easy enough; for which of us would not unhesitatingly choose riches? But if the question is, Which is the more dangerous to character? we must feign acknowledge with Johnson that

Wealth heaped on wealth, nor truth nor safety buys;
The dangers gather as the treasures rise.

G. I. S. Andrews.

RELATING TO BANK ACCOUNTS.

In suggesting, in the January number, that it might be mutually beneficial to accountants in country banks to cast their "theory and practice" into a common heap, through the medium of the AMERICAN COUNTING-ROOM, it was not my thought that any of us would have systems or methods differing in the main materially from those in use by our co-workers, but that by each or many of us bringing our methods side by side, some of us—and, perhaps, all— may by comparison be enabled to do our work more easily, and at the same time more thoroughly, practically, and intelligently.

I offer no apology for accepting your invitation to be the first to respond to my suggestion, and while I shall hope to assist in making some one's burden lighter, I expect to receive more than I impart.

In our work in all its departments the first aim is, clearness and accuracy; and this cannot be compromised in the least: the bank accountant's work must be complete in itself, without explanation, and *must* be *correct*. The second is, dispatch. As progression is now, and will continue to be, the watchword everywhere, we must gradually improve on the second without impairing the first; and as the practiced brain and hand in our day are, probably, not more rapid than in times past, this must be done by improving in our methods—being careful always that in the flood of methods offered we accept only such as *are* improvements.

Taking the headings suggested by you as nearly as convenient, we have, *first*, principal books: Teller's Book, Cash Journal, Deposit Ledger, General Ledger, Discount Ledger, Balance Books, Discount Register, Draft Register, Certificate of Deposit Register, Remittance Register, City Collection Register, Foreign Collection Register. The use of each will come up under the other headings except the first.

THE TELLER'S BOOK

Will have columns so arranged with printed headings that only figures will be required in making entry of every transaction affecting the Cash, and will enable the teller to balance his Cash without reference to cash journal, and will also afford a check on the correctness of every register, and, *vice versa*, every register will be a check on this book and—the teller.

The custom prevails in some (I think, many) banks of depending on the footings of the various registers and cash journals for cash balance. This has at least two principal objections: *first*, it makes the teller dependent upon figures made by others; and, *second*, in case of error there is nothing to indicate

whether in teller or book-keeper's work, often requiring each to go over his entire work in vain hunt for the other's mistake, when a comparison of footings on teller's book and totals, as carried to cash journal, would locate the error in a moment. Neither teller nor book-keeper can afford to have Cash dependent on other than the teller's figures, and it is imposing on book-keeper's time and good nature to require it. *Possibly* the teller may be allowed to count his money while cash journal is being balanced, and, if Balance agrees with his count, use his own discretion about striking Balance on his own book. It would seem unnecessary to say that the Cash should balance to a cent every night as truly as should the deposit or general ledger; but there are banks in which this is not attempted, strange as it may appear. There will be times when the Cash cannot be *made* to balance without *springing*. In this event enter discrepancy at once to "Cash, Short or Long" account, and from time to time close this into "Loss and Gain," or "Teller's Account," as may be agreed upon. Under this head let me say that where it is physically possible for one man to receive and pay out all the money he should do so. For two or three men to have a cash drawer—as, for instance, the man who writes New York and Chicago drafts, or the man who attends to collections—is a gross waste of time. A system of slips can just as well refer all money to its proper place at once, as for each man to count it in, make up his account at night, and turn over, to be recounted and put with general fund.

CHECKS AND DEPOSITS.

Enter initials and amounts on teller's book; at night add, and carry total checks paid and deposits received to cash journal, and from there to general ledger; assort checks and deposit-slips alphabetically, and post from them direct. I regard a "Check and Deposit Register" superfluous, for reason that the slips always remain in the bank for reference, and the checks until statement is rendered, and you can post more rapidly and with less liability to error from

JOHN DOE.

DATE.	TIME	WHEN DUE.	No.	PAYER.	WHEN PAID.	As Payer.		BALANCE AS PAYER.	SECURITIES.
						DR.	CR.		
1882. Jan. 1	30d	Feb. 3	4,276	Richard Roe.	1882.	1,000 ..		1,000 ..	John Smith.
Jan. 15	"	"	4,601	You (John Doe).		2,000 ..		3,000 ..	$2,000 U.S. 4 per ct. bds.
			4,276	Richard Roe.	Feb. 3		1,000 ..	2,000 ..	

DEPOSIT LEDGER.

DATE.	CHECKS IN DETAIL.	CHECKS.	DEPOSITS.	BALANCE.	DATE.	CHECKS IN DETAIL.	CHECKS.	DEPOSITS.	BALANCE.
1884. Feb. 4	100 120 300	520 ..	1,000 ..	480 ..					
Feb. 5	10 100 50 300 20 13	493 ..		13 ..					

DRAFTS DRAWN ON...
....

DATE.	IN FAVOR OF	No.	AMOUNT.	TOTAL.	EXCH'GE.	BY WHOM PURCHASED.
		00				
		01				
		02				
		03				
		04				

CERTIFICATE OF DEPOSIT REGISTER.

DATE.	No.	AMOUNT.	WHEN PAID.	BY WHOM DEPOSITED.	REMARKS.

CITY COLLECTION REGISTER.

DATE RECEIVED	PAYER.	OWNER.	RESIDENCE.	DATE.	TIME	INT.	OUR No.	AMOUNT.	REMARKS.

REMITTANCE OF DRAFTS TO NATIONAL PARK BANK, NEW YORK.

DATE OF DRAFT.	DRAWER'S No.	DRAWER.	ENDORSERS.	PAYER.	AMOUNT.	REMARKS.

checks and slips than from register, and can make statements much faster with items in detail on the ledger. I use ledger with space for two accounts to the page, and printed headings —

FORMS FOR NOTICES.

To *John Jones.*

Due *February 4, 1884.*

At SOUTH BEND NATIONAL BANK,

Account overdrawn,

$13.

To *John Jones.*

Due *Sight, 1884.*

At SOUTH BEND NATIONAL BANK,

S. M. Smith's Draft.

$100.

To *John Jones.*

Due *February 10, 1884.*

At SOUTH BEND NATIONAL BANK,

Your note to S. M. Smith,

$400.

[BACK OF THE THREE PRECEDING FORMS.]

"Please call at this bank and accept or pay draft as stated. If you have reasons for refusing acceptance or payment, please indorse such reasons hereon and return this notice to us, that we may report to our correspondent.	Not hearing from you by .... the collection will be returned with the information, "No attention given to our notice."	REMARKS.

"Date," "Checks in Detail," "Total Checks," "Deposits," "Balance"— using red ink for over-drafts, both on ledger and balance-book.

BALANCE BOOK.

I think that some of our city cousins would be surprised at the small percentage of country banks using a daily balance for deposit ledger, and would smile at the excuse sometimes given that want of time prohibits it. I am not quite prepared to say that it really saves time, although of that opinion, but am sure that it carries with it a feeling of confidence and security more than repaying the cost. For my discount ledger I use the method of adding to general ledger balance of yesterday the sum of all new balances for the day, and, substracting the sum of all old, the result to agree with new general ledger balance, but do not consider this quite "iron-clad" enough for deposit ledger. The old time balance-book affords absolute certainty; the necessity of carrying forward each day all unchanged balances before you can add, and of every two weeks carrying forward and re-writing all names, involves a great deal of work. I have arranged for myself a system of slips which enables me to commence adding the moment I am done posting names; and, unchanged balances never being carried forward, I add all balances, as, with the balance-book, is more convenient in posting, and affords paying-teller or cashier more ready reference.

A REMITTANCE.

Have correspondent's name printed at top of register. Use printed headings on single page of super-royal or imperial: "Date of Draft," "No. of Draft," "Drawer," "Indorsers," "Payer," "Amount," "Remarks." Register drafts to be sent, and carry total amount to Cash journal, and from there to general ledger. Check correspondent's account from register.

A DRAFT.

Use loose draft with printed numbers, and Draft Register with number printed — ∞ to 49 on left-hand page, and 50 to 99 on right-hand page. At night add on register, and carry to correspondent's credit, on cash journal, total drafts drawn, and to credit of Exchange total of exchange received. Check correspondent's account from the draft register. In checking up correspondent's account use harmonizing sheet with four headings—"We credit, they do not debit"; "They credit, we do not debit"; "We debit, they do not credit"; "They debit, we do not credit."

To "Our Balance" add the first two, and subtract the last two; the result will agree with "Their Balance."

A CERTIFICATE OF DEPOSIT.

When issued, enter on Register; at night carry from register to cash journal total certificates issued, and from teller's book total certificates paid. Then from certificates paid them, by number, to original entry on register and mark "paid," and you are ready to file. Proof that work is correct will be to occasionally see if certificates not marked "paid" in register equal general ledger balance. Do not make partial payments, but write new certificate when full amount is not wanted.

A COLLECTION.

City and foreign registers should be separate. I do not care to offer anything under this head, except that the city register is usually made to cover too much space—quite frequently two pages of super-royal—involving unnecessary work in keeping. This class of collections remaining in bank until paid or returned, correspondent's instructions, number, etc., will be noted on the paper, and do not need to be duplicated on register, as in case of doubt at time of payment the letter of instructions would be referred to anyway. If a draft, the paper shows for itself who is drawer; and the same as to indorsers, if a note or acceptance.

On single page of super-royal I would print headings—"Date Received," "Interest," "Payer," "Owner," "Amount," "Residence," "Date," "Time," "Our No.", "Remarks." "Our No." should be printed oo to 50, etc., and, coming next to "Amount," will facilitate checking "Paid or Returned."

A DISCOUNT OR LOAN.

Enter on discount register, at night foot register, and carry total to cash journal. From register also carry total discount received to cash journal; bills paid enter separately on cash journal as paid—or, if too numerous, use an auxiliary-book. Post discount ledger from register and cash-book, or auxiliary-book, if one is used. It is a matter of surprise that so many banks do without a discount ledger; but, knowing such to be the case, allow me to say a word in explanation and in favor. In this book is posted, under his own name, whether he be payer or not, all paper discounted for any customers. It affords ready reference concerning the amount of outstanding paper for which any customer is responsible, and the date of maturity of each note may be seen at a glance. The work of keeping the book posted is trifling as compared with the results. It is truly a joy forever. After getting forms from several banks, I have adopted, with slight change, those furnished by one of our city correspondents, and I like it. The headings are: "Date," "Time," "When Due," "No.," "Payer," "When Paid," "Dr.," "Cr.," "Balance," "Securities."

A CERTIFICATE.

Do not certify.

Myron Campbell.

ROBERT MORRIS AND CHARLES CARROLL.

At the January meeting of the Institute of Accountants and Book-keepers of New York a lecture was delivered, by Gen. R. W. Judson, upon "Eminent Characters in American History." The lecturer introduced to his audience, which was composed of members of the Institute and invited guests, several characters whose deeds in war and peace had made them eminent and crystalized their memories in the hearts of the American people. Although the interesting discourse, if published in full, would prove attractive to the general reader, and is well worthy of a prominent place in historical literature, we have found it possible only to give in these pages such extracts of the lecture as referred to persons whose deeds were closely coupled with the financial workings of the times in which they lived. Of the characters alluded to in the lecture the lives of Robert Morris and Charles Carroll are prominently those to which we look for commercial and financial incident. Both these men were possessors of great wealth, and with it served their country in its hour of peril and need.

We give the substance of what the lecturer said concerning the lives of these two eminent men.

ROBERT MORRIS.

Few men were more useful, or advanced the cause of liberty with firmer purpose, or with more determined energy, than the one I am about to name—not in deed upon the forum, or yet in the field, but in another and far different sphere.

The American people owe no greater acknowledgments to the thrilling eloquence of Patrick Henry, the negotiations of Benjamin Franklin, the fertile pen of Thomas Jefferson, or the conquering sword of Washington, than to the wonderful financial skill of Robert Morris—the great merchant and financier of the Revolution.

Money has always been the motive power of the world, and is likely ever to continue so to the end. And the want of money was the constant source of trouble, and the financial scourge of our army. Many times it threatened the annihilation of our army and the defeat of the Revolution. Upon May 10th, 1775, $2,000,000 of paper money were first issued by the Continental Congress, and they continued the issue until $200,000,000 were struck off, when, luckily, the old printing-machine broke down. Gold the Government had none; our currency was little better than rags. A common cotton pocket-handkerchief was ten dollars, and the poorest kind of brown or muscovado sugar was twenty dollars per pound, and other things in proportion.

Mr. Morris entered Congress in 1775, and at once took an active part for liberty, though an Englishman. The army was in great want of lead, and, fortunately, a large quantity had just arrived in port, and Morris gave fifty tons for the use of the army. The time of many of the soldiers had nearly expired, and money was needed to give a bounty of ten dollars in gold to induce them to remain. But what could be done? The military chest was empty—not a cent within its lids. Gen. Washington wrote to Morris explaining the wants of the army, and urging him to procure a loan. Mr. Morris was much troubled and perplexed, and remained at his store, pondering over the matter, until a late hour. On his way home he met a rich Quaker, who inquired the news. Morris replied that he had received a letter from Washington for $50,000, for bounty to soldiers, and added: "You must loan it." "What security canst thee give?" "My note and my honor," replied Morris. "Thee shall have it," said the Quaker. The next morning Morris rose early; wrote Washington sending the money; it was paid to the soldiers — they remained. Washington crossed the Delaware: fought the brilliant Battle of Trenton; captured a thousand Hessians; gained a signal victory at Princeton, and raised the drooping spirits of the patriots all over the land. Who shall say that Morris did not furnish the "sinews of war"?

Mr. Morris gave the army at one time several thousand barrels of pork and flour, and he it was who advanced the money and provisions for the army that, in 1781, gave the finishing blow to the war, in the capture of Lord Cornwallis at Yorktown. Mr. Morris had almost the entire charge of the financial affairs of the Colonies during the war.

It is a most singular fact, but nevertheless true, that for quite a long period the credit of Mr. Morris was greater than that of Congress itself. When all other resources failed Morris's individual credit supplied the need. He issued his own notes, at one time, for one million and a-half, for the use of the Colonies, and no one held a more responsible position, had more trials or difficulties to encounter, than Mr. Morris—scarcely excepting Washington himself! An honest, plain, practical, common-sense man, and an energetic, thorough, business-like merchant, he knew his place and his power, and kept the one and executed the other. He obeyed the ancient injunction:

"Act well your part :
There all the honor lies!"

How sad to reflect that one, who, by his wisdom, counsel, prudence and financial ability, acted so prominent a part in gaining our independence, should, in his old age, become heavily in debt, and actually imprisoned for several years—not for crime, but for debt! Neither his State nor his country that had received so much from him came forward to discharge their debt of gratitude! He had to beg of his friends not to write him as he had not a cent to pay postage.

By his severe public labors, and his many private misfortunes, he was worn out, and passed to his rest on the 8th of May, 1806, in his seventy-third year.

The true patriot will never forget the noble acts, or fail to honor the memory, of Robert Morris—the great merchant and financier of the American Revolution.

CHARLES CARROLL.

Charles Carroll, of Maryland, a devoted Catholic—a man of great wealth, and, it is sometimes said, was born with a silver spoon in his mouth. Sent to France at the age of eight years, for the purpose of obtaining an education, he remained abroad twenty years, and returned to America in 1764—a finished scholar and a polished man.

But such a long residence in foreign lands did not imbue him with a love of tyrannical institutions. He entered with great spirit into the controversy between England and the Colonies, and by his just views and strong opposition to the encroachments of kingly power, gained the confidence of the people and a leadership in their cause. As early as 1770–71 he published several able articles setting forth the rights of the Colonies, and they had great influence in molding the opinions of the people. About this time ne met Judge Samuel Chase, who said to him: "Carroll, we have the better of our opponents. We have completely written them down." "Do you think," said Carroll, "that writing will settle the ques-

tion?" "To be sure!" said Chase. "To what else can we resort?" "To the bayonet!" answered Mr. Carroll. How soon did this become true?

Soon after this time a vessel, with a cargo of tea, came to Annapolis; but the patriots would not allow the vessel to land, as they had solemnly pledged themselves, now and for ever, not to drink a drop of tea until the British duty was removed. Mr. Stewart, the owner, consulted Mr. Carroll; but he was no policy man—no half-way patriot—and he plainly told Mr. Stewart that he better not land or try to leave, but to burn his vessel and cargo. And within two hours, with his own hand, Stewart set fire to them, and, with sails and colors flying, the vessel and cargo were burned to the water's edge, to the great delight of a dense crowd of patriots.

With his fine voice, his choice language, and his graceful appearance, he was an able and eloquent orator—convincing many and pleasing all.

A member of the British parliament wrote to him ridiculing the idea of our resistance, and said that "6,000 English troops would march from one end of the continent to the other." "So they might," said Carroll; "but they will be masters of that ground only on which they encamp: for they will always find enemies before and behind them. Our resources will increase with our difficulties."

At the time the Declaration was brought forward Mr. Carroll was considered the richest man in the Colonies. To sign it was an important step to every individual member of Congress; for should the British arms prove victorious, confiscation of property and loss of life would be their certain portion. When asked whether he would sign it, he replied: "Most willingly"; and, seizing the pen, instantly traced the name Charles Carroll. A member standing near remarked: "There go a few millions; but when the hanging-time comes there are so many Charles Carrolls in Maryland they will not know which one to hang." Mr. Carroll at once took the pen with the ink yet wet, and added, "of Carrollton"—and was ever afterward known as "Charles Carroll, of Carrollton." What a noble act, and how grandly performed! Days of freedom and peace succeeded those of war and uncertainty. On July 4th, 1828, when ninety-one years of age, he laid the corner-stone of the great Baltimore and Ohio Railway.

It is a bright day in the dying autumn of 1832. An old man, in whose face is combined the maturity of intellect with the simplicity of childhood, is passing his last day on earth. Ninety-five years has he lived in the land; fifty-six years ago he was one of the noble band of fifty-six patriots who signed the Declaration of Independence. *He is the last survivor.* What must be his reflections at this time? *All gone but himself!* He has done a good work. The most ardent wishes of his patriotic heart have been more than gratified. The present is happy and joyous; the future big with promise. And now, at the sunset-hour, the silver cord is gently loosening, the golden bowl is breaking, and to Charles Carroll, of Carrollton — the last of the signers — death comes as a gentle sleep.

AS TO METHODS OF STATING THINGS.

Editor of AMERICAN COUNTING-ROOM.

I cannot keep my promise to furnish for your February number an article on Classification of Accounts. For this, thank God, on behalf of your readers. It may be true, as you say, that such an article could be made to set forth the ideas of a recent lecture before the Institute of Accountants "in a more comprehensive form than could be elicited from a repor." of the lecture itself; but the question still remains whether your readers care much for the ideas, however comprehensively they may be "set forth."

The lecture, if it may be dignified as such, was an informal and wholly unprepared talk before two blackboards, and in the presence of a body of intelligent accountants. The two blackboards, formed the basis of the classification, and enabled the lecturer to present two ledgers of skeleton accounts—or, rather, one ledger in two parts—the one part contained accounts which represented the activities of the *business,* and the other part those relating to *finance;* and the point of the lecture was to show that all the accounts required in any business can be ranged under these two heads. A good many interesting facts were brought under the microscope, and the lecturer convinced *himself* that his points were not only well-taken, but well sustained. He was not a little chagrined, however, to be told by one of his intelligent hearers that the nomenclature of his classification was stolen from that eminent author, Thomas Jones, who had also presented many of the lecturer's points in a little book, entitled," Paradoxes of Debits and Credits."

Upon a subsequent examination of this excellent *brochure,* I find a classification under the two heads, Business and Finance, varying from mine only so far as the proprietor's account is concerned ; and I am reminded of one of the literary exploits of Mark Twain, in which he dedicated a book to John Smith, under the plea that inasmuch as the person to whom a book is dedicated usually buys a copy, a large edition would be sold. He sent a complimentary copy of the book to Oliver Wendell Holmes, who returned him a copy of one of his own books, published years before, having *the identical form of dedication.* The humorous Mark was at first dumbfounded, but was able finally to account for the "strange coincidence " in the fact that while an invalid in the Sandwich Islands he had been restricted in his reading to a collection of Dr. Holmes's works — among them this book—and he had read and re-read them all,—absorbing them, as it were, and as a consequence had committed this unconscious plagiarism.

Whether my case is a similar one I do not know; but I do know, *first,* that I was honestly drawn to the nomenclature by the irresistible logic of my own convictions as to classification; and, next, that I would have adopted it out of Mr. Jones's own mouth had I received it thus; for, having once conceived it, no matter how, no other terms could have satisfied me.

And, innocent as I am of any intention to steal another man's thunder, I am quite willing to award to my respected friend all the honors which are his due. For certain it is that no other author of book-keeping of whom I have any knowledge can hold any comparison with Thomas Jones. I knew him intimately, and loved him dearly, as an honest Scotchman, a clear-headed, logical writer, and a modest man. He was always an inspiration to me; and radically as I differed, and do differ, with him concerning the position of the proprietor's account, I am one of his most sincere and earnest disciples.

What I attempted to illustrate on my two black-boards to that intelligent coterie of book-keepers was the intricate and complementary relation existing between the two classes of accounts; to show that what one class *asserted*, the other class recognized and *proved;* that when *business* declared a gain or a loss, *finance* immediately responded in exhibiting a corresponding increase or decrease in wealth. And beyond this, that while mere liquidating transactions, such as paying a debt or collecting what is due, could be recorded without touching the *business* accounts [thus requiring the use of but one board] *all* transactions looking to profit or loss, or marking the progress of the *business*, inevitably required the use of both boards, and a compensatory record in each of the two classes.

But I shall not further follow the line of the lecture, choosing rather to fill the space you have allotted me with some remarks on an entirely different subject.

I notice, in looking over the last few numbers of the COUNTING-ROOM, that some of your readers are strangely exercised concerning trial-balances. The questions are not unfrequently asked, " What is a trial-balance? and What does a trial-balance show?" In answer to the first query I would say that a trial-balance is a *trial*-balance; and, in answer to the second : What a trial-balance may *show* depends entirely upon what it *contains*. It is not at all likely that these answers will satisfy the querists—if any answers that I could give would; for I have discovered that most of the questions propounded to newspapers and other periodicals are, not for the purpose of eliciting replies from others, but to give a chance to the querist to ventilate some little pet theory of his own. As evidence on this head, have you never noticed that, however clear and conclusive an answer may be given to a question thus propounded, it never quite suits the propounder?

Take, for example, some of the simple and practical questions published in your October number as having been submitted to the competitors for the place of book-keeper in the Philadelphia Alms-house. Here is one : " When does Cash account close 'To Balance'?" Almost any intelligent person would have answered : "I don't know"; but this was far from being the answer which filled the mind of the questioner. Here is what he had in his mind : " Never. It sometimes has an appearance which would suggest to the inexperienced book-keeper that sort of treatment ; but an excess of disbursements over receipts to the experienced book-keeper is proof that he has either entered, as disbursements, moneys never paid out, or, what is more frequently the case, failed to record receipts, such as loans or overdrafts at bank by which payments were made which otherwise could not have been made."

Now, the beauty of this answer is, that it just fits the question, and nobody who had not had the practical experience which would enable him to ask that sort of a question could ever hope to concoct that sort of an answer. If I were to ask a question of this import I should be likely to blunder into something like this : " Is the credit side of Cash account ever larger than the debit side?" and most *theoretical* book-keepers would say, " No." Then would naturally follow the question, " Why?" and the answer, " Because we cannot pay out more money than we receive." Of course, no such replies would satisfy an Examining Board, who are furnished with questions and answers of the sort mentioned; and here is just where we are likely to fail in our attempts to reform the Civil Service.

The assertion made by the gentleman who furnishes this material that "text-books on book-keeping, as a rule, teach that Bills-payable account always closes 'To Balance.' has an air of freshness which is as amusing as it is interesting. It the first place, I know of no text-book that teaches that Bills-payable account *always* closes, in *any* way. Most of them recognize the better method of permitting the account to remain open so long as any of the "bills" are unre- deemed. The gentleman is right, how- ever, in assuming that no text-book on book-keeping has this information: "Many merchants discount their bills *and notes*, and largely increase their profits by so doing. *In their books, a Bills-payable account closing itself is not an infrequent occurrence.*" This is news in- deed, not only to authors of book-keep- ing, but, if I mistake not, to "many merchants." If it were generally under- stood by merchants that a system of book-keeping had been devised through which the Bills-payable account would "close itself," the person who should hold the patent of that system could or- der his Fifth Avenue mansion at once. The great solicitude with most of our financiers is to get their Bills-payable accounts into a condition to be handled at all. A *self-closing* account would dis- pose of the whole matter, and would be a boon that would turn Wall Street into an earthly paradise.

My experience with teachers and pro- fessional accountants, including myself, is, that we are apt to get into a rut, or, rather, into a good many ruts; and in- stead of trying to get out, we feel it- to be a duty that we owe to the world to pull others in after us. Most of us are "cranks" in one way or another, and we like to air our little conceptions, and shock people with the profundity of our researches and discoveries. Thus it is that we incline to verbosity and to hid- ing plain things under an avalanche of words. I am aware that the questions and answers given above were profess- edly put in this shape in order to "give the advantage to the experienced count- ing-house man as against the theorist"; but this could have been only for the reason that "the experienced counting- house man" is in a better mental condi- tion to probe a fiction than is a mere "theorist." No one can suppose for one moment that the questions were given then because they were business- like, or because they suggested business processes.

I trust no one will imagine that I am making an attack upon an individual. My only object is to point out a com- mon error of professional men, viz., the using of technical words and phrases to express plain truths. I often find teach- ers shaping their questions so as to "puzzle" the pupil; and under the plea of "making him think" they so hide the real meaning of the question as to ren- der an intelligent answer impossible.

I honestly think life is too short for this sort of thing, and I should be glad to see the time come when the line be- tween theory and practice, as we now un- derstand it, shall be obliterated. Theory which is not intimately related to prac- tice is false theory, and practice which does not both utilize and evolve theory is blind and foolish practice.

A ledger is a book of accounts. Each account has a distinct and personal rea- son for its existence. It stands in a recognized relation to the business, and is an essential part of the showing of the business. No account expresses anything when its sides are equal. Some accounts can have an excess of one side only; and some others may have an excess of either side. No ac- count ever "closes itself"; but any account may be made to "close," or cease to exist, by placing on the smaller side an amount which will make it equal to the larger side. No account is prop- erly closed "To" or "By" any other ac- count, or anything else, although the amount entered to make the sides equal may be transferred to some other place in the ledger. Generally, however, it is continued in the same account.

S. S. Packard.

SPECIAL PARTNERSHIPS IN PENNSYLVANIA ORGANIZED UNDER THE ACT OF 1836.*

It was early demonstrated in the history of the world that a combination of persons of different natural characteristics and abilities would be of mutual advantage, and add to the material prosperity of both; and that the association would be more profitable in its results than the sum of the individual efforts. There are persons who have natural qualifications for seeing farther into a millstone than others; and there are individuals who possess in a marked degree the faculty of discerning the right time and seizing the right moment for action; and it is a noticeable fact in history that these peculiar natural advantages have been almost uniformly bestowed upon those to whom, in the ordering of temporal affairs, a lesser share of this world's goods has been granted: and it is an evidence of the wisdom of the Creator that this has been the case, for how otherwise could the poor man ever be able to make for himself the place in the community that a man of ability is entitled to hold. Hence we find in the early centuries that men of different capabilities and of different pecuniary circumstances have consolidated their individual resources to their gain in commercial standing and their advantage in material prosperity. It was also discovered, in the days of early commercial enterprises, when voyages and travels by sea and land were matters—not of days and weeks, but of months and even years, and costly to an extent beyond our imagination, that by the association of several parties, none of whose individual means would warrant the venture, and where one, perhaps, was without capital, but possessed to a marked degree that combination of natural advantages before spoken of, and which is forcibly and clearly expressed in the language of the business community by the single word "brains," such operations could not only be successfully engaged in, but also that the profits of the trip would be so large that men who otherwise were outside of that class who in all history have claimed the exercise of the so-called Divine Right of sovereignty by virtue of "the aristocracy of birth" became members of a more worthy guild, who were aptly called "merchant princes"; for it has been to them that the kings, rulers, and high potentates, as well as the "effête aristocracy" have had to come to ask for the "sinews of war" and the bread to eat, and raiment to wear, in times of peace.

From these hasty remarks it will be readily seen that the formation of those business relations embraced in the several kinds of associations now known as partnerships has been but the natural sequence of events. The unequal distribution of the evidences of material prosperity now embraced under the general name of "capital" has also contributed largely to the formation of these associations. As men grew wealthy they learned that there was a limit to the capacity and endurance of one individual to attend to the multitudinous details of business, the supervision of an army of employés, and the watching of the state of the commercial market so as not to be left stranded with a full cargo when the tide should ebb: and also that the giving of an interest in the net gain was a wonderful stimulant to the energies of those who showed themselves to be of ability and discretion. And it also showed to those men who began early in life at the bottom of the ladder that there was a reward to those who made their employer's interests their own, and that by devotion to business they could in time win for themselves a place among those whose names were the backbone

* A Lecture delivered before the Book-keepers' Association of Philadelphia, by CHARLES W. SPARHAWK, January 7, 1884.
Vol. VIII.— 6.

of the financial industries of the nation. Hence partnerships between capital and skilled labor, where the wealth of the one was balanced by the business ability of the other, were common even in the days of the ancients.

But even in the early days of partnerships the unfortunate natural tendency of the superior mind to take advantage of his associate's weakness or want of capacity was developed. The earliest authentic history of any proceeding of this character is the sheep-raising partnership of Jacob and Laban, in the land of Canaan, 1750 years B. C., where in twenty years of joint partnership the terms thereof were changed ten times. If it were thus in the "good old days of the patriarchs" we cannot expect much better things now. It is noteworthy, also, that the above example shows that capital is not equal to "brains," and the relative position of these two elements remains so to this day. Experiences such as these showed that protection was needed to enable the man of average mercantile ability to engage in the battle of life with a fair chance of coming out of the struggle with something to show for his labor. Under general partnership law each and every partner is individually liable for the whole amount of the firm's indebtedness, and this can be collected from any one partner by the co-partnership creditors to the exclusion of the remainder — leaving the unfortunate man only the right of an action against his associates for contribution to make up their due proportion of the losses. In cases where all the pecuniary capital was furnished by but one partner, the result of an unsuccessful business operation was that the whole load fell on him, and he would probably have been better off had he never associated himself with the others.

And as trade and commerce increased, and large sums of money and many heads of brains were needed to successfully carry out the great enterprises which constitute the traditions of the business world, men found that some protection must also be given to "capital." Those who had the sinews of war and peace would not furnish them to brace the arms and sinews of the young giant, "commercial activity," without proper safeguards against fraud, rascality, maladministration, ignorance, or stupidity. Capital has always been proverbially cautious from the earliest times; hence companies were formed in which the liability of the partners was limited in various degrees, according to the nature of the business to be carried on. There are several forms of these institutions deriving their powers, authorities and restriction as to liability from the superior powers of the State; and they are all by law required to record the charters by virtue of which they hold their peculiar position in the community, where the eyes of all men who may do business with them may see what manner of being this is that seeks to enter into the commercial family on such favorable terms.

But there is a form of business association or partnership which has aimed to combine the best elements of the general partnership and the corporation systems; and it is with this that we now propose to speak. In the accomplishment of the object desired, this combination of systems has succeeded only in part. It has many desirable features, but it is impossible to frame any plan which will work satisfactorily under all circumstances. Many commercial enterprises can only succeed where large capital is backed by the unlimited liability of those who engage in it, for their transactions involve amounts beyond the powers of any but the Rothschilds and Barings to furnish; and others yet, venturing into untried fields, or into abandoned paths with inexperienced or unknown guides, require the strictest limitation of the liability of those who embark in the enterprise. Hence what are known as "limited"; or, since the term has come to be so universally applied to a class of quasi corporations, "special partnerships," have come to be almost universally known and met with.

The special features of this class of mercantile associations are:

That it shall be composed of two classes of partners — General and Special. The former may or may not be contributors of capital, but he or they are the sole managers of the financial and other affairs of the business, and his or their liability, in case of failure, is unlimited. The special partner, on the other hand, furnishes nothing but capital, and his liability for the results of the business is fixed by the amount he has contributed. For the use of this capital the general partners pay him lawful interest, and under certain circumstances he can participate in the profits; but woe to him if he shall attempt to interfere with or control the general partners in their management of affairs. "As a man makes his bed, so must he lie in it"; and if he attempts to step out he must take his chances on the floor among those who are not on the elevated position he had prepared for himself. Any interference by him in the affairs of the business renders him a general partner, with all of its duties and liabilities.

The State of Pennsylvania has always been noted for its conservatism, and our laws on this subject of Special Partnership are very full and clear — so eminently so that "he who runs may read," and any average business man can comprehend just what are the respective duties, privileges and liabilities of the respective classes of partners.

There has, however, been a recent decision by the Court of Common Pleas No. 3, of this county, which has changed the whole general understanding and construction of the statute as heretofore held by the business community, and it is by reason of this that I have selected this subject for my remarks this evening.

Before taking up this special case it will be well to review the law and decisions of our Courts upon the general subject.

The first and most important requisite for the formation of a special partnership is the finding of an individual with capital, who is willing to lend it for a business enterprise. "First catch your hare before you cook him." This being done, the agreements between the general and special partners as to what shall be the mutual duties of the former, what amount of capital (if any) they shall each contribute, and the other details of ordinary partnership, together with the agreement of the general with the special partner as to what rate of interest shall be paid on his capital and what proportion of profits he shall receive, if the latter is also the case, are all drawn and fixed privately, and with them the business community, at that time at least, has nothing at all to do. But the special partner, to protect himself and secure himself from unlimited responsibility, must place himself squarely before the business world and define his contemplated liability to it; and his duties in this direction are plainly laid down and expressed in the statute.

A certificate is drawn up, to which each partner, general and special, must affix his signature and make formal acknowledgment thereof before a proper officer. This certificate must specify the names and residences of all the general and special partners, the title of the proposed firm, the date of the formation of the partnership and its term of existence, the nature and place of business, the amount of special capital contributed and of what the same consists. If this special capital contributed is money, an affidavit that the full amount has been actually paid in in cash must be made by one of the general (not special) partners. If the special capital be contributed in the shape of merchandise or other assets, an application must be made to the Court of Common Pleas of the county within which the business is to be transacted for the appointment of a sworn appraiser, who shall examine said assets, and file an inventory showing the nature and appraised value thereof.

The formal certificate above referred to is to be advertised in full for six successive weeks in two or more newspapers published in the county within whose limits the business is to be carried on; and is further to be recorded, with its acknowledgments, affidavit, or sworn inventory and appraisement, in the office of the Recorder of Deeds for said county. It is further required that the publishers of the newspapers in which the certificate is advertised, shall make affidavit, giving dates of the publication, and that these affidavits shall also be filed with the recorder. The sign set up by the firm shall give, in addition to the declared firm-name, the names of all the general and special partners, stating the relation they bear to each other.

It is further provided that the name of the firm must consist of the names of at least two of the general partners, and that the words "and Company" must not be added unless there are more than two general partners. This prevents the use of the style "John Smith & Co." for a special partnership in which there is but one general partner, but which is otherwise legal in this State.

It is, however, expressly declared by the statute that no special partnership organized as above stated, can be formed for the purpose of carrying on the banking or insurance business.

The duties of the special partner now cease. His capital is locked up beyond his control, and until the time of the final settlement of the business he cannot handle or interfere with it without rendering himself liable as a general partner. His name must not be used in suits at law or equity by or against the firm, nor shall it in any way be connected with the business without the words "special partner" following it.

The duties of the general partners are, to carry on the business to its legal termination. They are not bound by the terms of the law, as the special partners are, for their liability is unlimited, and hence we may practically dismiss them from our consideration.

The next point for our attention is the nature of the partnership thus created as differing from the ordinary partnerships.

(1) This special partnership is in the nature of a charter for the term specified. It is not dissolved by the death of either a general or special partner, as ordinary partnerships are, unless expressly so provided in the original agreement.

(2) When insolvent or in contemplation of insolvency, it cannot prefer any creditor or class of creditors at the expense of the rest. If a judgment be confessed when in either condition, it will not only be stayed by the Court, but is expressly declared to be void *ab initio*.

(3) The interest of either a general or special partner, with consent of the remaining general partners, may be sold, transferred, or assigned by deed, duly acknowledged, to any other person.

(4) The interest of either general or special partner may be purchased by one or more of the other general partners without thereby working a dissolution or making the special partner a general partner. And the consent necessary for the carrying out of these two provisions may be given in advance, at the time of the formation of the partnership.

(5) The interest of either general or special partners may be devised by will, or sold by his administration, under direction of the Orphans' Court; and in any of the three last-mentioned cases the purchaser or assignee steps into the shoes of the original party and assumes his rights and liabilities; but this transfer of interest must be acknowledged, certified, recorded, and published, as in the original instance.

(6) Any renewal or continuation of the special partnership must have a new certificate acknowledged, advertised, and recorded, as in the original instance.

A special partnership, organized as above, can be dissolved only in one of the following ways:

(1) By mutual consent, after a notice of such dissolution shall have been filed in the recorder's office, and publication of the same for four weeks in a newspaper published in the county within which the said firm transacts its business.

(2) By the expiration of the term for which it was formed; but a dissolution for this cause need not be advertised. (*Haggerty* vs. *Taylor*, 10, 261.)

(3) By any alteration in the names of the partners (except where there has been a sale or transfer as above stated) or in the nature of the business, or in the capital or shares thereof, or of any other matter stated in the original certificate.

(4) By the admission of another general partner. But one or more new special partners may be admitted, and new special capital contributed, without thereby working a dissolution; but such changes must be acknowledged and recorded, as before stated.

We may now pass to the powers of the special partner.

(1) He may from time to time examine into the state and progress of the concern, and may advise as to the management, but he shall not transact any business for their account, nor be employed as agent, attorney, or otherwise. And it was held that where a special partner acted as agent in buying real estate for the use of the firm, which was paid for out of the joint capital, he rendered himself a general partner.

(2) He may receive, in addition to lawful interest on his special capital, a portion of the profits after all the debts are paid.

(3) No portion of the special capital shall be in any way liable for the debts of the general partners contracted previous to the formation of the special partnership.

(4) He may loan the firm money in addition to his contribution of special capital, and receive interest thereon without becoming liable as a general partner. (*Hogg* vs. *Orzil*, 34 Penn. State Reports, 344.)

(5) He may become the liquidating partner after dissolution, and distribute the assets among the creditors.

We may now pass to the special provisions by which a special partnership is converted into a general partnership, and the special partner rendered unlimitedly liable, as in ordinary cases.

(1) If he shall withdraw any portion of his capital—and it is expressly declared that if the special capital shall be impaired in the payment of interest to him, and he shall not immediately restore the same, he shall be liable.

(2) If he shall interfere in the management of the business otherwise than as before stated—and it was held in *Richardson* vs. *Hogg* (38 Penn. State Reports, 153) that where it was stipulated in the articles of agreement that the son of the special partner should keep the books and have a general superintendency of the business at a salary, and the general partners should sign no note or check without his knowledge and approval, that the special partnership was converted into a general partnership.

(3) If the partnership shall become insolvent or be in contemplation of insolvency, and shall make any transfer, assignment or conveyance, or confess any judgment, whether the same be done by either general or special partners, with the intent thereby to give a preference to any creditor or class of creditors of either the partnership or of any partner, said transfer, assignment, conveyance or judgment shall be void as against the creditors of the partnership; and if made by, or concurred in, or assented to, by the special partner, such action converts the special partnership into a general one.

(4) If any of the statutory requirements connected with the formation, the acknowledgment, recording and advertising of the certificate before referred to, shall be violated or omitted, or if any false statement shall be made in the certificate or affidavit thereof.

(5) If the special partnership shall change the nature of its business, or move its place of business into another county, without filing a new certificate in such county.

(6) If the names of the partners shall be changed (except by the entry of new special partners), or if any change shall be made in the nature of its business or in the capital or shares thereof, and the partnership be not immediately dissolved and wound up.

(7) If the special partner shall allow the use of his name upon the bill-heads, letter-heads, cards or circulars or sign of the firm, without the words "special partner" affixed thereto, thus lending his individual credit to the firm, and not defining his relationship thereto to the community.

(8) If the special partner shall contribute any portion of his special capital in goods or other assets, without the formal appraisal by the Court. (*Vandyke* vs. *Rosskam*, 67 Penn. State Reports, 330.)

Having thus considered the general provisions of the law and decisions of the Courts thereunder, we may now pass to the special before referred to.

It has always been the usage and custom of the mercantile community to consider the special capital as, in a certain sense of the word, to be a "trust fund," to be kept sacredly intact for the uses and at the risk of the business; and this special fund having been published to the world, the creditors of all special partnerships have come to regard it in the same light.

The firm of Gruber, Hoopes & Co. was formed in Philadelphia, July 1st, 1881. Henry Gruber and William P. Hoopes were the general partners, and Albert H. Hershon became the special partner, putting in twelve thousand dollars as special capital. It appeared afterward that this money was not his own, but was borrowed from his wife and her sister, to whom he gave his personal due bills. On July 1st, 1882, on taking a balance from the books, the firm found their net assets to be $12,098 — that is, after returning the special capital, the two general partners had exactly $98 as a fund from which to pay unforeseen losses, or, if none of those appeared, to divide between them. Mr. Hershon then prevailed upon the two general partners to assume his due bills to his wife and her sister, and to execute their judgment notes for the amount. In September, 1883, the firm failed, and these judgment notes were immediately entered up, and the stock in the store was seized by the sheriff under them. One of the merchandise creditors filed a bill in equity in the Court of Common Pleas No. 3 for the County of Philadelphia, and obtained a temporary injunction against the sheriff, and further prayed the Court to declare these judgments void as against the general creditors under the provisions I have before spoken of. The Court, however, (*Ludlow, J.,*) after hearing all the evidence, held that the firm was not insolvent at the time of giving the notes, and that contemplation of insolvency was not necessarily to be inferred; that the general partners had a right to assume the personal obligations of the special partner, as the firm had the use of the money; and therefore dissolved the injunction and dismissed the bill. The Court held, however, and it was admitted by all the counsel, that Mr. Hershon had made himself a general partner, and was, therefore, liable; but as he was not pecuniarily responsible, there was small consolation in that for the creditors of the firm.

Unfortunately, the case has not been taken up to the Supreme Court, and this decision, therefore, will not bind the other Courts of Common Pleas throughout the State, excepting in so far as the judges accept the ruling of their learned brother of No. 3 of this county. The decision, however, if sustained, will, it is feared, open the door to the perpetration of gross frauds upon creditors in that special partnerships can be formed in which the special partner, himself irresponsible, may put in borrowed capital, and by causing the firm to assume the debt very shortly after the formation of the partnership may, in case of disaster, remove the whole fund upon which the credit of the house is based beyond the reach of the creditors. The only protection against this is the decision that, where the special partner can be shown to be but a "man of straw" with another party behind him who manipulates affairs and receives the increment, the Court will compel the real partner to disclose himself and step into his proper position. This is a difficult thing to prove, however, and can be evaded by those skilled in concocting such schemes.

I have thus tried briefly to summarize the present status of our special partnerships. They have always been a favorite mode of business associations in our State, but, unfortunately, it is the case that this decision of Gruber, Hoopes & Co. has shaken their commercial position in the community. Framed by wise minds, as the law has been, we may hope for amendment to provide for the contingency I have stated as possible to happen; and we trust that equity, which governs the settlement of partnership matters, may yet be found to supply that protection for which "the law (by reason of its universality) is deficient."

COUNTING-ROOM CHATS.

[We desire to say to the readers of this department that in cases where correspondents request that we shall give an answer to their inquiry, and where we find it possible to do so, we follow their question with our reply ; but, in doing this, it is not our intention or wish to forestall others who may feel disposed to offer their views or suggestions on the subject inquired about. In many instances we expect the reply given will serve merely as an introduction, depending on our readers to take upon themselves the work of supplying the chief part of such information as is sought by the correspondent.]

What are the Functions of a Private Ledger?
From S. E. H., Philadelphia, Pa.

Will you please explain the use of the private ledger? Are the accounts kept in this book used to correct those kept in the general ledger, or are they separate accounts which do not appear in the general ledger? Please explain how they should appear on the balance-sheet.

REPLY.— It is sometimes the wish of proprietors to keep from the knowledge of their employees, or from all save some specially trusted employee, all knowledge of their partnership relations, and, sometimes, too, of the result of their business. In such cases, the private ledger is introduced. Say, for example, the proprietors of a concern do not wish to have it known, outside of themselves definitely, what the interest of each partner is in the business. The book-keeper who has in charge the general ledger keeps only an account with the proprietors under one general title, which may be Capital or Proprietorship, the special accounts of each proprietor appearing only in the private ledger. When the books are closed up, the results shown in the Profit and Loss accounts are carried to this General Proprietorship account, and from this the proprietors obtain the data with which to write up their special account in the private ledger. It is not necessary in this case that the accounts of the private ledger should appear in the balance-sheet. Then again, suppose it is the wish of the proprietors that all definite knowledge of the results of the business should be known only to themselves. They require of the book-keeper only to keep the accounts of individuals, and such other general accounts as do not show, particularly, any information concerning the results of their business, all information of that kind being kept in the private ledger. In this case, it would not be expected of the book-keeper to make out a financial exhibit showing all the profits of the business, and the results of the business at the close of the fiscal year, as is customary, but to report, as he would be called upon, the amount of the firm's indebtedness, the assets, so far as his ledger would show, and continue his books, from year to year, without any annual statement. There are many concerns in which it is not known outside of the proprietors themselves what the results of the business are. The inventories are taken in different departments, and by different persons, in such a manner that no one person will possess sufficient knowledge to enable him to determine what the amount of the inventory really is; but these separate parts of the inventory being all combined by one of the proprietors, and properly treated in connection with the accounts of the private ledger, enables them to arrive at the result.

Checks Dated Ahead.
From A. R. H., Philadelphia, Pa.

Some of our customers occasionally send checks dated one or two days ahead, and sometimes one or two weeks ahead, asking us to send a receipt in settlement of some bill of a certain date, or of the account in full, as the case may be. I want to ask, *first*, What is the proper form for a receipt to be given in return for checks dated ahead? *Second*, In case where a party sends a check dated ahead, and who dies previous to the date of the check, and where the check is protested when presented at the bank for payment, can the estate of the debtor giving the check be held liable for its payment?

REPLY.—We suggest, as a proper form for a receipt given in cases as above stated, that it would be well to specify that the payment was made by check bearing date so and so, as the

POLICY REGISTER.—FORM I.

Date.	In Whose Favor.	Property Insured.	Name of Company.	Pol. No.	Expires.	Premium.	Pol.&Surv.	Receipts.	Charged.	Paid or For'd.	Remarks.
Jan. 8	Snowbound R.R. Co., $10,000.	Freezing Point Depot.	North Pole.	17	1/6 85	15 ..	3 ..	12 ..	18 ..		Pg.91
Jan. 8	Penny, Wise & Co., $20,000.	Sausage Factory, Mince St.	Sure Fire, $10,000. Cold Blast, $10,000.	284 627	1/4 85 1/8 85	10 .. 10 ..	2 .. 2 ..	12 ..	12 ..		
			Forward		85 ..	15 ..	40 ..		45 98		

case might be. This would aid in demonstrating before a court that the check was given in payment of the bill or account as claimed, and dated ahead.

A bank is not permitted to pay checks presented for payment after its knowledge of the death of the depositor. If the check is presented before the knowledge of the death reaches the bank, and it is paid, the bank cannot be held by the estate as liable for such payment, and it is considered a valid payment. A check dated ahead, as stated, is evidence of indebtedness against the estate of the deceased person; but it would, perhaps, be the better way to present a regular bill for the amount, and use the unpaid check as an evidence that the bill had been admitted by the deceased before his death. The account, in connection with the unpaid check, should be filed with creditors' claims against the estate, but would have no preference over other claims placed in the hands of the administrator or executor.

Insurance Agency Accounts.
From INSURANCE, Saginaw, Mich.

I wish to receive, through the columns of the COUNTING-ROOM, some information as to the best method of keeping the accounts of insurance agents. In our business there are many small accounts, and it is desirable to so systematize the work that it may be done with the least labor possible. Have some of your readers valuable suggestions to offer?

*** It is not alone those who are engaged in the insurance business who seek information similar to that asked by our correspondent. In very many branches of business it is found necessary to keep petty accounts with a large number of persons. It is not the number of accounts, particularly, which gives rise to the seeming difficulty; but the fact that in themselves they are trifling, and yet absolutely essential. Some years ago we had occasion to organize a plan for keeping the accounts of a company somewhat similar in its workings to an insurance agency. There were a large number of persons dealt with, but in no case did the entire debits for a year exceed $50. They would not, perhaps, average half that amount. The entries were not frequent to the same accounts. The number of entries to any single account during the year being not more than six or eight, the plan adopted is one which

could be made to serve well in almost any similar business. We had a book made, the leaves of which were about 10 x 14 inches, opening at the end, as it were, instead of the side. The page was divided by horizontal rulings into eight spaces, of a little more than one inch each. Then the necessary perpendicular rulings for notations, numbers, dates and amounts were carried out, thus forming spaces for eight separate accounts on each page. Transactions of the day were written up in this book, which

the combined purposes of original entry, one part of the cash-book, and the ledger.

We have given in the annexed form, in addition to those for the purposes above recited, a few columns which would serve to simplify the cash account, and for enabling the agent to determine, at any time desired, the exact amount due him on personal accounts, or, rather, from customers to whom policies have been issued. A column, marked, "Paid or Forwarded," would serve to note the time of

LEDGERIZED INDEX.— FORM II.

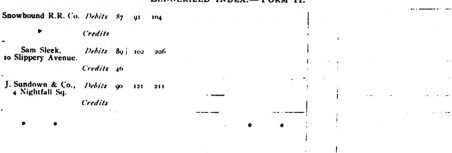

Snowbound R.R. Co.	*Debits*	87	91	104
	Credits			
Sam Sleek, 10 Slippery Avenue.	*Debits*	89	102	206
	Credits	46		
J. Sundown & Co., 4 Nightfall Sq.	*Debits*	90	121	211
	Credits			

formed a part of the regular cash entries; and instead of opening accounts with the persons to be charged, each of these transactions was indexed — the index, of course, being specially ruled for the purpose. The plan may be readily adopted in the insurance business, where, it seems, there would be as much saving of labor through it as in the case alluded to. In the insurance agency (fire insurance, we refer to) there would appear to be a uniformity of the transactions, certain information of a similar nature being connected with each transaction. The entry must show:

(1) In whose favor the policy was issued.
(2) The property insured.
(3) The name of the company issuing the policy.
(4) The number of the policy.
(5) The date of the expiration of the policy.
(6) The premium.
(7) Other charges, if any.

The form given herewith will serve better to illustrate the idea. The horizontal lines dividing the page into sections should, for the purpose of plainly separating each transaction, be ruled in red, thus making each entry serve as a distinct part of a ledger account. Instead of posting the entries they should be indexed, thus making the book we have described serve

payment, or the page to which the amount is carried—the payment appearing at that date in the register of cash receipts, an illustration of which is also given. If it is desired, the amount of each charge may be carried forward to the next entry of the customer. Thus, if the Snowbound R. R. Co., to which was issued a policy on January 8th, should take out another

46   DEBIT OF CASH-BOOK.—FORM III.

Date.	Title of Account and Items	Sundry Debtors	Reven- ues.	General Rec'pts
Jan. 8	Brought forward.........	486 ..	210 50	3,640 25
8	Policy-Register, 87	.. ..	10 ..	
8	O. Icicle & Son..........	18 50		
8	Bills-Receivable.........	.. ..	.. ..	240 40
9	Sam Sleek...............	12 ..		

policy before the premium and charges on this had been paid, the amount debited on January 8th could be carried forward to the next entry, and added to it, making the last entry show the total amount due from the company. Both of the transactions would be indexed. In making up a statement of an account where there were several charges, it would be necessary of course, to take the amount from the original entries, thus necessitating a reference to the index, and turning to the page upon which the entry appears; but in a business of this nature there are always so many accounts which have only a single item, or, at most, two or three items, the plan will be found to very materially diminish the labor which would be required in keeping a regular ledger.

For an example see the Ledgerized Index (Form II.). In making up a statement of the account of the Snowbound R.R. Co. it would be necessary to find the transactions on three different pages of the Policy Register. In the account of Sam Sleek it may be seen that it would be necessary to look upon two pages of the register as the first charge, viz., that on page 89 has been paid — the cash-book entry being on page 46; the perpendicular line placed after the page number (89) indicating that all charges previously made have been settled. To determine the amount due on account of policies issued, deduct from the total of the column of "Charges" in the register the total of the column in the cash-book, headed, "Sundry Debtors."

Circular Letters and Fac-similes.

From T. B. CAIN, Louisville, Ky.

We find it necessary in our business to frequently send out a small number of letters of a similar character, and have, heretofore, made it a practice to have them written. We use, generally, fifty to one hundred copies of the same wording, which applies to the class for which they are intended, with no changes excepting name and address of person to whom the letter is sent. Our objection to having them printed is the fear that they will not receive, from those to whom they are sent, the consideration that we desire them to have. There are a vast number of methods or devices in use for producing duplicate copies of letters, or fac-similes, but from the multitude, it is difficult to determine what is best to select. Can you, or any of your readers, offer suggestions which will aid us in making a selection? Information on this subject would be thankfully received.

REPLY.— This is a question which has confronted almost every business man who has endeavored to use the mails for conducting, systematically, a scheme of advertising, and who, like our correspondent, desires to communicate any special information to customers and others, where a circular could be made to answer the purpose. or nearly so, of a written communication. The devices for preparing circulars, of the kind alluded to, have grown so numerous that it is almost impossible to decide what particular one is preferable. It depends, of course, very much on the nature of the communication desired to be sent, the length of it, and the person to whom it is addressed, as to which style would be most advantageous.

Before the invention of the electric pen, and the gelatine pad, the lithographers had a monopoly in preparing circulars of this character. With the invention of the electric pen, and the various gelatine processes, such as the papyrograph, the hectograph, and various dry-copying processes, a new order of things has seemed to come into existence. Besides these, the invention of photo-engraving demands its share of public attention. In the lithographic processes, a special kind of prepared paper and ink are necessary; but when the copy is once made, and transferred upon the stone from which it is printed, almost any quantity desired can be produced. Where large numbers of fac-simile copies, or written letters, are desired, the lithographic process is, without doubt, the most economical. From a single writing, any number of transfers can be made upon a large stone, enabling the printer to strike off a number of copies at every impression. If, however, only a few copies are desired, this process would not be found so economical. The chief part of the expense would be the first transfer, which is somewhat costly; but where a large number, like ten thousand or upwards of any desired form, is wanted, this method, owing to its cheapness, possesses an advantage.

The electric pen is not much used at present. It was popular for a time after its invention, and before the invention of numerous other processes which have seemed to be more easily worked, and with better results. The process of photo-engraving possesses an advantage by being produced in metal, which can be used in any printing-office—the engraved reproduction of the writing being transferred to electric type or copper plates, which are used on an ordinary printing-press; but, in this method too, the first cost is somewhat expensive—a plate the size of an ordinary note-sheet costing from five to ten dollars. The press-work and paper, thereafter, are the only items of expense to be considered. Nearly all of the dry-copying processes, gelatine pads, etc., are more or less objectionable. Their use has become very common, and much of the work produced by them is of an inferior kind—blurred and indistinct. The type-writer furnishes a means which may, where a lithographic establishment is convenient, be adopted with comparatively small expense. By using a prepared ink, similar to that used by the lithographers in the work of photo-lithography, the print from a type-writer may be transferred upon stone, and from the transfer almost any desired quantity of *facsimile* copies may be obtained. We had occasion, recently, to examine what appeared to be a bundle of letters selected at random from the correspondence of a manufacturing company. The letters were attached together, but were of different makes of paper, and of various sizes. From the peculiar manner in which they were folded, showing creases, as apparently would appear if each had been inclosed in an envelope, they were made to have such a close resemblance to genuine letters that not one person in four, upon casual observation, would have supposed them anything different. But upon close examination they were found to be fac-similes. The firm, at whose expense they were made up, had obtained large numbers of testimonials concerning an article which they were manufacturing. These testimonials came from various business establishments in different parts of the country, and were, of course, very unlike in their general appearance. By judiciously imitating the paper upon which the letters were written, and in reproducing the writing by photo-lithography, the exceedingly close imitations were secured.

We believe the tendency is, or soon will be, to drift back to the ordinary type which, for the production of circulars, possesses very many advantages. Type, on account of its plainness and condensed form, is preferable to writing. The cost, too, of preparing circulars in this way is much in its favor. We were recently shown a font of type which represents exactly the work of an ordinary type-writer. A circular printed from such type, giving every appearance of having been produced on the "Remington" or "Caligraph" type-writers. And now, since the type-writer has been imitated by the type-founder, its popularity as a means of producing fac-simile copies for purposes of advertising, is very much lessened. We would suggest, in view of our knowledge

of the various processes, that either a well-written letter, or one printed with the ordinary plain type, would be the best. In neither of these cases is there any make-believe. The communication is exactly what it purports to be—either a written or a printed document. The day is almost passed when people of ordinary intelligence can be humbugged by the use of any of the devices which, for the preparation of fac-simile letters or circulars, are at present in vogue.

Measurement of Logs.

From JOSEPH RICHARD, New York.

I would like to ask "Nemo" for his rule in the measurement of logs. Have read with much interest his communications. Think that on this point he can give information of general interest to many of your readers.

REPLY (from "Nemo," De Land, Fla.)—The State Lumber Inspectors, for the port of Jacksonville, Fla., in reducing logs to board measure, use Preston's tables. Yellow pine logs are measured at the small end only by taking the diameter and the length. The table gives the contents in board measure. The market here is based upon the average of 3's (three logs to the thousand feet, board measure). To illustrate, I will give a raft settlement made recently. There were 241 logs measured, and by the tables the logs were found to contain 94.396 feet, B. M. By adding three ciphers to the number of logs, and dividing by the total number of feet, we find that it takes 3.09 of a log to make a thousand feet. The market price we will say, for example, is six dollars per thousand feet for 3 s. Since it takes more than three logs for a thousand feet, we deduct from the price the excess over three logs to the thousand, which is .09, leaving the price of this raft at $5.91 per thousand.

Memoranda for Drafts.

From FRANK MILLER, Sacramento, Cal.

The December number contains an inquiry as to memoranda for drafts.

The form herewith has been used for years with great satisfaction by a national bank. No other book is kept for references to outstanding collections. The stub is filled, except the lower lines, "When and how settled." The letter is then filled and detached, and mailed with the draft or note. The collector detaches

Date.......................188   No. *2500*

Owner...

Maker..

Payer...

Date...

Time.......................:.............Interest...............

Amount, $ ....Protest.................

Indorser...

....

To whom sent...

....

When and how settled.................................

. ...

4-83-1800.

NOT YET SETTLED.

...Perforated line...

NATIONAL BANK OF PATAGONIA.

....*,* 188

....

....

DEAR SIR:

Inclosed find for collection,

....

....

Please acknowledge receipt and return promptly if unpaid at maturity.

Respectfully,

PROTEST: FRANK MILLER, *Cashier.*
.... Perforated line........................

No. *2500.*

ON SETTLEMENT, PLEASE DETACH AND RETURN THIS SLIP TO
NATIONAL BANK OF PATAGONIA.

Please telegraph advice of all paper protested exceeding $500.

---

the lower end of the letter, and returns it with a check or the unpaid paper, often sending no letter of advice, which last is unnecessary. The clerk refers to the books and finds the proper stub, notes date on the lower lines, and then detaches the narrow margin marked "Not yet settled." The remaining and projecting margins give a rapid method of finding all outstanding papers. We use this as a form for transmitting deeds, and all papers of value. We have not found an index necessary. As it is essential that commercial paper must be protested, unless explicit orders to the contrary are given, the word "Protest" is inserted, and is never erased; but we often write "No" after it. The memorandum to telegraph advice of protested paper is valuable. The stub being found filled with the description of a draft, and the letter being detached and missing, the presumption is that it was properly mailed, as the whole operation is usually concluded without stop. We seldom put more than one item on a stub. Any clerk can use the book for transmitting or receiving collections. We commend the form to country bankers.

Overdraft of Partner.

From A READER, Lafayette, Ind.

Will you or some of your readers oblige me by replying to the following question?

A partner has overdrawn his account, and by agreement must pay interest on the amount withdrawn; how does he pay this interest? Should it be credited to Interest account, or placed to the credit of the other partner? Were it credited to the Interest account, would he not in that way receive back one-half, as he would share in the profit accruing from that account?

.. The interest on the overdraft or on the amount withdrawn should be credited to the Interest account. The partner paying the interest would certainly receive his share of the profit, and he would be entitled to it. The amount he overdrew was the firm's funds—not the funds of his partner. It was virtually a loan to him, the same as it would have been to any other person, and the other partner would be entitled to only his share of the profit accruing from interest on such loan.

A Seven-Account System Book-keeper.

From INQUIRER, Chicago, Ill.

Can you inform me what is meant by a "Seven-account system book-keeper"?

.. One would naturally suppose that a "seven-account system book-keeper" was one who could keep only seven accounts; but that would be a seven-account book-keeper. Now, let us see what is the special use of the word "system." Well, it may be a book-keeper with a system, who keeps seven accounts; but what

is the use of that system? Every book-keeper has a system: a digestive or an indigestive system; but this one has a seven-account system. Now, perhaps, it is meant that this particular kind of a book-keeper is one who carries every transaction into seven accounts. He certainly could not mean that he required only seven accounts for keeping books, because almost any business might have seven Joneses or seven Smiths, and each Jones and Smith would, of course, have to have a separate account. Now, if we have misstated it, and if Mr. Seven-Account System will himself arise and explain, we shall be very glad to place the information before our readers, and particularly before our Chicago correspondent.

A Loose Partnership Agreement.
From O. M. P., Chicago, Ill.

The following question recently arose in adjusting the profits of one of our large clothing houses.

A, having an established business with a capital of $50,000, admitted to partnership his son-in-law, B,—the son-in-law investing $5,000. According to agreement, the partners were to share in the gains and losses in the proportion of ¾ to ¼; there were no written articles of agreement, but it was understood between the partners that interest should be allowed at 6%, as a means of adjusting the difference in their investments. At the close of the year, the senior partner claimed that his account ought to be credited with interest on $4,500, and Interest account charged for that amount. The junior partner thought that the proper way would be to credit each partner with the interest on his entire investment—A to receive credit with interest on $50,000, and B with the interest on $5,000, Interest account being charged with the total amount. As will be readily seen, the difference between the two methods was about $400 (actually, it was more than this, as the amounts above stated were not as much as the facts of the case would show). What they now wish to know is, which, in the absence of any agreement, is the correct plan of adjusting the item of interest? The opinions of your correspondents are respectfully invited.

Departmental Accounts.
From BETA, St. Louis.

On page 229, in October number, I asked your readers for some hints as to ascertaining the profits and losses of different departments in the same business. Please, give your views on the subject; others, then, might follow with their ideas. I feel sure it would be a very natural question for a proprietor doing a mixed business to put to his book-keeper at this time. What have we made on our shoe department the past year?

⁎ In the communication referred to by our correspondent the question asked was relative to the apportionment of various expenses to the different departments of a business, where each department was kept in a separate account. In some cases it would be difficult to carry out the plan proposed or sought for in the communication. In other instances it would be a very simple thing to accomplish. To use the illustration cited by our correspondent—taking the case of a firm doing a business in carpets, upholstering, general dry goods, boots and shoes, furniture—it would seem to us that about the only way to arrive at an apportionment of the expenses among the various departments would be to ascertain the ratio of the general expenses to the entire sales of the establishment. Then from that form a ratio for dividing the general expense account among the various classes of goods handled, or special merchandise accounts.

Suppose the total sales of the establishment to be $200,000; the total expenses, $12,000; and the sales of the general dry goods department, $50,000; the example would be,

$$12,000 : 200,000 :: ? : 50,000$$
Ans., 3000

Then, to determine the profits from the dry goods account, it would be necessary to charge that account, out of expense account, with $3,000. There may be, in certain cases, some objection to this method. The cost of handling some kinds of goods is greater in proportion to the value than others; therefore it is difficult to establish any rule which would apply in all cases. The question is one which we shall be glad to see discussed by our correspondents, and we hope that all who can will favor us with the results of their practical experience.

Determining Personal Indebtedness.
From ORIOLE, Baltimore, Md.

Is there any short method for arriving at the personal indebtedness of a concern without going through the ledger, and making a statement of each debtors' account separately, and summing them up as in the case of a trial-balance?

REPLY.—There are various methods of arriving at this information. To attain the desired result it is necessary to commence the accounts in a systematic manner and upon a basis devised especially for the purpose. One plan would be to open an account, as an auxiliary to the general accounts, entitled. "Personal Debtors," or, as it is termed in Exhibit Book-keeping, "Anticipated Resources." Debit this account with the total amount of goods sold to time purchasers, and credit it with all payments made by such purchasers, and also with such other credits as the various debtors might be entitled to, as returned goods, rebates, discounts, and the like. In carrying this out it would be necessary to have in the sales-book a special column for the purpose for entering all amounts that would be carried to personal accounts in the ledger, and, in the cash-book, a special column for the credits given personal debtors. The footings of these columns should be posted to the auxiliary account of Personal Debtors, monthly, or such period as might be desired; and the balance of Personal Debtors would at any time show the exact condition of the ledger as to all such personal accounts.

The Best System of Shorthand.

From B. T. W., Sandusky, O.

Will you kindly inform me through your next number of the COUNTING-ROOM which is the best system of shorthand—Munson's, Pitman's, Graham's, or Burns's?

*** Feeling quite incompetent to answer this question decisively we consulted practitioners of the systems named. The practitioner of Munson's replied, "Munson's"; the practitioner of Pitman's system responded, "Pitman's"; the phonographer who uses Graham's style responds, "Graham's"; and a Burns's phonographer answered, "Burns." Of the Burns system we have but little personal knowledge, and know but few who practice it. Munson's, Pitman's and Graham's are the styles mostly used throughout this country. Pitman's is most largely used in England. It is also quite extensively used in the Western States. Munson's and Graham's

styles are more generally practiced in the East. They are all founded upon the original Pitman system, which was invented by Isaac Pitman, of Bath, England. A brother of Isaac Pitman, Mr. Benn Pitman, of Cincinnati, Ohio, is the recognized authority of the Pitman system in the United States.

Graham's and Pitman's closely resemble each other. Munson's style, founded upon the same general principles, possesses a more marked difference in its general features—one of the differences being that the dot-vowel-scale, as it is called, is reversed; and another feature of dissimilarity is that Mr. Munson adopts consonant strokes as word signs for short words, which in the Graham and Pitman styles are written with more abbreviated forms. Each author, of course, claims an advantage for his peculiar theory or practice. We think that the majority of professional reporters and shorthand writers use a combination of different systems, and many add devices of their own. There are, probably, very few who follow any one author in every particular, but gradually adopt practices based upon their individual experience.

One system may, perhaps, possess some advantages of legibility, while another will possess advantages of brevity and speed; but as to which of the systems would be the best depends much upon the natural ability of the learner. Now, we think, we have said quite sufficient without answering our correspondent's question, and if he can derive any satisfaction from our remarks he is entirely welcome.

Will the Manufacturing Account show Stock on Hand?

From ORIOLE, Baltimore, Md.

Is there any plan for ascertaining, from the Merchandise account, the value of stock in store? For example, suppose the establishment burns out on August 31st, is it possible to determine, from any manipulation of the Merchandise account, the value of the goods consumed? Your profits on sales vary, say, from 1% to 150%; or, in other words, if, when you have taken account of stock, can you prove the correctness of the result by any special manipulation of the Merchandise account?

*** We know of no process for manipulating a Merchandise account to make it show anything more than it should without manipulation. If there is such a wide range of profit as the correspondent refers to, and there has been no record made of the goods sold, it would be a difficult thing at any specified time to show precisely what the value of stock on hand would be, even twenty-four hours after an inventory had been made. The most feasible way that we could think of to arrive at such a result would be to ascertain, from the previous year, the profits on sales, and thus determine a percentage of gross profits, which would be reasonable to take as a basis for calculating a profit on the goods sold from the time the inventory was taken up to the date of the fire. In some kinds of business it is possible to keep what is called a "general stock-book," in which the goods are divided into classes, according to the percentage of profits, and in the carrying out of sales the division is also made under classified heads. In this way it is not difficult to ascertain, with reasonable accuracy, what the value of goods on hand is at any particular time, but it depends altogether on the nature of the business whether such a plan would be practicable.

This is a question which should elicit attention from our readers, and one, we think, deserving of discussion. Those able to offer suggestions will please avail themselves of the invitation.

Joint-stock Company Accounts.
From FRANK, Pittsburg, Pa.

In Vol. II., page 163, of THE BOOK-KEEPER, in giving a formula for opening joint-stock company's books, the author gives the following opening entry:

Stock Certificates
　　To Capital-stock

and says, "This shows the proper credit to the account of capital-stock, and the account of stock-certificates stands debited with the same amount. As certificates *are issued*, the account of stockholders is debited, and stock certificates credited through the journal entry, thus:

Stockholders
　　To Stock-certificates.

"As payment is made on the stock subscribed for, we have the entry, placing it in journal form, thus:

Cash
　　To Stockholders.

"When the stock subscribed for becomes fully paid up, the account of Stockholders will balance; and when all the stock of the corporation *has been subscribed for*, the account of 'Stock-certificates' will balance."

The italics are mine. This is equivalent to saying that Stock-certificates are issued as soon as stock is subscribed for and before it is paid for. Is it not the rule to issue certificates only to *paid-up* subscribers? Should 'Stock-certificates' account be closed before all the stock has been *paid* for? and if not, what entry should be made at the time stock is subscribed for? A little more light will oblige.

REPLY.—As a rule, stock-certificates are not issued until they have been paid for in full; but this is not invariably the case. There is no reason, if the certificate is properly worded and properly gotten np, to show the conditions upon which it is issued, for withholding stock-certificates from a subscriber, even though only a part of the amount subscribed for has been paid in. The account of stock-certificates has no special reference to the payments. If the stock has all been taken, there is no more to be subscribed for, and consequently the account of stock-certificates would be balanced or closed. As the account of stock-certificates is credited, the account of stockholders is debited, and the balance of the account of stockholders would show the amount remaining unpaid of the stock subscribed. The balance of the account of stock-certificates would show the amount unsubscribed for. If, in using the stock-certificates, where only an assessment has been paid in, the stock-certificate should read, in effect, that the person to whom it is issued has subscribed for, and agreed to take of the capital-stock of the corporation, a certain number of shares, and to pay therefor in assessments as he may be required so to do by order of the directors, or upon such other terms as it may be lawful for the stock to be issued. The certificate should also specify that all payments made on account of this certificate should be indorsed thereon.

The certificate is in one sense merely a receipt from the treasurer of the company to the subscriber, showing the amount of money paid in, and the purposes for which it was paid. At time the stock is subscribed for, the entry is made, charging the stockholder, and crediting the account of Stock-certificates. This simply shows a change in the condition of the assets of the company. Before the stock was subscribed for, the assets of the company embraced such of the shares of stock-certificates as were unissued. Now that the stock has been subscribed for, although not paid for, the form of the assets has changed, and the company holds the agreements of the stock-subscribers as an asset in place of stock-certificates. When this asset changes again by the payment of the amount subscribed, from an obligation of the stockholder to an actual cash value, the record shows the change in the assets by crediting the account of Stockholders, and charging Cash with it.

Deductions for "Wear and Tear."

From MILMAN, Philadelphia.

At our factory we deduct annually for "wear and tear" five per cent. from our Machinery account. Such being the case, is it not proper that the Machinery account should be charged with repairs made to machinery? Please ask your readers for their opinions on this subject.

_**_* The question is such an important one that we trust the readers of this department will give their ideas upon the practice which either they themselves have adopted, or belief as to the best method to be followed in such cases. It seems to us that the deduction of five per cent., from such a class of assets as machinery in active use, would scarcely be sufficient to cover its deterioration, together with the cost of keeping it in good working order. There are some kinds of machinery or tools, used in a manufacturing establishment, which, with ordinary usage, will last to do good work fifteen to twenty-five years; but much the greater part of the machinery in active use will not serve its purpose nearly so long as that. If the Repair account is not a large one, there could, probably, be no objection to charging such items directly to the general account of machinery; but if by so doing the Machinery account is increased, notwithstanding the deduction for deterioration, and irrespective of the addition of any new plant, it is evident that such a practice as the one referred to by our correspondent would not always be satisfactory. One suggestion that we should make is that, in determining the per cent. of deduction for "wear and tear," a careful estimate be made of the probable length of time the machinery will be practically useful. Most kinds of wood-working machinery will not last as long as that used in iron manufacturing.

Much of the machinery for the manufacture of woolen and cotton fabrics is of a nature that will be serviceable for many years. As a rule, we are in favor of keeping a separate account for repairs of machinery, charging that account off each year as an item of expense in conducting the business. Such practice must be exercised with judgment. If an old machine, through a large expenditure of money, is refitted or rebuilt so as to make it almost new, the item of cost would not properly form a part of the general Repair account. By the general Repair account we mean those essential repairs to machinery or parts of machinery which are necessary to replace broken parts, and keep the machinery in good running order. One prominent fault with manufacturers is their neglect to make proper allowances for the depreciation or deterioration of their manufacturing property—their buildings, tools, and various parts of the general plant. As a rule, however, we believe five per cent. is a reasonable deduction for deterioration of the plant of a manufacturing establishment.

Capital Stock Ablutions.

From CHAS. VINCENT, Baltimore, Md.

I have been informed that the Chamber of Commerce of New York made a thorough investigation into the subject of watering stocks of corporations, and sometime within the past few months took some definite action in regard thereto. Will you please inform me where I can ascertain what this action was, or give me through your columns some light upon the investigation referred to?

REPLY.—The Chamber of Commerce of New York appointed, during October last, a special committee on railroad transportation. This committee considered the subject, and investigated the stock-watering business of private corporations. The report of this committee was made November 1st, and in it the committee explained what it understood to be the meaning of the phrase "stock-watering." as referred to in the resolution under which its investigation had been conducted, which stated that it pertained to "corporations which perform public service under charters derived from the State or nation, and to which have been granted the power of eminent domain, and which, in some cases, enjoy large land grants and loans from the public purse. The question where and at what point the private rights of owners and managers of corporations cease, and the rights of the public begin, the committee conceded to be an exceedingly difficult one to decide. It, however, submitted the following proposition—the substance of which it believes should have a fair trial:

First, that stock-watering similar to the late issue of $13,000,000 of Manhattan Elevated Railway stock constitutes a grave offense against the community and should be made a misdemeanor by law.

Second, that capitalization of surplus earnings should be prohibited by law: that increase of capital, either by stock or bonded issues, should be defined by strict legal formulas, easily understood and only permitted for good and sufficient public reasons, and not because it can be shown that a corporation can be made to pay a fair dividend on an increased capital.

Third, that the public welfare requires that corporations should be subjected to Government supervision and control, "State or national, or both, as the case may be," by means of commissions or other methods.

Fourth, that such Government supervision should have power to regulate and control, within reasonable limits, the charges of these corporations.

Fifth, that ordinary differences arising between these corporations and their customers should be decided by Government Commissioners without the expensive and tedious delays incident to a lawsuit. That larger and more important questions should be, as now, referred to the Legislatures or the Courts.

Sixth, that there should be no fixed limit to the rate of cash dividend corporations acting under such supervisions as above indicated may pay to their stockholders, by reason of superior management of their affairs or of increased property, but such questions should be left to the legislative power which created them, to decide upon the necessarily varying conditions of each case.

"There is a painful distrust," say the committee, "pervading the public mind regarding the management of corporations." It is generally believed that corporations are managed in the private interest of a few large owners, with little regard to the interest of smaller holders and investors. Reports as to their true condition are only attainable by the few.

"No intelligent and disinterested man," the report continued, "will now pretend that com-

petition between different lines of railway or telegraph companies will sufficiently protect the public in the matter of rates. Pooling on through traffic has to a great extent abrogated competition, and local traffic, except at some favored points, and where water competition prevails, is necessarily deprived of the benefit of competition." The committee gave the following table of rates now in force on the Union Pacific Railroad as indicative of the necessity of Government interference to prevent its citizens from injustice:

	Per 100 lbs.
Rates from New York to San Francisco	2.25
Rates from New York to Salt Lake City	4.95
Rates from New York to Ogden City	4.65
Rates from New York to Dillon, Montana	3.45.

San Francisco is 850 miles beyond Ogden City. Dillon is 400 miles beyond Ogden City.

Cost of Production.

From M. C. FARNUM, St. Louis, Mo.

In view of the general depression in trade, and especially in the manufacturing branches, would it not be well to invite discussion on the subject of economy in the production of manufactured goods? From personal experience during several years, having examined the accounts of manufacturers in various lines of trade, the failures of very many should more properly be attributed to want of care and economy in the production of goods than what is commonly called "over-production of goods." Manufacturers, as a rule, apparently, have not yet acquired the necessary skill or prudence in the economic affairs of their business. Some have, of course, gone much further in this direction than others. As an illustration: in one establishment the estimated cost of making a certain piece of farm machinery was fully twenty per cent. greater than the estimated cost for manufacturing the same thing not a hundred miles distant. This difference could not have been in material, because both iron and wood were virtually of the same value in both places, and it must, therefore, have arisen in the minor details connected with the establishment. The item of labor alone could not have made any great difference—at least, not twenty per cent; but the *little things* connected with the business, which contributed to make up the general running expenses of the establishments, were the features which operated to effect this difference in the cost of production.

May it not have arisen from careless book-keeping? Are not manufacturers frequently, for want of well-kept and thoroughly systematized accounts, groping their way in the dark, unable to know just how they stand, until the season is passed and it is too late to remedy defects?

*** This is a very proper subject for discussion. The questions of our correspondent are pertinent, and call for the judgment and experience of our readers on the points referred to in the communication.

We have found in the *North American*, Philadelphia, a communication from Mr. Henry Kelly, F.C.A. (Fellow of the Chartered Accountants of England and Wales), in which he has very candidly and ably given an expression upon this subject. He says:

In these times of general business depression it may not be altogether out of place to introduce to the notice of manufacturers, merchants and other business men a subject that has presented itself to my mind, namely, that of exercising a more strict supervision over matters of account than is customary at the present time. Take, for example, the manufacturers ; in nine cases out of ten they never get at a scientifically analyzed cost of production, whereby they lose the opportunity of seeing whether such articles as they manufacture could, by strict economy and the introduction of an approved system, be produced at a less cost than is the case now. The profits on protected manufactures have in the past been such as to render it almost unnecessary to inquire very deeply into the matter, but I think the time has come when business men could with great profit to themselves devote some part of their attention to the pursuit of this subject, and so compensate themselves in a measure for the extremely low prices now ruling, both for manufacturers and for the expenditure on capital in money and brains by manufacturers and other business men engaged in the production of wealth. It has been asserted of the people of this country that they are too much given to "rush" in every business, without, however, sufficient reasons for the assertion. We are essentially a progressive people, working all the time at high pressure, but, individually, I cannot help thinking that it would pay us to give some thought to this matter, and others of a similar kind, the pursuit of which will suggest themselves to your readers.

Begging the insertion of these few remarks as an introduction to the subject in your valuable journal, should you deem the matter of public importance, I am, very respectfully, yours,

HENRY KELLY, F.C.A.

Something about Business-writing and a Teacher of it.

Editor of AMERICAN COUNTING-ROOM.

I am honored by your favor of January 30th, requesting a contribution from me on the subject of Business-writing. I would be glad to favor you were it not that my time is mortgaged for more than it. is worth. At some future time—within a few weeks, if you desire it—I will try to comply with your request. I will, however, at this writing, jot down a few "off-hand" thoughts from the book of experience, written in "muscular movement" at an average rate of thirty words per minute.

In 1852 I became disgusted with Greek and Latin, conic sections, star-gazing, etc., in my academical school-life. I left the academy and tne farm to make my way in the world. I secured a place in my uncle's grocery store in Wheeling, Va., as general clerk and book-keeper. Although, when I left school I was ready for Washington College, Pa, I discovered that I was not competent to make the bills, record the transactions, and keep the accounts of a retail grocery store. But I was determined to learn in the school of experience what the academies of the day had failed to teach me—how to do the ordinary every-day transactions of the world with dispatch and accuracy according to usage. With wonderful patience on the part of my uncle and his patrons, and great mortification and perplexity to myself, after a few months I succeeded in giving fair satisfaction.

From that day I commenced war upon the old methods and ruts of the schools, and have not yet ceased. I was a good writer; had taught writing at West Alexander Academy; Twinsburgh Institute; Western Reserve, O.; and other academies, to help pay my way. But my writing was as slow and precise as the graver of an artist, and I was in as deep a rut in penmanship as my teachers were in mathematics, science, language, etc. I was in demand as a teacher of penmanship—could write copy-lines equal to copper-plate, and as rapidly as an engraver; was as good as the average penmen of the day in fancy jim-cracks and spread eagles; astonished the rural natives with my wonderful specimens.

But I aspired to be an accountant, and entered Duff's Mercantile College, and graduated in nineteen days by actual count. My writing was in demand, and everybody appeared to like it, save myself. I was conscious that it was of no practical use. It was almost perfect in form for copy-lines, but entirely too slow for any other use. I put myself under the instruction of J. D. Williams and James W. Lusk, and I got more light on movement from Billy Miller, now of Packard's New York College, than from any other source up to that time — this was about the year 1857 or 1860, am not quite sure. Billy had the movement and he could throw some light on it, and tell his pupils how he did it. My dear Mr. Lusk was the best business-writer of any of the teachers of that day—the most rapid, the most legible, the most uniform, the easiest, plainest and freest penman, but I did not get the inspiration of movement from him. My dear departed teacher had it; he could write rapidly enough for any use, and beautiful and artistic enough. I was still groping in the dark, anxiously trying to write rapidly and legibly.

I was more and more in demand, and, as a teacher of book-keeping, mathematics and penmanship, held the position of Superintendent of Penmanship in Public Schools of Third and Fourth Ward, Allegheny City, Pa., and Superintendent of Duff's Mercantile College. After serving, as best I could, the venerable P. Duff, now deceased, the founder of business colleges in America, for about three years, as general superintendent of the college and professor of penmanship, I was offered the position as general book-keeper for the large wholesale drug, patent medicine, and white lead house of B. A. Fahnestock's Son & Co., Pittsburgh, Pa., where I remained about nine years. I hesitated several days to accept this position, for as I was conscious that although I had a fine reputation as a business penman and a teacher of penmanship, and had sold my slips of business-writing to several of the large business colleges as specimens, I was afraid I could not write rapidly enough for the business of that large concern. I accepted it, however, as my writing while at Duff's had increased wonderfully in speed—about fifteen or twenty words per minute; but I found it too slow. I had an opportunity, however, of watching the clerks and book-keepers, and still determined to write not only better than any of them, but excel them in speed also.

Now, for the first time in my life, about the year 1862, I began to discover the hidden springs of easy, rapid business-writing. I watched the

best writers, and studied closely their position and movement, and in a few months my speed was doubled with but little loss of legibility. I can now write an average of, perhaps, thirt words a minute in longhand, and two hundred words a minute shorthand; and with my able assistants, S. D. Everhart and Geo. I. Stahl, to teach the theory, and myself the practice, of business penmanship, we make no failures, or at least not more than one out of a hundred of the graduates of the commercial department of the Pittsburgh Central High School fail to become good, rapid, legible writers before they leave the schoolroom; and I here assert, without fear of successful contradiction, that in from one to three years after entering upon the active duties of clerks and accountants, taking age into consideration, that they are the best business-writers uniformly, and the best accountants in the city. The demand from the business firms of this city is now far in excess of the supply. They are in demand, principally, on account of their ability as rapid, legible, and beautiful business-writers. But every other part of a business education— book-keeping, rapid calculations, correspondence, business habits and customs, commercial law and English composition—is brought up to the highest degree of speed and accuracy.

There is no stock in trade so valuable to a young man as a good, rapid, clean cut, legible, uniform, and beautiful business hand, with the ability to add and extend rapidly and accurately, and express his thoughts on paper in comprehensive plain English. Put a young man in possession of a capital of this sort with a good character, and set him afloat in business, with a taste for self study, and, as a rule, he will out-distance your so-called "literary fellers" ten to one in the race to competence and influence. Our schools of to-day are almost as much of a failure as they were thirty years ago. They do not prepare the youth of the land to become intelligent merchants, manufacturers, farmers, artizans. We fail to educate for "the living present," and "let the dead past bury its dead." Greek was good enough for the Greeks, and Latin was good enough for Romans; but we cannot speak with them beyond the grave, or send them a letter in rapid business-writing. Imagine the Greeks and Romans, in the days of their prosperity, teaching the youths of their country a heathen English language yet unborn! Ridiculous! Their motto was "Teach youths that which they will practice when they become men." The time spent in most of our literary institutions in Greek, Latin, Hebrew, Sanscrit, and scores of approximate ology and doxy so-called sciences is ridiculous in the extreme, and worse.

If my old academical teachers were still living, and I could prove *malice prepense* against them for putting the straight-jacket of the schools on me, thus causing me to lose the best part of my time in life, I would vote to put the straight-jacket of a madman on them, and sentence them to imprisonment for life. But they were innocent. The straight-jacket of the schools has been inherited from generation to generation for more than two hundred years. It is hereditary insanity, difficult, very difficult, to eradicate.

For more than twenty years I have not accepted a single point in science on the faith in teachers and text-books. I first weigh it in the balance of experience and observation tested by my God-given faculties. I only accept on Faith the existence of an ever living God—the source of all Truth—and in His Dearly Beloved Son, the Saviour of the world. I do not accept half the dogmas of theologians.

BUSINESS COLLEGES.

The old established business colleges of the country, and the able, practical, progressive, wide-awake teachers in those schools, are doing more than all other causes combined to liberalize, modernize, and practicalize educational methods. They have been ridiculed and libeled by straight-laced, self-opinionated collegians; but these arrows fall harmless at their feet, without leaving even a trace of vengeance. The commercial colleges of to-day are quietly educating a grand army of, perhaps, fifty thousand young men for the live workers in the great world of commerce and industry, and they are fast becoming the leaders.

I have this moment received the following letter, which is the sixth young man called for within as many days past; but my supply is exhausted, and I hasten to grind them out. I have a place for every capable young man before he is ready.

OFFICE OF SCROBIE & PARKER,

Dealers in Implements and Fertilizers,

PITTSBURGH, PA., Feb. 4th, 1884.

PROF. C. C. COCHRAN.

Dear Sir: I would like to get a young fellow, say eighteen years of age, to help us in the office — a good, solid, earnest, industrious boy—good pen-

man, accurate in figures, etc. I am persuaded you turn out such boys at the High-school. Can you name one to me now? If he had some knowledge of shorthand he would please me better. To such a boy we could give a pleasant situation.

Your friend,

O. J. PARKER.

If any part of this very carelessly written and composed communication is of any importance to you as a preliminary for a series of topical papers on practical and industrial education, you are at liberty to use it. It will indicate how one gets into the straight-jacket of the schools, and the desperate struggle to become emancipated from its thralldom. In my future articles, which will be written with care, and embrace methods free from the scholastic tyrany, I will tell you how I got out and keep out of the ruts.

————— C. C. COCHRAN.

An Endorsement.

From PHIL. SCHROER, St. Joseph, Mo.

Having found the COUNTING-ROOM both interesting and profitable, I cheerfully acknowledge its merits. While it continues, and I wield the pen, you shall continue my name on its subscription-list. Some of the discussions, it occurs to me—for instance, those on averaging accounts—are sometimes too extended; but the entering into every detail is a characteristic of that patient class of mortals called "accountants" or "book-keepers."

"Howard's Art of Reckoning," which you sent me, is, I find, truly English, and needs to be Americanized. In its present shape it gives only moderate satisfaction.

₊*₊ It is an exceedingly difficult thing to determine precisely what quantity of any special line of discussion will prove sufficient for all readers. Among the many thousands of the regular readers of the COUNTING-ROOM there are, as we have learned, a large number especially interested in the full and complete discussions such as our correspondent alludes to—that of averaging accounts. We are well aware that for the majority of our readers the discussions on this subject are sometimes much more extended and technical than they care to read but it is not for those not especially interested in these discussions that they are published It is quite impossible to arrange a table of contents for a periodical of this or any other character so as to make all the articles alike instructive and interesting to all the readers. It has been our aim to furnish in each number something that will be of especial interest to every reader, and, therefore, we have widened the scope of subjects discussed and varied the style of discussion. There are comparatively few of our readers who, if they had the inclination, would have the time to carefully read and digest everything in each number of the periodical, although we endeavor, as far as possible, to present such subjects for discussion as will be found of unusual interest to the majority of our readers. It is as much a skill or tact to be able to decide at a glance what one should read, and what he should not read, as it is to make by application an advantage of what is read. We are thankful to our correspondent for his suggestions, and we know he is of a class that will be of service to us in making the various departments of the magazine still more valuable, instructive, and interesting.

Treatment of Property Accounts.
From HALIFAX, Nova Scotia.

Will you kindly inform me as to the proper method of treating the following two accounts? The first I will call "Property at C." This represents my place of business. The second I will call "Property at S," which represents my residence. Both of these properties I own in fee simple. During the past year I have made it a rule to charge to the General Expense account of my business all expenses connected with "Property at C," such, for instance, as taxes and insurance; but items of improvement to the property I have charged to the General Property account. I have charged to my Private account the expenses connected with "Property at S"—taxes, insurance, and the like. Improvements made there I have charged to the account representing that special property. By following this principle, I see that in the future the two accounts will grow beyond their actual value, and, therefore, what I desire is the method to adopt in such cases.

REPLY.—First, as to "Property at C," the only items, according to the correspondent, charged to this account are those of improvements. It might be that what he calls improvements are, in reality, repairs. If that is the case, the error lies in charging the Property

account with items that do not properly belong to it; but if they are, as he says, improvements, and are of that character which, from their nature, will increase the value of the property, there can be no objection—in fact, they should be charged directly to "Property account." One important thing which appears to have been overlooked is the deterioration, or, as it may be called, the wear and tear of the property—a subject elsewhere in this department commented upon.

There should be made each year some reasonable allowance for natural decay or deterioration of property. If such a course is pursued, our correspondent would find that, although charging the property with all improvements made upon it, yet, by crediting off each year a reasonable per cent. of its value, the account would not grow beyond its actual value, but would be gradually diminishing as an asset in his accounts. We believe that persons owning property which they carry in their accounts as certain valuable assets would find it very much to their advantage to adopt the plan of crediting off each year some reasonable per cent. or allowance for its depreciation. It is true that in some instances the appreciation of land upon which the improvements are located will counterbalance the natural decay of the improvements, and in such cases an allowance need not necessarily be made; but, as a rule, it would be better for property owners to have their accounts show an under-valuation rather than an over-valuation in their assets of this character.

In Vol. V. of THE BOOK-KEEPER, Nos. 55 to 59 inclusive, we published quite a large amount of interesting correspondence on the subject of "Real Estate Book-keeping," which very thoroughly discussed some of the points referred to by this correspondent, and which we would ask him to examine for further information on the subject.

In the case of "Property at S," the plan he adopts of charging to the property only the items of actual improvements is a correct one; but here, too, as in the other case, there should be an allowance for deterioration. The items of taxes, insurance, and others of that kind, which he charges to his Private account, are, in other words, rent of the property he occupies. To such items should also be added the deterioration of his private property, in order to arrive at the actual cost to him of rent.

Legal Miscellany.

DEALING IN "FUTURES."

In the case of *Cunningham* vs. *The National Bank of Augusta*, recently decided by the Supreme Court of Georgia, (November, 1883,) where a note was given to secure and make good any losses that might accrue from the purchase of certain cotton for future delivery, the intention and understanding being that the cotton was not to be delivered to, or received by, the defendant (the present plaintiff in error), but that there was to be a settlement at a future day, when the defendant was to receive or pay the difference between the contract price and the market price. On the day the settlement was to be made, it was held that such a transaction was in the nature of gaming, rendering the note void at the time it was given; and that the same could not be enforced even in the hand of a bona fide purchaser before maturity.

The Court in delivering its opinion said: "It is manifest that the consideration of the note sued on is for and on account of dealings commonly called 'Futures.'" . . . . But what is the transaction termed 'Futures'? It is this· One person says, "I will sell you cotton at a certain time in the future for a certain price." You agree to pay that price, knowing that the person with whom you have to deal has no cotton to deliver at the time, but with the understanding that when the time for delivery arrives, you are to pay him the difference between the market value of the cotton and the price you agree to pay if cotton declines; and if cotton advances, he is to pay you the difference between what you promised to pay and the advanced market price.

If this is not speculation on chances—a wagering and betting between the parties—then we are unable to understand the transaction. A betting on a game of faro, brag or poker cannot be more hazardous, dangerous, or uncertain, indeed. It may be said that these animals are tame, gentle and submissive compared with this monster. The law has caged them, and delivered them to their dens. They

have been outlawed, while this ferocious beast has been allowed to stalk about in open midday with gilded signs and flaming advertisements to lure the unhappy victim to its embrace of death and destruction. What are some of the consequences of these speculations on 'Futures'? The faithful chroniclers of the day have informed us that as growing directly out of these nefarious practices there have been bankruptcies, defalcations of public offices, embezzlements, forgeries, larcenies and deaths Certainly no one will contend for one moment that a transaction fraught with such evil consequences is not immoral, illegal, and contrary to public policy."

Such is the opinion of the Supreme Court of Georgia as to transactions in what are called " Futures."

There has been considerable legislation, as well as judicial decision, upon this subject. In the first place, it has been held that from the nature of the contract, and the circumstances attending it, it is apparent that the purpose was not to buy or sell the goods—that no delivery was intended, but at the same time appointed for delivery. The transaction should be closed upon the basis of the then market price of the goods, the losing party paying to the other the difference. The transaction is a wager, and, in the absence of any statute, it is void at common law. *Grizewood* vs. *Blane*, 11 Com. Bench, 73; Eng. C. L., 526. *Gregory* vs. *Wendell*, 39 Mich., 337. *Kirkpatrick* vs. *Bonsall*, 72 Penn. St., 155; also, 6 Bissell, 53; 65 Me., 570; 55 Penn. St., 294; 83 Ill., 33.

But a contract for the sale of goods to be delivered at a future day is valid, though at the time the vendor has not the goods in his possession, has not made any contract to obtain them, and has no expectation of acquiring them, otherwise than by a purchase at some time before the day of delivery. 3 Sandford, 230; 70 N. Y., 202; 11 Hun, 471; 39 Mich., 337; 82 Ill., 412; 72 Penn. St., 155; 65 Me., 570; 1 Bissell, 177; 7 do., 540.

In some of the States, statutes have been enacted especially directed against these gambling contracts. In Alabama, by § 2131 of the Code, all contracts founded in whole or in part upon a gambling consideration are void. And in the case of *Hawley* vs. *Bibb*, recently decided by the Supreme Court of Alabama (69 Ala., 52), a negotiable instrument, founded upon such a consideration, was declared void even in the hands of an innocent holder for value.

In Arkansas, by an Act passed March 30th, 1883, the buying, selling, or in any way dealing in "Futures" with a view to profit is declared to be gambling and a misdemeanor; and the first offense is made punishable by a fine of not less than $250, nor more than $500 for the second offense. In addition to the previous penalty, a sentence of imprisonment for thirty days in the county jail must be imposed.

By § 2638 of the Code of Georgia, a contract for future delivery, where both parties are aware that the seller expects to purchase, himself, to fulfill the contract, and no skill and labor, or expense, enters into the consideration; but the same is a pure speculation upon chances, is contrary to the policy of the law, and can be enforced by neither party.

In Illinois (Rev. Stat., chap. 38, § 130, p. 471): "Whoever contracts to have or give to himself or another the option to sell or buy, at a future time, any grain or other commodity, stock of any railroad or other company, or gold, or forestalls the market by spreading false rumors to influence the price of commodities therein, or corners the market, or attempts to do so in relation to any of such commodities, shall be fined not less than $10, nor more than $1,000, or confined in the county jail not exceeding one year, or both; and all contracts made in violation of this section shall be considered gambling contracts, and shall be void."

By chapter 78, § 6, Public Statutes of Massachusetts, it is provided that contracts written or oral, for the sale or transfer of a certificate or other evidence of debt due from the United States, or from an individual State, or of corporate stocks, shares, or interests, shall be void, unless the party contracting to sell or transfer the same is, at the time of making the contract, the owner or assignee thereof, or authorized by the owner, or assignee, or his clerk, to sell or transfer the certificate or other evidence of debt, share or interest so contracted for.

This alters the rule of the common law, previously stated that a contract for the sale of goods to be delivered at a future day is valid, even though the vendor has not, at the time, the goods in his possession.

In New York, previous to 1858, a similar statute existed; but by chapter 134 of the laws of that year, that statute was repealed, and such contract became valid. This, however, does not affect the force of the common law rule as to the invalidity of gambling and wager contracts.

And in Mississippi (Act March 7th, 1882), dealing in "futures" is declared unlawful; and any person convicted of buying or selling, either by agent or otherwise, any such contract, shall be fined not less than $50, and not over $500; and that no advance of money, nor any agreement for the payment of any sum for such purposes, shall be enforced in any of the Courts of that State.

Besides the statutes and the decisions already cited, there have been, in many of the States, other decisions involving the question, all upholding the doctrine that where no delivery is contemplated by the parties, the transaction is a wager contract and void. 4 Bradw. (Ill.), 594; 8 Bradw. (Ill.), 467; 97 Pa. State, 278; 52 Wis., 593; 1 Mo., App., 45; 6 do, 269; 48 Conn., 116; 65 Ga., 210; 9 Hun. (N. Y.), 429; 11 do, 471; 71 N. Y., 420; 77 N. Y., 612.

INNKEEPER — LIABILITY OF.

Plaintiff, the wife of General Hancock, sued the defendant, the proprietor of St. Clair Hotel, to recover the value of certain valuables taken from her rooms while sojourning at such hotel. The facts as to the occupancy of the rooms were as follows:

The husband of the plaintiff, General Hancock, an officer in the United States Army, in November, 1873, applied to the defendant for rooms and board at defendant's hotel for himself and family; and after some conversation, General Hancock agreed to occupy the rooms until the following summer, provided everything was satisfactory, and provided further that he was not sooner ordered away on military duty. The rooms were let less than transient rates, and the meals were to be taken at the defendant's restaurant connected with the hotel, and paid for as ordered. The family continued to occupy the rooms until June, 1874, and in March, 1874, the valuables were stolen.

It was contended on the part of the defendant that a substantial agreement had been made by General Hancock as to the length of time which he and his family should occupy said rooms, and that, therefore, he should be treated as a boarder or lodger, and not as a transient guest.

The referee refused so to find and gave judgment for the plaintiff; and on appeal to the Court of Appeals, (three judges dissenting), the judgment for the plaintiff was affirmed, and it was

Held, That under the facts, the plaintiff must be considered as a guest at the defendant's hotel, as to whom the defendant is an absolute insurer of the goods and valuables, and not as a boarder, in which case defendant would only be held to the exercise of ordinary care; and that as the defendant had failed to avail himself of the provision of the Statute of 1857, whereby, upon giving notice to deposit the valuables in his safe, he would be protected, he must suffer the loss.

Hancock vs. *Rand*, New York Court of Appeals, Nov., 1883.

SLEEPING-CAR COMPANY — LIABILITY FOR GOODS OF PASSENGERS.

Plaintiff, on a trip from Philadelphia to Pittsburgh, occupied a Pullman sleeping-car. On retiring, he put his watch and money in his vest, which he placed underneath the outside corner of the mattress of his berth. It was stolen during the night, and plaintiff sought to hold the company liable.

Held, That the company was bound to use reasonable and ordinary care to protect the property of its passengers; and whether or not such care has been exercised is a question of fact.

It being shown that the porter in charge of the car went outside for a few minutes to black boots,

Further *held*, That if the jury find that the theft would not have occurred if the watchman had been at his post, the company is liable.

Judgment for plaintiff.

Gardner vs. *Pullman Palace Car Co.*, Supreme Court of Pennsylvania, Nov., 1883.

JUDGMENT FIXING LIABILITY OF STOCKHOLDERS OF INSOLVENT CORPORATIONS—WHEN CONCLUSIVE.

K, a creditor of an insolvent corporation, brought suit against certain of its stockholders, H, B, and L, to enforce their individual liability for the debts of the corporation, and obtained a judgment against such stockholders,

respectively, for the amount found to be due by each. The execution issued against H in such action was returned unsatisfied, and, thereupon K filed a supplemental petition against B and L to recover the amount of the original judgment against H, alleging that H had acquired his stock by transfer from B and L at a time when all the debts of the company had been contracted, and prior to which time B and L were the owners and holders of the stock.

Held (reversing the judgment of the lower Court), That the original judgment was final, and could only be vacated, modified, or reversed in the mode prescribed by statute, and until thus vacated, modified or reversed, it was conclusive upon all the parties to the action as to all matters involved therein, and that section 5119 of the Revised Statutes does not authorize the filing of a supplemental petition after final judgment for the purpose of vacating, modifying or reversing such judgment.

Petition dismissed.

Bullock et al vs. *Kilgour*, Ohio Supreme Court, December 12th, 1883.

LIABILITY OF SURETIES FOR NOTE OF ADMINISTRATOR.

Boyd, the administrator of a solvent estate, purchased from M a monument for the deceased, giving in payment his negotiable note as administrator, and M giving him a receipt showing that the debt had been paid. Before the maturity of the note the accounts of B, as executor, were passed upon by the Probate Court, the receipt of M being treated as an actual payment, and allowed as a credit to B. The note was discounted by the bank before maturity—they having no notice of the settlement and allowance of credit to B. At maturity B was sued as administrator, and a judgment obtained against him to be satisfied out of assets in his hands. Execution was returned unsatisfied, and on B's refusal to pay the judgment this action was brought against the sureties on his bond, to recover upon the judgment.

Held, reversing the judgment of the lower Court, That the settlement of the account was the test and measure of the liability of the sureties; that the giving of a negotiable note as administrator was such a departure from his authority as to relieve the estate, and hence his sureties, from liability, and that whatever liability Boyd may have incurred individually upon the note or judgment, neither the estate nor the sureties were bound therein. *Curtis & Hill* vs. *National Bank*, Supreme Court of Ohio, December 18th, 1883.

MASTER AND SERVANT — CONTRIBUTORY NEGLIGENCE OF SERVANT.

Where an employee, engaged in coupling cars, failed to examine as to the nature of "deadwoods" upon cars, with which he had to do, and received an injury from such "deadwoods" while at work,

Held, If the appliances were dangerous, it was a risk of the employment which he took upon himself, and his failure to examine as to their nature constituted contributory negligence, and barred a recovery. *Hathaway* vs. *Michigan Central R. R.*, Supreme Court of Michigan, Oct., 1883.

MEANING OF "TWO-THIRDS'" VOTE.

The constitution of Minnesota provides: "The judicial power, etc., shall be vested in a Supreme Court, etc., and such other Courts, inferior to the Supreme Court, as the Legislature may establish by a *two-thirds'* vote."

Held, That this means a two-thirds' vote of all the members of each house, and not a two-thirds' vote of a quorum. *State* vs. *Gould*, Minnesota Supreme Court, Nov., 1883.

CONTRACT IN RESTRAINT OF TRADE— INJUNCTION.

One Brewer entered into a contract with Lamar, Rankin & Lamar, whereby, in consideration of $275, he surrendered his entire interest to the preparation known as "Brewer's Lung Restorer," and agreed never to use or permit his name to be used on any preparation which could be used for the same purpose as "Brewer's Lung Restorer"; and further agreed to keep secret from the balance of the world the recipe of the same. Subsequently, Brewer and other persons under the name of T. E. Brewer & Company made and sold a medicine under the name of "Brewer's Sarsaparilla Syrup," advertised and recommended for the cure of the identical disease for which "Brewer's Lung Restorer" was recommended.

Plaintiffs sued for an injunction, and defendant claimed the contract void, as being in restraint of trade and contrary to public policy.

Held, That such agreement was in partial restraint of trade only and was reasonable.

Injunction granted. *Lamar* vs. *Brewer*, Supreme Court of Georgia.

From Bradstreet's.

CONSTRUCTION OF WRITTEN INSTRUMENTS.

The construction of a written instrument is exclusively for the Court, except where it can be understood without reference to facts not within the writing, and then the jury are to judge of the whole altogether. So held by the Supreme Court of Pennsylvania in the recent case of *Foster* vs. *Berg*. This was a case in which the terms of a contract in controversy between the parties were to be gathered from letters and telegrams alone, the court holding that the interpretation of the contract was exclusively within its province.

RELEASE OF SECOND ACCOMMODATION INDORSER.

Where a joint judgment has been recovered against the first and second accommodation indorsers of a bill of exchange the second accommodation indorser will be released from liability by a valid tender by the first indorser to the judgment creditor of the full amount of the judgment in a currency which the creditor was bound by law to receive but refused. So held by the Supreme Court of Tennessee in the case of *Ewing* vs. *Sogg*, decided February 2d.

WHEN FEDERAL COURT WILL NOT GRANT INJUNCTION.

An injunction will not be granted by a federal court to restrain proceedings about to be taken in a State court on the ground that the State enactment under which these proceedings must be taken is an unconstitutional statute, according to the opinion of the United States Circuit Court for the district of Vermont in the recent case of *The Rennselaer & Saratoga Railroad Company* vs. *Bennington & Rutland Railroad Company*.

RECEIPT FOR PART PURCHASE-PRICE OF LAND NOT SUFFICIENT MEMORANDUM.

A memorandum of the sale of real property to be sufficient under the statute of frauds must be complete in itself, and must leave nothing to rest in parol, according to the opinion of the Supreme Court of Michigan in the recently decided case of *Gault* vs. *Stormont*. In this case a receipt for part payment of the purchase price of land expressing the full consideration was held not a sufficient memorandum under the statute.

NOTES AND COMMENTS.

We have commenced in this number a series of articles on building and loan associations. The author, Mr. R. B. Keys, has had an extensive and varied experience in the forming and in the accountantcy of such organizations in Philadelphia, and, judging from the many inquiries concerning the workings of these bodies which from time to time have been made of us, we believe the articles will prove unusually interesting and advantageous to our readers. Those having questions to ask, or suggestions to offer, while these articles are in progress, are informed that their communications will be placed before the author of the articles and receive his prompt consideration. This announcement is made upon his special request, and it is his hope that all who desire any further information upon the subjects treated than is given in the writings will forward their inquiries.

In making room in this number for the article on Building and Loan Associations it has been necessary to postpone until the next issue our series of articles on Public Moneys and Accounts. In connection with the latter we desire that persons having information of value to our readers, or wishing to obtain more explicit or any special information concerning the work and duties of public officials and public accounts, will communicate with us.

Our department of "Counting-room Chats" will, we believe, be found especially attractive in this issue, and we are glad to say that the interest manifested in the department and the correspondence reaching us are most encouraging evidences of its popularity and its growing usefulness. We repeat our invitation for contributions.

Pertaining to some special features in bank book-keeping we have been favored with an interesting communication, which is published as a general article, and to which the attention of all those interested in the subject of bank accounts is directed. We regret that another communication of a similar character, though treating upon quite a different branch of bank accountantcy, should have reached us too late for publication in this number, but it will appear in the March edition.

The Annual Meeting of the Institute of Accountants and Book-keepers of New York will take place on Friday, March 14th. The 15th of that month being on Saturday, the meeting will take place, according to the by-laws of the society, on the preceding Friday. It is expected that the meeting will be one of unusual interest. Officers are to be elected for the coming year, and it is proposed to have the usual annual re-union of members, and a pleasant time generally. Invitations have been sent to sister organizations in other cities, and hopes are entertained of having a large number of visitors present.

We have received the Annual Report of the Berkshire Fire Insurance Company of Massachusetts with the accompanying statement of the treasurer. It is a concise, business-like document, characteristic of the company from which it emanates. The figures given show a steady, wholesome growth over the business of previous years, conclusively proving what may be accomplished by honest business methods, careful management, and earnest, energetic work; and they cannot but be gratifying to officers and policy-holders alike. There has been a large increase in membership during the past year, and a proportionate gain in income and assets. The list of assets is singularly free from speculative or questionable investments, more than three-fourths being comprised in United States and Massachusetts Town Bonds, real estate and first mortgage loans.

The report contains among others the following items:

Total Assets, January 1st, 1884......$3,683,086.08
Total Receipts in 1883.............. 777,386.88
Surplus, Massachusetts Standard..... 448,209.13
Surplus, New York Standard........ 618,209.13

Embracing all the benefits of the Massachusetts non-forfeiture law, with an established record for fair dealing with its patrons during the thirty-two years of its existence, and under the able management of its experienced officers, there can be no doubt of its continued growth and prosperity.

The Massachusetts non-forfeiture law, under which the Berkshire Life Insurance Company, in common with its sister companies of that commonwealth, conducts its business, is something unique in the field of life insurance. It provides that no policy issued by a Massachusetts company shall become forfeited or void for non-payment of premium after two full annual premiums have been paid thereon; but upon a subsequent default the policy-holder *without any action on his part,* becomes entitled to an amount in paid-up insurance, proportionate to the amount of premiums previously paid, or to an amount in cash equivalent to the entire reserve value of his policy, less a small surrender charge allowed to the company: thus securing to the insured, by statute, absolute equity, and relieving him from the necessity of any negotiation whatever with the company to ascertain the amount which he should receive. This law went into effect on January 1st, 1881, and its beneficent results have been already felt, while the confidence it inspires in would-be insurers has largely increased the business of the companies over which its provisions are enforced.

NOVELTIES.

The Shannon Files and Schlicht's Indexes.

In its most popular form the (No. 4 A) Shannon File consists of a base made of combination woods to prevent warping and splitting,

Fig. 2.— Shows how papers are perforated.

to which is attached at the upper end a double-arched device for the reception of the papers. The double-arches open and close simultaneously by pressure of the movable part of either. At the lower end of the base is attached a perforator which is used to perforate the papers before filing, so that they pass freely over the arches, and form a compact mass of papers. An index to separate the papers alphabetically, and a cover (C. C. Cover), go with this kind of file. The Clague Compressor Cover (C. C. Cover) may be used on any Shannon File, and consists of a press-board sheet with tinned upper end, to which is attached a metal slide slotted to an angle of thirty degrees, and oper-

Fig. 3.— Shows File open and manner of removing a paper.

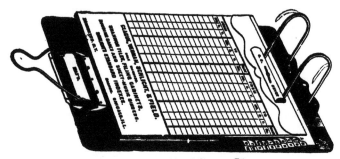

Fig. 1.—Represents No. 4A Shannon File.

ating freely on a rivet-shaped pin. To com-press the papers or lock the file it is necessary to press downward on the metal part of the cover, and push the slide to the left as far as it will go: to unlock the file, the slide is pushed to the right.

The files and binding-case are largely used by business men for filing letters, invoices, re-ceipts and other papers. These devices are also made in the form of a cabinet for con-cerns having large numbers of papers.

This filing system has features distinctive from all others in that papers are *held* in place

Fig. 4.
Shows how papers are transferred from File to Binding-case.

on the arches. Any paper can be conveniently examined, removed, and replaced, without dis-arranging the other papers. For invoices, it combines all the advantages of the old-fashion invoice-book, minus the labor of past-ing and indexing; and considering the slight cost of the binding-cases, it is cheaper by far.

Schlicht's Standard Index is a device for

rapid reference to names. Its advantages are that reference can be had to any name among tens or hundreds of thousands with almost equal facility, as names are classified according

Fig. 5.—Shows papers after having been transferred.

to the first syllable or part of the first syllable of surnames, and the first letter of given names. A more extended explanation will be given at another time.

The manufacturers of these Files and In-

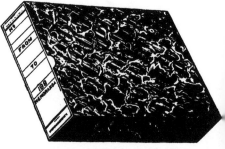

Fig. 6.—Shows Binding-case closed.

dexes are Messrs. Clague, Wegman, Schlicht & Field, of Rochester, N. Y.; Chicago, Ill.; Toronto, Canada; and Frankfort-on-the-Maine, Germany. The reader is referred to their advertisement, which appears in our advertising pages. Further information may be had on application to the above-named firm. Bardwell & Briggs, 318 Broadway, are the New York agents.

The "Complete" Check-book.

This is the name of a device patented by Mr. Myron Campbell, of South Bend, Ind. It is intended for a pocket check-book, and as such possesses several advantages over the various styles which are now in common use. In size it is only that of the check to be used, whatever that may be. It opens on the side, and is therefore less cumbersome when opened for use than those styles opening endwise. The space for entries and other memoranda is in more favorable form than ordinarily seen in the check-books for pocket use, as it affords a larger number of entries without carrying footings or balances forward than in the case where the entries are made in the ordinary manner, or even either of the styles manufactured by Hall & Co., of Providence, R. I., who furnish a large proportion of the pocket check-books now in use, especially in the larger cities. In the front part of Mr. Campbell's book are four leaves, all of which fold in from the four different directions,—that is, two fold in from the sides; one, from the back; the other, from the front; and two fold in from the ends—and from each end. The leaves give the space for entries and notations of the bank account, and are columnized with the following headings: "Date of Deposit"; "Amount of Deposit"; "Balances"; "Date of Checks"; "Number"; "In Favor of."

There is one suggestion we would offer upon the model furnished us by the patentee, viz., that the columns he has provided upon the blank pages should be reduced, and that the space for the name in whose favor the check is drawn should be increased. In the columns for amounts and balances he has provided sufficient room for $100.000, or even a million, while the space for the name is very limited, and would not be sufficient to write some names we have heard of, or, in fact, for some that we have occasionally to write. Following the blank leaves is a sheet of blotting-paper,

after which come the checks. The top of the check is attached to the back of the book—a perforated line running across the check. Persons desiring to examine this invention will, we presume, be supplied with models by addressing Mr. Campbell, at South Bend National Bank, South Bend, Ind.

The Web Tablet.

Under this name the Albany Perforated Wrapping Paper Company manufactures a very neat case for writing-paper. The paper is in a roll, which fits into a cylindrical case neatly finished in Russia leather and brass. This cylinder extends into a flat surface large enough to write a page on. This surface is provided with lines which show through the paper and guide the writer. The paper, as it is unrolled, passes under a metal strip which holds it firmly in

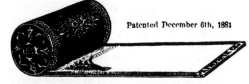

Patented December 6th, 1881

place, and also serves as a cutter for tearing off the completed page. The tablet is a very neat device for keeping the paper clean and ready for use. For writing on the lap, in traveling, etc., it would be quite convenient. We would suggest that there should be a ring at the cylinder end to hang it up by, and a roller in the cylinder to re-roll the paper.

Colton's Portfolio File and Scrap-book.

This is the name of an ingenious device for the systematic filing and preserving of private papers, notes, or clippings, which it may be desirable for one to place in the most convenient form of ready reference. As a receptacle for private papers, a business man has only to examine its construction and adaptability to become at once convinced of its usefulness. As an aid to public speakers, authors, and others, desiring to file away, in a classified order, memoranda, notes, or extracts, the portfolio will be found most admirably adapted. Its construction may be explained by saying that it consists of thirty-one large envelopes, fastened together by tapes passing through eyelets at the corners on the lower side, and protected by stiff cloth-covered boards on the outside, thus forming a book which, by lengthening the tapes, admits of being increased to any desired size. On the front side of each envelope rulings are made for writing, or giving a synopsis of, the contents of the envelope, and on the inside of the last cover is an index of subjects. To increase the capacity, as may be required, when the envelopes become filled, it is necessary only to lengthen the tape by unwinding it from the bottom; and to close the book, the thumb is placed on the edge of the back cover, as the back is thus pressed down, and the tape is drawn tightly, brought over the top of the book, and wound around the small brass button which holds it firmly.

THE LIBRARY.

BOOK-KEEPING FOR COUNTRY MER-CHANTS, AND VALUABLE INFORMA-TION ON VARIOUS BUSINESS TOPICS. By G. H. MOLL, St. Louis, Mo.

This is the title of a fifty-page pamphlet which, as its title indicates, furnishes some valuable information on various business topics. The purpose of the book is not, as the author says, to teach the science of book-keeping in all its branches, but simply and solely to give to country merchants and others doing a general merchandise business such instructions as will enable them, by means of double-entry book-keeping in its simplest form, to keep an accurate and systematic record of their business transactions. The first chapter is a brief exposition of double-entry book-keeping, giving a number of illustrations showing the manner of keeping a cash account, personal accounts, bills-receivable and bills-payable accounts, explaining the method of posting, and following with an explanatory set for practice. The cash-book, ledger, trial-balance, etc., follow in a second chapter. The author, presuming that the business he has illustrated has been destroyed by fire, makes up a "Statement of Fire Losses Sustained." which gives a very correct idea of the manner in which an exhibit of that character should be prepared. Several pages are devoted to business calculations, and then follow some pertinent remarks concerning "Commercial Paper," "Promptness," "The Evils of Buying from too many Houses" and "Overstocking," "Mercantile Agencies," "Counterfeit Money," etc. Altogether, the pamphlet is worthy of a careful perusal by business men — likewise, book-keepers. Price, fifty cents. Copies are supplied by the author, G. H. Moll, whose address is, care of Orr & Lindsley, St. Louis, Mo.

"The new edition of 'Students' Songs,' comprising the *twenty-first thousand*, has just been published by Moses King of Cambridge. This collection comprises over sixty of the jolly songs as now sung at all leading colleges in America. It has the full music for all the songs and airs. Compiled by Wm. H. Hills (Harvard, 1880). The price is only fifty cents." Orders may be addressed to the publisher, Moses King, Cambridge, Mass.

Magazines for February.

The North American Review for February contains a number of strong Papers of the highest interest to the American people. Mr. Carl Schurz contributes a Paper of much merit on the subject of "Corporations, their Employees and the Public." In this contribution the writer deals plainly and logically with his subject. He makes a strong argument in behalf of those employees who, for their own protection and the advancement of their interests, are obliged to resort to combinations and strikes for the purpose of securing what to them seems honestly to be their rights. The belief is asserted that corporations are under lawful obligation to perform their duties to the public, irrespective of what, in case of strikes among their employees, the cost may be. On the other hand, it is claimed, in behalf of corporations, that if they are to be bound to pay whatever wages their employees may demand, the employees may take undue advantage of this circumstance; that in view of the practical impossibility of filling their places with other competent persons at a moment's notice, the employees might feel encouraged to ask for more and more until, finally, their exactions would grow so exorbitant as to become utterly ruinous to the corporations, if complied with; that corporations should be permitted, in case of strikes, to go into the labor market and to supply themselves upon the best terms, even though thereby subjecting the public to damage and inconvenience. As a remedy for the existing evils, the writer thinks the suggestion is not only appropriate, but rapidly receiving favor — that the establishment of law tribunals of arbitration would act as a medium for adjusting difficulties arising between large corporations and their employees ; and it is claimed, in favor of the existence of such tribunals, that they would tend to make employers more careful and considerate in the treatment of their working-men ; and, on the other hand, would deter the men from countenancing foolish demands, for the reason that it would be distasteful to either of them to see their conduct publicly condemned by an impartial tribunal. The Paper is well worthy of careful and considerate study. Senator J. J. Ingalls contributes an exceedingly interesting article on "John Brown's Place in History." Of the many who have written concerning the services and peculiarities of this well-known character, probably no person is better able to furnish information and draw more logical conclusions than Mr. Ingalls. Prof. Andrew F. West presents a carefully prepared argument in favor of classical education. It is the side of the question that those opposed to his line of reasoning should, by all means, make themselves familiar with. "Race Progress in the United States" is an instructive treatise by Congressman J. R. Tucker. "Defects of the Public School System" is the title of a Paper by Rev. J. Savage, who takes the ground that the public school system of the country is being made too broad and too liberal ; that public schools should confine themselves to giving a thorough common education ; and he believes that the great mass of children will be greatly benefited by having education confined to these limits. Their necessities will never carry them beyond what a common education will supply. He believes, too, they should be well trained in the few essentials of good citizenship and those things that will fit them to lead self-sustaining, honest, and honorable lives. He argues that the common school, instead of being devoted to securing the largest good for the greatest number, has developed into an institution essentially aristocratic. One strong argument that he makes against the present system of public education is, that it fails to fit the great mass for real life by actually training large numbers into a positive distaste for what must be their real life-work. Artemus Ward stated, on a certain occasion, that "he tried to do too much, and did it," and this, it is claimed by Mr. Savage, "is just the weak point in our public school system ; it is trying to do too much, and, as a consequence, is doing very little thoroughly and well, while the things that ought to be of chief importance are certainly not accomplished." A discussion on the "Rival Systems of Heating," by Dr. A. N. Bell and Prof. W. P. Trowbridge, is an especially attractive feature of the number.

In the *Popular Science Monthly* Prof. Herbert Spencer contributes the opening article, "The New Toryism." Under the title, "College Athletics," by Prof. E. L. Richards, is a Paper taken up for discussion—the first part of which appears under the head of "Advantages," and forms a prominent contribution to this number. Dr. Felix L. Oswald contributes a Paper on the subject of "The Remedies of Nature." A practical discussion of "Dangerous Kerosene and the Methods for its Detection," by John T. Stoddard, professor of chemistry in Smith College, will be found useful and interesting. A Paper on "Right and Wrong," under the series of articles entitled "The Morality of Happiness," is a strong contribution upon an interesting question. Persons who doubt their ability to snore, sneeze, gap or cough properly, may find some very valuable information concerning these accomplishments by reading what Mr. Fernald has to say, and practicing the directions he sets forth, in his Paper on "How we Sneeze, Laugh, Stammer, and Sigh." Dr. William W. Jaques, the electrician of the American Bell Telephone Company, favors the readers of the magazine with the results of experiment and study on the subject of "Underground Wires." Mary C. Hungerford reports, in an article on "An Overdose of Hasheesh" (or Indian hemp), not only her experience, but some very pointed remarks on a subject that all persons who are troubled with headaches should lose no time in consulting. Hemp, taken in doses for a headache, notwithstanding what the writer has said, is far preferable to its exterior application, as many a victim would testify were he given an opportunity. A man being destroyed by an earthquake might have no particular interest in M. Daubrée's very learned contribution on the subject of their causes ; but those of us not yet destroyed are given an opportunity to ascertain what the professor has learned in a very extended tour of investigation. "Last Wills and Testaments," by Joseph W. Sutphen, should have a careful perusal. "Fifty Years of Mechanical Engineering," a Paper read before the Peoria Scientific Society, by A. C. Harding, forms an admirable contribution. Other articles, correspondence, and editorials, complete the number.

Lippincott's. The Paper on "Old Germantown," with which the February number opens, will be found of especial interest. It traces the early history of the town, calls to mind its prominent figures and characteristics in the past, and describes the existing relics. The accompanying illustrations are most admirably executed. An instructive article is that of Alfred M. Williams, which he entitles "An Indian Cattle-Town," and in which he relates his experiences while traveling extensively in the "Reservation." Miss Brewster describes the Breton Home of Madame de Sevigné, in a lively Paper entitled, "French Chateau Life, Past and Present." "A Pilgrimage to Sesenheim" is the title of a Paper by Horatio S. White. "On a Glass Roof" is an amusing description of winter fishing in Vermont, by Rowland E. Robinson. Dr. Felix M. Oswald contributes the second Paper on "Healthy Homes," which, we may justly say, should not be missed by any intelligent reader. The department of fiction in this number forms an excellent illustration of the many good qualities of the periodical. "Sebia's Tangled Web," a serial story by Lizzie W. Champney, portrays true character in an animated manner, and furnishes not only reading of unusual interest, but gives to the mind something that is well worthy of careful reflection. "A Mental Masquerade," by Ester Warren, and "Explained," by Alice Brown, are both bright and attractive stories. "The Great Jigtown Failure," by C. F. Johnson, is a realistic sketch most cleverly drawn. The various departments present their usual complement of very interesting reading.

Atlantic Monthly. "A Visit to South Carolina in 1860," from the pen of Edward G. Mason, is a contribution to historical events which, we believe, every reader of our magazine will be interested in. Mr. Mason relates a personal experience, heretofore unpublished, which furnishes some exceedingly valuable information on the condition of affairs in the South previous to the Civil War, and his very attractive manner of telling what he learned and saw adds very much to the interest of what is told. "The term abolitionist," says the writer, "had evidently been used to alarm the blacks, and the younger ones especially were firmly convinced that it meant a terrible creature, intent upon evil to them. Some waggish youths spread the story among the African members of the households in which we visited that we were what they called 'Bobolitionists.' For some time our appearance at the gateway of any of these houses was the signal for the instant disappearance of the crowd of young negroes, who but a moment before had been basking on the steps, or on the piazza, or in the dooı way ; and our entrance to the mansion was enlivened by the frightened glances of the sooty images hiding behind hat-stands, or peeping around corners. On one occasion, when a specially bright young darkey had been sent for to give us a specimen of a plantation dance and song, he bolted at the parlor door, and firmly refused to enter the room lest the 'Bobolitionists' should carry him 'Norf.'" This is a specimen of Mr. Mason's pleasantry, and the Paper abounds with many pleasing sketches of a similar character, and facts are related, also, concerning historical happenings at that time, rendering the Paper especially valuable. There are numerous interesting contributions to

this issue, and the revival stories are especially strong and inviting. "En Province," by Henry James; "In War Time," by S. Weir Mitchell; "A Roman Singer," by F. Marion Crawford ; and "Newport," by George Parsons Lathrop, are all continued, and fully sustain their interest. "The Confederate Cruisers," and "Mr. Trollope's Latest Character," are both timely and useful. "The Contributors' Club," and other departments, complete the attractions.

Century. In the February number Mr. George W. Cable contributes an elaborate and carefully prepared Paper on "The Convict Lease System in the Southern States." This subject has of late attracted unusual attention, and its able discussion by Mr. Cable will furnish those who are especially interested in it with valuable information. He first gives a brief sketch or pen-picture of a model prison—the State Penitentiary of the Eastern District of Pennsylvania. He discusses the theory of self-support, and depicts the evil principles of the lease system. For his information he goes into the State of Tennessee, where he finds the lease system carried out on its most favored principles. He then seeks for evidence in North Carolina, in Kentucky, in South Carolina, in Georgia ; reviews the pardoning power ; describes the condition of the system in Texas, in Alabama, in Arkansas, Mississippi, and Louisiana, and recites the various excuses for its introduction. In his concluding remarks, the writer says : "The lease system is itself the most atrocious mismanagement. It is in its very nature dishonorable to the community that knowingly tolerates it, and in its practical workings needs only to be known to be abhorred and cast out. It exists to-day in the twelve American commonwealths where it is found, because the people do not know what they are tolerating." Gen. Geo. B. McClellan contributes a Paper on "The Princes of the House of Orleans," which the readers of the *Century* will find of more than passing interest. The writer is familiar with his subject, and has made it highly instructive to the student of history. "Lieut.-General Sheridan" furnishes the subject of a very able sketch from the pen of Adam Badeau ; and a full-page portrait of the Lieut.-General forms an elegant illustration. The opening article of the number, which is most admirably illustrated, is concerning the life of "Gustave Courbet, Artist and Communist." Among the "Open Letters" is a lively discussion on "The Silver Dollar," which is entered into on the one side by Mr. John A. Grier, and on the other, by Mr. Horace White. Those interested in the silver question should not fail to read these communications. We should be glad, if space permitted, to give our readers an extended synopsis of each correspondent's views on this subject.

BUSINESS REVERSES.

Books.

I. S. McClintock, Palestine, Tex., reported closed by sheriff ; debts, $20,000.

W. E. Seebold, New Orleans. La., asks extension ; assets, $37,800 ; debts, $24,750.

H. G. Rasall & Co., blank-book manufacturers, Milwaukee, Wis., assigned ; debts, $16,078 ; nominal assets, $29,711.

Boots and Shoes.

A. Underhill & Co., Syracuse, N. Y., children's shoes, assigned ; preferences of about $23,500 ; estimated debts, $20,000.

W. P. Marsh, shoes, Springfield, Mass., failed ; debts reported at $16,000.

Carriages, Carts, Wagons, etc.

John Russell, Portland, Me. ; debts, $11,000 ; nominal assets, the same.

Clothing.

J. A. Anderson & Co., Atlanta, Ga., assigned ; debts, $42,000 ; assets, $50,000.

Julius Ashler, Augusta, Ga. ; debts reported at $10,000 ; assets, $5,000.

B. Davidson, Denver, Col., assigned ; debts, $89,290 ; assets, about $43,000.

Wade & Cumming, New York city, assigned, with preferences for $15,269 ; debts and assets, each about $50,000.

Commission.

M. Waterman & Co., San Francisco, Cal., assigned ; debts, $1,500,000 ; assets, reported at $800,000.

Gurley, Hardison & Co., Norfolk, Va., cotton and lumber, assigned.

J. H. Trowbridge & Son, Albany, N. Y., grain, assigned ; preferences for $34,500.

E. W. Coleman & Co., New York city, grain and flour, suspended, with preferences for $50,536 ; debts, reported, $300,000.

Lane & Son, New York city, grain ; schedules show : debts, $236,849 ; assets, $80,605.

B. R. Smith, New York city, cotton, suspended ; debts, $150,000 ; nominal assets, $200,000.

Chas. E. Hapgood & Co., wool, Boston, Mass., failed ; debts, $18,000.

Cotton.

Martin Van Sickler, Pittsfield, Mass., failed ; debts reported at $70,000.

Crockery and Glassware.

M. L. Navra, New Orleans, La., asks extension ; debts, $91,700 ; assets, $91,700.

Norton & Wieden, glass, paint, and colors, St. Louis, Mo. ; stock appraised at $88,000, and sold, by assignee, for $40,000 cash.

Dry Goods and Notions.

Jacob Schwed, Eufaula, Ala., failed ; debts, $100,000.

Irwin & Daniels, Fort Smith, Ark., assigned ; debts, $12,000.

Robert Moore & Co., Baltimore, Md., cloths, dissolved by limitation ; debts, $140,000.

A. Jordan, Milan, Tenn., failed ; debts, $16.000 ; assets, $12,000.

J. Jaros & Co., Nashville, Tenn., failed ; debts, $40,737 ; assets, $15,000 to $20,000.

Landram & Butler, Augusta, Ga., assigned ; preferences for $2,684 ; debts, $38,806 ; assets, $55,797.

Buckley & Co., Utica, N. Y., assigned, with preferences for $122,800 ; debts, reported, $200,000 ; ssets, $250,000.

Mayer Bros. & Co., Vicksburg, Miss., failed, and sold out ; debts, reported, $170,000 ; assets, $110,000.

James Manson, St. John, N. B., assigned ; debts, $80,000.

F. W. Chipman, Kentville, N. S., assigned ; debts, $50.000 ; assets, $70,000.

Wight, Forbes & Co., Boston, Mass., failed ; debts, $25,000.

M. R. Gossett, Independence, Mo., assigned ; preferences, $13,000 ; debts, $22,000 ; assets, $19,000.

Financial : Bankers, Brokers, and Capitalists.

Kenner & Moore, bankers, Morris, Minn., failed ; debts, $100,000.

City Bank of Leadville, Col., assigned.

First National Bank of Leadville, Col., closed ; receiver applied for.

Merchants' and Mechanics' Bank of Leadville, Col., suspended ; deposits, $250,000 ; surplus of $2,500.

Union Market Nat'l Bank, Watertown, Mass., suspended ; capital-stock, $200,000.

Flour.

A. Webb & Co., Portland, Me., dissolved ; debts, $43,000 ; available assets, $6,000.

J. W. Guernsey, Somerville, Mass., reported failed ; debts, $20,000.

General Store.

S. W. Wright, New Marlboro, Mass., failed ; debts, $30,000 ; assets, $15,000.

Ullman & Laub, Natchez, Miss., assigned ; debts, $22,000.

C. W. Savage & Sons, Miles City, Mont., assigned ; debts, $75,000 to $85,000 ; assets, $10,000 larger.

J. S. Bowman & Bro., Thompsonville, Ill., assigned ; debts, $41,000 ; assets, $28,000.

Bernhardt Bros., Salisbury, N. C., assigned, with preferences for $13,000.

G. W. E. Thorpe, Aiken, S. C. failed; debts, about $17,000.

M. Iseman, Marion, S. C., offers 33 cents; debts reported at $46,000.

Taylor & Hays, Schoharie, N. Y., assigned; assets, $200,000.

Rainley, Denton & Neale, Helena, Ark., attached for $28,000.

Darden Bros., Okolona, Miss., assigned; debts, $20,000.

J. A. Barnes, Eldorado, Ark., assigned; debts, $16,361; nominal assets, $23,547.

M. H. Hudgins, Hot Springs, Ark., attached, $10,000; stock on hand, $33,000.

Produce and Grain.

A. W. Thomas, Worcester, Mass., failed; offers 35 cents; debts, $21,000; assets, $12,000.

Grocers.

French & McKnight, Erie, Pa., judgments entered for $31,665; assets, $40,000.

Hamil & Hinton, Danville, Va., assigned; debts, $17,000; assets, $10,000.

Hains Bros., Augusta, Ga., sold out; debts, $35,000; assets, $28,000.

Rice Bros. & Co., Cincinnati, O., offers 50 cents; debts, $350,000; assets, $155,000.

B. Dub & Co., Augusta, Ga., groceries and hotel, failed; debts, $36,194; nominal assets, $40,471; preferences, $17,108.

J. T. Warren & Co., Cincinnati, O., gave chattel mortgages and assigned.

Hardware.

Lynch Bros., Des Moines, Iowa, chattel mortgage, and assigned; debts, $25,000; assets, $12,000.

Thomas Paryea & Slocum, Evansville, Ind., receiver appointed; debts, $34,000; probable assets, $43,000.

H. M. Burt, Lampasas, Tex., assigned; debts, $20,000; nominal assets, $17,500.

Hats.

M. Wolff & Co., New York city, assigned, with preferences for $52,043; debts, $291,761; actual assets, $79,683.

Iron.

Higgins & Morton, founders, Elizabethport, N. J., closed; debts, $20,000.

Lumber.

M. B. Rankin, Portland, Oregon, assigned; debts, $70,000; assets, $90,000.

George R. Wood, Sheffield, Pa., failed; executions issued.

Otis Eddy, Boston, Mass.; debts reported at $30,000; assets, $22,000.

Millinery.

H. Goldenberg, Frederick, Md., failed; debts, $21,465; assets, $10,000; offers 33½ cents.

Nunes, Jalkut & Robinson, St. Louis, Mo., assigned; assets, $12,000.

Friedberger & Strouse, Philadelphia, Pa., assigned; judgments entered, $51,058; execution issued; debts, estimated at $175,000 to $200,000; stock valued at $75,000.

Mrs. A. E. Davis, trading as A. E. Davis & Co., Columbus, O., assigned; debts, $54,000; assets, $25,000.

I. & H. Henley, Cincinnati, O., gave a chattel mortgage for over $13,000, and assigned.

James Alexander, Brooklyn, N. Y., assigned; preferences, $24,000; debts, $65,000.

Milling.

Joseph L. Augeny, Doylestown, Pa.; judgment entered, $12,525; execution issued on $525.

Gordon, Barker & Co., Sparta, Ill.; debts, estimated, $133,000; assets, $50,000; offer, 33½ cents, was favorably received by creditors.

Musical Goods.

The Chase Piano Company, Richmond, Ind., has given mortgage for $88,000; debts, about $90,000; assets, $76,000.

Ithaca Organ and Piano Company, Ithaca, N. Y., asks for extension; assets, about $540,000; debts, exclusive of capital-stock, about $280,000.

Paper.

Thomas B. Wheeler, New Haven, Conn., paper stock, failed; debts, $25,000; assets, $16,000.

N. W. Taylor, Chicago, Ill., assigned; debts reported over $150,000; assets probably more.

Cleveland Paper Co., Cleveland, Ohio, assigned without preferences; debts estimated at $350,000; assets, nominally, larger.

Joseph Stelwagon's Sons, manufacturers, Philadelphia, Pa., suspended; ask extension; debts from $60,000 to $90,000.

Printers.

Gunn, Curtis & Co., Boston, Mass., compromised at 35 cents cash; debts, $140,000.

Real Estate and Insurance.

Joseph Kuhn, Detroit, Mich., failed; debts, $195,145.

Tailors.

Osborn & Diver, Philadelphia, Pa.; judgments entered for $15,399, and execution issued.

Tobacco and Segars.

I. Rosenfield, Detroit, Mich., wholesale leaf-tobacco, assigned; debts, $60,000; assets, $17,000; offers 15 cents.

Warehouses.

Joseph W. Woolfolk, Columbus, Ga., failed; debts, reported, $200,000; nominal assets, $250,000. About $120,000 are in uncollectable claims on planters.

Woolens.

Eager, Bartlett & Co., Boston, Mass., failed; debts, $55,000; assets, $20,000.

Briggs Brothers, North Adams, Mass., offer 18 cents; debts, about $100,000.

Perine & Co., New York city, assigned; debts about $95,000; assets, $40,000.

Miscellaneous.

Knipe & Herrmann, Philadelphia, Pa., manufacturers of sheep, goat, and calves' kid; judgment entered for $29,409, on which execution was issued.

George F. Keller, New York city, provisions; schedules show: debts, $177,002; nominal assets, $192,990.

McKean Brothers, tanners, Watsontown, Pa.: owe $26,000; assets, $27,000.

E. Detrick & Co., bag manufacturers, San Francisco, Cal., assigned; debts, $376,746; assets, about $343,000.

H. W. Jenkins & Sons, Baltimore, Md., cabinet makers, offer 60 cents; debts, $56,000; assets, $48,000.

Goldsmith & Kuhn, New York city, diamonds, assigned, with preferences for $22,119; debts, $45,000; assets, $35,000.

W. E. Whitman, Winthrop, Me., agricultural implements, burnt out; offers seventeen cents; debts, $30,000; assets, $17,000.

Daniel F. Beatty, organ manufacturer, Washington, N. J., granted a partial extension; debts, $175,000; assets, $200,000.

Jeremiah B. Wadsworth, Morrisville, N.Y., cheese manufacturer, failed; debts, $72,000; assets, $40,000.

W. E. Phelps & Co., Elmwood, Ill., coal, brick, and foundry, failed; debts, $100,000; assets, $188,669.

Putnam & Phelps, curriers, Leominster, Mass., assigned; debts, $210,000; assets, $188,669.

DECEMBER TRADE REVIEW.

The general tendency of the month has been toward improvement. The increased movement of merchandise and an inclination to firmer prices has been so far maintained that a better feeling exists than was anticipated by many during the close of last month. The most marked activity in business has, perhaps, been manifested in New York and Chicago; in Boston there has been an increase in the volume of trade, though almost exclusively reported for immediate wants rather than for future uses. The movement at Cincinnati, it is reported, has been influenced to a degree by conditions of the weather. Large shipments from Philadelphia give signs of the appearance of better times in that locality. Baltimore, Cleveland, Milwaukee, and some other cities, have not yet commenced to feel the effects of an improvement in trade, but indications point strongly to its realization in all parts of the country before the close of February.

At the opening of the month of January the stock market was found in a seriously depressed condition. Soon after the first it commenced to show some signs of improvement, but the failure of the New York and New England Railroad, together with the report of the committee on Oregon Transcontinental affairs and Mr. Villard's resignation from the Northern Pacific, combined to depress stocks and stock operations. Notwithstanding these influences there existed a general feeling of confidence, which strengthened as the improved condition of affairs in commercial circles manifested itself.

Early in the month there was a strong bull movement, but before the 20th it had very nearly spent itself. Merchants throughout the country have been anxiously awaiting the statements in the hands of their accountants, though generally with the feeling that the information such statements would give would not be altogether agreeable to the

merchants' ambitions. Those who have been able to weather the storm during the last year are feeling more hopeful of the coming season. As there seems to be an abundance of loanable funds, at a small rate of interest, for those who have sufficient collaterals, the circumstance has had a soothing influence in some branches of business where it has been necessary to carry over large stocks. There has been, evidently, a large shrinkage in prices; but now the time for a slight turn in the tide of affairs having arrived, a better feeling is manifested, and we shall probably hear of fewer large failures than during the past six months.

The iron and nail mills which have been idle for some time will not, it is said, resume operations before the middle of February or, perhaps, the first of March. There has been a slight gain in iron, which is considered a turning point in the course of that commodity, and iron manufacturers are beginning to feel more hopeful of their situation. The tendency of the iron market has been downward during the past twelve or thirteen months, and the present favorable indications are received with strong hope for their continuance by all persons engaged in the iron industries. It is not expected that there will be any rapid advance in price, but a gradual improvement is looked for.

At Paterson, N. J., the operatives of the silk mills have begun a strike, and at Pittsburg, glass manufacturers have been having more or less difficulty with their employees; in fact, the strikes in the glass mills have been the cause of withdrawing from that industry a large amount of capital, which is now seeking investment in other directions.

The demand for wool and woolen fabrics has been reasonable, and the prices have been well maintained. The market for cotton, especially in New York, has been dull—at least during the closing days of the month.

MARKETS AND EXCHANGES.

(When no Figures are Given the Price Remains the Same as Last Quotation.)

Foreign Exchange.—Closing Rates for each Day in January.

	1.	2.	3.	4.	5.	7.	8.	9.	10.	11.	12.	14.	15.	16.	17.	18.	19.	21.	22.	23.	24.	25.	26.	28.	29.	30.	31.
London ....60 days	Holiday	482¼	483	....	....	483½	484	484½	....	484	....	484½	485	....	....	....	....	485½	....	....	....	486	....	....	486½	....	....
" ....3 "		485½	486	....	....	486½	487	487½	....	487	....	....	487½	488	....	....	....	....	....	....	....	488½	....	....	489	....	....
Paris, francs.........60 "		521¼	....	....	....	520⅝	520	....	....	....	....	519⅜	....	....	....	....	518¾	....	....	....	....	518⅛	517½	....	517½	....	516¼
" " ....3 "		518¾	....	....	....	517½	516¼	....	....	....	....	516¼	....	....	....	....	515⅝	....	....	....	515	....	514⅜	....	513¾	....	....
Geneva ....60 "		520⅝	....	....	....	520	519⅜	....	....	....	....	518¾	518¾	....	....	....	518⅛	....	....	....	517½	....	516¼	....	516¼	....	....
" ....3 "		517½	....	....	....	516¼	516¼	....	....	....	....	515⅝	....	....	....	....	515	....	....	....	514⅜	....	513¾	....	513¾	....	....
Berlin, reichmarks...60 "		94⅞	....	....	....	95	....	....	....	....	....	....	....	....	....	....	95⅛	....	....	....	....	95¼	....	....	95⅛	....	....
" " ...3 "		95¼	....	....	....	95⅜	....	....	....	....	....	....	....	....	....	95⅜	....	....	....	....	....	95⅝	....	....	96	....	....
Amsterdam, guilders 60 "		40⅛	....	....	....	....	....	....	....	....	....	....	....	....	....	....	....	....	....	....	....	40¼	....	....	....	....	....
" " 3 "		40⅜	....	....	....	....	....	....	....	....	....	....	....	....	....	....	....	....	....	....	....	40⅜	....	....	....	....	....

Government Bonds and Currency.—Closing Prices at the New York Board during January.

	Interest Periods.	1.	2.	3.	4.	5.	7.	8.	9.	10.	11.	12.	14.	15.	16.	17.	18.	19.	21.	22.	23.	24.	25.	26.	28.	29.	30.	31.
4½s, 1891 ....reg.	Q.-Mar.	Holiday	114¼	114¾	114½	....	114½	....	....	....	....	114½	....	....	....	114⅝	....	....	....	114½	....	114⅝	114½	....	....	....	....	....
4½s, 1891 ......coup.	Q.-Mar.		114½	114¾	114½	....	114½	....	114½	....	....	....	114½	114½	114⅝	....	....	114⅝	114⅝	....	114½	....	....	....	....	....	....	....
4s, 1907 ....reg.	Q.-Jan.		123⅝	123½	123⅝	....	....	123½	123⅝	...	123⅝	123½	123¾	124⅛	....	....	....	....	124	123⅞	123¾	....	...	....	123⅞	123⅞	....	123⅞
4s, 1907 ....coup.	Q.-Jan.		123½	123⅝	123½	123⅝	....	123¼	....	123⅞	....	123⅝	....	124	....	..	124⅛	124½	124	123⅞	....	....	....	123⅞	....	123⅞	....	....
3s, option U. S..reg.	Q.-Feb.		100¼	....	100	....	....	....	....	....	....	....	....	....	....	....	....	...	....	....	....	...	100⅛	100⅛	....	....	..	..
6s, cur'cy, 1895..reg.	J. & J.		128	....	130	128	....	...	..	....	...	128⅜	128⅜	...	....	....	....	....	....	....	...	....	....	129	....	....	....	..
6s, cur'cy, 1896..reg.	J. & J.		130	....	132	130	....	....	....	....	....	130⅜	130⅜	....	....	....	....	....	....	....	....	....	....	131	....	....	....	....
6s, cur'cy, 1897..reg.	J. & J.		132	....	134	132	....	....	....	....	....	132⅛	132⅜	....	....	....	132½	132⅜	.	....	....	....	....	133	....	....	....	....
6s, cur'cy, 1898..reg.	J. & J.		134	....	135	134	....	....	....	....	....	134⅛	134⅜	134½	....	134⅜	....	....	....	....	....	....	....	135	....	....	....	....
6s, cur'cy, 1899..reg.	J. & J.		135⅛	....	....	....	....	....	....	..	....	....	136⅜	136	136⅛	....	....	....	....	....	....	....	....	137	....	....	....	....
....	....		...	....	....	....	....	....	....	....	....	....	....	....	....	....	....	....	....	....	....	....	....	....	....	....	....	....

New York Stock Exchange.—Daily Highest Prices for January.

STOCKS.	1.	2.	3.	4.	5.	7.	8.	9.	10.	11.	12.	14.	15.	16.	17.	18.	19.	21.	22.	23.	24.	25.	26.	28.	29.	30.	31.
RAILROADS.																											
Atchison, Topeka & S. F....	Holiday	79⅞	....	....	....	80⅜	....	....	....	....	....	....	....	....	....	....	....	....	....	....	....	....	....	....	....	....	....
Boston Air-Line, pref.......		82¼	82½	....	....	81⅜	....	....	....	....	82⅜	....	82½	81½	....	....	....	....	....	....	....	....	....	....	....	82½	....
Bur., Cedar Rap. & No......		85	....	...	..	....	....	....	80	....	....	....	....	75	70	....	....	....	....	....	....	....	....	....	....	....	....
Canadian Pacific............		55⅜	57	....	57⅜	57¼	56⅛	....	56⅛	56⅛	56⅛	56⅛	....	56½	....	58¼	57⅜	57⅛	57⅜	58	57⅜	57⅞	57⅜	56⅞	56⅝	56⅛	55
Canada Southern............		51	52	....	53	53¼	52⅜	53½	....	52⅜	52⅜	52⅛	50⅛	50⅜	50⅛	51⅛	51	50⅛	50⅛	50⅜	....	51⅜	52½	....	53⅜	54⅛	54⅜
Central of New Jersey.......		85¼	86⅛	86⅜	86⅝	....	....	88	89½	90	....	89⅛	88½	88	87½	87⅛	....	87	86⅞	87⅛	....	86	86⅛	88	....	87⅛	87½
Central Pacific.............		64	64⅜	66⅛	66¼	....	65½	66⅛	67⅜	66⅜	66⅛	66⅛	65½	65	64⅛	65⅛	65⅜	64⅜	64⅛	65⅛	65⅜	63⅜	66⅛	66⅝	67½	67⅛	66⅝
Chesapeake & Ohio..........		15	....	14⅛	15⅛	15	15⅛	15	....	....	....	....	....	14	15	14⅜	....	14	15	14⅛	....	14⅜	15	13⅜	15	14⅜	....
Do 1st pref..		27	....	26	....	25⅜	24⅛	25	....	....	25⅛	26	....	23	25⅛	23	....	21	25	22½	23	....	23⅜	24	23⅜	24	....
Do 2d pref..		16¼	18	17⅛	....	17	15⅜	17¼	....	16⅜	17¼	....	16⅛	17¼	15	17	....	....	18	17	....	16	17⅜	17	....	17⅛	17⅜
Chicago & Alton.......		134½	134	133⅜	134	134½	136	135⅛	....	....	....	135	....	134⅛	135	....	....	....	135½	....	....	138	....	....	138½	139⅛	....
Chicago, Bur. & Quincy.....		120¼	121⅛	121	122¼	122⅜	121⅛	121⅜	...	121	121⅜	121	120⅜	120½	120	121½	120	119½	120	120¼	120⅜	121⅛	121⅜	122	123	....	122⅛
Chicago, Mil. & St. Paul ...		93¼	94½	93⅜	93⅛	....	93	93⅜	94⅜	92⅜	93	92⅜	89⅜	88⅛	88½	89	88⅜	86⅛	87	87⅛	87⅛	88½	88⅛	89⅛	90⅜	90⅜	89⅞
Do pref.		117	116⅜	117	116	116⅛	....	115¼	117	115⅞	115⅜	115⅛	114	114⅛	....	....	114	....	....	114⅛	115⅛	114⅛	....	114⅜	116½	116⅛	....
Chicago & Northwest.......		118	118⅜	118⅛	118⅜	118⅜	117¼	117⅞	118½	117⅜	117⅜	117⅛	116½	115⅜	...	116½	115⅛	114⅜	114⅞	115⅛	115⅛	116½	116⅜	117	118⅛	118⅜	118⅞
Do pref..		146	147	146¼	....	146⅜	145	145½	144⅜	145	....	143	142⅛	....	142	144	142½	142	141⅛	142⅛	141⅛	142⅛	143	145	145⅛	145⅜	145⅜
Chicago, R. I. & P		116⅜	117⅛	117½	116⅜	117⅜	117½	117⅜	....	117⅛	117⅛	117	116⅛	....	116	116⅜	116	115⅛	116	117	....	117⅛	117	117⅝	118	....	117⅝

Chicago, St. Louis & Pitts...
Chicago, St. P., M. & O... pref.
Do.   Do.   pref.
Cincinnati, Sand. & Cleve.
Cleveland, Col., Cinn. & Ind
Cleveland & Pittsburg, guar
Columbus, Chic. & Ind. Cen.
Delaware, Lack. & West.
Denver & Rio Grande.
East Tenn., Va. & Ga.
Do.   pref.
Do.   pref.
Evansville & Terre Haute.
Green Bay, Winona & St. P.
Hannibal & St. Joseph.
Do.   pref.
Harlem.
Houston & Texas Central.
Illinois Central.
Do.   leased line.
Indiana, Bloom'n & Western
Lake Erie & Western.
Lake Shore.
Long Island.
Louisiana & Missouri River.
Louisville & Nashville.
Louisville, N. Alb. & Chic.
Manhattan Elevated.
Do.   1st pref.
Do.   common
Manhattan Beach Co.
Memphis & Charleston.
Metropolitan Elevated.
Michigan Central.
Mil., L. Sh. & West. pref.
Minneapolis & St. L.
Do.
Missouri, Kansas & Texas.
Missouri Pacific.
Mobile & Ohio.
Morris & Essex.
Nashville, Chat. & St. L.
N. Y. Central & Hudson.
N. Y., Chic. & St. Louis.
Do.   pref.
New York Elevated.
N. Y., Lack. & Western.
N. Y., Lake Erie & W.
Do.   pref.
N. Y. & New England.
N. Y. & New Haven & Hart
N. Y., Ontario & Western.
N. Y., Susq & Western.
Do.   pref.
Norfolk & Western. pref.
Northern Pacific.   pref.
Do.   pref.
Ohio Central.
Ohio & Mississippi.
Do.   pref.
Ohio Southern.

Holiday

[Continued on next page.]

New York Stock Exchange.— Daily Highest Prices for January.— *Continued.*

STOCKS.	1.	2.	3.	4.	5.	7.	8.	9.	10.	11.	12.	14.	15.	16.	17.	18.	19.	21.	22.	23.	24.	25.	26.	28.	29.	30.	31.
RAILROADS.																											
Oregon & Trans-Continental	Holiday	31⅛	32⅜	32⅛	34½	34⅜	32¼	31⅛	31⅜	....	32	31⅝	30⅝	27⅛	26	....	25	23⅞	23⅜	21⅝	18⅜	19	20	23	24	25⅛	25⅛
Peoria, Decatur & Evansville		14	....	....	....	15	....	14	14⅛	13⅜	14	13⅛	13⅝	13⅜	13½	13⅜	13⅛	13½	13⅛	....	13	13⅝	14	14⅛	15⅝	15⅛	15⅜
Philadelphia & Reading		55⅝	57⅞	58⅝	59½	59⅛	58½	56⅝	59⅝	58	57⅞	57⅞	56⅝	55⅞	....	....	55⅝	54⅛	54⅝	54½	53⅞	54	54½	....	54⅛	55½	54⅛
Pittsburg, Ft. Wayne & Chic		132⅛	....	....	....	....	134⅛	132⅛	....	131⅛	....	....	....	....	132⅛	131½	....	....	....	131	....	132⅛	....	....	....	....	....
Richmond & Alleghany		6	....	....	....	....	....	4	....	5	....	....	....	....	....	....	....	4	....	....	....	....	....	....	....	....	....
Richmond & Danville		60	....	....	....	....	....	....	....	....	....	....	54½	52⅜	53⅛	....	55	....	....	....	....	....	....	56	....	....	....
Richmond & West Point		28⅛	28⅜	29⅛	31	30⅛	29⅛	27⅛	29⅛	29⅛	29	29⅛	28	....	27⅞	27⅛	....	27	27⅛	....	27⅛	27	26⅝	28	29	....	....
Rochester & Pittsburg		15	....	14⅞	15⅛	15⅜	15	15⅜	15⅛	15½	15⅜	15	14⅝	14½	....	14⅝	14½	14	14½	14⅝	14⅛	15	14⅝	15	15⅛	15½	15⅛
St. Louis, Alton & T. H		44	....	43	....	47	....	46	....	..	....	....	40	....	45	....	46	....	....	....	....	45	....	....	....	40	....
Do pref		87	88	89	....	92	88	90	....	....	....	....	....	....	....	....	....	88	....	...	....	91	....	....	....	....	....
St. Louis & San Fran		27	....	....	....	....	....	....	....	26	23	20⅛	27	20	....	....	....	....	....	....	....	....	22	....	....	....	21
Do pref		40	40⅛	43	41	41⅜	41⅛	42	42⅛	42	41⅛	40⅛	....	....	40	....	39	....	....	....	....	....	37½	39	....	....	....
Do 1st pref		90	....	....	....	....	....	91	....	90	91	....	....	....	90	....	87	....	....	....	....	....	....	....	....	85	84⅛
St. Paul & Duluth		34	....	....	....	....	....	32⅜	....	....	....	....	....	....	....	29⅜	....	....	....	....	....	....	....	....	....	....	....
Do pref		95	....	....	....	....	....	....	....	....	....	....	....	....	....	....	....	....	....	....	....	....	90	....	....	....	....
St. Paul, Minneap. & Man		95	96	97	98⅛	99	97	97⅛	98	97⅛	96⅝	96½	94⅜	95⅛	95	96	96½	88	89	87⅞	87½	88	87⅛	89	95⅛	93	....
Texas & Pacific		17⅛	18	18½	19⅝	20½	19⅝	19⅝	20½	19⅛	19⅝	19	17⅜	17½	17½	18½	16½	16½	17	17⅞	17½	17⅛	18	18⅛	19⅛	20⅜	20⅜
Union Pacific		71½	72⅜	73⅛	75	75½	74⅛	77⅛	78	77⅛	77⅜	77½	75⅛	74⅛	74⅜	75	74⅛	73⅜	74⅞	75⅜	76⅜	76⅛	76⅝	77⅛	78⅛	78⅜	78⅜
Wabash, St. L. & Pac		17⅛	18⅜	...	19⅛	19⅜	19½	18⅛	19⅛	19	18⅛	18⅜	17⅜	17⅛	17½	16½	15	14⅛	15	15⅝	15	15⅝	....	16⅛	16⅝	16⅝	....
Do pref		30⅛	30⅜	31	32	31⅜	30⅛	31	31⅛	30⅛	30⅜	30	29	....	28⅜	29	28	26	25½	26⅛	25½	25½	26⅛	26⅝	27	27⅝	27⅞
MISCELLANEOUS.																											
American Tel. & Cable Co		59⅛	60	....	61½	60½	61⅝	....	....	60½	61	....	60	59⅝	57⅞	60	....	59	....	60	....	....	....	....	....	....	59⅞
Bankers' & Merchants' Tel		121	121⅜	121½	121⅛	...	....	121⅝	121⅜	121⅛	121⅜	121⅝	121⅛	122	122½	122⅛	122⅜	122½	122⅝	....	122⅜	122⅝	123⅜	123⅝	....	123⅜	....
Colorado Coal & Iron		16⅛	15⅜	....	16⅛	....	16	....	15⅛	17	....	15	14	13⅛	13	....	11⅛	10⅛	11⅛	13	11⅝	11½	13⅛	14	....	....	13
Delaware & Hudson Canal		105⅛	105⅜	105½	105⅝	....	....	....	....	106	106½	....	105⅝	105⅛	105⅝	105⅝	....	105½	....	105⅛	....	106	....	107	107⅝	108	....
Mutual Union Telegraph		18	....	....	16½	17½	....	....	17⅝	....	....	....	16	14½	....	15⅜	....	....	16½	16⅛	17⅛	....	....	....	....	17	....
New Central Coal		10	....	....	....	....	....	....	....	....	....	....	....	....	....	....	....	....	....	....	....	....	....	....	....	....	....
N. Y. & Tex. Land Co		124	....	130	....	122½	....	132	134⅝	137½	138⅜	....	139	136	138	200	160	....	....	....	....	165	160	....	170	150½	160
Oregon Improvem't Co		65	61	....	....	65⅛	62	63	....	....	....	55	....	50	45	43	40	....	41	40½	44	40⅛	44	51	48	50	....
Oregon R'way & Nav. Co		96	98	101	103⅛	....	99⅛	99	101½	102	100	....	98	93⅛	92	91⅜	93⅛	91⅛	....	86⅝	82	83⅛	86	112	100	96	95
Pacific Mail		41	42	42⅜	43⅜	44½	42⅜	43⅜	....	43⅛	43½	43	41⅜	41⅝	41⅝	42	41⅝	41	42⅛	42½	42	42⅛	45	45½	45⅝	47	46⅛
Pullman Palace Car		114	115	....	115⅛	117	115½	115⅛	115	114⅛	113⅜	112	110	111⅛	109⅝	110	110	109	109⅛	111	110½	110⅝	110½	112	113⅛	115	....
Quicksilver Mining		6	....	....	....	....	....	....	....	....	....	....	5	5⅝	6	5⅛	5	4⅛	5	....	....	....	....	....	5⅛	6	5
Do pref		30	....	....	....	....	....	....	....	....	....	....	...	29⅝	30	....	27	25⅛	28	25	....	....	25⅛	30	29⅝	31	30
Standard Consol. Mining		6⅛	....	....	....	....	....	....	....	....	....	....	....	....	....	....	....	....	....	....	....	....	....	....	....	....	..
Western Union Telegraph		74⅜	75⅛	75⅛	76⅛	76⅛	75⅜	75⅛	76⅛	75⅜	75⅜	....	75½	74	73⅜	....	73½	72⅜	73⅜	73⅛	....	73⅜	73⅛	74½	74⅜	75⅜	76⅛
EXPRESS.																											
Adams		131	130	....	...	131	130	....	129	130	....	130½	130	129⅜	130	129⅝	129½	130	....	130½	130	....	....	....	129⅜	129⅛	....
American		92	....	91⅛	92½	92	93	....	....	92½	95	96	97	95⅝	94	95⅛	....	93	93⅛	94	93	94	95	96	95½	96	96⅜
United States		60	56	59⅛	60	....	....	..	...	...	....	....	59	60	57	59	60	....	59	....	60	61	60	61	....	60	....
Wells, Fargo & Co.		115	110	109⅛	...	110	112	109⅜	110	....	....	110½	110½	110	....	....	111	109	110	107	....	106	....	..	107	....	108

Petroleum.— Prices for each Day in January.

	1.	2.	3.	4.	5.	7.	8.	9.	10.	11.	12.	14.	15.	16.	17.	18.	19.	21.	22.	23.	24.	25.	26.	28.	29.	30.	31.
Pipe Line Certific's—highest	Holiday	114⅜	115⅛	115½	114⅛	115⅛	115⅛	115⅛	114⅜	113⅛	112½	112⅝	109⅛	109⅜	110⅜	109⅛	109⅝	109	109⅛	....	110⅛	110⅝	111½	111½	110⅛	112⅛	112⅜
" " lowest		112⅛	114⅜	114⅛	114½	114⅜	....	113⅛	112⅜	111⅝	111½	109½	107⅜	107	107½	107⅜	....	107⅝	107⅝	....	109⅜	110⅛	110⅛	109⅝	109⅝	110⅛	110⅜
Crude in bbls		8	8⅛	....	....	....	....	....	....	....	....	8½	....	....	....	....	....	....	....	8½	....	....	....	....	....	....	...
Naphtha		6½	6⅜	....	....	....	....	....	....	7	....	....	....	....	....	....	....	....	...	....	....	....	....	7½	....	....	....
Refined, cargo lots, 110 deg		9⅛	....	...	....	....	...	....	....	....	....	....	....	....	....	....	....	....	....	....	....	....	....	....	....	....	....
" 70 deg. Abel test		9⅜	....	9⅛	....	....	....	....	....	....	....	....	....	....	....	....	...	....	....	....	..	....	....	....	....	....	....

Grain.—Highest Prices for Future Delivery for each Day in January.

WHEAT—	1.	2.	3.	4.	5.	7.	8.	9.	10.	11.	12.	14.	15.	16.	17.	18.	19.	21.	22.	23.	24.	25.	26.	28.	29.	30.	31.
January	*Holiday.*	110⅝	....	111	110¼	....	109¾	108⅜	....	....	106⅞	104	104¼	105	104⅞	102⅞	102½	....	103½	103⅞	103⅝	105	105½	106⅞	105⅝	...	105⅜
February		112⅞	112⅞	113	112⅞	112½	111⅜	....	111	110⅝	108¼	106½	106⅝	106⅞	105⅞	104⅝	103⅞	103⅜	104¼	104⅞	104⅝	106	....	106⅝	106½	105¼	105⅜
March		114½	114¼	114⅞	114¼	....	113	....	113¼	113	110⅝	109¼	....	....	108¼	107⅞	106½	106½	107	107⅞	107¼	108⅜	....	109	108⅜	108⅛	....
May		118⅜	118¼	118⅜	118¼	....	116⅞	116½	117	116⅞	114⅜	113⅞	114	....	113½	112⅞	111⅜	111½	112	112⅞	112	113¼	....	113⅜	113⅝	112⅞	112⅞
April		....	....	....	....	....	....	....	....	....	....	....	...	111⅛	110⅛	109⅞	108⅞	108⅜	109¼	110	109¼	110⅛	....	111⅜	111	110¼	...
CORN—																											
January	*Holiday.*	64½	65¼	66⅜	66½	65¼	65⅜	....	65	64⅜	63	62½	62⅜	62½	62½	61	60¼	60⅝	61½	61⅜	61	61⅜	61¼	61	60⅞	....	60¼
February		65¼	66⅜	67¼	67	67⅛	66⅜	66	65⅞	65⅜	64	63½	63⅜	63⅜	62⅞	61⅜	61⅛	61⅜	61⅛	62½	61⅜	62	61⅜	61	60⅞	60⅞	60⅞
March		....	66½	67⅞	67⅜	....	66⅞	66½	....	65½	64⅛	63⅜	64⅜	....	....	....	....	62½	62⅞	63⅛	62¼	63⅜	62⅞	62¼	62⅜	61⅞	62½
May		67⅜	68¼	69⅛	69	....	68⅛	67⅞	..	67⅜	66¼	66	66⅜	....	66	65⅜	65½	65⅛	65¼	66½	65½	66¼	65⅜	65½	65	64⅞	65⅛
April		....	....	....	....	....	....	....	....	....	....	...	....	....	....	....	....	63½	63⅜	64⅜	63⅜	64⅜	64	63⅜	63	....	63¼
OATS—																											
January	*Holiday.*	40	40⅜	40⅜	40⅞	40⅜	40½	....	40⅜	40⅛	40½	40	40⅛	....	40	39⅞	39⅞	....	39⅜	40	39⅞	40	39⅝	39⅞	39⅜	....	39⅜
February		41	41⅜	41⅞	41⅜	41⅛	41½	....	....	....	40⅞	....	41	....	40⅛	40⅜	39⅞	39½	39⅜	40⅛	39⅜	40¼	40	39⅞	...	39⅜	....
March		42	42⅜	42⅜	....	42⅛	42⅜	42½	....	42⅜	41⅞	41⅞	42⅛	42	41⅞	41⅛	....	40⅞	40⅞	41⅜	41	41⅛	40⅞	....	....	....	40⅜
May		43⅜	43⅞	44⅜	44⅛	44	43⅜	....	. ..	....	43	42⅞	43⅜	....	42⅜	....	42⅛	42⅜	42⅜	43	42⅜	42½	42⅜	42¼	42½	....	....
April		....	....	..	....	....	....	....	....	....	....	....	....	43	42⅞	42⅜	....	42	42⅜	42½	42	42⅜	41⅜	42	41⅞	....	41⅜

Flour.—Closing Prices.

	First Quarter.		Second Quarter.		Third Quarter.		Fourth Quarter.	
No. 2 spring.......per bbl.	$2.00 @	2.75	$2.00 @	2.60	$2.00 @	2.50	$.... @	....
No. 2 winter	2.50	3.00	2.25	2.90	....	....	....	....
Superfine	2.80	3.35	2.60	3.35	....	....	....	....
Spring wheat extras	3.50	5.00	3.75	4.75	3.25	4.75	..	....
Minn. clear and straight	4.00	6.00	4.00	5.75	....	....	4.25	5.75
Winter shipping extras	3.35	3.75	3.25	3.60	3.15	3.40	3.20	3.40
Winter clear and straight	4.25	6.00	4.00	6.00	....	....	....	....
Patents, spring	5.50	7.00	5.50	6.85	....	....	....	...
Patents, winter	5.25	6.75	....	....	....	....	5.50	6.75
City shipping extras.......per bbl.	$5.15 @	5.55	$5.00 @	5.45	$5.15 @	5.35	$5.15 @	5.40
South'n bakers' and family brands	4.25	6.37½	4.25	6.25	....	....	....	....
Southern shipping extras	3.65	5.50	3.50	5.50	....	....	....	....
Rye flour, superfine	3.35	3.75	3.30	3.75	....	....	....	....
CORN MEAL—								
Western, etc	3.00	3.35	....	....	....	....	....	...
Brandywine, etc	3.35	3.45	....	....	3.30	3.45	....	...
Buckwheat flour.......per 100 lbs.	3.00	3.50	3.20	3.40	3.00	3.25	2.65	3.00

New York Coffee Exchange.—Spot Quotations on Rio Coffee for each Day in January.

	1.	2.	3.	4.	5.	7.	8.	9.	10.	11.	12.	14.	15.	16.	17.	18.	19.	21.	22.	23.	24.	25.	26.	28.	29.	30.	31.
Prime	*Holiday*	12.50	....	....	....	12.65	12.75	....	12.85	....	....	....	....	12.75	....	12.60	12.50	....	....	12.35	....	....	....	12.50	....	....	12.75
Good		12.25	....	....	....	12.40	12.50	....	12.60	....	....	....	....	12.50	....	12.35	12.25	....	....	12.10	....	....	....	12.25	....	....	12.30
Fair		12.00	....	....	....	12.15	12.25	....	12.35	....	....	....	....	12.25	....	12.10	12.00	....	....	11.85	....	....	....	12.00	....	....	12.25
Low Fair		11.70	....	....	....	11.85	11.95	....	12.05	....	....	....	....	11.95	..	11.80	11.70	....	....	11.55	....	..	....	11.70	....	....	11.95
G'd Ordi'y		11.35	....	....	....	11.50	11.60	....	11.70	....	....	....	....	11.60	....	11.45	11.35	....	....	11.20	....	....	....	11.35	....	....	11.60
Ordinary		11.00	....	....	....	11.15	11.25	....	11.35	....	....	....	....	11.25	....	11.10	11.00	....	....	10.85	....	....	....	11.00	....	....	11.25
LowOrd'y		10.50	....	....	....	10.65	10.75	....	10.85	....	....	....	....	10.75	....	10.60	10.50	....	....	10.35	....	....	....	10.50	....	....	10.75
St. G.Com		10.00	....	....	....	10.15	10.25	....	10.35	....	....	....	....	10.25	....	10.10	10.00	....	....	9.85	....	....	....	10.00	....	....	10.25
Good Com		9.60	....	....	....	9.75	9.85	....	9.95	....	....	....	....	9.85	....	9.70	9.60	....	....	9.45	....	....	....	9.60	....	....	9.85
Common		9.25	....	....	....	9.40	9.50	....	9.60	....	....	....	....	9.50	....	9.35	9.25	....	....	9.10	....	....	....	9.25	....	....	9.50

Sugar.— Highest Prices at Closing of each Day in January.

	1.	2.	3.	4.	5.	7.	8.	9.	10.	11.	12.	14.	15.	16.	17.	18.	19.	21.	22.	23.	24.	25.	26.	28.	29.	30.	31.
RAW SUGAR.																											
Com. to good refi. Cuba	Holiday	6 5/8	....	....	....	....	....	....	....	....	....	....	....	....	....	....	....	....	....	....	....	....	....	....	....	....	....
Com. to good refi. Porto Rico		6 1/2	....	....	....	....	....	....	....	....	....	....	....	....	....	....	....	....	....	....	....	....	....	....	....	....	....
Centrifugal		6 1/2	....	....	....	7 1/8	....	....	....	....	....	....	....	....	....	....	....	....	....	....	....	....	....	....	....	....	....
Manilla		6 1/8	....	....	....	....	....	....	....	....	....	....	....	....	....	....	....	....	....	....	....	....	....	....	....	....	....
Pernams		6 1/4	....	....	....	....	....	....	....	....	....	....	....	....	....	....	....	....	....	....	....	....	....	....	....	....	....
Bahia		6	....	5 7/8	6	5 7/8	....	....	....	....	....	....	....	....	....	....	....	....	....	....	....	....	....	....	....	....	....
Melado		....	....	....	....	....	....	....	....	....	....	....	....	....	....	....	....	....	....	....	....	....	....	....	....	....	....
REFINED SUGAR.																											
Cut loaf		8 7/8	8 7/8	....	....	....	....	....	....	....	....	8 1/2	8 1/2	....	....	....	....	....	....	....	....	....	....	8 7/8	8 1/4	....	....
Crushed		8 7/8	8 7/8	....	....	....	....	....	....	....	....	8 1/2	8 1/2	....	....	....	....	....	....	....	....	....	....	8 7/8	....	....	....
Cubes		8 1/2	....	....	....	....	8 1/2	....	8 5/8	....	....	....	8 3/8	....	....	....	....	....	....	....	....	....	....	....	....	8 1/8	....
Powdered		8 1/2	....	....	....	....	8 1/2	....	8 1/2	....	....	....	8 3/8	....	....	8 1/8	....	....	....	....	8 1/8	....	....	....	....	....	....
Granulated		7 7/8	7 7/8	7 3/4	7 13/16	....	....	....	7 3/4	....	....	7 13/16	....	....	....	....	....	....	....	7 3/4	....	....	7 13/16	....	....	....	....
Mould "A"		7 7/8	....	7 7/8	....	....	....	....	7 7/8	....	....	7 7/8	....	....	....	....	....	....	....	....	....	7 3/4	....	....	....	7 5/8	....
Confectioners' "A"		7 9/16	7 5/8	7 7/16	....	7 5/8	....	....	7 9/16	....	7 5/8	....	7 7/16	....	....	7 1/2	....	....	7 7/16	....	7 1/2	....	....	....	....	....	....
Coffee "A" standard		7 1/2	....	....	....	....	7 3/8	....	7 1/4	....	....	7 7/16	7 3/8	....	....	7 1/2	....	7 7/16	....	....	7 1/2	....	....	....	....	7 3/8	....
Coffee off "A"		7 1/2	7 1/2	....	....	....	....	....	7 3/8	....	....	7 1/2	....	....	....	....	....	....	....	....	....	....	....	....	....	....	7 1/2
White extra "C"		6 3/4	....	....	....	....	....	....	6 5/8	6 5/8	....	6 5/8	....	....	....	....	6 1/8	6 1/4	....	....	....	....	....	....	....	....	6 3/4
Extra "C"		6 5/8	....	....	....	....	....	....	6 5/8	....	....	....	....	....	....	....	....	....	....	....	....	....	....	....	....	....	6 5/8
"C"		6	....	....	....	....	....	....	6 1/2	....	....	....	....	....	....	....	6 1/8	....	....	....	....	....	....	....	....	....	6 1/2
Yellow		5 7/8	....	....	....	....	....	....	5 7/8	....	....	....	....	....	....	....	....	....	....	....	....	....	....	....	....	....	5 7/8
Yellow "C"		....	....	....	....	....	....	....	....	....	....	....	....	....	....	....	....	....	....	....	....	....	....	....	....	....	....

Lard.— Highest Price for Future Delivery for each Day in January.

	1.	2.	3.	4.	5.	7.	8.	9.	10.	11.	12.	14.	15.	16.	17.	18.	19.	21.	22.	23.	24.	25.	26.	28.	29.	30.	31.
January	Holiday	9.15	9.19	9.12	9.15	9.20	9.16	9.23	9.25	9.28	9.18	9.16	9.20	9.15	9.09	9.05	8.99	9.05	9.10	9.23	9.28	9.35	9.28	....	9.34	....	.. .
February		9.26	9.22	9.24	9.28	9.25	9.22	9.27	...	9.31	9.20	9.22	9.21	9.18	9.08	9.05	9.01	....	9.19	9.23	9.28	9.35	9.29	9.36	9.33	9.38	9.42
March		9.30	9.35	9.32	9.39	9.33	9.28	9.36	....	9.38	9.28	9.30	9.31	9.25	9.15	9.12	9.07	9.10	9.26	9.30	9.35	9.41	9.34	9.41	....	9.46	9.48
April		9.40	9.45	9.42	9.40	9.45	9.35	9.37	9.45	9.48	9.36	9.43	9.42	9.37	9.25	9.20	9.19	9.17	9.25	9.40	9.43	9.50	9.41	9.48	....	9.55	9.57
May		9.50	9.52	9.55	9.55	9.50	9.46	9.49	9.52	9.58	9.49	9.48	....	9.42	9.36	9.34	9.26	9.27	9.45	9.51	9.55	9.60	9.52	9.63	9.60	9.61	9.67
June		9.60	9.60	9.65	9.60	....	....	....	9.57	9.68	9.51	9.50	9.53	9.47	9.38	9.36	9.28	9.35	9.40	9.58	....	9.68	9.56	9.55	9.65	9.68	9.75

Pork.— Highest Spot Prices for each Day in January.

	1.	2.	3.	4.	5.	7.	8.	9.	10.	11.	12.	14.	15.	16.	17.	18.	19.	21.	22.	23.	24.	25.	26.	28.	29.	30.	31.
Mess	Holiday.	15.00	....	....	....	....	....	....	....	....	....	....	....	....	14.75	14.50	....	....	15.00	15.25	....	15.50	....	15.75	....	....	....
ExtraPrime		13.50	....	....	....	....	14.00	....	....	....	....	....	....	....	....	....	....	....	....	....	....	14.25	....	....	....	....	14.50
Prime Mess		15.00	....	....	....	....	....	....	15.50	....	....	....	....	....	....	....	....	....	....	....	....	15.75	....	....	....	....	...
Clear Back.		18.00	....	....	....	18.50	....	....	....	18.00	....	....	....	....	....	....	....	....	18.50	....	....	19.00	....	...	....	....	....
Family		16.00	15.50	....	....	16.00	....	15.50	....	....	....	....	....	....	....	....	....	....	....	15.75	16.37½	....	16.50	17.00	16.75	17.00	....

Cotton.—Current Prices for each Day in January.

	1.	2.	3.	4.	5.	7.	8.	9.	10.	11.	12.	14.	15.	16.	17.	18.	19.	21.	22.	23.	24.	25.	26.	28.	29.	30.	31.
UPLANDS. per lb.	*Holiday.*																										
Ordinary		8 7/16		8 3/8							8 7/16									8 3/8		8 7/16			8 3/8		
Strict Ordinary		8 11/16		8 11/16							8 11/16									8 11/16		8 11/16			8 11/16		
Good Ordinary		9 1/4		9 1/4							9 1/4									9 1/4		9 1/4			9 1/4		
Strict Good Ordinary		9 7/8		10							10									10		10 1/8			10 1/8		
Low Middling		10 3/8		10 3/8							10 3/8									10 3/8		10 3/8			10 3/8		
Strict Low Middling		10 3/4		10 3/4							10 3/4									10 3/4		10 3/4			10 3/4		
Middling		10 3/4		10 3/4							10 3/4									10 3/4		10 3/4			10 3/4		
Good Middling		11		11							11									11		11			11		
Strict Good Middling		11 1/2		11 1/2							11 1/2									11 1/2		11 1/2			11 1/2		
Middling Fair		12 1/2		12 1/2							12 5/8									12 1/2		12 5/8			12 5/8		
Fair																											
NEW ORLEANS. per lb.																											
Ordinary		8 7/16		8 7/16							8 1/2									8 1/2		8 1/2			8 1/2		
Strict Ordinary		9		9 1/8							9 1/8									9 1/16		9 1/8			9 1/16		
Good Ordinary		9 1/2		9 1/2							9 1/2									9 1/2		9 1/2			10		
Strict Good Ordinary		10 1/8		10 1/8							10 1/8									10 1/8		10 1/8			10 1/8		
Low Middling		10 3/8		10 3/8							10 3/8									10 3/8		10 3/8			10 3/8		
Strict Low Middling		10 3/4		10 3/4							10 3/4									10 3/4		10 3/4			10 3/4		
Middling		11 1/4		11 1/4							11 1/4									11 1/4		11 1/4			11 1/4		
Good Middling		11 1/2		11 1/2							11 1/2									11 1/2		11 1/2			11 1/2		
Strict Good Middling		11 3/4		11 3/4							11 3/4									11 3/4		11 3/4			11 3/4		
Middling Fair		12 5/8		12 1/2							12 5/8									12 1/2		12 5/8			12 5/8		
Fair																											
TEXAS. per lb.																											
Ordinary		8 7/16		8 3/8							8 3/8									8 3/8		8 3/8			8 3/8		
Strict Ordinary		9		9 1/16							9									9 1/16		9 1/16			9 1/16		
Good Ordinary		9 1/2		9 1/2							9 1/2									9 1/2		9 1/2			10		
Strict Good Ordinary		10 1/8		10 1/8							10 1/8									10 1/8		10 1/8			10 1/8		
Low Middling		10 3/8		10 3/8							10 3/8									10 3/8		10 3/8			10 3/8		
Strict Low Middling		10 3/4		11 1/8							10 3/4									11 1/8		11 1/8			10 3/4		
Middling		11 1/4		11 1/4							11 1/4									11 1/4		11 1/4			11 1/4		
Good Middling		11 1/2		11 1/2							11 1/2									11 1/2		11 1/2			11 1/2		
Strict Good Middling		11 3/4		11 3/4							11 3/4									11 3/4		11 3/4			11 3/4		
Middling Fair		12 5/8		12 1/2							12 5/8									12 1/2		12 5/8			12 5/8		
Fair																											
STAINED. per lb.																											
Good Ordinary		7 11/16		8 1/4							8 1/4									8		8 1/4			8 1/2		
Strict Good Ordinary		8 1/2		9 1/8							8 1/2									8 1/4		8 1/2			8 1/2		
Low Middling		9 1/2		9 1/2							9 7/8									9 1/4		9 7/8			9 1/4		
Middling		10 1/4		10 1/4							10 1/4									10 1/4		10 1/4			10 1/8		

UNITED STATES MAILS TO FOREIGN COUNTRIES.

Schedule of Steamers Appointed to Convey the United States Mails to Foreign Countries During the Month of February, 1884.

TRANS-ATLANTIC MAILS.

DATE OF SAILING.	NAME OF STEAMER.	NAME OF LINE.	PORT OF DESTINATION AND INTERMED'TE PORTS OF CALL.	Hour of Clos'g Mail at P.O. at Port of Departure.	MAILS TO BE CONVEYED.
			FROM NEW YORK.		
Feb. 2	City of Berlin	Inman	Queenstown	6.00 A.M.	Mails for Great Britain and Ireland; also French, Belgian, Netherlands, Swiss, Italian, Spanish, Portuguese, Russian, and Turkish closed mails; *also specially addressed correspondence for Germany, Austria, Denmark, Sweden, and Norway.*
2	Anchoria	Anchor	Glasgow	6.00	*Specially addressed correspondence for Scotland.*
2	Belgenland	Red Star	Antwerp	6.00	Mails for Belgium direct.
2	Rhein	North German Lloyd	Southampton and Bremen	11.00	Mails for Great Britain and Ireland; also German, Austrian, French, Belgian, Netherlands, Swiss, Italian, Spanish, Portuguese, Russian, Turkish, and Swedish closed mails via Southampton; mails for Germany direct; also Austrian, Danish, and Norwegian closed mails via Bremen.
5	Abyssinia	Williams & Guion	Queenstown	9.00	Mails for Great Britain and Ireland; also German, Austrian, French, Belgian, Netherlands, Swiss, Italian, Spanish, Portuguese, Russian, Turkish, Danish, Swedish, and Norwegian closed mails.
6	St. Simon	General Trans-Atlantic	Havre	10.00	Mails for France direct.
6	Pavonia	Cunard	Queenstown	10.30	Mails for Great Britain and Ireland, etc. (Same as Abyssinia.)
6	Zaandam	Netherlands Steam Nav. Co	Amsterdam	10.30	Mails for the Netherlands direct.
7	Gellert	Hamburg Am. Packet Co..	Plymouth and Hamburg	11.00	Mails for Great Britain; also German, Austrian, Belgian, Netherlands, Swiss, Italian, Spanish, Portuguese, Russian, and Turkish closed mails via Plymouth; mails for Germany direct; also Austrian, Danish, Swedish, and Norwegian closed mails via Hamburg; *also specially addressed correspondence for Great Britain and other European countries.*
7	City of Montreal	Inman	Queenstown	11.00	Mails for Germany, Austria, and Sweden via Southampton; mails for Germany direct; also Austrian, Danish, and Norwegian closed mails via Bremen; *also specially addressed correspondence for Great Britain and other European countries.*
9	General Werder	North German Lloyd	Southampton and Bremen	11.00	*Specially addressed correspondence for Scotland.*
9	Britannic	White Star	Queenstown	12.00 M.	*Specially addressed correspondence for Europe.*
9	Furnessia	Anchor	Glasgow	12.00	
9	Pennland	Red Star	Antwerp	3.00 P.M.	*Specially addressed correspondence for Europe.*
12	Wyoming	Williams & Guion	Queenstown	3.00 A.M.	Mails for Great Britain; also German, Austrian, Belgian, Netherlands, Swiss, Italian, Spanish, Portuguese, Russian, Turkish, and Swedish, closed mails via Southampton; mails for Germany direct; also Austrian, Danish, and Norwegian closed mails via Bremen; *also specially addressed correspondence for France.*
13	Fulda	North German Lloyd	Southampton and Bremen	3.30	
13	Gallia	Cunard	Queenstown	3.30	Mails for Ireland, etc. (Same as City of Montreal.)
13	St. Laurent	General Trans-Atlantic	Havre	3.30	Mails for France direct.
13	Schiedam	Netherlands Steam Nav. Co	Rotterdam	6.00	Mails for the Netherlands direct.
14	Republic	White Star	Queenstown	4.30	Mails for Great Britain and Ireland, etc. (Same as City of Berlin.)
14	Rhaetia	Hamburg Am. Packet Co	Plymouth and Hamburg	5.30	Mails for Great Britain and Ireland; also German, Austrian, French, Belgian, Netherlands, Swiss, Italian, Spanish, Portuguese, Russian, and Turkish closed mails via Plymouth; mails for Germany direct; also Austrian, Danish, Swedish, and Norwegian closed mails via Hamburg.
16	City of Chester	Inman	Queenstown	6.00	Mails for Great Britain and Ireland, etc. (Same as City of Berlin.)
16	Belgravia	Anchor	Glasgow	6.00	*Specially addressed correspondence for Scotland.*
16	Westernland	Red Star	Antwerp	6.00	Mails for Belgium direct.
16	Habsburg	North German Lloyd	Southampton and Bremen	11.00	Mails for Great Britain and Ireland, etc. (Same as City of Berlin.)
19	Nevada	Williams & Guion	Queenstown	8.00	Mails for Great Britain and Ireland, etc. (Same as Abyssinia.)
20	Amerique	General Trans-Atlantic	Havre	9.00	Mails for France direct.

[Continued on next page.

Date	Steamer	Line	Port	Time	Contents
Feb. 20	Scythia	Cunard	Queenstown	9.30 A.M.	Mails for Great Britain and Ireland, etc. (Same as City of Berlin.)
" 20	Leerdam	Netherlands Steam Nav. Co	Amsterdam	9.30	Mails for the Netherlands direct.
" 20	Donau	North German Lloyd	Southampton and Bremen	11.30	Mails for Great Britain and Ireland, etc. (Same as Rhein.)
" 21	City of Chicago	Inman	Queenstown	9.30	Mails for Great Britain and Ireland, etc. (Same as City of Berlin.)
" 21	Wieland	Hamburg Am. Packet Co.	Plymouth and Hamburg	10.00	Mails for Germany and Austria via Plymouth; mails for Germany direct; also Austrian, Danish, Swedish, and Norwegian closed mails via Hamburg; also specially addressed correspondence for Great Britain and other European countries.
" 23	Neckar	North German Lloyd	Southampton and Bremen	11.00	Mails for Germany, Austria, and Sweden, etc. (Same as General Werder.)
" 23	Celtic	White Star	Queenstown	11.30	Mails for Great Britain and Ireland, etc. (Same as City of Berlin.)
" 23	Bolivia	Anchor	Glasgow	10.30	Specially addressed correspondence for Scotland.
" 23	Switzerland	Red Star	Antwerp	1.30 P.M.	Mails for Belgium direct.
" 26	Wisconsin	Williams & Guion	Queenstown	2.00 A.M.	Specially addressed correspondence for Europe.
" 27	Werra	North German Lloyd	Southampton and Bremen	2.30 "	Mails for Great Britain and Ireland; also German, Austrian, Belgian, Netherlands, Swiss, Italian, Spanish, Portuguese, Russian, Turkish, and Swedish closed mails via Southampton; mails for Germany direct; also Austrian, Danish, and Norwegian closed mails via Bremen; also specially addressed correspondence for France.
" 27	Cephalonia	Cunard	Queenstown	2.30	Specially addressed correspondence for Europe.
" 27	Canada	General Trans-Atlantic	Havre	2.30	Mails for France direct.
" 27	Maasdam	Netherlands Steam Nav. Co	Rotterdam	4.00	Mails for the Netherlands direct.
" 28	Rugia	Hamburg Am. Packet Co.	Plymouth and Hamburg	4.30	Mails for Germany and Austria, etc. (Same as Wieland.)
" 28	City of Richmond	Inman	Queenstown	12.30 P.M.	Mails for Great Britain and Ireland, etc. (Same as Abyssinia.)
FROM BOSTON.					
Feb. 2	Marathon	Cunard	Queenstown and Liverpool	10.30 A.M.	Mails for Great Britain and Ireland; also closed mails for Belgium and France.
" 16	Samaria	Cunard	Queenstown and Liverpool	10.30	Mails for Great Britain and Ireland; also closed mails for Belgium and France.
FROM PHILADELPHIA					
Feb. 16	Illinois	American Steamship Co.	Queenstown and Liverpool	11.30 A.M.	Mails for Great Britain and Ireland.
" 23	Pennsylvania	American Steamship Co.	Queenstown and Liverpool	4.30 "	Mails for Great Britain and Ireland.
" 27	Vaderland	Red Star	Antwerp	8.30	Mails for Belgium direct.
FROM BALTIMORE.					
Feb. 14	Hermann	North German Lloyd	Bremen	2.00 P.M.	Mails for Germany.
" 28	America	North German Lloyd	Bremen	2.00 "	Mails for Germany.

MAILS FOR CANADA AND NEWFOUNDLAND.

Date	Steamer	Line	Port	Time	Contents
FROM BOSTON.					
Feb. 2	Carroll	Boston, Halifax, and Prince Edward Island	Halifax	11.00 A.M.	Mails for Nova Scotia.
			Yarmouth	7.00	Mails for Nova Scotia.
" 5	Cleopatra	Nova Scotia Steamship Co.	Halifax	11.00	Mails for Nova Scotia, Newfoundland, and Miquelon.
" 9	Carroll	Boston, Halifax, and Prince Edward Island	Yarmouth	7.00	Mails for Nova Scotia.
" 12	Cleopatra	Nova Scotia Steamship Co.	Halifax	11.00	Mails for Nova Scotia.
" 16	Carroll	Boston, Halifax, and Prince Edward Island	Yarmouth	7.00	Mails for Nova Scotia.
" 19	Cleopatra	Nova Scotia Steamship Co.	Halifax	11.00	Mails for Nova Scotia, Newfoundland, and Miquelon.
" 23	Carroll	Boston, Halifax, and Prince Edward Island	Yarmouth	7.00	Mails for Nova Scotia.
" 26	Cleopatra	Nova Scotia Steamship Co.	Halifax	11.00	Mails for Nova Scotia.
			Yarmouth	7.00	Mails for Nova Scotia.
FROM SAN FRANCISCO.					
Feb. 8	Mexico	Pacific Coast Steamship Co.	Victoria	9.00	Mails for British Columbia.
" 16	Queen of the Pacific	Pacific Coast Steamship Co.	Victoria	9.00	Mails for British Columbia.
" 24	Mexico	Pacific Coast Steamship Co.	Victoria	9.00	Mails for British Columbia.

MAILS FOR THE WEST INDIES, MEXICO, CENTRAL AND SOUTH AMERICA.

Date of Sailing.	Name of Steamer.	Name of Line.	Port of Destination and Intermed'te Ports of Call.	Hour of Closing Mail at P.O. at Port of Departure.	Mails to be Conveyed.
			FROM NEW YORK.		
Feb. 1	Acapulco	Pacific Mail	Aspinwall	10.00 A.M.	Mails for the South Pacific and Central American ports, and for the West Coast of Mexico via Aspinwall.
" 2	Newport	New York and Cuba Mail	Havana	1.30 P.M.	Mails for Cuba, and for the West Indies via Havana.
" 7	Valencia	Red D	Puerto Cabello, Laguayra, Maracaibo, and Curaçoa		Mails for Venezuela and Curaçoa.
" 7	Orinoco	Quebec Steamship Co.	Hamilton	10.00 A.M.	Mails for Bermuda.
" 7	British Empire	N.Y., Hav., & Mex. Mail	Havana	1.00 P.M.	Mails for Cuba, and for Porto Rico and Mexico via Havana.
" 8	Alene	Atlas	Kingston, Port Limon, and Savanilla	1.30 " 1.00 "	Mails for Jamaica, Port Limon, and the U.S. of Colombia, except Aspinwall and Panama.
" 9	Finance	U.S. and Brazil Mail	St. Thomas, Para, Maranham, Pernambuco, Bahia, and Rio de Janeiro	1.00 A.M.	Mails for the West Indies via St. Thomas, for Brazil, and for the Argentine Republic, Uruguay, and Paraguay via Brazil. Steamer receives mails from New York and Baltimore at Newport News, Va.
" 9	Colon	Pacific Mail	Aspinwall	10.00 "	Mails for the South Pacific, etc. (Same as Acapulco.)
" 9	Saratoga	New York and Cuba Mail	Havana	1.30 P.M.	Mails for Cuba, and for Porto Rico via Havana.
" 12	Santo Domingo	Clyde	Cape Hayti, Puerto Plata, Samana, St. Domingo City, and Grand Turk		Mails for Cape Hayti, Saint Domingo, and Turk's Island.
" 12	Muriel	Quebec Steamship Co.	Barbadoes	1.00 "	Mails for the Windward Islands.
" 12	Alpin	Atlas	St. John's	1.00 "	Mails for Porto Rico direct.
" 14	Cienfuegos	New York and Cuba Mail	Nassau and Santiago	1.00 "	Mails for the Bahama Islands, and for Santiago and Cienfuegos, Cuba.
" 14	City of Puebla	N.Y., Hav., & Mex. Mail	Havana and Santiago	1.00 "	Mails for Cuba, and for Porto Rico and Mexico via Havana.
" 16	Glenfyne	Red D	Puerto Cabello, Laguayra, Maracaibo, and Curaçoa	1.30 "	Mails for Venezuela and Curaçoa.
" 16	Niagara	New York and Cuba Mail	Havana	10.00 A.M.	Mails for Cuba, and for the West Indies via Havana.
" 19	Flamborough	Quebec Steamship Co.	Barbadoes	1.30 P.M.	Mails for the Windward Islands.
" 19	Alvena	Atlas	Port au Prince	1.00 "	Mails for Hayti.
" 20	City of Para	Pacific Mail	Aspinwall	10.00 A.M.	Mails for the South Pacific, etc. (Same as Acapulco.)
" 21	Orinoco	Quebec Steamship Co.	Hamilton	1.00 P.M.	Mails for Bermuda.
" 21	City of Alexandria	N.Y., Hav., & Mex. Mail	Havana	1.30 "	Mails for Cuba, and for Porto Rico and Mexico via Havana.
" 22	Athos	Atlas	Kingston, Port Limon, and Savanilla		Mails for Jamaica, etc. (Same as Alene.)
" 23	Newport	New York and Cuba Mail	Havana	1.00 "	Mails for Cuba, and for Porto Rico via Havana.
" 26	Antillas	Atlas	St. John's	1.30 "	Mails for Porto Rico direct.
" 27	Bermuda	Quebec Steamship Co.	Barbadoes	1.00 "	Mails for the Windward Islands.
" 28	Caracas	Red D	Puerto Cabello, Laguayra, Maracaibo, and Curaçoa		Mails for Venezuela and Curaçoa.
" 28	Santiago	New York and Cuba Mail	Nassau and Santiago	10.00 A.M.	Mails for the Bahama Islands, and for Santiago and Cienfuegos, Cuba.
" 28	City of Wash'gton	N.Y., Hav., & Mex. Mail	Havana	1.00 P.M. 1.30 "	Mails for Cuba, and for Porto Rico and Mexico via Havana.
			FROM NEW ORLEANS.		
Feb. 1	Whitney	Morgan Line	Vera Cruz	6.15 A.M.	Mails for Mexico.
" 2	S. J. Oteri	Oteri's Pioneer Line	Ruatan and Truxillo	8.00 "	Mails for Spanish Honduras and Bay Islands.
" 6	E. B. Ward, Jr.	Oteri's Pioneer Line	Ruatan and Truxillo	8.00 "	Mails for Spanish Honduras and Bay Islands.
" 7	Lucy P. Miller	Royal Mail Steamship Co	Belize, Puerto Cortez, and Livingston		Mails for British and Spanish Honduras, and Guatemala.
" 7	Hutchinson	Morgan Line	Havana	10.00 "	Mails for Cuba.
" 14	Morgan	Morgan Line	Havana	7.00 "	Mails for Cuba.
" 16	City of Dallas	Royal Mail Steamship Co	Belize, Puerto Cortez, etc.	7.00 "	Mails for British and Spanish Honduras, and Guatemala.
" 16	Whitney	Morgan Line	Vera Cruz	10.00 "	Mails for Mexico.
" 16	City of Mexico	N.Y., Hav., & Mex. Mail	Vera Cruz via Bagdad, Tam-	6.15 "	

Date	Vessel	Line	Ports	Time	Description
Feb. 21	Hutchinson	Morgan Line	Havana	7.00 A.M.	Mails for Cuba.
" 26	E. B. Ward, Jr.	Oteri's Pioneer Line	Ruatan and Truxillo	8.00 "	Mails for Spanish Honduras and Bay Islands.
" 28	Morgan	Morgan Line	Havana	7.00 "	Mails for Cuba.
" 28	Lucy P. Miller	Royal Mail Steamship Co	Belize, Puerto Cortez, etc	10.00 "	Mails for British and Spanish Honduras, and Guatemala.

FROM GALVESTON, Tex

Date	Vessel	Line	Ports	Time	Description
Feb. 2	Whitney	Morgan Line	Vera Cruz	....	Mails for Mexico.
" 17	Whitney	Morgan Line	Vera Cruz	....	Mails for Mexico.

FROM KEY WEST, Fla.

Date	Vessel	Line	Ports	Time	Description
Feb. 3	Morgan	Morgan Line	Havana	....	Mails for Cuba.
" 10	Hutchinson	Morgan Line	Havana	....	Mails for Cuba.
" 17	Morgan	Morgan Line	Havana	....	Mails for Cuba.
" 24	Hutchinson	Morgan Line	Havana	....	Mails for Cuba.

FROM BALTIMORE, Md.

Date	Vessel	Line	Ports	Time	Description
Feb. 9	Finance	U. S. and Brazil Mail	St. Thomas, Para, etc.	4.00 A.M.	Mails for the West Indies, etc. (Same as Finance above.)

FROM SAN FRANCISCO

Date	Vessel	Line	Ports	Time	Description
Feb. 1	Colima	Pacific Mail	Panama and Way Ports	8.30 A.M.	Mails for Mexico, and for the South Pacific and Central American ports.
" 6	Newbern	Cal. and Mexican SS. Co.	Ensenada, Cape St. Lucas, Magdalena Bay, La Paz, Mazatlan, and Guaymas.	11.00 "	Mails for the West Coast of Mexico.
" 15	San Jose	Pacific Mail	Panama and Way Ports.	8.30 "	Mails for Mexico, and for the South Pacific and Central American ports.

TRANS-PACIFIC MAILS.

FROM SAN FRANCISCO

Date	Vessel	Line	Ports	Time	Description
Feb. 1		French Contract Line	Papeiti	2.00 P.M.	Mails for Tahiti and Marquesas Islands. Mails close 4 p. m., January 31.
" 1	Mariposa	Oceanic Steamship Co	Honolulu	....	Mails for the Sandwich Islands.
" 7	Arabic	Occidental and Oriental	Yokohama and Hong Kong	10.30 A.M.	Mails for Japan, Shanghai, Hoog Kong and dependent Chinese ports, and the East Indies, except British India.
" 15	Alameda	Oceanic Steamship Co	Honolulu	2.00 P.M.	Mails for the Sandwich Islands.
" 15	City of Sydney	Pacific Mail	Honolulu, Sydney, Auckl'd	....	Mails for the Sandwich Islands, New Zealand, and Australia; for Fiji and Samoan Islands, and New Caledonia via Sydney, New South Wales.
" 20	City of Peking	Pacific Mail	Yokohama and Kong Kong	10.30 A.M.	Mails for Japan, etc. (Same as Mariposa.)

In case of accident to any steamer booked for departure at a particular date, another one is substituted to carry the mail at the time specified.

☞ Mails for Great Britain, and for the Continent of Europe *via* Great Britain, to be dispatched from New York as per this Schedule, are assigned to the fastest vessels available. Special directions on correspondence for Great Britain and the Continent for its dispatch from New York by particular vessels, merely with a view to celerity, are therefore unnecessary.

TELEGRAPHIC CABLE RATES.

Tariff to Great Britain, Ireland, France, and Germany.

Per word.

From New York City, Brooklyn, and Yonkers in New York, the New England States, New Brunswick, Nova Scotia, Ontario and Quebec.......... 50 cents.

From New York (except New York City, Brooklyn and Yonkers), New Jersey, Pennsylvania, Delaware, Maryland and District of Columbia....... 53 cents.

From Virginia, West Virginia, Ohio, Michigan, Kentucky, Indiana, Illinois, St. Louis in Missouri, and Milwaukee, Wisconsin...................... 55 cents.

From North Carolina, South Carolina, Georgia, Alabama, Mississippi, New Orleans in Louisiana,

Per word.

Tennessee, Denver and Leadville in Colorado, and Western Union offices in Florida............ 60 cents.

From Louisiana (except New Orleans), Texas, Wisconsin (except Milwaukee), Iowa, Missouri (except St. Louis), Arkansas, Minnesota, Dakota, Manitoba, Kansas, Nebraska, and Indian Territory.... 65 cents.

From Colorado (except Denver and Leadville), Wyoming, Utah, New Mexico, Idaho, Montana, Nevada, California, Arizona, Oregon and Washington Territory................................... 70 cents.

From British Columbia.......... .... 75 cents.

Senders can insure their messages being forwarded by any particular route, such as "via Siberia," "via Santander," "via Teheran," etc., by inserting the indication of route in the "Check." The indication is transmitted free of charge.
Messages destined for places beyond the lines of telegraph must contain instructions from the sender as to the name of the place from which they are to be posted. The postage to be charged is thirty-seven cents.

Rules for Atlantic Cable Business.

(1) The maximum length of a chargeable word will be fixed at ten letters. Should a word contain more than ten letters, every ten or fraction of ten letters will be counted as a word.

(2) Code messages must be composed of words in the English, French, German, Spanish, Italian, Dutch, Portuguese, and Latin languages. Proper names (*i. e.*, names of persons and places) will not be allowed in the text of Code Messages, except in the manner they are used in ordinary private messages.

(3) Groups of figures or letters will be counted at the rate of three figures or letters to a word, plus one word for any excess.

Rates from New York to	PER WORD	Rates from New York to	PER WORD	Rates from New York to	PER WORD
Aden, Arabia...	$1.43	Siberian rate shall be collected for messages to Japan.		from London: Rio de Janeiro and places north in Brazil, $2.41 per word; places south in Brazil, $2.61 per word. The words via *Government land lines* must be included and paid for.	
" via Bombay..............	2.20	Luxemburg......................	$ .56		
Africa—		Madeira, (Madeira Islands)......	.88		
Delagoa Bay..................	2.65	Malacca........................	2.05		
Mozambique	2.65	Malta	.64	Uruguay—	
Zanzibar......................	2.40	Mauritius—Telegrams for the Island of, can be posted at Aden.		Montevedio	$3.21
Africa (South)—				All other places in Uruguay..	3.21
Durban....................	2.65	Montenegro....................	.62	Argentine Republic—	
All other places in South Africa	2.75	New Zealand...................	3.40	Buenos Ayres..............	2.94
Algeria	.58	Norway.......................	.60	All other places in Arg'ne Rep	2.94
" via Falmouth..........	.77	Orkney Islands—Rules and rates same as Great Britain.		Chili	3.11
Australia, via Falm'th or Teheran	3.15			Peru—	
" " via Siberia	4.55	Penang, via Falmouth or Teheran	1.85	Arica	5.20
Austria	.61	" via Siberia..........	3.50	Arequipa...............	5.58
Belgium	.56	Persia	.90	Callao	6.30
Beloochistan	1.50	Phillipine Island, Luzon........	2.95	Islay	5.58
Benghazi — Messages posted at Malta.		Portugal	.65	Iquique	4.83
		" via Santander	.68	Lima......................	6.30
Burmah, Further India	1.80	Roumania	.62	Molendo	5.58
" " via Penang	2.30	Russia in Europe..............	.68	Puno	5.58
Bushire	1.18	Russia, Caucasus..............	.75	Tacna	5.20
Cape Verde Islands, St. Vincent.	1.48	Russia in Asia, west of Verkhnee Oudinsk	.90	Bolivia, Antofagasta........	4.83
Ceylon, via Falmouth or Teheran	1.75			Messages for South America can also be sent via the West Indies.	
Channel Islands—Rules and rates same as London.		Russia in Asia, east of Verkhnee Oudinsk	1.15		
Channel Islands via France......	.59	St. Vincent, Cape Verde Island .	1.48	Spain, via Falmouth or Santander	.66
China.........................	2.55	Scilly Islands. Same as London.		" via Gibraltar..........	.75
Cochin China—		Servia	.62	" via Marseilles..........	.65
Saigon, via Falm'th or Teheran	2.30	Sicily	.50	Sweden	.64
" via Siberia............	3.15	Sardinia.......................	.59	Switzerland....................	.56
Corfu	.64	Shetland Islands—Rules and rates same as Great Britain.		Tripoli	.79
Corsica	.59			Turkey in Europe..............	.64
Cyprus........................	.95	Singapore, via Falm'th or Teheran	2.08	" " via Falmouth....	.83
Denmark	.60	" via Siberia..........	3.25	" Asia—Seaports......	.70
Egypt—		South America, via cable from Europe:		" " via Falm'h	.88
Alexandria	.84	Brazil—		" " Inland......	.74
All other places in Egypt	.89	Maranham	3.52	" " via Falm'th	.93
Gibraltar	.68	Para	3.83	Turkish Islands................	.74
Greece........................	.66	Pernambuco	2.70	" " via Falmouth....	.93
Greek Islands..................	.70	Bahia and Rio de Janeiro....	2.91	Turkey, via Russia and Odessa Cable—Mess'es must be marked "via Indo," and sent via London. Rates are as follows:	
Heligoland	.65	Santos......................	3.11		
Holland.......................	.58	Santa Catherina	3.11		
Hungary......................	.61	Rio Grande do Sul..........	3.11		
India, via Falmouth or Teheran..	1.75	Other places in Brazil, north.	2.91	Turkey in Europe..............	.83
Italy	.59	" " " south.	3.11	" " Asia—Seaports......	.89
Java, via Falmouth or Teheran ..	2.20	Messages for Brazil can also be sent via Government land lines in Brazil at following rates *per word*		" " Inland......	.93
" via Siberia	3.50			" " Archipelago..	.93
Japan, via Falmouth or Teheran .	3.50			Tunisia.......................	.58
" via Siberia	2.80			" via Falmouth	.77
Unless specially directed, the					

To Cuba and West Indies.

VIA CABLE TO HAVANA, CUBA.

From New York City to the Following Places at the Rate of 50 Cents per Word:

Havana, Cuba	Consolacion*	Ciego de Avila*	Manzanillo‡	St. Dom'go (Coloniado*
Batabano, " *	Colon*	Guanaja*	Mariel*	Sagua*
Bajucal, " *	Cardenas*	Guines*	Pinar del Roi*	Santiago‡
Bemba, " *	Cienfuegos†	Guantanamo‡	Puerte Principe*	Santo-Spiritu*
Bayamo*	Caibarien*	Jignani*	Remedios*	Trinidad*
Bahia Honda*	Cabanas*	Matanzas*	San Antonio*	....

* Add to the rate of 50 cents per word 40 cents for each ten, or fraction of ten, words.
† Add to the rate of 44 cents per word $2.25 for first ten words or less, and 22 cents for each word over ten.
‡ Add to the rate of 44 cents per word $3 for first ten words or less, and 30 cents for each word over ten.

From New York City to

	Per word.		Per word.			Per word.		Per word
Antigua	$2.41	Grenada	$2.83	Porto Rico, San Juan	$2.08	St. Lucia	2.6
Barbadoes	2.84	Guadaloupe	2.51	" Other places	2.14	St. Vincent	2.7
Berbice	3.38	" Basse Terre.	2.49	St. Croix	2.22	Trinidad, Port of Spain.	2.9
Demerara	3.36	Kingston (Jamaica)	1.35	St. Thomas	2.17	" Other places..	2.9
Dominica	2.55	Martinique	2.60	St. Kitts	2.35		

To Mexico.

From New York City.

Messages to all places, except towns near the boundary line between the United States and Mexico, will be sent via cables of the Mexican Telegraph Company from Galveston, Texas. Important towns in Mexico near the frontier, sent via Western Union offices. For other places rates are as follows:

To Tampico, Mexico, $3.75 for ten words, and 33 cents for each word over ten.
To Vera Cruz, Mexico, $4.75 for ten words, and 43 cents for each word over ten.
To City of Mexico, Mexico, $5.25 for ten words, and 48 cents for each word over ten.
To Goatzacoalcos, Mexico, 62 cents per word.   To Salina Cruz, Mexico, 72 cents per word.
To Aspinwall, Colon, $1.00 per word.   To Panama, $1.00 per word.

To all other points in Mexico, on Mexican Government lines, the rate to Vera Cruz (no reliable inland line from Tampico) will be charged, and the Mexican Government rate will be added, as follows: 50 cents for ten words, and 5 cents for each word over ten.

To points on State or Private Line Stations, beyond the Government lines, the State or Private Line rate will be added to the Government rate.

The Date, Address and Signature are free.

To Central and South America.

VIA CENTRAL AND SOUTH AMERICAN CABLES.

Salvador.—LA LIBERTAD, 75 cents per word. Other offices in Salvador, 80 cents per word.

Guatemala.—All offices in Guatemala, 80 cents per word.   Honduras.—All offices in Honduras, 80 cents per word.

Costa Rica.—All offices in Costa Rica, $1.05 per word.

Nicaraugua.—SAN JUAN DEL SUR, $1.00 per word. Other offices in Nicaraugua, $1.05 per word.

South America.

Panama, $1.00 per word.   **From New York City.**   Aspinwall, Colon, $1.00 per word.

U. S. Columbia.—BUENAVENTURA, $1.52 per word. BOGOTA and other offices, $1.57 per word.

Ecuador.—ST. ELENA BAY, $1.77 per word. GUAYAQUIL, $1.77 per word.   Bolivia.—ANTOFAGASTA, $2.72 per word.

PERU.

	Per word.		Per word.		Per word.		Per word.
Arica	$2.52	Huanillos	$2.68	Mollendo	$2.47	Pisagua	$2.68
Arequipa	2.69	Iquique	2.57	Pabullon de Pica	2.68	Tacna	2.62
Callao	2.17	Lima	2.17	Payta	1.92		

CHILI.

	Per word.		Per word.		Per word.		Per word.
Caldera	$2.82	Copiapo	$2.93	Huasco	$2.93	Taltal	2.92
Carrizal	3.03	Coquimbo	3.03	Lota	3.18	Talcahuano	3.18
Chillan	3.18	Famaya	3.03	Ovalle	3.03	Tocopilla	2.83
Chanaral	2.93	Freirina	3.03	Santiago	3.18	Valdivia	3.18
Cobija	2.83	Guayacan	3.03	Serena	2.93	Vallenar	3.03
Concepcion	3.18	Higuera	3.03	Talca	3.18	Valparaiso	3.07

To Buenos Ayres and other places in the Argentine Republic, $2.92 per word from New York.

To Montevideo and all other places in Uruguay, $3.00 per word from New York.

BRAZIL.

	Per word.		Per word.		Per word.		Per word.
Bahia	$2.91	Para	$3.80	Rio	$2.91	Santos	$3.11
Pernambuco	2.70	Maranham	3.50	Rio Grande	3.11	Santa Catharina	3.11

All inland stations 15 cents per word in addition to tariff from nearest coast line station.

Nearly 400,000 pounds of dry bark were gathered from the cinchona trees in India last year.

Fifty-four railroads report their gross earnings for 1883 at the enormous sum of $261,530,078 !

The destruction of property by fire in this country last year reached the immense sum of $193,000,000.

Ground has been broken at Crystal Park, Colorado, for a railroad to the top of Pike's Peak, 14,200 feet above sea level.

Frensno Co., Cal., is building a canal 100 feet wide from King's river to irrigate 30,000,000 acres of hitherto dry and worthless desert.

Gossip is a sort of smoke that comes from the dirty tobacco pipes of those who diffuse it; it proves nothing but the bad taste of the smoker.— *George Eliot.*

Of 224 vessels laden with petroleum which cleared from the United States in 1882 for East Indies, China and Japan, only fifteen cleared from Philadelphia ! — a painful exhibit.

There are saline springs near Lake Manitoba, from which the finest salt has been made by the Indians from time immemorial. They used to sell the Hudson Bay Company about 150 bags a year of it in the olden time.

Much as Mr. Edison is interested in the practical working of electricity, he says that it is impracticable for propelling vessels through the water. The dynamo and batteries that would propel the Alaska at the speed it now makes would weigh 63,248 tons.

Salmon fishing on the Sacramento River is now very active, and is going on day and night, more than 2,600 men being employed in it. The California Fish Commissioners keep officers on duty to see that no nets are used with meshes less than 7½ inches long. During the past year eighty-four ar-

rests were made for violation of the law, and convictions were secured in nearly every case.

We have now in this country about 300,000 manufacturing establishments, employing nearly 4,000,-000 laborers, with $3,500,000,000 invested, and our manufactured products amount to nearly $6,000,-000,000 a year, or more than $1,000,000,000 more than those of Great Britain.

The conscientious editor of a Canadian journal, the Georgetown (Ontario) *Herald,* thus advertises in his paper : " We hereby notify the public that we will not do any printing for balls or other questionable entertainments. We have conscientious convictions which we are determined to adhere to strictly, even at the risk of giving offense."

Lieutenant Dick, of the Russian Army, is said to have discovered a new illuminating substance which is capable of imparting luminous properties to objects to which it is applied. It is in the form of powder and of three colors—green, yellow and violet, the latter being the most powerful. Water in a glass vessel is by this means converted into illuminating fluid. In a lecture recently delivered by the inventor at the Nicholai Engineering Academy, at St. Petersburg, he explained the application of the substance to military and industrial mining operations. The illuminating power lasts for eight hours, and the powder must then be renewed. The German Government is said to have lately been making experiments with Lieutenant Dick's invention.

It is reported the United States Circuit Judge, Thomas Drummond, of Chicago, will retire from the Bench in March next, after thirty-four years' service. He was appointed by President Taylor to the United States District Bench in 1850, and was made a Circuit Judge in 1869 by President Grant.

AMERICAN COUNTING-ROOM.

Vol. VIII.   MARCH, 1884.   No. 3.

COMMERCE AND ITS PROMOTERS.
ARTICLE I.

The origin of commerce may be traced directly to the wants of man. A love for beauty, utility and comfort is implanted in human nature, while in no one quarter of the globe are found all things to minister to it. Thus we see why it is that to-day "commerce is king," and reigns supreme throughout the world. As a natural consequence of the difference in climate and soil in different parts of the world no one country will produce everything required, while it is pretty sure to produce some articles in greater abundance than the inhabitants can possibly consume. This simple fact underlies all commerce; for, as some writer has said, "Had all nations found at home everything necessary and agreeable, it is impossible to conceive to what extent their mutual alienation might have proceeded. China and Japan help us to an idea of that which in such a case would have constituted nationality."

To trace the history of commerce, from earliest times down to the present: to study it in all its varied aspects, and to learn something of its promoters, is the object of these Papers. No subject which could be chosen is of more vital interest to the majority of mankind: for even those who disdain commerce and regard trade as something beneath their cultivated notice can no more live without it than those whose lives are spent in the counting-room or the warehouse.

An author may devote years of his life to writing some interesting or instructive book; but when it is finished, if it were not for commerce he could not give his cherished work to more than a few of his fellow-creatures, nor yet reap the substantial benefit for which, after all, most men' toil so unremittingly in every sphere of life.

The man of science may search among the hidden things of earth, and, possibly, bring to light facts of untold value to the world at large; but while he is so engaged he will do well to remember that he is dependent upon commerce for all the comforts which surround him, and that, were it not for the ceaseless revolutions of the wheels of trade, he would, probably, have to spend his time in far other occupation, supplying the primary wants of food, clothing and dwelling, of which he feels the need, in common with the rest of mankind.

The man of learning cannot do without the merchant any more than the merchant can do without the student. While we could more easily dispense with the poet, the artist, or the orator, than with the merchant, yet each of these is dependent on the other. Every class of men is dependent upon all other classes, and it would be more charitable and becoming if all would remember that the college and the warehouse are more nearly allied than at first sight might be supposed. Learning and Commerce are twin sisters, and hand in hand they lead the world in all knowledge. The merchant sends to every part of the world, gathering those things of which we have need from every country where they are to be found; and, besides the material things, he brings back information concerning all the various peoples and countries he has seen; and so he becomes an educator quite as much as the professor. Moreover, the merchant's field is a larger one, since it addresses the greater number of people with whom he comes in contact. But if, as we have seen, the learned profession cannot do without the merchant, we will find that to be properly equipped for his part in life the merchant is equally dependent upon the professor of learning. An ignorant man cannot be a successful merchant. This fact is so fully appreciated that to-day commerce is studied as a science, and lectures are delivered in all our colleges upon the principles governing commerce.

Cultivation is as much a necessity to the merchant as honor and integrity. The more he knows of history the better; for commerce connects the different events of history in all ages, and, as we shall see, *is* history in the fullest sense of the word. Then, too, he must study much concerning the manners and customs of the different people with whom he trades. Indeed, no branch of learning will be without its value to him; and the more he studies—not only in his youth, while preparing for the battle of life, but throughout his entire life — the more possibilities will there be for him in his business career.

Just in proportion as the influence of commerce increases, the need of a liberal mercantile education will increase also. No one will dispute the fact that commerce is the friend of culture and civilization — promoting science and art as well as giving very substantial assistance to the cause of religion. Commerce has always been the handmaid of religion. Looking back through the misty ages of the past we will begin our search for the earliest commercial nation. To us, whose homes are in this New World, the Old World seems venerable, indeed; but when Europe was a barren wilderness, peopled by wandering savages, a civilization existed which was even then ancient. Long before the pyramids reared their giant heads in the Egyptian desert, long before Abraham journeyed to the land which has ever since, in a peculiar sense, belonged to his descendants, these people were advanced in arts and manufactures. For the very *beginning* of commerce we must go the far east and visit that strange country, China. The very name is suggestive of commerce; for we are told it is derived from the word *tsan* (silkworm). "China is the home of the silkworm and the land of silk." It is the oldest nation upon earth; and to study its history is to study the development of its commerce; for in the Chinese nature is engrafted a love of trade, and from remotest times the bulk of the vast population of the country have been engaged in commercial pursuits. The Chinese possessed a knowledge of those things which we have been accustomed to regard as comparatively new inventions for very many centuries before the Christian era. When Europe was a barren waste, peopled with savages clothed in the skins of wild beasts, the Chinese understood the art of weaving, and wore garments of spun cloth, together with shoes of their own manufacture; they made paper, and understood the art of printing; they had clocks to measure the flight of time; they were even then, as they ever have been, noted for their porcelain, so that now the name has become synonymous with the ware; and, strangest of all, they possessed a magnetic compass and understood the manufacture of gunpowder. We are accustomed to look upon the Chinaman as an interloper; but if priority has any claim to be regarded, it is barely possible that we may be trespassing upon his domain; for there are learned men who think they have grounds for believing that the native North American Indian is directly descended from the Chinese who found their way to this continent across Behring Strait. At any rate, if so disposed, we may learn many a valuable lesson from this despised race — not only in their past history, but from their present example.

Little is known of the early history of India; but it seems certain, from what information can be gathered from their ancient writings, which were voluminous and have been carefully preserved, that the inhabitants of that country were, from time immemorial, highly commercial. The merchant was a highly respected member of society, and trade was an honorable calling. Of all countries in the world India is by far the richest in natural productions, and in all ages of the world's history it has been to the sunny plains of Hindostan that the merchant has turned his longing eyes; and in the dim past, when the science of navigation was wellnigh unknown, it was to this rich region that men of all nations directed their weary footsteps, toiling across the hot and sandy deserts of Arabia, to bring back the spices, gems, and other rare things which have ever been found there in profusion. In the inexorable march westward, which has marked the world's progress, India was early left behind; but it has never been forgotten; and, by and by, when we study the history of modern commerce, we will see why it has come to be regarded as the storehouse of the world. A simple list of the natural productions of India will at once amaze us by their extent and richness, and show us that it is her boundless wealth which attracts all nations to her shores.

And now, turning reluctantly from this bright and sunny land, let us spend a while with the grave and sombre people whose diligence and application reared those ponderous works of art — the obelisk, the sphynx, and the pyramid — which have puzzled all succeeding generations. One might be led to think that the same industry which enabled the Egyptians to erect such mighty and enduring monuments would have made them a busy, commercial people, too; but such was not the case. In point of fact, the Egyptians were an idle nation, and would not have worked as they did had they not been compelled to do so by the law of their land. But while their law coerced them to work, their religion decreed that they should not seek intercourse with other nations. These two facts — their idleness and their isolation — retarded the growth of commerce among them. At the same time, much is recorded concerning it which will be instructive for us to notice. From the earliest times of which we have any account, the Egyptians were well versed in the arts of civilization. We find them building their temples of marble, and living in homes of bricks made of mud and straw and baked in the sun; clothing themselves in garments of linen—showing that they understood the art of weaving, which is one of the earliest arts known to man— and manufacturing paper from the reedlike papyrus which abounded in their country. Corn was plentiful in Egypt, as we know from sacred writ; indeed, it is in the writings of sacred history that we gain much of our reliable information concerning the nations of antiquity. The corn of Egypt was wheat and barley—the word being then used in a collective sense to signify all kinds of grain, if, perhaps, we may except that to which the word is specifically applied to-day, and which, probably, was not known to the ancients. Indian corn is believed to be indigenous to American soil.

There were few animals in Egypt; but the people reared remarkably fine horses, which were exported in great numbers. In ancient times the horse was only used in war, and was not, in any sense, a beast of burden. We find, then, that the exports of Egypt consisted of corn, linen, paper, and horses; while they imported timber, metals, drugs, and spices — the latter being brought directly from India by the Arabian merchants, from which fact they were erroneously called the spices of Arabia. The consumption of drugs and spices was very great in Egypt, being used in the process of embalming the dead, for which the country was noted.

Egyptian trade was principally inland; for they constitutionally hated the sea, and, unlike the Chinese, they did not possess a compass. So, despite the fact that for several months in each year their country was under water, they seldom trusted themselves far from home, preferring rather to teach strangers the art of navigation, as far as they possessed any knowledge of it, and then rely upon them to bring them such things as they had need of. As we proceed in our investigations we shall find that navigation is a great factor in the development of commerce, and that those nations who fearlessly lead the way into unknown seas are the ones which attain the highest place in commercial eminence.

In proof of this fact let us cross from Egypt to Phœnicia, which was the greatest commercial nation known to antiquity, and combine with the study of her commercial history that of Carthage, with which she was so intimately connected.

Phœnicia was a narrow strip of land lying upon the western shore of Asia Minor. It was the smallest country we shall find occasion to discuss, in connection with the subject of ancient commerce; but its inhabitants made their power felt in the ancient world by reason of their love for the quiet and peaceful pursuits of commerce. The Phœnicians possessed many characteristics which are necessary to success in business: they were energetic and enterprising; they loved the sea; and while they avoided, as far as possible, warlike encounters with the nations around them, they were not afraid to court danger upon the mighty deep. We may learn much from this adventurous nation. Among other things, the advantages of establishing colonies, in connection with commercial pursuits — the Phœnicians having established more than forty colonies on the shores of the Mediterranean, the most celebrated of which was Carthage. From its illustrious parent this child of the sea speedily learned the science of commerce, and together they controlled the commercial interests of their time.

The two principal cities of Phœnicia were Tyre and Sidon. For our present purpose, however, it will be sufficient to trace some of the causes which led to the greatness of Tyre and Carthage. Their interests were identical, and what is said of one may be said of the other. We have already seen that to be a maritime power is one advantage, and to plant new colonies is another. The two others which we will notice are the following: skill in manufacturing, and the consequent increase in capital accruing therefrom. It is a well-known fact that Tyre possessed a knowledge of dyeing — the secret of which would give to a modern manufacturer untold wealth. The Tyrean purple was so rich and beautiful a color as to be a fitting emblem of royalty, and yet the manner of producing it is one of the lost arts. The dye is supposed to have been obtained from a certain fish which abounded in the Mediterranean Sea at that time, and the imprint of which is to be seen upon ancient Tyrean coins still extant. But, like many a merchant living to-day, the Phœnicians and Carthaginians delighted in keeping the secrets of their trade to themselves; and so this one, which would have been so highly prized by posterity, died with them. The other manufactures for which Tyre and Carthage were famous were, weaving, tanning, pottery, and working in metals. In the latter art the Carthaginians excelled; they employed 40,000 men in the mines of Spain, from whence they obtained gold, silver, copper, and tin.

The Phœnicians are said to have been the inventors of copper coins. As we have already learned, the Carthaginians and Phœnicians were the greatest commercial nations of antiquity. They extended their commerce into every known land: bringing, from Egypt, flax and paper; from India and the Red Sea, spices, frankincense. perfumes, gold, pearls and precious stones. They are also known to have penetrated to the interior of Africa, and to have traded with the dusky tribes there, although the records of their dealings are lost. But great as was their traffic upon land, it was exceeded by their commerce on the high seas. They pierced beyond the Pillars of Hercules, which were at that time the western boundary of the known world, and fearlessly explored the unknown and much dreaded region beyond. They were well rewarded for their courage and endurance, for they came upon a land rich in mineral wealth, especially tin. This country was no other than Great Britain, which at that time was peopled with savage tribes, living in rude huts, and engaged in hunting and fishing—little dreaming of the busy world far away to the southeast of them, or of the proud position which they were destined one day. to attain themselves.

With their characteristic secretiveness the Phœnicians and Carthaginians kept the knowledge of this discovery to themselves, and it is said that upon one occasion, when a strange vessel was seen following them, they proceeded to the length of casting themselves away upon the Spanish coast. Of course, the stranger followed their example and was wrecked. The home government richly rewarded the astute mariner who, rather than divulge the secrets of his State, sacrificed his own personal property. From Britain they brought away, tin, hides and wool; also, raw materials, which, in the hands of their skilled workmen, were enhanced an hundred fold in value, and thereby supplied them with increased wealth (capital), by means of which they continually extended their commerce.

With a list of those things which they exported, we will take leave of Tyre and Carthage. In exchange for the commodities which they brought from the East, West, North and South, they gave to the various nations with which they traded, corn, fruit, wax, honey, oil, skins of beasts, and manufactured goods in great variety: such as pottery, useful and ornamental goods in wrought metals, costly furniture, tapestries, etc.

In Greece we find many things which should have conspired to make her as great commercially as she was politically and intellectually. Small as the country really was, it possessed, in proportion to its size, a great extent of sea-coast, as well as numberless excellent harbors. Moreover, the land was extremely fertile, as well as rich in mineral wealth. The inhabitants, too, were noted for their activity and ingenuity. But as we proceed in our investigations, we will discover several reasons why they did not attain any especial commercial importance. Greece was originally a barbarous State, peopled, like the rest of Europe, by savage tribes. It is said to have been settled by colonists from Phœnicia and Egypt. Cecrops, the founder of Athens, is supposed to have been an Egyptian. At any rate, it seems certain that the civilization of ancient Greece had its rise in the commerce of Phœnicia. Greece was divided into numerous States, each one being quite independent of all others. Upon the slightest pretext these States were wont to declare war upon each other; and here already we have two good reasons for their want of commercial success. In no other calling in life is it truer that "union is strength" than that of commerce; and in all ages it has been found that war is its disastrous enemy.

In the early history of Greece little attention was paid to commerce; but as time went on, and their intercourse with Phœnicia became more extended, they became more interested in it, and we are told that Herodotus, Solon, and Plato were all merchants. The last-named sold oil in Egypt. This brings us to inquire what the country produced, and what it stood in need of; in other words, what it exported and what it imported. By the law of the land the Greeks were not allowed to export any article of which they did not possess a superabundance. In this fact we find another drawback to the growth of their commerce. The products of the country were thus sharply divided into two classes: those which they might exchange with foreign nations, and those which they might not. Among the former were figs and all kinds of fruits, wool and pitch; and among the latter were olives, honey, marble, and the products of their copper and silver mines. Olive oil and honey have ever been staple articles of commerce, and before butter and sugar were known must have been held in even higher esteem than they are to-day. Greece early possessed a knowledge of coining money, which they probably gained from the Phœnicians. They first used silver, and, afterwards, copper coins. In the course of time the Grecians themselves became adventurous, and, though unlike the Phœnicians, they never ventured beyond their own seas. They founded colonies on the western coast of Asia Minor and upon the countless islands of the Ægean Sea. Intercourse with these new possessions, which in time became as important a part of Greece as the main land, necessitated the building of ships; and as

Attica was a barren country, it is to her fleet, combined with her manufacturing interests, that Athens owed her greatness.

In early ages all merchants were engaged in the retail business, and sold their wares directly to the consumer. To facilitate this, periodical fairs were held, during the progress of which amusement was combined with business. Indeed, the Greeks were altogether too fond of pleasure, and the numerous holidays which they enjoyed sadly interfered with their more serious occupations. Moreover, they were deficient in business habits, being capricious and fickle, and lacking the application necessary to success in commercial pursuits. And so we see why it is that they cannot be said to have been a great commercial nation.

Rome is of little account in this history. She borrowed from all the nations around her, and gave very little in return: she imported everything, and exported nothing. Although Rome rose to such eminence among the nations of antiquity, it was rather through the power she possessed to imitate and appropriate than from any originality in her own people. The chief pursuits of the Romans were agriculture and war. Now, although commerce is to a large extent dependent upon agriculture, still the people who engaged in tilling the ground cannot at the same time be highly commercial, for the single reason that their avocation requires that they shall be scattered over so great an extent of territory that they do not have sufficient means of intercourse to develop commercial interests. Commerce always builds up large cities where those engaged in it do congregate. But we must not lose sight of the fact that agriculture promotes commerce as commerce promotes agriculture. We have already seen that war re-acts upon commerce. The ancient Romans were a warlike people, and extended their empire in all directions by the force of arms. Ruin and desolation follow everywhere in the train of war. The Roman conquests, however, ultimately resulted beneficially to the nations which they subdued; for in whatever country the imperial standard was planted, the arts of civilization, which the Romans had themselves learned from their neighbors, were introduced; roads were established, acqueducts and bridges were built, and cities were founded.

G. I. S. Andrews.

BUILDING AND LOAN ASSOCIATIONS.
ARTICLE II.

The loan to Mr. Ready having been made, it now becomes the duty of the secretary to place on record the various details connected therewith. The first of these is the record of the prior incumbrances that exist, which record, as will be seen from the following form, gives the name of the borrower, location of property, and other information necessary to enable the officers to see at any

RECORD OF INTEREST PAID ON PRIOR INCUMBRANCES.............18
BUILDING AND LOAN ASSOCIATION OF ———.

L. F	Name.	Locat'n of Property	Shares	Series	Am't of Interest.	When Due.	Receipt Presented	Date of Receipt.	Signature of President.	Remarks.

RECEIVED.....................188

of...

Secretary of the .... BUILDING AND LOAN

ASSOCIATION of .... the following papers con-

nected with the loan of Mr. ....

made by the said Association on .... shares of

their stock, viz.:

............Mortgage, for . . $... ...

............Bond and Warrant, $.......

............Bond of Indemnity, $.......

............Policy of Insurance, $.......

............Policy of Insurance, $.......

......set of Searches against...........

......set of Searches against...........

......set of Searches against...........

............Realease of Liens.

STOCK AS FOLLOWS :

....

....

....

Treasurer.

Memoranda of the surrender, etc., of the papers

of loan of Mr.....................by the BUILDING

AND LOAN ASSOCIATION of .... :

....

....

....

....

....

....

....

....

....

....

....

....

....

....

....

....

time the condition of the securities held by them. This book should be regularly and carefully examined as a safeguard against one of the snags which has wrecked many an association sailing apparently in a calm sea and under a favoring sky. For the borrower who is running at all behind is more apt to let his interest in first mortgage lapse than his building association dues, etc., where his shortcomings are noticeable month by month, till by and by the association is informed by its solicitor, if fortunate enough to have one who watches sheriffs' sales advertisements, that the property of so-and-so, who is a borrower, is to be sold, and the association is under the necessity of taking steps to protect its interests. It will be seen in the above blank that the provision made for the fulfilling of a requirement, which should be part of the terms of the loan, for the regular presentation of the receipts showing the payments of interest, and the certification of the president to the fact.

The next is the recording by the secretary of the various securities and collateral turned over by him to the custody of the treasurer, of which the above is one form. This blank scarcely needs comment, as it is so fully explained. The treasurer receipts on the one side for papers turned over to his care, and the borrower, his loan having been cancelled in due course, receipts on the other when they are returned to him. Following these various forms through, it will be readily seen that the record is complete of the transaction from beginning to end.

My next blank will show the record which the secretary makes of a more condensed exhibit of the business of the association with each of its members, and shows their name and address, the various forms of their indebtedness, from dues, interest, premium or fines, and the amount paid. (See illustration on next page.) This book can be made wide enough to take in a whole year or less, at the choice of the user; it can be varied by having, as some do, enough columns under the head of "Shares" to represent the numbers of series they are likely to run. There are still other variations according to the fancy of the secretary, but these are the *purposes* of the book—the modes of exhibiting the facts are many.

The secretary should also keep a cashbook, which should show on the Dr. side the various sources of income during each month, as assessments, dues, fines, etc., and the Cr. side the various kinds of expenditures, as expenses, loans, return premiums, dues (returned when there are withdrawals), etc., for each of

up promptly, have received somewhere as follows:

From Assessments	$150.00
" Dues	7,200.00
" Interest, say	263.00
" Premiums (@ 25%)	2,250.00
" Fines (as the case may be).	..
	9,863.00

And have paid out:

For Initiatory Expenses (say)	$300.00	
" Running Expenses	300.00	
" Loans (say)	9,000.00	9,600.00
Leaving in treasury	..	263.00

This would be as good a showing as it would be possible for it to make unless the rate of premium ran higher; and tak-

No.	Name and Address.	No. of Shares.	Assessments.	What For.	JANUARY.			FEBRUARY.				DECEMBER.			TOTAL.		
					Indebtedn's	Total Dr.	Total Cr.	Indebtedn's	Total Dr.	Total Cr.	•	Indebtedn's	Total Dr.	Total Cr.	Indebtedn's	Total Dr.	Total Cr.
				D. I. P. F.							•						
				D. I. P. F.							•						
				D. I. P. F.							•						
				D. I. P. F.							•						

which there should be an order or voucher. No payments ought to be authorized by the association, or passed by the auditors as correct, without proper vouchers.

The ledger should be first and chiefly of general accounts, *i. e.*, Cash, Dues, Assessments, Interest, Fines, Premiums, Initiatory Expenses, Expenses, Return Premiums, Loans, etc.

It will be seen that the secretary's duties are not trivial, and in the selection of an efficient and reliable secretary depends in a good degree the prosperity of the association.

An association of six hundred (600) shares, in the first series, loaning its money as it comes in every evening, will thus by the end of the year, if all pay

ing one-tenth of the premiums received as being carried for the current year, and charging one-tenth of the initiatory expenses in addition to the running expenses as incurred therein, would show a gain of $308 as the result of the year's business; that each share (having paid in $12) was worth in assets $15.89, and if it could be kept up would run the association out in eight years or less. But members will not always pay up; money will not always sell at 25% premium; there will be withdrawals; property may have to be bought in; treasurers or secretaries may decamp with funds; and other reasons may occur to keep down profits or make holes in the assets; and while nearly all of these contingencies may by careful watching be guarded against,

THE RAILROAD EMPLOYEES' LOAN & BUILDING ASSOCIATION OF PHILADELPHIA.

Fourteenth Annual Statement, for the Year ending December 31st, 1883.

RECEIPTS.

Dues..	18,393.00	
Interest..	4,837.99	
Fines..	251.59	
Entrance Fees (509 shares).................	50.90	
Loans repaid—		
35 shares, No. 2 series............ 7,000.00		
* * * * *		
Total, 78½ "	15,650.00	
Rent from real estate—		
No. 534 Silliman Street............... 121.00		
* * * *		
From sale of properties :		
No. 1623 Passyunk Avenue............. 221.97	1,076.00	
* * * * *		
	1,293.87	
Received from T. Comly Hunter, on deposit, in exchange for U. S. bond, as collateral for loan, account No. 792.	575.00	
Due W. H. Warder, account withdrawn stock.....	1,587.86	
Cash over at November meeting	1.00	
Balance in Treasury at last report.................	11,820.01	
Rent received from No. 1405 Clarion Street........	6.65	
	55,543.87	

DISBURSEMENTS.

Loans on 2½ shares, No. 4 series............ 500.00		
" 53½ " " 13 " 10700.00		
Total, 56 " "		11,200.00
Stock withdrawn, 354 shares....................		42,982.24

	Dues.	Allowance.	Total.
51 shares, No. 2's,	$12,268.00	$5,790.25	$18,058.25
* * * *			
354	$31,430.00	$11,552.24	$42,982.24

Interest on withdrawn stock.....................		84.97
Premium refunded on 13 shares..................		198.52
No. 534 Silliman Street..................... 84.09		
* * * *		
		681.38
Expenses :		
Secretary's salary......................240.00		
Rent of hall........................... 48.00		
Printing 32.50		
Books, etc............................. 20.50		
Building Association League dues. 1883. 5.00		
Advertising............................ 3.60		
Stationery............................. 3.25		
Year's subscript'n to *Legal Intelligencer* 3.00		
		355.85
Balance in Treasury this date..................		16.86
T. Comly Hunter's acc't, No. 792, Dec. payment..		24.05
		55,543.87

DR.	TREASURER.	CR.

To Balance in Treasury at last report.............	11,820.01	By orders paid...........................		43,283.51
" Cash received....	31,480.36	" Cash on hand this date		16.86
	43,300.37			**43,300.37**

DR.	PROFIT AND LOSS.	CR.

To No. 1623 Meehan Street..................	16.03	By No. 62 North Thirty-ninth Street	122.73
" " 1625 " "	10.33	* * *	
" " 1627 " "	13.21	" Undivided fractions at last report	.28
" Premium................................	198.52	" Entrance Fees.........................	50.90
" Expense................................	355.85	" Withdrawing Profits	4.26
" Stock..............	5,101.82	" Interest...............................	4,753.02
		" Fines.................................	251.59
		" Cash over.............................	1.00
	5,695.76		**5,695.76**

ASSETS.

Bonds and Mortgages at last report ......502 shares	100,400.00	
" " made this year... 55 "	11,200.00	
	558 shares	
" " " canceled this year. 78½ "	111,600.00	
		15,650.00
" " " at this date ...... 479½ shares		95,950.00
No. 62 N. Thirty-ninth St., subject to...	2,600.00	
" 204 Saunders Avenue, " ... 2,000.00	1,250.00	
" 534 Silliman Street, " ... 800.00	400.00	
" 536 " " " ... 800.00	400.00	
" 538 " " " ... 800.00	400.00	
" 1105 Morris " " ... 1,000.00	1,000.00	
	5,900.00	6,050.00
Outstanding Dues	776.00	
" Interest.....................	442.87	
" Fines.....................	6.14	
		1,225.01
Balance in Treasury...................		16.86
		103,241.87

LIABILITIES.

Third series, 60 shares ....@ 196.20			11,772.00
Fourth " 123 " ....@ 173.05			21,285.15
Fifth " 101 " ....@ 150.97			15,247.97
Sixth " 84 " ....@ 129.95			10,915.80
Seventh " 72 " ....@ 110.00			7,920.00
Eighth " 103 " ....@ 91.10			9,383.30
Ninth " 64 " ....@ 73.26			4,688.64
Tenth " 82 " ....@ 56.49			4,632.18
Eleventh " 43 " ....@ 40.77			1,753.11
Twelfth " 217 " ....@ 26.12			5,668.04
Thirt'nth " 466 " ....@ 12.53			5,838.98
1415 shares.			99,205.17
Paid in advance, Dues..... 19.00			
" " Interest ., 12.35			31.35
Unearned Premium on 207 shares.			1,904.69
Due T. C. Hunter (deposit for loan)			550.95
" W. H. Warder (for withdr'n st'k)			1,587.86
Undivided fractions..............			1.85
			103,241.87

continued prosperity can scarcely be expected by either individuals or associations.

The end of the year having come, it is now the duty of the auditors to make a careful overhauling of the books of the secretary and treasurer, and make their report. As a specimen report, the Fourteenth Annual Report of a Philadelphia association (see previous page) illustrates in a very striking manner many of the points I have presented herein.

It will be worth while, perhaps, to call attention to some of the more salient features.

Among the "receipts" will be found rents from various properties, as also sales, and among the "disbursements" some for account of these same properties.

These pieces of real estate were some that had, at various times, to be bought in to prevent worse loss.

There was at time of previous report over eleven thousand dollars on hand, showing that during 1882 the demand for money was considerably less than the supply.

Their Profit and Loss account shows a gain in disposing of some properties, and a loss on others, though these gains may have arisen from a judicious charging off against Profit and Loss, in former years, sums representing depreciation in value of any that seemed to demand it. This paring down of assets is a necessary part of the economic working of a really sound building association, as well as of any other corporation.

Their mode of ascertaining the values of shares in the different series is also worthy of careful scrutiny, though there is room for diversity of opinion as to the exact justice as between the series. However, it is a very good illustration of its kind, and, perhaps, in the long run is as equitable as any. It has stood the test of giving satisfaction to a large number of members for fourteen years, during which time two series have run out, and a third nearly so. It will also be noticed that this three series has been running eleven years, and will require three more months to complete it. The fourth series has a little more value ($173.05) than the third had at the last report ($170.69), so that this year, if as good as 1883, will close it out. It will also show that they "deduct for contingencies," so that if a member wants to withdraw before it runs out he has to pay a little something for the privilege, which deduction is explained as being based upon 10% of the net gain of each share during the year.

R. B. Keys.

TALE OF A BLOTTER.

" Poor boy! he had no one to defend him! I wonder if a blotter has such a thing as a heart? They say the heart does half of the thinking. I think and think all day long; all night, too. Humph! it's night all of the time now to me. I don't understand why that chap with pointed shoes and diamond stud threw me into this cupboard! Surely I wasn't inky enough to be entirely worthless. He only used me once. Then, he tossed me in here. I don't understand it. But I do wish someone would take me away from this dark place. Ugh! the spiders and mice have a fine time in here. They romp and cut up all day long; oh, what a fool I am! I go on talking about days, when it is night, nothing but night to me all of the time. I know I could clear up that mystery if some one would only take me out of this black place and examine me. Dear me! the door of this musty, old cupboard will never be opened. The fellow in peaked shoes and diamond stud made a big mistake when he put me in here. I'll turn against him yet; oh, I'll make him smart for—sending that poor boy to prison. How I pitied that boy. I used to hear him tell about his widowed mother and lame sister. He said they depended upon him for bread. I wonder what they'll do now? He can't work and earn money in prison. I know they, the members of the firm, were hard with him. However, that pretty fellow in peaked shoes and diamond stud almost, aye! *did* make them believe that the boy was guilty. Wait; when I do come out I'll make the villain smart. I'll pay him off for sending the boy to prison. Poor widowed mother and lame sister! Keep up stout hearts! I will stand by you; I will lift the burden from your souls, and bring sunshine again. I know it is hard for you; but the rod of affliction shall not rest much longer upon you both. The time will come, and soon too, when I shall give back to you the noble boy who suffers for what another did. How the guilty cur, the pretty fellow in peaked shoes and diamond stud quivered as he pressed me upon that page covered with the firm's name. He knew he was guilty; but he made the one great mistake of his life when he tossed me in here. If he had destroyed me, he would have been safe. He didn't, though. That proves to me that a merciful Providence watches over the weak.

Hello! someone's coming. What now! Ah!—thank Heaven! I'm out of *that* dark nest. Why, it's the eldest member of the firm. Ah! see how he examines me; how he calls the other member of the firm. They both are now examining me closely. Here comes an officer. They send him after the villain. Yes; you *were* hard with the poor boy.

You can say that over and over again, but it will not bring back the hours, days, and weeks he's passed in the lonesome prison. I wonder if you rich old chaps have had a thought for the widowed mother and lame sister? No; money, money, money; you live by money, you'll die by money; you can't take any money with you, though. Why don't that officer come back? He's been gone ten minutes—oh! here he comes with the pretty fellow in peaked shoes and diamond stud. They ask him if he's ever seen *me* before? See how his coward conscience smites him! His eyes seem ready to fall from their sockets; his face flushes red, then turns pale as marble. And now, the beads of sweat come out upon his brow, and he falters. But he's lost. They have read him through and through. They know his handwriting. *I* am the proof! Oh, so glad I am to prove him to be the guilty one, and not the poor boy in prison.

Hello! here I am in a nice frame upon the wall. No more lonely hours in the black hole with mice and spiders. There they stand, the boy, the poor boy just from the horrible prison a few days since. His arms are about the widowed mother and lame sister. He points toward me, and says, "*That saved me.*"

And the pretty fellow who wore peaked shoes and diamond stud—he's over on the Island now, breaking stones."

H. S. Keller.

PUBLIC MONEYS AND ACCOUNTS.

FOURTH ARTICLE.

GENERAL RECEIPTS OF CITY TREASURER.— *Continued.*

In the preceding (January number) was shown the form of a receipt for taxes to be used by the collector or treasurer of a city Government. With the stubs of such receipts forming an exact account of money received on account of taxes, it is a simple routine for the collector to write up his book of cash receipts after the hour for closing his doors. As the stubs are taken from the book they are entered, according to their order of number, consecutively, in the Register of Cash Receipts. (See pages 6 and 7.) First, the name or description of property, and then amounts in the columns under the heading "Receipts from Collection of Current Taxes." When all the stubs have been properly entered, the columns are footed and the cash counted to see that it corresponds with what is called for. The stubs are

TREASURER'S WARRANT REGISTER, FOR THE YEAR 18

Date.	No.	City Fund.	School Fund.	Poor Fund.	Highway Fund.	Lamp Fund.	Water Stock Fund.	Water Fund.	Public Debt Fund.	Special Fund.	Total.

filed away in such a manner as to form vouchers for the transactions. A good plan is that of having them numbered, and then if filed consecutively it will be found that they are ready for reference when needed. In case they are numbered, it would be necessary to add to the form of Cash Register a column for entering the number of each voucher.

In passing to a description of the Register of Cash Disbursements, I will state that the forms given have their objections as well as their advantages. The chief objection is that of size. A large book, and one having as many columns as these show must be large, is cumbersome and unwieldy. An improvement may be suggested. Instead of trying to concentrate all cash receipts into one book, and have that columnarized so as to save labor in posting and rewriting, there could be two or three smaller books. Instead of using a large book, such as these cash registers, I would advocate the introduction of several smaller ones. In the case of the Register of Cash Receipts, as shown on pages 6 and 7, January number, I would use three books instead of one. One book for "Receipts from collections of Current Taxes," another for "Redemption of Property sold for Taxes" and "Receipts account of Returned Taxes from City Attorney," and the third for "Re-

ceipts from Chamberlain" and "Miscellaneous Receipts." The first-named of the three books would be mostly used during the time for collection of current taxes. At this period there would be comparatively few entries in either of the other books, and after the time for adding the penalty to unpaid taxes this book of current taxes would be but little used. Through dividing the one book into three parts all the space would be economized, as one set of columns would not be filled up, while the other two were comparatively blank. This will apply to the form here given for the Register of Cash Disbursements.

In recording disbursements, the treasurer's work may be systematized and materially reduced by the use of a columnar ruled book, entitled, "Treasurer's Warrant Register." This is a record of warrants drawn on the treasurer, entered in the order of their payment. In the above illustration the funds upon which warrants are to be recorded as drawn are the more common titles found in city treasurers' accounts. The illustration is introduced more especially to explain general principles than to demonstrate any special feature. The Register, as will be seen, serves not only as a record of disbursements, but also as a ledger, at least as far as an account of the general funds is required.

S. R. H.

Known only to many as an appendage of England the name of India seldom suggests those principles and arts of life which in the West form the basis of modern civilization. Manufactures and trades are tacitly assumed in the West to be the peculiar heritage of the European and the American. Not a few claim them as the heaven-born gifts of the Anglo-Saxon. The people of the East it is generally thought in this part of the world have not been trained in the arts of commerce. The sages of India, some imagine, worked in the field or with the herd, and went clad in bark or rudest cloth; that the masses were half-naked and poorly sheltered; and that the land was· devoid of towns and cities where art struggled to help human curiosity. The old Brahmins it is supposed waited for Western enterprise to teach them the use of hands and brains in the conduct of affairs.

But India from the earliest days of history was a trading country. In its active intercourse with Europe in ancient and mediæval days it stands in strong contrast with the equally fertile empire of China, with the Arabian, or the Malayan peninsulas. The quick genius of its people, even more than its natural wealth and extensive seaboard, distinguish the land of the Hindoos from other Asiatic countries. Ancient Rome imported fine muslins from Bengal, and the Greek word for cotton (*sindou*) is the same as Sind or Ind. Philology has also proved that Solomon of Judah sent his merchant vessels to fetch fresh cargoes from the western shores of Hindostan. The first calico was printed in Calicut, on .the Malabar Coas: of India. The brilliant mediæval republics of Italy calculated to no small extent on the co-operation of Hindoo traders and manufacturers in acquiring their wealth in the markets of Europe. The high prosperity of the Portuguese and the Dutch stimulated these nations to seek Hindoo skill and industry in building up their commercial supremacy. Spices, drugs, dyes, rare woods, silk and cotton, gold and silver. were the temptations which allured to India adventurers from all parts of the world.

After the discovery of the passage round the Cape of Good Hope, in one of the attempts of which Columbus caught a glimpse of another unknown land, the European traders of the sixteenth century began to flock to the Indian coasts, finding there a state of commercial activity altogether unsurpassed in their own lands. In architecture and luxuries, in affluence and comfort of life, in the briskness and splendor of cities, in the conveniences of marts and fairs, the people of India were unrivaled. It was not till England began to call brute force and physical violence to aid in adjusting the relations of fair trade, and, incited by motives other than those of pure commerce, began to lay the hand of monopoly and absolute possession on the Indian soil, that a pall of inactivity has spread silence over the life of the country, and brought the tide of India to its lowest ebb.

It is true that India may be strictly described as an agricultural rather than a manufacturing country, yet not an insignificant portion of the population make their living by occupations requiring manual dexterity, or knowledge of arts, or combination of interests and organizing skill. There are no swarming hives of industry to compare with the factory centres of Lancashire or New England; nor is there a large. mining population living under the soil. India has not reached the modern stage of industrial development, which is based upon the use of coal and the discoveries of physical science. But it is rich in a great variety of the arts of civilized life, which employ skill of hand, or ingenuity of brain, or artistic taste. And the business methods throughout the country range from the simple rural economy of the interior village to the transactions of the most complicated trade-guilds of the seaport towns.

The *village system* of India, with its institution of caste, forms the original framework as well as the mainspring of the entire economic and social life of the people. It is necessary to note this fact, and that among the Hindoos economic relations and social morals go hand in hand, and are intimately blended. Each village and town in the country is an independent community, with a separate existence of its own, with its own peculiar interests, and having little more to do with the central Government than the payment of the annual revenue. Changes of government, rise and fall of empires, political revolutions, have swept over the face of the country without affecting the village policy of the people, or altering their social and domestic habits. A panic in one part of the country affects only those in the immediate vicinity. Religion, custom, and the ancient literature supply the band of union, all three of which have been handed down from the early fathers.

This village system is based upon division of labor, quite as much as upon hereditary caste. The organization and needs of Hindoo society demand that the necessary arts of daily life shall be practised in every village or community. The weaver, the potter, the brazier, the goldsmith, the blacksmith, the oil-presser, the shoemaker, just as well as the priest, the physician, and the general dealer, are each integral members of a community as well as inheritors of a family occupation. Our manufactures are thus all essentially domestic industries. The workman works with his own tools, at his own house in the paternal village. He is his own employer, and no keen-sighted capitalist is allowed to step in to make him a tool and a slave, or leave him only a remnant of his earnings. On the one hand, he has always a secure market for his wares; and on the other, his patrons have a guarantee that his trade shall be well learned. Simplicity of life and permanence of employment are thus happily combined with a high degree of excel-lence in design and honesty of execution. The shoemaker works at his leather with the same love and fidelity as the painter or the poet at their respective vocations. One half of his energies is not fretted away against the greed of the unscrupulous capitalist, nor the other half spent in doing his work ill, all the time vainly struggling to alter and improve his condition.

An overcrowded village relieves itself by the migration of bands composed of sufficient members of all the different classes or castes of the community to rear a settlement on a different spot. But there is another class of colonies scattered through the country, which are formed by skilled workmen who are noted for some speciality in their respective professions. Leaving their less ambitious brethren to minister to the ordinary needs of the paternal village, they settle in suitable localities to ply in the higher excellencies of their arts. The holy city of Benares has thus been made famous for its artistic braziery; and metal utensils being acceptable articles of gifts as well as valuable for use, the Benares coppersmiths are a thriving body. Similarly, the cotton looms of Dacca and Nuddea, in Bengal, turn out the best muslins, whilst Moorshevabad carries the palm in silk-weaving. The leather-workers of Cawnpore and Delhi supply the rich with embroidered harness and gilded shoes; and Monghyr blacksmiths have furnished northern India for centuries with firearms. The rule, however, that each producer is his own employer, and exhibits his goods side by side with those of his brother artisan, prevailed all through.

The pride and display of the rival kingdoms into which the country was, before the British advent, divided, gave birth to many arts of luxury which have not yet been entirely forgotten in the decaying capitals. Ivory-carving, the making of gold lace, and such other accomplishments, have not yet seen their last days.

The downfall, however, of the native courts deprived the skilled workmen of their chief market; while, on the other hand, the English capitalist has enlisted in his service forces of nature against which the village artisans in vain struggle to compete. The fortunes of India are now bound up with those of a country whose manufacturing interest depends upon a large export trade. There are no bars at the ports of British India for the protection of indigenous manufactures, and before the unrestricted strides of the giant princes of Manchester the fugitive native weaver exchanges his loom for the unaccustomed plough, and sits down to die in the first season of drought. Political economy, judging by the single test of cheapness, may rejoice at the result; but the philosopher will regret the increasing uniformity of social conditions, with a few billionaires and a mass of pauper slaves, while the loss to the world of numerous artistic industries can never be restored.

One of the earliest results of British rule in India was the growth of great mercantile towns. In the long list of races who have ruled the splendid empire it was reserved for the islanders of Great Britain to substitute the roar and din of commercial cities where the Hindoos had built their temples, the Musselman had raised palaces and tombstones, the Mahrattas their forts, and the Portuguese had followed with cross-crowned steeples. The older cities of India were either seats of royal courts, or resting-places of departed saints, where pilgrims flock from year to year and day to day. A commercial centre must grow of itself, and cannot be called suddenly into existence by the fiat of the wisest autocrat. It is in this difficult enterprise that the British in India have succeeded, after the Portuguese, the Dutch, and the French had successively failed. Still, however, so intimately is the village commune blended with the social economy of the people that the urban population forms a very small percentage of the whole. According to the report of the Registrar-general upon

the English census of 1871, "Any density of a large country approaching two hundred to a square mile implies mines, manufactures, or the industry of cities." But in India a density of thrice this limit is often attained throughout large districts entirely dependent upon agriculture. The 139 largest towns of British India represent, according to the census of 1871, in the aggregate of their population, less than four and one-half per cent. of the total; whereas the thirty-four principal towns in England and Wales showed an aggregate which was equal to thirty-two per cent. of the whole.

But the so-called "stationary stage" of Indian civilization (according to political economists of the Mill school) has disappeared; and there are perceptible throughout the country unmistakable signs of new conditions of supply and demand which are to rule its industrial capabilities. The Hindoo cultivator of the interior is beginning to learn to be keenly alive to the significance of each new variation in the mercantile atmosphere of the cities and ports.

Calcutta, Bombay, Gujerat, Karachi, and Rangoon are the principal outlets of the superfluous produce of India. The natural value of these seaports has been permanently confirmed and increased by construction of the main lines of railway communication. Trunk roads, rivers, and canals are also utilized to the purpose of transit from the centres of production to the sea-board, though much has yet to be done in this respect. The country sells more to foreign nations than it has to buy from them, and yet, strangely enough, the masses are becoming more and more indigent every day. The money of the people goes to fatten capitalists, office-holders, hangers-on, and parasites of other descriptions.

Amrita Lal Roy.

[*To be continued.*]

ANNUITIES.

In the general meaning of the word, annuities are fixed sums of money paid yearly for a consideration, either for a term of years or in perpetuity. Under this definition interest on notes or bonds are annuities. The different kinds of annuities which may exist are so numerous we cannot undertake to define them, but will confine ourselves to noticing such as are known as life annuities. In this country such are often established by a testator in his will, who desires to provide for parties of whose judgment or wisdom in the management of monetary affairs he may have doubt. But more especially shall we call attention to such as are erected by the payment of moneys to an incorporated institution.

We will suppose that A, having a sufficiency of this world's goods, and knowing that riches often take to themselves wings, desires to secure an income sufficient to meet his ordinary expenses in case all other resources fail. He at once pays into some incorporated company authorized to sell annuities, in whose soundness he has confidence, such a sum as they require, with an agreement on their part to pay to him yearly, during his lifetime, a certain amount. It will be readily seen that many factors enter into the calculation of annuities. On the one hand, there is the amount of interest the company can obtain for the money paid in, and, on the other, there are the age and state of health of the depositor. In some respects the same questions arise as in life insurance, and tables have been constructed to facilitate the calculations.

We append a table from the "Dictionary of Commerce," showing what amount must be paid at different ages to insure the payment of one hundred dollars a year during the life of the payer, calculated on the basis of interest at five per cent.

25	$1,512
30	1,453
35	1,385
40	1,307
45	1,216
50	1,112
55	995
60	866
65	732

Deferred annuities are such as commence a given number of years after the payment of the money, and continued during the life of the payer. These are purchased by those whose present income is more than they need, but who desire to prepare for possible adversity while they may.

Annuities on joint lives are sometimes purchased by husband and wife, payable until the death of the last surviving.

Annuities are less commonly purchased in this country than they would be had persons more confidence in the stability of the institutions selling them. Some of the European governments sell small annuities through their post-offices and savings-banks.

The interest on the National debt of England may be properly called a perpetual annuity that may be transmitted from one generation to another so long as the Government exists, for there is small probability that the principal will ever be paid. This, however, does not serve the purpose contemplated by annuities, as they are generally understood, in which it is expected that he of average life will receive back the amount he pays, with the accruing interest, less a fair amount as compensation for the corporation in keeping the accounts.

There are many classes in our country who could invest in a sound annuity company with advantage. Doubtless we all know people who are, for various reasons, unable to do much toward earning their own living, but who, fortunately, have sufficient property, the interest of which gives them a meagre support. They do not dare to draw on the capital, because that will lessen the annual interest, and they are really living in poverty while possessing wealth. Their capital, paid to an annuity company, would increase their yearly income and ensure them a continuance thereof during their lives, relieving them from the care of its management and the risk of losses by injudicious investment.

We have spoken of the want of confidence of our people in institutions that are authorized to sell annuities, but we see no reason why it should exist toward them more than toward any other investments; and our governments, both State and National, should take the utmost care to render deposits for annuities as nearly absolutely safe as possible. —*Phrenological Journal.*

PRACTICAL HINTS ON BOOK-KEEPING.*

I recognize the fact that I stand in the presence of book-keepers, cashiers and correspondents, sharpened by contact with the world, and matured and developed by experience; and I shall confine myself, during the time which I may occupy, to the making of such suggestions and the throwing out of such hints as have been prompted by the inaccuracies and imperfections met by me in the walks of business, and made by gentlemen filling acceptably to those who employ them positions of great responsibility.

At the outset it would be well for us thoroughly to understand one another as to the object of keeping books of account, and in such a presence as this I do not suppose that any two notions concerning the same will be found to exist. I hold, as has been forcibly observed by one of our Common Pleas judges, that the business man's books should be like the photographer's *camera obscura*, and should receive such a picture or record of what is doing, as a *camera* would receive of any object placed before it. As the photograph may be referred to in the future, so may the books, showing just what was done, for what purposes, and under what circumstances—all this being intelligible to a man of affairs without the presence of an interpreter to explain or to add to it. Entries should be made to show the present condition of the transaction, and should not include any circumstance, which it is expected, however confidently, may become a part of the same, the next, or any subsequent day. All of the record should be upon and within what are called and understood to be the books of account, whether they be principal or auxiliary. Papers or memorandums kept in the drawer, or carried in the pocket, and which are usually destroyed after the cash has been received

or paid, should not be made, nor will not be, by the careful and experienced book-keeper in recording business entrusted to his care.

Let me refer to the custom of exchanging promissory notes, which prevails to a greater or less degree in the business community, for the mutual accommodation of the parties to the transaction. I most earnestly urge upon your attention the necessity of recording the business done *just as it is done*, even though the record proposed may be opposed by the proprietor. His safety, no less than your reputation as a correct book-keeper, requires you not to pursue such a course; more especially is this necessary where the accommodation is exclusively on the one side, and where the liability upon the other side is the conditional liability which attaches to the indorser. Take, for instance, a case concerning which I was consulted within a day or two. A makes a note, and requests his friend B to indorse the same, and have it discounted at his, B's bank, for the purpose of giving A the proceeds. In such a case as this it is quite as important to have such entries made on the books as will show the character of the liability, as to show the other parts of the transaction. I recommended to my client to make an entry in his day-book, in which he would recite the transaction in such a way as to show clearly the relations between A and B, and from which he could post a debit to Bills-receivable account, and a credit to A's personal account. In the entry in the bill-book, I also advised that the fact that the transaction was made for the benefit and accommodation of A should be set forth, and that such an entry should be made in the cash-book as would discharge his Bills-receivable account for the note, and would charge A's account for the discount and for the

* A Lecture delivered before the Book-keepers' Association of Philadelphia, by THOMAS MAY PIERCE, March 3d, 1884.

Vol. VIII.—10

proceeds. You will observe that the books are now in a condition to receive any entry, easily and naturally, which the weakness of A at the time of the maturity of the note may occasion; for if the note should go to protest, the book-keeper would have but to charge back the note and the protest expenses to A's account, as in the case of any other account which had been previously closed by Bills-receivable.

Business men, I admit, are frequently sensitive on the subject of having transactions of a confidential character, and which are not connected with regular business paper, placed upon their books; but their safety, and for the books' sake, there should be made upon the books faithful records of what has been done, and no dependence should be placed upon memorandums which are kept for a while, and then destroyed.

This course I also urge the book-keeper to pursue in the case of an exchange of checks. If the exchange of checks does not involve the principle of a loan, but is an accommodation only in the respect of commanding the money at a more convenient point, as, for instance, a Chester manufacturer in Philadelphia, and desiring money himself, and having an ample supply to his credit in a bank in Chester, exchanges checks with a friend in Philadelphia — each check being dated the same day, and takes the check of his friend to his friend's Philadelphia bank and gets the needed money, a full entry of such a transaction, in the sense in which I am pressing upon your attention, could be made upon the stub of the check-book as an explanation why your check is drawn, and in your copy of your bank deposit is an explanation why the Chester check appears there. But if the essence or principle of a loan appears in the transaction, I would have it entered upon the cash-book, as well as upon the stub of the check-book, and in the copy of the deposit ticket. I do not suppose that it is necessary, for the information of many who are here, to say that if you take one's check to be used to-morrow that you should not accept it if dated to-morrow; but there may be some young members of our Association who have

not been as yet brought into contact with the disadvantages of accepting such a paper. The maker may not live until to-morrow. If you propose to give your check of to-day to a business friend, and have him return you the money to-morrow, the usual and the better course is to have him draw his check dated to-day, and accept your promise not to use it until to-morrow.

A kind of book-keeping which covers up and hides much that is done, and which requires the fullest investigation by one possessed of the largest experience and quickest perceptions, is, throwing transactions of this kind into a loan account in which the borrower is associated not only with other borrowers, but also with whatever lenders of money to you may be in existence. I would feel dissatisfied with myself if I failed to make use of the place to which your partiality and confidence have called me, to warn book-keepers from using such an account as a loan account, in which not only the identity of particular transactions is lost, but the individuality of those with whom you have made the transaction is sunk.

I have already anticipated one subject; but its importance is such, in my estimation, that even at the risk of repeating myself, I will call attention to it. It is that of preserving a copy of the deposit ticket which you send to bank with your deposit. I do not care to suggest to you to keep a special book into which to enter these copies, although I have met with such in several cases in which I have been professionally engaged; but I do very highly recommend the keeping of a copy of the deposit ticket, and respectfully suggest that it be copied on the stub of the check-book. The officers of the bank require us to write only the name of the drawee of the check or other paper deposited; but I would not only copy from the deposit ticket the name of the drawee, but I would also add, to the record of the same which I kept for my own use, the name of the maker, so that I could the more easily identify the check or draft deposited with the payment which had been made to me.

A short time since I was called into a

bank to take part in a discussion then going on among some of the officers of the bank, concerning the proper entries to be made in a certain case. I think it worth mentioning here, as it covers a subject of some importance. The bank had received in a deposit from one of its customers a sight draft, but had taken it for collection, and had not extended it into the money column with the other part of that day's deposit. The discussion arose as to the character of the entry that should be made by the book-keeper of the customer. It was contended, upon the one hand, that a sight draft was cash, and that the book-keeper should enter, on the debit side of his cash-book, this sight draft as money received from the drawee. Another contended that it was to be treated as a time draft, the drawee living at some distance, and some time necessarily being needed to hear from the draft. Another view was presented which I will not repeat, because I do not remember it with exactness. I have no hesitation in saying that there could be but one correct entry of the deposit of this draft, and that would be found on the stub of the draft-book, and the teller's entry in the bank-book. In due time it would be the duty of the book-keeper to request some action to be taken by the bank as to this draft which had been entered for collection, and if extended by the bank the book-keeper should add to his balance in bank on the stub of his check-book and increase his cash by so doing, and enter the same at that time upon his cash-book, and not until then. In case the bank would not, for sufficient reasons, extend the same, the matter would stand as a request for the payment of money which had not been complied with, and the books should present such a record.

But I will go further and change the case, and give you my views as to the changes required in the entry. Were the bank to accept the sight draft as cash, and extend it with the other part of the deposit, the book-keeper should certainly make the entry in the cash-book at once.

In settling the cash I would have the particulars of the balance on hand written on the face of the cash-book so clearly that each item could be identified. This practice has enabled me, in one or two cases in which I have been employed as an expert, to, trace with clearness and confidence monetary transactions. Another thought here suggests itself. It is, to enter receipts of money into a cash-book before you sign receipts, thus linking the act and the record of the act together, and avoiding mistakes occasioned by omissions of cash received. And, on the other hand, I suggest that if a bill is paid, particularly in money, that payment be entered into the cash-book before paying the same over to the collector.

A practice prevails, to what extent I know not, but I do know that to the least extent it is to be opposed, and we, as book-keepers, should set our faces resolutely against it — it is that of making use of the cash-book for other purposes than recording the cash received and the cash paid out. Many ledger results are produced by journalizing, through the cash-book, transactions in which no cash has passed either way. The least offensive form of this practice, and, perhaps, the simplest and most plausible transaction of this sort — the giving of a sight draft or order directly to the payee — I have seen entered into the cash-book on both debit and credit sides; crediting the drawee, and debiting the payee, although, as maker, cash was neither received nor paid out. But worse instances than this occur, particularly in the settlement of personal accounts, which are either discounted, or which may be the subject of a compromise. I object to such entries as make it appear that a debt of fifteen hundred dollars was paid entirely in cash, when there may have been by compromise a very large reduction, or by discounting a small amount thrown off the bill. I do not fancy breaking the entry of a transaction and dividing it between two books, as would be the case in such a transaction as this: A settles his account of fifteen hundred dollars by sending a fourteen hundred and twenty-five dollar check, and accepting from you a discount of five per cent., and entering into the cash-book the fourteen hundred and twenty-five dollars cash received, and into the day-book such an account of the matter as would cause A to receive credit for seventy-five dollars, and Discount account a debit for seventy-five dollars. I do not recommend this treatment, although I prefer it to the entry in the cash-book: to A, fifteen hundred dollars, and by discount, seventy-five dollars. That which I prefer would be made into a cash-book in which there is a discount column; then I would enter: to A, seventy-five dollars in the discount column, and fourteen hundred and twenty-five dollars in the cash column. A's account would show that there was but fourteen hundred and twenty-five dollars received by me in money, and the cash-book entry shows the transaction in its entirety. I would also recommend the cash-book containing a discount column for the case of Bills-receivable or Bills-payable discounted. But in the absence of this column I would prefer the entry in the cash-book: to Bills-payable or to Bills-receivable, as the case might be, for the face of the note, and by discount for the discount, to an entry made in both cash-book and day-book for the transaction.

I have no doubt that there are members present who are familiar with a plan which I will now propose, but which I name because there may be some present who have not met it.

Take the case of a jobbing-house, in which some of the members of the firm are successful salesmen, and to whom a small salary and an interest in the business is given, and the co-partnership lasts but for one year, and changes the next by some of the salesmen of the first year either drawing a different interest or none at all, or a new salesman being admitted to the firm. The plan is also useful in the case of a co-partnership for a period of years, in which the profits are divided differently year by year. Prior to dividing the profits in the proportions agreed upon, a certain percentage of the same is taken out or charged to the Profit and Loss account, and credited to a contingent fund for that year, out of which, or against which, losses of accounts made in that year are to be charged, as well as any unusual expenses in collecting them. In this way, the injustice that would otherwise arise by making men, who are not in the firm one year, but were in the succeeding year, bear any part of the loss arising from the failure to collect accounts of the preceding year, is avoided, as well as the injustice that would be done were the partners to remain the same, and the ratio of distribution were changed. For example, in 1881, A bought a bill of goods of a thousand dollars, the firm consisting of X, Y and Z, and dividing the profits equally, and the co-partnership continuing in 1882, but the profits divided thus: X one-half; Y and Z each one-fourth. If A did not pay his bill in 1881, and failed in 1882, and was unable to pay anything, it would be unjust to X to charge this account into Profit and Loss. Equity would require that it should be charged direct to the partners' account, each one-third, the proportion in which they participated in the profits in the year in which the account was created. Had there been, as I have suggested, and is usual in many houses, a portion of the profits of 1881 set over to the contingent fund, the loss would be chargeable to that contingent fund.

Still more manifest would the injustice be if X, who was in business in 1881, had gone out of business and W had taken his place, unless the contract between X and W had provided for such cases, and W had received compensation for the assumption of such disadvantages.

Another matter which our young book-keepers are apt to neglect is that of accounts charged into Profit and Loss. While the circumstances may be such as to make it the duty of the book-keeper so to close the account, he should preserve, in a list of suspended accounts, all such as have been closed into Profit and Loss, so that at any moment he may be able to show his employer the names and amounts that have thus been passed into the Profit and Loss account.

After closing the ledger, I suggest that it is quite as important to take off a second trial-balance as a check upon one's self and the correctness of one's work in making the closing entries, as it is to take off what is usually termed the trial-balance, but which, for the purpose of distinction, I speak of as the first trial-balance. If this second trial-balance is not taken off, it may produce much confusion, and impose much labor upon the book-keeper when he comes to close his ledger again. For if there should be a mistake which would be revealed by the second trial-balance, and which was not because such a trial-balance was not taken, it will appear on the next occasion of taking off the trial-balance, and may, before it is found, necessitate considerable extra work. Besides, if done immediately after the books are closed, the circumstances of the closing are not in any way connected with the business of the subsequent period, and they are much fresher and clearer in the mind of the book-keeper.

It occasions some book-keepers much perplexity to explain, particularly to an employer who is not a book-keeper, why his net capital appears upon the liability side of the second trial-balance. I will go a little further. I have heard a very philosophic, cultured and experienced, and popular author of a text-book on book-keeping, call this circumstance a paradox, and in what he calls an explanation of it he succeeded in enveloping it with no little mystery. If one will keep in mind that the books are the books of the business, and not of the business man, it will not be difficult to understand why capital invested in the business is due by the business to him who has invested it, and that the net capital embarked in the business should appear among the liabilities of the business as the amount due to him who has furnished it. The greatest difference between the business man's own account and accounts with third persons is, that accounts with third persons do not participate in the profits or losses of the venture, whereas the proprietor's account is credited for any profits that may be made, and is charged for any losses that may be sustained. To third parties the business and the proprietor constitute but one party, but in the relations of the business to the proprietor there are two parties. On the other hand, in case of adversity to such an extent as to produce insolvency, the amount of insolvency

will appear upon the debit or resource side in the second trial-balance. For the reason that the proprietor must pay into the business the amount of the insolvency to enable it to discharge its liabilities to third parties.

Another illustration: A loans you one thousand dollars, and you put it into the business and credit him for it. It is due to him no more than if you were to place one thousand dollars of your own money into the business; but you would be under the disadvantage, as compared with A, of not being able to get your money back until all other claims had been met, and for the reason that you would get more than your thousand dollars back in case of a prosperous condition of business.

Some little difference still exists as to what name to apply to the proprietor in writing the caption of his account in the ledger. There has come down to us by tradition the name of *Stock* to represent an individual proprietor. This may be, or may not be, an abbreviation of stockholder, but I am pleased to know that the tendency of the times is to use some other name for a proprietor's account. Stock account, while aged, always has the disadvantage of being liable to be associated with the stock of goods.

The present general usage seems to be to use the proprietor's own name, with, perhaps, the addition of the words *Capital account*, in order to distinguish it from an account kept with him, against which he is charged for the drafts made for personal expenses.

There are some business operations of such a character as to require the Expense account to be credited by an inventory before closing it. Take the case of a large manufacturing concern, which buys eight or ten thousand tons of coal in the summertime with the expectation that the amount will be sufficient to last until the next summer, and the books are closed on the 31st of January and contain no such account as Coal account, the coal having been charged to Expense account. It is very necessary that there should be an inventory taken of the coal on hand, and credited to the Expense account.

Again, suppose there is no account

kept for insurance, and the plant is large and the stock of raw material runs into the tens of thousands of dollars, necessitating an insurance of, say, from one to two hundred thousand dollars, which is placed in the fall of the year and the premiums paid for one year, and the books closed on the 31st of December, it would be very necessary to credit the Insurance account for the amount of premium paid for the time beyond the 1st of January, and that that amount should be brought down as a balance in the new Insurance account, or, in the new Expense account. There are other kinds of transactions involving the same principle, to which it may be readily applied.

It frequently happens that a payment in bulk is made to discharge a liability, which does not develope to its full proportions until a series of years shall have passed.

I will illustrate. A partner retired from a large jobbing-house, and arranged that he would withdraw his capital, which was quite large, in equal amounts, in three or four succeeding years, and he was to be allowed interest for that which remained. Afterwards, the remaining members of the firm agreed to pay him the interest at once, and the head of the house, who was quite noted for his exactness, devised entries to cover the case, and, being an intimate friend, discussed them with me and asked me to propose entries. As they contain a principle which is broad in its application, I will give them.

Cash, of course, was the creditor, and I made the current Interest account debtor for the interest due for the current year, say, 1879; interest account of 1880 for the interest accruing in 1880; Interest account of 1881 for its interest, and so on. When 1880 was reached in business, Interest account for 1880 was run into the then current Interest account; and when 1881 was reached, Interest account for 1881 was run into the then current Interest account, and so on. In this way, the Interest account of the year in which the payment was made was protected from undue charges, and the Interest account of succeeding years did not escape being charged with what properly belonged to them.

Of course, those before me thoroughly understand that when the footings of the two columns of the trial-balance are equal that the entire correctness of the books is not thereby proven. It is a very satisfactory condition of affairs, and is good as far as it goes; but there are two sides to the book-keeper's work, and his books may be correct by all the rules of the science, and yet the record may be an imperfect one. That is to say, his debts may be equal to his credits and yet one may be charged who is not in debt, and another may not be charged who is in debt to you.

Emphatically do I declare that the footings of the two columns of the trial-balance may be equal, and yet very grave errors exist. Mistakes may have been made in posting; but if the book-keeper made an entry upon the debit side in a wrong account when a debit of some kind should have been made, or make a credit in a wrong account when a credit in some account should have been made, a serious mistake would exist in two accounts, but it would not disturb the equality of the two columns of the trial-balance.

In general, mistakes in posting are not revealed by the trial-balance if proper amounts have been entered upon proper sides. Nor does the equality of the two columns of a trial-balance insure the correctness of our journalizing. The determination of the different debits and credits growing out of a transaction may be very bunglingly, awkwardly, incorrectly done, but if the debits are made equal to the credits the trial-balance will not indicate any error.

Duplications of transactions if correctly duplicated, or omissions of transactions which were done, may happen, and the equality of the two columns of the trial-balance will not be disturbed. Then how important it is that the book-keeper should have some other check — some other plan by which to assure himself of his correctness than the mere taking off of a trial-balance. Such other checks are furnished by the comparison of the cash actually on hand with the balance shown by the trial-balance. The comparison of the sum total of the notes receivable on hand and the balance shown by

Bills-receivable account — and the comparison of the sum total of one's own unredeemed promissory notes and acceptances as shown by Bills-payable book, with the balance in Bills-payable account; but, besides these, a very great assistance to the book-keeper in checking his books is the habit, now well-nigh universal, of sending out statements of accounts on the first of each month, by which we learn whether or not the books of our customers agree with our books, and receiving from those to whom we are indebted similar statements, we learn how our account appears on the ledgers of those to whom we are indebted, and thus is instituted a comparison between our accounts as they appear on their books, and their accounts as they appear on our books.

I bring this matter of sending out monthly statements quite prominently before you, because it is of assistance to the book-keeper in testing the correctness of his books, as well as for its importance to the financial management of the business.

I am not here for the purpose of obtruding any arbitrary notions of my own upon your attention, but I cannot close these remarks without referring to the use, by book-keepers, of red ink. I would recommend, however, that its use should be regulated by a principle—that its use should mean something. It may be used to distinguish between entries which come into the ledger from other books, and entries which are made on the ledger by reason of something already on the ledger. It were better not to use it at all, than to use it without a definite object in view. If, as is sometimes the case, closing entries are journalized, under the principle which I have mentioned, such closing entries should not be made in red ink. If the closing entries are not journalized, but made for the first time on the face of the ledger, they would under such circumstances be made in red ink, and transfers of the same in black. I urge upon you the importance of having a well-defined object in the use of red ink, and drop the subject and bid you good night.

THE MANUFACTURE OF BESSEMER STEEL.

The conversion of crude iron ore into steel, a metal having greater tenacity and closeness of structure, and far better adapted to the manifold uses to which it may be put than any other compound, involves processes upon which some of the world's ablest minds have expended a vast amount of research in bringing them to their present state of perfection.

The process was invented by Sir Henry Bessemer, who, in 1856, made what is technically called his first "blow."

To comprehend this term "blow," we must refer to the chemical constituents of the pig-iron, and to its manufacture into steel.

The crude ore is first melted in the blast furnace, and the molten iron resulting therefrom moulded into pigs, so-called. These are bars about four inches square and three feet long,

They contain, besides the iron, about four per cent. of carbon, three per cent. of silicon, .03 per cent. of phosphorus, .03 per cent. of sulphur, and .05 per cent. of manganese. These proportions apply to the average Crown Point iron of New York State, which is much used in Eastern mills. The small per cent. of sulphur in this compound adds to its value, as a larger proportion causes the steel to crack in the subsequent processes of rolling and forging.

We will now follow this pig-iron as it comes from the blast furnaces until it emerges at the other end of the mill in the form of finished rails. This steel is peculiarly adapted to the manufacture of rails; it is also slowly coming into general use for structural purposes, and is eminently suitable wherever wrought iron has been commonly used.

Imagine now this pig-iron hoisted by a hydraulic elevator to the top of a large, four-storied, fire-proof building, and dumped into the cupolas. These cupolas are made of wrought iron, and lined throughout with fire-brick; in shape, they resemble a long-necked bottle, and range from five to eight feet in diameter, and from twenty to forty in height. After the iron, follows a quantity of coal, with a small amount of limestone, the latter serving to flux the resulting coalashes. These operations go on day and night until the accumulation of cinder in the bottom of the cupola is so great as to impede the free exit of the melted iron, which is "tapped" or drawn out from a small hole in the bottom of the cupola. The "slag," *i. e.,* the impurities, by virtue of the superior gravity of the molten iron, rises to the top, and is drawn off at intervals through a hole in the side. On certain days there may be observed issuing from this hole what appears to be wool, but which on closer examination is shown to be cinder in the form of minute fibres: this may be placed in the flame of a gas-jet without even scorching.

As this mineral wool is very largely used, a more minute explanation may be interesting. It is made in large quantities from the blast furnace slag at Stanhope, N. J., by substantially the following process: The molten slag is allowed to run through an orifice of very small diameter, coming in contact with a jet of steam and air at right angles to the stream of slag, which blows it into the shape of exceedingly minute threads, which give it the woolly appearance. It is mainly a silicate of magnesia combined with other silicates in small quantities. It is used largely for non-conducting covering for steampipes, and is the best non-conductor of heat known, next to hair felt.

It is used in large quantities by the New York Steam Heating Company, and also by the Pullman Car Company, for filling the spaces around the sides and bottom of their palace and sleeping cars, as, in addi ion to its non-conducting properties, it answers admirably to deaden the noise. Put within the walls of a house, it serves to keep the rats out, as they never burrow in or through it.

To return to the subject: While the cupolas are being filled, a vast amount of air is forced up through them, by means of which a ready and perfect combustion is maintained.

About fifteen thousand pounds of iron are "tapped out" at once, weighed, and run into the "converter"; it rushes in a thick, molten stream through long, iron troughs, cracking and sparkling in its passage like so much water. The sight is beautiful, especially at night, when each of the flying sparks seems to burst like a miniature rocket.

These "converters," of which there are two, arranged side by side, are huge egg-shaped vessels; each is supported by two trunnions or bearings, on which it is rotated in a vertical plane by enormous hydraulic power. One of the trunnions is hollow, and serves to transmit compressed air into the space between the real and false bottoms of the converter, the latter being made of firebrick or ground stone, through which two hundred small holes are pierced for the passage of the compressed air.

Let us now suppose the converter turned to a horizontal position, and about eight tons of molten iron run in. The acute observer would notice a boy off in a corner of the mill turning a wheel rapidly, which opens a valve through which the compressed air rushes into the converter; at the same time the boy gives a certain lever a jerk which slowly turns this immense vessel upright. As it rises, the glowing ore within emits a volume of sparks of beautiful prismatic hues, which take their flight through the air in a beautiful luminous curve, and strike the opposite wall, fifty feet away, like a violent storm of hail. This is a grand sight, and when once seen, not soon forgotten.

The converter maintains its upright position about fifteen minutes, during which time the compressed air is rushing through the small holes in the false bottom, up through the molten iron, making it boil like a seething cauldron, with a roar that is almost deafening, and enveloping every particle in an atmosphere of oxydizing material.

In this respect the process is analogous to puddling, with the radical difference, in the rate of stirring, between the power of a man and that of the innumerable jets of air propelled through the mass by powerful engines.

When the blowing has continued fifteen minutes, there appears to the trained eye a slight difference in the color of the flame. It now presents a blinding, dazzling appearance, and rushes up through the stack in a body as large as a barrel, and sixty feet in height, lighting up the whole building with an unearthly, yellowish splendor, so great that the finest print may be read with ease a hundred feet away. If the metal is very hot, occasionally a huge mass will be violently hurled forth, falling in a cloud of fiery spray. The instant this change appears, a man, who has been standing near the valves before mentioned, shoves a lever down, and the converter rotates again to a horizontal position, emitting a beautiful cloud of molten sparks.

The blast is shut off, and a quantity of melted spiegeleisen, usually about one-tenth the entire mass of iron in the converter, is run into the metal, which has become partially oxydized. This spiegeleisen is a pig-iron containing a large per cent. of manganese and carbon. It takes up the oxygen, and returns to the metal a proper amount of carbon. Without the latter ingredient, the metal would become wrought-iron, or a similar unmalleable product. The reaction produces a brilliant, greenish flame for a moment.

The manufacture is now finished, and the product is poured into another ladle, thence into moulds, each containing about a ton and a half of this—Bessemer Steel. At this stage a small amount is reserved for the chemist, who ascertains by analysis the ingredients of each "heat," and the proportions in which they exist.

The steel ingots, after partially cooling in the moulds, are taken to another part of the mill, slightly re-heated and passed through a series of grooves or rolls driven by an engine of eighteen hundred horse-power. The ingot grows smaller and longer at each successive groove, until, at last, it becomes a bar about eight inches square and twenty feet long. Immediately the bar passes to a pair of shears which cuts it into pieces each the length of a rail about as easily as a boy bites off a stick of taffy. Off go these pieces to other furnaces, where they are again slightly re-heated, and passed through other rollers; these gradually form this short, square bar into a perfect rail. This bends and curls up as it nears completion, like an immense, fiery serpent, reminding the observer of Moses's brazen serpent in the wilderness. In an instant the ends are sawed off, sending out another shower of sparks, and the rail glides noiselessly, apparently by an unseen power, away to cool. Afterward it is straightened, and holes are drilled through the ends. The rail is now ready for market while yet warm, not having been allowed to cool from the time it went into the cupolas as pig-iron until this moment.

It will readily be seen that, in order to produce the greatest amount in the least time, everything must be done at the proper moment, and each man must be fully alive to the necessity of doing his part well and quickly. Such a condition is obtained in fact by paying the workmen by the ton, thus giving him a sense of responsibility, since he knows that the greater the out-put the greater will be his wages.

Altogether, the manufacture of Bessemer steel is a wonderful process. By the ingenuity of man a valueless compound has been converted into a valuable product in a simple and effective manner, thanks to the indomitable will and tireless energy of Sir Henry Bessemer.

As a matter of interest, I may state that the twelve hours ending at 6 A. M., Friday, December 7, there were forty-five "heats" blown, aggregating three hundred and fifteen tons. There were rolled, in the same time, eleven hundred and fifty-two rails, all at the works of the Lackawanna Iron and Coal Company, Scranton, Pa.

It should also be added that these works are the largest in the United States, and the second largest in the world.—*Dio Lewis's Monthly.*

COUNTING–ROOM CHATS.

[We desire to say to the readers of this department that in cases where correspondents request that we shall give an answer to their inquiry, and where we find it possible to do so, we follow their question with our reply ; but, in doing this, it is not our intention or wish to forestall others who may feel disposed to offer their views or suggestions on the subject inquired about. In many instances we expect the reply given will serve merely as an introduction, depending on our readers to take upon themselves the work of supplying the chief part of such information as is sought by the correspondent.]

On Banking Accounts.
From ALFRED SYNOLD.

In the January number of the AMERICAN COUNTING-ROOM you extend an invitation to bank book-keepers. I will reply in the order you put the questions, hoping that others may be benefited by my remarks as much as I hope to receive, through the columns of your magazine, practical points from my colleagues.

The books used in our bank are the following : general journal ; general ledger ; deposit journal ; deposit ledger ; certificate of deposit ; draft, collection and discount registers ; tickler ; and a daily general ledger balance-book, a deposit ledger balance - book, offering-book, discount ledger, and a monthly statement-book. The latter is a book presenting the business of the concern in a collective form.

But to begin with the first book named—the general journal. In this I enter all remittances in detail ; total amount of loans and notes discounted each day (which amount I get from the discount register) ; all discount, notes and loans paid (these I get from the tickler, and they are entered in the journal separately, with the total amount extended) ; all collections paid, when they belong to any of our correspondents (if collections belong to others we remit for them direct, and our draft register in this case completes the entry made of the item in our collection register) ; then all drafts drawn on our correspondents and entered in the general journal, and all other transactions, such as exchange, interest, expense, etc., making the closing entry of the general journal the footing of the deposit journal, that is, the total amount of checks paid, and the total amount of deposits received. Now, as my general journal is opened each day by bringing forward the cash-balance of the preceding day, all that remains to be done is to foot my journal, take the debit from the credit side, and the balance received must agree with the cash on hand.

The next morning I post ; and, as I go along, I carry the new balance of each account into my "daily general ledger balance-book," filling up with the old balances such accounts as are not charged. When I have all posted, I foot my balance-book, and, if the work is correct, the debit column must show the same footings as the credit column. This book is so arranged as to show the business of one week on a double page.

The deposit journal contains all checks and certificates of deposit paid on the debit side, and all deposits received and certificates of deposits issued on the credit side. The book-keeper begins to enter up in the journal on the afternoon, and post to his ledger at the same time, but without striking the "balance" of the account posted, for the reason that more entries may be made to the same account before the bank closes. He marks such accounts with a narrow strip of paper, extending out on the top of the ledger, which enables him to know which accounts have been posted. By three o'clock he has completed his journal entries, and has posted all amounts. After footing his journal and handing the amounts to the general book-keeper (as indicated above), he takes his ledger and begins to strike the new balances of the accounts posted, leaving the slips of paper to project out on top of ledger. He gets through with this work about the time when cash is balanced. The balances of all the depositors are now ready for the next day's business, and can be referred to instantly. The next morning he takes all the accounts posted in the previous afternoon and marked by the extending slips, and finds the difference between the old and new balances, as described by the inclosed sample of my "test sheet." This completes the work on the deposit book until the afternoon, when he begins entering as described above.

Since using my test sheet, we do not find

necessary to keep a deposit ledger balance-book any longer; but our book-keeper still takes a statement of all accounts, once in a while, only to see, however, that it was unnecessary, as the statement "comes out first pop."

Before describing our auxiliary books, I will say now (I forgot it before) that our ledgers are of the balance system; the general ledger has one account to a page with the following columns: Dr., Cr., Dr. balance, Cr. balance; while the deposit ledger is some wider and having two accounts to a page, with a Dr., Cr., and balance column, together with a space for entering the checks in detail, the total of which is carried in the Dr. column. To discriminate the kind of balance in the deposit ledger we use red and black ink — the former for Dr. balances, and the latter for Cr. balances.

In reference to the certificate of deposit register it is needless to say anything, as they are pretty much the same everywhere — likewise the draft register. As to the collection register, I will say that this book is used in two ways: *first*, all collections brought in by our customers to be sent away for collection are entered there, giving the owner's name, on whom drawn, where sent, amount, date, time, etc.; *second*, all collections received from our correspondents or elsewhere, excepting sight drafts, are entered there, giving owner's name (in this case it is the party's name who sent the item), on whom drawn, date, time, when due; then the collection is carried to the "tickler," and entered there under the day it falls due. When it is paid to us, we mark it so in the tickler, and credit our correspondent, or remit for it, as the case may be. With sight drafts received for collection, we make no record at all, but use the letter accompanying it instead. After presenting the draft to the party on whom it is drawn, we mark on the letter how it was disposed of — whether paid or returned. If it is paid, and belongs to one of our correspondents, we place it to their credit; if it belongs to some other party, we remit for it, and state this on the letter received with the collection. The letter is then filed. Besides this record, our letter-copying book shows the disposal of *all* collections received.

In discounting a note or making a loan, it is first carried through the discount register, giving name of payer and sureties, amount, time, date, and when due; then it is entered in the "tickler" under the day it becomes due.

When it is paid it is marked so, stating the day when paid. The tickler is the book showing what paper falls due on each day of the year, and is arranged upon the diary system. Our tickler when open shows six days or one week (on a double page) commencing with Monday and ending with Saturday, thus presenting at a glance all paper falling due through the week.

The offering-book is used for recording all loans and discounts on the day they are offered, for the purpose of showing the directors what paper has been offered and have them pass upon it. The discount ledger is a ledger in which an account is kept with each borrower showing his indebtedness to the bank. By these means the officers of the bank are always informed as to the amount that each borrower owes the bank, which enables them to control the loans and discounts in a way preventing the loaning of too much money to one man.

As soon as practical, I shall try to make a few improvements (which I have now in view) in the books of our bank, and shall mention them, with your permission, in the columns of the AMERICAN COUNTING-ROOM. I have yet to remark about certifying checks that when we certify we make a memorandum check of the one certified. This memorandum check is handed to the book-keeper who has charge of the deposit books; he takes a note of it in the account of the party drawing the check. When this check is finally paid, it is charged up like any other check, and the memorandum destroyed. The proper way, however, to treat certified checks is, I should think, to charge the party with it as if it had been paid, and credit "certified checks" account; then, when it is paid, charge the latter. In this way, the treatment would be similar to the certificate of deposit account, which is also credited when a certificate is issued, and charged when it is paid.

Calculating Interest on Bonds.
From JOSEPH HARDCASTLE, New York.

The January number of the COUNTING-ROOM contained a Paper, by Mr. W. P. St. John, president of the Mercantile National Bank, of New York, advocating the conversion of the existing Government bonds into 2% bonds having twenty years to run.

In his calculation to show that the Government would be a gainer by exchanging fifteen years' currency, 6% bonds — the Government taking these bonds at 124, and issuing, in their place, twenty years' 2% bonds — his estimate is as follows:

(10,000 — face value of bonds — is taken to illustrate the subject; $9,000 or 90% for the corresponding circulation; and tax, 1% per annum on circulation.)

Present Government obligation is 15 years' interest, at 6%; *i. e.,* one year's interest on 10,000, or 600×15......................	9,000	
Less 15 years' tax on circulation: 1 year's tax on 9,000, at 1%, is 90 ; 15 years' tax..............	1,350	
		7,650
Face of bond, payable at end of 15 years.......................... ..	10,000	
Present total obligation to pay.... ..		17,650
Against premium to be paid on $10,000 bond, at 124 (*i. e.,* 24 on each 100).....................	2,400	
Twenty years' interest, at 2%.....	4,000	
Face of the bond at maturing (twenty years hence).........10,000		
		16,400
Net cash gain to the Government by the purchase and exchange.. ..		1,250

The meaning of the above calculation is, that the net disbursements by the Government for $10,000 of these 6% bonds during the fifteen years of their existence will be $17,650. Mr. St. John calls this amount the present total obligation. A present total obligation is a sum of money paid at the present time in lieu of a future obligation; and this, according to rates of exchange, he proposes: viz., 124 is $12,400.

Next, that the disbursements by the Government (the proposed exchange being made) after twenty years will be $16,400. And he draws the conclusion that the Government by the operation will gain $1,250.

This reasoning is analogous to the following: He has my note, at six months, for $1,000, and I offer him my note at twelve months instead for the same amount.

The obligation to pay the 6 months' note is $1,000.
      "   "   12   "   "

Therefore the exchange is equitable.

The only way to compare obligations is to see what each obligation is worth at the present time, and the use of simple interest in such cases is simply an absurdity.

Mr. St. John's calculation above can only be considered as a rough approximation, and, consequently, entirely unreliable. I will substitute the following in its place.

The nature of a bond is as follows:

First. The Government agrees to pay every, say, half year an annuity to the holder of the bond until redeemed.

Second. At the redemption of the bond the Government will pay its face value.

Third. Money being worth, say, 3% per annum, payable, say, half-yearly, the present value of annuity + the present value of the face, equals the present value of the bond, which will vary little from the market-value.

The calculations are too laborious without the use of tables. The tables I shall use are the Mutual Life Insurance Company's.

The Government will pay us $300 at the end of each half-year for thirty half-years.	
The present value of $1 each half-year for thirty half-years, interest being 1½% per half-year (considered the interpretation of 3% per annum), by tables is 24.0158.	
Present value of an annuity of $300 = 24.0158 × 300 =..............	7,204.74
The present value of $1, to be paid at the end of thirty half-years at 1½% per half-year, is .6398.	
The present value of face of bond equals .6398 × 10000...........	6,398.00
Present total obligation..........	13,602.74

Therefore $10,000 6% fifteen years' bonds, when they have just fifteen years to run, and money being worth exactly 3% per annum, will be worth $13,602.74, or they will be quoted at 136, unless there be some slight disturbing cause in the money market, and then the price will not vary much from 136.

Let us now consider the tax on circulation. The circulation corresponding to 10,000 bonds is $9,000, and 1% on this is $90 per annum, payable annually. The holder, being a national bank, has to pay the Government an annuity, at the end of every year for fifteen years, of $90. But the present value of an annuity of $1, payable annually for fifteen years at 3% per annum, by table is $11.9379.

Present value of tax equals 11.9379 × 90 = 1074.41
The difference between present obligation of Government, $13,602.74, to bank, and bank's present obligation, if purchasing fifteen years' privilege (1074.41), is 12528.33.

Or the exchange value, money being at 3%, should be 125.28 — say, 125¼, not 124.

Similarly with the 2% bonds. • $10,000 bonds, 2%s, will yield $100 half-yearly for forty half-years, money being at 3%, as before.

Present value of interest — 29.9158 × 100 = $2991.58
" face of bond — .5513 × 10000 — 5513.00

$8504.58

Or the $10,000 bonds are worth now (money at 3% per annum) only 8504.28, or they should be 15 below par.

Finally, by Mr. St. John's proposition the Government received 10,000 6's, present worth 13602.74

The Government pays for premium in cash 2400

And gives to banks the 2's, worth at present 8504.58 10904.58

Net gain of Government $2698.16

If I am wrong in the above calculation, it is in assuming 3% as the rate for money. It is about the rate per cent. the Government can borrow money at, as is evinced by the 3's being at par.

Yet the proposition of Mr. St. John is to take at par the 2% bonds, whose value I have shown to be 15 below par. This is justifiable, for the two following reasons:

First. There is a tendency of the rate per cent. falling lower, and bringing the 2's to par.

Second. In purchasing $10,000 6% 15-year bonds, the bank will have to pay at the rate of 136, or $13,600 — on depositing which with the Government the bank will be allowed a circulation of $9,000; *i. e.*, $4,600 will yield the bank only three per cent., and the $9,000, tax off, will yield, say, 2% in addition to what the bank can make out of the $9,000 in its usual business.

National Institute of Chartered Accountants and Book-keepers.

From HENRY KELLY, Philadelphia.

Carefully reviewing the position of accountants and book-keepers in this country, it has occurred to me that an immense amount of good could be done in the way of elevating the members of the profession by the formation of a National Institute of Accountants and Book-keepers, and it would, undoubtedly, greatly promote the object of the *societies now formed* throughout the country if the members thereof were incorporated as one body (this

could be done without in anyway interfering with beneficiary associations, which the national association would not be, at any rate from an insurance point of view), as besides other advantages. Such incorporation would be a *public recognition of the importance of the profession*, and would tend greatly to raise its character, and thus secure for the country the existence of a class of persons well qualified to be employed in the responsible and difficult duties often devolving upon public and private accountants and book-keepers. It would be desirable, if incorporation by charter were obtained, that such conditions should be laid down as would require for the admission to membership of persons NOW already following the profession, long actual experience, or else the passing of appropriate examinations under the supervision of the corporation.

That with respect to the admission to membership of persons *hereafter* desirous of entering into the profession, I would suggest that, subject to future determination by the council or governing body of the corporation, a strict system of examination should be established, at the termination of the applicant's service (at least three years) under an accountant or book-keeper member of this Institute; or, if he (the applicant) has graduated in any of the universities of the U. S. A. one year.

That the examination would (subject to future determination of the governing body of the corporation) be of such a character as to test the knowledge of the candidates, not only in book-keeping and accounts, but also in the principles of mercantile law, and any other subject that might be deemed consistent therewith.

I believe that such a system would have an educational effect of a highly beneficial kind.

It would be desirable to obtain authorization to annex to the names of members letters indicating their membership. That the council upon the report of the examiners should grant to every person who has satisfactorily passed the examination a certificate to that effect. I would suggest that the first entrance-fee be fixed at $10.

That from the time when the first by-laws, made under charter, come into operation, every member of the Institute should, as long as he continues to practice the profession, obtain from the council, in every year, reckoned from such day as the by-laws of the Institute from time to time prescribe, a certificate of mem-

bership, and for every such certificate pay to
the council, for the use of the Institute, such
sum as might be prescribed in that behalf by
the by-laws of the Institute, say, not exceeding $5.

That, if any person, whilst he is a member
of the Institute (1) violates any fundamental
rule of the Institute applicable to him; or (2)
is convicted of felony or misdemeanor, or is
finally declared by any Court of competent
jurisdiction to have committed any fraud; or
(3) is held by council on the complaint of any
member of the Institute or of any person aggrieved to have been guilty of any act or default discreditable to an accountant or book-
keeper; or (4) is adjudged bankrupt, or, individually or as partner, makes an assignment
for the benefit of his creditors, or under any
resolution of his, or under the order of a
Court, or under any deed or document, has
his estate placed in liquidation for the benefit
of creditors, or makes any arrangement for
payment of a composition to creditors; or (5)
fails to pay any subscription or other sum payable by him to the Institute, under the charter
or by-laws of the Institute, for six months
after the same has become due, he shall be
liable to be excluded from membership, or suspended for any period not exceeding two years
from membership, by a resolution of the
council passed at a meeting specially convened
for that purpose, with notice of the object, at
which meeting there shall be present not less
than twelve of the members of the council, and
for which exclusion or suspension not less than
three-fourths of those present and voting shall
vote, and the members having first had an opportunity of being heard. But any such exclusion or suspension may be at any time
revoked or modified by the council at a like
meeting by such a majority as aforesaid, subject to such terms and conditions (if any) as
the council think fit, and notice of any resolution for exclusion or suspension shall forewith
be sent to the person affected thereby.

Determining the Aggregate of Personal Debtors without Detailed Statement.

From H. J. CARR, Grand Rapids, Mich.

I don't know that I have any real exception
to take to the editorial answer in AMERICAN
COUNTING-ROOM, for February, to the question
of "Oriole" as to short method for determining the personal indebtedness due a concern

(Account-receivable, etc.); since I myself use
a method somewhat similar to that indicated. But it has occurred to me that, perhaps,
the answer given does not go quite far enough,
nor cover all the ground that may possibly
have been expected from the not too explicit
query. For instance, in case information is
wanted quickly regarding the outstandings due
from customers at some certain period, from
account-books where the special treatment
suggested in the said answer has not been applied, or where the data for such application
is not conveniently obtainable.

In such case I can conceive of a method of
arriving at the desired results with a minimum
of labor, and a closeness of approximation dependent on the general correctness of the
ledger-accounts. In fact, I frequently make
such a computation as a check on trial-balance
work, and find it very feasible and satisfactory.
In the average mercantile books, the accounts
with customers form by far the largest proportion of all the accounts on the ledger; in some
cases from ninety to ninety-five per cent.—the
only other accounts being the usual general or
representative accounts, with occasional special
ones, and a minimum of purchase (or creditor)
accounts. And full as usually the latter are
grouped together in one part of the ledger, or,
if scattered among the customers' accounts,
can be picked out with tolerable ease. So, then,
all that is necessary to do is to make a trial-
balance of all such accounts on the particular
ledger, *except those with customers*. Finding
from such partial trial-balance the net aggregate balance (a *credit* balance, of course) that
amount will and must, by the laws of double-
entry book-keeping, equal the aggregate (*debtor*) balance due the concern from the remaining accounts; *i. e.*, the sundry customers'
accounts. And if the books are exact and
correct, a trial-balance of such customers' accounts in detail will prove it.

So of any section of accounts in a ledger;
the aggregate balance of the remaining accounts in the ledger will equal the net balance
of that particular section or group.

"We all knew that before," every reader may
say, of course; but candidly and on careful
thought, is the *application* of the fact as I
have suggested usually made?

The final agreement of Balance-account (if
made) with the balance of Stock-account, as
in closing a set of double-entry books, is an
instance of common use, and in the same train

of application as that which I have attempted to set forth. But for all that, do book-keepers usually see that the same thing is applicable to customers' accounts on special calls, as well as at stated periods? If so, I have not been able to learn of it, nor am I aware of having ever seen in the text-books any such application of double-entry principles. Despite considerable study on my part, and sundry years of practical work, I did not grasp this idea fully until a couple of years ago. I attempted at that time, in connection with some remarks on reverse posting, to show its practical use, but the types did not act just "square," and, coupled with possibly a defective statement of the point I aimed to make, gave me reason to doubt if I was entirely successful. in making it clear. And, too, the editorial comment upon the same article was so expressed as to make the doubt almost a certainty. (BOOK-KEEPER, Vol. V., page 357.)

Theoretically, the same point may be covered by the formulas suggested by Col. C. E. Sprague, in his logical articles on "The Algebra of Accounts," which added so much interest to the first numbers of Vol. I. of THE BOOK-KEEPER; and wherein he states the fundamental (or balance-sheet) equation to be, "What I have $+$ what I trust $=$ what I owe $+$ what I am worth." ($H + T = O + X$.) From which, may be deducted (although not specifically so expressed by him, I think,) $X + O - H = T$; which gives the result I have sought to set forth.

So, too, though less in detail, from his Paper on "The Fundamental Theory of Accounts," read before the Business Educators' Association at their last session at Washington. Possibly the same idea might be dug out of Folsom's "Logic of Accounts," if one could live long enough.

In actual business, Capital accounts (X), together with the Resource accounts (H), are not especially numerous. Creditors' Accounts (O) may be more numerous in some instances; in others, are replaced by two only, as Bills-payable and Accounts-payable. But the foregoing, taken altogether, make a number far short of Customers' accounts (T). Hence the practical feasibility of making a trial-balance of $X + O - H$, for the purpose of ascertaining a net amount equaling the aggregate of the far more numerous (T) accounts; and the use of same in every-day work, which I have sought to indicate above.

A case in point. A party (Smith, we will call him,) is interested in a certain concern doing a pretty large credit business, and having accounts with customers (retail and wholesale, in both city and country,) to the number of 2,800 to 8,000. Smith is engaged actively in certain parts of the business, but knows little or nothing of the accounts, the books being kept under the direction of another partner, who also manages the finances and collections, etc., but who is overworked by the excess of detail and numerous accounts and the like, and finds it a difficult thing to "keep both ends up," as the saying is.

A little commercial flurry strikes that locality, and A B C & Co. all at once find it "hard sledding"; yet don't think it can be possibly necessary to "go under," as they are confident that the business has been profitable. The accountant-partner is full of worry and trouble, and not having kept up collections any too well is inclined to "weaken." For, owing to the large failures of others and to certain liabilities as indorsers, etc., an immediate conclusion must be made and course of action adopted accordingly; so he calls in the other partners for a "closet conference." Of course, the first thing asked of him is a statement of the liabilities and resources. It so happens that the concern owes but few open accounts for purchases—notes having been given in the majority of that class. So the Bills-payable account, with the few Creditor accounts, soon tell the liability story, added to the bank notices for protested indorsements, etc. As to assets, however, and especially the outstandings due from customers, the answer does not seem so easy. Owing to press of work, no trial-balance has been attempted for three or four months, nor has any data been retained from the last one to admit approximate figures by adding sales, etc., and deducting credits for the intervening months. True, the books are posted up to date as close as possible, but it is certain that no detailed statement or trial-balance, can be made under twenty-four to thirty-six hours; while the information sought is wanted at once.

With such information, and the approximate knowledge of the value of the stock on hand, which Smith fortunately has, some satisfactory conclusion can be reached. Furthermore, a party whose aid is hoped for is willing to accept a lump valuation of the stock, which he himself can estimate also, but is not so willing to act upon the same treatment applied to the Accounts-receivable. Smith has a friend outside, it seems, with whom he has counseled at times, and, as a forlorn hope, calls him in and states the case, and asks, under the circumstances above stated, if they can get at a close, possibly exact, aggregate of the amount on their books due from customers? The books themselves are known to be worthy of confidence, and their showing correct, if that showing can only be arrived quickly as the case now demands. Easy enough, says Mr. Friend. Make a trial-balance of your representative accounts, together with all the accounts with creditors, which you say are not numerous. In other words, a trial-balance of every account in your ledger, *except* those with your customers; the net of that sectional trial-balance will be an amount equal to the aggregate which you have outstanding due from customers up to the date to which the books are written up. Happy thought! The computation is soon made, and the showing (barring the necessary allowances for doubtful debts, etc.,) is good; the margin of assets over liabilities meets the expectation of all parties, the despondent partner takes new courage, the asked-for financial aid is even more freely tendered upon showing, and A B C & Co. are speedily "out of the woods."

At the same time it is to be hoped that Mr. "Friend" took occasion to hint pretty forcibly that in the future their books would be *better kept*, and, to *more purpose*, if so arranged that just such information as was wanted in this instance might be given by them at any and all times without the need of special and extraordinary occasions to call forth such a flurry as that through which they had just passed.

Applying this to the "Balance-sheet of Y— and Z--," as given on page 19, Vol. I., let us see the result :

Y's capital...........	3,857.14	
Z's capital...........	5,142.86	9,000.00 = X.
P — (Due him)......	2,374.64	
O — "	3,273.29	
Bills-pay. outstand'g.	352.07	
		6,000.00 = O.
		15,000.00 = X + O.
Cash on hand........	2,344.25	
Merchandise on hand	5,655.75	
Real estate on hand..	2,000.00	
		10,000.00 = H.
	Net,	5,000.00 = T — (X + O — H)
U — Due from him...	3,999.23	
V — " " ...	109.32	
W — " " ...	891.45	5,000.00 = T — (X + O — H)

The Seven-Account System.
From W. H. H. Valentine, Chicago.

Permit me a few words in reply to "Inquirer." I have examined Parts I. and II. of a work entitled "The Seven-Account System of Book-keeping, by C. O. E. Matthern, Chicago," as claimed on the title-page, "introducing an original system of recording mercantile transactions under seven accounts, for the purpose of keeping constantly in view the condition or status of the business, without considering in detail the individual accounts." The seven accounts are as follows: Stock, Creditors, Merchandise, Expense, Customers, Cash, and Bank. Each of the seven has numerous factors, exhibited under distinct titles as a continuation of the same ledger.

The work issued in 1876 has not met a ready sale; and hence, no doubt, the non-appearance of Parts III. and IV. as promised. The author has an excellent central idea—but original only in name and in the manner of elucidation. In these two respects no thoughtful commercial teacher or practicing accountant, upon a careful examination of the work will dispute the author's claim to originality. The adoption of precisely seven accounts, through which to readily show the condition of the business, is purely arbitrary, and cannot be reasonably well adapted to general use. It would however, be possible to limit the number to two accounts—one for each of the two general classes. But this would also be of doubtful utility. The author of such a method might well term it "The Two-Account System of Book-keeping," and lay just claim to originality in name. But should explanations be made under an impression that the more obscurity the more philosophy, and the more philosophy the better the book, he would in this direction find the field already occupied.

In planning a system of record adapted to any business of considerable extent, and especially if involving many personal accounts, the aim should be to so arrange the books of original entry that all essential facts for readily showing the condition of the business, through a balance-sheet or equivalent forms, may appear on the ledger in the fewest accounts possible to an intelligent exhibit, and with the least possible labor in posting. This requires the use of special columns.

The chief aim should be to condense, under one title in the ledger, the personal accounts receivable; and under one title the personal accounts payable. These will be posted from the footings of the special columns kept for each class of personal accounts in the book or books from which the posting is done.

Each of the two distinct classes of personal accounts should then have a separate ledger, in which the individual accounts will appear: in the one, the Accounts-receivable; in the other, the Accounts-payable.

In this way the personal accounts are of easy access, and may be readily referred to for purposes of statements, etc., or taken to a daily or monthly abstract.

For the benefit of such of your readers as may desire to follow up the subject, the new Bryant & Stratton "Counting-House Book-keeping," (Set Eleven,) gives a most comprehensive and complete exposition of this system.

From O. E. MATTHERN, Chicago, Ill.

I am honored by your notice in the February issue of your valuable journal relative to a "Seven-account System Book-keeper," requesting a Mr. Seven-account System to arise and explain. Being the author of this system, I suppose your request solicits a reply from me direct; consequently, I take the liberty to acquaint all interested in the science of accounting with a few points relative to this new method of book-keeping thus freely tendered, for which accept thanks. You will also please find inclosed order for a yearly subscription to your magazine.

In reply to your first statement, namely, "One would naturally suppose that a Seven-account System Book-keeper was one who could keep *only* seven accounts," I remark that the understanding would have been correctly conveyed had it been said, "was one who kept seven *additional* accounts."

In reply to your second statement, namely, what is the special use of the word "system," it should have said, "is one who carries all transactions into one or another of seven accounts at certain intervals."

The Seven-account System of Book-keeping is a method of double-entry; by which all Ledger accounts are systematically classified for continual representation, monthly or daily, by seven fundamental accounts in preference to, and in advance of, taking a double-entry trial-balance. The seven accounts are: Capital ac-

count, Creditors' account, Merchandise account, Expense account, Customers' account, Cash and Bank account. These accounts balance by themselves, and control *all other* accounts in classes, namely, Capital class, Creditors' class, Expense class, and Customers' class, showing the summary of each class in advance, and thereby locating mistakes to each class separately.

The object of the system is two-fold: that is, to show two results from the same cause, both to be alike in the end, but arrived at in two different ways, one showing the result in advance of what the other is to end with.

The above results are arrived at from the same entry, which, in the first place, "according to double-entry," involves a debit or credit to one and another account, and in the second place by extending the amount into a proper column gives a debit and a credit to one and another of the seven principal accounts in the ledger, carried to them in total of the column at the end of the month, or daily, if desired, in a daily balance-book for that purpose.

I have mailed you various circulars on the subject, and beg to be excused if my explanation overtaxes your kind patience. Again accept thanks for bringing the subject before your patrons.

Checking Accounts.

From PACIFIC.

No doubt many readers will pass this article unnoticed, or at least unread, because its heading indicates that it relates to what many may consider a subject of slight importance. Everyone, doubtless, thinks it quite a simple matter to check an account, though all will agree that it is a tedious affair where the items are many and varied. But there is more in a check-mark than a great many have any idea of.

Has it never happened to you that, after carefully checking a very long account, you have found yourself unable to prove the balance of the checked items in your books with the balance of the statement checked? Doubtless it has so happened to everyone who has work of this kind to do.

If the amount of your difference should be, say, $100, and there are many items in your account of a like amount, you will be compelled to re-check all such items from the statement in order to discover the amount you may have checked in error. And even then are you certain to disclose the mistake? Most certainly not, if you use the ordinary check, thus: √

This simply has no value whatever to my mind; for as soon as it is dry it is quite the same as all the other checks, and you cannot *verify it* without great trouble, which becomes more of a task as the item so checked grows older.

It is often the case that it is desirable, and sometimes absolutely necessary, to know the date upon which your correspondent charged or credited you for a certain item. Perhaps a long time has elapsed since the transaction took place, and though you can find the item on your books with little difficulty, can you tell, from your check-mark, the date of entry on your correspondent's account? Certainly not, if you simply check as already shown (√).

I have had considerable of this work to do, and long since discontinued the use of this *useless* check-mark by substituting, alongside of the item checked, the day, month and year of entry on statement, thus enabling me to instantly verify any item so checked.

Suppose I check from statement, January 10th, 1884. I would mark item on my book thus: 1/10/84; and so on, in rotation, for the months, days, and years, thus: Mar. 16/83 — 3/16/83; Dec. 19/82 — 12/19/82. This takes but little time, and it in many ways repays a thousand fold the very trifling extra time needed. Try it and see.

"Wear and Tear."
From E. P. PALMER, Stockton, Cal.

In your February issue my attention was called to the inquiry of your Philadelphia correspondent as to "wear and tear" on machinery, and his custom of deducting each year five per cent; also, note your views on the subject and suggestions, which, in many respects, are correct both in theory and practice. There seems to be no universal rule among manufactories. Many keep no record of repair work, shouldering the expense on to their Merchandise account, and deduct, say from five to ten per cent. for wear and tear. With many machines after a few years' service, the yearly repairs place the machines at the end of year about as good as at commencement, and in many cases five per cent. is sufficient. Yet ten per cent. the first year is none too much, as the bases of value depends ofttimes on what the machinery would bring if sold, as well as what it is worth to the manufacturer, *i. e.*, what he

could replace it for; and a machine used six months or a year will not bring within twenty-five per cent. of cost, though worth more for service. As a matter of satisfaction it may pay to keep a Repair account, which ultimately goes to Expense or Profit or Loss; but it hardly pays, and I abandoned it several years since.

Too many accounts, which are not essential, increase cost of production, and should be dispensed with. The same principle holds good in book-keeping; the fewest entries and postings the better. I use but one line for every Merchandise account each month. One posting at end of month suffices for each party of whom I purchase. All merchandise purchases paid before end of month are not posted only in the aggregate at end of month. Employees' accounts never go in ledger, only as Labor account, and so on; but I have strayed from my subject. In conclusion, I do not think it wise to charge Machinery or Tool account with all the repairs made on each machine or tool, as we are apt to overlook it at end of year, and that ten per cent. will come nearer the per cent. than five per cent. I am generally governed by the condition of machine when taken in inventory.

From MANUFACTURER.

Your question, "Deductions for Wear and Tear" covers a very wide field. Repairs should be transferred to Profit and Loss, annually, or whenever the statements are made, because they do not represent value, but are merely necessary expenses, the same as pens, ink and paper, etc. Repairs do not increase the original cost or value; they restore only, or partly so. Excessive repairs, or, as I understand, the term, Betterments or Improvements, may be charged to Machinery account.

An inventory should be made of the machinery, tools, etc., by the superintendent, engineer, and foreman or others who are conversant with the condition of the machinery, etc.; and the book-keeper can then value the same with their help.

A five per cent. allowance is not sufficient.

If an annual allowance is made for wear and tear, I advise an actual valuation every third year, and a comparison made with the book-account.

If this is not done, the accounts are *nominal* assets—a word much used nowadays to denote what should be, but is not.

The book-keeper must bear in mind that the

actual value of the assets is required when making his statement.

After making the inventory, a depreciation should be made according to the nature of the machinery, the same as on the Book accounts, which may appear to be all good, and the doubtful ones weeded out, but some will turn out lame ducks. I call this, "Suspense account," for the Book accounts and· Bills-receivable, and "Contingencies for Machinery." Nothing is more liable to accidents than machinery and boilers, and they may happen after one year, and not the next.

The machine is a workman or mechanic, and you pay in advance. A first-class machine will live twice as long as a poor one, and the wages repairs will be less. The original cost will be more, but not proportionately so. The life of a machine is as uncertain as the life of a mechanic—all depending on care, nature of work, and constitution or quality. I close with this advice—undervalue rather than overvalue, and make no estimates when you can obtain actual values.

An Unexplained Entry.

From **CHARLES E. BREWER**, Brooklyn, N. Y.

Will you kindly express your opinion as to the correctness of the following entry?

> Cash Dr. to Capital-stock.
> Cash
> Plant

This is the formula of a record that recently came under my observation. The facts relating to the transaction are, that a certain firm on January 1st admitted, as partner, a person who advanced, as part capital, his foundry building, grounds, furnace, and appurtenances, and for the balance of his investment paid cash into the general partnership. I would like to ask if, in making an entry like the above, the book-keeper is governed by his employer, or if it is supposed that he follows the dictates of his own· judgment?

Your journal has always proved a most welcome visitor to our office, and has many times been a guide in the settlement of vexed questions.

REPLY.—The correspondent shows that the concern was a co-partnership. Why, then, should there be such an account as Capital-stock? There may have been properly a Capital account, which would be a representative element of the combined interests of the sev-

eral partners, presuming the partners separate or individual accounts to be kept in a special or private ledger. If it is meant that Capital-stock, as termed above, was Capital account, and there was in existence an account termed "Plant," it is possible that the entry would be admissible; that is, on the supposition that no cash-book was kept. If the firm kept a cash-book, the proper place for the cash feature of the entry is in that book.

As to the second inquiry, whatever may be our opinion, the fact is very apt to stare us in the face, that, if an employer wants an entry like the above made in some particular way, whether in the judgment of the book-keeper it may be good or bad, he is very apt to follow the directions of his employer. We do not say this because we think it always best that he should, and we believe that many book-keepers are not tenacious enough in allowing or demanding that their own judgment should have preference in matters which pertain especially to their calling. Should it prove that the entry made by the book-keeper, even by the direction of the principal, is erroneous, the book-keeper, and not the principal, will be very apt to shoulder the responsibility.

As the use of the journal gradually drifts out of practice, questions of the kind here alluded to grow less important. If, in the case alluded to, it is the desire of the concern that the foundry buildings, grounds, etc., invested by the incoming partner be closed, or carried in bulk into the general account termed "Plant," there should be no reason in saying that Plant should not be debited, and that the Capital account should not be credited. If the partners have separate and special accounts, the incoming partner, in the case alluded to, should be the one to whom the credit of the investment should be made.

Departmental Accounts.

From W. K. S., St. Louis.

"Beta," of St. Louis, on page 93 of February number, asks about determining profits and losses in departmental business.

If we could look into the details of the business, probably most of the expenses could be placed in the departments to which they belong. Take the shoe department, for instance; all the salesmen in that department can be determined, and their salaries charged to a Shoe Department Expense Account, and probably all large expenses, like insurance, advertising, etc., could be placed in the right departments, so that the only general expenses not distributed would be, rent, office salaries, postage, stationery, etc. The per centage would be small, and easily worked out. The sales of each department kept separate, together with the inventory of each department, would furnish the basis of gross profits. The expenses deducted would give net profits.

Joint-Stock Company Accounts.
From W. K. S., St. Louis.

On page 63, February number, "Frank" asks for more light on joint-stock accounts. The formula he quotes is not exactly correct, and has objectionable features. Instead of making entries to Stock-certificates and Stockholders, a better way is to deal with the individual stockholders and the Capital-stock account.

When the Capital-stock is subscribed for, charge the stock to the subscribers on the journal.

Sundries Dr. to Capital-stock —

    A B, 10 shares................1,000
    C B, 10   " 1,000

and so on to the end of the list. When A B pays for his stock, credit the money to his account, and give him a certificate. The Capital-stock account will then show how much capital has been subscribed, and the individual accounts will show the amounts they owe. If the above plan will take up too much room in the ledger he might save space by making an entry—

Stockholders Dr. to Capital-stock.

As the payments are made, credit them to stockholders' account. The last way saves opening numerous accounts.

If the stock is to be paid in installments, make a list of subscribers, and have columns for first, second, and third installments, and spaces to enter date of payment. Where the cash comes in on the call for the first installment, make the proper credit on the cash-book, and enter it also in the proper place in the installment-book. Give an installment receipt for the money, and when the stock is paid in full, issue certificates — that is, when A B has paid in full he returns the installment receipts, and takes a certificate in place of them. The rule is to issue certificates only for paid up stock; but there have been exceptions.

"Frank" asks if the Stock-certificate account should be closed before all the stock has been paid for. If he has already opened his books on the plan quoted, the account would remain open until the stock was full paid and certificates issued.

Ledger Footings.
From TACHYGRAPHER, St. Paul.

A late correspondent asks about footings and rulings on ledgers. I always show small pencil footings, and place balance, at end of month, before last date on Dr. or Cr. side, as the case may be. These pencil figures are very convenient for reference and in rendering statements. Where payments cover certain bills, black check-marks ($\checkmark$) on last line of date-columns, on both sides, show this fact.

When account closes to a late date, I rule a single red line just beneath pencil footings, beginning on first line of date column on Dr. side, and ending on last vertical line of Cr. side. But why not make this a black ink line? Black is much easier seen in bad light, and at all times is easier on the eyes.

ILLUSTRATION.

Sep, 25	M 6ods	734		45	95	Sep. 30	C	65	$\checkmark$	60	95
26	30	735	$\checkmark$	60	95	"	M	765		10	..
				100	90					70	00
						Oct. 5	C	163		35	25
										100	00

Distributing Labor in Time-book.
From B. F. Crow, Nebraska City, Neb.

I have been much profited by your "Counting-room Chats," and desire to ask my question.

Is there any formula for a time-book giving the distributed labor of, and the quantities completed daily by, employees in a manufacturing establishment, by which the unit cost of articles can be determined readily, and with the least possible labor? I inclose one which I have used, but think there may be others better.

In use, the distributed amounts are carried each month to a monthly distribution-sheet, which includes all the employees, having a column for each class of work on which labor was performed, and the total footings of this sheet are then grouped together under appropriate heads, which show the unit or sum-total cost of any piece or line of work. This gives very satisfactory results, but requires considerable labor.

The above is not given with a view to airing my scheme, but that in asking benefits from others I might also bring something into the general fund.

Manufacturing Accounts.
From SUBSCRIBER, Stockton, Cal.

I should like to hear, through your columns, from some of your experts who have settled upon the most practical method of keeping the accounts of a general manufacturing business: like many large incorporations in both the Eastern and Western States, who are manufacturing a varied line of goods — not specialties. I refer more particularly to arriving at the cost of making different articles.

I understand one institution charges up each department with all stock going in, adding to it all labor performed; and when it goes to the next department, it is charged to that, and the other credited, and so on throughout. It strikes me that might work when building but one or two articles, but when twenty or more are under way, it looks impracticable. Although ten years in the business, I have made but little progress beyond systems I adopted years since. I hear occasionally of some book-keeper who has a short method by which he can exhibit in one panoramic view the minutiæ and the whole business to the Board of Directors, showing stock on hand in each department, cost of construction of every machine throughout, and a general exhibit of their business; and doing it all himself. I have never seen it, nor have I faith that it can be accomplished. But I presume there are various improved methods. The question arises, what are they, and which is the best?

Discount on Partial Payments.
From PROGRESS, Chicago, Ill.

I would like to hear from some of my fellow accountants, through the medium of your valuable monthly, as to the custom of crediting discount on partial payments made on account of purchases. My employers lately told me that they thought my system of crediting discount on partial payments at time payment was received to be hardly proper, for reasons hereinafter explained.

For example, A pays $200 October 10th, on a purchase of $1,000, dated October 1st. On this payment he is entitled to six per cent. discount, according to the terms on invoice, which

is marked six per cent., ten days; five per cent., thirty days; or four per cent., sixty days. I enter in my cash-book: "Cash, $200; discount, six per cent., $12.75; total, $212.75." November 1st, A pays $300, being thirty days after date of purchase. I credit him with five per cent. discount, or a total of $315.75. December 1st, $300 is received on account, four per cent. being the discount at sixty days. I credit Cash and Discount, $312.50. Now, then, we will suppose A does not meet the balance of his obligation until some time after being due, or he fails before paying balance, here is where the question of the propriety of crediting discounts on partial payments, at time payment was made, arose.

In support of my practice, I maintain that an account should show, as nearly as possible, at a glance, what the balance is. Suppose I had not credited A with any discount, his account would show an indebtedness of $200, while really, he only owes $159, if his account is not past due, and then there may be interest due on the $159. The most of our customers pay their bills when due, or when discounted, as per such and such invoice; but some prefer paying $50, $100, $200, etc., at a time just as they have it to spare, regardless of amount of purchase, and frequently they desire to have their receipt sent to them for remittance, to show discount to which they are entitled. If any of the AMERICAN COUNTING-ROOM readers can enlighten me as to a more practical method than mine, it will be appreciated by "Progress."

Real Estate Accounts.
From C. W. H., Brooklyn, N. Y.

Should like to ask a few questions regarding the putting up of buildings. I will give my views, which, if incorrect, please point out the errors.

In starting a new building, all labor, material and expense, such as freight, cartage, labor putting up, and taxes, while in the course of construction, must be charged to Real Estate or Building (naming the place) for the cost of same; any repairs on same in after years to be charged to expense, it being supposed that everything is as good as new after repairs are made. When buying a building much out of repair, you charge Real Estate account for what you pay for same and expense of buying it. When you begin to repair it, you must charge the Real Estate account for these first repairs which shows the cost of the building in a good condition; but when same building comes again to repair, the repairs must be charged to expense as above. All alterations are to be charged to expense.

Commissions Subject to Special Terms.

From AN OLD MERCHANT, New York.

My agent, Henry Ruple, has sold, for my account, one threshing-machine for $600. He received therefor: cash, $100; notes, $500, payable with interest. Mr. Ruple, as my agent, is entitled to 20% of whatever is realized from the machine. Had he retained $20 in money and $160 in notes, the matter would have solved itself; but he sent home — cash, $80; notes, $500; and a statement of facts, which my book-keeper enters:

Sundries Dr. to Sundries.

| Cash.............. | 80 | Th'ing-machine acct. | 480 |
| Henry Ruple....... | 20 | Commission acct.... | 120 |

The contract between Henry Ruple and the concern states the facts.

The next entry must be:

Commission acct. Dr. to Henry Ruple........ 20
His share of money paid.

The next entry, as stated, is:

| Cash..............108 | Bills-receivable .....100 |
| | Interest acct........ 8 |

Which must be followed by:

Sundries Dr. to Henry Ruple.

Commission acct........ 20
Interest................ 1.60
—— 21.60

If Ruple waits for his money, he is entitled to the interest thereon, if the concern collects interest. There can be no doubt about that (?)

I have not your November number, and hence can only *see* what you state in the January number.

Post-dated Checks.

From ORIOLE, New York.

I kindly solicit information respecting checks which are dated ahead several weeks. My custom has been to record them in the cash-book when received, making note when payable as explanation, and pinning on check memoranda when due, and counting as so much money when balancing Cash. I have also credited them as Bills-receivable; but this to me seems inconsistent, as a check is not a promise to pay. Again; I have made no record in any book of the receipt of check, but have pinned a notice on check when payable, and held it out of my Cash until due, when entry would then be made in cash-book and acknowledgment sent. Can any of your readers suggest any better mode of recording checks of this character?

Foundry Accounts.

From A STUDENT, New York.

Will some of the older and experienced book-keepers be kind enough to explain or illustrate the best method of keeping a Foundry account, showing loss of metal and the actual cost price of the materials produced?

Bank vs. True Discount.

From JOHN H. RICORD, Jersey City, N. J.

When discounting notes for different parties by a concern, is it proper to deduct bank discount or the true discount for balance of unexpired time.

An Idea on Paging.

From TACHYGRAPHER, St. Paul.

By paging the books of original entry differently, explanation columns can be omitted on ledgers, thus gaining space for more accounts, and still showing, on ledgers, the character of each entry. I have pages on

Cash-book, 1 to 100
"   101 to 200

(Having two cash-books, gives cashier one, while book-keepers have the other.)

Journal, 201 to 500
All Sales, 501 to 1,000
Invoice,   "   "

With this arrangement, ledgers show whether items are Cash, Journal, or Merchandise, without wasting space or time on the usual " C," " J," and " M."

Question on Toll.

From QUIZ, Colliersville, Tenn.

A, who runs a cotton gin, and charges " one-tenth " for gining, takes 176 pounds toll from 1760 pounds brought to the gin by B. B claims that A is entitled to only 160 pounds, as he (B), by paying 176 pounds, would be paying toll on toll, which he would not do.

Irrespective of how the matter was settled,

it is now referred to the AMERICAN COUNTING-ROOM readers for an opinion.

Interest on Partner's Account.
From ROYAL COLON, Roseville, N. J.

Where a member of the firm is required to pay interest on the difference between the present worth of each partner, should the interest so cast be upon whole or one-half of such difference between their accounts?

Interest and its Cases.
From QUIZ, Colliersville, Tenn.

How many cases has Percentage, and what are they? Some mild authors, of still milder works, deal with the subject under four cases; others, five; while some prefer to treat it under seven heads. A reply to this will, perchance, be gratefully received by more readers than the writer.

Accounts of Stock-Certificates.
From FRANK, Pittsburgh, Pa.

Your reply to my question, published in your February number, answers only *one* of my three queries. In reply to the inquiry, " Is it not the rule to issue certificates only to *paid-up* subscribers?" you say, "As a rule, stock-certificates are not issued until they have been paid for in full; but such is not invariably the case." Then, instead of answering the questions, "*Should* Stock-certificates account be closed before all the stock has been *paid* for? and if not, what entry *should* be made at the time the stock is subscribed for?" you proceed to point out how the accounts may be kept where the *exceptional* practice is followed of issuing the certificates before they are paid for in full. Inasmuch, however, as the latter is the exception and not the rule, it is presumable that the method generally practiced is a better one. Will you or some of your readers be kind enough to give the plan used in *general* practice?

REPLY.—It was thought the question asked in the February number was answered by our reply, or at least would be when that reply had been coupled with what had been published in previous numbers bearing on the subject.

In answering the question above repeated, we say that Stock Certificates' account could not be closed until all the stock has been subscribed for. The payment of the stock would not affect the Stock Certificates' account, but that of stockholders. The account of Stockholders is debited, and that of Stock Certificates credited, at the time stock is subscribed for. When all the stock has been subscribed for, the Stock Certificates' account has its purpose, and is virtually wiped out. The account, then, of Capital Stock shows the proprietary liability of the company. If the stock has not been paid for in full, the account of Stockholders will show the amount due and unpaid for, which forms an asset of the company.

The correspondent asks if we will give the form used in general practice. If he means the method of keeping the accounts of a stock company, or making the entries concerning Stock Certificates and Capital Stock accounts, which is generally practiced, it would be difficult to comply with his request. There is such a variety of practices followed that one cannot well ascertain what the general method is. We believe it is not general to open or keep such an account as Stock Certificates. We have examined accounts of corporations where the amount of capital stock stood credited only to the amount of stock subscribed for, not the amount called for in the Articles of Incorporation.

Following that plan when stock is subscribed for, the account of Stockholders is debited, and Capital Stock credited, or, possibly, no entry is made until the stock is paid for, and the entry appears in the cash-book "Cash to Capital Stock." The plan offered in Vol. II., page 163 of THE BOOK-KEEPER, is one providing a means for recording the various steps in the organization of a company, and of showing in the accounts the precise condition of affairs.

A Loose Partnership Agreement.
From A. W. RAND, New York.

Under the heading, "A Loose Partnership Agreement" O. M. P. asks a question which brings up an oft-disputed point, though one that in the older countries and the older portions of this country has come to be well understood.

In this particular case it is very easy to write that B is correct and A wrong, but I suppose that O. M. P. would like such a presentment of the case as would satisfy both parties.

In order to fully understand the case let us see the result of each method of settlement. According to A, the entries would be:

Interest Dr. to A, 6% on $45,000, $2,700. A Dr. to Interest, ¼ of $2,700. B Dr. to Interest, ¼ of $2,700. Posting these amounts gives the following entries on the ledger:

INTEREST.

To A.............2,700	By A.............2,025
	By B............. 675
2,700	2,700

A.

To Interest........2,025	By Interest.......2,700
By Balance 675	
2,700	2,700
	By Balance........ 675

B.

| To Interest........675 | By Balance........675 |
| To Balance........675 | |

According to B the entries would be (and this is correct):

Interest Dr. to Sundries --To A, 6% on $50,000, $3,000. To B, 6% on $5,000, $300. Sundries Dr. to Interest — A, ¼ of $3,300, $2,475. B, ¼ of $3,300, $825. And, posting as before, gives us this result:

INTEREST.

To Sundries.......3,300	By A 2,475
	By B........... 825
3,300	3,300

A.

To Interest.........2,475	By Interest.......3,000
By Balance....... 525	
3,000	3,000
	By Balance 525

B.

To Interest........825	By Interest.........300
	By Balance........525
825	825
To Balance........525	

Showing that B, while correct, is so at the cost to A of $150. (By the way, how does O. M. P. make the difference 400?) The explanation of this difference is found in the fact that on the capital of $10,000, consisting of B's 5,000 and an equal portion of A's capital, B receives one-half, while he pays but one-quarter—that is, if their capital of $10,000 was share and share alike, while their profits were as 3 to 1, the account would be: "Interest Dr. to Sundries—To A, 300; to B, 300"; while Interest account would be balanced by "Sundries Dr. to Interest—A, $450; B, $150." The rule may be expressed that unless the proprietary interests of partners are, and continuously remain, in the exact ratio of their division of profits, all charges or credits should be made on the gross amounts and carried into Gain, where the final division can be made.

The writer recently had under examination a set of books where by failure to follow this rule certain losses had been charged directly to partners in one ratio, and gains from Profit and Loss in another — costing one partner $2,000.

From ALFRED SYNOLD, Columbus, O.

As I understand it, it seems to me that the only true way to adjust the difficulty is to credit both A and B with the interest on their respective investments, and charge Interest account with same. This being finally closed into Profit and Loss Account will naturally decrease the net profit of the concern, and in this way compel each partner to stand his proportionate share of this item of expense the same as they would shoulder all other expenses of the concern. After arriving at the *net profit*, then credit A with three-fourths and B with one-fourth. Thus each partner gets full interest on his investment, and also his share of profits. On the other hand, if A gets credit for interest on $45,000, and B gets no credit at all, then the statement of profit and loss is not a true one, as the concern pays interest on a capital of $45,000, while there were actually invested $55,000. In this case B might as well draw his $5,000 out of the concern, allowing A to draw the same amount from his investment. This will, no doubt, cripple the concern to some extent, taking away from it $10,000. But why should it remain if it is not worth the interest? Again, if $55,000 are invested (A, $50,000; and B $5,000), and A insists to be credited with interest on $45,000 (allowing B no interest), then the proportion of the profits on the $10,000, which is the difference between the interest-bearing capital and the capital actually invested should be equally divided between the two partners, and the remainder of the profits, which is the portion earned by the $45,000, should be distributed in proportion of three-fourths to one-fourth. This kind of caculating would only be justified in the event of A insisting on interest of $45,000; because, if he ignores the $10,000 in his interest calculations, he must make allowances for them in his profit and loss calculations, as the profits of the concern are due to this portion of the investment for its share, as well as to the $45,000. And since each partner contributed one-half of the $10,000, each partner should receive the proportion of the profits on this amount at the same rate.

This, as I said before, would only be justified under certain circumstances. The only true way is to allow interest on each partner's investment—at least I consider it so, but should be glad to be corrected if I am wrong.

From G. H. MOLL, St. Louis, Mo.

In answer to O. M. P. would say that in my opinion the view taken by B is correct. Interest should be allowed each partner on the full amount of his investment. The concern may be regarded as a borrower of the amount stated. It is immaterial whether the money is borrowed from members of the firm or outside parties. According to the agreement, profits and losses are to be shared in the proportion of three-fourths to A, and one-fourth to B. It would be unjust to let A balance B's capital with an equal amount of her own. If A were to offset B's $5,000 with $15,000 of his own, and receive interest on the remaining $35,000, it would be correct, and amount to the same thing as though the adjustment were made in the manner first mentioned.

Vowel Indexing.
From ALFRED SYNOLD, Columbus, O.

Would you please inform me what rule governs the indexing of names in an ordinary vowel index? I had a dispute about this. I claimed the first *vowel* after the initial letter in a name was the one under which vowel the name should be indexed; while the other party claimed that it was the first *letter* after the initial letter which indicated where the name should be indexed. For instance: "Brand" should be indexed in "O" he claimed, for the reason that "r" (first letter after the initial) comes after "O" in the alphabet. Who is right?

*** You are right, as the vowel index is ordinarily used. Your friend's index would not be a vowel index, but an index divided on the second letter—the following sets being grouped together: a to d, e to h, i to n, o to t, u to z. The vowel index is passing out of use, and more scientifically divided classification is taking its place where it is not entirely rejected for the card-index.

Repairs on Leased Property.
From A. H., New York.

I would like to have some one suggest how to make a charge of the following: A makes certain improvements on one of his buildings leased to B. B agrees to pay for half of the repairs in four yearly payments, but his lease runs but three years—the presumption being that it will be renewed. No open account is kept with the tenant. The conditions above mentioned are written across the face of the lease. Would this be considered a sufficient record—the rents being collected monthly?

Is a bank bound to pay a check in currency when funds are to the maker's credit, and other conditions regular, or is it a matter of courtesy?

Interest on Capital.
From MITCHELL.

I shall be thankful for an opinion as to the just distribution of interest to partners for capital invested under the following conditions:

A, B and C form a co-partnership. A is in debt. B and C pay A's debts, in lieu of the business he brings into the firm. In the articles of co-partnership is this paragraph:

"It is further agreed that each partner shall have the sum of five thousand dollars invested, and not have the privilege of drawing any thereof without the consent of the other partners first had and obtained: each partner drawing interest for all amounts invested above the said five thousand dollars."

The books were settled every six months, and interest for *full amount* of capital credited to B and C, and interest *charged* to A on his (debit) balance. A, having no other support than his business, which was merged in the partnership, made no objection at the time, not feeling strong enough to test the matter then. The partnership of ten or eleven years is now being settled. Should B and C have been credited with interest on full amount of their capital?

*** We shall be glad to receive the opinions of our readers on the above.

I. A. & B. C. M. U. S. N. A.

From Napoleon Taylor, Secretary.

De meetin habin been called to ordah, wid de president in de char, de minits ob de last meetin was red by de secretary amid brethless silence.

Brudder Pineapple was not present; he had met Brudder Pumroy at de door as he went home from de last meetin, and since den had felt de need ob complete rest.

Wen de minits had ben red, de president remarked dat dey met wid his approval, and onless some bigger man dan he was objected, dey would stand proved, and it was so ordahed.

De tresurer reported dat he had $10.28 and de note ob Brudder Jones fur fifteen cents, on demand wid interest, in de tresury. A bill fur de rent ob de rooms, amountin to $5, and one fur a inkstand and pen fur de secretary, amountin to $5, was presented and ordahed paid. De president took occasion to remark dat fur utter shiftlessness and total depravity de secretary took de cake; dat to go and spend $5 fur a inkstand was too much fur human natur to endure. Dat he was mighty glad to git a ten-cent bottle ob ink and a pen and holder fur two cents — in all, twelve cents — a clean savin ob four dollars and eighty-eight cents; dat he was strongly tempted to hab de things put on de presidential rostrum, where dey would be in keepin wid de dignitaries ob de office, and dat he would take de matter under prayerfully considerashun and report later. De secretary said dat he got de things to use; dat de pen jist suited his hand, and dat he would prognosticate dat de president would arribe at de conclushun dat he would leave dem where dey was, as he (de secretary) proposed to continue to use dem hisself. Havin wrasted wid de subject, de president came to de same turn ob mind and so announced.

De meetin den listened to a lecture, by Gen. P. Green Blunderbuss, on de subject, "Shall accounts in de ledger be ruled off wid one line or two?" De general remarked dat "dis was a grate country; dat one man was konsidered as good as another, and sometimes better. Dat de more money he had in his pocket de better a man was apt to konsider hisself. Dat he had seen de time when, habin plenty ob stamps, he wouldn't hab noticed any ob de members ob dis institoot ef he had met dem on de street, but dat now he had got so low dat he would shake hands wid any ob dem, and dat — " He

was here interupted by a whack on de side ob de hed from Brudder G. Washington Jones, which would hab nocked him down but fur de fack dat Brudder Smith gib him a left hander under de ear which stratened him up agen. He had jist arribed at a perpendickular posishun when Brudder Come-to-glory Brown introduced his shoemaker to him, and fur a moment de general seemed to be tryin to fly. Failin in de attempt, he was next tripped up by Brudder Charlemagne Victor Romeyn. Feelin dat de klimate was gittin too warm, and dat he needed air, he broke fur de dore, follered by all de movable furniture in de room. Ordah bein restored, de president made sum remarks about de deceitfulness ob riches, and urged de brudders not to be proud even ef dey was pore.

De Examinin Kommittee reported dat de turnups dey had received was not all good yet, and dat dey hoped dose ob de members as had not bought any would do so before dey was all gone; dey could recommend dem fur good turnups now, but couldn't say how long dey would remain so. Dey reported back fur de acshun ob de institoot de name ob J. Wilkinson Stewart; he had no money, and could only offer de kommittee, fur his inishiashun-fee, sum cabbages; but, as dey didn't none ob em like cabbage, dey reported conversely on de nominashun. He did not know nuthin bout bookkeepin, but dey could hab overlooked dat ef he had had de cash. De sense ob de meetin was dat de proposishun should be rejected with scorn; dat it was astonished dat so low-lived a nigger should hab attempted to thrust hisself on his superiors in such a way. De gemplum named bein present, habin been invited to hear de lecture, he rose to explane. He sed he had seen de depravity ob de kommittee, and had offered de cabbage jist as a feeler. Dat he had wid him money enuf to pay all de dews and fees, and hab twenty-fibe dollars left ober and abuv, and dat he was glad to find what a lot ob hippocrits he had missed gittin in wid. De president sed dat he was sure sum beefsteak had been made; dat he had known de gemman sum years, and always had thought him a man ob grate sense and judgment, and thought de institoot would meet wit a loss ef dey allowed such a man to miss becomin a member. Brudder Brown sed dat he had always konsidered Brudder Stewart a man ob large means and a man ob substance, and dat he stood agast at de temerity ob sum ob de men present speakin ob de brudder as dey did.

De Examinin Kommittee held a short konferance, and deported dat dey had found, on lookin over de record, dat de brudder had passed a better examinashun dan sum ob de members dat had talked so loud agin him; dat dey had nearly killed demselves laffin ober de cabbage joke, and dat dey proposed dat de gemman be elected ante bellum widout de konvenshun ob de ballot. De motion was carried by a large majority. De brudder, bein declared elected, paid his dews and fees in cash, and was thereupon chosen vice-president by brevet. De faces ob sum ob de members was a site to behold. De president gabe notis dat, onless prevented by de rumatiz, dat Brudder Gardner, ob de Lime Kill Club, would lecture at de next meetin.

Nuthin furder comin up, de meetin ajurned, and de members circumscribed to dere sweets ob apartments.

NOTES AND COMMENTS.

At a recent meeting of the New York Medico-Legal Society Dr. J. G. Johnson, of Brooklyn, read a Paper on "Poisoning by Canned Fruits and Meats." The Paper asserted that in some canning establishments muriatic amalgam is used in soldering on the lids of the cans. A theory advanced in explaining the cause of poisoning cases, was, that in applying with a brush the amalgam in the groove in which the lid fits, drops of the acid occasionally find their way into the can. There were present, representatives of the canned goods manufacturers, and among them were Mr. H. T. Going of the Canned Goods Exchange of Baltimore. Mr. Going said that the muriatic acid used in ceiling up the cans was so greatly diluted with water that a person could drink a small quantity without injury. Statistics were read showing that last year 60,000,000 dozen of canned goods were exported, and it was thought by Dr. Barrett, editor of *The Trade*, that if the goods were as dangerous to health as it had been reported, several millions of people would probably have been killed by their eating.

In summing up the discussion, it would seem that the manufacturers had rather the best side of the argument, and that the opponents to canned goods were unable to fully confirm their theories. The question is one of vital interest. It shall be an effort with us to gather all attainable facts and present them to our readers. If, as it is asserted by the manufacturers of canned goods, that their products are healthful and wholesome, contrary assertions are not only an injustice to the manufacturers and dealers, but a direct wrong and injury to consumers. Many thousands of people who use canned goods, would, if deprived of them, be unable to procure fruit of any kind, and, thereby, suffer a serious inconvenience, if not, indeed, an injury to health. Facts, and not blind theories, are what is wanted.

Among the powerful and beneficent organizations of this continent prominently appears the Woman's Christian Temperance Union. It embraces over five thousand local societies, while its membership numbers more than a hundred thousand. Of organizations, managed and composed entirely of women, it is the largest and strongest ever known. The thorough order and discipline manifested in all its operations, the carefulness and competency of its officers, superintendents and secretaries of departmental work are noteworthy examples of woman's capability and judgment. The society has made its influence felt in every nook and corner of the land. It is steadily growing in strength, while extending its lines of usefulness, charity and reform. May its work go steadily forward until its infinence covers the land as the waters cover the sea.

The Annual Meeting of the Institute of Accountants and Book-keepers of New York was held on Friday evening, March 14th. The officers elected were: *president*, Albert O. Field, of Naumberg, Kraus, Lauer & Co., 657 Broadway; *vice-president*, E. E. Griffith, of the Standard Collar Company, 21 Mercer Street; *treasurer*, A. Garrison, of George Mather's Sons, 60 John Street; *secretary*, J. H. Timmermann, Secretary of the Eleventh Ward Savings Bank; *financial secretary*, Joseph Rodgers, of Alfred Field & Co., 93 Chambers Street. Under the new by-laws the five general officers became, upon their election, members also of the Executive Council. This left nine other members of the Council to be elected. The following persons were elected: Joseph Hardcastle, Thomas B. Conant, Selden R. Hopkins, W.'B. Jaudon, T. I. Wiltshire, H. S. Ogden, Charles Dutton, Charles E. Cady, and Edward Griffin. A new Board of Audit was elected, consisting of Daniel T. Ames, W. J. Anderson, A. L. Woodworth. The committee on membership reported favorably on the names of Henry R. Kearns, William I. Hay, and Chas. W. Hamlin. The ballot was spread, and they were elected. Immediately after the election of members, a collation was served by the popular caterer, Terhune, and heartily enjoyed. A long list of toasts was offered and happily responded to. Among the guests present were Mr. James G. Keys and Prof. Thomas May Pierce, members of the Book-keepers' Beneficial Association of Philadelphia. The good wishes of the Institute for sister organizations in other cities were often alluded to, and the hope expressed by many in their remarks that there might be inaugurated a grand movement for a National Institute of Accountants and Book-keepers.

A prominent feature of the meeting, or rather the collation, was the absence of wine or other strong drinks. Lemonade and coffee only were served. Some of the speakers, in their response to toasts, expressed the opinion that toast-making on lemonade was a cool undertaking for book-keepers of New York. Champagne would, no doubt, have oiled up the tongues, warmed up the bodies, and thrown more enthusiasm into the speeches. But whether it would have added to the respectability, the culture, refinement, and goodnature of the occasion is a question of doubt. Rather, there can be no doubt that the stand taken by the Institute in banishing wine from its bill of fare at an annual dinner was one that will receive the hearty indorsement of the great majority of the profession in all parts of the land.

Among the members present at the Annual Meeting was Mr. Hugo Schumacher, of Akron, O. Mr. Schumacher came from Akron expressly to attend the annual gathering, and become personally acquainted with the members. It was his first opportunity to meet them, and

he received a hearty welcome. The visiting friends were escorted to the Metropolitan Hotel as the guests of the Institute, and a committee waited upon them until they were prepared on the following day to take their departure. At the Council Meeting, April 10th, the new board will take their places, and it is expected the various committees will be made up for the ensuing year.

A member of the committee on entertainment has handed us a reply to a request made of one of the members for a poem to be read at the Annual Meeting. The request was politely declined in the following lines:

> To think that you should ask *me*
> To write a fitting rhyme
> To read on an occasion
> So glorious and sublime
> As the Second Annual Meeting
> Of the I of A and B.
> I don't know how you did it—
> It's a mystery to me.

Just think of all the good things that ever yet were said—
The witty things, the brilliant things, by men of massive head,
And things appropriate to say on such a great occasion
As the gathering of the scribes to partake of a collation.
And fix it all in verses so beautiful and grand
That Alfred the Lord Tennyson will in amazement stand.
And then when it is perfect, and beautiful as day,
Then you can just imagine that is what I *meant* to say.

The poet of the evening was Mr. H. S. Ogden, who had prepared for the occasion, in response to the invitation of the committee, a very happy piece of verse, in which the name of every member of the association was brought fittingly into play.

According to the *Pall Mall Gazette*, trade in Great Britain is unusually dull and profitless. As a result, many once important commercial houses are tottering on the brink of bankruptcy. It is said that the contraction of values in almost every direction has created in that country almost wholesale insolvency. "But the evil day," says the journal, "is naturally put off as long as possible—the hope being that prices will rise, and enable holders to get rid of their stock of iron, wheat, rice or coffee, as the case may be. While failures are known to be impending, although the names of questionable houses are kept as quiet as possible, out of mistaken kindness, as persons of experience hold, the dullness deepens for want of confidence. Weak members of a trade usually make the trade itself weak." Would it not be well, we would ask, for the thought advanced here to be carefully considered by the commercial men of our own country? When we take into account the condition of the insolvents whose records appear in our financial papers, showing, in many cases, the resources of their concerns less than one-tenth of their liabilities, is it not an evidence that something is wrong in commercial circles? Why should a firm, when insolvency stares it in the face, continue to transact business as long as it is possible to secure credit, knowing, as they well must, that failure is inevitable? A glance through the long list of business failures and embarrassments should certainly prove a lesson to those engaged in business where it is essential that credit to those with whom they deal should be extended.

The Institute of Accountants and Bookkeepers of Chicago is, we are glad to note, coming gradually to the front among the beneficent and useful organizations of that city. As an outgrowth of that Institute there has been formed a Book-keepers' Building and Loan Association. This society is also meeting with cheerful encouragement. It was incorporated January 28th. Its officers are: Wm. S. Warren, *president ;* Rob. B. Kennedy, *vice-president ;* Chas. C. Nardin, *secretary ;* M. S. Woodward, *treasurer ;* Geo. C. Fry, *attorney.* We shall take pleasure in reporting the progress of these associations.

NOVELTIES.

Shannon Filing Cabinet.

In the February number we gave illustrations of the Shannon Files and Schlicht's Indexes, manufactured by Clague, Wegman, Schlicht & Field, of Rochester, N. Y. This firm manufacture also a cabinet, the arrangement of which is based upon the principles adopted in constructing the files and indexes. The advantages of cabinets over the ordinary files have frequently been referred to in these pages.

If the files are used without the cabinet, it is important to know something about the date of any particular letter or paper to be able to turn to it without hesitation. An ordinary file will hold only the letters of a month, or, say, two or three months at most, accumulating in a moderate size business-house. In a year or two a number of files will have been used, and the labor of searching for letters filed several months before begins to grow tedious. One advantage of the cabinet is that it will serve without changes a year, or, if desired, may be made to serve several years, according to the extent of the business and the size of the cabinet used. Using separate files, and

The Shannon File Drawer.

filing according to date, requires greater care and more time.

Fig. 1 represents the Shannon File Drawer

as it is taken from a cabinet. This drawer is similar in construction to the Shannon File, except that it has a drawer-front, held firmly in place by light iron brackets, and is not provided with a perforator. It is made to fit into a cabinet, desk or safe, and combines the advantages of both a drawer and a file. The file-drawers are made of well-seasoned wood, and present a handsome appearance. The metal parts are nickled or bronzed, and the handle is combined with a label-plate, which permits the easy removal and change of label.

The Filing Cabinet consists of a number of the File-drawers, provided with necessary indexes, and appropriately labeled. These cabinets are made to meet a diversity of wants. Some are arranged with the file-drawers divided according to the subject-matter of the documents or papers, and subdivided alphabetically; and others, so that papers may be filed in alphabetical order merely, and according to date. The cabinets are of various sizes, ranging from twelve to ninety-six file-drawers. They are constructed of well-seasoned black walnut, handsomely finished, and serve not only as a most useful piece of office-furniture, but as an ornament also. When desired, Sargent & Greenleaf

Twelve File Drawer Cabinet.

locks are placed on the drawers or any special drawer of the cabinet.

Figs. 1 and 2 show, respectively, a twelve and fifteen file-drawer cabinet. The former with doors; and the latter, without. The firm have prepared a handsome descriptive catalogue, beautifully illustrated, and containing much useful information for business men. Copies may be had by addressing Messrs. Clague, Wegman, Schlicht & Field, Rochester, N. Y., referring to this description.

Waterman's "Ideal" Fountain-pen.

This is neither a stylographic pen nor a fluid-pencil. It is an ordinary pen made into a fountain-pen by the introduction of a simple ingenious device for keeping the pen supplied with ink. It is an entirely new invention, so simple that one wonders why it was not long before discovered. Many people object to fountain-pens or fluid-pencils because they destroy the character of the hand-

Fifteen File Drawer Cabinet.

writing when one has learned to write with a pen and not a stick. We give herewith some illustrations which serve to show what the "Ideal" Fountain-pen is.

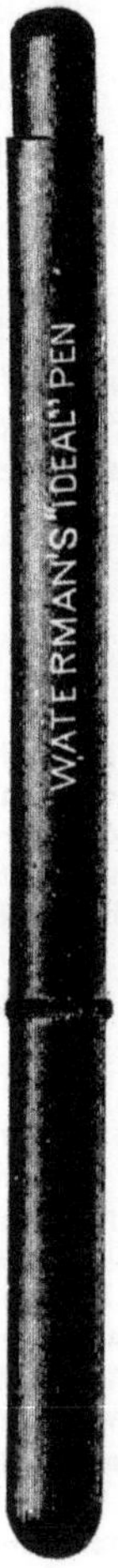

The handle is the reservoir for the ink, and it is made in two pieces, the point section, *C*, and the barrel, *D*, which have a screw-joint where the reservoir can be opened and filled without inking the fingers.

The pen, *A*, is held in the point section, *C*, by the feed-bar, *B*, which also carries the ink from the reservoir to the pen.

The fourth piece is the cap, *E*, which covers the pen to protect it from injury, and keeps the ink from drying when the pen is not in use. The cap can be put on the top of holder to make it longer while writing, or taken off when a shorter holder is desired.

Fig. 4 shows the part which feeds the pen. It fits to the underside of the pen, and extends up into the handle or reservoir.

The depth of the splits or fissures which run the whole length of the feed is shown by the dotted line in the feed-bar, *B*, Fig. 4, and their place below the corners of the groove, in Fig. 6.

The supply of ink is regulated automatically by the act of writing, in which the porous paper absorbs and draws the ink through the moving pen and feed from the reservoir; and the air to replace it is forced in by atmospheric pressure between the pen and the feed-bar. The air goes up to the groove on the side next to the pen, while the ink passes down in the fissures and next to them in the bottom of the groove, and each turns out for the other, thus permitting a continuous flow, but which stops when the pen is lifted from the paper. No shaking is required, for when the fissures are once thoroughly wet they never become empty or dry until after the last particle of ink is drawn from the reservoir.

A neat circular will be mailed free to our readers by addressing L. E. Waterman, manager, 10 Murray Street, New York. The manufacturers are an old New York house, well known and perfectly reliable. We commend them to our patrons.

• McGill's Patent Pin-fasteners.

The uses to which these fasteners are applied are innumerable. They are as useful and have grown to be as indispensable as pins. Their construction enables them to be applied with the fingers as pins are, and to be securely clinched by the same means. They consequently form the readiest as well as the very best binders for all description of papers; for sampling woolens, cottons, laces, ribbons, silks, plushes, wicks, and a thousand of other articles; for making paper and light wooden boxes, and for all descriptions of light binding; for fastening seed-bags

Fig. 1.—Pen closed for the pocket.

Fig. 2.—Pen with Cap on top ready for writing.

Fig. 3.—Sectional view of pen. *A*, gold pen. *B*, Feed bar. *C*, Point-section. *D*, Barrel. *E*, Cap.

Fig. 4.—Feed bar.

Fig. 5.

and sample packages that require opening, examination and re-fastening in transit through the mails, and for other purposes too numerous to mention.

Their usefulness and superiority has been recognized at home and abroad, and they promise soon to be an indispensable article of merchandise all over the world.

The Eyelet-fasteners enable documents bound with them to be sealed by having ribbons run through the eye in their heads. The shanks of these fasteners are made of pin-wire, with ground points, and may be inserted in the finest goods without injuring the fibre.

The manufacturers are Messrs. Holmes, Booth & Haydens, No. 49 Chambers Street, New York city. A handsome catalogue, containing descriptions and prices of a large variety of fasteners, and a fine copper-plate engraving of the firm's works at Waterbury, Conn., has been issued, and copies may be obtained upon application as above.

THE LIBRARY.

Magazines for April.

The *Century* presents in the April number an unusually attractive table of contents. The opening article on "The White House," which is beautifully illustrated, and may justly receive the indorsement of one of Mr. Smalley's most pleasing and graphic contributions to periodical literature. Geo. Alfred Townsend tells "How Wilkes Booth Crossed the Potomac." Sarah Freeman Clarke gives her second Paper, and the concluding one, of "Notes of the Exile of Dante." The article is superbly illustrated. What Walter Hill has to say about "Uncle Tom within a Cabin" is what everybody should know. Mr. Edward S. Wylde's article on "The New York City Hall," with its accompanying illustrations, is one of the prominent features of this number. "Progress in Fish-Culture," by Fred Mather, is admirably written and handsomely illustrated. In the department of "Timely Topics" appear some very appropriate notes upon the subject of "Mobs, and the Failure of Justice." The failure of justice, it is said, which makes room for the mobs and lynching is a greater disgrace than the savagery of the mobs. The fact that thirteen out of fourteen murderers escape the gallows is the one damning fact which blackens the record of our criminal jurisprudence. No American ought to indulge in any boasting about his native land while the evidence remains that the laws made for the protection of human life are thus shamelessly trampled under foot. No occupant of the bench and no member of the bar ought to rest until those monstrous abuses which result in the utter defeat of justice are thoroughly corrected." These are words which certainly ought to sink deep into the minds of American people who desire to see law and order established throughout the land, and receive such recognition and attention that good fruits may result from their sowing. The "Open Letters" are all especially interesting, and the Bric-A-Brac of the number pleasingly attractive.

There are fifteen important and instructive Papers presented in the *Popular Science Monthly* for April. The opening one is by Herbert Spencer, and entitled, "The Coming Slavery." Lieut. Bradley A. Fiske, U. S. N., writes on "The Electric Railway." "That the ideas as to what electricity can accomplish are visionary and impracticable," says the writer, "may seem to be the case to some. That they are so in reality is not believed by many who have given the subject impartial study. Some of these believe that in the very near future electric cars will supplant the horse cars, and upon short lines like elevated roads, steam locomotives; but it will not be practicable for many years to run electrical cars upon long lines. Such may be the case. But it should be remembered that in most instances in the history of industrial progress the practical developments of meritorious systems have surpassed in rapidity the expectations of even impartial men. A very high scientific authority in England once spoke very favorably of the idea of using steam-vessels for short distances, and for river navigation, but laughed heartily over the suggestion of their ever going to sea, and offered publicly to eat the boilers and engines of the first one that should cross the Atlantic. Probably there are not many men who, in the light of what has recently been accomplished, would promise to eat the motor of the first electric car that should run from New York to Chicago. Persons who complain of the intrusion of drummers and book-agents may be interested in reading what Dr. E. F. Brush has to say on "The Faculty of Speech." "I have said the faculty of speech resides in the anterior lobes of the brain. But the evidence gleaned from pathology is convincing that the faculty is confined to a comparatively limited portion of the frontal lobe of the left cerebral hemisphere. This localization of a function to a single side of the brain is a curiously interesting fact. But when it is known that the left side of the brain presides over the motions and sensations of the right side of the body, it may be conceived that because we are right-handed we are left-minded. Why we are right-handed involves a discussion which would be beyond the limits of the present essay. But that the left side of the brain is almost always larger than the right is a well-known fact, and this asymmetry of the encephalon was prominently brought before the public during the Guiteau trial, with its prominent ghastly rhombocephalic. . . . The highest and best result of education is to form our ideas into words, to crystallize them into speech. We all feel that here we fail. Our thoughts swell up and almost burst their limits, but faulty speech will not give the color and glow which the soul infuses into the thoughts."

In the April number of the *North American Review* Dr. Felix L. Oswald contributes an important Paper on "The Changes in the Climate of North America." The article goes to illustrate the importance of forests to climatic influences; and not only climatic influences, but upon the results of rain-falls and other causes which lead to destructive freshets and swollen rivers. In a part of the Paper the writer discourses somewhat upon the subject of agriculture, and points out to our husbandmen many truths of our agricultural resources and possibilities. "An acre of ground planted with bananas," he says, "will feed as many persons as thirty acres of the best potatoes, or twenty-five acres of wheat. In many parts of Southern Europe the chestnut is the bread plant. A most prolific variety which is cultivated in the highlands of the Appenines would thrive as far north as Connecticut. A single tree often produces several thousand sweet and mealy half-ounce nuts, which the Italians grind like corn, and use for various palatable farinacious preparations, in nutritive value far superior to the potato and rye-bread diet of their northern neighbors. Olive-trees live six centuries, and after the tenth year an olive garden produces fourteen times as much oil as the same area of any

annual plant. . . . Extensive tree-plantations,". the writer asserts, "though at first perhaps dependent upon irrigation, would soon begin to generate their own rain, and modify the climate of the surrounding country. . . . Orchards," it is thought, "will probably open the campaign against the desert, and forest-trees will be added only to utilize the soil of the northern mountain regions." Orchards and forests, it is the belief of the writer, will so materially affect rain-fall and the melting of ice and snow, causing disasters such as have recently been seen along the Ohio, will seldom be heard of. The subject of replanting trees, where much of the country has been shorn of its forests, is thoughtfully considered in the Paper, and some satisfaction may be gleaned from the fact that our statesmen have already begun to think that laws upon the subject are needful. "The total damage of the flood of 1882 has been estimated at $12,000,000 in Ohio and Indiana; of that of 1883 at $22,000,000 in Ohio, $8,000,000 in Indiana, and $6,500,000 in Western Kentucky." These figures are certainly sufficient to start thought in the direction of earnest inquiry to ascertain if remedies are possible. "The Decline of American Shipping" is very forcibly discussed in the number, and very agreeably, too, by N. Dingley, Jr., M.C., and Mr. John Codman, and the "Development of Religious Freedom" is an especially strong Paper, by Rev. Dr. Phillip Schaff. Prof. C. A. Egbert makes "A Plea for Modern Languages," which is well worthy of careful perusal. Julian Hawthorn contributes a sound and sensible Paper on "Literature for Children." A discussion on "Recent Discussions of the Bible," between Rev. A. G. Mortimer and Rev. Dr. R. H. Newton, forms a contribution which cannot fail to attract attention.

In the *Atlantic* for April Mr. Oliver T. Morton discusses the subject of "Presidential Nominations," an interesting topic at this time. In the commencement of his Paper Mr. Morton quotes, *first*, M. de Tocqueville; and, *second*, John Stuart Mill. M. de Tocqueville visited the United States during the administration of Andrew Jackson, and expressed his opinion that there was much more distinguished talent among the subjects of this country than among the heads of the Government. "It is a well-authenticated fact," he said, "that at the present day the most able men in the United States are very rarely placed at the head of affairs; and it must be acknowledged that such has been the result, in proportion as democracy has outstepped all its former limits. The race of American statesmen has evidently dwindled most remarkably in the course of the last fifty years. This is as much a consequence of the circumstances as of the laws of the country." A portion of the quotation from John Stuart Mill is, "In the United States, at the election of President, the strongest party never dares put forward any of its strongest men, because every one of these, from the mere fact that he has been long in the public eye, has made himself objectionable to some portion or other of the party, and is therefore not so sure a card for rallying all their votes as a person who has never been heard of by the public at all until he is produced as the candidate. Thus the man who is chosen, even by the strongest party, represents, perhaps, the real wishes only of the narrow margin by which that party outnumbers the other. Any section whose support is necessary to success possesses a veto on the candidate." Mr. Morton, while admitting that Mr. Mill and M. de Tocqueville are right in their views, asserts that in their conclusion lies a fundamental error. "If democracy is responsible for the colorless character of its Presidents," he says, "it is a sin of omission, and not of commission." In summing up, the writer offers a plan for nominating the chief magistrate, which, if followed, he believes would be attended with beneficent results — remedying many of the evils existing under the present system. George Parsons Lathrop writes on "Night in New York." Maria Louise Henry contributes an interesting chapter on "Madame de Longueville." N. S. Shaler furnishes an interesting Paper on "The Red Sunsets." The department of fiction is well sustained. Henry James continues "En Province," which has reached the seventh chapter. F. Marion Crawford presents the nineteenth and twentieth chapters of "A Roman Singer." Edith M. Thomas writes on "The Return of a Native." S. Weir Mitchell continues the interesting story, "In War Time."

In the April number of the *Phrenological Journal* we find a noteworthy sketch, with portrait, of Wendell Phillips. The article adds an important page to the biography of one of our ablest of departed statesmen and orators. Under the title of "Collins's Ode to the Passions" is furnished an unusually spicy and agreeable description of our personal emotions: fear, terror, anger, despair, jealousy, and mirthfulness. Major-Gen. Chas. G. Gordon, who at the present time is figuring so prominently in the British soldiery, furnishes the subject of a sketch written from a phrenologist's point of view. The article is accompanied by a portrait, which adds to its attractiveness. "Causation and Prevention of Insanity" is discussed in an able article by Dr. Reynolds, of Maine. This is a subject that cannot be too carefully considered. "Advancement of civilization," says the writer, "brings no relief from insanity. On the contrary, insanity has increased with the advance of civilization, and is increasing to-day faster than ever before." Dr. Geo. M. Beard is quoted as saying, "Insanity is a barometer of modern civilization. Though existing in all recorded ages, and among all peoples, and known under various and inconsistent names and superstitions, yet is rare, and always has been rare, with the savage, the barbarian, and the partly enlightened. There is no race, no climate, no institution, no environment, that can make insanity common, save when united with, and re-enforced by, brainwork and in-door life." This certainly should be a powerful warning to our class of readers. Let us study the causes of insanity, and the means for the prevention of this greatest misfortune which can befall any human being. Many things can be done with little care or cost that will aid to fortify the system against danger.

BUSINESS REVERSES.

Agricultural Implements.

V. J. Williams & Co., Dubuque, Iowa, attached for $12,633; debts estimated at $39,000.

Books and Stationery.

McCarthy, Carlton & Co., Richmond, Va., assigned; debts about $12,000; assets, $15,000.

Boots and Shoes.

Peter L nsing, Deer Lodge, Mont., assigned; debts, $24,000; assets, $26,000.

Joseph S. Smith, manufacturer, Philadelphia, Pa., suspended; debts about $18,000; assets, $12,-000.

Charles Emerson, manufacturer, Stoneham, Mass., assigned; debts reported at $30,000.

T. P. & S. S. Smith, manufacturers, Philadelphia, Pa., suspended; offer 15 cents in two and four months; debts, $48,000; assets, $43,000.

Clothing.

Henry Lewis & Co., Hartford, Conn., assigned; debts, $11,000; assets, $6,000.

Henry J. Woodrich, Chicago, Ill., closed by sheriff; debts, $22,000; assets, $16,000.

Commission.

B. Blake & Co., Baltimore, Md., grain and flour, assigned; debts estimated, $23,000; assets, $16,-000.

W. Waterman & Co., San Francisco, Cal., grain; schedules show debts, $942,011; actual assets, $866,238; offer 50 cents.

Edward Pilsbury's Sons, New Orleans, La., cotton, failed ; debts, $135,867 ; nominal assets, $152,-700.

E. W. Coleman & Co., New York City, flour and grain ; schedules show debts $758,660 ; actual assets, $56,752.

D. L. Mowry & Son, cotton, Charleston, S. C., failed ; debts reported at $150,000 ; nominal assets, $225,000.

Crockery and Glassware.

T. & E. Jaeger & Co., wholesale crockery, Chicago, Ill., assigned ; debts, $67,000 ; assets, $50,000.

Dry Goods and Notions.

M. K. Bitterman, Junction, Kan., dry goods and clothing, assigned ; debts, $9,000 ; nominal assets, $24,000.

Quinn Bros., Little Rock, Ark., failed ; debts estimated at $40,000 ; actual assets about $23,000.

Joseph Freeman, importer, New York City, assigned ; giving preferences for $44,801.

Delane & Hickok, Augusta, Ga., assigned ; debts, $83,985 ; assets, $72,548.

W. L. King, Brockport, N. Y., assigned ; debts, $18,000 ; assets, $10,000 ; preferences, $9,000.

Financial : Bankers, Brokers, and Capitalists.

Central Bank of Upper Sandusky, Ohio, suspended ; debts, $60,000 to $100,000.

J. Hodges, banker, Plattsville, Wis., assigned ; debts, $124,000 ; assets, $226,000.

Geo. R. Curry, Augusta, Ga., banker, assigned ; debts about $220,000 ; assets nominally the same.

McGinnis Bros. & Fearing, bankers and brokers, suspended ; debts over $150,000 ; assets probably larger.

Merchants' and Mechanics' National Bank of Leadville, Col., receiver appointed.

Furniture.

Riverside Furniture Co., Wheeling, W. Va., assigned ; debts, $76,000.

General Store.

Bennett & Wishon Mercantile Co., Sullivan, Mo., assigned.

E. D. Putney, Antrim, N. H., failed ; debts reported at $18,000 ; nominal assets, $10,000.

Gleaves & Averill, Redding, Cal., failed ; debts about $29,000 ; assets, $22,000.

Thomas & Hart, Rocky Mount, N. C., assigned ; debts, $20,000.

J. C. Smathers, Turnpike, N. C., assigned ; debts, $16,000 ; assets, $13,000.

Allen & Martin, Albany, Oregon, reported failed ; debts about $30,000 ; assets, $20,000.

Produce and Grain.

Henry McEwen, Morris, Ill., failed ; debts, $62,000 ; assets, $46,000 ; preferences, $29,394.

C. F. Kingsley, Fall River, Mass., failed ; debts about $26,000 ; actual assets, $7,000.

Grocers.

W. F. Burns, Santa Cruz, Cal., attached ; debts, $14,000 ; assets, $5,000.

F. H. Stilling, Augusta, Ga., failed.

Hardware.

Davis & Ketcher, Little Rock, Ark., assigned, and receiver appointed ; debts, $14,000 ; assets, same.

Iron.

Higgins & Morton, Elizabethport, N. J., assigned ; debts, $27,000 ; nominal assets, $22,000.

Jewelry.

W. A. Smith, Boston, Mass., assigned ; debts about $200,000.

Lumber.

Watertown Lumber Co., Boston, Mass., failed ;

John O. Terry & Sons, New Orleans, La., ask extension ; debts, $41,914 ; assets nominal, $79,000.

J. O. Sullivan, St. Louis, Mo., assigned ; assets, $30,000.

Notions, Fancy Goods, and Novelties.

B. A. Dryer, New York City, confessed judgment ; debts about $20,000.

Oils and Lamps.

H. Koster, San Francisco, Cal., failed ; debts, $26,000 ; assets, $15,000.

Paper.

Thomas & Bossel, Philadelphia, Pa., failed ; debts, $24,000.

Silk.

Geo. L. Broomhall, Paterson, N. J., manufacturer, obtained extension ; net capital about $20,-000.

Miscellaneous.

Lea & Cresson, Philadelphia, Pa., Albion Print Works, assigned.

Glessner & Ross, cracker and confectionery manufacturers, Kansas City, Mo., attached for $29,000 ; debts, $14,000.

Wm. S. Fogg & Son, New York City, bedding, assigned ; debts, $37,776 ; actual assets, $22,309.

George Parsons, fireworks, New York City, assigned, with preferences ; debts, 35,000 ; assets, $20,000.

The Jones Car Manufacturing Co., Schenectady, N. Y., receiver appointed ; debts, $200,000.

J. M. Jones' Sons, car manufacturers, West Troy, N. Y., assigned, with preference.

Hofberg Brewing Co., West Berkeley, Cal., offer 40 cents ; accepted ; debts, $40,000 ; assets, $22,-000.

U. S. Smelting Co., Philadelphia, Pa., failed ; debts about $165,000.

MARKETS AND EXCHANGES.

(WHEN NO FIGURES ARE GIVEN THE PRICE REMAINS THE SAME AS LAST QUOTATION.)

Foreign Exchange.—Closing Rates for each Day in February.

	1.	2.	4.	5.	6.	7.	8.	9.	11.	12.	13.	14.	15.	16.	18.	19.	20.	21.	22.	23.	25.	26.	27.	28.	29.
London .... 60 days	486¼	....	....	....	....	....	....	....	....	....	....	....	....	....	....	486¾	487	....		....	....	....	....	487½	....
" .... 3 "	489	....	....	....	....	489½	....	....	490	....	....	....	....	....	....	....	490½	....		....	....	....	....	....	....
Paris, francs .... 60 "	516¼	....	....	....	....	....	....	....	....	....	....	....	....	....	....	....	....	....		....	....	....	....	....	516¼
" " .... 3 "	513⅞	....	....	....	....	....	....	....	....	....	....	....	....	....	....	....	....	....	Holiday	....	....	....	....	....	....
Geneva .... 60 "	516¼	....	....	....	....	....	....	....	....	....	....	....	....	....	....	....	....	....		....	....	....	....	....	515⅝
" .... 3 "	513⅜	....	....	....	....	....	....	....	....	....	....	....	....	....	....	....	....	....		....	....	....	....	....	513¾
Berlin, reichmarks .... 60 "	95⅜	....	....	....	....	....	....	....	....	....	....	....	....	....	....	....	....	....		....	....	....	....	....	....
" " .... 3 "	96	....	....	....	....	....	....	....	....	....	....	....	....	....	....	....	....	....		....	....	....	....	....	....
Amsterdam, guilders .... 60 "	40½	....	....	....	....	....	....	....	....	....	....	....	....	....	....	....	....	....		....	....	....	....	....	....
" " .... 3 "	40⅜	....	....	....	....	....	....	....	....	....	....	....	....	....	....	....	....	....		....	....	....	....	....	....

Government Bonds and Currency.—Closing Prices at the New York Board during February.

	Interest Periods.	1.	2.	4.	5.	6.	7.	8.	9.	11.	12.	13.	14.	15.	16.	18.	19.	20.	21.	22.	23.	25.	26.	27.	28.	29.
4½s, 1891 .... reg.	Q.-Mar.	113½	113⅝	113⅞	113⅜	....	113½	....	....	....	113¼	113½	....	113⅜	....	....	....	....	113½		....	....	113⅜	....	....	113⅜
4½s, 1891 .... coup.	Q.-Mar.	114½	114⅝	....	....	114½	114⅝	....	....	....	....	....	....	....	....	114½	114⅝	114½	....		114⅝	....	....	....	....	....
4s, 1907 .... reg.	Q.-Jan.	123⅜	123⅜	123⅜	....	....	....	....	....	123⅜	....	....	....	123⅜	....	123⅜	124	123⅜	....		....	....	....	....	....	....
4s, 1907 .... coup.	Q.-Jan.	123⅜	....	....	....	....	....	....	....	....	....	123⅜	....	123⅜	....	....	....	....	....	Holiday	....	....	....	....	....	....
3s, option U. S. .... reg.	Q.-Feb.	100¼	....	....	....	....	100⅝	100¼	100¼	100⅝	....	101	....	....	....	....	100⅝	....	....		....	101	....	....	....	....
6s, cur'cy, 1895 .... reg.	J. & J.	129	....	....	....	....	....	....	....	129½	....	....	129	....	....	....	....	....	....		....	....	....	....	....	....
6s, cur'cy, 1896 .... reg.	J. & J.	131	....	....	....	....	....	....	....	131¼	....	....	131	....	....	....	....	....	....		....	....	....	....	....	....
6s, cur'cy, 1897 .... reg.	J. & J.	133	....	....	....	....	....	....	....	133½	....	....	133	....	....	....	....	....	....		....	....	....	....	....	....
6s, cur'cy, 1898 .... reg.	J. & J.	135	....	....	....	....	....	....	....	135½	....	....	135	....	....	....	....	....	....		....	....	....	....	....	....
6s, cur'cy, 1899 .... reg.	J. & J.	137	....	....	....	....	....	....	....	137½	....	....	137	....	....	....	....	....	....		....	....	....	....	....	....

New York Stock Exchange.—Daily Highest Prices for February.

STOCKS.	1.	2.	4.	5.	6.	7.	8.	9.	11.	12.	13.	14.	15.	16.	18.	19.	20.	21.	22.	23.	25.	26.	27.	28.	29.
RAILROADS.																									
Atchison, Topeka & S. F.	80⅜	....	....	....	....	....	....	....	....	....	....	....	....	....	....	....	....	....		....	....	....	....	....	....
Boston Air-Line, pref.	81½	....	....	....	....	....	....	82½	....	....	82	....	....	....	....	....	82½	....		82⅝	82½	....	....	....	82⅝
Bur., Cedar Rap. & No.	70	75	....	....	....	....	....	....	....	....	....	....	....	....	....	....	....	....		....	....	....	....	....	....
Canadian Pacific	56¼	55⅜	56½	55⅞	55¾	54¼	55½	56	55⅞	55½	55	55⅜	55½	56½	55⅜	55	56½	55⅞		55⅛	55⅜	55⅛	55	54½	54⅝
Canada Southern	54½	55½	56	55⅜	55½	55⅛	56¼	56⅞	57⅛	56⅞	56¼	56¼	57⅛	57⅜	56½	56	56¼	56⅛		56	55½	55⅛	54⅜	53⅞	53½
Central of New Jersey	87	87⅞	88	87½	89	88½	89⅝	89⅞	88⅜	87½	87	87⅛	87¾	88¼	87½	88⅝	89⅛	90	Holiday	89⅝	89¼	....	88¼	88½	87½
Central Pacific	64	65⅛	....	64⅛	64½	63⅞	63⅛	63⅜	63½	62⅝	....	63	63¼	63⅜	63¼	62⅝	63	62⅞		62⅝	62	61⅛	60⅝	60⅛	61
Chesapeake & Ohio	15	14⅝	14⅜	14	15	14⅝	14	13⅞	14	14⅛	....	....	....	....	....	....	14⅜	14⅛		14⅛	14	....	14⅛	14	13⅝
Do 1st pref.	23⅞	26⅛	27⅛	26⅝	27	....	27½	28	....	....	27½	28	....	27⅛	....	26⅛	26	25½		26½	27	26⅛	27	26⅛	25
Do 2d pref.	16	17⅜	....	16	18	....	17	18	....	17	16⅝	17⅛	15	17	....	....	....	....		17⅛	17	....	....	....	16⅛
Chicago & Alton	140	....	141	140½	....	139	....	....	139½	....	....	139	....	135	136	134⅝	136	135½		136	....	135⅜	133⅞	134½	....
Chicago, Bur. & Quincy	122½	124½	....	126¼	125½	125½	126	126⅝	127⅛	127½	126⅝	127½	....	127⅝	127	126⅝	127½	127⅞		126⅛	127½	126⅛	124⅛	123½	123
Chicago, Mil. & St. Paul	90⅝	92	92⅛	92½	91⅞	91½	93½	93⅜	94⅛	93⅝	93⅝	93⅝	93⅜	94½	93½	92⅝	93¼	93⅜		93	92⅝	92½	91½	90⅞	90⅝
Do pref.	117	....	118	117½	117½	....	117	118	118¼	118¼	118	118¼	....	119	118½	117½	118	117½		117⅝	....	117	117⅞	117	116
Chicago & Northwest	119	120½	121⅜	121½	120½	120⅝	121½	122½	123½	124	122½	123½	....	123½	122⅜	122⅛	....	122½		122	121⅝	121½	120	118⅝	118⅛
Do pref.	145⅜	147½	....	....	146½	145⅛	147	148	148⅜	149½	148½	149½	148⅛	148⅜	146½	146	146½	147½		....	146	145	....	144½	142½
Chicago, R. I. & P.	118	119	120	120⅜	119⅞	119	119½	122½	126⅝	125¼	124½	124½	125⅝	126	125	124	124½	....		124½	123½	123½	122	121½	121

Holiday

Chicago, St. Louis & Pitts.																		
Do pref.																		
Chicago, St. P., M. & O. pref.																		
Do pref.																		
Cincinnati, Sand. & Cleve.																		
Cleveland, Col., Cinn. & Ind.																		
Cleveland & Pittsburg, guar.																		
Columbus, Lack. & Ind. Cen.																		
Delaware, Lack. & West.																		
Denver & Rio Grande.																		
East Tenn., Va. & Ga.																		
Do pref.																		
Evansville & Terre Haute.																		
Green Bay, Winona & St. P.																		
Hannibal & St. Joseph pref.																		
Harlem.																		
Houston & Texas Central.																		
Illinois Central.																		
Do leased line.																		
Indiana, Bloom'n & Western.																		
Lake Erie & Western.																		
Lake Shore.																		
Long Island.																		
Louisiana & Missouri River.																		
Louisville & Nashville.																		
Louisville, N. Alb. & Chic.																		
Manhattan Elevated.																		
Do 1st pref.																		
Do common.																		
Manhattan Beach Co.																		
Memphis & Charleston.																		
Metropolitan Elevated.																		
Michigan Central.																		
Mil., L. Sh., & West.																		
Do pref.																		
Minneapolis & St. L.																		
Do pref.																		
Missouri, Kansas & Texas.																		
Missouri Pacific.																		
Mobile & Ohio.																		
Morris & Essex.																		
Nashville, Chat. & St. L.																		
N. Y., Central & Hudson.																		
N. Y., Chic. & St. Louis.																		
Do pref.																		
New York Elevated.																		
N. Y., Lack. & Western.																		
N. Y., Lake Erie & W.																		
Do pref.																		
N. Y. & New England.																		
N. Y., New Haven & Hart.																		
N. Y., Ontario & Western.																		
N. Y., Susq. & Western.																		
Do pref.																		
Norfolk & Western.																		
Do pref.																		
Northern Pacific.																		
Do pref.																		
Ohio Central.																		
Ohio & Mississippi.																		
Do pref.																		
Ohio Southern.																		

[*Continued on next page.*]

New York Stock Exchange.—Daily Highest Prices for February.—*Continued.*

STOCKS.	1.	2.	4.	5.	6.	7.	8.	9.	11.	12.	13.	14.	15.	16.	18.	19.	20.	21.	22.	23.	25.	26.	27.	28.	29.
RAILROADS.																									
Oregon & Trans–Continental																			Holiday						
Peoria, Decatur & Evansville																									
Philadelphia & Reading																									
Pittsburg, Ft. Wayne & Chic.																									
Richmond & Alleghany																									
Richmond & Danville																									
Richmond & West Point																									
Rochester & Pittsburg																									
St. Louis, Alton & T. H.																									
Do pref.																									
St. Louis & San Fran.																									
Do pref.																									
Do 1st pref.																									
St. Paul & Duluth																									
Do pref.																									
St. Paul, Minneap. & Man.																									
Texas & Pacific																									
Union Pacific																									
Wabash, St. L. & Pac.																									
Do pref.																									
MISCELLANEOUS.																									
American Tel. & Cable Co.																									
Bankers' & Merchants' Tel																									
Colorado Coal & Iron																									
Delaware & Hudson Canal																									
Mutual Union Telegraph																									
New Central Coal																									
N. Y. & Tex. Land Co.																									
Oregon Improvem't Co.																									
Oregon R'way & Nav. Co.																									
Pacific Mail																									
Pullman Palace Car																									
Quicksilver Mining																									
Do pref																									
Standard Consol. Mining																									
Western Union Telegraph																									
EXPRESS.																									
Adams																									
American																									
United States																									
Wells, Fargo & Co.																									

Petroleum.—Prices for each Day in February.

	1.	2.	4.	5.	6.	7.	8.	9.	11.	12.	13.	14.	15.	16.	18.	19.	20.	21.	22.	23.	25.	26.	27.	28.	29.
Pipe Line Certific's—highest																			Holiday						
" " lowest																									
Crude in bbls.																									
Naphtha																									
Refined, cargo lots, 110 deg.																									
" 70 deg. Abel test.																									

Grain.—Highest Prices for Future Delivery for each Day in February.

WHEAT—	1.	2.	4.	5.	6.	7.	8.	9.	11.	12.	13.	14.	15.	16.	18.	19.	20.	21.	22.	23.	25.	26.	27.	28.	29.
February	105	105⅝	106½	....	107¼	107⅞	107⅞	107⅝	109	108¼	109	....	108⅝	108⅞	....	108⅝	108⅝	....	Holiday.	107⅞	....	....	....	....	....
March	107⅝	107⅝	108½	108	109	109⅝	108⅝	109⅝	110¼	....	110⅜	110¼	109⅝	110¼	109⅝	....	109⅜	109⅞		108⅜	108¼	108⅝	108⅛	108½	108
April	109⅞	110	110¼	110⅜	111⅝	112	111	111½	113¼	....	113⅜	113¼	112¼	112⅝	112¼	112	....	111⅛		111⅛	110⅜	110⅜	....	110¼	110⅜
May	112½	112⅛	113	112⅞	114	114⅝	113¼	114⅝	115⅝	....	116	115⅝	114⅝	115¼	114¾	...	114¼	113⅜		113¾	113	113½	113⅛	112⅞	112⅝
....	....	....	....	....	....	....	....	....	....	....	....	....	...	....	....	....	....	....		....	....	....	....	....	....

CORN—	1.	2.	4.	5.	6.	7.	8.	9.	11.	12.	13.	14.	15.	16.	18.	19.	20.	21.	22.	23.	25.	26.	27.	28.	29.
February	60⅝	61	61½	61½	62	62⅛	61⅝	....	63⅜	63⅛	64	64⅛	63⅞	63⅛	....	63	62⅛	..	Holiday.	62¾	62	62⅛	....	62⅛	62⅝
March	61⅝	....	62⅛	62½	63	63⅛	62⅝	....	63⅝	63⅝	64½	65⅛	64	64⅝	63⅜	63⅛	63⅛	62⅜		62⅝	62⅛	62⅝	....	....	62⅛
April	63½	....	64	63⅝	64⅛	65	64½	....	64⅝	....	65⅜	66½	65¼	65⅝	65⅛	64⅛	64⅝	64⅛		63⅝	63⅝	63⅜	....	63⅝	63⅛
May	64⅝	65	65⅛	65⅝	66⅛	66⅛	65⅜	65⅝	66⅛	66⅞	67⅝	67⅞	66⅛	67	66⅛	66	65⅝	65⅛		65⅜	65⅛	....	....	65	64⅝
....	....	....	....	....	....	....	....	....	....	....	....	...	....	....	....	....	....	....		....	....	....	....	....	....

OATS—	1.	2.	4.	5.	6.	7.	8.	9.	11.	12.	13.	14.	15.	16.	18.	19.	20.	21.	22.	23.	25.	26.	27.	28.	29.
February	39⅝	39⅝	39⅞	....	40⅝	40¼	40½	40¼	41	41½	41⅝	....	....	....	41⅛	42⅝	41½	41	Holiday.	40⅝	....	....	....	....	....
March	40⅝	40⅝	....	....	41½	....	41	41⅛	41⅛	....	42	....	....	....	41⅝	....	41⅛	41		40⅝	....	40⅛	....	....	....
April	41½	....	....	41⅞	42½	....	42	42⅛	42⅝	....	43	....	....	....	42⅝	....	42½	42		41⅝	....	41⅛	....	....	....
May	42⅛	42½	....	42⅝	42⅞	42⅞	42½	43	43⅛	43¼	43⅝	....	43⅛	....	43½	43⅛	42⅞	42⅝		42⅛	42	42⅛	....	....	42⅛
....	....	....	....	..	....	....	....	....	....	....	....	....	....	....	....	....	....	....		....	....	....	....	....	....

Flour.—Closing Prices.

	First Quarter.		Second Quarter.		Third Quarter.		Fourth Quarter.	
No. 2 spring .... per bbl.	$2.00 @	2.50	$.... @	....	$2.10 @	2.50	$2.25 @	2.60
No. 2 winter	2.25	2.80	....	....	2.25	2.85	2.40	3.00
Superfine	2.65	3.35	2.75	3.35	2.75	3.35	2.75	3.40
Spring wheat extras	3.50	4.50	....	....	....	....	3.50	4.75
Minn. clear and straight	4.50	5.60	4.50	5.75	4.50	5.65	4.50	5.75
Winter shipping extras	3.15	3.50	3.35	3.50	3.15	3.50	3.25	3.60
Winter clear and straight	4.00	6.00	4.50	6.00	....	....	4.50	6.00
Patents, spring	5.50	6.75	5.50	6.85	....	....	5.75	6.85
Patents, winter	5.50	6.90	5.50	7.00	5.50	6.90	5.40	7.00

	First Quarter.		Second Quarter.		Third Quarter.		Fourth Quarter.	
City shipping extras .... per bbl.	$5.15 @	5.40	$5.25 @	5.50	$5.15 @	5.50	$5.10 @	5.50
South'n bakers' and family brands	4.50	6.25	4.50	6.00	....	....	4.60	6.25
Southern shipping extras	3.50	5.50	3.50	5.25	....	....	3.65	5.50
Rye flour, superfine	3.40	3.75	....	....	....	....	....	....
CORN MEAL—								
Western, etc	3.00	3.25	3.00	3.30	....	....	....	....
Brandywine, etc	3.30	3.45	3.35	3.45	....	....	....	....
Buckwheat flour .... per 100 lbs.	3.25	3.50	3.00	3.25	2.75	3.00	....	....

New York Coffee Exchange.—Spot Quotations on Rio Coffee for each Day in February.

	1.	2.	4.	5.	6.	7.	8.	9.	11.	12.	13.	14.	15.	16.	18.	19.	20.	21.	22.	23.	25.	26.	27.	28.	29.
Prime	12.90	....	....	....	....	....	12.75	....	....	....	....	....	12.90	12 80	....	....	....	....	Holiday.	....	....	....	12.90	....	....
Good	12.65	....	....	....	....	....	12.50	....	....	....	....	....	12.65	12.55	....	....	....	....		....	....	....	12.65	....	....
Fair	12.40	....	....	....	....	....	12.25	....	....	....	....	....	12.40	12.30	....	....	....	....		....	....	....	12.40	....	....
Low Fair	12.10	....	....	....	....	....	11.95	....	....	....	....	....	12.10	12.00	....	....	....	....		....	....	....	12.10	....	....
G'd Ordi'y	11.75	....	....	....	....	....	11.60	....	....	....	....	....	11.75	11.65	....	....	....	....		....	....	....	11.75	....	....
Ordinary	11.40	....	....	....	....	....	11.25	....	....	....	....	....	11.40	....	....	....	....	....		....	....	....	11.50	....	....
LowOrd'y	10.90	....	....	....	....	....	10.75	....	....	....	....	....	10.90	....	....	....	....	....		....	....	....	11.00	....	....
St. G.Com	10.40	....	....	....	....	....	10.25	....	....	....	....	....	10.40	....	....	....	....	....		....	....	....	10.50	....	....
Good Com	10.00	....	....	....	....	....	9.85	....	....	....	....	....	10.00	....	....	....	....	....		....	....	....	10.10	....	....
Common	9.65	....	....	....	....	....	9.50	....	....	....	....	....	9.65	....	....	....	....	....		....	....	....	9.75	....	....

Sugar.—Highest Prices at Closing of each Day in February.

	1.	2.	4.	5.	6.	7.	8.	9.	11.	12.	13	14.	15.	16.	18.	19.	20.	21.	22.	23.	25.	26.	27.	28.	29.
RAW SUGAR.																									
Com. to good refi. Cuba	6⅜	....	....	....	....	....	....	....	....	....	....	....	....	....	....	....	....	....	Holiday	....	....	....	....	....	....
Com. to good refi. Porto Rico	6¼	....	....	....	....	....	....	....	....	....	....	....	....	....	....	....	....	....		....	....	....	....	....	....
Centrifugal	7¼	....	....	....	....	....	....	....	....	....	....	....	....	....	....	....	....	....		....	....	....	....	....	....
Manilla	6⅛	....	....	....	....	....	....	....	....	....	....	....	....	....	....	....	....	....		....	....	....	....	....	....
Pernams	6¼	....	....	....	....	....	....	....	....	....	....	....	....	....	....	....	....	....		....	....	....	....	....	....
Bahia	5⅜	....	....	....	....	....	....	....	....	....	....	....	....	....	....	....	....	....		....	....	....	....	....	....
Melado	....	....	....	....	....	....	....	....	....	....	....	....	....	....	....	....	....	....		....	....	....	....	....	....
REFINED SUGAR.																									
Cut loaf	8½	....	....	....	....	....	....	....	....	8⅛	....	8⅛	8⅛	....	....	....	....	8		....	....	....	7⅝	....	7⅝
Crushed	8½	....	....	....	....	8⅛	8⅛	....	....	8⅛	....	8⅛	8⅛	....	....	....	....	8		....	....	....	7⅞	....	7⅝
Cubes	8⅛	....	8	8⅛	....	....	....	....	....	8	....	....	7⅞	....	....	....	....	....		....	7⅝	....	....	....	7⅝
Powdered	8⅛	....	8	....	....	....	....	....	....	....	....	....	7⅞	....	....	....	....	....		....	....	....	7⅝	....	....
Granulated	7 13/16	....	7⅝	....	....	....	....	7⅝	7⅝	7 11/16	....	....	....	....	....	7⅝	....	7 9/16		....	7½	....	....	....	7⅝
Mould "A"	7⅝	....	....	....	....	....	....	....	....	7½	....	....	....	7½	....	7⅝	....	....		....	7⅝	....	....	....	7⅝
Confectioners' "A"	7½	....	7 7/16	....	....	....	7½	....	7 7/16	7⅝	....	....	....	....	....	....	7 5/16	7½		....	....	....	7 7/16	7½	....
Coffee "A" standard	7⅝	....	....	....	....	....	....	....	....	7½	....	....	....	....	....	....	....	....		....	....	....	7⅜	....	....
Coffee off "A"	7⅛	....	7	....	....	....	....	....	....	6⅞	....	....	....	....	7	....	....	....		....	6⅞	....	6⅞	....	....
White extra "C"	6⅝	....	....	6 9/16	....	....	....	....	....	....	....	....	6⅛	....	....	....	....	....		....	....	....	6⅝	....	....
Extra "C"	6⅛	....	....	....	6 7/16	....	....	....	....	6⅝	....	....	6⅛	....	....	....	....	....		....	....	....	6⅛	....	....
"C"	6⅛	....	....	....	....	....	....	....	....	6	....	....	5⅞	....	....	....	....	....		....	....	....	5⅝	....	....
Yellow	5⅜	....	....	....	....	....	....	....	....	5⅝	....	....	....	....	....	....	....	....		....	....	....	5⅛	....	....
Yellow "C"	....	....	....	....	....	....	....	....	....	....	....	....	....	....	....	....	....	....		....	....	....	....	....	....

Lard.—Highest Price for Future Delivery for each Day in February.

	1.	2.	4.	5.	6.	7.	8.	9.	11.	12.	13.	14.	15.	16.	18.	19.	20.	21.	22.	23.	25.	26.	27.	28.	29.
February	9.39	9.48	9.60	9.95	9.80	9.75	9.70	9.75	10.00	10.10	10.03	10.25	10.15	10.20	10.10	9.99	9.87	9.95	Holiday	....	9.93	9.90	....	....	....
March	9.46	9.57	9.72	9.85	9.89	9.84	9.77	9.83	10.04	10.13	10.24	10.26	10.24	10.21	10.16	9.99	9.90	9.98		10.00	9.96	9.90	9.85	9.73	9.78
April	9.53	9.30	9.80	9.92	9.98	9.92	9.85	9.92	10.14	10.22	10.28	10.32	10.30	....	10.24	10.03	9.93	10.04		10.08	10.05	9.98	9.93	9.83	....
May	9.61	9.75	9.92	10.06	10.10	10.02	9.96	10.03	10.25	10.34	10.37	10.38	....	10.36	10.30	10.12	10.02	10.12		10.14	10.12	10.06	10.00	9.89	9.90
June	9.68	9.78	9.95	10.12	10.18	10.10	9.99	10.05	10.30	10.36	10.42	10.45	10.44	10.40	....	10.15	10.03	10.15		10.20	10.17	10.05	10.03	9.93	9.98
July	9.73	....	10.00	10.15	10.22	10.10	10.05	10.10	10.35	10.45	....	10.52	10.45	10.50	10.45	10.20	10.10	10.20		10.25	....	10.08	10.12	9.97	9.95

Pork.—Highest Spot Prices for each Day in February.

	1.	2.	4.	5.	6.	7.	8.	9.	11.	12.	13.	14.	15.	16.	18.	19.	20.	21.	22.	23.	25.	26.	27.	28.	29.
Mess	15.75	16.00	17.00	....	....	16.50	16.62½	16.75	17.00	17.50	18.25	....	....	....	18.00	18.25	18.00	....	Holiday	....	....	....	....	15.75	....
Extra Prime	14.50	....	15.50	....	....	....	16.00	....	16.50	....	17.50	....	....	....	....	....	17.25	....		....	....	....	....	....	....
Prime Mess	15.75	....	....	....	....	....	....	....	....	....	....	....	....	....	....	....	....	....		....	....	....	....	....	....
Clear Back	19.00	19.50	20.00	....	....	19.50	20.00	....	20.50	20.75	21.00	....	....	....	20.50	....	....	....		....	21.00	....	....	....	....
Family	17.00	19.50	18.00	....	18.25	....	....	19.06	19.50	....	20.00	....	....	....	....	....	....	....		....	....	....	....	....	....

Cotton.—Current Prices for each Day in February.

	1.	2.	4.	5.	6.	7.	8.	9.	11.	12.	13.	14.	15.	16.	18.	19.	20.	21.	22.	23.	25.	26.	27.	28.	29.
UPLANDS.																									
Ordinary.....per lb.	8 1/4	....	....	....	....	....	....	....	....	....	....	....	....	....	....	....	....	....	Holiday	....	....	8 9/16	8 1/4	....	....
Strict Ordinary	8 11/16	....	....	....	....	....	....	....	....	....	....	....	....	....	....	....	....	....		....	....	9	9 1/16	....	....
Good Ordinary	9 1/4	....	....	....	....	....	....	....	....	....	....	....	....	....	....	....	....	....		....	....	9 13/16	9 5/8	....	....
Strict Good Ordinary	10 1/8	....	....	....	....	....	....	....	....	....	....	....	....	....	....	....	....	....		....	....	10 3/16	10 1/4	....	....
Low Middling	10 3/8	....	....	....	....	....	....	....	....	....	....	....	....	....	....	....	....	....		....	....	10 7/16	10 1/2	....	....
Strict Low Middling	10 9/16	....	....	....	....	....	....	....	....	....	....	....	....	....	....	....	....	....		....	....	10 5/8	10 11/16	....	....
Middling	10 3/4	....	....	....	....	....	....	....	....	....	....	....	....	....	....	....	....	....		....	....	10 13/16	10 7/8	....	....
Good Middling	11	....	....	....	....	....	....	....	....	....	....	....	....	....	....	....	....	....		....	....	11 1/16	11 1/8	....	....
Strict Good Middling	11 1/4	....	....	....	....	....	....	....	....	....	....	....	....	....	....	....	....	....		....	....	11 5/16	11 3/8	....	....
Middling Fair	11 5/8	....	....	....	....	....	....	....	....	....	....	....	....	....	....	....	....	....		....	....	11 11/16	11 3/4	....	....
Fair	12 3/8	....	....	....	....	....	....	....	....	....	....	....	....	....	....	....	....	....		....	....	12 1/16	12 1/8	....	....
NEW ORLEANS.																									
Ordinary.....per lb.	8 3/8	....	....	....	....	....	....	....	....	....	....	....	....	....	....	....	....	....		....	....	8 13/16	8 5/8	....	....
Strict Ordinary	9 3/16	....	....	....	....	....	....	....	....	....	....	....	....	....	....	....	....	....		....	....	9 5/8	9 5/16	....	....
Good Ordinary	10	....	....	....	....	....	....	....	....	....	....	....	....	....	....	....	....	....		....	....	10 3/16	10 1/4	....	....
Strict Good Ordinary	10 3/8	....	....	....	....	....	....	....	....	....	....	....	....	....	....	....	....	....		....	....	10 7/16	10 1/2	....	....
Low Middling	10 5/8	....	....	....	....	....	....	....	....	....	....	....	....	....	....	....	....	....		....	....	10 11/16	10 3/4	....	....
Strict Low Middling	10 13/16	....	....	....	....	....	....	....	....	....	....	....	....	....	....	....	....	....		....	....	10 7/8	10 15/16	....	....
Middling	11	....	....	....	....	....	....	....	....	....	....	....	....	....	....	....	....	....		....	....	11 1/16	11 1/8	....	....
Good Middling	11 1/4	....	....	....	....	....	....	....	....	....	....	....	....	....	....	....	....	....		....	....	11 5/16	11 3/8	....	....
Strict Good Middling	11 5/8	....	....	....	....	....	....	....	....	....	....	....	....	....	....	....	....	....		....	....	11 9/16	11 5/8	....	....
Middling Fair	11 7/8	....	....	....	....	....	....	....	....	....	....	....	....	....	....	....	....	....		....	....	11 15/16	12	....	....
Fair	12 3/8	....	....	....	....	....	....	....	....	....	....	....	....	....	....	....	....	....		....	....	12 5/16	12 3/8	....	....
TEXAS.																									
Ordinary.....per lb.	8 3/8	....	....	....	....	....	....	....	....	....	....	....	....	....	....	....	....	....		....	....	8 13/16	8 5/8	....	....
Strict Ordinary	9 3/16	....	....	....	....	....	....	....	....	....	....	....	....	....	....	....	....	....		....	....	9 5/8	9 5/16	....	....
Good Ordinary	10	....	....	....	....	....	....	....	....	....	....	....	....	....	....	....	....	....		....	....	10 3/16	10 1/4	....	....
Strict Good Ordinary	10 3/8	....	....	....	....	....	....	....	....	....	....	....	....	....	....	....	....	....		....	....	10 7/16	10 1/2	....	....
Low Middling	10 5/8	....	....	....	....	....	....	....	....	....	....	....	....	....	....	....	....	....		....	....	10 11/16	10 3/4	....	....
Strict Low Middling	10 13/16	....	....	....	....	....	....	....	....	....	....	....	....	....	....	....	....	....		....	....	10 7/8	10 15/16	....	....
Middling	11	....	....	....	....	....	....	....	....	....	....	....	....	....	....	....	....	....		....	....	11 1/16	11 1/8	....	....
Good Middling	11 1/4	....	....	....	....	....	....	....	....	....	....	....	....	....	....	....	....	....		....	....	11 5/16	11 3/8	....	....
Strict Good Middling	11 5/8	....	....	....	....	....	....	....	....	....	....	....	....	....	....	....	....	....		....	....	11 9/16	11 5/8	....	....
Middling Fair	11 7/8	....	....	....	....	....	....	....	....	....	....	....	....	....	....	....	....	....		....	....	11 15/16	12	....	....
Fair	12 3/8	....	....	....	....	....	....	....	....	....	....	....	....	....	....	....	....	....		....	....	12 5/16	11 3/8	....	....
STAINED.																									
Good Ordinary.....per lb.	8 1/4	....	....	....	....	....	....	....	....	....	....	....	....	....	....	....	....	....		....	....	8 3/16	8 1/4	....	....
Strict Good Ordinary	8 13/16	....	....	....	....	....	....	....	....	....	....	....	....	....	....	....	....	....		....	....	8 5/8	8 11/16	....	....
Low Middling	9 1/4	....	....	....	....	....	....	....	....	....	....	....	....	....	....	....	....	....		....	....	9 1/16	9 3/8	....	....
Middling	10 3/8	....	....	....	....	....	....	....	....	....	....	....	....	....	....	....	....	....		....	....	10 5/16	10 3/8	....	....

UNITED STATES MAILS TO FOREIGN COUNTRIES.

Schedule of Steamers Appointed to Convey the United States Mails to Foreign Countries During the Month of March, 1884.

TRANS-ATLANTIC MAILS.

Date of Sailing.	Name of Steamer.	Name of Line.	Port of Destination and Intermed'te Ports of Call.	Hour of Clos'g Mail at P.O. at Port of Departure.	Mails to be Conveyed.
			FROM NEW YORK.		
Mar. 1	Adriatic	White Star	Queenstown	5.30 A.M.	Mails for Great Britain and Ireland; also French, Belgian, Netherlands, Swiss, Italian, Spanish, Portuguese, Russian, and Turkish closed mail; *also specially addressed correspondence for Germany, Austria, Denmark, Sweden, and Norway.*
" 1	Rhynland	Red Star	Antwerp	5.30 "	Mails for Belgium direct.
" 1	Saller	North German Lloyd	Southampton and Bremen	11.00 "	Mails for Great Britain and Ireland; also German, Austrian, French, Belgian, Netherlands, Swiss, Italian, Spanish, Portuguese, Russian, Turkish, and Swedish closed mails via Southampton; mails for Germany direct; also Austrian, Danish, and Norwegian closed mails via Bremen.
" 4	Arizona	Guion	Queenstown	8.00 "	Mails for Great Britain and Ireland; also German, Austrian, French, Belgian, Netherlands, Swiss, Italian, Spanish, Portuguese, Russian, Turkish, Danish, Swedish, and Norwegian closed mails.
" 5	Servia	Cunard	Queenstown	8.30 "	Mails for Great Britain and Ireland; also German, Austrian, Belgian, Netherlands, Swiss, Italian, Spanish, Portuguese, Russian, Turkish, Danish, Swedish, and Norwegian closed mails; *also specially addressed correspondence for France.*
" 5	France	General Trans-Atlantic	Havre	8.30 "	Mails for France direct.
" 5	Edam	Netherlands Steam Nav. Co	Amsterdam	10.00 "	Mails for the Netherlands direct.
" 6	Baltic	White Star	Queenstown	10.00 "	Mails for Great Britain and Ireland, etc. (Same as Adriatic.)
" 6	Lessing	Hamburg Am. Packet Co.	Plymouth and Hamburg	10.00 "	Mails for Germany and Austria via Plymouth; mails for Germany direct; also Austrian, Danish, Swedish, and Norwegian closed mails via Hamburg; *also specially addressed correspondence for Great Britain and other European countries.*
" 8	City of Montreal	Inman	Queenstown	11.00 "	Mails for Ireland; *also specially addressed correspondence for Great Britain and other European countries.*
" 8	Rhein	North German Lloyd	Southampton and Bremen	11.00 "	Mails for Great Britain; also German, Austrian, French Belgian, Netherlands, Swiss, Italian, Spanish, Portuguese, Russian, Turkish and Swedish closed mails via Southampton; mails for Germany direct; also Austrian, Danish, and Norwegian closed mails via Bremen; *also specially addressed correspondence for Ireland.*
" 8	Circassia	Anchor	Glasgow	1.00 P.M.	Mails for Scotland direct.
" 8	Waesland	Red Star	Antwerp	1.00 "	Mails for Belgium direct.
" 11	Abyssinia	Guion	Queenstown	2.00 A.M.	Mails for Great Britain and Ireland, etc. (Same as Arizona.)
" 12	Pavonia	Cunard	Queenstown	3.00 "	Mails for Great Britain and Ireland, etc. (Same as Servia.)
" 12	Labrador	General Trans-Atlantic	Havre	3.00 "	Mails for France direct.
" 12	P. Caland	Netherlands Steam Nav. Co	Rotterdam	5.00 "	Mails for the Netherlands direct.
" 13	City of Paris	Inman	Queenstown	12.30 P.M.	Mails for Great Britain and Ireland, etc. (Same as Arizona.)
" 15	Britannic	White Star	Queenstown	5.00 A.M.	Mails for Great Britain and Ireland, etc. (Same as Adriatic.)
" 15	Anchoria	Anchor	Glasgow	5.00 "	*Specially addressed correspondence for Scotland.*
" 15	Belgenland	Red Star	Antwerp	5.00 "	Mails for Belgium direct.
" 15	Main	North German Lloyd	Southampton and Bremen	5.00 "	Mails for Great Britain and Ireland, etc. (Same as Saller.)
" 18	Wyoming	Guion	Queenstown	6.30 "	*Specially addressed correspondence for Europe.*
" 19	Werra	North German Lloyd	Southampton and Bremen	7.30 "	*Specially addressed correspondence for Great Britain;* also German, Austrian, Belgian, Netherlands, Swiss, Italian, Spanish, Portuguese, Russian, Turkish, and Swedish, closed mails via Southampton; mails for Germany direct; also Austrian, Danish, and Norwegian closed mails via Bremen; *also specially addressed correspondence for Ireland and France.*
" 19	Gallia	Cunard	Queenstown	7.30 "	Mails for Great Britain and Ireland, etc. (Same as Servia.)
" 19	St. Laurent	General Trans-Atlantic	Havre	7.30 "	Mails for France direct.
" 19	Amsterdam	Netherlands Steam Nav. Co	Amsterdam	8.30 "	Mails for the Netherlands direct.
" 20	Republic	White Star	Queenstown	8.30 "	Mails for Great Britain and Ireland, etc. (Same as Adriatic.)

Date	Ship	Line	Port	Time	Mails for
Mar. 20	Gellert	Hamburg Am. Packet Co.	Plymouth and Hamburg	9.30 A.M.	Mails for Great Britain and Ireland; also German, Austrian, French, Belgian, Netherlands, Swiss, Italian, Spanish, Portuguese, Russian, and Turkish closed mails via Plymouth; mails for Germany direct; also Austrian, Danish, Swedish, and Norwegian closed mails via Hamburg.
" 22	City of Chester	Inman	Queenstown	10.00	Mails for Great Britain and Ireland, etc. (Same as Adriatic.)
" 22	Furnessia	Anchor	Glasgow	10.00	*Specially addressed correspondence for Scotland.*
" 22	Pennland	Red Star	Antwerp	10.00	Mails for Belgium direct.
" 22	Donau	North German Lloyd	Southampton and Bremen	11.00	Mails for Great Britain and Ireland, etc. (Same as Salier)
" 25	Nevada	Guion	Queenstown	1.00 P.M.	*Specially addressed correspondence for Europe.*
" 26	Fulda	North German Lloyd	Southampton and Bremen	8.00 A.M.	Mails for Great Britain and Ireland, etc. (Same as Salier.)
" 26	W. A. Scholten	Netherlands Steam Nav. Co	Rotterdam	4.00	Mails for the Netherlands direct.
" 26	Bothnia	Cunard	Queenstown	1.00 P.M.	Mails for Great Britain and Ireland, etc. (Same as Servia.)
" 26	Amerique	General Trans-Atlantic	Havre	1.00	Mails for France direct.
" 27	Celtic	White Star	Queenstown	1.30	Mails for Great Britain and Ireland, etc. (Same as Arizona.)
" 29	Oregon	Guion	Queenstown	4.00 A.M.	Mails for Great Britain and Ireland, etc. (Same as Adriatic.)
" 29	Bolivia	Anchor	Glasgow	4.00	*Specially addressed correspondence for Scotland.*
" 29	Westernland	Red Star	Antwerp	4.00	Mails for Belgium direct.
" 29	Neckar	North German Lloyd	Southampton and Bremen	11.00	Mails for Germany, Austria, and Sweden via Southampton; mails for Germany direct; also Austrian, Danish, and Norwegian closed mails via Bremen; *also specially addressed correspondence for Great Britain and other European countries.*
" 29	City of Chicago	Inman	Queenstown	12.00 M.	Mails for Great Britain and Ireland, etc. (Same as Arizona.)

FROM BOSTON.

Date	Ship	Line	Port	Time	Mails for
Mar. 1	Catalonia	Cunard	Queenstown and Liverpool	9.30 A.M.	Mails for Great Britain and Ireland; also closed mails for Belgium and France.
" 15	Marathon	Cunard	Queenstown and Liverpool	9.30	Mails for Great Britain and Ireland; also closed mails for Belgium and France.
" 29	Samaria	Cunard	Queenstown and Liverpool	8.30	Mails for Great Britain and Ireland; also closed mails for Belgium and France.

FROM PHILADELPHIA.

Date	Ship	Line	Port	Time	Mails for
Mar. 1	Pennsylvania	American Steamship Co.	Queenstown and Liverpool	9.30 A.M.	Mails for Great Britain and Ireland.
" 12	Ohio	American Steamship Co.	Queenstown and Liverpool	7.30	Mails for Great Britain and Ireland.
" 19	Indiana	American Steamship Co.	ueenstown and Liverpool	4.30	Mails for Great Britain and Ireland.
" 26	Illinois	American Steamship Co.	Queenstown and Liverpool	6.30	Mails for Great Britain and Ireland.
" 26	Zeeland	Red Star	Antwerp		Mails for Belgium direct.

FROM BALTIMORE.

Date	Ship	Line	Port	Time	Mails for
Mar. 6	Hohenstaufen	North German Lloyd	Bremen	2.00 P.M.	Mails for Germany.
" 13	Weser	North German Lloyd	Bremen	2.00	Mails for Germany.
" 20	Nurnberg	North German Lloyd	Bremen	2.00	Mails for Germany.
" 27	Habsburg	North German Lloyd	Bremen	2.00	Mails for Germany.

MAILS FOR CANADA AND NEWFOUNDLAND.

FROM BOSTON.

Date	Ship	Line	Port	Time	Mails for
Mar. 1	Carroll	Boston, Halifax, and Prince Edward Island	Halifax	11.00 A.M.	Mails for Nova Scotia.
" 4	Cleopatra	Nova Scotia Steamship Co.	Yarmouth	7.00	Mails for Nova Scotia.
" 8	Carroll	Boston, Halifax, and Prince Edward Island	Halifax	11.00	Mails for Nova Scotia, Newfoundland, and Miquelon.
" 11	Cleopatra	Nova Scotia Steamship Co.	Yarmouth	7.00	Mails for Nova Scotia.
" 15	Carroll	Boston, Halifax, and Prince Edward Island	Halifax	11.00	Mails for Nova Scotia.
" 18	Cleopatra	Nova Scotia Steamship Co.	Yarmouth	7.00	Mails for Nova Scotia.
" 22	Carroll	Boston, Halifax, and Prince Edward Island	Halifax	11.00	Mails for Nova Scotia, Newfoundland, and Miquelon.
" 25	Cleopatra	Nova Scotia Steamship Co.	Yarmouth	7.00	Mails for Nova Scotia.

FROM SAN FRANCISCO.

Date	Ship	Line	Port	Time	Mails for
Mar. 2	Queen of the Pacific	Pacific Coast Steamship Co.	Victoria	9.00 A.M.	Mails for British Columbia.
" 10	Mexico	Pacific Coast Steamship Co.	Victoria	9.00	Mails for British Columbia.
" 18	Queen of the Pacific	Pacific Coast Steamship Co.	Victoria	9.00	Mails for British Columbia.
" 26	Mexico	Pacific Coast Steamship Co.	Victoria	9.00	Mails for British Columbia.

[Continued on next page.

MAILS FOR THE WEST INDIES, MEXICO, CENTRAL AND SOUTH AMERICA.

DATE OF SAILING.	NAME OF STEAMER.	NAME OF LINE.	PORT OF DESTINATION AND INTERMED'TE PORTS OF CALL.	Hour of Closing Mail at P.O. at Port of Departure.	MAILS TO BE CONVEYED.
			FROM NEW YORK.		
Mar. 1	Acapulco	Pacific Mail	Aspinwall	10.00 A.M.	Mails for the South Pacific and Central American ports, and for the West Coast of Mexico via Aspinwall.
:: 1	Saratoga	New York and Cuba Mail	Havana	1.30 P.M.	Mails for Cuba, and for the West Indies via Havana.
:: 4	Reliance	U.S. and Brazil Mail	St. Thomas, Para, Maranham, Pernambuco, Bahia, and Rio de Janeiro	1.00 A.M.	Mails for the West Indies via St. Thomas, for Brazil, and for the Argentine Republic, Uruguay, and Paraguay via Brazil. Steamer receives mails from New York and Baltimore at Newport News, Va.
:: 4	Creole	Quebec Steamship Co	Barbadoes	10.00 "	Mails for the Windward Islands.
:: 4	George W Clyde	Clyde	Cape Hayti, Puerto Plata, Samana, St. Domingo City, and Grand Turk		Mails for Cape Hayti, Saint Domingo, and Turk's Island.
:: 6	Orinoco	Quebec Steamship Co	Hamilton	1.00 P.M.	Mails for Bermuda.
:: 6	City of Merida	N. Y., Hav., & Mex. Mail	Havana	1.00 "	Mails for Cuba, and for Porto Rico and Mexico via Havana.
:: 8	Niagara	New York and Cuba Mail	Havana	1.30 "	Mails for Cuba, and for Porto Rico via Havana.
:: 10	Colon	Pacific Mail	Aspinwall	10.00 A.M.	Mails for the South Pacific, etc. (Same as Acapulco.)
:: 11	Ailsa	Atlas	Kingston, Port au Prince, Savanilla, Greytown, and Port Limon		Mails for Jamaica, Hayti, Greytown (Nic.), Port Limon, and the United States of Columbia, except Aspinwall and Panama.
:: 13	Valencia	Red D	Puerto Cabello, Laguayra, Maracaibo, and Curaçoa	1.00 P.M.	Mails for Venezuela and Curaçoa.
:: 13	Cienfuegos	New York and Cuba Mail	Nassau and Santiago	10.00 A.M.	Mails for the Bahama Islands, and for Santiago and Cienfuegos, Cuba.
:: 13	British Empire	N. Y., Hav., & Mex. Mail	Havana	1.30 "	Mails for Cuba, and for Mexico via Havana.
:: 14	Alps	Atlas	St. John's	1.00 "	Mails for Porto Rico direct.
:: 15	Newport	New York and Cuba Mail	Havana	1.30 "	Mails for Cuba, and for the West Indies via Havana.
:: 18	Flamborough	Quebec Steamship Co	Barbadoes	1.00 "	Mails for the Windward Islands.
:: 18	Therisina	Red Cross	Para, Maranham, and Pernambuco	7.00 "	Mails for Brazil; and for the Argentine Republic, Paraguay, and Uruguay via Brazil. Steamer sails from Baltimore.
:: 20	City of Para	Pacific Mail	Aspinwall	10.00 A.M.	Mails for the South Pacific, etc. (Same as Acapulco.)
:: 20	Orinoco	Quebec Steamship Co	Hamilton	1.00 P.M.	Mails for Bermuda.
:: 20	City of Puebla	N. Y., Hav., & Mex. Mail	Havana	1.30 "	Mails for Cuba, and for Porto Rico and Mexico via Havana.
:: 21	Alvo	Atlas	Port au Prince	1.00 "	Mails for Hayti.
:: 22	Glenfyne	Red D	Puerto Cabello, Laguayra, Maracaibo, and Curaçoa		Mails for Venezuela and Curaçoa.
:: 22	Saratoga	New York and Cuba Mail	Havana	10.00 A.M.	Mails for Cuba, and for Porto Rico via Havana.
:: 25	Muriel	Quebec Steamship Co	Barbadoes	1.30 P.M.	Mails for the Windward Islands.
:: 25	Santo Domingo	Clyde	Cape Hayti, Puerto Plata, etc	1.00 "	Mails for Cape Hayti, St. Domingo, and Turk's Island.
:: 25	Alene	Atlas	Kingston, Savanilla, Greytown, and Port Limon	1.00 "	Mails for Jamaica, etc. (Same as Ailsa.)
:: 26	Advance	U. S. and Brazil Mail	St. Thomas, Para, etc	1.00 A.M.	Mails for the West Indies, etc. (Same as Reliance.)
:: 27	City of Alexandria	N. Y., Hav., & Mex. Mail	Havana	1.30 P.M.	Mails for Cuba, and for Mexico via Havana.
:: 28	Alpin	Atlas	St. John's	1.00 "	Mails for Porto Rico direct.
:: 28	Santiago	New York and Cuba Mail	Nassau and Santiago	1.00 "	Mails for the Bahama Islands, and for Santiago and Cienfuegos, Cuba.
:: 29	Niagara	New York and Cuba Mail	Havana	1.30 "	Mails for Cuba, and for the West Indies via Havana.
			FROM NEW ORLEANS.		
Mar. 1	Whitney	Morgan Line	Vera Cruz	6.00 A.M.	Mails for Mexico.
:: 3	S. J. Oteri	Oteri's Pioneer Line	Ruatan and Truxillo	5.00 P.M.	Mails for Spanish Honduras and Bay Islands.
:: 6	Hutchinson	Morgan Line	Havana	7.00 A.M.	Mails for Cuba.
:: 8	Lucy P. Miller	Royal Mail Steamship Co	Belize, Puerto Cortez, and Livingston	10.00 "	Mails for British and Spanish Honduras, and Guatemala.
:: 9	City of Mexico	N. Y., Hav., & Mex. Mail	Vera Cruz via Bagdad, Tampico, and Tuxpao	7.00 "	Mails for Mexico.
:: 13	Morgan	Morgan Line	Havana	7.00 "	Mails for Cuba.

Date	Ship	Line	Destination	Time	Mails
Mar. 16	Whitney, jr.	Morgan Line	Vera Cruz	6.00 A.M.	Mails for Mexico.
" 16	E. B. Ward, jr.	Oteri's Pioneer Line	Ruatan and Trujillo	5.00 P.M.	Mails for Spanish Honduras and Bay Islands.
" 19	S. J. Oteri	Oteri's Pioneer Line	Ruatan and Trujillo	5.00 "	Mails for Spanish Honduras and Bay Islands.
" 20	Hutchinson	Morgan Line	Havana	7.00 A.M.	Mails for Cuba.
" 20	City of Dallas	Royal Mail Steamship Co	Belize, Puerto Cortez, etc	10.00 "	Mails for British and Spanish Honduras, and Guatemala.
" 27	Morgan	Morgan Line	Havana	7.00 "	Mails for Cuba.
" 29	Lucy P. Miller	Royal Mail Steamship Co	Belize, Puerto Cortez, etc	10.00 "	Mails for British and Spanish Honduras, and Guatemala.
" 30	City of Mexico	N. Y., Hav., & Mex. Mail	Vera Cruz via Bagdad, etc.	7.00 "	Mails for Mexico.

FROM GALVESTON, Tex.

Date	Ship	Line	Destination	Mails
Mar. 3	Whitney	Morgan Line	Vera Cruz	Mails for Mexico.
" 17	Whitney	Morgan Line	Vera Cruz	Mails for Mexico.

FROM KEY WEST, Fla.

Date	Ship	Line	Destination	Mails
Mar. 2	Morgan	Morgan Line	Havana	Mails for Cuba.
" 9	Hutchinson	Morgan Line	Havana	Mails for Cuba.
" 16	Morgan	Morgan Line	Havana	Mails for Cuba.
" 23	Hutchinson	Morgan Line	Havana	Mails for Cuba.
" 30	Morgan	Morgan Line	Havana	Mails for Cuba.

FROM BALTIMORE, Md.

Date	Ship	Line	Destination	Time	Mails
Mar. 4	Reliance	U.S. and Brazil Mail	St. Thomas, Para, etc.	4.00 A.M.	Mails for the West Indies, etc. (Same as Reliance above.)
" 19	Theresina	Red Cross	Para, Maranham, & Pernam co	4.00 "	Mails for Brazil; and for the Argentine Republic, Paraguay, and Uruguay via Brazil.
" 26	Advance	U.S. and Brazil Mail	St. Thomas, Para, etc.	4.00 "	Mails for the West Indies, etc. (Same as Reliance.)

FROM SAN FRANCISCO

Date	Ship	Line	Destination	Time	Mails
Mar. 1	Granada	Pacific Mail	Panama and Way Ports	8.30 A.M.	Mails for Mexico, and for the South Pacific and Central American ports.
" 6	Newbern	Cal and Mexican SS. Co	Ensenada, Cape St. Lucas, Magdalena Bay, La Paz, Mazatlan, and Guaymas.	11.00 "	Mails for the West Coast of Mexico.
" 15	San Blas	Pacific Mail	Panama and Way Ports	8.30 "	Mails for Mexico, and for the South Pacific and Central American ports.

TRANS-PACIFIC MAILS.

FROM SAN FRANCISCO

Date	Ship	Line	Destination	Time	Mails
Mar. 1		French Contract Line	Papeiti	2.00 P.M.	Mails for Tahiti and Marquesas Islands. Mails close 4 p. m., February 29.
" 4	Mariposa	Oceanic Steamship Co	Honolulu	10.30 A.M.	Mails for the Sandwich Islands.
" 8	Oceanic	Occidental and Oriental	Yokohama and Hong Kong		Mails for Japan, Shanghai, Hoong Kong and dependent Chinese ports, and the East Indies, except British India.
" 14	Australia	Pacific Mail	Honolulu, Sydney, & Auckl'd		Mails for the Sandwich Islands, New Zealand, and Australia; for Fiji and Samoan Islands, and New Caledonia via Sydney, New South Wales.
" 15	Alameda	Oceanic Steamship Co	Honolulu	2.00 P.M.	Mails for the Sandwich Islands.
" 27	C. of Rio de Janeiro	Pacific Mail	Yokohama and Kong Kong	10.30 A.M.	Mails for Japan, etc. (Same as Oceanic.)

In case of accident to any steamer booked for departure at a particular date, another one is substituted to carry the mail at the time specified.

☞ Mails for Great Britain, and for the Continent of Europe *via* Great Britain, to be dispatched from New York as per this Schedule, are assigned to the fastest vessels available. Special directions on correspondence for Great Britain and the Continent for its dispatch from New York by particular vessels, merely with a view to celerity, are therefore unnecessary.

TELEGRAPHIC CABLE RATES.

Tariff to Great Britain, Ireland, France, and Germany.

Per word.

From New York City, Brooklyn, and Yonkers in New York, the New England States, New Brunswick, Nova Scotia, Ontario and Quebec.......... 50 cents.

From New York (except New York City, Brooklyn and Yonkers), New Jersey, Pennsylvania, Delaware, Maryland and District of Columbia....... 53 cents.

From Virginia, West Virginia, Ohio, Michigan, Kentucky, Indiana, Illinois, St. Louis in Missouri, and Milwaukee, Wisconsin..................... 55 cents.

From North Carolina, South Carolina, Georgia, Alabama, Mississippi, New Orleans in Louisiana,

Per word.

Tennessee, Denver and Leadville in Colorado, and Western Union offices in Florida........... 60 cents.

From Louisiana (except New Orleans), Texas, Wisconsin (except Milwaukee), Iowa, Missouri (except St. Louis), Arkansas, Minnesota, Dakota, Manitoba, Kansas, Nebraska, and Indian Territory.... 65 cents.

From Colorado (except Denver and Leadville), Wyoming, Utah, New Mexico, Idaho, Montana, Nevada, California, Arizona, Oregon and Washington Territory................................... 70 cents.

From British Columbia.......... .... 75 cents.

Senders can insure their messages being forwarded by any particular route, such as "via Siberia," "via Santander," "via Teheran," etc., by inserting the indication of route in the "Check." The indication is transmitted free of charge.

Messages destined for places beyond the lines of telegraph must contain instructions from the sender as to the name of the place from which they are to be posted. The postage to be charged is thirty-seven cents.

Rules for Atlantic Cable Business.

(1) The maximum length of a chargeable word will be fixed at ten letters. Should a word contain more than ten letters, every ten or fraction of ten letters will be counted as a word.

(2) Code messages must be composed of words in the English, French, German, Spanish, Italian, Dutch, Portuguese, and Latin languages. Proper names (*i. e.*, names of persons and places) will not be allowed in the text of Code Messages, except in the manner they are used in ordinary private messages.

(3) Groups of figures or letters will be counted at the rate of three figures or letters to a word, plus one word for any excess.

Rates from New York to	PER WORD	Rates from New York to	PER WORD	Rates from New York to	PER WORD
Aden, Arabia...	$1.43	Siberian rate shall be collected for messages to Japan.		from London : Rio de Janeiro and places north in Brazil, $2.41 per word ; places south in Brazil, $2.61 per word. The words via *Government land lines* must be included and paid for.	
" via Bombay..............	2.20	Luxemburg............................	$ .56		
Africa—		Madeira, (Madeira Islands)......	.88		
Delagoa Bay....................	2.65	Malacca..............................	2.05		
Mozambique	2.65	Malta................................	.64		
Zanzibar	2.40	Mauritius—Telegrams for the Island of, can be posted at Aden.		Uruguay—	
Africa (South)—				Montevedio	$3.21
Durban........................	2.65	Montenegro........................	.62	All other places in Uruguay..	3.21
All other places in South Africa	2.75	New Zealand.......................	3.40	Argentine Republic—	
Algeria..........................	.58	Norway............................	.60	Buenos Ayres................	2.94
" via Falmouth........	.77	Orkney Islands—Rules and rates same as Great Britain.		All other places in Arg'ne Rep	2.94
Australia, via Falm'th or Teberan	3.15			Chili.............................	3.11
" via Siberia	4.55	Penang, via Falmouth or Teheran	1.85	Peru—	
Austria	.61	" via Siberia..............	3.50	Arica	5.20
Belgium	.56	Persia	.90	Arequipa	5 58
Beloochistan	1.50	Phillipine Island, Luzon.........	2.95	Callao.........................	6.30
Benghazi — Messages posted at Malta.		Portugal..........................	.65	Islay	5.58
Burmah, Further India.........	1.80	" via Santander	.68	Iquique	4.83
" " via Penang..	2.30	Roumania	.62	Lima...........................	5.58
Bushire..........................	1.18	Russia in Europe..................	.68	Molendo	5.58
Cape Verde Islands, St. Vincent.	1.48	Russia, Caucasus..................	.75	Puno	5.58
Ceylon, via Falmouth or Teheran	1.75	Russia in Asia, west of Verkhnee Oudinsk	.90	Tacna	5.20
Channel Islands—Rules and rates same as London.		Russia in Asia, east of Verkhnee Oudinsk	1.15	Bolivia, Antofagasta...........	4.83
Channel Islands via France......	.59	St. Vincent, Cape Verde Island ..	1.48	Messages for South America can also be sent via the West Indies.	
China	2.55	Scilly Islands. Same as London.		Spain, via Falmouth or Santander	.66
Cochin China—		Servia	.62	" via Gibraltar.	.75
Saigon, via Falm'th or Teheran	2.30	Sicily	.50	" via Marseilles.........	.65
" via Siberia........	3.15	Sardinia	.59	Sweden..........................	.64
Corfu	.64	Shetland Islands—Rules and rates same as Great Britain.		Switzerland......................	.56
Corsica	.59	Singapore, via Falm'th or Teheran	2.08	Tripoli	.79
Cyprus	.95	" via Siberia.......	3.25	Turkey in Europe..............	.64
Denmark	.60	South America, via cable from Europe:—		" " via Falmouth..	.83
Egypt—		Brazil—		" " Asia—Seaports ..	.70
Alexandria	.84	Maranham	3.52	" " " via Falm'h	.88
All other places in Egypt	.89	Para	3.83	" " Inland........	.74
Gibraltar	.68	Pernambuco	3.70	" " " via Falm'th	.93
Greece	.66	Bahia and Rio de Janeiro....	2.91	Turkish Islands..................	.74
Greek Islands...................	.70	Santos.....................	3.11	" " via Falmouth..	.93
Heligoland......................	.65	Santa Catherina	3.11	Turkey, via Russia and Odessa Cable—Messages must be marked "via Indo," and sent via London. Rates are as follows:	
Holland.........................	.58	Rio Grande do Sul..........	3.11	Turkey in Europe..............	.83
Hungary.........................	.61	Other places in Brazil, north.	2.91	" " Asia—Seaports	.89
India, via Falmouth or Teheran.	1.75	" " " south.	3.11	" " " Inland.......	.93
Italy............................	.59	Messages for Brazil can also be sent via Government land lines in Brazil at following rates *per word*		" " " Archipelago..	.93
Java, via Falmouth or Teheran ..	2.20			Tunisia	.58
" via Siberia..............	3.50			" via Falmouth............	.77
Japan, via Falmouth or Teheran.	3.50				
" via Siberia	2.80				
Unless specially directed, the					

To Cuba and West Indies.

Via Cable to Havana, Cuba.

From New York City to the Following Places at the Rate of 50 Cents per Word:

Havana, Cuba	Consolacion*	Ciego de Avila*	Manzanillo‡	St. Dom'go (Coloniado*)
Batabano, " *	Colon*	Guanaja*	Mariel*	Sagua*
Bajucal, " *	Cardenas*	Guines*	Pinar del Roi*	Santiago‡
Bemba, " *	Cienfuegos†	Guantanamo‡	Puerte Principe*	Santo-Spiritu*
Bayamo*	Caibarien*	Jignani*	Remedios*	Trinidad*
Bahia Honda*	Cabanas*	Matanzas*	San Antonio*	....

* Add to the rate of 50 cents per word 40 cents for each ten, or fraction of ten, words.

† Add to the rate of 44 cents per word $2.25 for first ten words or less, and 22 cents for each word over ten.

‡ Add to the rate of 44 cents per word $3 for first ten words or less, and 30 cents for each word over ten.

From New York City to

	Per word.		Per word.		Per word.		Per word.
Antigua	$2.41	Grenada	$2.83	Porto Rico, San Juan	$2.18	St. Lucia	2.66
Barbadoes	2.84	Guadaloupe	2.51	" Other places	2.14	St. Vincent	2.73
Berbice	3.38	" Basse Terre.	2.49	St. Croix	2.22	Trinidad, Port of Spain.	2.94
Demerara	3.36	Kingston (Jamaica)	1.35	St. Thomas	2.17	" Other places..	2.96
Dominica	2.55	Martinique	2.60	St. Kitts	2.35		

To Mexico.

From New York City.

Messages to all places, except towns near the boundary line between the United States and Mexico, will be sent via cables of the Mexican Telegraph Company from Galveston, Texas. Important towns in Mexico near the frontier, sent via Western Union offices. For other places rates are as follows:

To Tampico, Mexico, $3.75 for ten words, and 33 cents for each word over ten.

To Vera Cruz, Mexico, $4.75 for ten words, and 43 cents for each word over ten.

To City of Mexico, Mexico, $5.25 for ten words, and 48 cents for each word over ten.

To Goatzacoalcos, Mexico, 62 cents per word.   To Salina Cruz, Mexico, 72 cents per word.

To Aspinwall, Colon, $1.00 per word.   To Panama, $1.00 per word.

To all other points in Mexico, on Mexican Government lines, the rate to Vera Cruz (no reliable inland line from Tampico) will be charged, and the Mexican Government rate will be added, as follows: 50 cents for ten words, and 5 cents for each word over ten.

To points on State or Private Line Stations, beyond the Government lines, the State or Private Line rate will be added to the Government rate.

The Date, Address and Signature are free.

To Central and South America.

Via Central and South American Cables.

Salvador.—La Libertad, 75 cents per word. Other offices in Salvador, 80 cents per word.

Guatemala.—All offices in Guatemala, 80 cents per word.   **Honduras.**—All offices in Honduras, 80 cents per word.

Costa Rica.—All offices in Costa Rica, $1.05 per word.

Nicaragua.—San Juan del Sur, $1.00 per word. Other offices in Nicaragua, $1.05 per word.

South America.

Panama, $1.00 per word.   **From New York City.**   Aspinwall, Colon, $1.00 per word.

U. S. Columbia.—Buenaventura, $1.52 per word. Bogota and other offices, $1.57 per word.

Ecuador.—St. Elena Bay, $1.77 per word. Guayaquil, $1.77 per word.   Bolivia.—Antofagasta, $2.72 per word.

PERU.

	Per word.		Per word.		Per word.		Per word.
Arica	$2.52	Huanillos	$2.68	Mollendo	$2.07	Pisagua	$2.68
Arequipa	2.69	Iquique	2.57	Pabullon de Pica	2.68	Tacna	2.63
Callao	2.17	Lima	2.17	Payta	1.92		

CHILI.

	Per word.		Per word.		Per word.		Per word.
Caldera	$2.82	Coplapo	$2.93	Huasco	$2.93	Taltal	2.92
Carrizal	3.03	Coquimbo	3.03	Lota	3.18	Talcahuano	3.18
Chillan	3.18	Famaya	3.03	Ovalle	3.03	Tocopilla	2.83
Chanaral	2.93	Freirina	3.03	Santiago	3.18	Valdivia	3.18
Cobija	2.83	Guayacan	3.03	Serena	2.92	Vallenar	3.03
Concepcion	3.18	Higuera	3.03	Talca	3.18	Valparaiso	3.07

To **Buenos Ayres** and other places in the Argentine Republic, $2.92 per word from New York.

To **Montevideo** and all other places in Uruguay, $3.00 per word from New York.

BRAZIL.

	Per word.		Per word.		Per word.		Per word.
Bahia	$2.91	Para	$3.80	Rio	$2.91	Santos	$3.11
Pernambuco	2.70	Maranham	3.50	Rio Grande	3.11	Santa Catharina	3.11

All inland stations 15 cents per word in addition to tariff from nearest coast line station.

Pen-wipers.

When a cat sings, it is done for a purr-puss.

A man has to be "quick" in order to look alive these times.

A strange transformation—when a rooster finds a grain of corn and makes an-oat of it.

Though a ship may apparently leave port with perfect freedom, it generally goes out with the tide.

No matter how much of a sham there is about a fire, the firemen always like to find the hose reel.

"No, Charlie, you mus'n't call on me; I'm engaged, and Jim won't like it." "Well, he calls on you and I don't like it. I guess I've got as good a right to worry him as he has to worry me."

There is a statement going the rounds that three times around an elephant's foot is the hight of the animal. Once around a mule's hind foot is about fifteen or twenty feet to the man who tries it.

"Is virtue a thing remote?" inquired Confucius. If Con. had lived in the present day he never would have asked such a foolish question. Remote! Well, we should remark! It's about the remotest commodity in the market.

Always Condemned.

Letters of administration have recently been taken out in Baltimore on the estate of Elizabeth Carlotta Petronella Bath Hendrickson Van Boetzelaer Van Dubbledam, widow of Christian Willem Johann Baron Van Boetzelaer Van Dubbledam. Great Scott! Here is a case where profanity was not only excusable, but necessary. What a relief to the weary clerk who did the writing to get off the concluding name with a flourish.

Elizabeth and so forth was once courted by Chris. Willem,
Who asked her if she'd marry him and be his loving wife ;
She said she'd face the duties and would do her best to fill 'em,
Although she must submit to being Dubbledamed for life.

But her fate's far worse than e'er she thought ; for though she's dead and planted,
Whoever has to write her name to Tophet sure would jam her,
By all who speak of her she's on to realms Infernal canted ;
It can't be helped, with such a name, they have to Dubbledam her.

Time Too Short.

"Mr. Johnson," said Mr. Banks, "the money is all right, isn't it?"

"Oh, yes, Mr. Banks."

"Then there is nothing more to do than for you to give me your note for sixty days."

"Give you my note—what for?"

"Simply as an evidence of the debt."

"Why, Mr. Banks, you ain't afraid to trust me, are you?"

"Certainly not."

"You don't think I'm dishonest?"

"Why no, but you might die."

"Ha, ha, ha, I knew you was joking. Die! Who ever heard of a man dying in sixty days?"

VOL. VIII.   APRIL, MAY, JUNE, 1884.   Nos. 4–6.

METHODS OF BANK CLEARINGS.*

Banking, as practiced among the ancients, was merely the loaning of money at usury. It is unknown when money came to be received on deposit, although, from the parable of the talents, it must have been the custom in our Saviour's time. The early history of banking is involved in obscurity; no organization appears to have been attempted until the latter part of the twelfth century (1171), when the Bank of Venice, the first institution of its kind in Europe, was founded. It owed its existence to the Crusades and the necessity of the Government obtaining money to conduct those wars, and continued for upwards of six centuries. The Bank of Genoa, the Bank of Amsterdam and the Bank of England, all owed their origin to the wants of the governments that gave them life, and not only did they sustain those governments through long and exhausting wars, but they formed important aids to the development of industry and the advancement of commercial prosperity.

In the early days of banking, deposits were not subject to check, but could be transferred only on the books of the bank. As commerce increased, and credit was introduced, this regulation proved inadequate to meet the demands of business. To relieve this inconvenience, deposits were then allowed subject to draft; and these orders, now called bank-checks, proved so popular that they began insensibly to absorb the principal elements and qualities of bills of exchange, and were given and accepted in payment of debts. Although each succeeding year enlarged the sphere of their utility, their use on an extended scale is of comparatively recent origin. In England and the United States they have reached their widest development, for in most of the continental nations banking, as an instrument of trade, is unknown. Victor Bonnet, a recent French writer, says: "The use of deposits, bank accounts and checks is still in its infancy in this country. They are little used even in the great cities, while in the rest of France they are completely unknown." The Comptoir d'Escompte used the greatest efforts to induce French merchants to adopt English habits in respect to the use of checks and the keeping of bank accounts, but in vain; as M. Pinard, the manager, says: "They would not because they would not"; their prejudices were immovable. The savings of the French peasants are kept in their homes, and hoards put in the traditional stocking; they have no faith in banks. The deposits in all the savings-banks in France are not equal to the deposits in the savings-banks of New York city alone.

*A Lecture delivered before the Book-keepers' Association of Philadelphia, by CHARLES F. WIGNALL, April 7th, 1884.

When the economy of the check system had caused the innumerable daily payments of a community to be effected by a comparatively small amount of money, the next and culminating step was to allow payments among the banks themselves to be effected by off-setting one amount against another. This principle appears to have been first understood and acted upon — not by bank managers, but by the messengers, who, in their endeavors to lessen their labors, resorted to the expedient of meeting at some convenient place and exchanging checks. From this beginning has resulted the present admirable system of bank clearings. Representatives of banks widely separated in a city are thus brought to one common centre, and in the liquidation of debts between them both time and money are economized. Widely known by name, the bank clearing-house is an institution whose operations are imperfectly understood by the commercial world. While its influence is felt, and its results accepted, except to a comparatively few its workings are a mystery.

In the United Kingdom, Edinburgh enjoys the honor of first adopting the clearing system, although on a limited and imperfect scale.

In 1775, some of the private banks in London organized the first clearing-house in that city. The actual clearing-house, as it exists at present, dates only from 1860; and it was not until 1864 that the Bank of England and the joint-stock banks were admitted. Its operations, compared with our own, are complicated, and require the attendance of a clerk from each bank the greater part of a day. The morning exchange begins between 10 and 11 o'clock, and is usually over at noon.

The checks to be cleared are entered in a book called the "out-clearing book,"

and sent to the clearing-house, where they are distributed, entered by the representative of the bank receiving them in the "in-clearing book," and sent to his bank for payment. The afternoon exchange begins at half-past 2 o'clock, when the process of the morning is repeated as frequently as the receipt of checks at the bank warrants it. At five minutes past 4 o'clock the doors are closed, and the delivery ceases. Checks not good must be returned to the clearing-house before 5 o'clock, except on stock-settling days and the 4th of each month, when, on account of the exceptionally large transactions, the time is extended until quarter past 5. At the close of the exchange, at 4 o'clock, the "out-clearing" books are taken to the clearing-house, a comparison made with the "in-clearings," and a balance struck with each bank. A clearing-sheet, being a summary of the day's proceedings, is made out, and, to prove its correctness, compared with that of each bank. As all of the private banks have accounts at the Bank of England, the balance, if debtor, is paid by an order upon that institution transferring the amount from the account of the debtor bank to the account of the clearing-house; and the creditor banks, by a similar order from the inspector of the clearing-house, have their balances transferred from the clearing-house account to their own. All the transferring is done on the books of the Bank of England, no money entering in any manner into the operation.

In the United States, the first clearing-house was established in New York city, and went into operation October 11th, 1853. It is composed at present of sixty-three banks, with a capital and surplus aggregating $101,320,000. As most of the disbursements of the United States are made in New York, to facilitate the transactions of the Government with the various banks the Sub-Treasury is admitted to membership. They have but one clearing a day, at 10 A.M. During the year 1883 the clearings amounted to thirty-seven billions, and the balances paid, to one and one-half billions.

The clearing-house in Philadelphia was organized January 25th, 1858, and opened for business March 22d, 1858. The exchanges for the first day amounted to two millions of dollars. The average clearings for 1884 amounted to nine millions, showing an increase in twenty-six years of 350%. The total exchanges for the year 1883 were two billions of dollars, and the balances, two hundred and forty-one millions. There are two exchanges daily: one, at 8.30 A. M., known as the "Morning Exchange," and confined to items received by the banks the day previous; the other, at 11.30 A. M., known as the "Runner's Exchange," confined to items received in the morning mail and to notes and acceptances due on that day. The preparation for, and the manner of, conducting the morning exchange is as follows:

At the close of business, the checks on the various banks which have been received during the day are placed in envelopes, one for each bank, securely gummed and sealed with wax, with the aggregate amount of the inclosed checks written on the outside. The amount of each package is entered upon a sheet called the "Clerk's Package Statement," and the total of these various packages will be the total credit of the bank at the clearing-house the next morning. Prior to half-past eight o'clock, the next morning, the representatives of the various banks assemble — each bank being represented by a receiving and a delivery clerk. The receiving clerks having taken their respective desks, promptly at half-past eight o'clock, the line of

delivery clerks begins to move, distributing among the various banks their respective packages, and taking receipts therefor from the various receiving clerks on the package statement. On a paper called the "Settlement-sheet" each receiving clerk places the amounts of the various packages he has received. The difference between the aggregate of packages received and those delivered is the debtor or creditor balance of the bank.

The delivery clerks now return to their respective banks with the packages they have received; the checks are examined, and, if correct, posted to the various accounts. Should any of these checks be not good or informal, they must be returned to the bank sending them before 12 o'clock. Should such return invalidate any items sent by the bank making the claim, or by any other bank to the bank upon whom the claim is made, the bank refunding shall have the right to return such invalidated items before one o'clock the same day, if accompanied by a statement of the facts from the president or cashier of the bank making the claim. If a depositor have insufficient funds to his credit to pay all of his checks received in the same exchange, the bank has no legal power or right to select or choose from among them certain ones which it will honor and certain ones which it will dishonor. Those having the earliest dates cannot be selected, for priority of presentment, not of date, secures priority of payment; and since through the medium of the clearing-house checks are all presented at the same time, all or none must be paid. I am aware that a contrary practice prevails in some banks, and that the paying-teller frequently makes a selection to suit his convenience; but such a course has no legal sanction, and renders the bank liable to the holders of the dishonored paper.

To revert to the progress of the exchange. Each receiving clerk remains at the clearing-house, and furnishes to the manager a ticket bearing the total debits, total credits, and the amount of the balance of his bank. From these figures the settlement is made. A duplicate slip is made and passed among the various clerks who enter the amounts on the settlement-sheet opposite the name of the bank furnishing the slip. By this method each bank secures a record of the day's clearings. The receiving clerks must remain until the clearings balance; and to those who have arrived late, been disorderly, or made errors in their settlements, fines are generously distributed by an impartial manager.

Under penalty of a fine, the debtor banks are compelled to pay their indebtedness before 12 o'clock noon; after which time the creditor banks are entitled to receive their balances. At present all balances over five thousand dollars must be paid in treasury or clearing-house certificates. If the amount be under five thousand dollars it is settled by bank due bill. Treasury certificates, for clearing-house purposes, are issued, under Act of Congress, by the Assistant-Treasurer of the United States, in denominations of five and ten thousand dollars, for similar amounts of legal tender notes deposited with him. Clearing-house certificates are issued by the manager of the clearing-house, in denomination of five thousand dollars for United States gold coin deposited with him. Both of these certificates are negotiable only between members of the clearing-house association, and are redeemable at any time upon presentation at the proper depository. No notes issued by a national bank, nor any certificate based

upon them, is receivable in payment of clearing-house balances; everything is based upon the gold or paper currency of the United States.

The second or runner's exchange is held at half-past eleven o'clock, for the exchange of checks received in the morning mail, and notes and acceptances due that day. The packages are prepared and entered on a sheet called the " Runner's settlement." But one representative from each bank is needed in making this exchange. The packages are distributed by him, and those received entered on the debtor side of the runner's settlement, and a memorandum of the totals and balance furnished the manager. The runner's sheets are passed among the various clerks for their signatures. After the clearings balance, the debtor banks pay their indebtedness by due bill, which is charged and returned to them in the next morning's exchange from the Philadelphia National Bank. The creditor banks receive the manager's check on the same bank for the amount of their credit. Items in the runner's exchange not good or informal must be returned before three o'clock. An exception is allowed in the case of certain of the banks, who, on account of their distance from the business centre, have the privilege of returning items at any time before three and a-half o'clock, upon giving notice before three o'clock of their intention to return.

The runner's exchange is merely supplementary to the morning exchange, and to me appears perfectly unnecessary and useless. Why Philadelphia, whose volume of business is much smaller, its banking capital infinitely less, and its movements much slower, than New York, must have two daily exchanges, while New York city, with its activity in business and greater number of banks, finds one amply sufficient, I am at a loss to explain ; unless it be due to the natural conservatism of Philadelphians, who, after having adopted a system, are loth to modify or change it for another, no matter how much more rapid and progressive the new system may be.

Under clearing-house rules depositors are responsible as indorsers for the nonpayment of checks upon members of the association, deposited as cash, until the close of the business day next succeeding that upon which such checks are deposited. No bank outside of the clearing-house is under any obligation to observe these rules, and, consequently, can have no remedy against a member for breach of them ; unless it can be shown that by virtue of an express or implied understanding a contract was made in reference to such rules and usages.

The responsibility of the association is limited to the faithful distribution by the manager, among the creditor banks, of the sums actually received by him, and any losses occurring while the balances are in his custody shall be borne and paid by the associated banks in proportion to their capital. The expenses for operating the clearing-house, with the exception of the expense for printing, are apportioned in a similar manner among the various banks.

As collateral security for their daily settlements, each bank deposits, in proportion to its capital, certâin securities approved by the clearing-house committee. In case of the default of any bank in the payment of its balance, these securities are applied to its payment, and the surplus, if any, held as collateral security for any other indebtedness to members of the association.

That their workings may, to a certain extent, be open to the inspection of their associates, each bank furnishes to the clearing-house a daily statement of its condition at the close of the business, giving its loans, discounts, deposits, etc. A weekly statement of the average of these amounts is furnished every Monday morning, and by order of the clearing-house published in the newspapers of the next day, and a copy furnished each bank. This publication is an important element in keeping credit transactions within due control, and preventing the over-zealous from outstepping the bounds of prudence. There is nothing good but what can be perverted to evil ; and it is to be regreted that this publication of the bank's condition is so unscrupulously used by the "bulls" and "bears" in their manipulations of the stock-market.

Such is the operation of clearinghouses, as they exist in the principal cities of the United States. The difference, if any, is in the minor details ; the general working is similar to the type I have explained.

In addition to the regular *city* clearing, the London clearing-house takes under its wing all checks of *country* banks which have for their agent some of the clearing-banks of the metropolis. This country clearing is from twelve o'clock until quarter past two. The balance is found the same as in the city clearing, but is not settled for until three days have elapsed ; so that the balances paid each day are in reality the balances resulting from transactions three days previous. The clearing-banks send these checks without delay to the country banks, when, if not good, the checks are returned. There is no similar system on this side of the Atlantic, although a strong demand and necessity for one. Depositors are constantly complaining of the delay in advising, and the expense of collecting, country items ; and when you consider the circuitous course many checks travel before reaching their destination, these complaints are not without reason. Checks on Norristown are sometimes sent to New York; others, on places in New Jersey not thirty miles from Camden, are returned to Philadelphia before reaching their destination. These are but specimens of a large number of country checks and drafts which are sent from bank to bank and town and town to escape the payment of a small collection charge. Thus valuable time is lost, which, in the case of a promissory note, might delay it beyond its maturity, and release the indorsers. The clearing-houses of the principal cities are derelict in their duty to the public in delaying the establishment of some method similar to that of London. It would require concerted action, but would not be difficult to establish. Each of the country banks keeps its reserve funds in one of the principal cities, and it would only be necessary to divide the United States into districts, and have each of the principal cities clear for its nearest district. Such a system would be a great improvement upon our present method, in saving time, labor, and expense.

The association of banks in the principal cities has been productive of the most beneficial results. They have given uniformity in the conduct of banking, and, by assisting their weaker associates, and preventing at every little stringency the precipitation of a financial panic, have given stability to the commercial world. In all periods of public distrust they have stood as the bulwarks of credit. The concerted action of the banks of Philadelphia and New York did much to give confidence to the Government in the dark days of the Civil War; and it was through the powerful influence exerted by the clearing-houses of Boston, New York and Philadelphia that a general suspension of the banks in 1873 was prevented.

An examination of the reports of the clearing-house is a never-failing index of the growth and prosperity of a community. In Philadelphia, since 1858, the number of banks in the clearing-house has increased from seventeen to thirty; the capital, from eleven millions to seventeen; the loans, from twenty-one millions to seventy-six millions; and the daily exchanges, from two millions to an *average* of nine millions. Surely such figures as these, while not so large as our metropolitan neighbor's, are of sufficient magnitude to entitle us to being considered as something more than a mere provincial village.

COMMERCE AND ITS PROMOTERS.

ARTICLE II.

In our last Paper we found that the old Romans devoted themselves chiefly to agriculture and war. Although such was the case we are not to suppose that commerce was unknown among them; on the contrary, we learn that ancient Rome was a great commercial centre, and that there, as to-day, in London or New York people from all over the known world might be found who were just as keen to strike a good bargain as their modern representatives. Rome was cosmopolitan in its character. The trade carried on there was extensive; but it consisted chiefly in the exchange of commodities brought by merchants from foreign lands. We have already seen that Rome had little or nothing to give in return for all the precious things which her luxurious mode of living rendered necessary to her existence, and which she derived from far off India and China, from Egypt and from the neighboring oriental countries. Commercial pursuits were looked upon by the aristocratic element of ancient Rome with contempt; although we do read of notable instances where very eminent men did not disdain to derive their wealth from so lowly a source.

Coined money was first used as a means of barter and sale a few centuries before the Christian era: it was not long until the Romans learned the advantage of loaning money out at interest, and they speedily became notorious usurers. The records of their transactions are so infamous that it is no wonder the practice was considered disreputable, and that many centuries afterwards there still existed a strong prejudice against money-lenders. The ancient Romans were a practical, business-like people, and the nucleus of many of the avocations which now attention engage were found among them. The study and practice of law was their delight. They possessed a system of banking in many respects similar to that now practiced, and it is probable that they also originated the idea of the modern system of insurance, for they were wise enough, we learn, to insure the valuable cargoes sent to foreign ports, although it seems not to have occurred to them to protect their lives or property in that way.

Besides banking and insurance we may look to the Romans for the first accountants spoken of in history; they learned arithmetic and book-keeping from the Phœnicians. The law of the land compelled those who dealt in money—the usurers, or bankers—to keep books; ere long *everyone* engaged

in business in Rome followed their example, and they earned for themselves the right to be called a "nation of book-keepers." How unwieldy were the implements with which these ancient business men did their work, compared with all the conveniences in which the modern book-keeper revels! Their books were waxen tablets, while the Roman numerals, it will be found by anyone making the experiment, cannot be as easily handled—added, multiplied or subtracted—as those in use now. Indeed, among thoughtful people it has been a matter of conjecture how they manipulated their figures at all.

The fifth century of the Christian era brought sorrow and distress to Europe. A mighty, cruel, relentless, horde of barbarians came surging in upon the civilized world, and, like the angry waves of the sea dashing again and again upon some weak and unprotected coast, swept everything before them. Before the close of the century the grand old Roman Empire, already tottering to its fall by reason of the insidious vice and luxury which had undermined it, was finally overthrown. In its ruins were buried nearly all the countries which for more than five hundred years had owned the imperial sway of Rome. The names of Alaric and Attila, "the scourge of God," have become synonymous with all that is cruel and bloodthirsty. With fire and sword they laid desolate the whole European continent. The various pursuits of civilization, arts, science and commerce languished, and were all but crushed out of existence. Then followed the Dark Ages, when for centuries all the energies of Europe were paralyzed, trade was interrupted, and nations were separated. During the period that followed there must have been little or no commercial intercourse among European countries, and of what little did exist no record has been kept.

By reason of her position and fortifications Constantinople was enabled to withstand the attacks of the barbarians more successfully than the rest of Europe. In that city, more highly favored by nature than almost any other on the face of the earth, were preserved the remnants of the old civilization and the nucleus of the future commerce of the world.

Emerging from the darkness which for two hundred years hung like a pall over Europe we find, towards the close of the seventh century and the beginning of the eighth, that anarchy prevailed to such a degree that anxiety was felt for the safety of commerce. Then arose in the Eastern or Byzantine Empire one of those strong characters who always seem to appear upon the stage of history just when most needed. Leo III., a man of humble birth, rose by force of arms and genius—first to be the ablest general in the land; and, finally, to be the ruler of the Empire. He saw that the only hope of the nation lay in its commerce, and set himself the task of collecting the scattered fragments of commercial enterprise. So remarkable that for four hundred years the entire trade of Europe was completely centered in Constantinople. The situation of Constantinople, just on the confines of Europe and Asia, is a happy one: it is the key to both these great continents, and was destined by nature to be the capital city of a mighty nation, had it but fallen into other hands. All authentic records of Byzantine commerce are lost, but it is certain that during the eighth, ninth, tenth and eleventh centuries this nation towered far above all competitors in the commercial world. The monopolies and restrictions which existed previous to the eighth century

were broken up during the wise administration of Leo III. Duties were made uniform and moderate enough to encourage trade. The anarchy that had prevailed, in one way, resulted in good to the commercial men of the time, for it relieved them of many fiscal oppressions under which they had been laboring.

Monopolies are a drawback to trade, while liberty and freedom are essential to commercial prosperity. And now once more liberated from prison we find commerce making rapid strides. Although a portion of the Byzantine nation were imbued with the Roman notion that trade was derogatory, the greater part, after the manner of Arabian and Eastern merchants, regarded it as honorable, and engaged in its pursuit. Their mercantile fleets sailed upon the waters of both the Black and Mediteranean seas, while their extensive caravan trade found its way from Cherson (Sebastopol in the Crimea), along the northern shores of the Black and Caspian seas, to China, and, through Armenia, to India, bringing thence all the rich and precious things of which they, in common with all the nations which followed them, have felt the need. They learned from the Chinese the manufacture of silk, and introduced that art, in which they soon excelled, into Europe. They were also skilled in the manufacture of linen and woolen goods, and their rich and oriental tastes found expression in the beautiful tapestries which they wrought. Among their exports were these manufactured goods, as well as wine, oil, needles and cutlery. These latter were manufactured at Damascus, and were justly celebrated for their admirable qualities. Damascus steel was, until very recent times, considered the finest in the world, and the art of manufacturing it was greatly coveted by other nations. Damascus blades played a prominent part in the Crusades—wars instituted to wrest the Holy Land from the grasp of the infidels and Turks into whose hands it had fallen. The process of manufacture whereby the steel was so highly tempered, simple though it probably was, has ever remained a mystery.

Commerce is a source of wealth to a nation. Therefore it is not surprising to find that during the period which we are considering, the Byzantine Empire attained the zenith of its fame, and was the richest country in Europe. Constantinople not only distributed to Western Europe all the commodities gathered from the East, as well as the products of her own country, but for several centuries supplied it with all the coin in circulation.

When the barbarians swept down upon the Roman Empire and demolished it, a certain colony of fishermen fled from the inevitable bondage which they saw staring them in the face, and established themselves on the lagoons at the head of the Adriatic Sea. Here they lived in peace, and, occupied with their daily pursuits, had little thought of the beautiful and powerful city which it was their privilege to found. On the spot where these men settled rose that proud mistress of the sea—Venice.

Several other cities in Northern Italy had also been gradually growing, until in the eleventh and twelfth centuries the sturdy young republics or free cities of Pisa, Florence, Milan, Genoa and Venice became formidable rivals for some of the trade so long centred in Constantinople. The Venetians rendered valuable assistance to the Emperor Alexius I. in time of war, for which services they were very liberally rewarded. A whole street of warehouses in Constantinople was given to

them, and they were accorded the freedom of the seas as far as the entrance to the Black Sea. In this fact may be traced the beginning of the decline of commerce in the East and its extension in Western Europe. Venice was not slow to avail herself of her important privileges, and ere long the Venetian suburb, called Galata, was the busiest commercial point in all Constantinople. The Byzantine Empire still reserved to itself the right to trade exclusively in the Black Sea, but as the Italian Republics became more powerful they were forced to further concessions. Several commercial treaties were made, some of which are still in existence. The various Italian cities were at continual enmity with one another, each in turn struggling for supremacy. Genoa and Venice were the most important, commercially, and, for our present purpose, it will be sufficient for us to learn something concerning them. Jealousy sometimes works wonders, and in this particular case the success which Venice had achieved in the East speedily led Genoa to emulate her example. She obtained similar immunities, and soon maintained an independent settlement at Pera. From there we find these energetic little republics pushing their way into Asia, as well as establishing commercial colonies in the Crimea. Indeed, they displayed an amount of enterprise that would be commendable among modern merchants.

We have previously noted the fact that war has a disastrous effect upon commerce. Such is usually the case, but an exception must be made in favor of the Crusades. These wars, which lasted during the twelfth and thirteenth centuries, were far-reaching in their results, and changed the whole social and political character of Europe. Interesting, however, as it might be to study the question in all its bearings, it is only in our province to inquire what effect the Crusades had upon commerce. The answer is an easy one, for the benefits were numerous. The Crusaders procured supplies, and fitted out naval armaments, while resting in the maritime Italian cities. The merchants consequently grew so rich that ere long they vied with the nobles of the land. As their wealth accumulated, civilization and refinement increased in proportion, and an intense thirst for knowledge seemed to take possession of men. The merchant princes in Italy became the friends and patrons of learning, and lived in friendly union with the artist and the man of letters. The progress of the world in all ages has been due, in a very large degree, to the energy and enterprise of its commercial men. The interchange of ideas, which was one of the immediate results of the Crusades, inspired men with a passion for travel, and they were no longer content with the monotonous existences they had previously lived. In the interests of commerce men undertook journeys which, in an age when steam was an unknown agency in travel, must have been formidable indeed. The wonderful civilization of the Far East came to be better known than at any time since the Dark Ages, like a thick cloud, had come in between Europe and Asia; and the marvellous stories that travelers like Marco Polo (who was also a merchant) told of what they had seen in China and Hindostan seemed almost like a revelation from another world.

Just here let us tarry a moment to ask what the chief exports and imports of the Italian cities were, and then we may proceed to inquire what three discoveries which led to the extension of commerce were made about this time. Porcelains, silks, and various oriental commodities, such as precious stones, pearls, spices and exquisitely fine cloths, were imported by the Venetians from the East, while, in return, they exported timber, brass, tin, lead and precious metals, oil, saffron and other Italian productions, as well as some wool and woolen goods. Silk-weaving was introduced into Italy, by Roger Guiscard, in 1148, and it soon became a staple article of manufacture, as well as commerce. The invention of the compass has been ascribed to a native of the Italian town Amalfi, but this statement is not generally credited; in point of fact a knowledge of the polarity of the magnet was early known, and the application of it to purposes of navigation dawned upon the minds of men so gradually that no name can be identified with a discovery which has done more to further commercial interests than any other the world has ever seen. As we have already noted, the Chinese were acquainted with the properties of the magnet from the earliest times, and the Phœnicians also possessed a compass. These facts lend color to the theories of those historians who allege that Europeans derived their knowledge of the magnetic needle from those travelers before alluded to, who, in all probability, brought it, together with other rare and curious things and much useful knowledge, back home with them from the Far East, where they spent so many years of their lives.

At any rate it was not until early in the fourteenth century that the compass began to be generally used by European mariners, and more than another century elapsed before men were found brave enough to sail westward in search of new fields of enterprise. In the meantime the commercial countries of Southern Europe, following their new-found guide, which pointed with such never-failing precision in one direction, steered their vessels fearlessly northward, towards England and Flanders, and thus began that extension of the world's commerce which has gone on ever since.

Before leaving the shores of the Mediterranean, about which we have lingered so long, it will, perhaps, be as well to trace the progress of commerce in its westward march, from the Gulfs of Venice and Genoa, toward the Strait of Gibraltar, whence it soon after spread its wings, and sailed to the furthermost parts of the earth. It is a notable fact that while the use of the compass proved an inestimable benefit to commerce in general, and consequently to the world at large, it robbed the countries lying about the Mediterranean of that prestige which had so long been theirs, and which they have never since regained. The fourteenth and fifteenth centuries were the most splendid in the annals of Genoese and Venetian commerce, and, during that time, the French cities on the Mediterranean shared their prosperity. In even a greater degree did their activity and energy extend to Spain. In the fifteenth century Barcelona excelled in all commercial pursuits; her vessels traded in every part of the Mediterranean and the English Channel; and it is to Spanish enterprise that the first important discovery which followed the use of the mariner's compass in Europe may be attributed.

Christopher Columbus, having read "The Adventures of Marco Polo" and other works of a like character, conceived the idea that it would be possible to reach the Far East by crossing the unknown waters of the Atlantic. Believing himself commissioned by God to undertake the task, he sought aid at the various European courts, and was finally befriended by Queen Isabella, of Spain. In the summer of 1492 he set sail from Palos, and a few months later, when on the verge of despair and about to abandon his long-cherished dream of finding a new path to India, he stumbled on our continent. Emulating his example, Vasco de Gama, a Portuguese, a few years later, made another equally important discovery: in 1498, with a fleet of three vessels, he succeeded in rounding the Cape of Good Hope, thus establishing a water-route to India, and thereby revolutionizing the history of commerce. Most of the newly-discovered continent, especially in South America, was, as a matter of course, claimed by the Spaniards. The great quantities of silver and gold found there so far enriched Spain that she speedily advanced to the foremost ranks among European nations, and for a time her commercial importance and naval power were second to none. But her easily-acquired wealth proved fatal to her best interests. The gold which flowed so freely into her coffers created monopolies, always disastrous to commerce, luxury crept in, and idleness followed in its wake. These were in turn succeeded by social degradation and misery, and almost as quickly as she rose to eminence Spain sank out of sight again. The contrast between Spain and that of the northern nations of Europe, to which we will next turn our attention, is very marked, and leads us to the conclusion that the possession of gold is, in itself at least, a questionable good. As Dr. Lord says: "Gold is not wealth; it is the exponent of wealth. Real wealth is in farms, and shops and ships—in the various channels of industry, in the results of human labor."

G. I. S. Andrews.

The former articles treated mainly of that branch of "The Premium-full-paid Plan," which showed the "many series," the "premium deducted," and the "interest paid upon the full value," except in the case of the Railroad Employees' Association Report, concerning which, *en passant*, I see the printer, for the sake of his space, has left off that portion which shows their mode of ascertaining the values of shares in the different series, and to which I invited "careful scrutiny," so I append it herewith:

plan when first started created quite a furor among its advocates, and was thought to be the *ne plus ultra* of all schemes by which borrowers and non-borrowers were both to be benefited in an extraordinary degree. The plan may perhaps be best understood by the following extract from the Constitution of one of them, in its article on "Loans," as follows:

Sec. 1. Each and every stockholder (except those named in Article II.), for each and every share of stock that he or they may hold in this Association,

	3d Series.	4th Series.	5th Series.	6th Series.	7th Series.	8th Series.	9th Series.	10th Series.	11th Series.	12th Series.	13th Series.
Paid in per share..................	132.00	120.00	108.00	96.00	84.00	72.00	60.00	48.00	36.00	24.00	12.00
Gain on each share..................	64.20	53.05	42.97	33.95	26.00	19.10	13.26	8.49	4.77	2.12	53
Present value of shares..................	196.20	173.05	150.97	129.95	110.00	91.10	73.26	56.19	40.77	26.12	12.53
Value at last report..................	170.69	149.06	128.44	108.84	90.25	72.67	56.11	40.56	26.03	12.51	..
Increase for the year..................	25.51	23.99	22.53	21.11	19.75	18.43	17.15	15.93	14.74	13.61	12.53
Deduct dues for the year..................	12.00	12.00	12.00	12.00	12.00	12.00	12.00	12.00	12.00	12.00	12.00
Net gain per share for the year..................	13.51	11.99	10.53	9.11	7.75	6.43	5.15	3.93	2.74	1.61	53
Present value per share..................	196.20	173.05	150.97	129.95	110.00	91.10	73.26	56.49	40.77	26.12	12.53
Deduct for contingencies..................	..	5.31	4.30	3.40	2.60	1.91	1.33	85	48	1.40	53
Withdrawing value, December 31st, 1883........ ...	196 20	167.74	146.67	126.55	107.40	89.19	71.93	55.64	40.29	24.72	12.00

Stockholders in all of the series, with exception of the third (the oldest), will be allowed to withdraw their stock, upon the basis of a deduction of ten per cent. of the net gain upon each share, as shown by the last preceding annual report, together with whatever dues may have been paid in since said report, with the addition of interest, at the rate of four per cent. per annum, upon the withdrawing value of each series, as ascertained above. Stockholders who have borrowed shall receive an equivalent value for their shares in repayment of loans.

This Association charges interest only on the amount received, *i. e.*, the principal less the premium; and this constitutes one phase of the "interest upon the reduced value" plan. Other associations count the premium as well as the dues as payments on account of the principal; and once a year estimate the amount remaining due as a new principal on which interest is to be paid. ·

II. *The interest-in-advance plan.*—This

shall be entitled to receive a loan of two hundred dollars from the Association.

Sec. 2. Whenever the funds in the treasury shall warrant, the preference for the loan of one or more shares shall be disposed of in open session of the Association, and the stockholder who shall bid interest in advance for the longest period of time, shall be entitled thereto, and all profits and interest arising therefrom shall inure to the mutual advantage of the stockholders.

Sec. 3. A loan shall not be made under par, and in the event of the funds of the Association laying unproductive for the space of two months, the directors shall be empowered to loan what may be on hand, to others than stockholders, or stockholders who have borrowed out all of their shares, for a premium to the highest bidder, for any term not exceeding one year, the interest to be paid monthly ; and should there be no demand for such unproductive fund, to invest it in some safe interest-bearing stock, such as Government, City, etc.

Sec. 4. Whenever any stockholder shall have bid successfully, and become thereby entitled to a loan or loans, he shall either pay or allow to be deducted the interest bid for the same, and for which he shall receive a receipt, and he is, by the said payment, relieved from payment of interest monthly for the period of his bid ; but before receiving the loan, he or they shall secure the re-payment thereof to the Association, by judgment, bond or mortgage, and a policy of fire insurance on all buildings offered as security, and for every loan of two hundred dollars, shall transfer one share of stock to be held as collateral security, the directors to be satisfied that the security is good and sufficient. In case of failure to give satisfactory security for such loan within two months from the date of purchase, the interest will be charged to such purchaser, and the money revert to the Association.

Sec. 5. Loans may be made on the stock of this Association whenever the Association or Board of Directors shall deem the same sufficient security to warrant the loan, and a stockholder obtaining a loan on his stock shall likewise give his judgment bond, conditioned for the payment of his dues, interest and fines.

The plan here may be illustrated by supposing a case : a stockholder wants to borrow $1,000, or on five shares. He may have paid in one month's or more dues. He makes his bid, say, one hundred months (on the principle that the Association will "run out" in about that time); if his bid is the highest, he takes the loan. Sec. 4, it will be noticed, provides "the interest bid is to be deducted (or paid by him)"; consequently he gets —on his one hundred months' bid—just one-half the five shares principal, or $500. He has no interest to pay, *provided the series runs out in one hundred months;* but has given his bond and security for $1,000, and in the one hundred months will have paid in, in dues, just the amount he received. If he had been paying in several months' dues before

he bid and bought out, those payments would be taken out of the number of months bid—month for month—and he would receive so much more apparently of his principal sum. If the series did not run out in the one hundred months, at the expiration of that time he would be called upon to commence paying interest upon the full principal, *i. e.,* in this case stated $1,000, when it will be readily seen his prospects are not nearly so brilliant as they were. I have known none of this character, depending solely upon this plan as stated, to succeed ; where any Interest-in-advance Associations have, it has been by uniting some other scheme of making earnings along with their legitimate one of simply loaning to their stockholders—one that I knew of, united that of banking and brokering. Indeed, some associations under this plan seemed to have been formed principally with a view to the greater facilities afforded for some unscrupulous managers to get and use the funds of their unsophisticated stockholders, without giving any adequate security. In many cases the only security held was stock in the same or kindred associations.

III. *The premium-paid-monthly plan.*— Under this plan the bidder for money, instead of offering a percentage as in the first, or paying interest in advance for a certain number of months as in the second, bids so much per share, *i. e.,* if he wants to borrow on five shares (for instance) he bids, say, twenty-five cents per share; and, if successful, has to pay in his dues, $5 ; his interest, $5 ; and his premium, $1.25, every month—the idea being so to divide the payment of the premium as to give the borrower (1st) more principal, and (2nd) an easier method of paying his premium. Comparing this with the case of Mr. Ready in Article I., who received in cash $750, this borrower receives $1,000; Mr. R. paid $250 premium: this one pays $1.25 per month; if for ten years, he will have paid $150 (this of course would be changed if the rates are different, but it would require about forty-two cents per share per month for ten years to amount to the $250), with the advantage of time in his favor in making the payments. The advantages to the Association collectively would be found in the long run to be about the same in either case, as the premium adjusts itself always to the law of supply and demand, and borrowers calculate closely as well as lenders.

There are, again, variations upon this plan, one of which is very similar to a variation upon the "premium-full-paid," and consists in giving the borrower credit upon his principal indebtedness, with all payments made (except interest), and at the end of each year stating a sum thus reduced, upon which the borrower pays interest. In one set of asso-ciations of this latter kind they profess to exclude the borrower from all participation in the profits on the principle that he has no interest therein, having drawn out all his capital, and has nothing to do but to fulfill his contract and pay in his money as he has stipulated. When he has so paid in all his indebtedness his bond is to be returned to him and his shares cancelled. This, of course, makes the non-borrowers take all the risk of losses, as is proper when theirs is all the gain. In these, also, the members are known only by a number, and the loans are reported as made to—No. 620, or whatever the borrower's number on the roll might be; the delinquents are reported the same way; so that the affairs of each individual member are solely between him and the officers, and not made known to his fellow members. This is claimed as being an important improvement in the method of running. I present here a report of a company of this kind at the end of its first year:

THE PROTECTIVE BUILDING AND LOAN ASSOCIATION.

Dr.	CASH.	Cr.
To Dues, interest and premiums....................		By Loans to stockholders.	19,900.00
" Fines and assessments........................ 19,857.77		" Return with interest, Stockholder No. 14.......	1,025.00
" Loan from stockholder No. 14.......... 1,000.00		" Charter...............................	81.75
" " " " No. 4.................. 1,500.00		" Treasurer's bond.........................	28.12
" " " " No. 233.......... 1,000.00		" Interest on money advanced	32.47
		" Books, advertising, rent, and running expenses.	580.35
		" Withdrawals...........................	257.50
		" Balance in treasury......................	1,452.58
Total......................... 23,357.77		Total.........	23,357.77

Dr.	PROFIT AND LOSS.	Cr.
To Expense........................ 722.69		By Interest	605.96
" Interest paid, Book 14.............. 25.00		" Assessments and fines.......	512.15
" Balance 379.46		" Withdrawals...........................	9.04
Total.................. 1,127.15		Total......	1,127.15

Dr.	STOCK.	Cr.
To Withdrawals.................... 584.25		By Dues.	19,435.00
" Balance.... .... 19,452.72		" Premium..............................	222.51
		" Profit and loss....	379.46
Total.................. 20,036.97		Total......	20,036.97
		" Balance..........................	19,452.72
To 1,376¼ shares, 1st series; value, $12.27, or...... 16,889.66			
" 78 shares, 1st series, borrowed; value, $12, or.. 936.00			
" 209 shares, 2d series; value, $6.07, or.......... 1,268.63			
" 21½ shares, loaned on; value, $6, or............ 129,000			
" Premium of borrowers....... .... 222.51			
" Undivided.... .... 6.92			
Total............... ..... 19,452.72		Total...........	19,452.72

ASSETS.		BALANCE.		LIABILITIES.
Bond and mortgage........................	19,900.00	Due stockholders, No. 4 and 233....................		2,500.00
Due by stockholders....	696.14	Due advance.........................		96.00
Balance in treasury.........................	1,452.58	Balance capital-stock........................		19,452.72
Total................................	21,048.72	Total........................		21,048.72

DR.					BOND AND MORTGAGE.			CR.

No. Book.	Order.	Series.	Shares.	Amount.	Amount Paid. Dues.	Premium.	Total Cr.	Amount Due.
188	11	1	50	10,000.00	600.00	182.25	782.25	9,217.75
194	28	1	10	2,000.00	120.00	26.10	146.10	1,853.90
1	32	1	2	400.00	24.00	50	24.50	375.50
..	..	..	.. ..	.. ..	.. ..	.. ..	.. ..	.. ..
Stock Loans...................			99½	19,900.00	1,065.00	222.51	1,287.51	17,612.49

UNPAID AND ADVANCE.

No. Book.	Unpaid.	No. Book.	Advance.
33	15.20	3	24.00
47	114.18	176	60.00
60	10.10	183	4.00
..	..	230	8.00
	696.14		96.00

Also another one in its eleventh year:

THE RANDOLPH BUILDING AND LOAN ASSOCIATION.

DR.		CASH.		CR.
To Balance, Annual, 1883.........................	9,934.26	By Loans..........................		5,900.00
" Loans repaid......	3,700.00	" Withdrawals..........................		18,071.75
" Rents, less commission..................	646.00	" Water and ground rent..................		104.76
" Real estate sold........................	3,581.82	" State tax		245.65
" Dues, interest, and premium...	17,678.77	" Property tax..........................		129.50
		" Running expense..................		411.31
		" Matured stock..........................		9,635.50
		" Interest paid on M. S..................		201.90
		" Balance in treasury.....................		840.48
Total................................	35,540.85	Total........................		35,540.85

DR.		PROFIT AND LOSS.		CR.
To Expense	891.22	By Interest		4,377.50
" Interest allowed M. S.	281.90	" Premium.........................		374.67
		" Fines..........................		32.10
		" Withdrawals..........................		629.53
		" Rents collected, less commission		646.00
		" Premium on M. S		66.50
" Balance.........................	5,015.90	" Real estate.................,......		62.72
Total................................	6,189.02	Total........................		6,189.02

DR.		STOCK.		CR.
To Withdrawals..........................	19,402.70	By Balance, 1883..........................		95,798.80
" 142 shares Matured..................	28,400.00	" Dues..........................		13,529.50
" Balance..........................	66,541.50	" Profit and loss..........		5,015.90
Total................................	114,344.20	Total........		114,344.20
		By Balance		66,541.50
To 18 shares, 2d series; value, $181.22, or..........	3,261.96			
" 77 shares, 3d series; value, $153.34, or..........	11,845.68			
" Undivided..........	.03			
Total........	66,541.50	Total.........................		66,541.50

ASSETS.	BALANCE.	LIABILITIES.

Assets		Liabilities	
Bond and mortgage........................	69,309.00	Stockholders in advance............................	320.20
Real estate.........	5,734.39	Matured stock..	12,200.00
Due by stockholders..	3,264.83	Interest due M. S....................................	78.00
Balance in treasury............	840.48	Balance capital......................................	66,541.50
Total..................	79,139.70	Total................................	79,139.70

BOND AND MORTGAGE.

No. Book.	Series.	Shares.	Amount.
235	2	5	$1,000
315	3	5	1,000
331	3, 4	18	3,600
..	..	..	..
			$69,300

UNPAID THIS DATE.		STOCKHOLDERS IN ADVANCE.		MONEY DUE. FIRST SERIES STOCKHOLDERS.	
No. Book.		No. Book.		No. Book.	
235 .. .. 45.30		331 300		10 3,700	
331 .. .. 2,128.58		407 10		40 1,000	
.. .. ..		.. .. ..		.. .. ..	
3,264.83		320.20		12,200	

These specimens of the results of various forms of working will suffice to give a tolerably clear idea of the main differences in building associations. Many other variations there are: such, for instance, as in the value of a share and amount of dues payable; some doubling the amount I have stated, and others halving it: the one gives the value of a share full-paid, $400, and dues, $2 per month; the other making it $100, and dues, 50 cents per month. One of this last-named kind has lately been started in Chicago, in connection with the Institute of Accountants and Book-keepers in that city, with some new features in it; but they are all in the main, as I have said before, likely to result in the end about the same, both to borrowers and non-borrowers. With a few words upon the other points intended to be touched in these articles, I will, Messrs. Editors, trespass no longer on your time and space.

The value that may be derived from such organizations depends upon the character of the community. In most of the cities and towns of our land they could not fail, rightly administered, to be beneficial. More especially is this the case where land is cheap, and the laboring classes are seeking homes. In cities like New York, where capital is abundant, land is high, and every inch of available space is desirable for business purposes, where men do not have homes, they could not possibly thrive; but where the ability to secure a home must depend upon years of constant savings, there is room for the beneficent work of this kind of savings-bank. But in doing this it must not be forgotten that there are risks that may be incurred, which can and ought in great measure to be avoided. As in the case of freedom, the price of which is eternal vigilance — so, for the success of an enterprise of this kind, no careless trustfulness, no thoughtless leaving the vital interests of the many in the hands of the few, will suffice. Know well your officers and directors, have frequent and full examinations, demand clear and explicit statements of all transactions. Elect auditors who know their business, and see to it that they do *audit* — not merely sign their names to a report prepared for them. Have every member's book presented for examination and settlement at least once a year. Pay your secretary and treasurer for their services, and do not allow them, as is sometimes the case, to use the funds until wanted. With all the care you can exercise you may not altogether escape loss, for bad times will come, fires will occur, and other ills that humanity is liable to suffer must be looked for; but with them you will be the better for a well-conducted building association.

R. B. Keys.

BUSINESS IN INDIA.— *Concluded.*

The *internal* trade of India greatly exceeds its foreign commerce. This includes, of course, the wholesale business connected with the export trade in all its stages. Besides cotton, jute, indigo, tea, oil-seeds, the export of wheat from India has increased steadily and with marvelous rapidity during the last decade, until it fairly threatens to drive the American grower from the European marts; and as soon as cheaper and more convenient means of transit have been established in the interior of the country, it promises for years to come to stand unrivaled in the wheat trade of the world.

Europeans control the shipping business, and have a share in the collection of some of the more valuable staples of export, especially wheat; but by far the greatest part of the internal collection of the products, their accumulation at the central marts, and their final despatch to the seaboard, are in the hands of the natives. On the other hand, manufactured articles from abroad are distributed in the reverse direction, through the same channels; the adaptation of the supply to the demand of the consumer naturally falling to those who are best acquainted with the native wants. There is also the interchange of commodities of native growth and manufacture between the several districts and provinces. Most of the retail shops, even in the metropolitan cities, are owned by natives.

The Vaisya, or merchant caste, has now scarcely a separate existence, but its place has been filled by off-shoots and well-marked classes. On the western coast, the Parsees, by the boldness and extent of their operations, tread closely upon the heels of the great English houses. There are the Banias and Marwaris in the Bombay Presidency and Central Provinces; while, in Bengal, representatives of all the different castes have devoted themselves to the wholesale trade.

Local trade is conducted in the permanent *bazars* of the large towns, at weekly markets in the rural villages, and at periodical gatherings for religious purposes, known as fairs, or *melas*. The traveling broker or agent also handles certain departments. The town *bazars* are extensive market-places, where traders of every description have their booths. The greatest part of the shopping is done in these places, and their number varies according to the size of the town. Beside these there are special bazars, as of brass-works, pottery, cloth, fruits of the season, etc., which afford choice from larger collections of the different articles, as, also, they supply the booth-holders of the general bazars. Isolated specialty shops are rather rare. The Hindoo cannot do business unless he can carry on a chat with his neighbor across the passage-way.

Outside of town, the traveling broker or agent plays an important part. The cultivator himself, who is the chief producer, and, also, the chief consumer, as well as the rural gentry, know little of large cities, and expect the dealer to come to their own doors. Each village has at least one resident trader, who usually combines in his person the functions of money-lender, grain merchant, as well as seller of Manchester and home-spun cloths. The simple system of rural economy depends upon the dealings of this man, who is sometimes decried as a usurer, but who is often the one thrifty person among an improvident population. Under the protection of English law there are, undoubtedly, occasional abuses of the money-lender's privileges; specially as now the force of the moral sense of the community is diminishing in its effect. In districts where the staples of export are largely grown, the cultivators sell their crops to the traveling brokers, who resell to larger dealers, and so on until the commodities reach the hands of the great shipping houses. The wholesale trade thus ultimately rests with a comparatively small number of persons, who have agencies or branch firms at the central marts.

As the general dealer of the village is the money-lender of his neighbors, so the wholesale traders and traveling merchants have been, and still are to a certain extent, the great bankers of the country. Their character for integrity and honesty has always been deservedly held at high esteem. Being also hereditary traders by families, the guarantees of safety were regarded as both morally and actually strong. Letters of credit and exchange, transported by agents from one part of the country to another, have been in use for a long time in India, when means of communication were scarce and insecure. These individual "money-men" are now giving place to corporate banking institutions.

At this part of my subject I may properly mention what presumably will have special interest to the readers of the COUNTING-ROOM, that book-keeping is a high art among my countrymen. The system of double-entry has been in vogue for many centuries; and it is fairly debatable whether the Italians did not first acquire their knowledge of it in Indian counting-rooms. The caste of accountants ranks next in order of dignity to those of the priest and the physician, and is above that of the merchant and trader. Book-keeping is looked upon as the handmaid of the science of arithmetic, which, with poetry and medicine, form the three-fold gift of Brahma (the Creator) to his children. Unfortunately, as they say, the saint is not known in his own country, and the conscientious child of the quill is the occasion of much good-humored fun. By the light-headed youth of the village he is known as the over-scrupulous lean gentleman who burns a pound's worth of oil to balance half a penny's worth of account, and whose better-half is in a perpetual rage because of his incurable habit of staying out late.

The subject of business in India must not omit to say a few words upon the most characteristic phase of buying and selling, as also the most interesting and pleasant that is seen either in that country or anywhere else in the world. It is at the great religious fairs, or *melas,* which are held periodically at certain spots in most districts, that one sees, as if in a variety show, the kaleidoscopic mingling of Indian life in all its aspects. Religion is the original pretext of these gatherings, and they are always the occasions of bathing in the holy water of the river Ganges, and of practising ceremonies and almsgiving. But not the least important part — to foreigners the most—is the excuse afforded by religion for secular business. The *melas* last through several successive days, and take place under the auspices of the prince or landlord of the district, though rich and poor, old and young, male and female, vie with one another in extending patronage to the motley traders.

A *mela* is at once an exhibition of industry, a glorification of religion, and a public recognition of social feelings. Petty traders bringing all those miscellaneous articles which can be packed into a pedlar's wallet, the rich merchant with his wagon-loads of shawls and valuables—in short, all imaginable classes of dealers—exhibit to curious holiday-makers articles of every description that money can buy or curiosity desire. Everyone feels bound to enjoy, even to the extent of rapture, and the whole scene presents, with its many colored tints of dress and canopy, a bright spectacle of hopefulness, and success and joy. Long lines of booths and stalls, with toys and sweetmeats, stretch far away into pine and cedar groves, all teeming with looking-glasses, beads, necklaces and rings, armlets and anklets, brooches, pins and ornaments for the head; whilst the cook-shop sends forth pleasant odors, and sweetmeat men display their wares in tempting luxuriance. Farther away in the groves, horses, mules and asses, camels and elephants, panthers and cubs, are picketed about in thousands, and grooms and muleteers are lying under the trees, sleeping off their fatigue. On another side might be seen the bright tents, where courteous-tongued merchants are discoursing upon shawls and silks to admiring spectators. Here the bookseller is reciting some passage from a popular author; and there the seller of musical instruments is blowing a pipe. On a remote spot will be seen even forbidden fruits and drinks, such as canned biscuits (said to be made with porcine lard), soda water and lemonade.

One feature of distinction, however, from similar gatherings in the West is to be found in the absence of drunkards and drink-shops. In the midst of the many-tongued confusion there is respectable sobriety and orderly behavior. Nobody jostles intentionally against somebody else; nor are there mischievous wags seeking to create annoyance to young girls, and flirtation seldom goes farther than a distant ogle. At the end of the fair, it is not clear whether the nasal pedlar or the busy sweetmeat vender has not made as much out of the juvenile customers as the sedate shawl merchant or the *nonchalant* horse-dealer from their fathers.

The gentlemen who ply the nimble fingers find, too, good reasons for congratulation; while the itinerant devotee, with his idol on his shoulder, draws many a penny for the building of a house to his god. All agree in returning home pleased and happy, and a great many money-makers do little else for the succeeding days than making ready for the next occasion.

In view of the troubles between employers and employed, which are of such common occurrence in the business world at the present day, I must not conclude without noticing one characteristic aspect of the system of caste artisanship in India, beside what has been already said in regard to its general economical functions, and that is, the part which the several castes play as naturally and strongly organized trades unions. The members of a trade in a village are scions of the same stock, and are bound together by ties of relationship and sympathy. No outsider can enter into their body, nor can a member leave them without risking the certainty of his social position. Every single class is, in the very nature of things, rigidly defined in its outlines, and compact in its organization. Thus, by their natural combination, the Hindoo artisans are always able to command a higher price for their commodities than they could in what is called a free market. It is a universally known fact in India that traders are able to maintain, and often do maintain, two prices for the same article in the same bazar. Obnoxious customers have always a hard time of it. Englishmen, particularly high-paid civil or military officers and *protégés* of the Government, have, all the days of their life in India, to pay higher prices, sometimes two or three times as much, as the ill-paid Hindoo, for almost every article of necessity or luxury. This plan is not adopted and pursued surreptitiously, but is openly acknowledged and defended. At one of the fairs, a horse-dealer told an Englishman who wanted to buy the second of a pair of horses — the first and comparatively superior one from which had just been taken by a native — that the *Sahib* (same as lord, used to designate Englishmen) must pay half as much again — not only because he could better afford to, but, as he naively declared, European baggage consists of hard, heavy, angular, close-packed boxes, much more likely to gall the poor beast than the soft, bulky, round and lighter bundles of his native brother. The pious heathen concluded with a homily to his white brother of the Church, to the effect that kind feeling toward our fellow-creatures should always have more weight with us than considerations of mere gain, which is a cardinal principle of virtue, as was taught by the wise men of old.

Amrita Lal Roy.

TRAITS OF THE SUCCESSFUL.

What *is* success? Ask a dozen people this question, and you will probably find that no two of them will answer you in exactly the same manner. Each individual, however, has his own idea as to what constitutes success, though it may not always be easy for him to define it even to himself. Success, like poverty, is a relative term. That which will satisfy one man will fail to satisfy another. A modest competence, with but few of the good things in life, will suffice for one, while another aspires to wealth or fame. All men are striving for something: whether consciously or unconsciously, they desire certain conditions which they do not possess, and fancy that could they but reach the ideal which they have set before them, they must be better off and happier than they are to-day. How many are satisfied when they do attain that for which they work so hard?

In the common acceptation of the term, success in life, means the accumulation of money. It is to this end that most men bend their best energies; and he who can amass the largest fortune is accounted by his fellows the most successful man. To be rich in this world's goods is what everyone desires, despite the fact that it remains an open question, whether or not the possession of wealth is an unmixed good. True happiness does not consist in the abundance of the things possessed, but, rather, in a contented mind, which, as we are told by the highest authority, is great riches. This is fortunate, indeed, for comparatively few men ever rise above mediocrity. The wealthy may be sharply divided into two classes: those who have inherited their money, and those who have made it for themselves. The former, in the majority of cases, do not possess any very marked characteristics, and, under less favorable circumstances, would, possibly, never have risen to the surface at all, so that we must look to the latter for an answer to the question, What are the elements of success in life?

Self-made men are to be met with everywhere in this country. They are the bone and sinew of the nation which owes its present proud position in the world to the energy and enterprise they have displayed in developing its resources. Self-made men, as we know, rise from obscurity and, possibly, extreme poverty, to be an influence in society, and to be possessors of wealth in a greater or less degree. Their characters are as various as their number is great, but they must all possess some traits in common which enable them to push to the front ranks in the battle of life. The object of our present inquiry is, What are these traits?

To emunerate a list of the elements of success in life, and then ascribe all of them to any *one man* would be folly, for, as has just been intimated, the qualifications which men possess for making their way in the world are numerous and varied. Still, the question will be a profitable one for us to study, and may lead to our cultivating each one for himself some of those traits in which he feels himself deficient. At the head of the list let us place knowledge. It is true that very many ignorant men rise, but it cannot be denied that "knowledge is power"; and in these days of free schools and good, cheap literature even the poorest among us can, if he so desires, obtain a liberal education to start out with. This obtaining an education is something that cannot be delegated to another: a man can, if he have the money, pay other people to do much for him, but no man can study for another; *that*, each man must do for himself. Moreover, the very act of acquiring knowledge implies several of the requisites which will go to swell the stock in trade of him who aims at success. He must have perseverance and industry, and an innate love for work, for it is an old and true saying that "There is no royal road to learning." It is evident, then, that children may learn some useful lessons for life while at school. Teach them to persevere industriously in their work for the sake of the reward that the possession of knowledge brings with it. A love of work for its own sake is natural to very few; but all can and ought to be taught very early in life that useful occupation is the surest road to happiness, to say nothing of success.

When labor becomes a pleasure, then a good foundation is laid, and it will be comparatively easy to build the superstructure. Children should also be taught the value of money: when they reach a proper age it is a good plan, for those who can do so, to give them an allowance, more or less as the case may be, and require them to provide themselves with certain necessaries. Let them have absolute control of the money, only stipulating that they shall get themselves specified things or go without, and they will soon learn that they must handle it thoughtfully and carefully. And thus another element of success — economy — will be inculcated.

And now take a youth who has learned to work because he likes it. He works diligently, and in spite of discouragements perseveres to the end of his task. If, with all this, he has learned to lay out money wisely, he is tolerably well-equipped, and ought to succeed. But does he not want something more? Yes; it must be impressed upon him that "Honesty is the best policy." Without integrity of character he can never hope to make a success in life; and to be worthy to be trusted will surely be the desire of every noble nature. Self-esteem—that is, a proper respect for one's self—is necessary. To have faith in one's self is a good thing, while courage and determination go a long way too. The man who knows and feels that he is capable of doing a certain thing, and who resolves that nothing shall deter him from accomplishing his purpose, has that within him which will assist him in his laudable effort, "For they can conquer who believe they can." But it is not enough for a man to be upright and honorable in all his dealings; industrious and per-severing in all he undertakes, and thrifty and economical in his habits of life. There are some less noble attributes to be found among the successful men of the world, which we must, however unwillingly, point out.

The economy, which is perfectly proper and, indeed, most desirable and necessary when practiced within certain limits, often degenerates into covetousness and avariciousness, so that it is not an uncommon thing to meet with very rich men, especially among those who have made their own money, who are exceedingly parsimonious. Self-conceit will further a man's interests however distasteful to those around him his assertions of it may be, and assurance, or what is vulgarly called "cheek," will do him good service in his struggle with the world. There is, also, a certain shrewdness—call it *meanness* if you will—that makes a man sharp enough to get the advantage, if there happen to be one in the bargain he is striking, which will further his cause; although shrewdness should not, perhaps, be classed among the less desirable elements of success in life. Necessity often stimulates to success; an early and happy choice of occupation contributes in a great degree to the same end, while good business habits are indispensable.

Kate Kanada.

LEGAL-TENDER PAPER MONEY.*

It is impossible to approach the topic involved in this proposed constitutional amendment without being confronted by the recent decision of the Supreme Court of the United States on the subject of legal-tender money. We have reached a crisis in our judicial history. It has been proclaimed by the highest judicial tribunal in the land—that tribunal which was created to be the arbiter on constitutional questions—that it is constitutionally competent to the legislative power to make any form of paper currency a legal-tender in the payment of private debts; that there is not one fixed and immutable standard of value in this

* An Address by George Ticnor Curtis, advocating an amendment to the Constitution in regard to the issue of Legal-Tender paper money. Made to the Judiciary Committee of the House of Representatives, Forty-eighth Congress, April 15th, 1884.

country; that no matter what may have been the medium of payment agreed upon between creditor and debtor, it is within the power of Congress to force into private contracts, as a medium the tender of which is to discharge the debt, anything that Congress chooses to call money; and that what Congress shall enact to be money for the payment of all debts is a matter of legislative discretion, incapable of being revised or controlled by the judicial power.

In reaching this stupendous conclusion, the Court has announced a doctrine respecting the incidental or implied powers of Congress that is so sweeping, and so entirely at variance with all formerly received ideas of the nature of this Government, that sober and reflecting men stand amazed and bewildered. I shall speak of this decision with the utmost respect for the judges who have made it. With me the habit of reverencing the judicial power, and especially that high tribunal in which is lodged the interpretation of the Constitution for the purpose of administering justice, has become a second nature. My whole life since I came to manhood has been passed in courts of justice and in the studies appropriate to my profession; and I do not now need to learn how necessary it is to speak and think of the men who sit in that exalted place with perfect respect for their personal characters and their public function.

But, sir, I know, or believe that I know, for what purpose that tribunal was created; and I cannot express what I felt when I heard promulgated from that bench doctrines which amount to a renunciation of the function that it was created to fulfill. Nay, sir, when I heard the practices of European Governments used as a kind of measure of the powers of this limited American Government of ours, my patriotism suffered a shock that I cannot describe. I had been accustomed all my life to believe that here great discoveries in the science of Government had been made and put into operation by our ancestors; that they had not only founded these institutions upon the principle that all government derives its authority from the will of the people, but that they had discovered and put into practical operation that other principle, that the people limit their Governments and limit themselves by public compacts in which the whole of society covenants with every part, the majority with the minority, the strong with the weak, the

whole collective body of the people with every individual. I had learned from long study of these institutions how private rights are protected from oppression; how the acknowledged powers of a written constitution are to be interpreted by a fixed rule; how the admirable machinery which gives definite operation and certainty to that rule was devised, and how it works; how just and how well-founded was our boast that these institutions were distinguished by a broad line of demarkation from all other Governments that rest for their title on conquest, or on the domination of a class or of classes, and on unlimited and unrestrained powers. When, therefore, we were virtually told from the supreme bench that all this boast is a mistake; that all this pride in the institutions of our country is a false sentiment; that the people have imposed no restraints on the power of a majority; that there is an armory of implied legislative powers from which the majority can extract any instrument that they may choose, to be wielded as they choose, I could not help asking myself whether I still lived under the Constiution of the United States.

No one, I suppose, will impute to me a desire to exaggerate. I shall take care that no one can justly impute to me such a purpose. I shall make a careful and exact statement of the doctrine lately promulgated by the Supreme Court, and shall contrast it with the doctrine of their predecessors.

Mr. Chairman, when the men who made the Constitution put into it a clause giving to Congress authority to pass all laws necessary and proper to carry into effect the specific powers enumerated and granted in the preceding clauses, they established a measure of the legislative authority. If they had done nothing more it might have been a reasonable inference that the limits of the legislative authority were left to legislative discretion. But they did a great deal more, and what they did renders it absolutely certain that Congress is not the final judge of the extent of its implied powers. A judicial department was created; a Supreme Court was created; and to that tribunal, as the final arbiter, was committed the intrepretation of every part of the Constitution on which any question may arise in any controversy capable of taking the form of a suit at law or in equity. The measure of the legislative powers, therefore—what laws are necessary and proper to carry into effect the enumerated powers of the Constitution, what means may be used for the accomplishment of given ends—was taken out of the unlimited discretion of Congress and was subjected to a judicial test. This has ever been regarded as a remarkble proof of the completeness of our polity. There is nothing like it in any of the other modern or the ancient Governments. It is that which makes a written constitution practically successful; that which secures the constitutional rights of individuals and of States against the power of a mere democracy of numbers, and reconciles popular government with rights which no Government can be allowed to invade if liberty is anything but a name. It was a great discovery in the science of free government; far greater than the establishment of the principle that all power resides in the people, important and unquestionble as that principle is.

The rule of determination which measures the legislative authority of Congress in the choice of means for the execution of its acknowledged powers necessarily supposes a certain relation between the means employed and the end that is to be accomplished. What that relation is was first considered by the Executive when Congress passed the bill to charter the first bank of the United States. In the great argument written by Alexander Hamilton, which convinced the mind of Washington that to create a banking corporation would be constitutional, because such an instrument would bear a certain relation to the execution of one or more of the acknowledged powers of the Government, it is not claimed or pretended that there is an unlimited choice of means open to the legislature.

It was conceded by Hamilton that the means selected must bear some direct relation to the end that was to be reached by using it. In the opposing argument made by Jefferson, it was not denied that there are some implied powers comprehended in the general grants of the objects to which the legislative power of Congress was to extend; but it was denied that a banking corporation bore to any one or more of those objects the relation which the rule of interpretation required. The controversy about the precise meaning of the words " necessary and proper," as descriptive of the laws that may be passed, did not lead to the conclusion on the one hand that the whole question is referred to the discretion of Congress, or to the conclusion on the other hand that Congress has no discretion to exercise. Hamilton did not deny that there must be a direct relation of means to ends. Jefferson did not deny that within certain limits Congress has a range of choice as to the means or instrumentalities which it will employ for the execution of its acknowledged powers. These great men differed on the fact of whether a banking corporation bore the requisite relation as an instrument to any constitutional power that was to be executed as the end.

It was when, in 1819, the great mind of John Marshall formulated in a judicial decision the true doctrine of incidental or implied powers that the measure of the legislative authority received its judicial interpretation. It was then, in the case of McCulloch *vs.* Maryland, that two great branches of one comprehensive rule were exhaustively and accurately defined. Marshall's doctrine was, that while for the execution of the principal and acknowledged powers of the Government there is a certain range of means or instruments open to the discretionary choice of Congress, yet these means or instruments must have certain qualities or characteristics, otherwise the field is unlimited and undefined. He defined the objets or ends for which an implied power may be exercised as those legitimate objects or ends which are comprehended in the principal and enumerated powers of the Government. These, of course, are described in the Constitution in general terms; but they are each of them stated, appropriately described, and specifically granted. It is upon his definition of the implied powers that there has been so much misconception; and yet he described and defined them so lucidly, so exactly, and in such unmistakable terms, that it is marvelous how men can understand him. He defined the essential qualities and characteristics which every incidental or implied means must have as being these three: *First,* the means or instrument chosen for the execution of an acknowledged power of the Government must be appropriate and plainly adapted to the end; *second,* it must not be prohibited by the Constitution; *third,* it must be consistent with both the letter and the spirit of the Constitution. To whatever variety of means or instrumeuts *all* these qualities and characteristics belong the legislative discretion of choice extends; and of the degree of necessity at any particular time for resorting to one of these defined means or instruments, rather than to another, Congress is the final judge. But, outside of this defined range of legislative choice, there is no legislative discretion and no legislative power to pronounce that a thing is necessary at a particular time, or at any time. The legislative discretion embraces the degree of necessity only when the means proposed to be used bears the defined relation to one or more of the principal powers of the Government as the end.

It follows as an inevitable inference from this plain doctrine that the question whether a particular means or instrument possesses the defined qualities and characteristics—bears the defined relation to the end involved in the execution of one of the known specific powers of the Government—is not committed to the final decision of Congress. It is not a political question. The political question is confined to the degree of necessity for resorting to one means rather than to another when both possess the requisite qualities and characteristics. Whether they do possess those qualities and characteristics is, as a final question, a judicial question. It was to determine this juidcial question that the judicial power was created.

It would be difficult for any human intellect to frame a rule of interpretation plainer and safer than this. It left nothing to be complained of by the strict constructionist, for it gave him a rule which measures by well-defined limits the nature of the incidental or implied powers. It left nothing to be complained of by the broad or liberal constructionist, for it allowed to the legislative discretion all the range of choice that is consistent with the terms of a written constitution, while it also permitted the legislative department to judge finally the degree of necessity at any particular juncture for resorting to any means that has the defined qualities and relations to any particular power of the Government.

This was one of those consummate statements of constitutional doctrine which, when they are first announced, seem to be the product of individual genius, and therefore to partake somewhat of the positiveness of individual authority. But the more this rule of interpretation is studied, the more clearly does it reveal its logical consistency and its conformity to good sense. Marshall left to his judicial successors, by the announcement of this rule for measuring the implied powers of Congress, a very plain task, and they have in general applied it with a wise accuracy. It has often been said that

he molded our constitutional law. If by this is meant that he shaped it arbitrarily, the assertion is not true. If it is meant that he molded it by interpreting the Constitution upon sound principles—principles which make it equal to any emergency and at the same time make it consistent with liberty—the praise is eminently his due. But it must be remembered, also, that he had associates of great authority, for with him sat Story and Bushrod Washington, and Thompson, who concurred in his reasoning and his conclusions.

It is sixty-five years since Marshall and those who sat with him laid down the rule which defines the nature and limits of the incidental or implied powers; and this great rule has never been completely departed from until now, although it has within the past twenty years been much encroached upon. Bnt now it is overthrown, so far as one judicial decision by the same tribunal can overthrow the doctrine of a former decision. It is impossible to reconcile Marshall's rule of interpretation with the late decision. His rule cannot be found in the late decision. I do not say this for any purpose of reproach; I say it because one of two conclusions is inevitable : Either Marshall and his associates were wrong, or the present judges are wrong. It is the same Constitution with which the judges in 1819 and the judges in 1884 had to deal, so far as the measure of the implied powers is concerned. But the results to which they have respectively come are widely asunder.

But before I state the substance of the late decision, I desire to remind you of what took place during the forty years which followed the year 1820. After the adoption of the Constitution, it was seen by enlightened men in Europe, and even by many of the less educated classes, that here had been established a Government under which property and personal rights were to enjoy guarantees such as had never been enjoyed in any other country. It was seen that here there could be no arbitrary interference by Government with the obligation of contracts ; that here there was to be one uniform and fixed standard of values; that paper money, as a medium of compulsory payment of debts, which had been the bane of our previous social condition, was now for ever discarded ; that whatever a man might bring with him to this country, or send here for investment, or whatever he might earn after he arrived here, would be measured as to its pecuniary value by a fixed standard, and that in no state of circumstances, under no condition of public affairs, could any public authority compel him to discharge a debt by accepting a species of currency that was not within the terms of the contract. The consequence was a vast emigration to our shores; for here the capitalist and the laborer were alike assured that in all contracts the only legal measure of value was to be in accordance with the standard of value recognized throughout the world, when the contract called for that measure of what the debtor was to pay.

After the Supreme Court of the United States had, in 1819, laid down the great rule which, while it admitted of the creation of a National bank, defined the nature and extent of the implied powers of this Government, and it was further seen that it was for the judicial power to exercise some restraint upon the discretion of the majority as represented in Congress, capital began to flow in here from foreign countries to an enormous extent.

From 1820 to 1860 we became a people of debtors for untold millions, in every variety of form; and to the foreign capital thus intrusted to us, and to the labor that accompanied it, we largely owe the development of our country. If the constitutional doctrines now promulgated by the Supreme Court are not encountered by an amendment to the Constitution, all our debts of every description, whether they be bonds held by a millionaire or the wages due to a day laborer, may at any time, in the naked discretion of a majority of Congress, be discharged in a medium of payment never contemplated in the contract, and incapable of satisfying its value.

I shall now state with precision what was recently decided by the Court. The exact question that was before the Court was, whether in time of profound peace, and without any reference to the supposed exigencies of the public safety or the public necessities peculiar to a state of war, it is constitutionally competent to Congress to enact a law making the promissory notes of this Government a legal-tender in the payment of private debts. This attitude of the question enlarged its scope beyond all the peculiar necessities of a state of war. It was not to the power to make or to carry on war that the interference with or the effect on private contracts was now to be referred as an incident. It was to other powers that it was to be referred; powers which exist

at all times, and are to be exercised under all circumstances—such as the power to borrow money, or the power to pay the debts of the United States, or any of the other specific powers of the Government which may require to be executed at all times and under all circumstances. This being the attitude of the question, bringing into view the nature and extent of the incidental or implied powers on a subject of transcendent importance to the public welfare, we might well have expected to see a consistent application of the doctrine of Chief-Justice Marshall and his associates so accurately made that if the power in question was to be asserted by the Court to have a constitutional basis it would be done by a clear exposition of its conformity with the ancient and established rule of interpretation.

Now, what has been the reasoning, or the line of argumentation, adopted and followed out in this recent decision? It is this: To issue Government notes, for circulation as money, and to affix to them the quality of being a compulsory tender in payment of debts, is an incident of political sovereignty. Many Governments do it. The Governments of the States before the Constitution did it, and the Congress of the Confederation upheld them in it. It is not expressly prohibited by the Constitution of the United States. Therefore, although it is not specially authorized by the Constitution, it may be regarded as an incidental or implied power, to be referred to one or more of the enumerated powers of the Constitution as a means appropriate and conducive to their exercise. There is some argument resorted to in the opinion of the Court to show that this means bears the requisite relation to the power, for example, to borrow money. Thus it is said that lenders of money will be more likely to lend it to the Government if the Government notes with which they are furnished in contracting the loan have a legal quality by which all creditors can be compelled to receive them from all debtors.

Does it require any man to be a constitutional lawyer, or a lawyer of any kind, in order to see that this incident, or feature, or quality of the note does not make them bear the requisite relation as a means to the power of borrowing money as the end? What is the requisite relation? One part of it is, according to Chief-Justice Marshall's definition, that the means employed shall be something that directly executes the principal power for which it is chosen. There is a power to make war. A particular military engine, although it did not exist when the Constitution was made, may be employed as a means of making war, because its employment directly executes the power to carry on war. A bank may be created, not because the creating of a bank is an incident of sovereignty, not because other Governments create banks, but because a bank may be an instrument that will directly execute the specific power to borrow money, or the specific power to collect and distribute revenue. But can this be said of an instrument which, when it is delivered by the Government to a person from whom the Government borrows money, is to become in other hands than his a medium which all creditors can be compelled to receive from all debtors? The question answers itself to any unsophisticated mind.

The quality of legal-tender in all private contracts does not, as a means of executing any one or more of the specific powers of the Government, bear to those powers the relation required by the rule which Marshall laid down. This, it may be said, is a matter of opinion; and the Court is of opinion that it does not bear the requisite relation. But there is a revising opinion, even in regard to the decisions of the Court, although that revising opinion cannot judicially enforce its conclusions. That revising tribunal of opinion is the intelligent judgment of the country; and this judgment is quite competent to see that a law which forces all creditors to receive from all debtors a medium of payment that was not contemplated in their contract, cannot be an exercise of the Government's power to borrow a sum of money from any one who has money to lend, and who chooses to lend it to the Government.

I come now to that other quality which every incidental or implied power must have, according to the doctrine of Marshall and his associates. This is, that the means chosen for the execution of one of the principal powers of the Government must be consistent with both the letter and the spirit of the Constitution. I have studied the late opinion of the Court most attentively, in order to discover, if I could, how it reconciles legal-tender paper money with either the letter or the spirit of the Constitution. It is useless to say that such money is not expressly prohibited to this Government by the Constitution, unless you can go farther and show that it is consistent with the letter and the spirit of the Constitution. If

it is not, it is just as effectually excluded as if it were in so many words expressly prohibited. The framers of the Constitution did not expressly prohibit it, because the letter and the spirit of the Constitution are both inconsistent with it, and therefore an express prohibition was unnecessary. Look, for a moment, at the letter of the Constitution. When its framers prohibited the States from making anything but gold and silver a legal-tender for private debts, they at the same time conferred on this Government the power to make coin, and to regulate its value and the value of foreign coin that might be in circulation here. There you have the letter of the Constitution on this whole subject of legal-tender. How does the Court reconcile legal-tender paper with the coinage power? I have looked in vain through its opinion for such reconcilement. All men who are not blinded by some fanciful theory will admit that the coinage power was exclusively vested in this Government for the purpose of establishing a legal and constitutional measure of value, that would operate uniformly throughout the country.

There is a previous history of the state of our metallic circulation before the Constitution, which has not been adverted to by the Court, but which is of the highest importance. Before the Constitution, some of the older States had been in the habit of coining small silver pieces and a little copper. But the great bulk of the metallic money in circulation here consisted of foreign silver coins and a few foreign gold coins. There are persons now living who, like myself, can remember that this condition of our metallic circulation lasted until the year 1820, and a little later. The foreign coins were, in my boyhood, in all the tills of the shop-keepers, in the leather pouches of the farmers, in the contribution-boxes of the churches, in all trade of every kind in which small change was required. Larger payments could be made in the notes of specie-paying banks, of which there were only a few. But the value of this foreign coinage varied in different parts of the country. It was not entirely driven out until the United States Mint had supplied our own coin in sufficient quantity to meet the internal wants of the country. It was to change all this condition of the metallic currency, and, at the same time, to vest in this Government an exclusive power over it, so as to establish a fixed standard of value in all payments, by means of a uniform metallic measure of value, that the coinage power was bestowed on this Government in 1788.

I find no reference to this purpose of the coinage power in the late opinion of the Court. I find it asserted that legal-tender paper is consistent with the letter and the spirit of the Constitution ; but how it is to be reconciled with the purpose of the coinage power I am unable to discover. If it was the object of the coinage power to establish one uniform and unvarying measure of value by a metallic standard of value—and all our judges, publicists, and statesmen prior to 1862 have so accepted it— then a law which compels all creditors to receive from all debtors a medium of payment which may be of less value than the metallic measure, according to varying circumstances, is not reconcilable with the letter, as it is far from being reconcilable with the spirit, of the Constitution. The only argument I can find in the opinion of the Court, in support of its conclusion, is this : The power to make paper a legal-tender is not prohibited to this Government in the Constitution. It is an incident of sovereignty, and has been employed by many Governments. In our Government it is a power "analogous" to the exclusive power of coining money and regulating the value thereof and of foreign coins. Therefore, the conclusion is, this Government has two powers— one an incidental or implied power to issue paper and make it a legal-tender in payment of all debts, the other an express power to make metallic money and regulate *its* value in all payments. I need not say that this idea that the power to make legal-tender paper is "analogous" to the power to make coin and *fix its value*, excludes the whole purpose for which the coinage power was conferred on this Government. How can there be, in a commercial country, two standards of value, two measures of value, one of which, when the medium of payment is tendered, may be ten, fifty, or sixty per cent. below the other? Who ever before heard that under our Constitution an incidental or implied power is "analogous" to an express power when they relate to things diametrically opposite? Who has ever before imagined that a paper currency, the value of which no legislation can fix, is "analogous" to a metallic currency the value of which legislation can fix?

Mr. Chairman ; it is, after all, in the doctrine of the Court respecting the implied powers of this Government over private contracts that

the misfortune of this decision chiefly consists. I wish, in all sincerity, that the learned judges had recollected that, with the exception of the prohibition against impairing the obligation of contracts, direct cognizance of contracts between private individuals are matters of State concern ; and I wish they could have pointed out to the country where, aside from the bankruptcy power, this Government gets its authority to dictate what my neighbor shall receive from me or from my estate, in discharge of a debt that I owe him. I can understand how the exercise of the acknowledged powers of this Government often incidentally and injuriously affect the contracts which men make with each other. Most men, even the laboring classes, often understand and feel this, to their cost. It is one of those indirect consequences which flow from all the operations of government, and men must bear it as they can. But how this Government gets its authority to inflict a direct loss upon private individuals, by a direct enactment that all creditors shall receive from all debtors something that is not gold or silver, or of the value of gold or silver, is what I cannot understand. It has not been explained to the satisfaction of the country. It is not capable of being so explained.

It has been loudly complained in the public press that the Court has abdicated its constitutional function. It pains me to say that the complaint is substantially well founded. For, sir, of what avail is it to say, and to say truly, that the degree of necessity for a law is, in some circumstances, a political question to be determined by Congress, if, in the same breath, in arguing that a law is within the incidental and implied powers of the legislative department, the Court does not adhere to the limits and definitions of those powers laid down in former decisions? It was said by a Senator, in debate quite recently, that there is now no kind of law which Congress cannot pass, falling within its incidental or implied powers. Whether he said it regretfully or otherwise, I do not know, but according to the recent decision of the Court, it is true. I do not suppose that the Court would allow a law to take effect that violated an express prohibition of the Constitution. But their doctrine that incidental or implied powers which are not expressly prohibited have no limits but those incomplete, shadowy, and ill-defined qualities on which they have rested this one, does in effect relegate the whole question to the discretion of Congress, and will hereafter prevent the judicial power from fulfilling one great branch of its constitutional function, unless the people, by an amendment of the Constitution, shall adopt a different law of interpretation. Permit me to add that there is one thing which the country should be made clearly to understand. According to the doctrine now laid down by the Supreme Court, there is no quality whatever that a bare majority of Congress may not at any time give to a paper currency, issued by, and under the authority of, this Government. The notes can be made payable centuries hence, or they can be issued without any time for their redemption, without any provision for their redemption, and without any designation of the medium of payment. This follows as a necessary consequence from the doctrine that the qualities to be given to such a currency are matters resting in the legislative discretion; and, therefore, what is called, in the jargon of our day, "fiat money," is, according to the effect of the judgment of the Supreme Court of the United States, completely within the legislative powers. To affix the quality of legal-tender to Government notes, whenever an exigency for it arises, is, says the Court, a constitutional power, and to determine when the exigency has arisen, is a political question.

It is, therefore, a political question whether an exigency has arisen calling for the issue of notes having any quality whatever annexed to them, or having any quality whatever withheld from them, which, in the judgment of Congress, is needful to be given or to be withheld. Any one who will carefully examine the opinion of the Court will see that it has not limited the power to give the quality of legal-tender to notes of the Government that are on their face made redeemable or payable in gold. The Court has not founded the legal-tender quality on the fact that the notes issued under the Act of 1862, and reissued under the Act of 1878, were made payable in coin. Far from it. The reasoning by which the Court supports the power to make the notes of the Government legal-tender, in the payment of private debts, goes wholly beyond any consideration of the time or the medium in which the notes are to be redeemed. The argument and the conclusion are that to give the quality of legal-tender to Government notes is an incident of

sovereignty, and is a power that many sovereigns have exercised. History tells us it has been exercised by other sovereigns without making the notes redeemable in gold as often as it has been when they were so made redeemable.

In its opinion the Court says: "It [the power to borrow money on the credit of the United States] includes the power to *issue*, in return for the money borrowed, the obligations of the United States *in any appropriate form of stock, bonds, bills, or notes.*"* But when the Court came to the giving of legal-tender quality to any of these forms of obligation, it did not limit *that* power to forms made redeemable in gold, or show that a form so made redeemable was what they meant to include in the decision, and that a form not so made redeemable was one that they meant to exclude. In short, the whole tenor of the opinion negatives the idea that the legal-tender quality rests on the time or mode of redemption of the notes; and there is not a word of limitation in the opinion which confines that power to notes made redeemable at a particular time or in a particular medium. If it was intended that the power should be understood as so limited, why was not that limitation carefully made in the opinion? The dissenting judge manifestly understood his brethren as I have understood them, namely, that the power to give the quality of legal-tender to the notes of the Government is not founded on or limited to notes made redeemable in gold, but that it extends to all forms of Government obligations which Congress may deem "appropriate" issues.

I will detain you, sir, with only one other consideration. Let no one suppose that this legal-tender question is exclusively or chiefly a question for the rich or for what are commonly called the business interests, deeply, as they are concerned in it. It is likewise a poor man's question. The rich and prosperous can often manage to protect themselves against the consequences of the ordinary measures of Government. Too often, perhaps, they suffer from these measures, but they are rarely brought to utter ruin or very near or very near to it. But no man, be his resources what they may, can protect himself, or those who are to come after him, against a governmental power which will render all his wealth of no appreciable value, or of no value at all, whenever

---

* I have italicised these words in order to give them prominence.

caprice or phrensy shall put that power in operation. While this is true, it is true also that on the laborer, on all who work with hand or brain without other capital than their skilled or their unskilled labor; these are the men and the women on whom the measures of Government fall with the greatest severity, and especially when they are paid for their labor in a depreciated currency. A single illustration will make this apparent. The labor of a soldier is one of the most arduous and the most dangerous of all the forms in which muscle, guided by intelligence is ever employed in great masses. The price of no labor of any kind ever advances as fast or as far as the cost of the necessaries of life advances, when all payments are made in a depreciated currency. In our late civil war the average pay of a common soldier in the Federal armies was $13 per month; sometimes he got a bounty, ranging from $100 to a higher sum, according to the ability and liberality of the community which first raised his regiment or his company. But he had to receive both pay and bounty in a depreciated currency; and all the while his family at home had to pay in that currency for the necessaries of life at rates enormously enhanced by the depreciated medium in which payments were made. Your doors are now besieged, or very soon will be, by thousands of brave men asking for some equalization of the war bounties and some further just compensations for their services.

What has happened once, in consequence of your depreciated paper currency, will always happen to the laboring classes, whenever that process is repeated. It is an inexorable law, which no legislation can countervail, no sovereignty, be it limited, or unlimited, can control that the wages of labor do not and cannot rise in proportion to the rise in the necessaries of life which is entailed by a depreciated currency. By all the motives, therefore, that ought to actuate statesmen, you are called upon, I respectfully submit to devise the only measure by which the late decision of the Court can be encountered, so as to cut off effectually the power which the Court has declared to exist. Here is a question that appeals to all men from the possessor of millions, down through all grades and condiitons of men, to the man or woman who goes home on Saturday night with a few dollars earned in the course of the week and who has nothing else

on earth but what he or she may earn in the week to come.

The Constitution has devolved on the two houses of Congress the initiation of amendments, by proposing them to the States, or the calling of a convention of the States for the same purpose. The latter would now be a hazardous and imprudent step. The former you can take without unduly agitating the public mind. You can put it to the people of the States to determine whether they will interpose, will define the extraordinary power that may be exercised over the currency in time of war, and prohibit its exercise at all other times.

I have only to add that I presume you will report an amendment, which, while it will allow of the exercise of this extraordinary power in time of foreign war, legally declared, or in time of civil war legally proclaimed to exist, will yet place a limit somewhere by which its exercise may be terminated, and will give the authority only to two-thirds of both houses. And further, I presume that you will render it impossible, hereafter, for Congress to exercise this power in time of peace. This is all the suggestion I have to make to your superior wisdom concerning the form of the amendment.

Mr. Chairman: There was a period in the history of England, not very remote, when doctrines were maintained, very honestly maintained by some, which, if they had not been checked, would have transformed that Government from a limited to an absolute monarchy. We are in some danger, great danger, of a corresponding catastrophe; for there are tendencies at work which may easily transform this political system from a Constitutional Government of checks, balances and limitations, to an absolute tyranny of an uncontrolled majority. Happily, such a revolution may be averted by peaceful means, because we possess, in the process of amending our Constitution, the means of correcting any departure from its fundamental principles that may have been brought about by erroneous judicial decision or any other wrongful public action.

It has been asked by some who entirely disapprove and deplore the late decision of the Court, whether it is necessary to put in motion the process of amending the Constitution in order to encounter it. Why not leave it to time and to better judicial consideration to correct this great judicial error? Why not look to the Court itself to correct its own mistakes? Under ordinary circumstances this would be the best course. But those who reason in this way on this momentous subject seem to me to overlook some very important and vital considerations. They overlook the judicial history of this question. At first we had a decision, concurred in by five judges out of eight, that at no time could Congress constitutionally give the quality of legal-tender to the notes of the Government. Then we had this decision reversed, after the number of the judges had been increased to nine, and it was held by a bare majority of the Court that in time of war, as a measure of overruling public necessity, this power could be exercised. Now we have it held that the time, an extraordinary public emergency, is not an element in the case; that this power is not confined to a state of war, but may be exercised at all times upon any kind of exigency that Congress shall consider to be an exigency. This tremendous decision, abolishing all the former distinctions, has been concurred in by eight judges, and there was but one dissent.

This progress of judicial opinion is a most remarkable fact. Without making the least reflection upon the personal consistency of any one of those learned persons, I think that this growth of judicial opinion, this expansion of the judicial mind into the realms of boundless authority, and into the doctrines of consolidation, is a thing that should attract—it does attract—the attention of the country. It will require that at least one generation shall pass away, probably more than one, before we can look for a judicial reversal of these doctrines. They permeate the atmosphere in which we are living. They are acceptable to many who hunger and thirst for what they call a strong Government. They fall in with plans which individuals and communities are forming and pushing forward. To wait until the judicial pendulum has swung back and found its equilibrium, so that it will beat in harmony with the great mechanism of which it ought to be the controlling power, is to wait for what this generation is not likely to see. The true remedy is for the people of the States, speaking through an amendment of the Constitution, to say, and to say *now*, that this Constitution shall not be construed, by any of its functionaries, upon the principle that its implied powers have no limitations but the flexible, indeterminate, and undefined attributes which are all that this decision leaves to them. We may take example from our forefathers. When the Constitution, as first promulgated to them, appeared to them to have created a Government not limited by sufficient safeguards of the rights of persons and of States, they immediately amended it. When afterwards it appeared by a judicial decision that a State could be sued by an individual in the Federal tribunals, they immediately cut off, by an amendment, a power which they considered as derogatory to the State sovereignties. So now, the people will, if you shall afford them the opportunity, be ready to interpose and put an end to an interference by this Government with private contracts at a time when no great public exigency calls for it, and when none but an imaginary exigency can ever be pretended to exist.— *Rhodes's Journal of Banking.*

COUNTING-ROOM CHATS.

[We desire to say to the readers of this department that in cases where correspondents request that we shall give an answer to their inquiry, and where we find it possible to do so, we follow their question with our reply ; but, in doing this, it is not our intention or wish to forestall others who may feel disposed to offer their views or suggestions on the subject inquired about. In many instances we expect the reply given will serve merely as an introduction, depending on our readers to take upon themselves the work of supplying the chief part of such information as is sought by the correspondent.]

Concerning Trial-balances.

From S. WALLER, Seneca Falls, N. Y.

Herewith please find a form of making trial-balances showing what employers want and need to know. A few questions which can be readily answered from this form are : the cost of merchandise bought, amount cost of labor, amount expenses, amounts due from, and to, individuals, and amount of sales in each and every month in the year. A comparison showing the amounts of each of these and other items, in each corresponding month of every year the business has been carried on, can also be made at a glance. At the end of each year, when an account of stock is taken, if for a manufacturing business, the amount and per centum of the cost of each kind or class of materials used, that of labor, and that of each kind of other expenses entering into the aggregate cost of production for any given year. All these and other important items are placed in the order required by the nature of the business, so that their import and bearing are easily seen and comprehended. This information so readily given, makes a "trial-balance" of the very greatest value in every manufacturing and trading business. The detection of errors in posting and footings is also of value.

In these examples the last month in the year's business is taken ; then, after the inventory is made out, the accounts closed and those open are shown in the Balance account of each class of business accounts.

The statements showing the amounts of sales, profits and other particulars, are made up from the items contained in the trial-balances, and agree with the Balance accounts.

Presuming these examples and statements, in the forms given, to be sufficiently clear of as to render unnecessary further explanation, I will submit them without further comment; if not, I will try to answer questions which any one may wish to ask.

A form of a record ledger, in which an account of the cost of each kind of material used in a manufacturing business can be easily kept, which has several times been called for, will be forwarded as soon as possible.

I think Mr. Packard's remarks on trial-balances are not of much, if any, value.

New Form for Merchandise Account.

From G. H. MOLL, St. Louis, Mo.

I wish to submit a method for keeping Merchandise account so that the debit side will show the net amount of inventory and purchases, and the credit side the net amount of sales. The ledger pages intended for Merchandise accounts of this character should be provided with three amount columns on each side. In the explanation we will take, first, the debit side of the account, Into the outer, or right-hand column of this account, carry the amount of the inventory; into the middle column, post the purchases. The first column is intended to contain the credit entry for goods returned, and for reclamations made by the house; also the credit entry for discounts received. Deduct from the purchases the sum of these two items, and carry the remainder into the outer column. On the credit side, follow the same plan, but post the sales into the middle column. Where there are two or more entries of sales, such as cash or time sales, it is necessary only to post one into the middle column; the other directly into the outer. The debit entries for goods returned, and for reclamations against the house, and discounts allowed, are posted into the first column. Deduct these from the sales, and into the outer column carry the remainder.

In the accompanying illustration, the entries are made so as to represent both the ordinary and the proposed method. In the representation of the ordinary plan, both sides of the account are shown to be $1,000 larger than by representing the proposed arrangement. The balance is, of course, the same in both. In the proposed plan is exhibited the actual net purchases and sales, while under the usual method these can be arrived at only by taking out the items from oposite sides. It may, at first, seem a little awkward to post credit entries to the debit side, and debit entries to the credit side, but when it is considered that return and reclamation discounts are, in fact, reductions of purchases and sales, it seems to me that the method is not only justifiable, but strongly correct.

Percentage and its Cases.

From C. E. Cady, New York.

In the March number of the Counting-Room "Quiz" asks: "How many cases has percentage?" and says some mild authors treat it under four, others five, and some use seven, heads. The average younker sees at least as many as seven heads, ten horns, and the objective case every time! The milder the better it seems to me, for three cases cover all

Any two of these being given the other may be found.

Formulas.

1. $B \times R = P.$
2. $P \times B = R.$
3. $P \div R = B.$

Many formulas in addition to these may be stated, as

$B + P = A.$
$B - P = D.$
$B \times (1 + R) = A.$
$B \times (1 - R) = D.$

Beyond the first three cases the method of finding the unknown elements is so apparent that in general a formula is not necessary. For example, suppose it were required to find the base, the rate and amount being given. It must be understood that the processes of percentage are those of comparison, and in order to compare numbers they must have a definite relation to each other, or have some elements in common. The rate bears no necessary relation to the amount any more than to any other number whatever. The base, being the founda-

Terms used in	Base.	Rate.	Percentage.	Amount.	Difference.
Percentage .... Profit and Loss	Cost.	Per cent. of Gain or Loss.	Gain or Loss.	Selling Price with Gain.	Selling Price with Loss.
Commission	Value of goods bou't or sold	Rate of Commission.	Commission.	Value of Goods and Commission.	Goods less Com.
Insurance	Sum Insured	Rate of Insurance.	Premiums.	......	......

the ground that is usually contained in the text-books, however many divisions the author prefer.

Without going into unnecessary technicalities, suppose we consider the word "case" to mean a division or branch of the subject. The ordinary text-book on arithmetic is too limited in scope to treat the subject completely, and in order to cover the salient features, authors give only the principal cases, not all that are possible, nor those that are self-evident.

In order to a clear understanding I will quote the usual terms, their symbols, and the formulas for work:

Terms.   Symbol.

Base.—The number on which the percentage is calculated .... B.
Rate.—The number of hundredths taken .... R.
Percentage.—The product of base by rate .... P.
Amount.—The sum of base and percentage .. A.
Difference.—The difference between the base and percentage .... D.

tion number, is 100 per cent., and we can assume a term not generally used in the text book, viz., the base per cent., which of course must be 100. It follows that the amount per cent. must be 100 plus the rate. The amount being composed of base and percentage, evidently bears some relation to the amount per cent., and we have a problem which comes under formula three above given; for it is clear that the amount per cent. bears the same relation to the amount that the rate does to the percentage. Formulated, the statement would be: $A \div (100 + R) = B.$ (100 is here used in the sense of 100 per cent., or 1.00.) By a similar process of reasoning we derive the formula to find the base when the rate and difference are given: $D \div (100 - R) = B.$

Since technicalities are dry without their application, it may be well to prolong this already too long answer to the question by showing the equivalents of these terms on the practical bearings on the problems of profit and loss, commission, insurance, etc. All calculations based on the hundred are amenable to the rules of percentage, hence its applications are not limited to the examples given, but they are sufficient for illustration:

Those who are sufficiently interested to pursue this subject to the bitter end, might profit by sending twenty-five cents for a copy of "Thirty Possible Problems of Percentage" to Bardeen, publisher, Syracuse, N. Y.

Discounts on Partial Payments.
From GEORGE H. CLEMENS, Louisville, Ky.

Put me down as in favor of the manner of calculating, and the time of crediting, discounts allowed on partial payments of bill, before maturity, as stated by "Progress" in your March number. I have calculated and disposed of discounts in that manner ever since I had occasion to discount a bill. It is based on the principle that $100, less the rate of discount, will cancel $100 of the debt; and as for crediting the party the discount, I do not know of a better time than when the discount is earned, and that is when the money is paid. There can be no objection to the crediting of the discount at the time the money is paid that would not apply to the crediting of the money itself. It is absolutely necessary that it should be credited then, that the account on its face may show its true condition.

From EQUITAS, Camden, N. J.

Referring to the matter of "Discount on Partial Payments," in your March number, page 165, allow me to suggest to your correspondent "Progress" that it would seem, on the face of the matter as he has presented it, that he is in error. In the first place he is doing business for his employers, and they have the right to instruct him how they wish that business done—the question of it being satisfactory or not to customers is theirs to answer.

In the next place, the firm made the terms on which they are willing to sell goods, and *their* meaning and interest therein should certainly govern the book-keeper in his entries. And next, "Invoices marked 6 per cent. ten days, 5 per cent. thirty days, or 4 per cent. sixty days," would not necessarily, nor without special understanding to that effect, to

my mind, even impliedly refer to partial payments. A merchant might be *willing*, for various reasons, to encourage customers to pay in advance, even on account, and to that end hold out inducements in the shape of a premium for so doing; but on the other hand, he may say, "I offer you this premium for paying your bill in advance of when I may demand it of you (meaning its entirety); not for paying a part at a discount of 12 to 15 per cent. per annum to leave the balance to run over time on which I can only claim interest at 6 per cent. per annum." It thus appears as a question of agreement, of which both parties have a right to a full and fair understanding.

If it becomes one of equity, I think the case he cites would be clearly not in his favor.

Accounts of Real Estate.
From JOSEPH HARDCASTLE, New York.

In the March number, A. H., of New York, asks for information, if I understand his communication aright:

1st. As to how the Real Estate account for the piece of property in question should, in the books of the landlord, be kept.

2d. As to whether it is sufficient that a memorandum of certain improvements to be made by the landlord, who is to be re-imbursed in part by the tenant, be written across the face of the lease.

The majority of book-keepers, when a piece of property is bought, open an account for it, debit the account with the purchase price and all incidental expenses of purchase, then with cost of improvements, repairs, insurance and taxes, and credit it with the rent.

I think it is better to have two accounts: one for the cost of improvements, or betterments as they are sometimes called; and the other for the rents, repairs, insurance on building and taxes; the former gives the cost of the property to us, and the latter the net income on the same.

We make a similar division of accounts in the case of money loaned, and interest paid for its use.

Rent is nothing but payment for the use of property.

Since improvements and repairs are to be charged to different accounts, it is necessary that there should be some means of distinguishing them.

An improvement is such a change. in the structure or to the property, as to render it of more value.to the landlord ; a repair is a change in the property entirely for the benefit of the tenant or to keep the property in good order.

I will now proceed to offer my suggestions.

Debit the Real Estate account with purchase price, and cost of improvements and credit it with payments as they are made by the tenant at the end of the first, second, third and fourth years respectively.

The landlord in making his agreement with the tenant for these improvements, no doubt considers the improvements to his property at the end of each of these years with the difference between the amount paid by him and the re-imbursement for the tenant, so long as the agreement is in force, and at the end of the fourth year to be worth to him half of what it cost him.

The Rent account should be credited with the rent received, and debited with repairs, taxes and insurance. The balance of this account will be the net income from the property.

Now, as to the second point in A. H.'s communication.

I do not consider it sufficient to merely write the conditions of agreement for the improvement across the face of the lease, for the following reasons :

1st. This agreement is quite independent of the lease.

2d. The agreement remains in force one year after the lease has expired.

3rd. All contracts should have a consideration expressed—the lease being an exception, and in it the consideration is implied.

There should be an agreement or contract drawn up, and signed by both landlord and tenant, stating that the tenant agrees to pay these yearly installments in consideration of the landlord improving the property for the benefit of the tenant, and at the end or other sooner termination of lease, the improvements are to become the landlord's property.

Question on Toll.

From Quizzed, Plainfield, N. J.

I think that under this question Quiz is acting toward his brother accountants in a method worthy of his name. I wonder if he is the originator of the series of questions of this sort which have been going the rounds of the papers

lately. Evidently he has not given us all the information on this subject that is in his possession. " B claims A is entitled to only 160 pounds." Why not only 150, or only 60, or only 16. Whether, as in his question, it is cotton to a gin, or, as in some of its cousins now running riot in the country presses generally, it is wheat to a grist mill, or logs to a saw mill, or cream to a creamery, or beets to a sugar factory, there would seem, to an eastern man who never saw a cotton gin, creamery, or sugar factory, and only a few times in his life a grist mill or saw mill, only one answer to the whole batch. Gross toll from gross receipts before manufacture. Net toll from net product of the manufacture.

Post-dated Checks.

From "Kays," Wingtown, D. C.

In reply to "Oriole's" request for information as to the proper treatment of checks dated ahead, allow me to premise that such checks are not good business, though I know they are issued and received, and no doubt will continue to be, and hence his inquiry is a very pertinent one, and the difficulty he finds as to what to do with them is a real one. They are not money, strictly speaking ; they are not due bills ; they are not bills receivable ; and yet very often a receipt is given for them as if they were money. And here lies the clue to the proper answer, How did you receive it ? If you received it as cash and gave a receipt for it that way, it ought to go into your cash-book and count as part of your cash on hand, unless you treat your cash settlement in such a manner as to show such items treated as cash, which are not really so, in a place by themselves thus :

Cash in bank.................$——
Cash in checks bankable.......$——
Cash in checks dated ahead.....$——
Cash in memorandums........$——
Cash on hand.................$——

The plans of entering as bills received, or making no record, are open to the objections specified ; and in the latter case, stated of "not sending acknowledgment until due," is not likely to be satisfactory to the sender of the check.

The best plan, it seems to me, would be to enter in cash-book, and if there are many of them, and they have to be carried for any length of time, to open an account called "post-dated checks" if you choose, or any other name to indicate its character; and if you keep a diary for your bills receivable, payable, etc., on the plan of a bank tickler, record under the due dates so that they may not be overlooked. If they are few and for not long time, counting as cash is as good as any.

From Church St., New York.

Oriole "wants to know, you know" what to do with post-dated checks, and then suggests three ways of treating them, All of them are unsatisfactory, but not more so than is the evil itself.

When the millenium comes, if we continue to trade, probably there will be none, but in the meantime each individual case will have to be treated on its merits. The scientific way would be to open an account for post-dated checks, and "waste" them to the debit of that account, and the credit of the maker; but as Sam Weller said of the alphabet, " I doubt if it is worth going through so much to learn so little."

Probably his last method is, all things considered, the best; but, then, care must be taken not to forget their collection. If his bill-book is as in some forms, simply a record of the items composing his bill accounts, this can be secured by entering them in red. If, however, his bill-book is of the modern form, and is the basis of his credits to dealers and charge to bill accounts, difficulties will arise.

I heard of one bank, in this city, having a large " Bulls Head " trade, that used to discount largely the butchers' " five day checks " out of their legal tender reserve and count them as legal tenders, but this was attended with some "tall scratching" when the examiner came around.

Perhaps the most satisfactory way of treating them would be to go for the maker with a big club. To that, however, his employer's salesmen would object even if his employer did not.

Give it up; give us an easier one.

Interest on Partners' Account.
From Veteran, New York.

Royal Colon, Roseville, N. J., asks: "Where a member of the firm is required to pay interest on the difference between the present worth of each partner, should the interest so cast be upon whole or one-half of such difference between their accounts?"

Presumably the inquirer refers to a case where the profits are divided equally, and the interest is adjusted as stated. I should say that it would be correct to charge the minor capitalist with interest on the whole difference, crediting interest accounts; or, equally correct, to charge him, and credit the major capitalist, with interest on half the difference; and that these two procedures would result in precisely the same balances:

For

100..............Minor | Interest............100

and

100...........Interest | Minor...............50
$\qquad\qquad\qquad\quad$| Major...............50

is precisely the same, when reduced, as

50...............Minor | Major...............50

It seems to me that there is much to be said in favor of the latter method, because the former (through Interest account), gives an appearance of earnings which are not earned.

From Stylos.

Three men form a partnership. Each contributes $50,000 capital. Each to have $2,000 salary. Any partner overdrawing his salary to be debited with five per cent. upon the overdrawn amount at end of each year. Partner A lives within his salary. Partner B overdraws $1,000 yearly. Partner C overdraws $2,000 yearly. Queries: what entries should be made in debiting the five per cent.; and what disposition is to be made of the constantly augmenting overdrawn accounts of partners B and C? According to a recent paragraph in your journal, in such circumstances the five per cent. should be credited to Interest account. I object, on the ground that the apparent profits of the business would thus be augmented by the amount of the five per cent., which is not part of the *bona fide* earnings of the business, but simply an item employed to equalize the accounts of the partners equitably. It may be replied that interest is a legitimate item of profit. In some cases this is true. But where, for example, a trading concern has accumulated a surplus which is invested outside the business, say in five per cent. Government bonds, it will not be contended that the dividends on these bonds are part of the actual working profits of the concern. And if a portion of the said surplus were drawn out by a partner in excess of his salary, why should the five per cent. chargeable to him be accounted a legitimate item of profit any more than the dividends on bonds?

In the course of ten years partners B and C will have overdrawn $30,000, which will have been increased by compound interest at five per cent to nearly $50,000. How is this $50,000 to appear in the balance-sheet? Let us suppose that partners B and C have nothing to show for this large amount. It has all been eaten up in family expenses. Would it not, therefore, be misleading and improper to include such a sum in the list of Accounts-receivable, forming part of the firm's assets? I am aware that this is the usual practice, but I think there is a more sensible way. I would suggest the following method:

Let each partner have a Capital account to which is carried the profits and losses of each year; and a Personal account, in which he is debited with all cash or goods withdrawn, and credited with his salary. Let these Personal accounts be squared off each year at the time of stock-taking by carrying their respective balances to the corresponding Capital accounts. This should be done before calculating the five per cent. chargeable upon overdrawn accounts. The five per cent. may then be reckoned upon the differences between the several partner's Capital accounts, and charged accordingly. Just before stock-taking at the end of the first year, after carrying the balances of the partners' Personal accounts into the respective Capital accounts, the balances of the latter will be as follows:

```
To the credit of partner A........$50,000
    "       "       " B......... 49,000
    "       "       " C........ 48,000
```

The original capital of partners B and C is thus reduced by the amounts overdrawn by them. Now make the following Journal entries.

```
Partner B, Dr............$50.00
    To partner A.............$16.66
    "    " B.............. 16.67
    "    " C.............. 16.67
```

Being five per cent. on $1,000 difference between partner A's and partner B's Capital account.

```
Partner C, Dr...........$100.00
    To partner A.............$33.44
    "    " B.............. 33.33
    "    " C.............. 33.33
```

Being five per cent. on $2,000 difference between partner A's and partner C's Capital account.

By posting these entries, and repeating the same process year by year, exact partner's rights are preserved without an entry in Interest account, or a constantly increasing fictitious amount appearing among the assets in the balance-sheet. If this plan is unscientific or misleading in any particular I hope some brother accountant will be kind enough to point out its defects, and to indicate a better method.

Manufacturing Accounts.

From "ADVANCE," Philadelphia, Pa.

The question started by "Subscriber," of Stockton, Cal., as to the most practical method of keeping the accounts of a general manufacturing business so as to arrive at the cost of making different articles, opens up a large field of inquiry well deserving of attention, and one which I hope will bring free and full answers from those (and there must be many of them among your subscribers) who either from choice or the necessities of their position, have worked out a solution wholly or partially successful. It is too broad in the manner in which it has been stated, for a very satisfactory answer in the short space you can give to it in this department. I propose now only to say that I do not at all agree with "Subscriber' in his lack of faith in the fact (for it is a fact) that there can be such an exhibit made which will show any firm all that it needs to know both as to cost of manufacturing and stock on hand in any and every department, and were it advisable or desirable, the cost of any particular machine, though as to this last it might come up for decision as to whether the labor spent in attaining that, repaid in results its cost.

I purpose at some future time to prepare for your magazine some of my experience and conclusions, and in the meantime hope to see others coming forward with theirs. By this means we can mutually benefit each other and add to the interest of your already valuable work.

Bank vs. True Discount.

From A. W. RAND, New York.

Mr. H. Ricord's questions under this head in March number can only be answered, "That depends." If one of the "different parties" is the maker of the note to be discounted, it is well to bear in mind that in most of these

United States any method which produces to the lender more than legal interest on the *sum invested* is usury, entailing penalties more or less barbarous from imprisonment down, and this just the same for a clerical mistake in the calculation of a legal method as for the correct computation of an illegal method.

If, on the other hand, the note is already the property of one other than the maker, and is untainted, and is discounted by the "concern" for the holder, the question of usury does not arise, and the method may be selected which being customary is most profitable to the lender. In this city the reckoning would be made by deducting from the face of the note interest for the unexpired time, actual days, and each day one three hundred and sixtieth part of the year.

When H. R. can in every case determine what is usurious and what is legal, his education in this respect will be completed.

From "QUERY," New York.

Mr. Ricord asks in regard to discounting notes, whether "is it proper to deduct bank discount or the true discount for balance of unexpired time?"

It does not seem to me that there ought to be any question as to this. The concern discounting the note may need, and ought to so consider the possible necessity, to put the paper into bank for discount, when they would certainly have to stand bank rules; and why should their customers, who for any reason choose to come to them in preference to the bank, stand the same?

The Seven-account System.
From W. S. GAGE, Cincinnati, O.

I read with much interest what the two correspondents had to say in the March number concerning the "Seven-account System of Book-keeping." Having read and studied to some extent the little work entitled "Manual of Exhibit Book-keeping," which I purchased in the spring of 1880, I was forced to the conclusion that the principal features embodied in the Seven-Account System were borrowed from or patterned after the idea carried out in the small Manual. The theory of grouping or classifying accounts so as to show definite results in a book outside of, and, I may say, irrespective of, the ledger is fully explained and

demonstrated in a systematic manner in the work I allude to. It was the first treatise of the kind I ever saw, though I have since come across several works which make some advances in that direction.

From the understanding I get of Mr. Matthern's discription of the Seven-account System, the plan adopted in the work on Exhibit Book-keeping is, in many respects very much superior. I should judge that both offer advantages over the ordinary circuitous double-entry day-book, journal and ledger routine. If left to follow the dictates of my own judgment I would certainly adopt some system based upon principles similar to those advocated and enunciated in the little work I have referred to.

Interest on Capital.
From "PARTNERSHIP," Grovestend, N. J.

"Mitchell" presents in your March number the case of a partnership of three, with a statement of circumstances hardly full enough to elicit an intelligent answer to his inquiry. He says "A is in debt. B and C pay A's debts in lieu of business he brings into the firm;" and further, that in the articles of copartnership, "it is further agreed that each partner shall have the sum of five thousand dollars invested," etc. Did B and C each put in five thousand dollars, and out of that sum pay A's debts, and was the amount so paid charged to A's account and *thus* form the debit balance on which interest was charged to his account, or did they advance him in addition enough to make up his five thousand dollars and charge that to his account, or did they give him credit with "the business" in lieu of which they paid his debt? etc.

But the statement of the case that it being agreed that "each partner draw interest for all amounts invested *above* the said five thousand dollars, and then that "interest for *full amount* of capital was credited B and C," answers for itself the question whether or not that should have been done. Evidently there was intended to be some equity in favor of A's "business" as against their capital to that extent—that that capital was not to draw interest, but only the excess.

Business Educators' Convention.
From C. E. CADY, President Business Educators' Association, New York.

As many of the readers of the COUNTING-ROOM give more or less attention to educational affairs, it may interest them to know that the Sixth Annual Convention of the Business Educators' Association of America will be held in the city of Rochester, N. Y., from the 17th to the 23d of July next. This association is composed largely of the principals and teachers of business colleges, and represents an important division of the educational system of the country.

The meetings of this body are of interest not only to those who are actively engaged in the work of teaching, but they should have a special interest to all who have to do with books of account, while the business college is in a sense a book-keeping school, the accomplishment of this study does by no means circumscribe its actual work. Receiving its students in their teens, largely from the public schools, with little or no knowledge of business methods and customs, it aims to give them such technical knowledge of the counting-room and office as will enable them at once to render effective service. It is not necessary at this time to say how well this work is done; the question is fully answered in the constant and increasing demand of business everywhere for trained assistants.

That there should be an earnest, active sympathy between the business community and commercial schools, it seems to me no one can doubt. The book-keeper and correspondent need reliable assistance no less than the employer. The business novitiate sustains a relation to the manager, the accountant or correspondent, similar to that which he holds to his principal; each demands the same accountability from his assistants, and neither can afford to lay aside active duty to become an instructor.

Since business constantly demands new blood, it becomes a matter of prime importance to those interested to know through what channels that blood flows. The results of the commercial school are bound to be felt in the counting house, hence the business man cannot afford to be an indifferent spectator of their work. His experience is valuable, his counsel is solicited, and his criticisms do not offend the live teacher. He is welcomed as a visitor in their school, and as an attendant at the Convention. Those attending the Convention can get reduced rates of board both at hotels and private boarding-houses, by addressing Mr. L. L. Williams, Chairman Executive Committee, Business University, Rochester, N. Y. Reduced railroad fares from the west and southwest can be secured by addressing Mr. G. W. Brown, of Jacksonville, Ill. From the east all the railroads sell excursion tickets at most accommodating rates.

A WALL-STREET FAILURE.

The schedules of the firm of Grant & Ward, who failed and made an assignment for the benefit of creditors, have been given to the public. As the facts come to light it becomes evident that the failure should have been no surprise. It is only another case where reckless book-keeping, or, we may say, the disregard of book-keeping, has produced consternation among the principals composing a suspended concern.

The report of the assignee will make interesting reading, and serve to explain why the failure should have been no surprise to any one closely connected with the business affairs of the concern. The liabilities are shown to be $16,792,647 72, the nominal assets $27,139,098 56, and the actual assets $67,174 30. The assignee makes an explanatory statement, in which he says : " Every endeavor has been made to comply with the rules of this court relative to a statement of the nominal and actual value of the assets and the annexing of a recapitulation to the schedules. It has been impossible, however, to ascertain who were the owners, first, of all the securities in possession of Grant & Ward at the time of their failure, or, second, of all the securities pledged by them and held by creditors as collateral to loans. It has been impossible to ascertain what was the actual value of the interest of Grant & Ward in the securities found in their possession or pledged by them as collateral to loans. The books of the firm of Grant & Ward do not show with any degree of completeness or accuracy the transactions of the firm. No cash-book or journal has ever been kept by the

firm since its inception, and no balance-sheet has ever been taken from the books that were kept, as the assignee is informed by their employes. No reliable or complete list of their assets appear either upon their books or among their papers. The assignee has been obliged to a very great extent, in making up his inventory and schedules, to rely upon information obtained from the statements of members of the firm of Grant & Ward, and information obtained from those claiming to hold obligations of the firm of Grant & Ward, or who have had dealings with them, and from loose memoranda or indorsements upon envelopes. The assignee has not felt justified in relying upon this information with such a degree of certainty as to make positive statements based upon it to a greater extent than is shown by the schedules.

In nearly every case in which the firm of Grant & Ward has had dealings with either customers or pledgers of securities the stocks and bonds left in their custody have been either sold or rehypothecated for amounts bearing no reference to the value of the interest of Grant & Ward in those securities. No satisfactory or complete record of those transactions appears upon the books of Grant & Ward. No satisfactory or complete book of bills payable or bills receivable was kept by the firm. In cases where securities had been rehypothecated they have been generally rehypothecated for larger amounts than have been loaned by Grant & Ward upon them. In the rehypothecation of securities by Grant & Ward no attempt has been made to keep together securities which had been pledged together to secure a single sum loaned by Grant & Ward, or to keep the securities of one individual from being mingled with those of another. On the contrary, a portion of the securities pledged by one individual was frequently placed with a portion of the securities pledged by several others, individuals or corporations, to form a security upon which Grant & Ward borrowed money.

Many of the loans apparently outstanding on May 6th were closed out either in whole or in part shortly after that date by sales of the securities held by the pledgees. Many of such loans are still outstanding in whole or in part, and in many of such cases of both classes the assignee has been unable as yet to obtain definite information as to what has been done by the pledgees, by reason of their neglect to impart such information to him after application had been made to them for statements. For these and other reasons the assignee has been unable to present a more complete and satisfactory summary of the assets and liabilities of Grant & Ward than those herewith presented. From the best information that the assignee has been able to obtain, he believes that upon the closing out of the loans made to Grant & Ward, secured by pledge of collaterals, no amount exceeding $10,000 will be found due to the assignee for which specific claims will not be made by those whose securities have been rehypothecated for amounts greater than the amounts loaned to them by Grant & Ward.

Nearly all the securities of any substantial value, which came into the possession of the assignee on May 8th, 1884, are claimed by third parties as their property. Many of these securities, the assignee claims, are subject to the payment by pledgors of the amounts loaned

to them thereon. In nearly every case the amount of these claims is in dispute. In the case of a claim made against the Buffalo, New York, and Philadelphia Railroad Company for the amount of $177,142 89 loaned upon 310 of the first mortgage bonds of that road, which bonds appear upon the amended schedules, not only does the railroad company claim that on a settlement of its accounts with Grant & Ward no sum is due to secure which these bonds can be held, but two distinct and specific claims are made by other persons for whatever interest Grant & Ward may have as pledges in these 310 bonds.

Very large pecuniary transactions in the name of Grant & Ward, and with funds of Grant & Ward, were carried on by the assignors, Fish & Ward, during the years 1882, 1883, and 1884, of which no record whatever appears upon the books of the firm, and the only evidence of which is found in the individual check books of the assignor, Ward, and in memoranda in private books kept by the assignor Ward, and by the assignors Fish and Ward jointly.

The assignment, by its third paragraph, directs the assignee to pay, by way of preference, to the persons named in a schedule thereto annexed, marked schedule "A," the debts owing to them by said firm, by reason of their holding or owning instruments bearing the firm name of Grant & Ward, in the nature of guarantees for the performance of certain contracts therein referred to; said instruments also containing promises to pay money, or of holding or owning any instrument for the payment of money bearing said firm name issued in connection with the instruments heretofore referred to. Since the assignment was executed and delivered to the assignee, and since he has taken possession of the estate of the assignors, information has come to the assignee, by the statements of the assignor Ward and otherwise, to the effect that the contracts referred to in the said instrument were fictitious, and that no such contracts in fact existed; that said Ward and said Fish represented to various parties that the firm of Grant & Ward had contracts with the United States Government and other parties which were exceedingly profitable, and that the said Fish and the said Ward borrowed immense sums of money from various parties for the alleged purpose of investment by the firm of Grant & Ward in such alleged contracts, and that the said firm of Grant & Ward, through said Fish and Ward, agreed with persons advancing money for the purpose aforesaid, to compensate them for the use of their money by paying them certain proportions of the expected profits from the contracts, which profits were guaranteed to be certain amounts. The assignee is therefore advised and believes that so far as the transactions aforesaid are concerned, or so far, at least, as the relations of the said firm of Grant & Ward to such transactions are concerned, the same were nothing more nor less than borrowing money at usurious rates of interest and upon fraudulent representations.

The assignee is advised and believes and understands the law to be that so far as the defence of usury is concerned the firm of Grant & Ward have waived that defence by entering these particular persons in schedule "A" annexed to the assignment; but the assignee does not admit that any of the parties named in schedule "A" are entitled to receive from the estate, or to claim as creditors against the estate of Grant & Ward, more than the amount actually advanced by them less the amounts received by them from the firm of Grant & Ward on account of the transactions in question:

and the assignee will therefore submit to the court the question, in the proper time and in the proper mode, as to the amounts, if any, of the debts actually owing, in law or in equity, to the various persons named in schedule "A" annexed to said assignment. The assignee has also received evidence since the said assignment was made, and since he has assumed the duties of assignee, which leads him to believe that one or more of the parties named in schedule "A" are debtors of the firm of Grant & Ward and not creditors.

The assignee, while stating the foregoing facts and submitting them to the court as part of the records of the case, further states that he belives that the intention of all the parties to the general assignment, at the time when it was executed, delivered, and recorded, was to provide for the payment only of the just and lawful debts, and the assignee is advised and believes that the assignment as drawn provides for the payment only of such amounts as shall prove to be just and lawful debts, and that the assignment was not drawn with any intent to secure payment of any fraudulent or fictitious claims; that the precise amounts due to any of the parties, or the state of the accounts between them, or the nature of the transactions with them, were not, as the assignee is informed and believes, known to any of the parties to the assignment except the assignor, Ferdinand Ward, and whether or not all of said facts were known even to him at that time the assignee is not informed. On the 8th day of May, 1884, the assignee took possession of the assets of Grant & Ward.

On the 9th day of May, 1884, a suit was commenced in the Supreme Court by John H. Morris, as assignee of James D. Fish, for the benefit of his creditors, against U. S. Grant and the other members of the firm of Grant & Ward and the assignee, for the purpose of setting aside the assignment. On the 9th day of May, 1884, in that suit the undersigned was appointed receiver, *pendente lite*, of the assets of Grant & Ward without prejudice to any claim to any of the property which might thereafter be made by him as assignee claiming under the assignment to him by answer in the cause. A bond in the penal sum of $50,000 was given by the receiver, and since the 9th of May, 1884, he has been in possession of the assets of Grant & Ward, and in the discharge of his functions as receiver. The assignee has answered in the cause, insisting upon the validity of the assignment and his title, as assignee, and has retained counsel for the purpose of defending that suit, and intends to defend it in good faith and with diligence. At the present time the undersigned is not in possession of any of the assets of Grant & Ward, as assignee, but is in possession of those assets as receiver in the suit above mentioned. The assignee begs leave to file supplemental schedules when his information relative to the matters assigned to him is more complete and accurate.

JULIEN I. DAVIES, Assignee.

The liabilities are made up in the following manner:

CLASS A.
Creditors preferred in assignment holding instruments described in assignment.....................

CLASS B.
Preferred creditors for deposits and loans, as set forth in assignment. $1,396,435 69

CLASS C.
Subdivision I—Secured creditors... 12,684,037 50
Subdivision II — Unsecured creditors. Not holding notes: I..... 653,174 53
Not holding notes. II............
Subdivision III.—Unsecured creditors holding notes.............. $2,059,000 00

CLASS D.
Contingent........................   ....

$16,792,647 72

The assets are made up as follows:

	Nominal Value.	Actual Value.
Schedule 1.........	$2,813,520 62	$27,473 40
Schedule 2.........	45,205 00	4,680 00

(2) Being claimed by assignee of Ferdinand Ward, also claimed by Sheriff under attachment.

Schedule 3	84,134 00	14,384 00
Schedule 4.........	18,216 85	14,941 85

(4) Being claimed by assignee of Ferdinand Ward, also claimed by Sheriff under attachment.

Schedule 5.........	1,637,107 00	374,571 25

Title to almost all of these securities in dispute.

Schedule 6.........	9,090,322 69	14,905 65
Schedule 7.........	321 25	321 25

which makes the nominal value of the assets claimed or in dispute to be $1,700,528 85, and nominal value of those not in dispute and not claimed, $11,988,288 56, and the actual value $57,174 30.

Schedule 8 shows

rehypothecations.	15,150,800 00	10,000 00

Whether this amount will be realized is doubtful.

This makes the complete figures to

be assets, nominal value.........	$27,139,098 56
And actual value.................	67,174 30

Class "A" of the schedules show the preferred creditors named in schedule "A" annexed to the assignment. They are not secured, and the amounts due are unknown. These creditors are:

Edward C. James, New York City.
James Henry Work, New York City.
William B. Warner, New York City.
Jerome B. Chaffee, New York City.
Frank F. Wood, Brooklyn, N. Y.
Edward L. Short, all claims released, N. Y. City.
Edward L. Wilmerding, New York City.
Charles P. Britton, New York City.
Ezra A. Tuttle, New York City.
James C. Gardiner, New York City.
Frederick D. Grant, Morristown, N. J.

These claims are for "holding or owning instruments bearing the firm name of Grant & Ward in the nature of guarantees for the performance of certain contracts therein referred to; and instruments also containing promises to pay money; or holding or owning instruments for the payment of money bearing said firm name issued in connection with said instruments heretofore referred to."

CLASS B.

Preferred creditors who have made loans or deposits of money or securities not secured by collateral:

Davis, Work & McNamee............	$300 00
Erie Railway Co., special account.....	40,000 00
Mrs. U. S. Grant....................	2,763 75
Frederick D. Grant.................	533,763 85
Jesse R. Grant......................	113,415 50
Almon Goodwin....................	1,792 08
Mexican Southern Railway...........	83 34
Edward N. Tobey...................	13,377 68
W. S. Warner, treasurer.............	124 74
W. S. Warner, trustee...............	55 00
W. W Smith........................	21,913 57
W. H. Tyler.......................	99 42
Thomas B. Medary..................	705 57
Mrs. K. S. Leavitt..................	2,000 00
Wyandotte Water Co................	5,572 45
J, Nelson Tappan	513,750 00
J. B. Chaffee.......................	30,870 85
N. H. Shephard.....................	513 32
N. C. Fitzsimmons..................	3,039 50
William A. Boyd....................	4,181 25
Charles P. Stone....................	374 28
C. Lowery..........................	599 75
S. F. Moriarty......................	21 27
Armourdale Water Co................	492 00
E. E. Doety........................	4,767 68
Henry Green.......................	3,255 93
L. B. Howe.........................	15 00
James R. Jessup....................	31,828 00
William J. McBride.................	400 00
Freeman Clarke, registered bond account............................	1,610 42
B. H. Smith........................	Unknown,
William C. Smith...................	64,777 73

Some of these amounts are believed to be incorrect, and others are believed not to be due or only a portion of them, while some of these creditors have stock still held for their account.

Among the secured creditors are:

Marine National Bank, money loaned..	$269,000
Fourth National Bank of New York, money loaned......................	370,000
J. & W. Seligman & Co., money loaned	644,500
Equitable Life Assurance Co., money loaned............................	1,050,000
Bank of the Republic, money loaned....	315,000
James R. Smith, money loaned........	125,000
Oriental Bank, money loaned.........	280,000
United States National Bank, money loaned............................	150,000
Continental National Bank, money loaned............................	125,000
Merchants' Bank of Canada, money loaned............................	125,000
First National Bank, money loaned....	90,800
National Park Bank, money loaned....	75,000
National Shoe and Leather Bank, money loaned.........................	150,000
Mutual Benefit Life Insurance Company of New Jersey, money loaned..	800,000
C. P. Britton, money loaned..........	25,000
B. N. Smith & Co., money loaned.....	40,000
National Bank of Commerce, money loaned............................	750,000
United States Trust Company, money loaned............................	1,050,000
Drexel, Morgan & Co., money loaned..	250,000
American Exchange National Bank, money loaned......................	125,000
Metropolitan Trust Company, money loaned............................	200,000
Mutual Life Insurance Company, money loaned............................	100,000
Martin Leaske & Co., money loaned...	50,000
Lardlow & Co., money loaned........	100,000
Bank of Montreal, money loaned......	150,000
Mechanics' National Bank, money loaned............................	50,000
Arend & Young, money loaned........	30,000
Mercantile Trust Company, money loaned............................	1,250,000
Phenix National Bank, money loaned..	75,000
Herzfeld & Co., money loaned........	10,000
New York Life Insurance and Trust Company, money loaned...........	205,000
E. St. John Hayes & Co., money loaned	50,000
American Loan and Trust Company, money loaned......................	50,000
Bank of New York, N. B. A., money loaned............................	50,000
Worden & Co., money loaned........	50,000
M. Morgan's Sons, money loaned......	25,000
Union Trust Company, money loaned.	150,000
National Bank of the State of New York, money loaned......................	100,000
City National Bank of Hartford, Conn., money ioaned......................	25,000
City Bank of Brooklyn, money loaned.	25,000
Long Island Loan-Trust Company, money loaned......................	50,000
National Iron Bank of Morristown, N.J., money loaned......................	70,000

In order to verify the often-published statements that grave irregularities have long been practiced upon the Government by dishonest importers, the New York *Commercial Advertiser* recently went into a long and careful examination of the work in the appraiser's office and in the various departments connected with the New York Custom House, which resulted in the publication of facts of such especial interest to merchants and manufacturers as well as importers, that, for the benefit of our readers, we quote following extracts :

"That a clear understanding of the situation may be reached, it may not be out of place to trace briefly the growth of the United States Custom House, and the system by which importations are appraised and duties are assessed. The laws relating to the customs and the administration of the tariff regulations make a vast library in themselves ; but copious and intricate as are these regulations they all take their inceptive from a hog-skin bound little book printed in 1798.

"Alexander Hamilton, the father of American finance, is generally credited with being the founder of the customs system in this country. However this may be, it is certain that while Mr. Hamilton was in the Treasury Office he caused the English revenue system to be thoroughly examined, and adapted it to the needs of the United States. A comparison of the laws of 1798 demonstrates the close resemblance to the regulations existing in the mother country.

" The machinery used for collecting the revenue in the early years of the republic was exceedingly simple. All the more important cities were made centres of customs districts, over which appraisers ruled. Even several of the Hudson River and Long Island towns had each its customs departments. It was in July, 1866, that the present system of consolidation at the port of New York was adopted, and the abuses that are complained of have grown up under this gigantic machine.

" The Act of July, 27th, 1866, provided, among other things, that in lieu of the old Board of Appraisers then existing at the port of New York, there should be an appraiser appointed by the President, by and with the advice and consent of the Senate, who should have had experience as an assistant appraiser, or practical acquaintance with the quality or value of one or more of the chief articles of import subject to appraisement.

" The same Act also provided that in lieu of the assistant appraisers then authorized by law for the port of New York, the Secretary of the Treasury should appoint not more than ten assistant appraisers who should have had experience as assistant appraisers, or be practically acquainted with the quality and value of one or more of the chief articles of importation, to examine and appraise which they should be respectively assigned, and who should be empowered to appraise goods according to law under the direction and supervision of the appraiser, and each of whom should be required to take an oath diligently and faithfully to examine goods and report to the appraiser.

"The Secretary of the Treasury was

also empowered, on the nomination of the appraiser, to appoint such a number of examiners as he might determine to be necessary, and to fix their compensation, which should not exceed $2,500 a year, upon the recommendation of the appraiser. The examiners were required to be experts in their specialties, and to aid the assistant appraisers in forming their opinions of the value of imported goods. Upon the Secretary of the Treasury, also, was made to devolve the appointment of the clerks employed under the appraisers, and the fixing of their salaries.

"The law of 1866 also provides as follows : 'It shall not be lawful for the appraisers, assistant appraisers, examiners, clerks, verifiers, samplers, measurers, or others employed in the department of the appraiser to be at the time engaged or interested in any commercial or mechanical business, or acting for any person engaged in such business.'

"One of the most important clauses of the law of 1866 is that which directed that one assistant appraiser should be appointed with special reference to his qualifications to perform the duties and to act in the place of a special examiner of drugs, medicines, and chemicals ; and that another assistant appraiser should be detailed by the appraiser for supervision of the department for the examination of merchandise damaged on the voyage of importation, and, as far as practicable, to make examinations and appraisement of any other merchandise as the appraiser might direct, and in all cases truly to report to the appraiser the extent of the damage, and also the true value of the merchandise. This damage appraisement is subject also to the revision, correction or approval by the Appraiser in Chief.

"For some reason the Revised Statutes, while incorporating the main features of the law of 1866, omit the clause empowering the Secretary of the Treasury to appoint the appraiser, and substitute a provision giving the President the power of appointing the assistant appraisers, thereby greatly increasing the duties of their office.

"Immediately after the passage of the Act of 1866, the Hon. Thomas McElrath was appointed appraiser at the port of New York. He at once proceeded to organize the assistant appraisers in conformity with the law. He divided the department into ten divisions, each under an assistant appraiser. This organization is maintained to this day, excepting in such minor transfers and changes in various lines of goods from one division to another as has from time to time been made by his successors. Appraiser McElrath remained in office until after the inauguration of President Grant in 1869, when the Hon. Charles A. Dana, of the New York *Sun*, was appointed to succeed him, but Mr. Dana wished to be Collector of the Port of New York, and did not wish to be appraiser, and Mr. McElrath was requested to act until General George W. Palmer, now Deputy Collector of the Seventh Division of the Custom House, was confirmed General Palmer became identified with the Liberal Republican movement in 1872, and upon the re-election of President Grant was removed from office and superseded by the Hon. William A. Darling. Mr. Darling's appraisership continued until the spring of 1875, when he resigned, and was succeeded by the Hon. Stephen B. French, ex-member of Congress from Long Island, and now president of the Board of Police Commissioners of this city.

"During the following summer an unsuccessful effort was made by the friends of the late E. D. Morgan to nominate him for Governor, and Mr. French, by taking an active part in the State Convention as a friend of Governor Morgan's, called down upon himself the enmity of A. B. Cornell, who succeeded in getting the nomination. After his election Governor Cornell demanded and received the head of Appraiser French just prior to the expiration of President Grant's second term.

"The Hon. S. B. Dutcher succeeded to the office. He served during the administration of President Hayes, and resigned the office in 1880 to accept the appointment of Superintendent of Public Works of the State of New York, tendered him by Governor Cornell.

"President Hayes, in January or February following, appointed John Q. Howard, a henchman of his, to succeed Mr. Dutcher. Howard had come from Ohio to New York in very reduced circumstances and been appointed by Hayes an examiner in the department, and then advanced to an assistant appraisership. His management of the Appraiser's Department calls for a more extended notice than that of any of his predecessors. He was removed from office under charges in 1883 by President Arthur, and was succeeded by General Alexander P. Ketchum, the present incumbent, who had been general appraiser—an entirely distinct officer, and semi-judicial—for many years.

"The abuses which we are about to describe took place under the administration of John Q. Howard, the Ohio henchman of President Hayes. Under Appraiser Howard each of the ten assistant appraisers acted in great measure independently of the appraiser, who contented himself with receiving and certifying to their reports. The better to understand these matters, a brief statement of the basis of subdivision and classification of importations is now necessary. The first division is presided over by the chief of staff of the appraiser. He is the most responsible subordinate officer in the department. The present incumbent is Major Fowler, who succeeded Stephen N. Simonson, and is the head of the Damage Allowance Department. He is charged with a variety of duties that make it easy for him to hold the importer at his mercy. He controls the Barge Office at the Battery, and is charged with the examining and appraising of all dutiable articles found in the baggage of cabin passengers and immigrants, and the appraisement of all dutiable articles seized for violations of the custom-laws. He is also charged with the examination and appraisement of all packages arriving from abroad by express, known as 'packed packages,' of all household and personal effects, of all live animals, of building material, of coal, gutta percha and India rubber, of hides, horns, ivory, shells, oakum, paper stock, skins (not furs), spars and spiling, and cabinet woods. He has charge also of the United States Sample Office, in which all samples of merchandize are examined and passed, including the branch United States Sample Office for coffee at Bartlett's Stores, Brooklyn.

"The heads of the remaining nine divisions have superintendence of the following goods and wares:

"SECOND DIVISION.

"The Second Division, Assistant Appraiser Stevens — Albums, antiquities, artist's materials, bronzes, clocks, such merchandise as is known by name as fancy goods; fancy boxes, gold and silver ware; jewelry, including diamonds; small manufactures of marble and spar, Mosaics, musical instruments, optical, philosophical, and photographic apparatus, paintings, precious stones, printed matter, stationery, statuary, toys, and works of art.

"THIRD DIVISION.

"The Third Division, Assistant Appraiser Kent—Braids and binding, button materials cut for that purpose, embroideries (except of gold and silver), hatters' plush, laces and lace goods of every description excepting lace curtains, tidies, mosquito and other nets, silk wearing apparel, silk (raw), manufacturers of silk and trimmings.

"FOURTH DIVISION.

"The Fourth Division, Assistant Appraiser Birdsall, who, in addition to his other duties, is also special deputy appraiser. Mr. Birdsall examines and appraises bags, bagging, binding, curtain holders, manufactuers of gutta percha and India rubber, excepting toys, ladies' linen and cotton wearing apparel, lace curtains, linen and cotton tape, manufactures of cotton, flax, grass, hemp, jute, or articles of which either of these articles shall be a component of chief value, excepting carpets, matting, and oil cloth, mosquito and other nets, rope and cordage, school-bags of hemp, grass, and jute, linen or cotton thread, tidies, twine, and webbing.

"FIFTH DIVISION.

"The Fifth Division, Assistant Appraiser Dr. Auerbach -— Baskets, bonnets, bunting, corsets, corset laces, feathers (crude and ornamental), artificial or natural dyed and dried flowers, gloves, hair braids, hats, hosiery, hoods, knit goods, millinery goods, parasols, regalias, straw braids, umbrellas, willows and willowware, German and English worsted dress goods, woollen yarn.

"SIXTH DIVISION.

The Sixth Division, Assistant Appraiser Wickham—Shoddy, wool, and all materials which enter into or form a component part of textile fabric, except cotton and silk, bristles, carpets, carpeting, esparto and sisal grass, fibre flax flocks, furs and all manufacturers of fur,

hair of all kinds, hemp, jute mats, matting, marble monuments, oil-cloth, palm leaf ratan, shawls (except cotton and silk), lithographic stones, grind, flint and polishing stones, upholstery goods of wool, worsted or hair, whalebone, all manufacturers of woollen cloth, wool worsted or hair, and French worsted dress goods.

"SEVENTH DIVISION.

"The Seventh Division is Assistant Appraiser Dr. Gregg's—Anatomical importations, apothecaries' glassware, asphaltum and bituminous substances, cardomen, seeds, chalk, chemicals of all kinds, chemical apparatus, clay, corks, cork tanbark, dextrine, drugs of all kinds, dye woods and dye stuffs, earths, extracts, gelatine and gums, gypsum, isinglass, leeches, lime and lemon peel, medicines, minerals and mineral water, mustard seed, paints, perfumery, plaster of Paris, printing ink, pumice stone, quicksilver, resinous substances, saltpetre, toilet soap, specimens of botany and natural history, sponge, punk, surgical instruments, sulphur ore, varnishes, vanilla beans, vinegar, wax (bees'), vegetable and water colors (moist and dry).

"EIGHTH DIVISION.

"The Eighth Division, Assistant Appraiser Hay—Alabaster, glassware, porcelain, and manufacturers of boots and shoes and leather ; bricks, confectionery, crockery, drain pipe, earthenware, glass, glassware, glucose, honey, leather melado, molasses, Parian and porcelain ware, and sugar.

"NINTH DIVISION.

"The Ninth Division, Assistant Appraiser Biglin, who appraises asbestos, blacking, bronze powders, buttons (except worsted and silk), carriages, coach hardware, cutlery, Dutch metal, emery, epaulets, gold and silver leaf, gold and silver galloon, gold-beaters' skins, hardware, harness, iron and manufactures of

PERSONALITY OF HANDWRITING. 241

iron, jews harps, machinery, metals, mica, models, needles, ores, pen tips and holders, pins, saddlery, steel and manufactures of steel.

"TENTH DIVISION.

"The Tenth Division, Assistant Appraiser Sturges—Beverages, ale porter, cigars, cigarettes, cocoa, coffee, cordials, fireworks, food, fruits, furniture, grain, grease, groceries (except molasses and sugar), gunpowder, hops, lemon and lime juice, malt, nuts, nutmegs, oils (except medicinal and painters'), plants, seeds, soap (not toilet), soap stock, sopaline, spirituous liquors and snuff.

"BUREAUS.

"In addition to the divisions already mentioned, there are connected with the Appraiser's immediate office four bureaus, besides the chief clerk's office:

"The Law Clerks' Bureau, in which are examined all the suits brought against the Collector in the United States ports, growing out of the various litigated questions under the tariff. A report in each case is written out, properly recorded, and signed by the Appraiser personally.

"The Invoice Bureau, in which are received, entered of record, and distributed all the invoices and other papers. The officer in charge reports direct to the Appraiser.

"The Tea Bureau, in which are examined and tested for purity all teas arriving at the United States. The examiner in charge reports direct to the Appraiser.

"The Chemists' Bureau, or United States laboratory, in charge of the different analytical chemists, who also report in person direct to the Appraiser."

[To be continued.]

PERSONALITY OF HANDWRITING, AND EXPERT EXAMINATIONS.*

Of the necessity for expert examination of handwriting you all are familiar. The frequent occurrence of cases in courts of justice in which the identity of handwriting is involved, has called into service a class of persons who are supposed to possess superior experience and skill in the examination of handwriting. Respecting the value of testimony based upon such examinations there is among jurists a wide diversity of opinions. This results from various causes. First, cases differ widely in the character and extent of writing called in question. There are cases which, from the great skill employed by the forger or the limited extent of his work, well-nigh defy detection; while others, of great magnitude, or perpetrated with less skill, are detected with almost a certainty. Second, it often happens that unskilled or mercenary persons are called as experts

when, through their blundering or transparent knavery, the very idea of expertism is brought under suspicion, if not into disrepute.

The question, then, often arises: Is there any reliable dependence to be placed in scientific examinations and comparisons of handwriting when conducted by persons of acknowledged skill and integrity? We believe that there is. Every adult handwriting possesses peculiar personal characteristics, unconsciously established through the force of habit, that become unavoidable, and which mark the identity of handwriting as conspicuously and certainly as does physiognomy the identity of the person. No two persons, writing naturally, in accordance with habit, can ever write in all respects alike. Different writings may, as will different persons, present a general resemblance so close as to deceive

* An address delivered by Mr. D. T. Ames, of New York City, Author and Expert of Handwriting.

the unfamiliar observer, and yet really have little or no characteristic resemblance.

Persons writing naturally do so without thought respecting the peculiar construction of their writing. The hand operates the pen as it were automatically through the sheer force of habit, by which all the innumerable personalities are unconsciously imparted to writing. Learners and forgers *think* respecting their writing, and hence, the more stiff and formal style of their work; there is wanting the easy, graceful flow apparent in thoughtless or habitual writing. Lines show more of nervousness and hesitancy while the whole construction of the writing is more exact and formal; and, besides, every different handwriting abounds in wellnigh numberless habitual peculiarities, of which the writer himself is unconscious, and cannot, therefore, avoid. Thus, two other insurmountable difficulties are placed in the way of the forger: first, to observe and imitate all the characteristics of the writing he would simulate; and, second, to note and avoid all the habitual characteristics of his own hand. Habit in writing becomes so fixed and arbitrary (not to mention the great artistic skill required to exactly imitate an unpractised hand), that I do not conceive it to be possible for any one to simulate the writing of another, or to so dissemble his own writing, in any considerable quantity, as to defy detection through a really skilled expert examination.

Forgeries are mostly of autographs, and are perpetrated by various methods —one of which is to place the paper upon which the forgery is to be made over the signature to be copied, when, by holding the same to the light or to a window, the writing to be copied may be seen through so that an outline may be traced with a pencil, which is then carefully traced with a pen. Another method of obtaining an exact outline is to place over the signature or writing to be copied a piece of thin transparent paper, upon which is traced with a pencil the outline of the writing which appears underneath; after which the side of the paper opposite the tracing is blackened over with a soft pencil crayon, or other similar substance, when the traced paper is placed upon the sheet where the forgery is to be made, and then, with some smooth-pointed instrument, the penciled outline is retraced with sufficient pressure to cause an offset of the coloring matter to the paper underneath, sufficiently to present a distinct outline of the writing as made upon the tracing. A forgery perpetrated in this manner is sure of detection; when subjected to a skilled examination it will be manifest —first, in the shaky and hesitating quality of the ink lines, as the result of being carefully drawn to follow the traced outline; second, in unnatural rests and retracing, occasioned by stops to study the original writing; and third, in the retouchings of the shaded strokes, which can seldom be made of the proper strength the first time passing over the tracing with the pen, and therefore require subsequent modification. All subsequent touches of the pen, rests, and retracings are certainly detected when subjected to microscopic examinations. Yet forgeries made in this manner are very likely to deceive unskilled or unsuspecting persons, since if made with a tolerable degree of skill they will be in outline and general appearance a close reproduction of the original. Another and, perhaps, the most dangerous signature is where a skilled artist places before himself the signature to be forged, and practises upon it as from a copy until his hand has become so accustomed to its formation and movement as to reproduce it to a great degree of accuracy with the natural movement of the pen. When this is done by a really skilled imitator a signature which presents no extraordinary and difficult-of-imitation personalities is often reproduced wellnigh to perfection—so near as to render very difficult, if not baffle, all expert examinations. The lines and movement, of course, are correct, and the only basis for the expert is in the variations of the forgery from the *characteristic* forms of the original writing. These will vary according to the skill of the forger. Should his skill be very great, the variations may be so slight as to scarcely exceed the ordinary variations between genuine autographs; in which case even skilled experts may fail to discover any tangible or convincing proofs of forgery, and may honestly differ in their opinions.

[The speaker here made a skillful use of the blackboard for illustrating his subject—first, by writing a name in a natural manner, and then making a copy of the same in imitation of a tracing, and afterward touching in the shades in imitation of the manner of forgery.]

No two genuine signatures are ever exactly alike. They vary, as do different kernels of the same grain, in size and outline, while they are characteristically identical; and a person is no more likely to be mistaken respecting the identity of his autograph than he would his coat, hat, or the faces of his relatives and friends. When apparently two autographs are found that appear exactly alike, and when superimposed one is found to exactly cover the other throughout, the forgery of one or both is certain.

I was lately called into a bank in Brooklyn. As I entered I met the cashier about going to his dinner. He returned to his desk, and from it handed me a package of several hundred checks, with a request that I look them over while he was gone. I was without the slightest clue to his object, but presumed that within the package there was a suspected forgery, and so at once began an examination. I at first passed them through my hands, and any one that in the least degree excited my suspicion I placed on one side. I thus selected half a dozen or more. These I again passed through my hands, laying out those most suspicious.

In a very few minutes, and long before the cashier returned, I found remaining in my hands two checks, the signatures to which appeared exactly alike, and different to a considerable extent in their style from all of the others. I placed one over the other and held them to the window, and they so correctly covered over each other as to appear one signature. I then examined them with my glass, and was convinced that they were both forgeries. One for $1,800, had been paid by the bank; and the other, for $1,750, would have been paid had it not exceeded the deposit, which caused a delay, and notice to be sent to the depositors, who denied its genuineness.

When the cashier returned I handed to him the two checks and said: "I think those checks are what trouble you." "You surprise me!" he said. "How in the world did you ascertain that?" I then explained, and he admitted that I was correct.

The writing of the person suspected of the forgery was obtained and identified with that in the forged checks, so as to lead to conviction and imprisonment.

Where the original writing or signature of any forgery, made by tracing, can be found for comparison, the forgery is easily and certainly proved. Most forgers understand this, and hence either destroy or conceal the original, or purposely vary their forgery from the exact outline of the original.

MR. H. C. SPENCER: How does a photograph, when enlarged, aid in detecting a forgery?

MR. AMES: It is no aid as a means of detection. A direct examination of the writing, with good glasses, is a much better and more reliable method. The photograph is of value where access cannot be had to the original, and for purposes of illustration, by placing duplicates of the writing in question in the hands of the court and jury, that they may better understand and appreciate any expert testimony and explanations given.

MR. C. H. PEIRCE: When diamond cuts diamond—*i. e.*, when the skill of the forger is equal to that of the expert—do you not believe that a forgery may be so perfectly executed as to defy detection?

MR. AMES: I would not presume to define the possible or impossible. I believe that it would be, to say the least, rare that a forger would do his work so perfectly as to leave absolutely no indication of ungenuineness.

MR. PEIRCE: When you have expressed your opinion fully, and taken sides in a case, do you feel bound to sustain that side in case further developments should show you to be in error?

MR. AMES: By no means. It is the sole duty of an expert to discover and present facts, without regard to whether they may or may not sustain any theory he may have formed, and should he, at any time, find that he has been misled or deceived into giving an erroneous opinion, he should say so, and frankly state his reasons for the change of opinion; and in any case where he is in doubt he should so admit, giving his reasons *pro* and *con;* and when under cross-examination, he should admit

frankly any fact which he may believe to exist, tending to controvert his expressed opinion. An expert witness should, in my opinion, have no facts to conceal or about which to quibble.

MR. H. C. SPENCER: You have stated that one genuine autograph differs from another. You also disprove the genuineness of an autograph by pointing out its differences from your genuine standards. How are you to determine that the variations noted result from the inability of the forger to correctly reproduce an autograph, rather than from the incidental variations between genuine autographs? or, in other words, whether they are the natural variations in writing, or imperfections in copying?

[In reply, Mr. Ames requested a member to write his autograph twice upon the blackboard, and another member to copy it as perfectly as possible, and then write his own.]

MR. AMES said: When a person writes his own autograph, it is without thought, from force of habit; and, if repeated, although with variations in form, size, etc., there is a perfect ease or thoughtless freedom of line, and a homogeneousness which stamps both as the result of one writing habit. Peculiar shades, turns, spacings, and the nice personal characteristics which impart a personality to writing, are reproduced with a natural ease. Not so in a forged writing.

[Turning to the blackboard, Mr. Ames gave a very elaborate analysis of the genuine autographs—pointing to their apparent differences, and comparing them in their nature and degree with those in the counterfeit. He made it very apparent that the differences between the genuine were slight, and of very different character than were those between the genuine and forged writing. He pointed to many instances where it was very apparent that the force of habit had asserted itself, and caused the copyist to impart his own personality, rather than that of the original. Loops were differently turned and proportioned, letters differed in the manner of their construction, shades were misplaced and different in degree, and letters were differently joined and proportioned. It was clearly shown how these were radical differences, resulting alike from the inability of the copyist to observe and reproduce the writing habit of another, and to avoid his own. In these comparisons the speaker made it very apparent how such differences as he pointed out must be the result of an entirely different habit, rather than of the acci dental variations of the same habit. It is a matter of much regret that full illustrations, as used upon the board by Mr. Ames, cannot accompany his lecture ; but for that, very elaborate and numerous drawings would be required.]

ILLUSTRATIONS AND ANALYSIS.

The annexed cut and analysis, which were furnished by Mr. Ames for this report, are practically the same as those given before the Convention, and will serve to convey an idea of those used on that occasion:

The force of habit and the difficulties in the way of forgery are illustrated in the cut shown. The first two lines represent genuine autographs : the third, a skillfully executed forgery, and to the casual observer it is a *fac-simile* of the genuine, and would pass as such. Yet, under a scientific examination it differs very widely—in fact, has scarcely a characteristic resemblance—while as proof of its ungenuineness no less than thirty characteristic differences may be cited—twenty-five of which are indicated by numerals in the cut. (1) The staff of the *F* in the genuine terminates at the base line with a round, free movement, while in the forgery it is broken at the base and horizontal at its terminal. (2) The *F* is crossed with a curved line, while in the g it is straight. (3) The initial line to the cap of the *F* is longer and farther from the second, and not so nearly parallel, making a differently formed and larger space than in the f. (4) The loop is larger and more egg-shaped in the g. than in the f. (5) The cap of the *F* in g. is far above the top of the stem, and close to it in the f. (6) The shade of the loop is chiefly below the middle in the g., while it is above that point in the f. (6) It is a more graceful and better balanced curve than in the g. (8) The initial to the *R* begins with a well-defined right curve in the g., and a compound one in the f., and (9) the shade is low down toward the base in the g., while it is near the top in the f. (10) The top portion of the *R* is larger and more round in the g.

than in the f., and (11) it is less shaded in the g. than in the f. (12) The last stroke of the *R* is shaded lower down in the g. than in the f.; while the centre loop points straight upward in the g., and nearly horozontal in the f. (13) The finishing turn of the *R*, the lower turn of the *u*—in fact, all the turns of the g. are more round and full than in the f. (14) The *ss*'s in the g. are more round and open at the top; and have for the down stroke a simple right curve, and (15) terminate with a triangular form; while in the f. these letters are closed and pointed at the top, have a compound curve in down-stroke, while they termi-nate with well-turned graceful loops. (16) The *ll*'s in the g. cross less than one-fourth of their height from the base; in the f. above, one-eighth; and (17) all the *l*'s are angular in their top turns in the g., and round in the f.; while from habit the first *l* in the g. is shorter and thinner than the second, while they are in all respects alike in the f. (18) In the g. the *l*'s terminate with a straight down-ward movement; in the f., with a turn and upward right curve. (19) In the g. the loop at the base of the *L* is much larger and broader than in the f.; (20) while the staff is more sloping, with the shade much lower down in the g. than in the f. (21) The *y* in g. is angular in the top of the first part, and round in its turn at the bottom of loop; while the first part in the f. is round, and the turn of the loop angular. (22) In the g. the connecting line to the *o* approaches at an angle near the base, while in the f. it approaches on nearly a parallel move-ment, and much higher, while the whole letter in the g. is much more narrow and contracted than in the f. (23) In the g, the *n* is round at the top, also the first turn at base is round and open, while both these turns in the f. are sharp angles. (24) The terminal lines in g. are

compound curves, while in the f. it is curved only slightly to the right. (25) All the punctuation points in the g. are very delicate points, while in the f. they are conspicuous curved dashes.

It is apparent from its character that the above forgery was perpetrated with-out tracing, and upon nearly the natural movement, as the lines are smooth, graceful, and none of the shaded lines show retouching, and all the variations noted in the foregoing analysis result from the power of habit asserting itself on the part of the forger, and a failure to note many of the nice habitual character-istics of the genuine autograph. It is also apparent that the forger was a more skilled artist with the pen than the writer of the genuine. This appears in the better balanced lines in the top of the *F*, compound curves of the *ss*'s, the more graceful loops, better rounded *o*, and more nicely turned *n*; and the whole movement appears quite as free as the genuine, while it must have been thought-fully and carefully written; hence it is a fair inference that when writing with en-tire freedom from thought and without effort to copy there would have been manifest additional grace and skill.

In answer to a question, Mr. Ames re-ferred to the Morey-Garfield letter. He said that one of the conclusive reasons which led him at the first sight to pro-nounce the famous letter a forgery, was the fact that the dot intended for the *i*, in Garfield, was to the left of the *f*, and over the *r*. I did not believe it was possible that General Garfield had not learned where the *i* was in his auto-graph, or that a habit so long and oft-repeated should make such a mistake. Had the dot been omitted entirely, I should have thought that a possible over-sight; but such a misplacement could only be the blunder of a copyist.

Late Legal Decisions.

NEGLIGENCE—INJURY TO A CHILD—DYNAMITE.

The plaintiff's father was engaged in the cultivation of a farm owned by the defendant. The foreman of the defendant had left a parcel of dynamite in a temporary shed near the place where the plaintiff's father was working, and the plaintiff, who was eight years of age, having taken him his dinner, went into the shed, and, seeing one of the exploders, struck it with a stone, shattering his hand. An action was brought to recover damages, and the jury were instructed to find for the defendant, on the ground that it was the duty of the parent to take care of his child, and see that it did not commit trespass. On appeal, this judgment was reversed, and the Court

Held, That the defendant was guilty of negligence, in permitting such a dangerous explosive to lie unguarded; that children, wherever they go, are expected to act upon childish instincts and impulses, and others who are chargeable with a duty of care and caution toward them, must calculate upon this, and take precautions accordingly. If they leave exposed to the observation of children anything which would be tempting to them. and which they, in their miniature judgment, might naturally suppose they were at liberty to handle or play with, they should expect that liberty to be taken.

Powers *vs.* Harlow, Supreme Court of Michigan, April, 1884.

CONTRACT TO MARRY—CONSIDERATION.

Plaintiff, Mrs. Connor, entered into a contract with defendant's intestate, one Jarvis, in June, 1882, to marry "within a reasonable time hereafter," and Jarvis, in consideration of the agreement of the plaintiff, promised therein to give plaintiff, on or before the day of such marriage, certain bonds of the value of $10,000. Jarvis died in December, 1882, the marriage never having taken place, and plaintiff brought this action to recover from the administrator the value of the bonds, alleging that she was at all times ready and willing to marry as aforesaid, but that Jarvis refused. Judgment was given for the defendant, and plaintiff appealed. The higher Court reversed the judgment, and

Held, That the promise and conduct of the plaintiff constituted adequate and valuable consideration for the promise of Jarvis, and she is justly and legally entitled to receive it. The circumstance that the marriage was not in fact consummated is immaterial. It was not consummated because of the fault of Jarvis, and it is a maxim of the law that no man shall take advantage of his own wrong.

Judgment reversed.

Connor *vs.* Stanley, Supreme Court of California, April, 1884.

MUTUAL INSURANCE COMPANY—DIVISION OF SURPLUS.

A surplus had been accumulated by the Southern Mutual Insurance Company, the company having, for several years previous, retained from the premiums paid in a certain amount as a reserve fund. It filed a bill in equity, alleging this surplus and praying for a decree directing how the same should be divided.

Held, That all those persons who had paid premiums and held policies during the years in which the fund was being accumulated were entitled to a *pro rata* share of the division, and that it should not be divided simply among those who held policies at the time the bill was brought.

Carlton *vs.* Southern Mutual Insurance Company, Supreme Court of Georgia, decided June 10, 1984.

LOTTERY BUSINESS—LIBEL—NO RECOVERY.

Plaintiff was the manager of the Louisiana State Lottery Company, and sued the defendant as publisher of the Philadelphia *Times* for libel, by reason of the publication of the following:

"Mr. M. A. Dauphin, the agent of the Louisiana Lottery, to whom deluded lottery victims addressed their remittances, and whose correspondence has been excluded from the mails, has decided that he is a bigger man than Dorsey or Brady, and that he must have damages if he can't publicly and insolently defy the laws. Mr. Dauphin will fail in his attempt to recover damages from a cabinet officer for the offence of honest fidelity to the laws; but the lesson is worthy of the study of the nation. It is the dying shriek of one of the most stupendous public robberies of our history, and will shed exceptional lustre upon the character of Postmaster-General Gresham, who is honored with the last ebullition of malignity of a long omnipotent, but now overthrown, organized crime."

Plaintiff claimed that he had been brought into public scandal and disrepute by reason of this publication, and had been injured in his business. A defence was interposed that the business of the plaintiff was an illegal one, both under the laws of the United States and under the laws of the State of Pennsylvania, where the publication was made, and that, therefore, no recovery could be had.

The Court held that no action for libel could be maintained where the business as to which an alleged libel was published was an unlawful one, and that acting as agent for a lottery was such an unlawful business.

Dauphin *vs.* the *Times* Publishing Company. U. S. Circuit Court, E. D. Pennsylvania, decided April 30, 1884.

SAVINGS BANK—DEPOSIT IN WIFE'S NAME.

Plaintiff, being a depositor in a savings bank, and desiring to open another account, deposited money in the name of his wife, the bank usage not permitting two accounts to be kept open in the same name. After the death of his wife, the bank refused to recognize his right to the money, and in an action brought to recover the deposit, the Court

Held, The fact that a depositor has money deposited in the name of another does not affect his right to the deposit.

Davis *vs.* Lenawee County Savings Bank, Supreme Court of Michigan, decided March, 1884.

(From Bankers' Magazine.)

Notes Drawing Interest Due Annually.—In case of non-payment of interest *annually* as provided, must a note drawn as follows be protested in order to hold the indorser liable for the interest?

$5,000.　　　　　NEW YORK, July 1, 1883.

Five years after date I promise to pay to the order of John Dakin, Five Thousand Dollars, at the State Bank, Chatham, N. Y., *with interest annually.*　　　　　JOHN DOE.

Reply.—Protest is unnecessary. Where a note is payable in installments, whether of principal or interest, an action may be maintained by the holder against all parties liable upon the note for each installment as it becomes due. Oridge *vs.* Sherborne, 11 Meeson & Welsby 374; Cooley *vs.* Rose, 3 Mass. 221. Between an installment of principal and of interest there are, however, in other respects, marked differences. An installment of principal bears grace, is subject to protest and notice to indorsers, and non-payment of it is a dishonor of the whole note, which puts it at once in the category of overdue paper. But, as is said by the Supreme Court of Massachusetts, in the case of National Bank of North America *vs.* Kirby, 108 Mass. 501, " In its effect upon the credit of a note, it is manifest that a failure to pay interest is not to be ranked with a failure to pay principal. Interest is an incident of the debt, and differs from it in many respects. It is not subject to protest and notice to indorser, or days of grace according to the law merchant. Interest is not recovered on overdue interest, and the statute of limitations does not run against it until the principal is due. The holder of a note with interest payable annually loses no rights against the parties to it, whether makers or indorsers, by neglecting to demand it; and he has the election to do so, or wait and collect it all with the principal."

Indorsement of Checks.—I have a controversy with certain banks, and was referred to you for a decision of the matter. I am General Agent of a life insurance company. My business and bank business—*i. e.*, my bank account—I do under my proper name, A. L. R. Checks or indorsements of checks are given me and received by me, made to A. L. R., General Agent of the ——— Company, which I indorse with my name only as A. L. R., which our banks refuse to accept, claiming that I must sign the stated qualification to my name. I hold such to be unnecessary; and the signing of my name, doing my business (*i. e.*, keeping my bank account) under my proper name, A. L. R., duly to be sufficient, and legally so to all intents and purposes. I have consulted legal advice here, and find myself sustained, while all the banks hold to the contrary.

Reply.—The requirement of the paying-banks is in accordance with the general custom of bankers. It may be technically true in this case, that a check payable to " A. L. R., General Agent, etc.," is not payable to the company of which he is agent, but is payable to A. L. R., as an individual ; that the words "General Agent" are mere words of general description of no particular legal effect, and that his individual indorsement is sufficient to pass the title to it. This, however, is not conclusive of the matter. It should be remembered that the banks upon which the checks are drawn are under no liability or duty *to the holder* to pay them. Their sole duty is to their *depositors*. It may be that the words "General Agent, etc.," upon the face of the check are mere words of description, without legal effect, or the reverse. Of this the paying bank can have no knowledge when the check is presented, unless it takes time to inquire. It sees, however, that the drawer of the check has attached some importance to the capacity in which A. L. R. is to receive his money, by writing it on the face of the check, and he may at least desire A. L. R.'s acknowledgment, by his indorsement, that he has received it in that capacity. It is, therefore, in our opinion, a reasonable requirement on the part of the paying banks, in the conduct of their business, that such checks shall be indorsed in full, and one in which they will doubtless be sustained by their depositors, to whom only do they owe any duty in the matter. They are bound at their peril to see that all checks paid by them are paid only to those properly entitled to payment, and they are accordingly entitled to demand that checks shall be so indorsed as to be complete vouchers, and carry with them full proof that the money was paid and received, as the drawer intended:

Checks to Order of Bearer.—Ought a paying-teller to ask for a written indorsement on a check payable "to the order of bearer," or a check payable "to the order of self or bearer," when presented at the counter by the drawer or any one else?

Reply.—We regard it as good banking practice, in cases of this kind, to require an indorsement. The indorsement will serve as a receipt to identify the party receiving the money, and will generally be given, if asked

for. We do not know that it has ever been decided that the bank has a technical right to demand an indorsement, or, in other words that it would be justified in refusing to pay solely for want of one. At the same time, the form of the check is somewhat ambiguous, and the teller should err in such cases, if at all, upon the side of safety. In this city, even if a check is payable absolutely to bearer, most tellers, owing to the frequency of forgeries, require an indorsement; and if the amount is large, they will require the identification of the bearer. It should be remembered that when a check is presented for payment, a bank has always the right to take time to satisfy itself that payment is proper ; and it may properly regard itself as waiving this right for the convenience of the check-holder, in consideration of his indorsing the check or procuring himself to be identified.

[*From Bradstreet's.*]

Authority of Agents. — Where a principal puts it in the power of his agent to make contracts or to do acts apparently within his authority, which result in injury to innocent third persons or to the principal, the law will impose the loss upon the latter. So held by the Texas Court of Appeals in the recently-decided case of the New York Insurance Company *vs.* Rohrbrough et al.

Commission added to Interest not Usury. —The payment of an amount to a loan broker as commission by the borrower of money, which, added to the current interest upon the amount of the loan, largely exceeds legal interest, does not show usury in the loan without proof that the broker acted as the agent of the lender, according to the decision of the Supreme Court of Illinois in the recently-decided case of Brown et al. *vs.* The Scottish-American Mortgage Company.

Indorser not discharged when money refunded by indorsee.—Where an indorsee of a note payable at a bank received from a bank payment thereof, the bank officers being under the impression that the maker had on deposit sufficient funds to meet the note, and on the same day, the bank having discovered its mistake and demanded the money back, repaid it, the Supreme Court of Pennsylvania held (in Meredith *vs.* Haines) that the indorser was not discharged from liability to the indorsee.

Creditor as Quasi Trustee.—A creditor holding the property of a corporation in order to apply the profits thereof to the reimbursement of himself and the payment of its other debts is analogous to a trustee, and must return to the stockholders the remnant of the property in his hands after the purposes of his quasi trust have been subserved. So held by the United States Circuit Court for the District of California in the recently-decided case of The Pioneer Gold Mining Company *vs.* Baker.

State Legislature have authority to close navigable rivers.—The case of Lee *vs.* Young et al., decided by Judge Nelson in the United States District Court at Boston on the 13th inst., arose upon a libel for demurrage caused by the obstruction of Charles river in repairing Warren bridge. It appeared that the libellant, a master of a schooner having on board a cargo of coal, was prevented from proceeding up the Charles river to the Charles river wharf by reason of the act of the defendants, contractors employed by the city of Boston to repair Warren bridge, in closing the navigation of the river. The defendants, acting under the authority of an Act of the Massachusetts legislature and the license of the harbor commissioners, closed the river for three days while the repairs were going on. The court held that, in the absence of any legislation by Congress prohibiting it, the work done under the authority of the Act of the legislature was lawful, and, there being no evidence of unnecessary delay in doing the work, he dismissed the libel with costs.

Charitable Institutions a "Business" within the meaning of the Law.—The case of Rolls *vs.* Miller, decided some time ago by the Chancery Division of the High Court of Justice (England), involved the question whether carrying on a charitable institution was a "business" within the prohibition of a covenant in a lease providing that the lessee should not carry on nor permit to be carried on upon the premises leased any trade or business whatever without the consent of the lessors. It appeared that the defendant was about to use the property for the purpose of a charitable institution, from which however no profits were derived by the managers. The court at that held that the proposed employment of the house would be a breach of the covenant referred to, and declared that in its opinion a "business" would still be a business

although no profit was made. This view of the law has just been affirmed by the Court of Appeal. In a decision rendered on the 28th ult., on an appeal from the judgment above mentioned, Lord Justice Cotten, in affirming the judgment, said that the object of the covenant was that the house should be used only as a private residence, though there were no express words to that effect. But there was no doubt that a business was carried on—namely, the business of keeping a lodging-house. The fact that no profit was made or sought to be made did not make any difference. In fact, if any business at a profit had been meant there would scarcely have been occasion for the use of the word "trade."

Nail Rods not Bar Iron.—The case of Abbott et al. *vs.* Worthington, recently decided in the United States Circuit Court at Boston, was an action brought against the collector of the port of Boston to recover duties paid under protest. It appeared that the collector assessed duties at the rate of 1½ cents per pound on an importation of Swedish iron nail rods, under schedule E., section 2504 Revised Statutes, as bar iron, rolled or hammered. The plaintiffs claimed that the articles were only liable to a duty of 1¼ cents per pound, either as a description of rolled or hammered iron not otherwise provided for or as coming under the similitude clause section 2499 of the Revised Statues, as resembling scroll iron. Judge Colt, in ordering judgment for the plaintiffs, said that the evidence showed that the articles imported were known commercially as nail rods, and that in a commercial sense nail rods were not bar iron, and further added: "The article is made and used for a special purpose, and known in commerce by a distinct name. It further appears that in the Act of 1842, and in some previous Acts, nail rods are specially designated as such, so that Congress in the tariff laws has recognized nail rods as distinct from bar iron or iron in bars. Nail rods, having acquired a specific commercial designation among traders and importers, and having been designated by a specific name in previous tariff legislation, would not properly come under the general term bar iron in the Revised Statutes, but should be classified as a description of rolled and hammered iron not otherwise provided for, and so subject to a duty of 1¼ cents a pound."

NOTES AND COMMENTS.

Are we a nation of gamblers? This question, it seems is quite as pertinent as that discussed in the *North American Review*, "Are we a nation of rascals?" Are not the two questions closely allied? Does not gambling beget rascality? Is it not, in fact, one of the chief stepping-stones to all kinds of fraud? The disposition to get something for nothing is one of the crying evils of our nation. By it we are being rapidly borne into the destructive tide of dishonor and disgrace. Just how to draw the line that defines where gambling begins and where it ends may be difficult. To accurately define it may not be an easy task. But percision in drawing the lines or hair-splitting dispute over the use of words in a definition are not important features for discussion in condemning the practice. The man who in June bets on the price of wheat or cotton in October is as properly considered a gambler as he who stakes his money on a horse-race. The man who puts up a hundred dollars to pay for margins on a thousand dollars' worth of stock is as much a gambler as the one who stakes his money on a faro-table or a game of poker. That one is more genteel than the other, we shall readily admit. That the gamblers of one class are more respectable than the others cannot be denied. But who will undertake to excuse either? The man who buys stocks and pays for what he buys, buying at a price to-day which enables him to sell at an advance to-morrow, is doing as legitimate a business as the merchant who buys sugar at one price and sells at another. There is a difference between buying stocks and paying the market value, and buying options or advancing on margins. If speculations in stocks were confined to actual purchases and sales, with completed transfers in each case, the stock operations of the country would be diminished several hundred per cent., but fewer people would meet with financial ruin, and the record of commercial failures would be materially decreased.

The cause of a large proportion of bank failures may be either directly or indirectly traced to stock gambling speculation. The amount of injury resulting from the failure of a bank is inestimable. It is not alone the gambler who is ruined, or the stockholders and depositors who suffer, but the damages spread in all directions and the effects are felt more or less throughout the whole community. The depositor who loses his money is compelled to disappoint those whom he owes, and they in turn disappoint their debtors. He who wagers his money on a game of chance or a horse-race is, as a rule, the principal sufferer by the act, and his loss is oftentimes confined to himself and those dependant upon him.

———

We can scarcely pick up a newspaper without having our attention attracted to some case of defalcation or embezzlement, of which, when the facts have been sifted to the bottom, the announcement comes, "gambling the cause." If a book-keeper is short in his cash, or a trusted employee proves himself a defaulter, the natural inquiry is "Did he gamble?" Is it possible to discover a remedy for this deplorable state of affairs? One plan only can be relied upon. Total abstinence. Let it be distinctly understood that any person who will bet or wager anything to the value of a farthing on a game of chance, trial of strength or speed, future values of stocks or products, or on the result of any election, is wholly unfit for a position of trust. Brand every person who bets or patronizes lotteries as a gambler. Treat him with the suspicion that enshrouds a knight of the green cloth. The treatment may be considered severe, but it is one that will go far towards speedily eradicating a mighty curse and a powerful antagonist to uprightness and morality.

———

A change in the proprietorship of the AMERICAN COUNTING-ROOM took place in January, 1884. The magazine passed at this time into the hands of the present owners, the Counting-Room Company, Limited, a joint-stock corporation, organized under the laws of the State of New York. At the time the Company was formed the following persons were elected officers: Charles E. Sprague, President; George B. Packer, Vice-President; Selden R. Hopkins, Secretary and Treasurer. In March following, Mr. Hopkins resigned his position as Secretary and Treasurer, and Mr. J. M. Abbott was elected to fill the vacancy for the unexpired term. This position Mr. Abbott has continued to hold ever since. With the exception of Mr. Abbott, the stockholders had been, before the organization of the corporation, either directly or indirectly interested in the publication and the business connected with it. Their investment in the Company was in proportion to their interest in the business prior to the formation of the corporation. The arrangement with Mr. Abbott provided that he should become a subscriber to the capital-stock of the Company to the amount of about one-fourth of the entire capital. This amount was to form a working fund which, it was estimated, would be sufficient to procure the necessary stock and machinery for placing the Company and the publication in a strong financial condition. Soon after this arrangement was undertaken and before Mr. Abbott had paid in the amount proposed under the agreement, there came a series of financial crashes in New York. Though not directly affecting the business, these financial disturbances had their detrimental influence upon the Company. Mr. Abbott met with annoyances which interferred with the arrangements he had entered into. As a consequence, the business of the Company has suffered, and patrons of the magazine have been put to unpleasant inconveniences and disappointments. Instead of being able to assume full business management of the establishment as contemplated, Mr. Abbott has been obliged to look after other interests, and the managing editor, with a multiplicity of other duties and with little or no assistance, has been left to " hold the fort " as best he could.

The publication of the magazine was interrupted. The business was left practically without a head. The management by the editor was more assumed than authorized. Neither the President nor Vice-President of the Company were empowered or authorized to transact business. Neither were able to be present and look after affairs had they been authorized. As day after day passed, and week followed

week, an improvement in the situation has been almost hourly expected. A better feeling in financial affairs has been looked for, but the little that has come to business in general has brought no special relief in this instance. Though that part of the business which includes the publication of the magazine has been almost at a standstill, yet the amount of necessary correspondence has been unusually large, much of which, under the circumstances, has had to be neglected. Patrons who have received short and delayed responses, or possibly none at all, to inquiries which should have entitled them to prompt and courteous replies, will, it is hoped, accept a general apology for dereliction of duty, with the understanding that the fault was not the result of carelessness but rather the force of circumstances.

It is the expectation of the publishers to go ahead with the magazine. It is hoped the lost ground will be fully recovered, and that patrons will not lose interest in the publication. A spirit of forbearance on the part of subscribers is asked for. It is probable that the next issue will combine the first three numbers of the following volume, viz., for July, August and September.

The political questions this year are more worthy than usual the attention of business people. The number of candidates furnishes a variety in choice, so that the most fastidious should not complain of being forced to forfeit his right to the ballot for want of some one to vote for who meets his exceptional or special theories. The Free Trade Republican and Protectionist Democrat seem to be as much favored as the Protectionist Republican and the Free Trade Democrat. Then the Prohibition Democratic-Republican Suffragist is provided with a candidate who fills the niche according to his approved ideas of political reform. Without engaging too rashly in speculation over the result, it is safe to say that since there are 401 electoral votes to be cast, the candidate receiving 201 of the number will be elected. Owing to the general mixture, it is difficult to make a political estimate that will be pleasing to all parties. The COUNTING-ROOM is not in any sense a political journal. The editors, as a matter of course, have political views, and probably as strong ones as any of their readers. If any direct or special good would probably come to the class whose interests this magazine endeavors to espouse through a discussion of politics, these columns would be found "red-hot" with political lore. If it was in either the power or the heart of one party more than another to raise the appreciation of and respect for the services of this hard-working, trade-ridden class, the pages of this issue and all forthcoming issues of this book would be made to burn with political argument.

There is at least one thing political that the patrons of this magazine feel a deep interest in. And not alone should these readers be interested in it, but all persons desiring good government, and, especially all tax-payers. It is to see that positions where the official is expected to have a knowledge of accounts is filled by competent and able accountants. One of the chief political burdens of the country is the elevation to office of men who are entirely incapable. In every case where the incumbent is entrusted with public finances he should be a person familiar with accounts. Such officers as city and county treasurers or comptrollers should in all cases be chosen with special reference to their fitness as account-ants. If the civil service reform is to be a true reform, here is a field where it should be brought into practical use. Let persons seeking offices of this kind, before being nominated, prove their efficiency and worthiness by passing a severe examination before a board composed of experienced and qualified examiners. The adoption of such a reform would enable the electors to vote intelligently. But, under the present circumstances, in local affairs let voters cast their ballots for the man who is known by his experience as best qualified to fill the place, irrespective of party. To insure the vote of the party, let those who attend the nominating conventions and meetings understand that it is necessary in all cases to choose persons especially fitted for the positions they are to fill. The tax-payers of the country are being robbed annually of a large per cent. of what goes into the public purse, because of the ignorance of those they elect to positions of trust. It is not always the officials, but as often those employed by the officials, who commit the thefts. The officer whose business

it is to examine the books and see that all funds are properly accounted for is a novice with books of account, and consequently, before he is hardly aware that such a thing as fraud is possible, the treasury is robbed. In some instances the loss is from sheer incapacity of the official. Let accountants, wherever they have a voice in making nominations, demand that for all financial positions those of known fitness and ability should be nominated.

But now the approaching election is not far off, and we are expected to use our best judgment in placing good men in office. It is too late, this time, to talk about the conventions. That must be reserved for another season. We have been asked to publish an estimate of the strength of the two great parties, furnished by an old subscriber. This speculation is given in the form of a table. The author, while claiming wisdom as to how nearly every State will go, seems to admit an inability to classify four States. Two of these, New York and Indiana, are important ones. It is difficult to foresee just what cyclones are in the political atmosphere, ready to break forth and upset the calculations of the veteran prognosticators. We give the table for what it is worth. It may be of some service to those who like to see what others think:

STATE.	REP	D'M	p	STATE.	REP	D'M	p
Alabama	—	10	—	Missouri	—	16	—
Arkansas	—	7	—	Nebraska	5	—	—
California	8	—	—	Nevada	3	—	—
Colorado	3	—	—	N. Hampshire	4	—	—
Connecticut	—	—	6	New Jersey			
Delaware	—	3	—	New York	—	—	36
Florida	—	4	—	N. Carolina	—	11	—
Georgia	—	12	—	Ohio	23	—	—
Illinois	22	—	—	Oregon	3	—	—
Indiana	—	—	15	Pennsylvania	30	—	—
Iowa	13	—	—	Rhode Island	4	—	—
Kansas	9	—	—	S. Carolina	—	9	—
Kentucky	—	13	—	Tennessee	—	12	—
Louisiana	—	8	—	Texas	—	13	—
Maine	6	—	—	Vermont	4	—	—
Maryland	—	8	—	Virginia	—	12	—
Massachusetts	14	—	—	W. Virginia	—	6	—
Michigan	13	—	—	Wisconsin	11	—	—
Minnesota	7	—	—				
Mississippi	—	9	—	Total	182	153	66

The paper of Mr. Charles F. Wignall, which forms the opening article of this number, will be found worthy of preserving. The methods described might have been contrasted with the routine practiced in some of the cities thirty years or more ago. Such a contrast would illustrate how methods connected with banking have kept pace with the advancement in mechanics, arts, and sciences. It was customary for each bank to send a porter to the other banks. These porters were provided with a book of entry, and each carried the money for the banks upon which he called. The paying-teller of the receiving bank took the exchange and entered it on the credit side of the book; then he entered on the debit side the return exchange, and gave it, with the book, to the porter. In their rounds the porters crossed and recrossed each other's footsteps frequently. They often met in groups of half-a-dozen at the same bank, and thus interfered with each other. They seldom completed the circuit in less than one or two hours. Instead, as now, of having the counting of the exchanges in the morning, the porters returned so as to bring this work in the middle and after-part of the day, when the general business was pressing.

Instead of attempting a daily adjustment of accounts, which would have caused a waste of labor, an agreement was made between the banks, providing for a weekly settlement. This took place on Friday, after that day's exchanges. This gave an opportunity for sharp practice. Money could be borrowed on Thursday to meet the exchanges on Friday. When the loan thus made was returned on Saturday, the bank stood again on the debit side of the weekly account. Banks located at a distance from the commercial centre managed, under this practice, to carry an inflated line of discounts based on debts due to other institutions. It became an affair of cunning management by some to run a small credit of two or three thousand dollars with each of thirty or forty banks, giving them a handsome capital on which to do a discounting business. As a result, the Friday settlements proved to be a wide pathway to unfair dealings. In an effort to obviate the bad system which had grown up, the cashier of each bank, as soon as the " Exchange Balance List " had been completed, would send out porters with checks to draw every dollar due from other banks. This process caused great confusion. Disputes over errors arose, and blunders seemed unavoidable. After all the draft-drawing was over, came the settlement of the porters among themselves. A *porters' exchange* was held on the steps of one of the prominent banks, at which, among themselves, they accounted for

what had been done during the day. This general settlement was thus described by an author, many years ago:

" Thomas had left a bag of specie at John's bank to settle a balance which was due from William's bank to Robert's; but Robert's bank owed twice as much to John's. What had become of *that?* Then Alexander owed Robert also, and William was indebted to Alexander. Peter then said that he had paid Robert by a draft from James, which he (James) had received from Alfred on Alexander's account. That, however, had settled only half the debt. A quarter of the remainder was cancelled by a bag of coin which Samuel had handed over to Joseph, and he had transferred to David." It is safe to say that the bank officials could not themselves have easily untangled these complications. Each porter had his tally, and by liberating from the net-work first one and then another, in their order of simplicity, the settlement was finally completed. Not the least irritating feature of the case was that a single small draft involved a commotion. If time were allowed, the debtor banks would finally be obliged to pay the liquidating bolance; but the hour of closing arrested the process, and the banks where the demand was then in force were obliged to disburse the coin. It was not unusual for a debtor bank, with its debt doubled, to add fifty thousand dollars to its specie at the close of the day. Another bank, with half a million to its credit in the general account, would often find itself at three o'clock depleted of one or two hundred thousand dollars of coin. Various questions were discussed looking to a plan for removing these difficulties. But, owing to a diversity of opinion, any attempted innovation was reluctantly considered. According to Mr. James S. Gibbons, at one time cashier of the Ocean Bank, of New York, the subject of a new method was discussed in all its bearings at informal meetings of bank officers, and steps were taken to obtain general co-operation in some partial and experimental plans. " Such, however," he says, "was the diversity of opinions, even among those most anxious to promote the object, that nearly a year passed before it was thought expedient to issue notices to take decisive action upon it. Then it encountered much silent and determined opposition. Those banks which had profited most by enforced

NOTES AND COMMENTS.

255

credit balances feared the restraint and domination of others; and these had prejudices to overcome, and a long score of annoyances to forget; but it was manifest that the subject could be deferred no longer. A plan was adopted and went into effect October 1, 1853. Its complete success soon banished all feelings but those of gratification and common interest."

The question of the liability of railroad companies on bills of lading is attracting attention. The law on this subject has been found wholly inadequate to meet the exegencies constantly arising. As it now stands, bills of lading issued by shippers who have not received the property specified, are worthless as securities. Justice to the commercial public demands that bills of lading should be so protected by law, that questions of value as to negotiability could not arise. The present law which fails to hold shippers to a strict accountability for the acts of their representatives is extremely damaging to commercial interests. Measures are under way to try and secure the desired reformation. Referring to this subject the editor of *Bradstreets* says the New York Board of Trade and Transportation have "adopted resolutions recommending the adoption for the use of all transportation companies and freight lines a uniform bill of lading, which will, in clear and unequivocal language, declare who is liable for loss and damage, and not leave it in the power of the company by refusing to give necessary information, or otherwise to throw unsurmountable obstacles in the way of an action at law by which parties aggrieved may have the justice of a claim determined."

Mr. Frank S. Gardner, Acting Secretary of the New York Board of Trade and Transportation, in a letter to the above named journal says:

"One question is the liability of a railroad company or any common carrier for a bill of lading, issued by the anthorized agent of said company or common carrier, for all expressed in the bill of lading, whether the goods represented to be shipped have been actually shipped or not.

"The other question is the necessity for a uniform bill of lading by all freight lines, and an amendment to them such as will declare who is liable to the consignor or consignee in case of loss or damage to the goods shipped. This question is quite fully explained in the report of our Committee on Arbitration and Claims, of which I inclose a copy.

"The first-named question arose last Fall in the case of the Blue Line, New York, Boston and Philadelphia firms having advanced on bills of lading which, although signed by the regular agent, were fraudulent, no goods having been actually shipped. Also a similar case in connection with the Missouri Pacific Railroad. The claim against the Blue Line was settled; the latter was not.

"In face of this danger, which threatened to unsettle all commercial transactions with carrying companies, and recognizing the present absence of any satisfactory law on the question, our Board referred the matter to the National Board of Trade last January.

"At the request of our delegates, subsequent to the National Board meeting, Simon Sterne, Esq., drafted a bill. The bill was referred to our Committee on Legislation, approved by them, reported to the Board, and on Friday last, at a special meeting of our directors, unanimously adopted and forwarded to Washington for immediate introduction in Congress.

"The bill is framed on the theory that it would be unjust to the railroad companies to make them liable for all bills of lading, fraudulent or not, unless some scheme was permitted by which they could protect themselves and speedily discover fraud. The plan proposed in the bill gives the companies room for the adoption of any scheme which to them seems to answer the purpose, but they are required to hold themselves liable for all bills unless they designate at the point of destination some person who may be applied to by the merchant or banker for a certification of the correctness of the bill of lading. Several plans by which a company may place checks on their agents have been suggested, that will, with little or no additional expense to it, give absolute security. This part, however, is for the companies to elaborate. The person designated in the bill of lading who will certify at the point of destination may be the agent of the connecting line. The expense of the inquiry is to be paid by the person offering the bill of lading for certification.

"We have requested the New York Cotton Exchange and the New York Produce Exchange to give the bill a most careful and critical consideration, and we are informed that a committee of each organization has the bill before them. While the bill has been carefully considered, amendments may be found to be desirable before it should be passed. Early in December we will make application for a hearing before the committees of Congress having the bill in charge, and a strong effort will be made to secure its passage.

" In regard to the other question (the liability for loss or damage and the amendment of bills of lading), we referred this matter to the Railroad Commissioners, believing that if the proposed amendment was adopted by the companies over which a State commission had jurisdiction, it would lead to its adoption by all other lines. The fairness of the amendment proposed, we think, will commend itsslf to the commissioners and to all merchants and shippers, and perhaps to the freight lines also."

The series of instructive articles on " Building and Loan Associations," by Mr. R. B. Keys, which close with this number, will be found of marked value to persons interested in such co-operative bodies. The writer, an experienced accountant, has for several years had much to do with the practical workings of a number of these associations in Philadelphia. Many thousand persons in the Quaker City, now owners of their homes, can attribute this part of their good fortune to the beneficent results of co-operation. It is one of the pleasant features of stability in that city. There are few prominent cities in the United States which will compare with Philadelphia as places where men of moderate incomes enjoy the satisfaction of living under their own roofs. It is to be regretted that so few in all cities are permitted this privilege. As the working people of cities, artisans, merchants and those engaged in any of the industrial professions, become owners of buildings in which they live, prosperity and stability advances. As a matter of industrial economy, so far as dollars and cents, it cannot be argued that the welfare of this class are always enhanced by owning their homes. Many instances may be cited where homes are rented at less than the interest would be on their value. Then there are cases where, owing to the irregularity of employment, occasional changes of residence are necessary. This would necessitate a sale of the home and such sale would usually result in a loss. However, tak-

ing all things into consideration, it is far better that the family should own the dwelling in which it lives. Such ownership will prove a strong feature in the advancement of civilization, morality, and good government. Men of wealth in large cities would find it much to their interest to foster and encourage a disposition leading in this direction.

The address reported in another department of this number on " Personality of Handwriting and Expert Examinations," will be found replete with valuable information. A recent case before the courts in Western New York gave evidence of the importance to be attached to expert testimony. It was a case in which the executors of an estate refused a claim, based upon a note, said to have been given by the deceased several years before his death. Suit was brought by the holder of the note. Two similar notes had been presented to the executors and by them allowed. This, the third note, when presented was objected to on the ground that it had not been presented in accordance with the law, and was therefore uncollectable. At last suspicions were aroused, and Mr. Ames, the expert, was consulted. The signatures to the notes which had been allowed were pronounced by Mr. Ames as forgeries. His services were at once employed, and, upon careful examination, he decided that the note in question was also a forgery. On the day of the trial, after the plaintiff had introduced a prominent bank official to prove the genuineness of the signature to the note, recess was taken. During the recess the witness, who had testified to the genuineness of the note, was asked if he had ever examined the writing referred to with the aid of a magnifying glass. He had not. Would he like to do so? Certainly. The most careful examination was made, and when the writing was compared with that of the person in whose favor the note was drawn, the witness could understand how he had been deceived. Being an honorable man and becoming fully convinced that he had been deceived, he went back upon the witness-stand and corrected his testimony. Having made a careful examination of the writing with the aid of a powerful glass he had come to the conclusion that he was not competent to testify that the signature was genuine. That, in fact, he had doubts of it genuineness. This was followed up by furthe evidence, and the executors were enabled to save the estate many thousand dollars. Sympathy for the guilty party alone saved a criminal prosecution and probably a term in a State institution. This is only an illustration of many instances in which expert testimony has proven of immense value. As an expert in handwriting, Mr. Ames stands at the head of his profession. He has won a reputation which makes his services sought after far and near. Standing entirely above reproach in character and integrity, it is well known that his services cannot be procured except in cases . where he is morally certain that the means at his command has enabled him to form a just and truthful conclusion.

Many of our readers will study with interest the series of papers, prepared especially for the COUNTING-ROOM, entitled "Commerce and Its Promoters," the second of which is printed in this number. Many lessons of importance to-day may be learned by a study of what took place centuries ago. One of the prime objects in the preparation of these papers, however, is to furnish those having little time for study with a careful review of historical events which relate in any way to the commercial and industrial affairs of all civilized nations. Those who have not made commercial history a study, and thereby become versed in the events upon which the series treat, will find the papers a valuable condensation of useful knowledge. If, while the articles are being presented, there should arise with any a desire for further information concerning the subjects treated, they are invited to forward letters of inquiry. An effort in such cases will be made to secure the information desired and give an intelligent reply.

Mr. John W. Francies, of Philadelphia, offers his services to the public as a professional accountant. Long experience in the management of accounts and business interests has qualified him for the work he proposes to do. His location at 1020 Arch Street is central, and being well connected and favorably known, he will soon win a prominence in his specialty. We esteem it a pleasure to refer to him in these columns.

We give in this number the concluding portion of a paper on "Business in India." The writer, Mr. Amrita Lal Roy, is a Hindoo gentleman, a native of Calcutta. His familiarity with the history and conditions of the people and customs upon which he writes makes the information valuable for its reliability. The peculiarities of trade and traffic among the nations of the East are just now particularly interesting. Information of this character will prove serviceable to a thorough comprehension of reports concerning affairs in that part of the globe.

It might have a salutary effect on dishonest bank officials in this country to occasionally apply the penalty that was prescribed in France for the directors and managers of the Banque of Lyons et Loire which failed some years ago. The trial was concluded recently. M. Savary, ex-deputy, and at one time Under Secretary of State, was sentenced to five years in prison, to pay a fine of 20,000 francs, and to suffer for ten years a suspension of his civil and political rights. M. Zielinski, the manager, was sentenced to five months in prison and to pay a fine of 8,000 francs ; M. Bellantan, sub-manager, four months in prison, with a fine of 5,000 francs. The rest were only fined, the amounts ranging from 1,000 to 10,000 francs.

THE LIBRARY.

WOMAN'S SERIES FOR THE MODERN LANGUAGES:
FIRST GERMAN BOOK; SECOND GERMAN BOOK;
FIRST FRENCH BOOK; SECOND FRENCH BOOK;
FIRST SPANISH BOOK.

A. S. BARNES & Co., New York and Chicago.

We are glad to welcome any works which facilitates the study of languages if they are based on correct principles of instruction. This series has greatly pleased us. In each, the language taught is itself made the medium as well as the subject of the teaching. The German book is entirely in German, the French course in French, and the Spanish language is taught in Spanish. And it is intended that the supplementary explanations of the teacher shall be in the foreign tongue, not in English. He is aided by beautifully and apposite illustrations, and must do the rest by the universal language of sign and gesture, until the stock of words, scanty and crudely used at first, becomes by growth and deft moulding so plastic that any new idea is readily fitted with its appropriate word-clothing, and any new word is, by the skilful handling of the words already known, made alive with meaning. This is how we learned our mother tongue, and we cannot improve upon the processes of nature. So progressive is the course of either of these books, that an intelligent reader would scarcely need a teacher, exeept to give the true pronunciation.

We must somewhat disagree with the author's opinions, as stated in the preface, on the introduction of grammatical terms and paradigms. We think that should, at least with children, be left for a later stage. He speaks of a paradigm as if it were a natural organism, not a mere conventional classification, like that of botany. The power to call up at will any grammatical form in its appropriate connection is what is needed—not the power to give a symmetrical list of all possible forms. It is just so with other tables. The person who can give instantly the product of any two digit-numbers need not trouble himself to learn the multiplication table, and he to whom the idea "they would have loved," brings to the tip of his tongue "amavissent" need not grieve because he has not reached that point through the route of "amo, amas."

In all other respects these little books call for the highest commendation. The outward appearance is very attractive.

St. Nicholas.

The young people have a magazine of which they may well be proud. St. Nicholas for June is as usual, and the older members of the family will learn much if they too will turn over its pages. The sixth spinning-wheel story by Miss Louisa M. Alcott, entitled, "The Banner of Beaumanoir," is a pretty story of devotion and heroism. How much good one little boy may do even though he be delicate, or a cripple like Tommy Glen, or apparently a dunce like Johnny Haven, may be learned by reading "Two Boys of Migglesville," by W. W. Fink. Miss Susan Anne Brown suggests a charming idea for little girls, in "Margaret's Favor Book." A most interesting and instructive article entitled, "Queer Game," by Mrs. S. B. Herrick, relates to the "little busy bee" and its habits. Several serials are continued. The illustrations throughout are good, one sketched by a little girl of ten deserving special mention. Not the least charming poem in the number is one contributed by little Paul Hoffman, who is only eleven years old.

St. Nicholas for July is brimful of reminiscences of Revolutionary days, and ought to prepare the little folks for a patriotic celebration of Independence Day. An illustrated article on "The Bartholdi Statue," by Charles Barnard, is particularly interesting. Some pretty poems grace the number; among them one entitled "Gold-Robin," by Celia Thaxter.

Phrenological Journal

for June is a good number. An article on "Texas and San Antonio," by Lydia M. Millard, gives us a glimpse of that vast State which the writer tells us is "more than twice as large as England, Scotland and Ireland combined, with a territory nearly six times as great as the State of Pennsylvania, her breadth from north to south is nearly one thousand miles." Dr. C. L. Carter contributes an article on "Man in Geological Eras." Two biographical and phrenological sketches find place in the number; the subject of the first being Henri Milne Edwards, the eminent naturalist, who is now nearly eighty-four years of age, though "still fresh, mentally, seeming in most respects to retain the ardor of youth, having for study and research his old earnestness, and for progress a most cordial co-operation." The subject of the second sketch is Savorgnan de Brazya, the explorer and diplomat, who, although still a young man, has already achieved for himself a proud position. He has given to the scientific and geographical world much useful knowledge by his explorations on the Dark Continent. Several other good articles form interesting reading, while much that is instructive concerning such vital topics as those of health, training of children, etc., make a valuable number. A paper on " Why so many women fade early " will also interest many.

Atlantic

for June is pleasant reading. It contains some excellent papers on widely different topics. One entitled " Paris Classical Concerts " is very interesting. There are thousands of lovers of music in America who would gladly welcome the establishment in our larger cities of just such musical societies as those described as having achieved snch popularity in Paris. I. S. Wood contributes an article on the " Trail of the Sea-serpents," in which he gives a detailed account of all the well authenticated sea-serpent stories that have been published from the middle of the seventeenth century down to the present time. He says, " According to the old adage there is no smoke without fire, and as from earliest times the existence of a gigantic sea-snake has been asserted by sailors as a fact which no one would think of controverting, it is not likely that there was no foundation for their belief." Many noteworthy facts are elicited in his treatment of the subject, not the least interesting of which is, that the mysterious monster has been known to visit a certain spot on the New England coast more frequently than any other locality in the known world, excepting, perhaps, the Norwegian coast. The secend installment of Mr. Richard Grant White's series, " The Anatomizing of William Shakespeare " is an important paper. He makes a digression from his subject, and devotes the article to answering two adverse criticisms which appeared respectively in the New York *Times* and the *Evening Post.* He disposes of his opponents in a masterly manner, and at the same time contributes a large amount of useful information which will prove of value to Shakesperian students. " Penury not Pauperism," by D. O. Kellogg, shows conclusively that to give the poor pecuniary assistance is to deprive them of their independence. While an article entitled "Washington as it should be," by O. B. Frothingham, will find many interested readers.

Century

is interesting and instructive throughout. " What is a liberal education," by Charles W. Eliot, is an able argument in favor of the extension of the present curriculum of college study. Important studies, like English, French, German, history, political economy and natural science, receive little or no attention in the colleges of our land, when, in the opinion of the writer, they ought to be placed side by side with the older, though, perhaps, not more necessary, branches already considered essential to a liberal education. Mr. Eliot makes a strong plea in favor of the revision of the present list of college studies, and shows that it will be necessary in order to make provision for the youth of the twentieth century. "The Use and Abuse of Parties," by Washington Gladden, is a short but timely article, and will furnish excellent reading for every man interested in the politics of this country. The writer claims that it is the duty of all good citizens to enter into politics, and further to their best abilities the good of the nation to which they belong. Good men must enter into politics if they desire to preserve their liberties. "Not to attend the caucus," Mr. Gladden says, "is to neglect the supreme duty of citizenship." He closes an interesting paper with the following encouraging remarks : "The abuses of party will cease when good men use the parties instead of being used by them, An article on "Commerce in the Colonies," by Dr. Eggleston, is a prominent feature in the number. It contains very much useful information on the subject of early commerce in this country. Julian Hawthorne contributes a valuable paper on " American Wild Animals in Art." " The Diary of an American Girl in Cairo during the war of 1882," is a unique but particularly interesting paper. It is written by Miss Nannie Stone, whose father, General Stone, served in Egypt during the war of 1882. The young lady's simple recital of the horrors of that seige, show us how on occasion delicately matured and tenderly cared for women can rise to heights of heroism undreamed of under ordinary circumstances. "An Average Man," by Robert Grant, is concluded in this number. It is an average story without any very exciting incidents or dramatic situations ; the more true to life on that very account. The Average Man, in these prosaic days, it is to be feared more often than not marries for money, and usually wrecks his own and his wife's happiness thereby.

Lippincott.

The second paper on "Shapespeare's Tragedies on the Stage," by John Foster Kirk, is devoted to a discussion of the relative merits of the three actors, Forrest, the elder Booth and Macready. The first named, Mr. Kirk says, possessed more physical advantages than any other actor, not excepting Salvini—a symmetrical figure, a handsome face and a voice "so powerful and clear that its lightest tones fell upon the distant ear as if there were no intervening space, and when unstrained it had the fullness and mellowness that belong only to the finest organs." And yet he failed to make the use of his gifts. The defects which marred the performance of this celebrated actor are carefully pointed out. In his best impersonations, Booth displayed a harmonious blending of physical and mental attributes which was grateful to the spectator, sparing him "the necessity of scrutinizing his own conceptions." Mr. Kirk speaks highly of the actor's elocutionary powers, and also of his ability to sink his own individuality in that of the character he was representing. "No tragedian," he says, "whom I have seen, displayed this power in the same degree as Booth." Iago was his best character. In some Shakesperian plays, Booth was a complete failure, but this was when the part "lay beyond the proper scope of his powers." "No actor," Mr. Kirk says, "ever achieved quite the same pre-eminence on the English stage as Macready," and yet he, like Lebrun, had to pass through a long period of discipline, a persistent and arduous struggle against certain innate tendencies and natural defects. In early life his acting was crude as well as being characterized by "a general lack of physical charm." As a proof of what perseverance and patient study will do, the writer tells us that "in later years no actor knew better how to regulate the display of emotion," while "his attitudes," as his French critics remarked, "were those of Greek statuary." His chief fault was that "it could never be said that his own personality was merged in that of the character." A comparison is drawn in this respect between Booth and Macready as well as in the quality of their voices. The paper is attractive, and will be read with profit by all lovers of Shakesperian tragedy.

Lippincott's Magazine for July opens with an illustrated paper on "Some Suburbs of New York." Bergen Hill, or Jersey City Heights, still retains much of its primitive appearance. The most remarkable and interesting house in the village is the "Sip House, which has an interest unique in this country, to the best of the writer's knowledge and belief, in being now the residence of the descendants, in the seventh generation of its builders, by whose family it has been continuously occupied." Short Hills, New Jersey, is also described at some length. James S. Whitman gives an entertaining account of a sojourn of "Three Months in Chili," while the first of two papers on "Life in a Prussian Province," by Sara M. S. Pereira, is equally interesting. One may learn much of foreign lands without traveling themselves. Frank Bellew paints in his "Recollections of Ralph Waldo Emerson," a pretty word picture of Emerson in his own house. And Dr. Os-

wald gives many valuable hints in his sixth paper on "Healthy Houses."

North American Review.

The opening article in the July number of this ably conducted magazine is one on "Juries and Jurymen," by Judge Robert C. Pitman. In a clear and concise manner that gentleman advocates the necessity of elevating the character of juries and providing them with better accommodation and treatment. The advisability of permitting juries to separate for the night, even though they may not have agreed upon a verdict, is suggested, also, that in certain cases it would be better not to require a unanimous verdict. The reforms suggested, though radical, would perhaps be beneficial. Prof. Van Buren Denslow contributes a powerful article entitled "American Economics." Free-traders will find food for thought in its perusal, while protectionists will take pride in learning that a full third of all the annual increase in wealth now going on in the world is occurring in the United States. The weak points in the divorce laws in this country are pointed out in a paper on "Marriage and Divorce" by Justice Noah Davis. He believes that "uniformity of the grounds of divorce ought to exist throughout all the States," and maintains that only for one single cause should absolute divorces ever be granted. The article on "The Annexation of Canada," by Dr. P. Bender, will direct attention to a subject which has heretofore been deemed of little importance. It will surprise many to learn that Canada possesses an extent of territory within about 300,000 square miles as great as that of the American Republic ; that the route from Japan to Liverpool, *via* British Columbia and Port Hudson, Hudson's Bay, would be over 2,000 miles shorter than that *via* San Francisco and New York ; that the extraordinary fertility of the soil in the Canadian Northwest has earned for it the title of "the future granary of the world;" that the country is rich in timber, fisheries, and mineral wealth, and that it possesses an unusually healthy climate. Altogether, Dr. Bender will convince those who read his paper that the vast extent of territory to the north would be a valuable acquisition to the United States. Reciprocity in trade, at least, between the two countries would be desirable. Prof. D. McG. Meares, in his paper on "Government Telegraphy," gives some weighty reasons why it would not be well to place the system of telegraphy in the hands of the Government. "The Future of the Negro" is discussed in a number of interesting letters contributed by various persons, the majority of whom seem to think that American negroes will ever remain in those Southern States where they have so long been domiciled, and in the course of ages will become a cultured and influential class.

New Englander.

The *New Englander* is a bi-monthly review published by William L. Kingsley, New Haven. The numerous excellent articles to be found in the July number indicate the high character of the magazine. Prof. Francis W. Kelsey contributes an article on "Taxation in the United States," in which he treats of the tariff question. "The present high rate," he says, "was imposed upon the country by the War of the Rebellion, and having out-lived its usefulness ought to be done away with." The burden of the article is, that "foreign competition is not a common enemy," but would have a salutary influence upon the commerce of the country. "The Genesis of Modern Free Institutions," by the same writer, is an interesting paper. The free institutions which we enjoy to-day, it is alleged, had their origin in the earliest times, and may be traced through the various epoch, of their existences from Paganism to Christianity, which "has done more to advance the cause of civil rights than any other agency." Prof. H. W. Farnam, of Yale College, writes in a forcible manner on the "Manual Training of Boys." It is to be hoped the day [is] distant when instruction in industrial oc[cupations] will be included in the list of studies in [publi]c schools. Those interested in this im[portant] subject will read Prof. Farnam's paper [wit]h interest. The following articles also [find pl]ace in the number: "Civil Service Re[view] by Elial F. Hall; "The Charter of Con[necticut], and the Charter of Yale College," by [Joh]n Bliss; "Milton's Angels," by John A. [...]; "Teaching of the Twelve Apostles," by [...] E. Edwin Hall, and "The Contest as it is [toda]y," by Rev. M. E. Dwight.

Pulpit Treasury.

[T]he *Pulpit Treasury*, a new Evangelical monthly, has established so good a reputation for itself in the one year of its existence, that the *Southern Pulpit*, a magazine of similar character, has joined its forces with it. Hereafter the editors will work together. The July number contains several able sermons by eminent clergymen, and a variety of useful and interesting matter on church topics. The publication is non-sectarian, and with such a splendid list of contributors as it possesses, must surely commend itself to ministers and theological students generally.

Popular Science.

The *Popular Science* monthly for July is rich in good things. In the opening words of the first paper, "The Great Political Superstition," Herbert Spencer gives the key to the article when he asserts that "The great political superstition of the past was the divine right of kings. The great political superstition of the present is the divine right of parliaments." Samuel A. Fisk, M.D., paints "Colorado for Invalids" in such glowing colors as will tempt many a one afflicted with throat or lung troubles to try what its bracing air will do for them. The so-called "New Theology" is discussed at length by Rev. George F. Lyon. A very ably written article on "The Feints of Manual Training," by Prof. C. M. Woodward, Ph.D., Washington University, St. Louis, will attract attention. The experiment of introducing the teaching of industrial occupations into schools and colleges is a comparatively new one, but seems already to be giving promise of a rich harvest. Dr. Woodward speaks authoritatively as he has had charge of both kinds of schools—those devoted to intellectual training only, and manual training-schools as well. His opinions carry weight with them. Other useful and instructive papers will find interested readers.

Who Art Thou, Man?

Man that is married of woman is of many days
    and full of trouble.

In the morning he draweth his salary, and in the
    evening

Behold! it is gone. It is a tale that is told.

It is vanished, and no one knoweth whither it
    goes.

He riseth up clothed in the chilly garments

Of the night,

And seeketh the somnambulent paregoric,

Wherewith to soothe his infant posterity.

He cometh up as a horse or an ox,

And draweth the chariot of his offspring.

He spendeth his shekels in the purchase of fine
    linen,

Wherewith to clothe the bosom of his

Family.

Yet himself is seen in the gates of the city

With one suspender.

Yea! he is altogether wretched.

Man born of woman is of few days and no teeth.
And, indeed, it would be money in his pocket
sometimes if he had less of either.

As for his days, he wasteth one-third of them;
and for his teeth, he has convulsions when he cuts
them, and, as the last one comes through, lo! the
dentist is twisting the first one out, and the last
end of that man's jaw is worse than the first, being
full of porcelain and a roof-plate built to hold black-
berry seeds.

He buyeth Northwestern at 110, when he has
sold short at 96, and his neighbor unloadeth upon
him Iron Mountain at 63⅜, and it straightway
breaketh down to 42¼.

He riseth up early and sitteth up late, that he
may fill his barns and storehouses, and lo! his
children's lawyers divide the spoils among themselves, and say, "Ha-ha!"

He growleth and is sore distressed, because it
raineth; and he beateth upon his breast and sayeth, "My crop is lost!" because it raineth not.
The late rains blight his wheat, and the frost
biteth his peaches.

If it be so that the sun shineth, even among the
nineties, he sayeth, "Woe is me, for I perish";
and if the north winds sigheth down in forty-two
below, he crieth, "Would I were dead!"

If he wear sackcloth and blue jeans, men say,
"He is a tramp"; and if he goeth forth shaven
and clad in purple and fine linen, all the people
cry, "Shoot the dude!"

He carrieth insurance for twenty-five years, until
he has paid thrice over for all his goods, and then
he letteth his policy lapse one day, and that same
night fire destroyeth his store.

He buildeth him a house in Jersey, and his first-
born is devoured by mosquitoes. He pitcheth his
tents in New York, and tramps devour his substance. He moveth to Kansas, and a cyclone carrieth his house away over into Missouri, while a
prairie-fire and ten million acres of grasshoppers
fight for his crops. He settleth himself in Kentucky, and is shot the next day by a gentleman,
colonel and a statesman, "because, sah, he resem-
bles, sah, a man, sah, he did not like, sah." Ver-
ily, there is no rest for the sole of his foot, and if
he had it to do over again, he would not be born at
all, for "the day of death is better than the day of
one's birth."

The Cigarette Plague.

Cigarettes, like the world itself in Words-
worth's sonnets, are too much with us. They
are universally excused and suffered on the
same plea as that urged by the young mother
of a contraband baby—that it was a very little
one. Cigarettes are so attenuated in their di-
mensions, and have the credit of being s⦿
mild and light in the incense they sprea⦿
they are permitted or encouraged wh⦿
and coarser methods of tobacco cor⦿
would be tabooed. A cigar is an unc⦿
A pipe, while eminently suitable for ⦿
and the cloister, is not suitable for ⦿
ments abroad. Fifty years ago, Joh⦿
Croker complained that the ambulat⦿
had superseded the sober, sedentary cla⦿
he lived now, he would have written cig⦿
The air is full of a sort of miasma of ⦿
ettes, because they can be discussed so ⦿
and thrown away so lightly—because ⦿
smoking of them may be a matter of ⦿
minutes or of one. The cigarette is ub⦿
tous. It prematurely infests the dining-ro⦿
it is not excluded from the boudoir; ⦿
sanctioned in the drawing-room—on the ⦿
ciple, perhaps, that those who have commi⦿
a few social peccadillos are not excluded fr⦿
the pale of society, because it is regarded ⦿
weak rather than wicked.

There is not a theatre or place of amus⦿
ment in London whose corridors or precinct ⦿
are uncontaminated by the taint of the cigar—
ette. As the popularity attained by cigars in ⦿
England during the first three decades of this ⦿
century may be traced to the revolutionary ⦿
wars in which our troops were engaged, so the ⦿
first impetus given to cigarette-smoking was ⦿
the larger acquaintance we made with Turkish ⦿
ways and customs during the Crimean war, o⦿

nearly thirty years ago. But it is less than fifteen years ago that royal patronage gave the cigarette the vogue which now belongs to it. There are, of course, cigarettes and cigarettes. When the tobacco of which they consist is fresh and the best of its kind, and the paper in which it is inclosed is of delicate manufacture, there is nothing positively offensive in their smell. But the majority of cigarettes consumed in England, and consequently of the cigarette smoke as it assails a majority of our nostrils, is insufferable. The tobacco is stale and of an inferior quality, the paper is coarse, and its aroma is clearly perceptible; while the general impression produced upon our olfactory organs is that of a mephitic fume such as might ascend if crushed straw, sprinkled over with cayenne pepper, and interspersed with small fragments of brown paper, were ignited on a dish. There is no reason why cigarettes should be ostracised from polite society, but if a reaction is not to be excited against them, their consumption ought to be regulated. As it is, we groan under a tyranny of cigarettes, and, for the most part, exceedingly bad cigarettes, too. It was a Scotchman who said, "Whisky is a bad thing—especially bad whisky."—*The World* (London).

For Product Safety Concerns and Information please contact our EU
representative GPSR@taylorandfrancis.com
Taylor & Francis Verlag GmbH, Kaufingerstraße 24, 80331 München, Germany